KENT HISTORY PROJECT

6

KENT IN THE TWENTIETH CENTURY

KENT HISTORY PROJECT

ISSN 1352-805X

Already published

Traffic and Politics: The Construction and Management of Rochester Bridge, AD 43–1993, ed. Nigel Yates and James M. Gibson

Religion and Society in Kent, 1640–1914, Nigel Yates, Robert Hume and Paul Hastings

The Economy of Kent, 1640–1914, ed. Alan Armstrong

Faith and Fabric: A History of Rochester Cathedral, 604–1994, ed. Nigel Yates with the assistance of Paul A. Welsby

Early Modern Kent, 1540–1660, ed. Michael Zell

Volumes in progress

The Government and Politics in Kent, 1640–1914, ed. H. C. F. Lansberry

Kent to AD 800, ed. John Williams

Early Medieval Kent, 800–1220, ed. Richard Eales

Later Medieval Kent, 1220–1540, ed. Nigel Ramsay

KENT IN THE TWENTIETH CENTURY

EDITED BY

NIGEL YATES

with the assistance of
ALAN ARMSTRONG, IAN COULSON
and ALISON CRESSWELL

THE BOYDELL PRESS

KENT COUNTY COUNCIL

First published 2001
The Boydell Press, Woodbridge, and
Kent County Council

ISBN 0 85115 587 1

The Boydell Press is an imprint of Boydell & Brewer Ltd
PO Box 9, Woodbridge, Suffolk IP12 3DF, UK
and of Boydell & Brewer Inc.
PO Box 41026, Rochester, NY 14604–4126, USA
website: http://www.boydell.co.uk

A catalogue record for this book is available
from the British Library

Library of Congress Cataloging-in-Publication Data
Kent in the twentieth century / edited by Nigel Yates ; with the assistance of
Alan Armstrong, Ian Coulson, and Alison Cresswell.
p. cm. – (Kent history project, ISSN 1352–805X ; 6)
Includes bibliographical references and index.
ISBN 0–85115–587–1 (alk. paper)
1. Kent (England) – History. I. Yates, Nigel. II. Series
DA670.K3 K45 2001
942.2'3 – dc21   00–046851

This publication is printed on acid-free paper

Printed in Great Britain by
St Edmundsbury Press Ltd, Bury St Edmunds, Suffolk

Contents

Appendices

Plates

Dust jacket illustration
Promotional photograph of the new Larkfield Leisure Centre opened in 1981.

Maps

Figures

Tables

Notes on Contributors

Alan Armstrong was Professor of Economic and Social History at the University of Kent, having previously taught at the Universities of Nottingham and Warwick, and was the editor of *The Economy of Kent, 1640–1914* (1995) in the Kent History Project. He has also published *Stability and Change in the English Country Town: A Social Study of York, 1801–51* (1974), *Farmworkers: A Social and Economic History* (1988) and several contributions to multi-author volumes and learned journals on aspects of demographic and rural social history.

Brian Atkinson was Lecturer in History at the University of Kent where he continues to teach students registered for the Diploma in Kentish History and the Certificate in Modern History. His previous publications include *Trade Unions in Bristol* (1982) and he has also contributed the nineteenth-century political chapter to *Government and Politics in Kent, 1640–1914* in the Kent History Project.

Alan Booth is Lecturer in Economic and Social History at the University of Exeter, having previously been Lecturer in Economic and Social History at the University of Sheffield. In 1998/9 he was Visiting Professor at the Institute of Historical Research, Hitotsubashi University, Japan. He is the author of *British Economic Policy, 1931–49* (1989) and co-author (with Melvyn Pack) of *Employment, Capital and Economic Policy* (1985) and (with Sean Glynn) of *Modern Britain: An Economic and Social History* (1996).

Ian Coulson is Inspector and Adviser for History for Kent County Council, a member of the Lord Chancellor's Advisory Council for Public Records, and Fellow of the Schools History Project at Trinity and All Saints' University College. He is the author of fifteen text books for schools and has been involved in producing the A-Level syllabus for the Cambridge History Project.

Alison Cresswell is Research Archivist in the Centre for Kentish Studies at County Hall, Maidstone. She is the author of *A Kentish Cookery Collection* (1978), *A Kentish Herbal* (1984) and *The Dering Love Letters* (1994). She has also catalogued several manuscript collections and produced the texts of two tapes, on Ightham Mote and Uppark, for the National Trust.

Gerald Crompton is Lecturer in the Canterbury Business School at the University of Kent, having been previously Lecturer in Economic and Social History at the same university. His recent publications include an article on rail nationalisation in the *Journal of Transport History* (1999) and contributions to *The Dynamics of the International Brewing Industry* (1998) and the *Proceedings of the Twelfth International Economic History Congress* (1998).

Robin Gill is the Michael Ramsey Professor of Modern Theology in the University of Kent and an Honorary Canon of Canterbury Cathedral. Before moving to Kent he held the William Leach Research Chair in Applied Theology at the University of Newcastle. Amongst his books are *The Myth of the Empty Church* (1993) and *Churchgoing and Christian Ethics* (1999).

Paul Hastings was Inspector for History for Kent County Council and has taught in both schools and colleges of education as well as for university extra-mural departments and the Open University. He is the author of more than fifty books and articles, including several contributions to the Kent History Project, and has also written three programmes for BBC Television.

Lord Kingsdown (Robin Leigh-Pemberton) is Lord Lieutenant of Kent, a post he has held since 1982. He is a former member of Kent County Council (1961–77, Chairman 1972–75), Chairman of the National Westminster Bank and Pro-Chancellor of the University of Kent (1977–83) and Governor of the Bank of England (1983–93).

Michael Rawcliffe was Principal Lecturer in History at Stockwell College of Education in Bromley and later Head of History at St Olave's School in Orpington. In 1972 he was exchange Professor of History at Markato State University in Minnesota. His publications include 'Bromley, Kent Market Town to Victorian Suburb' in F. M. L. Thompson (ed.), *The Nature of Suburbia* (1982).

Nigel Yates is General Editor of the Kent History Project and Senior Research Fellow in Church History at the University of Wales, Lampeter. He was the co-author (with Felicity Stafford) of *The Later Kentish Seaside* (1985) and (with Robert Hume and Paul Hastings) of *Religion and Society in Kent, 1640–1914* (1994), and has published several other books on religious history including *Buildings, Faith and Worship* (1991, 2nd edn 2000) and *Anglican Ritualism in Victorian Britain, 1830–1910* (1999).

Foreword

The Rt Hon Lord Kingsdown

Anyone who embarks on a history of the twentieth century, whether it is of Kent or anywhere else, will be confronted by the challenge of recording and evaluating change on a scale never known before. I have no doubt that the experienced and conscientious contributors to this history of our county will surmount this challenge, each in their own subject and in their own way.

For me in writing this foreword the challenge takes a different form, for I am no expert and have undertaken little special research in seeking to set the scene for what follows. In venturing to give my impressions of the county over the last century I can draw on my own experience for much of it and on the impressions I gleaned from my parents and their contemporaries for the remainder. As for the future, my surmises will be no more than submissions to be tested against those of others; but they come from someone who has lived in the county all his life and has been involved, in one way or another, in its public life for nearly all of the post-war period.

I think the most significant change of the twentieth century in Kent is the relief from manual labour for the vast majority of people. Whether on the land, in the brick fields, in the chalk pits, down the coal mines, in industry or even in domestic service, the vast majority of men and women in 1900 lived by the sweat of their brow and the toil of their hands. I believe then that more people were engaged in agriculture and domestic service than in any other activities; and we only have to look at those two activities now to see what a liberation this change represents and what a fundamental social change. Modern domestic appliances are taken for granted by our present generation but they have been tremendous liberators of all members of the family, not least the mother or housewife, in terms of freeing time for a wealth, a bewildering even confusing wealth, of alternative activity. The fact that the modern farm will probably nowadays only require one pair of hands, where at many times of the year ten were required a century ago, has had a profound effect on country villages and rural population.

This, combined with the recent serious deterioration in the profitability of farming, presents sharp uncertainty about what life in the countryside will or ought to be like in the future. The problem for the countryside in the agricultural depression of the 1930s lay in abandoned farmland, derelict buildings, declining employment and no investment: the problem for the twenty-first century looks like being the reconciliation of increasingly sophisticated agriculture with anyone's idea of what the countryside should look like. It is tempting for preservationists, even the more positive version of that cult the conservationists, to strive to recover a countryside that existed at some time and in some ideal form in the past, that was as God made it in all its natural beauty. Yet any brief consideration shows that the countryside's appearance has always been changing in response to man's demands on it. The twentieth century has seen these demands veer from neglect to intensive use and I am sure the next century will see increasing anxiety about reconciling conflicting demands upon the land from which we derive our life.

It is, incidentally, worth recalling for a moment the fundamental change in the public's attitude towards planning. When the first substantial Town and Country Planning Act was introduced in 1947 it was seen as a serious attack on the liberty of the individual to do as he liked with his own property; now we are all experts at participating in any decision affecting our neighbourhood and see it as our right. 'Planning' in a densely populated country must be inevitable but it is something our ancestors at the start of the century would find strange and see even as interference rather than the positive co-operative function it is supposed to be.

If planning went through a period when it was felt to be primarily negative in its function and effect in its early days, it will represent in the future an increasing challenge not only for national government but, more important for us, also for county and district government. This is going to be increasingly the medium through which the prospects for Kent's economy, employment and prosperity is projected; positive, pro-active planning as a joint function of government and the private sector. Once again our predecessors would be surprised, if not disapproving, of such intrusion. After all, they would claim, they established the business where the demand and resources dictated: the great chalk pits and cement works of north-west Kent; the brick fields on the brick-earth deposits on the north coast and Weald (and, as a consequence, that fleet of red-sailed barges for ever conveying thousands of tons of Kentish clay and chalk in the form of bricks and cement to London and its outskirts); the paper mills where the water and easy access from Scandinavian forests pin-pointed. Perhaps we are the inheritors of some eyesores as a result, but those were not the days of development grants encouraging investment where it might not otherwise have gone; and, when we see the scale of some modern industry in Kent, we must not cavil at such grants or our share of them.

When one looks back over the century, however, more of what the world associates with Kent and what seemed to be its lively characteristics has departed than has been replaced: holiday-makers crowding each weekend up and down the meagre roads to Thanet; paddle-steamers plying between London and Margate; even Gravesend early in the century an elegant resort for Londoners; houses by the thousand round the coast let to families for their annual fortnight at the sea; and the great annual exodus from East London in the autumn in the form of an invasion of working holiday-makers in the hop-gardens. Now, somehow, this colourful routine no longer stops within the county, and Kent is seen from outside as a county of passage to the continent of Europe and of mechanised agriculture.

The unique combination of the conurbation of London on the north-west and the channel ports in the south-east does appear to dominate our county at present. No doubt this has always been so, to a greater or lesser extent, ever since Roman times, with Watling Street bringing with it what are now Canterbury and the Medway Towns with their cathedrals and history along its way. The colossal growth in cross-channel traffic in the later part of this century has, however, put a new complexion on this feature. This growth has had to be accommodated and, with the completion of the fast rail link in the wake of the Tunnel and its concomitant motorways, I believe will be. Many people regret this and will probably never be reconciled to it; others, however, will see it as the dominating influence and opportunity for the county's economic future, located as we are between London and the great markets of Europe. What a challenge to ensure that this is all for the best and not a gradual erosion of the garden of England! I am optimistic about this; I believe that, with skilful improvement of communications by rail and road laterally from the main spines of the motorways and the new railway, those parts of the county which now languish economically should have as good a chance of transformation as anywhere in England, and with good planning and design should not lose their character.

One change, which an observer over the century will notice, is the drastic reduction in the armed services in the county. My generation was brought up to assume the presence in Kent of the great naval bases in Chatham and Sheerness, with warships lying off the coast of Sheppey; the Royal Marines at Deal; the Royal School of Military Engineering in Gillingham; the depots of the two county regiments in Maidstone and Canterbury respectively with their home battalions alongside them; the garrison at Shorncliffe and the School of Infantry at Hythe; and this list is far from complete, I suspect. It is interesting to reflect, however, that until the war of 1939–45 people in Kent were not so aware of the Royal Air Force as of the Navy and the Army. This was suddenly corrected in 1940 when the fighter stations became household names – Biggin Hill, Detling, West Malling to name but some of them.

The main point though is to remind us of the influence of the armed services in the days I am describing, both socially and economically in Kent life; how dependent some towns were on the establishments and how prolonged have been the efforts to restore their economies after the closures by the introduction of modern development, something that is now largely complete and successful. But there is a gap in the life of these towns compared with 'garrison' days; the military tradition was genuinely felt and was a source of pride. Kent, nevertheless, remains fortunate in retaining more than its numerically fair share of major military establishments and I like to think there will continue to be some reality behind the feeling of being Great Britain's front-line county. For this indeed is what Kent has been. While it may have been our lot to be the first to welcome, if that is the word, the Romans and to have had to negotiate a successful deal with the Normans on Swanscombe Hill, the Cinque Ports, the Martello Towers and, in this century, the Dover Patrol, the Dunkirk Evacuation and the Battle of Britain are poignant reminders of our front-line position. May it never take this past and historic form again! I do not believe it will, but in another form I am sure it must be in the forefront of the country's life, as communications with Europe intensify and cross-channel trade and transport grow in volume.

Many people view this prospect with horror, associating it with acres of concrete spreading over green countryside. I have to say that we need to recognise that it is in this sphere of activity that our future lies. Kent has moved away from the old industries and military establishments to being a centre for the best in modern industrial and commercial development; whether it be in pharmaceuticals, service industries – as in office development at Kings Hill – or a wealth of sophisticated small and medium-sized enterprises which are increasingly appearing as internal communications in the country improve. The opportunities for well-paid employment are, I believe, great; what may be the problem is producing enough well-qualified young people to fulfil this need, much though our centres of higher and further education are developing.

I believe this history will provide an important record of Kentish life in this last century, with all its changes, which will help us all to understand what has made Kent so special and to appreciate what lies ahead of us. The economic opportunities seem to me to be very favourable. The challenge is going to be exploiting them in a way that enables social stability and a still beautiful county to match material progress; Kent may not be very different from other counties in this respect but there was a stability amongst those who lived and worked by the sweat of their brow which we, relieved of that but surrounded by all our modern distractions, may be losing. It will be upon this anxiety, I believe, that those responsible for our county in the next century will most have to concentrate.

May the record of the past, which this history presents, help them: the best of Kentish life and traditions are still vigorous and we can be proud of them. Long may they last!

Acknowledgements

The original team of contributors for this volume was signed up by Alan Armstrong and myself during 1991. Although there have been a few changes since then I am delighted that we have been able to assemble such a strong and distinguished group to produce this volume. I am particularly grateful to all the contributors who have met my strict deadlines for their contributions and who have not raised too many objections to my stylistic preferences and editorial methods. I am especially grateful to Alan Armstrong and Ian Coulson who have contributed much more to this volume than their individual chapters. At a much later stage I was able to recruit Alison Cresswell as a research assistant and she has done most of the work in assembling illustrations for the volume as well as contributing the population figures for Kent towns in Appendix I and dealing with a number of other specific queries relating to factual information in the text. I am also grateful to the Leisure Services Officer of Tonbridge and Malling Borough Council for permission to reproduce the original publicity photograph for the opening of the Larkfield Leisure Centre as the dust-jacket illustration for this volume. Further debts of gratitude are owed to Lord Kingsdown for contributing the foreword; to the Centre for the Study of Cartoons and Caricature at the University of Kent for providing copies of the political cartoons used as illustrations in this volume; to the Planning Department of Kent County Council for reproducing the Ordnance Survey maps of Ashford; and to the Education and Libraries Department of Kent County Council and the Court of Wardens and Assistants of Rochester Bridge who between them have provided the substantial subsidy towards the costs of publication that a volume of this sort requires.

Nigel Yates

Introduction

Nigel Yates

In his foreword to this volume Lord Kingsdown has rightly pointed to the many fundamental changes that have taken place, affecting the lives of every single member of society, in the twentieth century. Change has certainly been more rapid in the past hundred years than in any previous century but these changes had been made possible by the slightly slower but, in many respects, even more fundamental changes of the second and third quarters of the nineteenth century. These had produced, for the first time, a politically and religiously pluralist society, and had begun the undermining of the *ancien régime*, so ably assessed and described by Jonathan Clark and Linda Colley,[1] and of the landed estates that had provided the basis of economic, political and religious power in Kent, as in the rest of England. The declining power and influence of these landed estates, and of their aristocratic or gentrified owners, has continued apace throughout the twentieth century.[2] It is noticeable that whereas up until the Second World War Kent County Council was still largely dominated by the owners of large estates, such men or women have taken little part in local politics in Kent in more recent years, and within even the Conservative party it is the interests of commerce and the professions that have become the dominant ones.

There is no doubt that the growing centralisation of government throughout the nineteenth and twentieth centuries has meant that the individuality of the different parts of England has become less noticeable, to the extent that it is almost impossible to tell one town centre from another, since the range and names of the shops are virtually the same. However, in so far as local identity has been preserved, that of Kent in the twentieth century has been very much shaped by the Conservative party, which has dominated the political representation of the county at Westminster, at County Hall and in the local town halls throughout much of this period. In a sense this domination has been misleading. It has been achieved, partly at least, by the fragmentation of the political opposition to the Conservative party. Although there has been much philosophical division within Conservatism throughout the century, whether over tariffs and free trade in the early years, over attitudes to the welfare state in the period after the Second World War, or over Britain's role in the European Union in the last decade, there has been no formal split within the party since the middle of the

---

1   J.C.D. Clark, *English Society, 1688–1832*, Cambridge 1985; L. Colley, *Britons: Forging the Nation, 1707–1837*, New Haven and London 1992.
2   D. Cannadine, *The Decline and Fall of the British Aristocracy*, New Haven and London 1990.

nineteenth century when an alliance of Peelites, Radicals and Whigs was bought together to form the modern Liberal party. By contrast, the Liberals split in the 1880s over Irish Home Rule and again, between 1916 and 1945, partly as a result of the personal divisions between Asquith and Lloyd George. On each occasion part of the former Liberal party, the Liberal Unionists in the 1880s and the Liberal Nationals in the 1940s, was absorbed into the Conservative party.[3] The divisions within the Liberal party were of enormous benefit to the emerging Labour party which finally replaced it as the main opponent of the Conservative party in most parts of the country during the 1920s.[4] Although the Labour party has never suffered such disastrous splits as the Liberal party, it was greatly weakened for several years by the establishment of the Social Democratic Party in 1981. The result has been that there have been several periods during the twentieth century in which the Conservative party has benefited electorally from the divisions among its opponents, especially during the 1920s and 1980s; in Kent, as elsewhere, this meant that Conservatives have been able to win seats at both parliamentary and local-government elections with minority support among the electorate, because the votes of their opponents did not go over-whelmingly to Labour or Liberal candidates but were divided more equally between them.

Throughout many of the chapters in this book, the results of Conservative domination in Kent are only too clear. In the 1920s and 1940s it resulted in a determined reluctance to implement government recommendations for social reform, partly on grounds of cost but more importantly because they were regarded as philosophically unacceptable. In the 1960s and 1970s Kent resisted government pressure for comprehensive education, believing that the retention of selection offered choice to parents and better standards for the academically gifted, though both these alleged benefits were challenged at the time, and have continued to be challenged thereafter, by independent research. The strength of political Conservatism in Kent led to the Conservative party locally adopting policies which, whilst acceptable to rank and file Conservatives, had been largely rejected by the party hierarchy between 1945 and 1975.[5] Some of the initiatives, especially in the field of social services, were to be adopted by the incoming Conservative government after 1979. Whereas the first three-quarters of the twentieth century had witnessed the growth of power by both central and local government, which had taken on responsibility for many services that had previously been left to the private or voluntary sectors, the last quarter has seen government policy being directed towards a withdrawal from public-sector provision and a return to a greater role for both the private and voluntary sectors. This has been achieved by a mixture of forced privatisation, particularly in respect of the nationalised industries, and legislation to either compel, or at

---

[3] C. Cook, *A Short History of the Liberal Party*, 2nd edn, London 1984, pp. 63–136.
[4] The main exceptions were South-West England and parts of rural Scotland and Wales.
[5] E.H.H. Green, 'Thatcherism: A Historical Perspective', *Transactions of the Royal Historical Society*, 6th Series, ix (1999), pp. 17–42.

least to encourage, local authorities and other public bodies to put the provision of specific services out to competitive tender. The determined attempt by central government between 1979 and 1997 to reduce the size of the public sector has resulted in local authorities employing fewer staff, maintaining fewer buildings and, in real terms, raising less revenue from the local community. That, however, is not the way that it has been perceived by many local council-taxpayers, who have tended to complain of having to pay more and more for ever poorer services.

The 'Thatcherite Revolution', which has been accepted, with some reservations, by the Conservative party's main political opponents, has permeated every aspect of public life, affecting schools, libraries, recreation, policing, the public utilities and the National Health Service. It was Thatcherism that prevented the public investment necessary to secure the provision of a new rail link between London and the Channel Tunnel and which has created many crises for cultural organisations and other contributors to the overall quality of life, which cannot generate sufficient income to ensure their survival. These are the negative effects of Thatcherism; but it has undoubtedly had its positive benefits as well; most public organisations, including local authorities, and those no longer in the public sector, have become both more efficient and more cost-effective. It remains to be seen how much of this legacy will survive or whether, in future years, there will be pressure for central and local government to begin to recover some of the functions that were lost in the 1980s and 1990s, and for the state to start to involve itself more in areas where the dominance of the profit motive is thought to be inappropriate.

The political developments of the twentieth century have had an enormous impact on the citizens of Kent, but there have been others equally important. The impact of two World Wars, and the enormous number of casualties that they created, have had a profound effect in both the long and the short term. It was the experience of unemployment and social deprivation in the inter-war period and the inability, or reluctance, of existing agencies to provide adequate relief that led to the creation of the welfare state after the Second World War. It was the destruction of communities, in both Britain and Europe, during the Second World War that led to the setting up of the Common Market and the European Union, which has provided both political stability and economic opportunity for Britain in the last quarter of the twentieth century, though not without some concerns being expressed from time to time about loss of sovereignty and the uncertainties of change. The twentieth century has witnessed, in Kent as for Britain as a whole, the continued decline of religion in the lives of people, a movement already well under way during the nineteenth century, but at the same time a massive increase in personal possessions, luxury goods and opportunities for employment. At the end of the twentieth century most people work far fewer hours for much greater financial reward, even when inflation is taken into account. Far more people own their own homes and are able to take holidays. Some sectors of the economy, such as leisure and recreation, have greatly expanded, though manufacturing has declined. Whilst it is not the case that poverty has been eliminated, it has been greatly reduced and there is universal provision for retirement and state pensions, which barely existed before 1900.

All these, and many other, themes are explored in the chapters that follow. There is in some, perhaps inevitably, a greater concentration on the first seven decades of the century than the last three, and for good reason. It is not the job of the historian to forecast the future and many of the significant developments of recent years cannot yet be viewed with objective impartiality or perspective. We can objectively assess the decline of agriculture and horticulture in Kent over the century, but it is still too early to assess what the impact of that will be on the countryside and those who live there. We can chronicle the reorganisation of the National Health Service but we do not yet know whether this will lead to improved health care in the future. It is difficult also to write about contemporary events – for which the historian shares all the same prejudices as any other member of the public – in a totally unbiased manner. Whilst all the contributors to this volume have endeavoured to put both sides of the contemporary arguments, their personal views cannot always be totally concealed, nor should they be. Nevertheless it is hoped that this survey of Kent in the twentieth century will present a balanced assessment of the events and personalities of the last hundred years, and prove to be of benefit both to those living in Kent now and to future generations of the county's inhabitants, as well as to the wider academic community.

1

Population

MICHAEL RAWCLIFFE

In the years covered in this chapter, the boundaries of north-west Kent registered several changes. Deptford, Greenwich, Lewisham and Woolwich had been incorporated into London under the Local Government Act 1888, which created the London County Council (LCC). Both this, and the creation of the Greater London Council (GLC) in 1964 reflected the outward expansion of suburbia. Within the boundary of the GLC the newly formed London Boroughs of Bexley and Bromley were created, with a combined population of half a million people. In 1988 the GLC was abolished, but the London Boroughs remained with enhanced powers. Many of the inhabitants of these two large suburban boroughs still like to add Kent to their address, feeling more affinity with the county than with south-east London.

Much of this chapter is based upon the printed decennial census statistics published between 1911 and 1991, and upon the statistics of birth, marriages and deaths. No census was taken in 1941 because of the Second World War, and so, where necessary, the mid-year estimates for 1939 have been used.

The census is usually conducted in April when the population is relatively stable. However, due to a strike, the census in 1921 was delayed until 19/20 June. This, combined with an abnormally warm summer, inflated the population figures for the Kentish seaside resorts. Thus we need to be cautious when comparing the figures for 1911 with those for 1921, and likewise 1921 with 1931. In addition the male losses in the First World War, and the deaths from influenza in 1918–19, must be borne in mind. If a census had been held in 1941 it would have revealed a considerably reduced civilian population, especially in the vulnerable coastal towns of Kent.

Because of the hundred-year rule, only the printed census statistics are available to a researcher of the twentieth century before 2002 (when the 1901 returns are due to be released). In spite of this the census volumes contain a wealth of general detail, and the questions asked have not only increased in number and range, but have also been refined in the light of experience. For example, in the last two censuses those present and those usually resident have been distinguished, making exact comparisons with earlier censuses difficult. Also, to take account of the loss of Bexley and Bromley, previous census figures for Kent have been adjusted to the new boundaries (see Table 1).

Table 1

Population Growth in Kent, the Boroughs of Bexley and Bromley, and England and Wales, 1911–91

	A		B				C	
	Administrative County minus Bexley and Bromley	% increase or decrease	Former Kent boroughs of Bexley and Bromley and London Boroughs from 1.4.69		% increase or decrease		England and Wales	% increase or decrease
Year			Bexley	Bromley	Bexley	Bromley		
	(000s)		(000s)	(000s)			(000s)	
1911	868.9		15,895	33,646			36,070	10.9
1921	938.1	8.0	21,457	35,052	35.0	4.2	37,887	5.0
1931	958.7	2.2	32,652	47,698	52.0	36.1	39,952	5.5
1951	1,090.2	13.7	88,791	64,179	172.2	34.6	43,758	9.5
1961	1,198.6	9.9	89,550	68,252	0.85	6.3	46,105	5.4
1971	1,399.5	16.8	217,076	305,377			48,750	5.6
1981	1,463.3	0.45*	214,800	294,500	-0.11*	-0.37*	49,634	1.8
1991	1,493.9	0.21*	211,404	282,920	-0.16*	-0.40*	51,100	3.0

* per cent per year

It is believed that in the 1921 census the population of the county was overestimated by 3.6%. The population of Margate MB was the most distorted, by 40.3%, followed by that of Broadstairs and St Peters UD by 28%.[1] The result was that, whilst Kent's population growth between 1901 and 1911 had been rather lower than England and Wales, the growth between 1911 and 1921 was shown to be nearly double.[2]

Kent's population and development was, and is, clearly linked with that of London. Between 1901 and 1921 the LCC's population was relatively static. The real development came in Greater London where the dormitory population resided. For example between 1911 and 1921 the largest population increases were in Bexley UD (35%) and Crayford UD (91.3%).[3] Other areas which saw considerable growth were Bromley RD (21.5%) and Penge UD (21.5%). By contrast Canterbury CB and Cranbrook RD each declined by 5.7%.

The population in 1921 was most densely concentrated in the north-west of the county, and the Medway towns. In total numbers, Gillingham, with a population of 54,026, was the largest borough, followed by Margate, 46,480, and Chatham, 42,013. Interestingly Chatham's population had fractionally declined (by 0.6%) since 1911. This was no doubt caused by the reduction in naval personnel and dockyard workers after the First World War. The loss by migration of 4,476 outweighed the excess of births over deaths by 237. This large migration loss was also seen in Dover MB (7,650), Gillingham MB (4,153) and Rochester MB (2,334).

During the decade 1911–21 Kent's population increased by 9.2%, nearly double that of England and Wales. In the next decade there was a 6.8% increase, compared with 5.5% for England and Wales. Whilst the 9.2% may have been exaggerated due to the June census, the 1921–31 increase may well be an underestimate.[4]

The 1931 census reveals considerable growth in the dormitory or suburban boroughs of north-west Kent, compared with the modest growth of 1911–21 (see Table 2). By contrast Margate MB and Broadstairs and St Peters UD declined by 34.1% and 16.6% respectively. Of even more significance is the continued relative decline of the rural districts. By 1931 the municipal boroughs and urban districts contained 72% of the population. Meanwhile the north-west Kent suburbs were attracting most of their migrants from the more densely populated areas of London,[5] but also some from Kent itself. By contrast Maidstone MB had grown by 14.4% between 1921 and 1931, drawing most of its

1   *Census of England and Wales 1921: County of Kent*, London 1923, p. viii.
2   *Ibid.*, p. ix.
3   Crayford's increase was aided by the transfer of 2,455 acres from Dartford RD on 1.10.1920.
4   Kent's population includes Bexley MB and Bromley MB, and thus the percentages are higher than in Table 1; *Census of England and Wales 1931: County of Kent*, London 1933, p. vii.
5   Penge UD with a high density, more typical of Inner London, had a loss by migration of 0.5%.

Table 2

Growth of Selected MBs and UDs in NW Kent,
1911–21 and 1921–31

	1911–1921 % growth	1921–1931 % growth
Kent	9.2	6.8
Beckenham UD	5.2	31.4
Bexley UD	35.0	53.5
Bromley MB	4.2	29.4
Sidcup UD	5.3	38.2

migrants from Kent.[6] At this stage the growth of Gillingham and Chatham MBs was below the county average, at 5.7% and 2.3% respectively.

Because of the Second World War the census for 1941 did not take place, and thus the 1951 census encompassed a considerable period of change. The introduction to the published 1951 census statistics[7] divided the two decades into four useful sections:

a. 1931–1939. During this period the expansion of suburbia is clearly seen, with the Greater London area continuing to increase at an even greater rate. This rate was much greater than for the county as a whole. Thus we see the expansion of Kent by 17% with the Outer Ring[8] expanding by 23%. Within the latter Beckenham MB expanded by 48.4%. This expansion of the suburbs of north-west Kent was at the expense of Inner London. The period saw the continued development of large estates, and the desire of people to move out into areas of lower density. Other areas of noticeable growth were the Medway Towns of Chatham, Gillingham and Rochester, which rose by 16%, and the coastal areas of Broadstairs UD, Deal MB, Herne Bay UD and Whitstable UD, which rose by 13%. These coastal towns continued to attract those retiring from the built-up areas in Kent, and other counties. Other towns such as Maidstone MB, Sevenoaks UD and Tonbridge UD rose by only 11%. By contrast Margate MB and Ramsgate MB saw little growth (5.5% and 4%) and the rural districts as a whole grew by only 4%.

b. 1939–1941. This period coincided with heavy air attacks. The suburban areas near London, Thameside, the Medway towns and the coastal towns most liable to invasion, saw the biggest decreases through migration or evacuation, especially in 1941. Interestingly there was movement into the inland rural districts, and into Maidstone, Sevenoaks and Tonbridge. Overall, Kent saw a larger decrease in population than the country as a whole.

---

[6] As late as 1951 Maidstone had 66.9% of its population born in Kent; *Census of England and Wales 1951: County of Kent*, London 1954, Table 18, p. 93.

[7] *Ibid.*, p. xiii.

[8] The Outer Ring was the area immediately outside the administrative County of London.

c. 1941–1948. Apart from 1944, when Germany launched its rocket offensive, the population began to return to their homes, and the pre-war pattern was resumed. With demobilisation, the population of Kent increased to about its 1939 level, but the greatest increases remained in the north-west Kent suburbs.

d. 1948–1951. The final three years saw the continuation of the trend, and there is some evidence to show that several of those who had been evacuated from Inner London were reluctant to return and instead remained in the suburbs and other less densely populated parts of Kent.

The 1961 census shows a yearly increase of 0.84% in Kent's population over 1951. Some 0.77% of this was accounted for by internal migration. The largest administrative unit was Bexley MB, where the population had reached 89,550, a yearly increase of 0.9%. Most of the available building land in the suburbs had been developed before 1939, and thus it was the areas slightly further out that saw the largest increase. For example Dartford RD (3.56%), Gravesend MB (1.43%), Maidstone MB (1.01%), Maidstone RD (1.16%), Orpington UD (3.56%), Rochester MB (1.33%) and Strood RD (3.26%)[9] all saw gains in excess of the Kentish suburbs. This suggests that migrants were attracted to areas where communications were good for those commuting, and house prices were sufficiently low to compensate for the cost of travel. Maidstone may be the exception, for both the MB and the surrounding RD expanded, reflecting not only migration from the surrounding area but also the development of housing estates for its indigenous population. Maidstone therefore had both commuters and many who were employed in the locality.

For the first time the RDs saw a greater growth than the MBs and UDs. The former grew at 1.35% per year, compared with the MBs and UDs (0.7%).[10] However, some areas saw a population loss. These were Eastry RD (–0.22%), Queenborough MB (–0.3%), Lydd MB (–0.28%) and Sheerness UD (–1.41%).

As a result of the creation of the GLC, most of the north-west Kent suburbs, with a joint population of just over half a million, were transferred from the county. Overall, Kent increased its population between 1961 and 1971 by 16.8%, compared with 9.9% in the previous decade (see Table 3).[11]

Between 1961 and 1971 the percentage of people living in MBs and UDs declined by 3.3%, but still nearly two-thirds of the county lived in them. However, the densities of some of the RDs had distinctly urban characteristics, especially in certain wards. The largest decennial increases were seen in Ashford UD (24.3%), Lydd MB (48.1%), New Romney MB (30.4%), Sittingborne and Milton UD (27.2%), Tonbridge UD (34.2%) and Whitstable UD (26.2%). Conversely Folkestone MB (–0.8%) and Southborough UD (–0.2%) declined over the decade.

Once again, wards in rural districts contiguous to urban areas saw considerable development. For example the population of Ashford UD increased by

9   All per-year increases.
10   Kent grew at an annual rate of 0.84% between 1951 and 1961.
11   Figures adjusted to incorporate new boundaries of the county.

Table 3

The Population of Kent, the MBs and UDs, and RDs, 1951–71

	Population			% increase per decade	
	1951	1961	1971	1951/61	1961/71
Kent	1,091,153	1,198,564	1,399,463	9.9	16.8
MBs and UDs	751,144	810,813	917,194	7.6	12.4
RDs	312,192	357,336	449,093	13.5	23.1

24.3% in 1961–71 whereas adjacent West Ashford RD saw an increase of 41.4% (see Maps 1 and 2) Meanwhile in the newly created London Boroughs of Bexley and Bromley the decennial increases were only 3.4% and 4% respectively.

In the 1981 census the distinction was made between those who were 'present' and those who were temporarily away on census night. In order to maintain comparison with earlier census figures, only those 'present' have been included in the population figures given for 1981 and 1991.

Between 1971 and 1981 the county as a whole experienced a 4.9% population increase, whilst Dartford (6%) and Sevenoaks (10%) saw an even greater one. During this period the population of England and Wales increased by only 0.5%. Direct comparisons over time within the county are complicated by local government reorganisation in 1973/4 whereby all the existing boroughs, UDs and RDs were merged to form fourteen districts. The boundaries of the former local authorities and of the new districts are shown in Maps 3 and 4.

Compared with 1961–71, when the county had increased its population by 200,899, an increase of 1.56% per year, the 1981–91 increase was only 1.7% over the decade. As Map 4 shows, Canterbury (5.9%) and Ashford (6.6%) had the largest decennial increases, whilst in the western districts the population actually fell, with Gravesham seeing the largest decrease (4.5%). The district of Rochester-upon-Medway had the largest population despite an overall decline of 0.6%. By contrast, the second largest population was in Maidstone which had increased its population by 2.9%. Gillingham was by far the most densely populated district with 11.9 persons per acre (29.4 per hectare).[12] At the other end of the scale was Ashford, which was the most thinly populated district, with only 0.6 persons per acre, as against the county's 1.6 (4 per hectare) and 1.3 (3.2 per hectare) in England and Wales.

Similar declines over the decade to those of Kent's western districts were to be found in adjoining Greater London, which had a 4.9% loss of population. Bexley and Bromley were both losing population, but the other former Kentish boroughs of Lewisham and Greenwich were suffering an even greater loss. In fact Greater London had declined from 8,197,000 inhabitants in 1951 to

---

[12] One hectare = 2.471 acres. Whilst the Census now uses hectares, acres have been retained so that comparisons may be made from 1921.

6,692,200 in 1991. This can be seen as part of the continuing movement outward from Inner London to Greater London and into the outer suburbs, with a similar, but less strong pull inwards from the county into the less densely populated suburban fringe. Bromley was the least densely populated London Borough, with 7.7 persons per acre (19.1 per hectare) against an average for Outer London of 13.4 per acre (33.2 per hectare).

In conclusion one must note that throughout the period under consideration, growth was unevenly divided within and between the units of local government. For example between 1911 and 1921 Bromley MB had risen in population by 1,406. However, of the six wards, the two most densely populated, the Town and the adjoining Martin's Hill wards had declined, whilst the others had increased. Similarly, in the larger London Borough of Bromley in the 1991 census four of the wards had increased whilst five had declined since 1981.[13]

(1) Births and Deaths

Professor Alan Armstrong[14] has demonstrated that in no five-year cycle between 1851 and 1911 did the death rate in Kent fall below 12.8 per 1,000 (the figure in 1906–10), while there was a peak of 20 per 1,000 in 1866–70. In the period since 1914 the overall average is much lower, and is within the parameters of 10.5 in 1923 and 16.1 in 1918.[15] One must note the effect of the two World Wars. The Registrar General differentiates between those who died as civilians, and those civilians killed as a result of enemy action. Those who died in active service were excluded. It may seen odd that the civilian death rates for the war years 1915–18 are higher than any subsequent figures. This may be due to two factors. Firstly, many males volunteered for active service before conscription was introduced in 1916. This may well have taken away the healthiest male group, having the effect of raising the overall death rate. Secondly, 1918–19 saw the most severe influenza epidemic in modern times, and this affected both sexes.

The first influenza outbreak was between July and September 1918, the second from October to December 1918 and the third from January to March 1919. The areas hit most severely are listed in Table 4. In Kent, Folkestone had the highest number of deaths in the first wave, Bromley in the second, and Chatham in the third. Bromley had the highest number of overall deaths, closely followed by Erith.

Influenza is a viral infection which strikes very quickly, usually within three days. As yet there is no known cure. In addition, influenza can also lead to other diseases such as pneumonia, which may increase the risk of death amongst the old and frail as a result of its debilitating tendencies. It has been estimated that

13   *Bromley in 1991*, Bromley 1993, vol. 1, table 2.2.
14   *The Economy of Kent, 1640–1914*, ed. W. A. Armstrong, Woodbridge 1995, p. 42.
15   The statistics are drawn from *The Registrar General's Statistical Review of England and Wales for the Year 1923*, London 1925, table LXXX, p. 141.

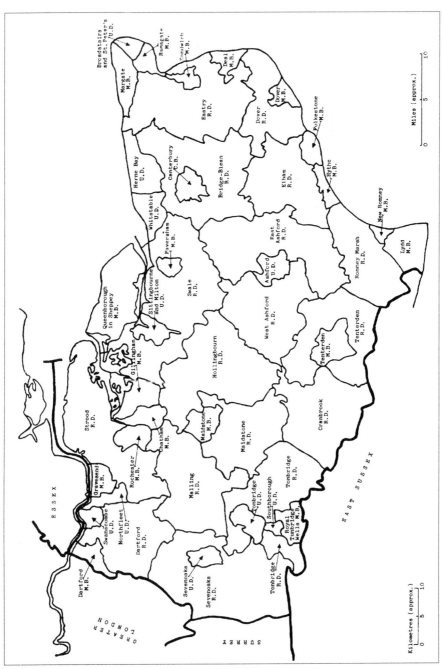

Map 3. Map of Kent showing local authority boundaries, 1971 (*Census of England and Wales 1971: County of Kent*, Part I, London 1973, p. x).

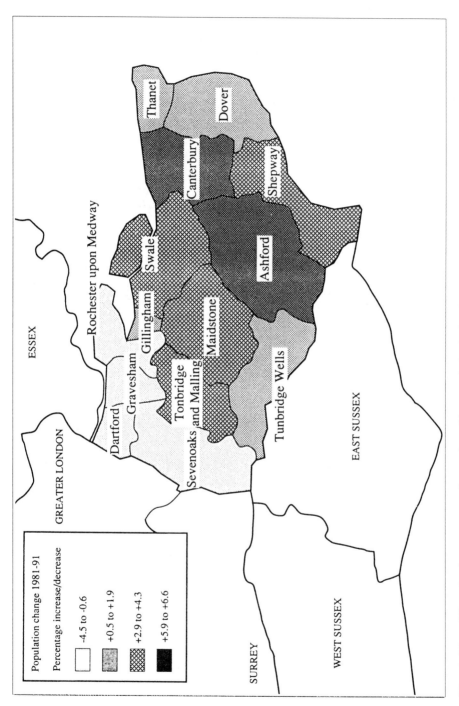

Map 4. Map of Kent showing percentage changes in resident population by local authority district, 1981–91 (*Census of England and Wales 1991: County of Kent*, Part I, London 1993, p. 12).

Population change 1981-91

Percentage increase/decrease

- -4.5 to -0.6
- +0.5 to +1.9
- +2.9 to +4.3
- +5.9 to +6.6

ESSEX

GREATER LONDON

Rochester upon Medway

Dartford

Gravesham

Gillingham

Swale

Thanet

Canterbury

Dover

Shepway

Ashford

Maidstone

Tonbridge

Sevenoaks and Malling

Tunbridge Wells

SURREY

WEST SUSSEX

EAST SUSSEX

Table 4

Deaths from Influenza in Kent – Sixteen Highest Local Authorities, 1918–19

	July–Sept 1918	Oct–Dec 1918	Jan–Mar 1919	Total Deaths
Beckenham UD	114	128	33	275
Bromley MB	148	134	111	393
Canterbury CB	77	17	43	137
Chatham MB	95	5	150	250
Dartford UD	137	9	114	260
Dover MB	89	95	95	279
Erith UD	94	125	148	367
Folkestone MB	154	124	60	338
Gillingham MB	95	102	138	335
Gravesend MB	130	77	120	327
Maidstone MB	114	23	67	204
Margate MB	148	26	123	297
Penge UD	137	95	87	319
Ramsgate MB	101	94	74	269
Rochester MB	114	24	26	164
Tunbridge Wells MB	130	57*	95	292

* 51.7% of all deaths recorded

more people died of influenza in Europe in 1918–19 than were killed on active service in the First World War. The Registrar General considered it of such importance that several pages of the 1919 Annual Report were devoted to it. The Kent figures would suggest that areas near London, those which were ports, with access to the continent, and areas with a high percentage of elderly people suffered most. Folkestone, which fitted into two of these categories, had the most influenza deaths in July to September 1918. The sixteen areas listed in Table 4 had 4,496 deaths, at least one-third of the total deaths in Kent. The random nature of the outbreaks is both clear and puzzling. Whilst Erith suffered a progressive increase in the number of influenza deaths, other areas such as Bromley[16] and Ramsgate saw a successive decline, whilst Chatham, Dartford and Margate had significant lows in the second wave. Perhaps the only generalisation which may be made is that all the areas listed had close contacts with other areas: commuters in Beckenham, Bromley, Dartford and Erith; ports such as Dover, Folkestone, Margate and Ramsgate; and market towns such as Canterbury and Maidstone.

16 There are only two references to the influenza in the *Bromley and District Times*. The first, on 1 November 1918, noted: 'The "flu" has been responsible for a good deal of staff disruption, our own staff among the numbers.' The second, on the 6 December 1919, implies that a shortage of glass bottles made the epidemic worse. The article said that materials such as Bovril were available, but could not be dispensed sufficiently. It called for the early demobilisation of glass-factory workers.

Table 5

Birth Rates per 1000 live births in Kent by Selected Areas, 1911–71

	England and Wales	Kent	Bromley	Chatham	Sevenoaks RD	All urban districts	All rural districts
1911	24.3	21.1	19.5	26.3	18.7	21.2	20.8
1921	22.4	20.0	17.9	23.4	17.6	19.4	20.2
1931	15.8	14.9	13.6	18.0	15.0	14.9	14.9
1941	13.9	15.0	13.1	18.8	12.9	15.1	14.4
1951	15.5	14.8	14.2	15.8	14.7	14.7	14.9
1961	17.6	16.4	14.2	20.6	15.3	16.2	17.2
1971	15.9	16.1	14.0	23.1	13.0	16.2	15.8
1911–15	23.6	20.4	18.5	20.8	18.1	20.0	20.6
1916–20	20.1	19.4	18.1	23.6	18.2	18.8	19.5
1921–25	19.9	18.0	16.2	21.4	17.0	17.7	17.9
1926–30	16.7	15.5	17.0	19.2	15.2	15.4	15.5

Deaths in the Second World War hit suburban north-west Kent the hardest. In 1941 Kent lost 638 civilians, Bromley accounting for 95 of them. In the following year, 1942, there were 238 deaths, with the following areas suffering the greatest loss – Beckenham 81, Bexley 66, Bromley 62, and Penge 86.

Unlike the death rates, birth rates in Kent followed a more discernible downward pattern between 1911 and 1991. Comparing figures for 1911 and 1971 there was a 40.3% decline in the birth rate in Kent, and comparable declines in the areas selected in Table 5. The real fall came between 1921 and 1931 when the birth rate for Kent fell by 25.5%. This was mirrored by the rural districts, and even boroughs such as Chatham, which had a birth rate well above the Kent average, saw a decline of 23.1%. The years following both World Wars experienced a rising birth rate. In 1920 the birth rate rose to 23.9 which was higher than for each of the three pre-war years of 1911–13 (average 20.8). Chatham experienced a similarly brief rise, but this was followed by an almost progressive decline. Chatham's birth rate by 1936 was not dissimilar to the Kent average (see Table 6).

The end of the Second World War shows an increase in the birth rate for Kent to 21.2 in 1946, but by 1951 it had declined to 14.8. Whilst there are increases to 16.4 and 18.2 in 1961 and 1966, the 1970s saw a decline to 16.1 in 1971 and 12.3 in 1976. Subsequently the Kent birth rate has not registered above 13 per 1,000.[17] It seems clear that the trend towards later marriage and smaller families has had its effect on the birth rate.

[17] Chatham's birth rate in 1971 was 23.1 per 1,000, seven points above the Kent rate.

Table 6

Birth Rates per 1000 live births, in Kent, Chatham MB,
UDs and RDs 1921–36

	Kent	All UDs	Chatham	All RDs
1921	20.0	19.4	23.4	20.2
1922	18.6	18.7	22.4	18.5
1923	18.2	18.3	21.1	18.2
1924	16.5	16.5	19.7	16.6
1925	16.5	16.5	20.3	16.3
1926	16.2	16.3	20.2	16.1
1927	15.4	15.5	21.2	15.1
1928	15.4	15.3	18.1	15.3
1929	15.3	15.3	18.0	15.1
1930	15.2	15.2	18.6	15.2
1931	14.9	14.9	18.0	14.9
1936	14.6	14.6	15.5	14.6

(2) Sexes, Ages and Marital Condition

The census of 1921 gave the first clear indication of the effects of the First World War upon the population, with a decline in the number of males aged 20–39, many of whom had died on active service.[18] War losses therefore offset the expected increase in population resulting from a higher birth rate between 1880 and 1900. In addition, male deaths in the war led to an increase in the number of women who were single or widowed. In 1921 there was an excess of 57,490 females over males, an increase of 31,851 on that of 1911.

The impact of the First World War continued to be demonstrated long after it was over. In the 1931 census the number of widowed women in Kent between the ages of 30 and 38 was 2,467, though the sex ratio is reduced from 1,106 to 1,087 females per 1,000 males. It will be noted that this was still above the 1,063 of 1911.

The 1931 census also showed a decline in the number of children under the age of ten compared with 1921, reflecting a falling birth rate, whilst the rise since 1921 in the number of males between ages 20 and 39 was probably due to movement into north-west Kent of new migrants and their families. Some came

---

[18] Once the Armistice had been declared in November 1918, newspapers begun to publish lists of the war dead by town, village, church and association or school. War memorials today are a living reminder of how the First World War affected virtually every community, however small. With conscription in 1916, the impact of war transcends social class. The war memorial at Goudhurst was unveiled on Sunday 30 November 1924. A year earlier the Goudhurst branch of the Loyal Men of Kent had honoured the nineteen members killed in the war. See A. W. Tiffin, *The Goudhurst Coronation Book*, Tunbridge Wells 1937, p. 505.

Table 7

Population by Age Groups, 1931–51

Age last birthday	Kent			England and Wales
	1931 persons (000s)	1951 persons (000s)	% increase or decrease 1931–51	% increase or decrease
All ages	1219.3	1564.3	28.3	9.3
0–4	88.3	135.6	53.6	24.4
5–9	99.1	115.5	16.5	−4.6
10–14	97.8	101.0	3.3	−11.3
15–24	200.1	191.8	−4.1	−19.0
25–34	188.8	214.5	13.6	−1.3
35–44	166.5	236.6	42.1	23.0
45–54	153.4	215.9	40.7	21.3
55–64	118.8	164.0	38.1	22.7
65 and over	106.5	189.3	77.8	61.6

to live in the suburbs to commute to work elsewhere; others to work locally in the building industry and allied trades.

Because of the Second World War, the next census was not taken until 1951. The two main factors affecting the age distribution in Kent were the decline in fertility and the heavy inward migration from other areas, including London. As we have noted earlier, the latter not only occurred between 1931 and 1951 but had been a trend from the end of the nineteenth century. Thus numbers in the middle age-groups tended to be larger than the younger age-groups because of earlier high birth rates. The numbers in the 0–4 age-group were proportionately higher than the next two groups because of the high post-war birth rate in 1946 and 1947. In both years Kent reflected the national trend.

The effects of this changing fertility was masked by internal immigration into the county, especially into north-west Kent. This accounted for the higher numbers in certain age-groups than would have been expected to have survived since the 1931 census. Thus the number in the 25–34 age-groups in Kent in 1951 was higher than that in the 5–14 group in 1931, and even at 55–64 the numbers were higher than if deaths in the intervening years were the only consideration (see Table 7).

The extent to which Kent was a net gainer from inward migration between 1931 and 1951 is shown by comparing the percentage increases for Kent with that of England and Wales. In spite of the fact that there was only one age-range where there was a maximum 0.8% difference between the Kent figures and those of England and Wales, Kent's population increased by 28.3% compared with the national increase of 9.5%. The table shows that Kent had gained a considerable number of young or middle-aged adults, and their families, by migration.

Table 8

Age Distribution in Selected MBs and UDs in Kent, 1951

Administrative area	% distribution by age group		
	15	15–64	65+
Chatham MB	24.5	54.9	10.7
Chislehurst and Sidcup UD	25.2	66.7	8.1
Crayford UD	24.8	67.1	8.3
Deal MB	24.1	63.3	12.6
New Romney MB	24.5	61.7	13.8
Orpington UD	24.1	65.5	10.4
Queenborough MB	26.2	63.0	10.8
Rochester MB	24.2	65.4	10.2
Kent	**22.5**	**65.4**	**12.1**
Beckenham MB	19.8	67.9	12.3
Bromley MB	20.5	56.9	12.6
Folkestone MB	20.6	64.7	14.7
Herne Bay UD	19.3	59.5	22.5
Hythe MB	20.2	61.5	18.3
Royal Tunbridge Wells MB	19.4	62.0	18.6
Sevenoaks UD	18.7	64.9	14.4
Whitstable UD	20.2	59.0	20.8

Note: The Kent average is placed in the middle of this table. Those areas with a percentage distribution by age under 15 of over 24% are placed in the upper part of the table, those with a percentage distribution of less than 21% in the lower part.

The effects of the First World War were still to be seen in the 1931 and 1951 age and sex differences. In 1931 the males in the 35–44 age-group were under-represented[19] and thus in 1951 there are only 31.9% in the male population in this age-group. Conversely the males in the 55–64 age-group saw only a 15.4% increase, compared with a female increase of 29.4%. The Second World War deaths were roughly half that of the First, and their effects are less noticeable. The female numbers in the younger age-groups are also depleted due to wartime marriages and subsequent emigration.

The 1951 figures also demonstrated the ageing of the Kent population. In that year, 12.1% of the population were 65 and over, compared with 8.7% in 1931. These percentages were higher than for England and Wales which were 7.4% in 1931 and 10.9% in 1951. The 1951 figures also showed fewer persons in the younger working category of 15–34 years. By 1951 it had been reduced to 26% from 32% in 1931.

Between 1931 and 1951 there was a significant increase in the number

[19] The 600,000–700,000 deaths in the First World War had hit this age-group in 1931 very hard.

Table 9

Percentage of Persons 65 and over in Selected Coastal Towns, 1951–71

Administrative area	1951 (%)	1961 (%)	1971 (%)
Broadstairs and St Peters UD	19.0	26.4	28.0
Deal MB	12.6	15.9	19.0
Folkestone MB	14.7	19.3	22.0
Herne Bay UD	22.2	26.8	31.8
Hythe MB	18.3	22.2	25.4
Margate MB	16.0	19.3	26.2
Whitstable UD	20.8	25.2	23.3

married in the younger age-groups. In 1951 Kent had more married over the age of fifteen than nationally. This may well have been due to the number of younger couples moving into the county to live. Whilst the number of young married couples increased, so also did the divorce rate with a fivefold increase since 1931. This represented 6.3 per 1,000 for those over 15, as against a national rate of 6.0.

If one looks at the age distribution between the various areas of Kent in 1951, one sees considerable variation. Table 8 highlights the differences in the under-15 age-group in the new outer suburbs of north-west Kent (Chislehurst and Sidcup, Crayford, Orpington) and the Medway towns, with the older suburbs (Beckenham and Bromley) and the coastal resorts. Conversely those 65 and over were concentrated on the coast. More than one in five of the population of Herne Bay and Whitstable were in this category. This contrasts with Chislehurst and Sidcup, and Crayford, where only 8.1% and 8.3% respectively were over the age of 65. Of those in the working age-range, 15–64, both Bromley (56.9%) and Chatham (54.9%) were well below the county figure of 65.4%. This may well reflect the ageing of earlier migrants to the area in the 1920s and 1930s.

By 1961 the population aged 65 and over in the county had risen to 13.2% from 12.1% in 1951 whilst the under 15s had risen marginally from 22.5% to 23% in the decade. The trends noted in the 1951 census for the over 65s by area were continued; whilst those in the commuter areas remained roughly similar, there was a marked increase in the already high rates for the coastal resorts (see Table 9). Direct comparisons with 1981 and 1991 are difficult because of the grouping into districts. Nevertheless the districts revealed further development of the 1951–71 pattern. In the pensionable group,[20] in the fourteen districts all but three showed an increase between 1981 and 1991. Clearly within some coastal towns the percentage of pensioners was even larger. The largest increase was in the over-75 age-range with some areas showing a 25% increase.

---

[20] Defined as men 65, women 60.

Table 10

Population by Age in Kent and its Districts, 1981 and 1991

	Under 15		Pensionable age (65m and 60w)	
	1981 (%)	1991 (%)	1981 (%)	1991 (%)
Kent	22.7	20.1	18.4	19.3
Ashford	23.6	21.3	17.9	18.8
Canterbury	20.5	18.7	24.7	24.8
Dartford	22.0	19.5	16.2	16.9
Dover	21.1	19.4	20.7	21.7
Gillingham	24.8	23.0	14.1	14.5
Gravesham	23.9	20.8	14.7	16.8
Maidstone	23.4	20.1	16.2	17.2
Rochester upon Medway	25.2	22.0	13.4	14.4
Sevenoaks	22.8	20.0	15.7	18.2
Shepway	20.0	18.6	25.2	24.7
Swale	24.3	21.5	16.8	17.3
Thanet	19.4	18.6	28.2	27.7
Tonbridge and Malling	24.0	20.2	14.5	16.1
Tunbridge Wells	22.1	18.9	19.9	19.5

Conversely, every district had a decreased percentage of those fifteen and under, though the under fives increased in all but one of the districts. The exception was Gillingham which stayed at 7.6%, whilst remaining the district with the highest percentage of under 15s (see Table 10).

(3) Households

Family size brings together many of the previous statistics on population. In 1921 private families[21] accounted for 91.1% of the population of Kent. The major reasons for the decline in family size are mainly attributed to earlier household formation, young people leaving home earlier and establishing separate households, increasing longevity and the rise in the number of separations and divorces.

Whilst the average size of families fell radically between 1921 and 1931, the number of private families increased by 22.6%, whilst the population in private

---

[21] *Census 1921 Kent*, p. 3. A private family is defined thus: 'any person or group of persons included in a separate return as being in separate occupation of any premises or part of premises is treated as a separate family for Census purposes'.

families increased by only 9%. This can be explained by the high marriage rate and the decline in the death rate. Thus, between 1921 and 1931 there was a decrease in the number of families containing five persons or more and an increase in families of up to three in number. Two- to three-person families in 1931 accounted for 48.1%, compared with 37.2% in 1911, and 40.1% in 1921. The largest families of eight and over saw a considerable decrease, and in 1936 they accounted for only 3.6% of all families. As we shall see in Chapter 6, the consequences of the combination of a rising number of families/households and their decreasing size were to have a significant effect upon housing needs in Kent and elsewhere.

Another feature evident from the 1981 census was the number of households in Kent where there were one or more children under 16 living with one adult over 16. In Kent as a whole, 5.2% of children lived in such households, varying from 4% in Sevenoaks to 8.3% in Thanet. Expressed in another way, 1.8% of all households in Kent were in this category, with Sevenoaks and Tonbridge and Malling at 1.5% and Thanet at 2.4%.[22] In the 1991 census the percentage of single parents had risen to 3%, with the highest incidences in Gillingham (3.6%) and Thanet (3.9%).[23]

A further feature of the smaller family was the number of households with people living alone. In 1981 they accounted for 20.5% and by 1991 the figure had risen to 24.7%. The highest incidences in both years were in Thanet, and the lowest in Tonbridge and Malling.

In the *Planning Strategy for Kent*, published in 1990, it was shown that in 1986 one-person households were most common in east Kent, of which Thanet formed a part. Here they accounted for 25.8% of all households. Mid-and west Kent and north Kent accounted for 20.9% and 20.0% respectively. The planners envisaged that the percentages would increase over the period 1986 to 2001 as follows: mid- and west Kent 41.9%; north Kent 47.3%; and east Kent 31.3% – an overall figure for Kent of 38.5%. This will have clear implications for future housing provision. Many of those living alone were pensioners. In 1981 28.3% of pensioners living in Kent were in this category.[24]

The number of two or more pensioner households was 11.2% of all households in 1981 and 10.7% in 1991. Thanet, which included Margate and Broadstairs, contained 42.9% of households in this category, decreasing to 35.2% in 1991. Conversely Rochester-upon-Medway had the lowest such figures: 19.1% in 1981 and 19.9% in 1991. The high incidence of pensioners, and their increasing longevity, has considerable implications not only for housing, but also for the provision of health and social services.

Another factor which became evident from the census questions in 1991 concerned births outside marriage. In no district was the illegitimacy rate less

[22] *Kent County Monitor*, London 1981, table D, p. 5.
[23] *Kent County Monitor*, London 1991, table 1, p. 23. The County Monitors were published both separately and also incorporated into each County Report. The numbering is the same in each case.
[24] *Kent County Monitor*, 1981, p. 5.

Table 11

Births outside Marriages in Selected Areas, 1991

Administrative area	Births outside marriage %	Unmarried couples with children at same address %
England and Wales	30.2	–
Kent	27.9	65.2
Dartford	23.9	71.4
Dover	28.2	60.4
Gravesham	27.7	59.0
Sevenoaks	21.9	68.3
Shepway	33.3	69.8
Swale	30.9	65.9
Thanet	38.5	59.7
Tonbridge	21.5	73.7
Tunbridge Wells	22.1	72.7
Greater London		
Bexley	25.2	65.5
Bromley	24.4	63.7
Greenwich	40.1	57.1
Lewisham	44.8	52.2

than 20%; many of these parents were single mothers. Significantly, however, 65.2% of children in Kent were born to parents of different surnames living at the same address (see Table 11). Some of these couples may later have married, but both sets of figures show that marriage is far from being considered a prerequisite for the development of a family.

(4) Migration

In spite of the problems involved in plotting migration into or out of the county with any real accuracy, certain trends are clear.[25] Whilst migration into the county between 1911 and 1921 was minimal at just over 1%, the growth of suburbia and general movement outwards from London was reflected in the period 1931–51, with most of the growth taking place before the war. Whilst there were boundary changes which make direct comparisons difficult, the suburbanisation of north-west Kent beyond the Victorian boroughs of Bromley and Beckenham was remarkable (see Table 12).

[25] The problem of inflation in the 1921 figures make comparisons with 1911 and 1931 difficult. Also the loss of Bexley and Bromley in the 1960s and the district reorganisation of 1973/4 create difficulties for analysis of the second half of the century.

Table 12

Gains by Migration in Selected Areas of Kent, 1931–51

Administrative area	Total increase (%)	By births and deaths (%)	Balance by migration (%)
Kent AC and CB.	28.3	9.5	18.8
Municipal Boroughs and Urban Districts	31.8	10.0	21.8
Bexley MB	172.2	35.7	136.5
Chislehurst and Sidcup UD	208.8	31.1	177.7
Orpington UD	145.0	28.1	116.9
Crayford UD	72.2	25.7	46.5
Rural Districts	18.1	8.4	9.7

Nevertheless the average growth in Kent over the two decades was 18%. Bexley, Chislehurst and Orpington increased at a considerably greater rate. Meanwhile the urban districts and municipal boroughs as a whole expanded by 21.8% and the rural districts also experienced modest growth. This was frequently in the rural districts surrounding towns, such as Maidstone (see Table 13). It will be noted that between 1951 and 1961, whilst migration into Kent and also into the MBs and UDs had been considerably reduced, migration into the RDs had increased. The rapid expansion of both Bexley and Chislehurst and Sidcup had slowed dramatically, reflecting the fact that most of the easily available land had been developed between 1931 and 1939. However, the two areas adjoining had seen a considerable inflow of migrants. Both Dartford MB and Orpington UD had seen increases well above the average for MBs or UDs, whilst Herne Bay UD, Broadstairs UD and Tenterden MB had experienced a dramatic rise of between 15.1% and 21.7%. Given the fact that all three areas saw deaths outnumber births, reflecting an already older population, the new migrants may well have been of retiring age at Broadstairs and Herne Bay, though not so at Tenterden.

The post-war trend was confirmed in 1991 with the four districts of Seven-oaks, Dartford, Gravesham and Rochester-upon-Medway experiencing a decrease in population, whilst the rest saw real growth, with Ashford and Canterbury growing by 6.6% and 5.9% respectively. Table 14 considers not only the growth in each district but also the part played by migration. Several of those districts with a negative natural increase saw considerable internal migration. Canterbury saw a 6.6% growth, a 4.2% balance of deaths over births, compensated by 10.1% internal migration. In general, districts with a large percentage of older people, and an excess of deaths over births, still attracted a substantial number of migrants. In many cases these were no doubt pensioners retiring to the coast and/or to cheaper housing areas. Conversely, the Medway towns saw a loss of population, though the younger age structure resulted in an excess of

Table 13

Decennial Increases or Decreases by Selected Areas, 1951–61

Administrative area	1931–51 % growth per year	Increase or decrease in 1951–61 (+ or -) % per year		
		Total	By births and deaths	Balance of inward or outward migration
Kent	1.26	0.84	0.37	0.48
MBs and UDs	1.39	0.70	0.37	0.33
Rural Districts	0.83	1.35	0.34	1.01
Bexley MB	5.14	0.09	0.44	−0.35
Chislehurst and Sidcup UD	5.81	0.36	0.69	−0.33
Broadstairs UD	0.85	1.19	−0.32	1.51
Dartford MB	1.76	1.22	0.16	1.05
Herne Bay MB	1.17	1.49	−0.67	2.17
Orpington UD	4.59	2.39	0.75	1.63
Tenterden MB	1.01	1.53	−0.64	2.17
Tonbridge UD	0.67	1.41	0.41	1.01
Elham RD	0.21	0.64	−0.70	1.33
West Ashford RD	0.96	−0.66	0.55	1.21

births over deaths. Nevertheless, one may assume from the table that the area was no longer attractive to migrants, or, conversely, that families, once established, were moving out into less densely populated areas of Kent.

(5) Place of Birth

For reasons of economy, classification by birth place by individual county was omitted from the 1921 and 1931 printed tables and does not reappear until 1951. In 1951 all the counties of England and Wales as places of birth are represented in the Kent population. Also, those born within the United Kingdom (excluding Eire) accounted for 95% or more of the Kent population up to and including the 1981 census. In 1991, with the first ethnic census, 97.7% of the Kent population was classified as white.[26]

Table 15 takes one beyond the general statistics for Kent, bringing out clearly the diverse birth place profile of the north-west Kent suburbs, Gillingham, Chatham and Maidstone, and the rest of Kent in 1951. Overall, 39.6% were Kent-born, but the figures are much lower in the areas adjoining London, with

---

[26] *Kent County Monitor*, table J, p. 24.

Table 14

Percentage Population Increase or Decrease in Kent
and its Districts 1981–91

Area	Total	By births and deaths	Migration and other changes
Kent	**1.7**	**1.3**	**0.4**
District			
Ashford	6.6	2.5	4.1
Canterbury	5.9	–4.2	10.1
Dartford	–3.3	1.1	–4.4
Dover	1.3	–0.3	1.6
Gillingham	0.5	7.1	–6.6
Gravesham	–4.5	4.0	–8.5
Maidstone	2.9	1.9	1.0
Rochester-upon-Medway	–0.6	7.4	–8.0
Sevenoaks	–0.8	1.9	–2.7
Shepway	4.3	–4.1	8.4
Swale	4.3	3.2	1.0
Thanet	1.3	–6.0	7.3
Tonbridge and Malling	3.5	3.7	–0.2
Tunbridge Wells	1.9	–1.1	3.0

only just over one in four in Chislehurst and Sidcup UD being born in the county. Significantly, 44.7% were born in London. This contrasts with Canterbury CB where 65.9% were born in the county, and Maidstone MB where the figure was 66.9%. Conversely the birth-places of those in the north-west Kent suburbs show clearly the twin pull of those suburbs, receiving migrants from the more densely populated areas of inner London, and also those moving into suburbia from the outlying areas of Kent. Whilst migrants were attracted to Kent from all parts of the United Kingdom, the majority of migrants were born within London and the south-east region.

In 1991 a new question was asked about those who had a different address one year before the census. It was found that 9.6% of the Kent population had moved a year before the census. Short-distance movement within a ward and movement between wards and within a district accounted for the majority of moves. Whilst there is an obvious overlap between categories, it is safe to assume that the vast majority of moves took place within the county. However, we have already noted the regional differences within Kent and the fact that towns such as Canterbury and Maidstone attracted many from the surrounding

Table 15

Place of Birth of those Resident in Kent, 1951

Male and female (%)

	London and SE including Kent	Kent born	London	Other counties and regions	UK	England and Wales
Kent	77.7	39.6	17.2	10.2	91.5	87.9
Canterbury CB	77.9	65.9	6.3	17.4	96.6	95.3
Beckenham MB	76.4	30.0	33.6	19.9	96.4	94.2
Bexley MB	80.4	31.0	40.5	11.6	97.0	92.0
Bromley MB	77.4	38.1	30.2	16.5	95.8	93.9
Chislehurst and Sidcup UD	79.2	26.1	44.7	14.8	95.9	94.0
Orpington UD	76.6	33.6	31.9	17.7	95.6	93.3
Gillingham MB	71.5	58.9	7.4	21.3	95.9	92.8
Maidstone MB	78.5	66.9	6.3	12.9	92.9	91.4
County remainder	77.9	58.4	11.6	16.0	95.7	93.9

areas. Overall, probably four out of five migrants moved within the London and south-east region.

If we analyse the migrants by age-group, though several of the categories overlap bringing the total to more than 100%, we find that those aged between 20 and 24 are the most likely movers within each category (19.8%). This is probably the most mobile group, perhaps leaving home, setting up in a flat, getting married or cohabiting, or finding new accommodation. If we add the next three categories, some 41.5% to 51.7% in each group had moved between the ages of 20 and 34, probably incorporating the births of children and perhaps moving to larger accommodation, or moving to a different job. Some 18.4% of those 14 and under moved in the preceding year, as part of a family. Of these, 8.4% were in the 0–4 age-group, many of whom were probably the cause of the decision to move. At the pensioner end of the scale, significant numbers are still moving. In this case the family is probably shrinking, as children grow up and leave home. At a later stage the house itself may be too large, and illness or the loss of a partner may lead the remaining occupant to seek sheltered accommodation or a nursing home. It is noticeable that after the age of 70 the majority moving are women, probably after being widowed. Although the printed census does not divide the county into districts, it is clear that the latter profile fits several of the coastal resorts such as Herne Bay and Broadstairs, whereas the former typifies areas such as Maidstone and the north-west Kent commuter areas.

A study of direct relevance to Kent was *The Householders and Commuters' Survey of Mid and North Kent*, published in 1990. The study focused on two north Kent districts, Dartford and Gravesham, and mid-Kent, and the results were based on over 1,000 returns in each area. The two showed considerable variations. In mid-Kent, 22% of heads of household had been resident in the local area for less than two years. This compared with 10% for Dartford and Gravesham. In the latter, two-thirds of heads of households had been resident for more than ten years, compared with 54% in mid-Kent. The compilers of the report suggested that Dartford and Gravesham's 10% reflected a downturn in the housing market, which reduced the flow of migrants from London. Also the area was subject to greater constraints upon housing as it was within the Metropolitan Green Belt. Conversely mid-Kent had more available building land and had a substantial and sustained building programme which attracted new migrants.

In Dartford and Gravesham, 61% had moved from within five miles of their current residence, compared with 47% in mid-Kent. In Dartford and Gravesham, 16% had relocated from London, compared with 17% in mid-Kent. The study confirmed the earlier conclusion that mid-Kent drew migrants more widely than Dartford and Gravesham from within Kent and further afield. In the case of Dartford and Gravesham, 50% of the movement from Greater London was from the former Kent boroughs of Bexley and Bromley.

(6) Migrants Born outside the United Kingdom

In 1951 those born in the Old and New Commonwealth, and in British colonies and dependencies, averaged 1.5% for the county. By 1971 this had risen to 1.9%, whilst the total of those born outside the United Kingdom rose between 1951 and 1961 from 2.4% to 2.9%. In 1961 Indian migrants accounted for 0.5% of the Kent population, but 0.9% in Gillingham.

The 1971 census showed that whilst 95.9% of the Kent population were born in the United Kingdom, Old and New Commonwealth immigrants were concentrated in north Kent. Gravesend with 5% and Gillingham with 3% were above the Kent average of 1.9%.

Figures taken after local-government reorganisation in 1973/4 show that the trend of Old and New Commonwealth immigrants moving into north Kent and the areas of Kent adjoining London still continued. In 1981 Gravesham had 6.8% of heads of household born in the Old and New Commonwealth compared with only 1% in Dover and a Kent average of 2.3%. As was the case with earlier white immigrants, north Kent and the Medway towns, with smaller, cheaper and more easily available housing attracted many from the more densely populated areas of London.

In 1991 questions were asked for the first time about ethnicity. The north Kent districts of Dartford (95.9%), Gillingham (96.1%), Gravesham (91.6%) and Rochester-upon-Medway (95.6%) had the lowest percentage of white resi-

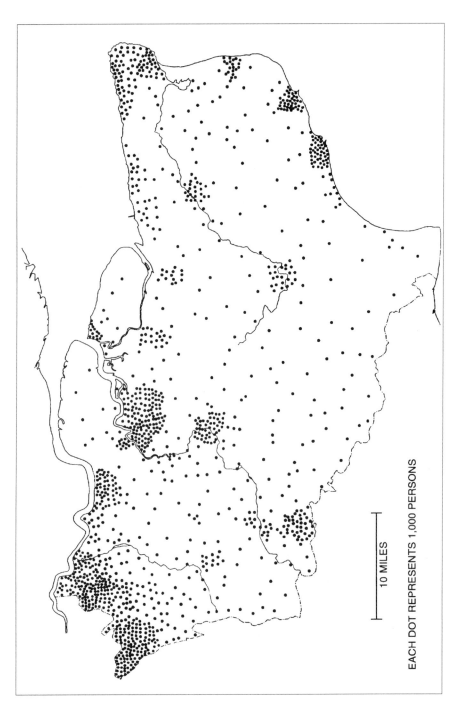

EACH DOT REPRESENTS 1,000 PERSONS

10 MILES

Map 5. Map of Kent showing distribution of population, 1948 (*Planning Basis for Kent*, Kent County Council, Maidstone 1948).

dents. Migrants, both from the UK and abroad, have tended to move first into the inner cities or towns where there was cheaper housing and a greater variety of jobs. Those that were able then moved by stages into areas of lower densities and further job opportunities.

(7) Population Density

Between 1921 and 1991 the density per acre of the county increased from 1.2 to 1.6, with the municipal boroughs and urban districts rising from 6.5 to 6.8 per acre, and the rural districts from 0.4 to 0.5 per acre between 1921 and 1961. With the creation of the London Boroughs, and the loss of Bexley and Bromley, the density of the remainder of Kent went down to 1.5 per acre in 1971. Perhaps more significant is that, during the same period, the densities of the rural districts rose to 0.6 per acre.

As has been noted earlier, the 1921 census included many visitors, which distorted the population and the densities of many seaside resorts in Kent. It must also be noted that the overall density included parks, playing fields and other open spaces. In a rural area a ward containing a village nucleus is likely to have a much higher density than the surrounding area. Densities alone do not give any indication of the quality and type of housing. Equally the term municipal borough, in Kent, for historical reasons, contained a very disparate group. For example, the municipal boroughs of Lydd and Tenterden had very low densities of 0.2 and 0.4 per acre in 1921, and remained low until they were subsumed into the new county districts in 1973/4.

In considering densities, one must also be aware of local circumstances. In 1921 many hospitals still contained those injured in the First World War, and there were airforce bases and newly acquired pits, e.g. in Eythorne and Chislet wards. However certain features do show through. For example Penge UD, on the fringe of densely populated London, had a density of 34.1 per acre in 1921. This high density remained, and Penge still has the highest density per acre in the London Borough of Bromley.

The period 1921–51 saw a slight overall increase in the densities of the MBs, CBs and UDs from 6.4 to 6.6 per acre. However this slight increase disguised real suburban growth. Bexley density rose from 4.3 to 18.2, Beckenham from 8.6 to 12.5, Crayford from 4.9 to 11.0, and Chislehurst from 3.2 to 9.4 per acre. It should be noted that the rural districts did not experience depopulation but rather a small increase from an equally small base. Of those rural districts with densities of 0.3 per acre or less, only Swale had fallen between 1951 and 1961 from 0.32 to 0.3 per acre. The overall population densities within Kent in 1948 are shown in Map 5.

The 1971 census reflects a further steady accretion in densities, with Tonbridge UD (4.8 to 6.7 per acre) and Sittingbourne UD (4.8 to 6.3 per acre) seeing the most rapid gains. The areas fringing London, north Kent, the Medway towns, Folkestone, Maidstone and Ramsgate all had densities of ten or more persons per acre. Similarly, rural areas within the orbit of the leading towns were also developing.

Whilst the overall density for Kent remained at 1.6 persons per acre in 1981 and 1991, eight of the newly formed districts increased their density, two went down and four remained the same. Regionally, of those nearest London, Dartford and Gravesham declined, while Tonbridge and Malling and Tunbridge Wells remained constant. Elsewhere all the districts in the north and central areas of Kent increased in density. To the south, Ashford and Dover remained the same while Shepway saw a marginal increase. Overall there was very little movement between 1981 and 1991 except for the rise of Gillingham from 11.6 to 11.9 and Thanet from 4.6 to 4.9 persons per acre. By 1991 Gillingham's density was very nearly that of Outer London's 13.4, and above that of the less populated London Borough of Bromley with its 7.7 persons per acre.

2

The Economy of Kent: An Overview

ALAN BOOTH

The economic development of Kent in the twentieth century is essentially a story of the continuing relative contraction of agriculture which had begun in the 1870s,[1] growth and crisis in manufacturing, and growing domination of the service sector. In every respect, the economy of Kent has been buttressed by the proximity of London. The pattern of Kentish agricultural production, of the manufacturing industries of north Kent and of the service sector benefited profoundly from the closeness to either the wealth and scope of the London market or the levers of power and the discretionary spending of the government machine. There are, however, some major discontinuities in Kent's economic development since 1900. The twentieth century has seen the rise and fall of the Kent coalfield; the growth and collapse of the long-established arms producers; and the revitalisation of Kent's manufacturing sector followed by late and steep 'de-industrialisation'.

(1) Change at the Sectoral Level

The most basic data on economic change can be gleaned from the census, providing we remain aware of the limitations of the source. Early censuses did not distinguish clearly between 'occupation' and 'industry' (so the censuses for both 1901 and 1911 contain a large class of 'labourers' unattached to any specific industry) and the census years might have been chosen to cause maximum discomfort to historians. The year 1921 saw the steepest recession in British industrial history; the census of 1931 was taken in the depths of the 'slump'; in 1951, the pattern of demand and hence employment was still greatly shaped by government controls which were designed to help the British economy overcome its immense financial and economic problems after 1945. Administrative changes will also leave their mark on census figures. The county boundary of Kent was redrawn in the 1960s with the loss to Greater London of the areas that formed the London boroughs of Bexley and Bromley, representing in population terms roughly one-sixth of the county. The changing definition of

---

[1] G. Mingay, 'Agriculture', *The Economy of Kent, 1640–1914*, ed. W.A. Armstrong, Woodbridge 1995, pp. 78–9.

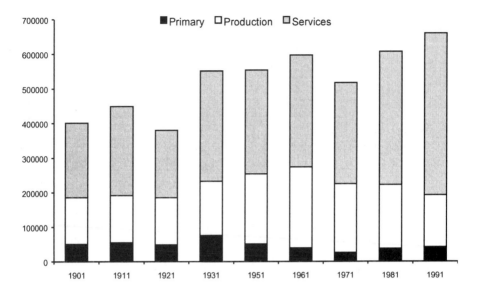

Figure 1. Changes in employment in Kent since 1901

Notes
1   Unclassified 'labourers' identified in the censuses of 1901 and 1911 have been allocated to the production industries.
2   Primary industries are 'agriculture, forestry, fishery' plus 'energy and water'; production industries are classed as 'manufacturing' plus 'construction'.

Source: *Census*, Industrial Tables.

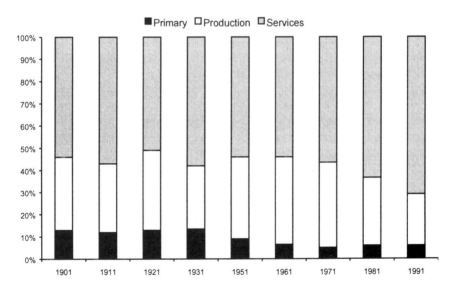

Figure 2. Sectoral patterns of employment in Kent since 1901

Notes and Source: as Figure 1.

the age at which juveniles enter the labour market (ten years of age before the First World War; fourteen years between the wars; fifteen and then sixteen since the Second World War) has also affected the data.

With these considerations in mind, Figs 1 and 2 show the changes in sectoral patterns of employment in the county during the twentieth century, in terms of both actual numbers employed (Fig. 1) and the proportional distribution (Fig. 2). There have clearly been three major trends: the steady contraction to the 1970s of the proportion of the workforce in the primary sector; the rejuvenation of the 'production industries' after 1945; and the substantial growth of the services both in the inter-war years and after 1971. The shrinking of the primary sector (from approximately 13–15% of the workforce before the Second World War, to 6–7% since 1961) has been caused in large part by a substantial decline in Kent's agricultural workforce from roughly 50,000 between 1901 and 1939 to 14,000 in 1991. Our understanding of the dynamics of change within manufacturing and construction are not at all helped by the holding of the inter-war censuses in years of deep recession, but the figures suggest substantial problems in the 1920s and early 1930s which seem to have been resolved after the war, with the upturn beginning in the middle 1930s (see below). Numbers employed in the production industries rose by roughly one-third between 1931 and 1951 and there was further expansion into the 1960s, with the biggest contribution coming from substantial growth in manufacturing employment. Industry remained prosperous into the 1970s (the fall in industrial employment between 1961 and 1971 being largely explained by the loss of parts of north-west Kent to Greater London in the 1960s) but hit real problems in the 1980s. Finally, there appears to have been major shifts of employment from the production to the service industries in both the inter-war years and since the 1970s. Whereas manufacturing employment stagnated from the end of the First World War to the mid-1930s, the number of service jobs expanded by roughly two-thirds, and even more intense forces have been at work since 1971, with more than one-third of manufacturing jobs disappearing at the same time as service-industry employment rose by half.

The economic structure of Kent has been disproportionately geared to both the primary and service sectors compared with that of the UK as a whole, though the distinctiveness has lessened over time (see Table 16). Since Kent is customarily described as 'the garden of England', the weight of agricultural employment should come as no surprise. The very big commitment to service-sector employment even from the start of the century is less easily explained, though an attempt is made below to present the inter-war years as a transition from a traditional to a modern service economy at a time of high unemployment in manufacturing which encouraged workers into low productivity services. The post-war rejuvenation of Kent's industrial base slowed the growth of the service sector and as a result, Kent's pattern of employment tends to converge with that of the country as a whole; even the big contraction of manufacturing in Kent after 1980 only mirrors national trends.

To go much beyond these broad generalisations, we need to look at a more

Table 16

Distribution of the Workforce, Kent and the UK, 1921–91[1]

	Primary[2]	Production[3]	Services
	UK		
1921	14.1	48.5	37.4
1931	11.9	37.0	50.6
1951	8.9	43.6	47.4
1961	6.6	44.3	48.7
1971	4.3	42.9	52.8
1981	3.2	35.3	61.5
1991	1.9	26.9	71.2
	Kent		
1921	12.9	35.9	51.3
1931	13.7	28.6	57.7
1951	9.1	36.8	54.1
1961	6.5	39.3	54.2
1971	5.0	38.5	56.5
1981	6.2	30.4	63.7
1991	6.3	22.9	70.9

Notes

1 The figures for the UK to 1961 contained a further column, 'not known' which in no year amounted to more than 0.5% of the total workforce.

2 'Primary' is defined as 'agriculture, forestry, fishing, mining and quarrying' up to 1971 for both Kent and the UK and from 1981 as 'agriculture, forestry, fishing, coal, oil and natural gas extraction and processing' for the UK and as 'agriculture, forestry and fishing plus energy and water' for Kent.

3 'Production' is defined as 'manufacturing; gas, water, electricity, construction' up to 1971 and from 1981 as 'manufacturing plus gas, water and electricity plus construction' for the UK and 'manufacturing plus construction' for Kent.

As a result of the different definitions of 'primary' and 'production' in 1981 and 1991, the figures for Kent and the UK as a whole are not directly comparable for these two years. These problems do not of course extend to the definition of the service sector, where the figures are comparable throughout.

Sources: B.R. Mitchell and P. Deane, *Abstract of British Historical Statistics*, Cambridge 1971, p. 60; *Annual Abstract of Statistics*, various years; *Census*, Industry Tables.

disaggregated picture. Since Alan Armstrong's chapter deals in depth with changes in the agricultural sector, the remainder of this chapter will focus only on coal-mining, the production industries and the service sector.

(2) The Coal-mining Industry

Although geologists began to suspect from the middle of the nineteenth century that coal measures might be found in Kent, it was not until 1890 and the sinking of a borehole on the foreshore below Shakespeare Cliff, 1½ miles south-west of Dover, that these expectations were confirmed. By 1914, and forty boreholes later, workable coal seams had been found in a substantial part of the south-east corner of Kent, comprising some 240 square miles of which fifty were under the sea. The land area covered runs roughly ten miles inland from Richborough, almost to Canterbury, and then south to Folkestone. The best seams were found at very deep levels. Most of the coal was soft and friable and suitable for gas-making or for firing steam boilers but, critically, was soon thought to be too soft for mechanical cutting and of insufficient quality for household use.[2] Production from the Shakespeare pit began in 1912, and in the following year two further collieries began to raise coal (at Snowdown and Tilmanstone in the centre of the coalfield about halfway between Dover and Canterbury). In 1914, coal was located in economically viable quantities at Chislet in the north-western part of the coalfield.

The discovery of coal in the south-east of England was exciting, raising the prospect of supplying the enormous and prosperous markets of southern England at low transport costs and prompting plans for major economic development of the county, with new railways, docks, iron and steel works and urban centres.[3] But by the mid-1920s, it became clear that Britain's coal-mining industry was characterised by at best stagnant demand, over-supply, excessive competition, pressure on profit margins and increasing government intervention. It was possible to develop new coalfields with great success, as the example of the Dukeries clearly demonstrated, but conditions in Kent were more difficult and the coal of poorer quality.[4] As in the Dukeries, Kent's coal deposits were relatively deep, but even Kent's best seams were relatively thin and faulted and there were major additional problems in the heat and the amount of water in the rock strata above and below the coal seams. The Kent coalfield was difficult, expensive and unremunerative. As Table 17 shows, the Kent coalfield expanded rapidly in the late 1920s and early 1930s, despite the very difficult conditions facing the coal industry and the wider national economy. The Kent coalfield in fact reached its peak of employment in 1936, but it remained small in scale, at no stage producing as much as 1% of the nation's coal or employing as much as 1% of the industry workforce. The economic significance of the Kent coalfield was therefore limited, both nationally and locally. However, during the Second World War the Kent coalfield was to claim a prominent role in British industrial relations history, and to understand wartime events it is necessary to note some features of the development of the coalfield.

[2]   W. Johnson, 'The Development of the Kent Coalfield, 1896–1946', Kent PhD 1972; E.A. Ritchie, *The Kent Coalfield: Its Evolution and Development*, London 1919; J. Preston, 'Industry, 1800–1914', Armstrong, *op. cit.*, pp. 122–3; C.J. Stubblefield, 'The Kent Coalfield and Other Possible Concealed Coalfields South of the English Midlands', *The Coalfields of Great Britain*, ed. A. Trueman, London 1954, pp. 154–66; W. Ashworth, *The History of the British Coal Industry. Vol. 5: 1946–1982. The Nationalized Industry*, Oxford 1986, p. 14.

[3]   P. Abercrombie and J. Archibald, *East Kent Regional Planning Scheme*, 2 vols, London 1925 and Canterbury 1928.

[4]   R.J. Waller, *The Dukeries Transformed: The Social and Political Development of a Twentieth Century Coalfield*, Oxford 1983, pp. 237–41.

Table 17

Output and Employment in the Kent Coalfield, 1913–46

	Production (000 tons)	Employees (000)	Kent's share of UK coal output (%)	Kent's share of UK employment (%)
1913	59	1.1	0.02	0.10
1923	488	2.1	0.18	0.17
1924	330	1.7	0.12	0.14
1925	368	1.9	0.15	0.17
1926	214	2.1	0.17	0.19
1927	637	2.8	0.25	0.27
1928	930	3.6	0.39	0.38
1929	1,149	4.3	0.45	0.45
1930	1,292	5.1	0.53	0.55
1931	1,586	5.7	0.72	0.66
1932	1,824	6.4	0.87	0.78
1933	1,928	6.6	0.93	0.84
1934	2,030	7.1	0.92	0.90
1935	2,089	7.3	0.94	0.95
1936	2,026	7.4	0.89	0.96
1937	–	7.3	–	0.99
1938	1,771	6.6	0.78	0.84
1939	1,865	6.4	0.81	0.84
1940	1,572	5.7	0.70	0.76
1941	1,377	5.0	0.67	0.72
1942	1,322	5.3	0.65	0.75
1943	1,388	5.5	0.71	0.78
1944	1,313	–	0.72	–
1945	1,213	–	0.71	–
1946	1,301	–	0.74	–

Source: R.J. Waller, *The Dukeries Transformed: The Social and Political Development of a Twentieth Century Coalfield*, Oxford 1983.

The creation of the Kent coalfield confronted entrepreneurs with the classic managerial problems: how much capital to invest and how to form the labour force. The initial development of the Kent coalfield suffered from capital shortages and it was only the formation of a new amalgamation (Pearson, Dorman Long) which promised sufficient capital to develop large-scale mining at Betteshanger. Capital costs were formidable because of the depth and faulting of the seams, and the oppressive conditions underground. The rather uncertain quality of the coal was an additional unwanted handicap. Pearson, Dorman Long sought and obtained Treasury guarantees for much of its investment. These difficulties were paralleled by the problems in assembling a settled mining workforce far from the established coalfields. High unemployment in the older, export-oriented coalfields such as South Wales, Northumberland and Durham provided a ready supply of potential migrants and the provision of modern housing at affordable rents was a further incentive for unemployed miners to move to Kent, but it was difficult to create a settled workforce. There were deep and lasting frictions which reflected the regional differences among the immigrant miners.[5] These regional frictions were exacerbated by the 'butty system' of underground sub-contracting. It had been brought to Kent by migrants from the Midlands coalfields but was regarded as exploitative by those from other coalfields.[6] These instabilities were superimposed upon a high labour turnover which was common in all new coalfields but was worsened in Kent by the physically demanding nature of the work underground.[7] Many of the immigrants had been unemployed for some time and were totally unprepared for the hot, wet and extremely strenuous work in the Kent pits.[8] In such conditions, it was extremely difficult to create stable institutions, a problem which was exacerbated by the hostility between the miners and the local community.[9] High labour turnover and isolation from other coalfields created a general shortage of labour in the Kent pits, which made the companies wary of using the sack to impose tight discipline over the workforce.[10] The Kent companies could not pick and choose their employees and imported labour militancy with their miners with the result that the Kent Miners' Association became a relatively militant union.

These conflicts bubbled over during wartime. Coal was the main wartime energy source but national output and productivity fell steadily, particularly during the first two years of war.[11] Miners became increasingly frustrated that government controls over the wartime labour market prevented them from leaving an industry whose pay levels were falling behind those in the munitions and other booming industries and whose working conditions were poor.[12] These problems were particularly starkly illustrated in the Kent coalfield where working conditions remained bad, institutions were still underdeveloped and where the threats of German invasion were highest (during the summer of 1940 when France was staggering to her fall, ministers contemplated the evacuation of the Kent coalfield and the loss of all its output[13]). During 1941 industrial relations at the Betteshanger colliery were strained because of conflict over

---

5   G. Harkell, 'The Migration of Mining Families to the Kent Coalfield Between the Wars', *Oral History*, vi (1978), pp. 98–113.
6   R.E. Goffee, 'The Butty System and the Kent Coalfield', *Bulletin of the Society for the Study of Labour History*, xxxiv (1978), pp. 41–55.
7   Johnson, *op. cit.*; Waller, *op. cit.*, pp. 237–8.
8   Goffee, *op. cit.*, p. 50.
9   Harkell, *op. cit.*, p. 108.
10   Waller, *op. cit.*, p. 238.
11   W.H.B. Court, *Coal* (UK Official History of the Second World War: Civil Series), London 1951, pp. 107–77.
12   L. Harris, 'State and Economy in the Second World War', *State and Society in Contemporary Britain: A Critical Introduction*, ed. G. McLennan, D. Held and S. Hall, Cambridge 1984, pp. 56–70.
13   Court, *op. cit.*, p. 133.

special payments for working a very difficult seam.[14] The dispute was referred to arbitration which essentially backed the management's proposals, prompting approximately 4,000 Betteshanger miners to strike. Although wartime regulations banned strikes, the local union officials backed their men. The government, faced with an unappealing choice between imprisonment for all the strikers for breaking wartime regulations, or a better offer to get the miners back to work, decided on a middle way and arrested the 1,000 underground workers with whom the dispute had begun. All those arrested pleaded guilty and were fined, but three leading union officials were imprisoned with hard labour. Only nine men paid their fines and the strike continued. The only men who could resolve the dispute were in gaol, where ministers were forced to go to recommence negotiations. After eleven days the officials were set free and the miners returned to work, and the court reluctantly agreed not to enforce the unpaid fines. Although the Betteshanger dispute was relatively short lived it has become an important landmark in the history of British industrial relations. The episode was recounted to the first major post-war investigation of British industrial relations, the Donovan Royal Commission on Trade Unions and Employers' Associations, as evidence that legal sanctions on strikers were most likely to be inoperable, and even the Thatcher governments' legislation on trade unions did not propose imprisonment for strikers, but opted instead for heavy fines on unions combined with sequestration of their assets.

After the war, Kent continued to produce relatively costly coal, not least because high wages were needed to attract and retain miners in the diverse and relatively prosperous Kent economy and thin faulting seams were unattractive for mechanisation.[15] The National Coal Board managed to develop new markets for Kent coal – the original plans for industrial (cement-making, paper manufacture), steam raising (for the Southern Railway), electricity generation (at the Richborough power station) and household uses were rethought when oil invaded the traditional industrial uses and gas began to erode the household market. New uses were found in steel-making and the power stations on the Thames, and the Kent pits rather uncertainly survived the first big colliery-closure programme of the later 1950s. Snowdown and Betteshanger even attracted new investment in the 1960s, but the NCB was beginning to concentrate its largest investments on pits with greater long-term potential and the gap between Kent's and national productivity widened.[16] The first casualty was Chislet, which closed in July 1969, but Kent's relative position deteriorated. In 1968, productivity in Kent had been three-quarters of the national average, but by 1975 it had fallen to less than half.[17] The Kent coalfield was living from hand to mouth. The demand for its product showed no strong underlying growth despite the efforts to process Kent coal into household smokeless fuel, and the NCB was reluctant to commit

[14] B.J. McCormick, *Industrial Relations in the Coal Industry*, London 1979, pp. 42–5.
[15] Court, *op. cit.*, p. 346; Ashworth, *op. cit.*, p. 294.
[16] *Ibid.*, pp. 235–65.
[17] *Energy Statistics*, 1976.

investment funds. Tilmanstone and Snowdown were on the NCB list of small, high-cost pits for closure in the early 1980s but won a temporary reprieve in 1981. But this was only a stay of execution. Snowdown ceased production after the 1984–5 strike and was finally closed in October 1987; Tilmanstone ceased production in October 1986; and even Betteshanger closed in August 1989. The last years of the Kent coalfield were marked by bitter industrial relations, but its fate was ultimately sealed by the huge recession after 1981 in the British steel industry, which had been the last strong user of the particular grade of coal which Kent alone could produce.[18]

(3) The Production Industries

There is nothing quite so dramatic in the history of the production industries in Kent in the twentieth century. We know from the work of James Preston[19] that Kent lacked a real manufacturing heartland, but at the risk of gross over-simplification we may identify four separate (or largely separate) elements in the county's industrial base. The obvious foundation is that part of industry which is needed to meet the basic needs of the local community. It would include the food and drink processors, construction, those parts of the metals and engineering sector concerned with the manufacturing, servicing and repair of agricultural machinery and equipment and, at a pinch, parts of the leather and clothing industries. In very general terms, activity in this part of Kent's productive economy was small in scale, often in family enterprises, with a high turnover of firms, and is consequently extremely inaccessible to historians. Much food and drink manufacture, for example, has always been conducted on a very small scale in dispersed locations and often as part of retailing (bacon curing, confectionery making, the baking of bread); and agricultural-machinery making has connotations of blacksmiths' shops and rural craftsmen. Almost by definition this form of economic activity is labour intensive and operates at low levels of productivity. Some more substantial and durable activity has taken place and has attracted the attention of historians but for the most part we can make only reasoned suppositions about what has happened to this part of the economy in the present century.

We know a little about the brewers. From 1900 to approximately 1970 there has been a steady concentration of the industry into larger, more capital intensive units of production and the steady closure of small local and then regional breweries. The number of breweries in the Medway towns fell from five in 1900, to one in 1918 which was subsequently closed in 1938.[20] The wave of concen-

18 Much of the information in this paragraph is taken from the 'Kent coalfield' file of press cuttings held at Deal Library.
19 J.M. Preston, *Industrial Medway: An Historical Survey: Industrial Development of the Lower Medway Valley with Special Reference to the Nineteenth and Early Twentieth Centuries*, Rochester 1977; *idem*, 'Industry, 1800–1914'.
20 Preston, *Industrial Medway*, pp. 145, 185, 200.

tration since the 1960s associated with the spread of pasteurised beers, brought even regional breweries under the control of the biggest national companies and production processes were changed. Beer is, however, not typical of the industry as a whole, as the figures in Table 18 will demonstrate. There have been countervailing tendencies at work as numbers employed in food and drink manufacture have been relatively stable since 1920. Clearly much of the activity in this industry in Kent, though small in scale, has established niche local markets and has resisted the revolution in food retailing (similar to that in brewing) which has seen the inexorable rise of branded, nationally advertised goods produced by ever more mechanised methods and sold through ever more dominant chains, first of grocers and subsequently of supermarkets.

In the other part of this 'local' economy, similar trends have been evident. In building, numbers employed appear to have remained very stable (apart from the inexplicable recorded fall in 1921) and a rise in 1991 (not included in Table 18) no doubt associated with civil-engineering work in connection with the Channel tunnel, which at the peak of the construction effort employed more than 8,000 workers on the British side.[21] At the county level this was largely an industry dominated by small family firms engaged in local house-building and repair. In agricultural engineering, the county boasted in Aveling & Porter of Rochester a company which had been highly successful in the second part of the nineteenth century and became one of the major firms in the industry. It produced steam-driven machinery, initially for agricultural work but subsequently for civil engineering (primarily road-rollers) but poor decision-making after 1918 led to increasing difficulties and failure to develop new product lines, notably its diesel engines, rapidly enough.[22] The Rochester factory closed in 1933, but agricultural engineering continued in the county on a much smaller-scale and with dispersed works. However, numbers fell consistently from 1,800 in 1951 as the big international firms began to dominate the market in the 1960s and 1970s. Thus, this 'local' economy has been relatively resilient during the twentieth century, in so far as we can tell from the limited information available. Resilience is only to be expected, as these activities supply basic support for both agriculture and urban life, but resilience in the sector as a whole almost certainly masks a high turnover of individual firms, since small firms with limited reserves of capital and experience tend to have high birth and death rates. This type of small-scale enterprise will be found everywhere and plays a vital if frequently overlooked role in the economic life of the nation and region.

Once we move beyond the local economy, we inevitably concentrate on industries in which Kent has specialised. The first such sector is building materials, cement- and brick-making. Cement-makers need ample supplies of chalk or limestone and shale or clay, as well as access to ample supplies of fuel and power. Kent had traditionally had great locational advantages in this industry as

---

[21] *Independent*, Saturday 6 October 1990. See also the *Financial Times* 'Survey' (Friday 6 May 1994) which describes the complexity of the electronic and mechanical engineering work in the Tunnel.
[22] J.M. Preston, *Aveling and Porter, Ltd.*, Rochester 1987.

Table 18

Numbers Employed in the Production Industries in Kent, 1901–71

	1901[1]	1911[1]	1921	1931	1951	1961	1971
Food, drink, tobacco	8,709	8,497	11,257	13,291	11,856	11,850	10,490
Chemicals	2,293	3,503	4,848	5,406	8,749	13,820	11,320
Metal manufacture	1,104	1,399	1,591	1,687	1,772	2,080	2,050
Mechanical engineering[2]	18,321	19,216	14,591	13,053	20,171	25,310	20,480
Electrical & precision engineering[2]		5,076	6,269	8,963	15,562	29,150	17,380
Shipbuilding & repairing	5,636	5,602	15,592	13,603	14,392	9,300	8,240
Vehicles	3,566	4,639	6,614	8,981	16,746	8,700	7,490
Other manufacturing[3]	3,514	291	785	1,963	8,345	11,980	16,970
Textiles	973	1,439	1,195	1,715	2,295	2,410	1,240
Leather	1,692	1,778	1,233	1,394	897	630	530
Clothing	18,720	19,196	9,087	9,138	5,802	3,590	3,760
Bricks, cement, glass	12,902	10,309	12,816	5,517	11,111	13,440	10,040
Timber & furniture	5,196	5,380	11,007	4,739	5,257	6,190	7,000
Paper, printing, publishing	7,931	10,880	13,159	22,306	25,859	35,530	31,340
Manufacturing	90,622	97,205	110,044	111,756	148,814	173,980	148,330
Construction	42,654	35,736	18,967	38,221	43,679	49,480	41,300
Total	133,281	132,941	132,194	149,977	192,511	223,460	189,630

Notes

1 In both the 1901 and the 1911 censuses 'general labourers' are recorded separately but have been real-located among the production industries in proportion to the numbers recorded in those industries; and 'dealers' are included in the industry classifications but have been excluded here, on the grounds that they are part of the distributive trades.

2 Electrical engineering was not shown as a separate group within the wider metals and engineering group in 1901. Precision engineering, including jewellery, has been assigned throughout to the electrical engineering industry.

3 This is a residual category. Nothing should be read into changes in the numbers employed in this group before 1931.

Source: Census, Industrial Tables.

chalk and London clay were found close together in the lower Medway valley. The raw materials for brick-making were also found in the area. The proximity of London, both as a market and as a supply source for coke fuel for cement and domestic ash for brick-making gave Kent enormous advantages during the nineteenth century. The pre-eminent position of Kent in the building materials sector has not, however, continued into the twentieth century, even though employment has remained relatively buoyant apart from the slump years of the early 1930s, as Table 18 indicates. Residential house-building declined in the Edwardian period, especially in and around London and when building activity revived after the First World War Kent's brick-makers suffered from cheaper sources of supply with the development of the Bedford and Peterborough brick-fields and the production of 'Fletton' bricks, which required less fuel than other types of brick and permitted greater mechanisation of production.[23] Flettons were aimed initially at London builders, making competition extremely difficult for Kent producers.

Technical progress in cement-making led to concentration of production and the ability to exploit raw materials inferior to those found in the Medway valley. The advantage in the industry shifted towards larger producers who could mobilise the capital required for investment in the most modern technology, and the optimum size of plant continued to rise through much of the first half of the century as instrumentation brought more accurate control of production processes. The combined effects of long-lived plant, increasing capital costs per unit of output, rising productivity and increasing fuel efficiency as kiln size increased led inevitably to the disappearance of all of Kent's small-scale cement works, not least because in the period 1900–35 concentration was expedited by efforts to cartelise the industry.[24] The first significant concentration in the industry, the formation in 1900 of Associated Portland Cement Manufacturers Ltd, was primarily a combination of Medway producers, but the progress of technology rapidly allowed producers in other parts of the country to exploit their own raw materials and APCM's share of the growing national market steadily contracted.[25] Further efforts at concentration had similar effects, so that the Medway valley cement-makers became much smaller in number, but with much larger, more efficient works, and Kent remained the biggest regional producer whilst retaining a steadily diminishing share of the national market. The Kent producers suffered in the 1930s when excess capacity in Europe made London a target for dumping of excess cement at below market price, but continuing modernisation and re-equipment gave the Medway cement-producers an edge when more favourable conditions returned in the early 1950s with the massive post-war rebuilding programme not only in Britain but in continental Europe. However, Medway producers found their export markets more difficult from the early 1960s when increasing fuel costs coincided with rising tariff barriers in many developing countries as governments protected their own cement-makers as part of an import-substitution programme. At this point, cement-making became a much more international and global activity, and its more recent history is examined below with equally 'globalised' sectors, paper-making and oil-processing.

The third sector of Kent's economy is in many ways the most interesting, the

[23] Preston, *Industrial Medway*, pp. 164–75; R. Evely and I.M.D. Little, *Concentration in British Industry: An Empirical Study of the Structure of Industrial Production, 1935–51*, Cambridge 1960, pp. 224–7.
[24] B.R. Williams, 'The Building Materials Industry', *The Structure of British Industry: A Symposium*, ed. D. Burn, Cambridge 1958. M. Compton and E.M. Bott, *British Industry: Its Changing Structure in Peace and War*, London 1940, pp. 72–4; Preston, *op. cit.*, pp. 166–75; P.L. Cook, 'The Cement Industry', *The Effects of Mergers: Six Studies*, ed. P.L. Cook, London 1958, pp. 36–95.
[25] *Ibid.*, pp. 28–54.

Plate 1. Railway workers at entrance to Eastern Station, Ashford, c.1910.

Plate 2. Ashford haulage contractor, c.1920.

Plate 3. Erecting shop at Ashford Railway Works, 1947.

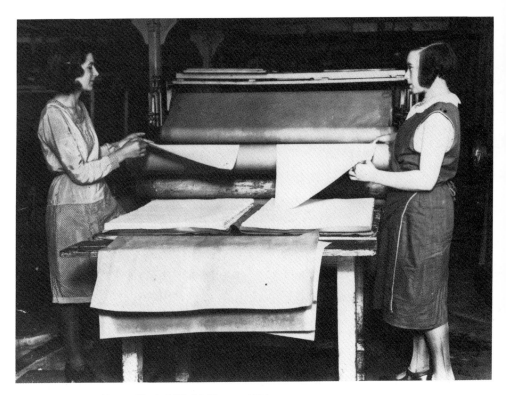

Plate 4. Paper making at Hayle Mill, Maidstone, 1931.

Plate 5. Medway Brewery at Maidstone showing the river in flood.

Plate 6. Aerial view of power station on the Isle of Grain, 1972 (© Topham Picturepoint).

armaments and engineering sector of north-west Kent. The munitions industry was long established in Kent, notably in the naval dockyards at Chatham and Sheerness, the Royal Arsenal at Woolwich, a major gun-powder producer at Faversham and the North Kent Iron Works which produced shells, but there were substantial new developments in the late nineteenth and early twentieth centuries, with the establishment of factories owned by Vickers at Crayford, Erith and Dartford, and the location of Shorts aircraft factory (eventually) at Rochester.[26] Foremost among the powerful engineering firms was the Siemens factory at Woolwich, whose main interests shifted after 1918 from submarine cables to telephone equipment and marine communications, much of which had military applications and resulted in great expansion of activity during both world wars.[27] The growth of interest in this sector flows from historians' growing interest in the foundations of industrial competitiveness and alternatives to the so-called 'Fordist' system of mass production of standardised goods by capital-intensive methods. Among the most studied options to 'Fordism' is 'flexible specialisation', a production system which reverses the principles of mass production by combining skilled, adaptable workers and general-purpose (rather than specialised) machine tools to manufacture a wide and changing range of semi-customised goods.[28] Although mass production probably had its origins in the manufacture of small arms, the Kent munitions firms were able, and required, to turn their attentions to the production of a wide variety of goods, as will be seen.

North-west Kent had two great advantages for the arms producers. First, government defence research and production establishments were concentrated in the area (in addition to Woolwich, Chatham and Sheerness, there was the Royal Aircraft Factory, later the Royal Aircraft Establishment, at Farnborough). The private arms manufacturers collaborated closely with government research establishments on new weapons and equipment for the services.[29] Secondly, these state and private arms producers created a pool of highly skilled labour, capable of working to fine tolerances and on highly complex tasks. Some private firms, notably Siemens, had very strong education and training programmes to develop skilled workers and professional electrical engineers, but others, Short Brothers, for example, relied heavily on recruiting skilled workers and professional engineers from Chatham naval dockyard and Shorts' construction methods were deeply imbued with the Chatham ethos.[30]

In general terms, Kent's arms makers prospered in both world wars. The Vickers factories produced machine guns, specialised equipment for the navy and aircraft parts. Siemens' Woolwich works made telephones, field-telephone

26 Preston, 'Industry, 1800–1914', pp. 110–13; J.D. Scott, *Vickers: A History*, London 1962; C.H. Barnes, *Shorts Aircraft since 1900*, London 1967.
27 J.D. Scott, *Siemens Brothers, 1858–1958: An Essay in the History of Industry*, London 1958, pp. 205–44.
28 M. Piore and C. Sabel, *The Second Industrial Divide*, New York 1984.
29 Scott, *Vickers*, p. 117; Barnes, *op. cit.*, pp. 16–28.
30 Scott, *Siemens*, pp. 225–9; Barnes, *op. cit.*, pp. 22–3.

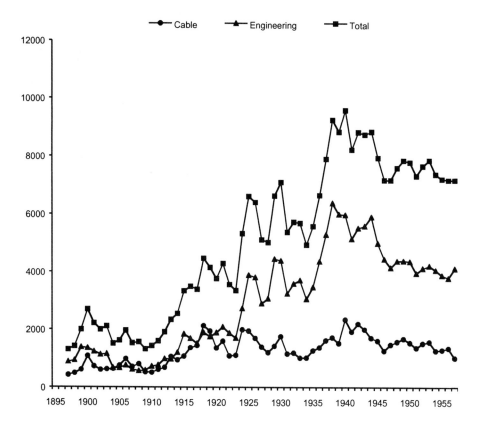

Figure 3. Number of employees at Siemens' Woolwich Works, 1897–1957.

Note: Total number of employees includes those described as 'staff' as well as those in the 'Cable' and 'Engineering' departments.

Source: J.D. Scott, *Siemens Brothers, 1858–1958: An Essay in the History of Industry,* London 1958, pp. 266–7.

equipment and power cables in both wars, components for radar and special equipment in the second; Fig. 3 shows clear peaks of employment in the rearmament and wartime period. There were also huge increases in employment in the Woolwich Arsenal (50,000 employees during wartime, compared with roughly 5,000 in peacetime) and the Chatham dockyards (to 11,000 in the First World War and 10,500 in the Second).[31]

After the wars, however, they tended to go their separate ways and showed that the north-west Kent arms firms were better when pursuing flexible speciali-

[31] Scott, *op. cit.*, pp. 225–9; Preston, *op. cit.*, p. 111; Preston, *Industrial Medway*, p. 197; P. Inman, *Labour in the Munitions Industries* (UK Official History of the Second World War: Civil Series), London 1957, p. 82.

sation than mass production. After 1918, the Vickers factories turned to a variety of peacetime operations: Crayford to sporting guns, sewing machines and motor car parts; Erith to matchmaking machinery, machine tools, cardboard-box-making machinery and gas meters; and Dartford to furniture, wooden toys and washing machines.[32] Short Brothers gained from the Air Ministry's parcelling out of orders to protect a select group of plane-makers, but the firm needed to make a variety of coach-work products (pram bodies, motor car bodies, lightweight bus bodies) and small boats to preserve a nucleus of skilled workers in the face of the vicissitudes of the aircraft market.[33] Siemens was the best placed of all the Kent engineers because the firm began to concentrate heavily on telephone development and began to shift its centre of gravity from the manufacture of submarine cables (Fig. 3). For all those firms which had been able to preserve their physical and human capital stocks, the rearmament programme of the late 1930s brought renewed prosperity and a major recovery of their major production lines, but a further, ultimately less successful process of readjustment took place after 1945.

With the return of peace, Vickers looked to manufacture new products which called for great accuracy in manufacture and close control in production systems to retain its substantial pool of highly skilled labour which had during wartime undertaken precision work on guns and naval gun-control systems. The Vickers board saw the manufacture of punch-card accounting machines as a suitable work for their Crayford factory and its machine fitters and acquired a major share-holding in Powers–Samas, office machine makers. This business expanded rapidly and in 1952 also took over the Dartford factory, which had been producing petrol pumps and a variety of machine tools.[34] But the shift to 'less flexible' specialised production (once Powers–Samas became a wholly owned subsidiary of Vickers in 1955 and when the Crayford factory also turned to these machines) failed in 1958 after an enormous but inadvisable expansion in the mid-1950s.[35] The Siemens factory at Woolwich experienced huge growth in the demand for telephone equipment, on which it had increasingly specialised since the 1920s.[36] However, the major restructuring of the British electrical-engineering industry in the 1950s and 1960s almost certainly postponed modernisation of the Woolwich factory until the middle 1960s. The scale of the capital programme required at this time created a heavy dent in the profits of AEI (which had merged with Siemens in 1954) and in turn made it a take-over target for GEC. When GEC eventually gained control of AEI one of its first

32 Scott, *Vickers*, p. 144.
33 P. Fearon, 'Aircraft Manufacturing', *British Industry Between the Wars: Instability and Industrial Development, 1919–1939*, ed. N.K. Buxton and D.H. Aldcroft, London 1979, pp. 222–6; Barnes, *op. cit.*, pp. 28–9.
34 Scott, *op. cit.*, pp. 308–9, 311, 323; M. Campbell-Kelly, *ICL: A Business and Technical History*, Oxford 1989, pp. 147–9, 151–2.
35 *Ibid.*, pp. 171–90.
36 Scott, *Siemens*, p. 211.

decisions in 1968 was to close the Woolwich factory; this was largely completed in 1970 with the loss of 5,000 jobs.[37]

The final element in the sorry tale of Kent's private arms manufacturers concerns the removal of Short Brothers from Rochester to Belfast. In the early years of the Second World War (just as in the First), there was a 'crisis of munitions production' following military reversals which led to a broadly based criticism of Britain's industrial leaders.[38] With its traditional skill- and managerial-base from the Chatham dockyard, Short Brothers was less well-placed than many aircraft producers to handle the pressures of mass production, and its performance record was consistently poor; Shorts produced the Stirling, one of the least successful heavy bombers of the war, very unsuccessfully. The Ministry of Aircraft Production wanted the firm to switch to the manufacture of the Lancaster bomber, but the senior management was so obstructive that in January 1943 it was first replaced and two months later the firm was nationalised.[39] After the war the government rationalised Shorts' activities at Belfast and the removal of plant and machinery from Rochester was completed in 1948.

Perhaps the biggest blow to the tradition of munitions-making in Kent has been the closure of the royal dockyards. Sheerness closed in 1957 and Chatham in 1984. Sheerness launched its last ships at the turn of the present century and remained as a small repair and refitting yard which was extremely vulnerable when the post-war retreat from Britain's imperial role led to substantial cuts in the size of the navy. Nevertheless, Sheerness remained a substantial operation into the late 1950s, with over 1,000 workers transferred to Chatham when the yard closed. Chatham, however, seemed to have found a more permanent place with its increasing concentration on submarine building and refitting. Chatham continued to build a range of naval vessels in the twentieth century, but it launched its first submarine in 1908 and came increasingly to specialise in this type of vessel.[40] Chatham's dry dock facilities have also been important in the refitting programme for surface and submarine vessels. Some naval strategists expressed concern after both the First and Second World Wars about Chatham's vulnerability to artillery and air from Europe but Chatham retained its position, and employment was remarkably steady in peacetime periods (see Table 19).

Chatham appeared to have secured itself a lasting place in the national defence economy with its specialisation in the repair and refitting of nuclear submarines from the 1960s, but the increasing severity of public expenditure problems from the mid-1960s, and disappointment with the economic performance of the Royal Ordnance Factories and naval dockyards, led to a series of defence reviews which attempted to make the public-sector arms producers

[37] K. Williams, J. Williams and D. Thomas, *Why Are the British Bad at Manufacturing?*, London 1983, p. 152.
[38] J. Hinton, *Shop Floor Citizens: Engineering Democracy in 1940s Britain*, Aldershot 1994, pp. 27–52.
[39] D. Edgerton, *England and the Aeroplane: An Essay on a Militant and Technological Nation*, London 1991, pp. 73, 78–9; Hinton, *op. cit.*, pp. 95, 138; Barnes, *op. cit.*, pp. 29–32.
[40] P. Banbury, *Shipbuilders of the Thames and Medway*, Newton Abbot 1971, pp. 92, 98–9.

Table 19

Numbers of Workers in Chatham Naval Dockyard,
selected years 1900–66

1900	5,670	1933	8,098
1914	9,930	1938	11,079
1918	12,117	1961	8,832
1920	11,033	1966	7,614
1926	9,166		

Source: Hansard, various issues.

more commercial in attitude and approach.[41] The election of a Conservative government in 1979, which was antipathetic to public-sector activity in general and which also faced a mounting public expenditure crisis, prompted an extremely radical defence review in 1981 which paid particular attention to the working of the naval dockyards and recommended the closure of Chatham.[42] The conclusion of naval work at Chatham brought severe disruption to the local economy but its full impact will take some time to be revealed. One of the great strengths of the industrial economy of north-west Kent has been its base of highly skilled managers and workers who have either been trained directly by the Ministry of Defence and its predecessors or who have worked to the exacting standards imposed by the Ministry on private-sector defence contractors. Chatham naval dockyard was one of the principal suppliers to the local economy of trained managers and workers, with a long-established reputation for technical excellence.[43] The closure of the dockyard made many more highly skilled workers available to local employers in the short term, but the longer-term position and the future of highly skilled engineering work in the county must be more uncertain.

The fourth main part of Kent's industrial economy is the processing of imported raw materials. The main constituents of this sector are paper-making and oil refining. Paper-making has had a long history at various sites in the county and provided everything from the high-quality white papers for ledgers and banknotes to the mass-produced common papers from the mechanised mills which began to appear early in the nineteenth century.[44] The main development after 1900 was the consolidation of the production of newsprint on the north Kent coast as newspaper publishers began to buy up mills to process imported pulp. The first newspaper publisher to realise the need for such backward integration was Edward Lloyd, publisher of the *Daily Chronicle*, who in 1902 estab-

41   K. Hartley, 'The Defence Economy', *Britain in the 1970s: The Troubled Economy*, ed. R. Coopey and N. Woodward, London 1996, pp. 228–9.
42   Secretary of State for Defence, *The United Kingdom Defence Programme: The Way Forward*, London 1981, Cmnd 8288.
43   Banbury, *op. cit.*, p. 75.
44   Preston, 'Industry, 1800–1914', p. 117.

lished the then biggest paper works in the world at Sittingbourne to manufacture 1,000 tons of newsprint and other paper per week. Associated Newspapers, publishers of the *Daily Mail*, adopted a similar policy, founding a mill at Gravesend in 1910 and in 1919 buying a further mill at Greenhithe. The great advantages of the Kent coast were good access from the sea to bring in pulp and good communications with London and Fleet Street. Finally, in 1914 Bowaters, a firm of paper merchants from London, acquired a site on the Thames at Northfleet near Gravesend to manufacture newsprint, but as a result of wartime and post-war disruptions this did not begin production until 1920.[45] The history of these three firms became intertwined during the inter-war years as joint ventures were begun and abandoned and mills changed hands, notably a new mill at Kemsley, near Sittingbourne which was begun by Lloyds, sold to Allied Newspapers, owned by Sir William Berry and subsequently to Bowaters, which in 1936 became the largest newsprint enterprise in Europe and produced, largely from the mills at Northfleet, Sittingbourne and Kemsley, 60% of all the newsprint manufactured in Great Britain.[46] Thus by the mid-1930s five great paper mills were established in the county and each of these mills produced a range of other products in addition to newsprint. Other Kent paper-makers had also been expanding in the later 1920s, notably the Reed paper mill producing wrapping papers and the Townsend Hook works. Thus by 1939 paper-making in Kent had acquired a capital-intensive, high-volume, high-productivity sector which relied on the importing of raw materials and proximity to the final user in London.

Another similar industry was oil refining which expanded rapidly in the post-war years. In the 1930s Berry Wiggins had established a small refinery at Kingsnorth on the north Kent coast to make tar products, but oil refining capacity expanded enormously after the war as a result of significant changes in government policy. The war had exposed gaps and vulnerabilities in Britain's industrial capacity, among the biggest of which was oil refining. The Attlee and Churchill governments used import quotas very aggressively to protect domestic producers and plug the gaps.[47] The Thames estuary was a favoured location for new oil-refining capacity, and in 1953 BP built its Isle of Grain refinery, one of the largest in the country in the 1950s.[48] By 1961 Kent boasted more than 3,000 oil-refinery workers. The growth of oil refining in the county encouraged the diversification of the chemicals industry (which was also protected by import quotas); Table 18 shows considerable expansion of employment in the 1950s. Import quotas were also imposed on newsprint, paper and board, all of which were produced in the large paper mills on the north Kent coast inducing considerable new investment in the county, notably by Bowater (at Northfleet, Kemsley, Sittingbourne, and a new packaging factory at Gillingham in 1960)

---

[45] W.J. Reader, *Bowater: A History*, Cambridge 1981, pp. 12–42.
[46] *Ibid.*, p. 118.
[47] A.S. Milward and G. Brennan, *Britain's Place in the World: A Historical Enquiry into Import Controls, 1945–60*, London 1996.
[48] D. Burn, 'The Oil Industry', *The Structure of British Industry*, ed. D. Burn, p. 185.

and Reed (at Snodland). However, Bowater in particular paid insufficient heed to the growth in the early 1960s of world-wide excess capacity in both newsprint and packaging. It discovered that its Kent mills were inefficient by international standards and it cut back production significantly.[49]

Cement-making also became a more globalised industry in the post-war period and followed a similar path to that of the paper-makers. As cheap cement became more generally available from many countries in the 1980s, Kent's main cement producers, Blue Circle and Rugby Portland, turned more to imports, resulting in the closure of two of Kent's four integrated cement works and other related facilities during the decade.[50] However, in 1989 Blue Circle also negotiated long-term quarrying permissions in the Medway valley to sustain the Rochester works. Thus the Kent cement industry has entered another substantial recession as the industry has once again become 'globalised', but on a more extensive scale than in the 1930s.

Drawing these elements together, Kent's industrial base came under a series of pressures after 1918. There were a number of significant casualties in the 'local' economy, especially among the small number of large firms. At the same time, at the national level technological change and concentration in building materials undermined the pre-eminent position of Kent's producers, especially in the London market and the county's arms producers were scratching around to find suitable work. The cable makers (not only Siemens at Woolwich but also firms established at Gravesend and Greenwich) were being forced to switch from submarine cables to power and telephone cable.[51] The period 1918–35 was a difficult one for Kent's industrial producers. Conditions improved markedly in the second half of the 1930s. Rearmament clearly boosted the defence economy, the electrical engineering firms benefited from the 'electrification' of the UK, and the paper-making industry began to see the maturing of the big new investments in newsprint mills on the north coast. This renaissance of Kent's industrial base continued after the Second World War. Two vivid illustrations make the point quite clearly. First, during the war Medway workers and radical industrialists led by George Dickson, the unorthodox managing director of Winget Engineering of Rochester, expressed alarm about post-war employment prospects.[52] These anxieties were multiplied in 1946–8 when the government insisted that Shorts' plane-making interests be transferred from Rochester to Belfast. The local economy was, however, only temporarily damaged. The removal of Shorts created the necessary factory space for the movement of new firms into the area, among them Blaw Knox, makers of construction plant and

[49] Reader, *op. cit.*, pp. 272, 295; Preston, *Industrial Medway*, p. 205.

[50] T. Moyes, 'Corporate Behaviour and Locational Change in the UK Cement Industry, *Geography*, lxxviii (1993), pp. 297–301.

[51] R.E. Catterall, 'Electrical Engineering', Buxton and Aldcroft, *op. cit.*, p. 270; Preston, 'Industry, 1800–1914', p. 116; Scott, *Siemens*, pp. 123–42, 191–210.

[52] Hinton, *op. cit.*, pp. 133–9.

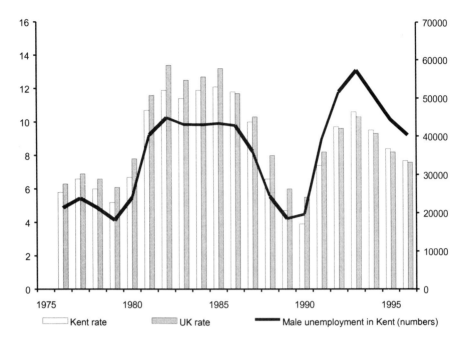

Figure 4. Unemployment in Kent and the UK, 1976–96.

Source: Department of Employment, *Gazette*, various issues.

steel-works equipment.[53] Secondly, Siemens was forced after 1945 to find new factory space in the north of England because labour was so scarce at Woolwich factory, several thousand below actual requirements.[54] In the long post-war boom which lasted from 1945 to the early 1970s, Kent and the south-east more generally was double-blessed. Closeness to the huge London market, with its disproportionate numbers of affluent consumers, clearly helped the consumer-oriented parts of Kentish industry. But Kent was also favoured because of the structural changes which had taken place in local firms earlier in the twentieth century. Investment in the building materials industry during the 1930s clearly paid off in the 1950s and 1960s with the reconstruction of Britain's cities and infrastructure. The expansion of Kent's engineering industry, which came in part from the recovery of the defence economy, produced a base of human and physical capital to respond to changed market conditions after 1945. These advantages were accentuated by government determination to broaden Britain's industrial base after the war. Kent drew disproportionate benefit from the operation of import quotas on a variety of industries which governments fostered for strategic reasons. With such obvious signs of excess demand in the economy,

[53] *Ibid.*, pp. 136–9; Preston, *op. cit.*, p. 205.
[54] Scott, *op. cit.*, p. 215.

upsets like the collapse of Powers-Samas in 1958 and the closure of the Woolwich telecommunications factory in 1968 could be absorbed – not without difficulty or severe localised disruption – but the economy of Kent powered forward
until the more substantial problems of the 1980s. We have noted the closure of
Chatham dockyard and the downturn in both paper- and cement-making during
that decade, but unwelcome changes hit manufacturing in Kent more widely in
the 1980s. Two forces interacted to create particular problems for Kent's manufacturers. The very high exchange rate for sterling at the start of the 1980s not
only made life difficult for exporters and those firms competing with imports in
the domestic market, but also encouraged companies with global interests to
source production from outside the UK. The scale and dynamics of change can
be detected in the local labour market. During the long boom, Kent's unemployment rate lay well below the national average, but that advantage disappeared, as
can be seen in the bar charts in Fig. 4.

Figure 4 also shows changes in male unemployment in Kent, which can be
used as a rough guide to the state of the local production industries. Not all
unemployed males came from manufacturing and construction, but employment
in this sector was overwhelmingly male and was hit especially hard during the
slumps of the early 1980s and 1990s. In Kent, male unemployment almost
doubled in 1980–1 and more than doubled in 1990–1. There is no doubt at all
that Kent's manufacturing suffered a huge crisis in these two slumps, and falling
male unemployment in Kent after 1986 represents shifts of unemployed production workers into services and changes in the official definitions of unemployment rather than recovery in building and manufacturing. Other statistics
confirm this picture. Approximately 30% of employment in Kent was in the
manufacturing sector in 1961 and 1971, but by 1991 the figure had fallen to
14%. This was clearly the low point of Kent's industrial economy, and at the end
of the twentieth century Kent's economy was clearly more heavily dependent on
the service sector than at any time in its history.

(4) The Service Sector

As is evident from Table 16, Kent's economic structure has been dominated by
the service sector throughout the twentieth century. Kent's dependence on services was clearly much greater than that of the UK as a whole at the turn of the
present century, but the differences narrowed steadily from the First World War
to 1981 and the proportions were more or less identical in 1991. There seem to
be two questions to be posed of these trends: why was Kent's economy so
distinctively biased towards the service sector in the first half of the century; and
what has caused the relative expansion of the service sector at both the national
and local levels throughout the twentieth century?

To answer these questions it is necessary to consider briefly the role of services in the national economy. There are two 'models' which might help. The
first, more obvious, is the developed economy pattern in which the growth of

the service sector reflects a 'professionalisation' of national economic and social life. In all developed countries the demand for doctors, teachers, social workers, lawyers, managers, scientists and technicians has grown. As incomes have risen, the pattern of consumer expenditure has changed. Economists have identified a shift in consumer expenditure from basic foodstuffs to manufactured goods as wealth increases and a second shift from manufactures to services as living standards rise still further, though it would be unrealistic to assume that these processes are fully understood.[55] In most developed countries, this expansion of demand for service-sector workers has been roughly balanced by a decline in the number of workers in the primary sector – particularly from agriculture – so that in the 1950s and 1960s the production industries typically accounted for 40–50% of total employment with the balance in primary and service activities. There has been a limit to this process, however; from the mid-1960s signs of 'de-industrialisation' have spread in many rich countries with a steady decline in the proportion of the workforce in manufacturing employment while the service sector continued to absorb new workers as consumer expenditure on services and world trade in services grew very rapidly. Typically, this last phase involves the employment of increasing numbers of women in service-sector occupations at all levels. A good part of the explanation of the growth of the service sector is thus involved in a process of economic and social modernisation, a natural development in growing economies as incomes rise, economic and social life becomes more complex, family size falls and the roles of women change. There is, however, also a 'traditional service sector' which requires mention, and is found in its most clear-cut form in low-income, less-developed countries (LDCs). Employment patterns in such countries tend to be dominated by very large agricultural sectors, but many LDCs also have a surprisingly large service sector. The typical LDC has very high income inequality and over-plentiful supplies of cheap labour. There are few constraints on employers, and wealthy citizens making lavish use of personal servants to undertake tasks which would be simply uneconomic in countries where average incomes are higher and wealth more equally distributed. In addition, most LDCs simply do not have either enough jobs to employ the population of working age or any form of social security for the mass of the population, leaving the unemployed and under-employed little option but to congregate in low-income, low-productivity services (such as the infamous 'squeegee merchants', scavengers and street pedlars) to make some contribution to household income when full-time employment is unavailable.

At the broadest level, both models apply to Kent in the twentieth century. The forces underlying the modernising, developed-economy model should be particularly powerful in areas like Kent where living standards are boosted by the proximity of the capital city and the concentration therein of professional,

55 S. Glynn and A. Booth, *Modern Britain: An Economic and Social History*, London 1996, pp. 1–47, 273–6.

managerial and administrative functions. On a national level, service-sector employment has been heavily concentrated in south-eastern England at least since the 1850s.[56] On the other hand, there have also been aspects of the 'traditional service sector' in Kent, especially before 1939. In the early 1900s, economic and social conditions in Kent were very far removed from those found in classic late twentieth-century LDCs, but the county's distinctive economic and social geography (notably the presence of a very substantial upper-middle, servant-employing class and a large rural hinterland still dominated by agriculture which was far from prosperous before 1939) encouraged some parts of a traditional service sector to remain prominent well into the twentieth century. In short, the disproportionately large service sector in the county before 1939 cannot be fully explained persuasively in terms of the modernisation hypothesis outlined above.

A little more flesh can be put on these very broad approaches to the role and growth of the service sector by reference to Table 20 which compares the proportion of Kent's workforce in certain service activities with that in the UK as a whole. 'Domestic service' represents the quintessentially traditional part of the service sector. The wealthy have been able to purchase private services not through the market but by employing workers directly as domestic servants, especially when income distribution is highly unequal and when labour is cheap relative to the cost of the capital equipment (vacuum cleaners, washing machines, central-heating systems) which can supply the same benefits to the consumer. A recent historian of the service sector has argued that employment in domestic service grew rapidly in the Victorian period but collapsed in the first half of the twentieth century: 'Upstairs/Downstairs is a pre-1914 world.'[57] 'Commerce', as defined in the censuses before 1951, embraced financial services and (from 1921) parts of the distributive trades. At one level, commerce is a modern service as the demand for financial and retailing services seems to rise with average income, but classic LDC experience also suggests that distribution is an activity into which the under-employed can flock if the supply of labour greatly exceeds demand. There is good evidence, on a national scale, that unemployed industrial workers entered the distributive trades (in inefficient corner shops and in labour-intensive activities as retailers began to compete on standards of service) and other parts of the service sector in the depressed inter-war labour market.[58] 'Public administration and defence' is also something of a hybrid. The growth of public administration reflects the professionalisation of British economic and political life, but large numbers in 'defence' is more redolent of the 'pre-professional' phase when soldiers and sailors could be recruited easily and cheaply from urban and rural districts. 'Professions' is the archetypal

---

56 C. Lee, 'The Service Industries', *The Economic History of Britain since 1700. Vol. 2: 1860–1939*, ed. R. Floud and D. McCloskey, Cambridge 1994, p. 125.

57 *Ibid.*, p. 122.

58 D.H. Aldcroft, *The Inter-war Economy: Britain, 1919–1939*, London 1970, pp. 230–6.

Table 20

Service Sector Employment in Kent and Great Britain, 1901–31

	1901	1911	1921	1931
		Domestic Service		
Kent	15.5	14.6	12.3	11.3[1]
GB	9.5	9.1	7.0	7.2
	Public Administration and Defence (Public Administration only)			
Kent	8.8	8.6	9.7	12.0
	(1.6)	(2.3)	(n/a)	(7.1)
GB	2.4	3.0	3.7	2.9
	(1.4)	(1.8)	(2.4)	(0.7)
		Commerce[2]		
Kent	3.0	3.7	13.4	16.8
GB	4.1	4.9	7.7	11.0
		Professions[3]		
Kent	4.8	5.4	3.5	4.1
GB	4.1	4.4	4.1	4.4

Notes

1 As figures for domestic service are not given separately for Kent in the Census of 1931, this figure has been calculated on the assumption that the proportion of domestic servants within the wider enumeration group 'Personal Service' was the same in 1931 as in 1921, when separate figures were given for sub-categories. Calculations were made for males and females separately.

2 As defined in each successive census. The main change is the inclusion of clerical workers in 1901 and 1911, who are distributed by industry of employment from 1921.

3 As defined in each census. The main change is the inclusion of entertainers and sportsmen in 1901 and 1911, and exclusion thereafter.

Sources: Census, Industry and Occupation Tables; C. Lee, 'The Service Industries', *The Economic History of Britain since 1700. Vol. 2: 1860–1939*, ed. R. Floud and D. McCloskey, Cambridge 1994, pp. 122–5 (for the numbers of domestic servants in Great Britain); Mitchell and Deane, *Abstract of British Historical Statistics*, pp. 59–61.

modern service, though measurement problems (outlined in the notes to Table 20) limit the term's usefulness. In very broad terms, it is clear that before 1939 Kent's service-sector employment was so large because a modern service sector was growing when traditional service activities remained very resilient.

The really big component in the Kent service sector before 1939 was the 'traditional' activity of domestic service. More than one-tenth of all workers (and more than one-quarter of all service-sector workers) in Kent were in domestic service in the census years before 1931. 'Upstairs/downstairs' clearly did not disappear from Kent with the First World War but remained until the Second. Domestic service represents low-paid and low-productivity work and in many ways illustrates the dead weight of depression in the agricultural and industrial economy of the region between the wars.[59] In a depressed general-labour market and with limited employment opportunities for females, domestic service offered a very traditional avenue of work for the unskilled unemployed. The two hybrid categories show a similar pattern of development. There was very strong growth in commercial activity, both in Kent and more generally. In part, the rapid expansion of employment resulted from 'modernising' forces. There was strong growth in retailing in the north-west of the county around London. The number of separately enumerated workers in financial services grew rapidly (2,310 in 1901, 3,878 in 1911, 4,245 in 1921, and 8,887 in 1931) but comprised an insignificant part of the total workforce (less than 0.05% of Kent's total workforce in 1931). On the other hand, commerce undoubtedly acted as a reservoir for those who lost their agricultural or industrial jobs. Employment in distribution roughly doubled between 1921 and 1931, and did not reach this level again until well after the Second World War. Employers in distribution exploited the slack inter-war labour market. Public administration and defence also illustrate the dual character of the service sector in Kent. The scale of central- and local-government employment was marginally higher in the county than in the nation as a whole before the First World War, but the Kent boroughs clearly expanded their workforces after the war and especially in the slump in ways which were not generally paralleled. On the other hand, Kent was undoubtedly heavily garrisoned, as one might expect given its strategic position. The census does not give figures for each of the three services, but the number of RAF personnel clearly grew rapidly alongside the much longer established naval and army bases in the county. Thus, both 'traditional' and 'modern' service-sector activities saw employment growth in the inter-war years.

Although the Second World War did not entirely sweep away the traditional service sector, the much tighter labour market after 1945, rising living standards and the growth of a more diversified female labour market ensured that the more modern services would flourish and the traditional would wilt. Domestic service contracted dramatically; in 1951, domestic servants comprised 4% of the county's workforce (much lower than the inter-war figures given in Table 20, but still above the 2.2% in the nation as a whole). The contraction of the number of armed-forces personnel in Kent came more slowly, but the ending of conscription in the late 1950s and the reduction of Britain's overseas defence role and with it the size of the navy reduced the number of defence personnel in Kent. On the other hand, the local economic and social structures have become more 'professionalised' since 1951. At the broadest level, there has been substantial growth in the number of managerial and professional workers in the county, and even changes in census definitions cannot mask the general trends (see Table 21).

---

[59] In agriculture, the number of casual workers almost halved between 1921 and 1931, with smaller, though noticeable falls in the number of 'regular' male and female workers over the same period. Aggregate employment in manufacturing remained steady over the decade 1921–31, but a very large increase in employment in paper-making tended to cover steady falls elsewhere: G.H. Garrad, *A Survey of the Agriculture of Kent*, London 1954, p. 227; see also Table 18 above.

Table 21

Professional and Managerial Employment in Kent, 1951–81[1]

	1951	1961	1971	1981
Number	67,899	116,750	124,090	122,580
Proportion of those economically active (%)	12.2	19.6	20.3	20.0

Notes
1   Defined here as 'employers', 'self-employed', 'managers', 'foremen' and 'professional workers'.

Source: Census, Occupational and Industrial Tables.

Within this broad category, the number of workers in education trebled between 1951 and 1971, rising from 2.1% to 6.6% of the total county workforce. Similarly, the creation of the National Health Service and the subsequent growth of public expenditure on health have been reflected in a near doubling of the numbers of workers in medical services in the county (to comprise 5.0% of the county workforce) over the same period. Finally, mention must be made of the growth of employment in financial services in the present century. The growth in personal and corporate wealth in the twentieth century has stimulated an enormous expansion in the banking and financial sector to manage the growth of assets. Employment in the financial-services sector has risen dramatically from the negligible levels in 1901 noted above to more than 92,000 in 1991, representing 13.9% of the county's workforce, and much of that great rise has occurred since 1971.

This broad shift in occupations has reflected and stimulated a shift in the gender balance of employment. The service sector, in both its traditional and modern forms, is a major employer of female labour. In 1951, four in every ten service-sector workers were female; by 1991, more than half the much expanded services workforce was female. There has been a considerable expansion of female employment at the same time, as jobs in manufacturing (which tend to be for males) have disappeared because of the closure of manufacturing firms and the normal processes of technical change. This change has been concentrated in the period since 1951, as Table 22 illustrates.

The figures suggest relative stability in the female labour market in the first half of the century. Women made up roughly 27–8% of the workforce before 1951 and the proportion of working-age women who were economically active changed little, certainly before the Second World War. In some respects, this is surprising. The very slow contraction of the 'traditional' service sector and the rapid expansion of the 'modern' noted above might have produced rather more obvious growth of female employment, but the shift of female workers into the service sector has occurred largely in the second half of the twentieth century. The rising participation ratio after 1951 has clearly been founded upon the increasing tendency for women to return to employment after marriage and

Table 22

Female Labour Force Participation in Kent since 1901

	Percentage of workforce female	Percentage of female workers married	Female participation rate[1]	Proportion of female workers employed part-time
1901	27.1	20.6[2]	28.0	–
1911	28.0	12.4	28.9	–
1921	28.0	11.7	28.5	–
1931	26.6	–	29.1	–
1951	29.2	38.5	32.8	12.9
1961	39.0	32.8	45.9	24.6
1971	41.1	65.0	51.9	–
1981	38.8	66.5	57.6	36.6
1991	43.0	63.9	67.0	33.0

Notes

1   The definition of the participation rate changes over time. Before 1921, the participation rate is calculated as the proportion of females aged ten and who are over economically active. In the inter-war
censuses, the denominator is the number of women aged 14–60, and after the Second World War
changes in the minimum school-leaving age have been taken into account.
2   The percentage married and widowed, as the 1901 census does not separate the two groups.

Source: Census.

childbirth. Falling family size, the increasing ability of women to control their
fertility, fundamental changes in attitudes which have made work more socially
acceptable for married women, and girls' improved performance in education
have all underwritten this very fundamental change in the labour market.[60] The
economic mobilisation of women with family responsibilities has also been
facilitated by the growth of part-time employment; indeed, more than two-thirds
of the increase in total employment in Kent since 1951 can be explained by the
growth of part-time female employment. This development can be interpreted
as either evidence of the exploitation of females in low-paid, insecure jobs with
few promotion prospects, or a happy match between employers' demands for
cheap, flexible labour and women's desires to mix work and family responsibilities in innovative ways.[61] Whatever the final judgement, the female labour
market at the end of the twentieth century in Kent appears to be rather more
prosperous than that faced by males in the county. The strong growth of female
employment has been underpinned by comparatively low unemployment, when
compared with male workers. Figure 5 shows the number of claimant unemployed by gender since 1976. Throughout the period covered, males have made
up roughly 60% of the county workforce and females approximately 40%. The

[60]   S. Dex, *The Sexual Division of Work*, Brighton 1985.
[61]   O. Robinson, 'The Changing Labour Market: The Growth of Part-time Employment and Labour
Market Segmentation in Britain', *Gender Segregation at Work*, ed. S. Walby, Milton Keynes 1988.

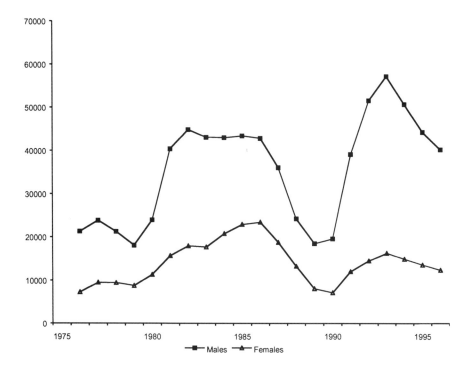

Figure 5. Numbers unemployed in Kent since 1976.

Note: Figures relate to July each year.
Sources: *Employment Gazette* and *Labour Market Trends*, various issues.

differential exposure to unemployment is all too clear. As noted above, male unemployment has risen sharply during recessions. Female unemployment, on the other hand, is subject to less severe cyclical fluctuations and runs at much lower levels than among males. In general, the service sector has shown strong underlying expansion since 1951 (as is evident from Figures 1 and 2) and this has increasingly favoured the growth of jobs for women and has supported the local economy through the very difficult times it experienced in the 1980s and 1990s.

(5) Conclusion
Four main trends are evident in the economy of Kent since the First World War. First, the twentieth century has seen the rise and decline of the Kent coalfield, a development which has been both exciting and frustrating in the sense that hopes were raised of a major industrial transformation of the south-east of the county, only to be thwarted by the difficulty of the underground conditions and,

in the longer term, by fundamental changes in the energy market. Secondly, the manufacturing base, which appeared to be in a rather parlous state in the 1920s and early 1930s, was rejuvenated by rearmament in the later 1930s, which aided the long-established arms economy of the north-west of the county, and also by the transformation and expansion of the material processing industries (cement, paper, oil) which increasingly moved to coastal locations within easy reach of the London market. This strengthening of Kent's manufacturing economy lasted into the 1980s, when a combination of high interest rates, national economic mismanagement, cuts in defence expenditure and the pressures on materials processors from more intensive global competition dealt a severe blow to the production sector from which it has not yet fully recovered. The local economy has, however, retained some of its buoyancy with the strong growth of the service sector since the Second World War, which reflects the particular advantages of Kent, in terms of proximity to the administrative hub of London and good transport links for the county's commuters, but also more generally in the forces of professionalisation of British economic and social life and the switch of expenditure into services as incomes rise. Finally, the second half of the present century has witnessed the growing economic mobilisation of women and a major shift of female employment from domestic service to many other parts of the service sector, notably the professions, the 'leisure industry' and financial services. This great growth of the service sector has not, however, been able to sustain Kent's relative prosperity. The unemployment rate, which remained consistently below the national average throughout the long post-war boom, has exceeded the national average since the early 1990s and the return to boom conditions depends upon another fundamental restructuring of the local manufacturing base into areas of greater long-term potential.

3

Agriculture and Rural Society

ALAN ARMSTRONG

On the eve of the Great War, the chief crop grown by British farmers was grass. This reflected the increased importance attaching to livestock products from the 1870s, the consequence of rising living standards and large-scale imports of cereals in which overseas, especially North American, producers enjoyed a considerable comparative advantage. Approximately one-third of British consumer expenditure on food in 1913 was spent on imported goods, and the contribution of agriculture to the national economy was in relative decline. Although some observers, notably A.R. Hall, sometime principal of Wye College, reckoned to discern sure signs of improvement from 1908 (reflecting a modest price recovery), at no time since the late 1870s had it been easy to make a good living from farming; there was a marked tendency to look back to the mid-Victorian period as a 'golden age', which in all probability could never be recovered. Kent was not immune from the difficulties of these years, as is shown vividly by a 37% decrease in agricultural rents between 1873 and 1911 – a fall exceeded in only six other English counties. Here, as elsewhere, output adjustments were the order of the day, the area of land given over to arable falling from 436,000 acres in 1875 to 294,000 in 1914, and the amount of permanent pasture rising across the same period from 290,000 to 439,000 acres. Those branches of production that contributed most to the public perception of Kent as the 'Garden of England' experienced varying fortunes. The area of land given over to the cultivation of hops – always a risky venture and vulnerable to foreign competition – halved between the late 1870s and 1914. However, fruit production, encouraged by enhanced purchasing power, rose steadily, approximately doubling in terms of acreage between 1888 and the early 1900s.[1]

For all its difficulties, and there were many, agriculture remained the most important single economic activity of Kent on the eve of the war. According to the 1911 census, the number of farmers and graziers (4,881) was exceeded in only twelve other English counties, and that of agricultural labourers (31,591) in only three. The number of people employed per thousand acres, or per holding

---

[1] For an elaboration of these remarks, see the chapter on 'Agriculture' by G.E. Mingay in *The Economy of Kent 1640–1914*, ed. A. Armstrong, Woodbridge 1995, esp. pp. 76–81.

was extremely high, being matched or exceeded only in Middlesex, Surrey and Lancashire, while a multiplicity of tradesmen and shopkeepers depended on the custom of agriculturalists and formed an integral part of rural society.[2] As elsewhere, Kentish villages were 'still dominated by that powerful traditional triumvirate of squire, large farmer and parson' so that, at least superficially, rural life went on as it had always done.[3] In its last pre-war issue, the *Kentish Gazette* devoted half a column to the 'threatened great European War' but nearly equal space to the Petham and Waltham Flower Show and more to the East Kent Art Exhibition and to its Poultry Notes.[4] The British people expected a war of short duration and had little to guide them other than recollections of the Boer War, fought thousands of miles away against colonial guerrillas, and folk memories of the Battle of Waterloo. There was no way of foretelling the horrors that lay ahead, or indeed the ways in which the war would impact on economy and society.

(1) The Wartime Experience, 1914–18

The first effects noticed in rural Kent, apart from bustling troop movements, involved the requisitioning of farm horses, which gave rise to some delays in the getting in of the 1914 harvest, and a drain of men volunteering for military service. Landed proprietors were zealous in encouraging their employees to sign up. From Chevening, Colonel Borton, too old to serve himself, conveyed his cowman, footman and butler to Maidstone to enlist; at Mereworth, Lord Torrington induced several young men to follow his example by joining the ranks; while the tiny hamlet of Knowlton produced no fewer than twelve recruits (out of a total population of 39), thereby winning the *Weekly Dispatch* competition for 'the bravest village in Britain'.[5] However, as early as April 1915 it was acknowledged at the Maidstone depot of the Royal West Kent Regiment that enthusiasm had definitely abated, even as the need for more servicemen continued to escalate. Under arrangements concluded in August 1915, a national register was drawn up of all men aged between fifteen and sixty-five, with those engaged in essential civilian work 'starred' (i.e. they would neither be accepted for military service nor solicited for it). Farmers, and some specialist agricultural occupations were included in this category, though not the all-round men. There followed in March 1916 the Military Service Act ushering in conscription for all men aged 19–30, although starred individuals were to be allowed temporary exemption in order to allow time for substitutes to be found. Individual

2   W.A. Armstrong, 'Kentish Rural Society during the First World War' in *Land, Labour and Agriculture 1700–1920*, ed. B.A. Holderness and M. Turner, London 1991, p. 110. Much of what follows is based upon this chapter, which may also be consulted for fuller references.

3   Mingay, *op. cit.*, p. 81.

4   *Kentish Gazette*, 1 August 1914.

5   P. Horn, *Rural Life in England in the First World War*, Dublin 1984, p. 28; *South Eastern Gazette*, 15 September 1914; *Kentish Gazette* 1 April 1916.

cases were decided by local tribunals, initially based on district councils, dominated in the rural areas by farmers and later by the War Agricultural Committee
(see below); appeals against their decisions (on behalf of the men concerned, or
by the military authorities) were determined by two county tribunals sitting in
Canterbury and Maidstone. Inevitably, conscription was an invidious business,
for the machinery appeared to many to be capable of being manipulated by
farmers to the advantage of their sons. In official correspondence, the Chairman
of the West Kent Appeals Tribunal remarked in 1918 that 'the automatic exemption of the young farm labourer is a cause of serious discontent in the villages,
not merely among the relatives of men serving but among the men who have
returned home . . . owing to wounds or sickness. . . . As a rule the employer is
the father.'[6]

Thus, the pattern of military recruitment had a direct bearing on labour availability and also offers an insight into the texture of social relationships during
the war. On behalf of farmers, it must be acknowledged that they faced genuine
problems in finding substitute labour, for enormous numbers were absorbed into
the war construction and munitions industries, as well as into the armed forces –
these included the creation of a seaport at Richborough where at one point
20,000 men were at work on the project; the construction of approximately fifty
airfields in the county; and the covering of the Isle of Hoo with batteries and
forts. Moreover, it is fair to mention that many farmers' sons did serve with the
colours and never sought to avoid military service. The contrast drawn in Sir
Charles Igglesden's novel, *Crimson Glow,* between the farming families of the
Pattendens (whose son, having volunteered, is missing in action) and the
Flowerdews (whose son is exempt) had substance in fact as well as in fiction.[7]
And people in other walks of life, as the surviving papers of the East and West
Kent Tribunals show, exerted themselves no less strenuously to obtain exemp-
tion for their sons – though with much less chance of success.

The first response of farmers to labour scarcity was to seek to prise boys of
twelve and over out of school. This reflected a widespread and long-standing
suspicion that, as the Chairman of the Ashford branch of the National Farmers'
Union (NFU) put it, 'education was no good to them at all; it unsettled them and
they were much better off on the farm'.[8] The Kent Education Authority (against
the background of a persuasive Board of Education circular) gave way in March
1915 and by the end of the war over 4,000 Kent children were 'licensed' to be
released for agricultural purposes. Kentish agriculture had always relied on the
contribution of women and continued to do so, though the extent to which they

---

[6]   CKS C/A2/15/1. Correspondence of Clerk to West Kent Appeals Tribunal with Government Departments. Copy letter dated 4 February 1918.
[7]   Sir C. Igglesden, *Crimson Glow,* 2nd edn, Ashford 1925. While its literary merits are decidedly
limited, this novel accurately reflects many aspects of rural life in Kent during the war. R.K.I. Quested,
*The Isle of Thanet Farming Community. An Agrarian History of Easternmost Kent:Outlines from Early
Times to 1992* (privately printed 1996), pp. 171–2 has brought to light a number of instances of farmers'
sons fighting and dying in the conflict.
[8]   *South Eastern Gazette,* 2 February 1915.

were prepared to become virtually full-time, rather than seasonal, workers was said to be hampered by higher wages in munitions works, by income derived from billeting soldiers, and by separation allowances which some contemporaries thought too lavish. Later in the war, Kent became one of the main users of the Women's Land Army, constituted in 1917, accounting for 10% of the national total. Towards the end of hostilities, prisoners of war were extensively used but a major source of replacement labour was soldiers not currently required for military purposes. These men were charged for by the War Office at rates which farmers initially demurred at, but reliance on this source became well established from 1917, and by the autumn of 1918 some 3,000–4,000 were at work on Kentish farms, performing their tasks with varying degrees of expertise and enthusiasm, since relatively few had prior experience of farm work. By ordinary peace-time standards, the agricultural labour force was a motley crew, but by a combination of these expedients the aggregate input of labour into Kentish agriculture was probably more or less maintained.[9]

Indeed, it was vital to do so, as events unfolded. During the first phase of the war, no special attention was given to agriculture and farmers were left free to follow whatever lines of production suited them. However, a poor harvest in 1916 and losses of ships from submarine attacks – both of which threatened to exacerbate existing price inflation and to cause industrial disruption – brought about a sea-change in policy. Asquith's government gave way in December 1916 to a coalition headed by Lloyd George, pledged to resolute action in the prosecution of the war and in the direction of the civilian economy, from which came the power to sustain the war. A food production programme was set in hand to control cropping and to push it firmly in the direction of the growing of more cereals and potatoes, since it was appreciated that a given area of arable land would feed more people than the same area given over to livestock. To this end, farmers were encouraged to plough up grassland by a totally unprecedented system of guaranteed prices, under the Corn Production Act of 1917. The local implementation of the policy was entrusted to the county and district war agricultural committees. It was their task to visit every farm, to schedule land for ploughing and in the last resort to recommend the ejection of unsatisfactory farmers in favour of more efficient replacements, or they could farm holdings on their own account. The county committees also took charge, via subcommittees, of the allocation of labour and other scarce supplies such as fertilisers and farm machinery including American tractors and tractor ploughs which typically made their debut on British farms during the last year of the war.[10]

[9] As it was nationally, according to the calculations of P.E. Dewey, *British Agriculture in the First World War*, London 1989, p. 139, who estimates that with these various forms of replacement labour, the shortfall was 9% in 1916 and 4% in 1918.

[10] On this subject see G.A. Garrad, 'The Work of the Motor Tractor in Kent', *Journal of the Royal Agricultural Society*, lxxxiv (1918), who stresses the experimental nature of their introduction and the problems involved.

Table 23

Acreage devoted to principal arable crops in Kent, 1914–18

	1914	1916	1918	% Increase 1914–16	% Increase 1916–18
Wheat	46,464	53,325	76,830	15	44
Barley	28,925	24,903	29,515	−14	19
Oats	41,106	46,003	57,857	12	26
Peas and Beans	17,764	13,994	30,449	−21	118
Potatoes	16,220	15,080	24,479	−7	62
Total	150,479	153,305	219,130	2	42

Source: CKS CC/R46. *Report of Work Done by the Kent War Agricultural Committee from its Formation until December 31st, 1918*, p. 76, quoting acreage returns published by the Food Production Department.

In Kent, the War Agricultural Committee issued over 3,000 ploughing orders and in only a small minority of cases was prosecution necessary. As a consequence, the acreage devoted to arable crops was dramatically increased (see Table 23); indeed, the rise in the acreage devoted to wheat was exceeded in only five other counties and, in the case of potatoes, only one. Naturally, the output of other farm products fell back. Although the number of cattle increased by 17% between 1914 and 1918, there was a decrease of 15% in the number of sheep, and even greater falls for pigs and poultry. Land given over to small fruits fell by 35% and in the case of hops by even more, for during the war the government took a series of steps to curtail beer consumption and brewing with the consequence that the hop requirement was greatly reduced. It was at the instigation of growers that, in 1917, the government took measures to compel them to confine themselves to no more than 50% of their 1916 acreages, with a hop controller to oversee these arrangements.[11]

The effects of the war on the main elements of rural society were varied. Least well-known is its impact on rural tradesman and craftsmen. Much depended, no doubt, on their locations. Brisk business might follow the establishment of troop encampments. On the other hand some shopkeepers lost custom (such as a grocer of Shalmsford Street who attributed his failure to the grubbing-up of hops and the consequent reduction of pickers). Several blacksmiths are known to have downed their tools and entered government employment, at Dover and the Chatham dockyard, and there is evidence from Thanet that small-holders, market gardeners and some rural tradesmen were forced out of business as a result of the sometimes wayward decisions of the military tribu-

[11] *Idem, A Survey of the Agriculture of Kent,* County Agricultural Surveys No. 1, Royal Agricultural Society, London 1954, pp. 104, 114, 131, 144, 157, 162.

nals. On the whole though, the rate of attrition of such rural businesses seems to have been no higher during the war years than in peacetime.[12]

Much more information is available concerning farmworkers and the indications are that cash wages increased by between 1s and 3s during the first two years of war, to reach an average of 22–23s early in 1917. Later that year, statutory minima came into effect for the first time, linked to the Corn Production Act, and in January 1918 the cash wages of ordinary labourers in Kent ranged from 25 to 30s, rising to 33s in May. Earnings (taking account of piecework, overtime and Michaelmas money) appeared from small-scale enquiries to add perhaps 2–4s a week, and on fruit and hop farms, 4–7s a week, to these time-wage rates.[13] However, it is improbable that the remuneration of farmworkers rose by more than about 50% up to 1918, while even the boost that came with the application of the Wages Board minima still left their incomes somewhat short of achieving a doubling. This level of pay was insufficient to match increases in the cost of living, which between 1914 and January 1919 rose by some 122%, though there must have been wide variations of individual experience. Single men, living in, were to some extent protected from increases in the cost of living, and among their married counterparts much depended on the family profile:

> a man who has four or five children of school age . . . will probably lose more by the rise in prices than he will gain by the rise in wages; but a man who no longer has any young children, but two or three aged 14–18 and a wife with more leisure to work on the farm will probably gain more by the rise in wages than he will lose by the rise in prices.[14]

The combination of unusual security in employment, with pressure on real wages, encouraged the spread in the later stages of the war of agricultural trade unionism, particularly by 1918 when the appearance of branches of the National Union of Agricultural Workers (or its rival, the Workers' Union) were noted – at Penshurst, Ashford, Paddock Wood, Lenham, Boughton, Selling, Faversham, Chilham, Chartham, Wye and Sissinghurst among other places.[15]

At the other end of the rural social spectrum, landowners had even more reason to rue the effects of the Great War. Already before 1914, landlords were conscious of some erosion of their social and political influence as a class, and for many members of the rural elite the war had disastrous effects. At the heart of their problems was the war-time stasis in rents. It was not customary to raise

12 Armstrong, *op. cit.*, pp. 124–5; Quested, *op. cit.*, pp. 173, 187–8; and see C. Grilli, 'The Effects of the First World War on the Survival of Craftsmen and Traders in Twenty-four East Kent Villages', BA Dissertation, University of Kent, 1990.
13 PP 1919 (Cmd 25) IX. Board of Agriculture and Fisheries. *Wages and Conditions in Agriculture*, II, *Reports of Investigators, Kent* (by B.H. Holland), pp. 124, 125, 128. See also E.J. Mejer, *Agricultural Labour in England and Wales, Part I, 1900–1920*, University of Nottingham School of Agriculture 1949, p. 32.
14 *Wages and Conditions in Agriculture*, pp. 131–2.
15 *South Eastern Gazette*, 5 March 1918; 26 March 1918; 2 April 1918; 9 July 1918.

the rent on a sitting tenant and to attempt to do so, in wartime, would have been considered ungentlemanly and unpatriotic. Moreover, from 1917 rent increases were effectively prohibited under the terms of the Corn Production Act. Consequently, rent revenues stagnated, at a time of brisk inflation and considerably increased rates of direct taxation. The economic pressures of the times were in some instances exacerbated by the loss of heirs on the field of battle, weakening the resolve of many great landowners to continue. Kent was considerably affected by such changes. Sales that occurred early in the war suggest some hesitancy on the part of prospective purchasers, evidenced in late 1915 when the bidding was slow at the dispersal of the Hartridge Manor estate (Staplehurst), while in February 1916 the East Sutton estate of Sir Robert Filmer (killed in action) achieved mixed results, some farms being bought by their tenants but half a dozen remaining unsold. However, there were signs, later in the year, that the market was beginning to move: part of this property, bought by Henry Gurr of Chatham for £10,750 and comprising land at Newington and Hartlip was resold for £14,530 in July. The following year, 1917, saw the disposal of the Badsell and Tudeley estates by order of Lord Falmouth and of well over 2,000 acres by William Deedes in the parishes of Postling, Saltwood, Aldington, Sellindge and Lympne, the purchasers again including some sitting tenants.[17] The year 1918 saw even more feverish activity in the land market. Land put up for sale in that year, and noted in the local press, included outlying portions (at Wingham and Elmstone) of the Street End estate of the Baker White Family in April; in the following month, an attractive hop and arable farm near Malling fetching £7,000; farm properties at Minster, Hartlip and Milstead on behalf of gentlemen such as Colonel Baldock, Major Locke and Captain Tylden; and the disposal of fruit freeholds at Sandwich, the property of Miss F.J. Lang ('every lot sold'). In August, the Arpinge estate at Newington near Hythe was sold up and great interest was shown in the Eastwell Manor sale ordered by Lord Gerard. September saw reports of the sale to tenants of a valuable fruit farm near Yalding by Colonel Cornwallis; the disposal of nearly the whole of Lord Harris's Sittingbourne estate and the Lee Priory Estate at Littlebourne – in both cases by private treaty with the tenants. In October the *South Eastern Gazette* remarked that 'the estate market was never so active as in the present year' and forecast that although the market must be 'about at its top', more would follow.[18]

No doubt the motives behind the numerous sales varied according to the individual circumstances in which landlords were placed. Not all of the vendors, by any means, were forced into selling, but business logic no doubt prompted others to recognise the wisdom of adjusting their landholdings 'while the going was good and the land-market hungry', perhaps in order to diversify their investments, and bearing in mind that no tax was payable on the capital proceeds of

16 *Ibid.*, 9 January 1916; 22 February 1916; 25 July 1916.
17 *Kentish Gazette*, 8 September 1917; 15 September 1917.
18 *Kentish Gazette*, 6 April 1918; 18 May 1918; 24 August 1918; 12 September 1918; *South Eastern Gazette*, 14 May 1918; 6 August 1918; 10 September 1918; 17 September 1918; 1 October 1918.

the sale of farms. Although there was some speculation, the striking feature common to most cases was the purchase of their holdings by one-time tenant farmers, corroborating the widespread impression that they had done well out of the war by dint of revenues that far exceeded their increased costs.

Writing a few years later, A.G. Street, a Wiltshire farmer and author, opined that 'it was impossible to lose money at farming just then'.[19] A few cases have been detected where Kentish farmers managed to do just that, and were bankrupted during the war years,[20] but the vast majority, it was commonly assumed, were prospering greatly. Certainly this view was widely held among their labourers, according to B.H. Holland of Harbledown Lodge, Canterbury, who compiled the Kent report on *Wages and Conditions in Agriculture*. It is unfortunate that few farm records survive to test such assertions in detail, although one accessible set shows what could be (though not always was) achieved. Francis Chambers was the fortunate owner of fruit farms at Lested Lodge and Redwater, near Maidstone: despite increases in various outlays (including labour), his profits rose from an average of £608 (1911–13) to £1,765 (average of 1914–15) reaching £3,943 (1916–17), followed by a second peak of £4,904 in 1918–19. Against this background he had no difficulty in replacing the 20 horse power Ford motor car, initially purchased in 1913, with a more expensive Overland model in 1916, while early the following year we find him buying a further farm at Egerton for £3,300.[21] No better illustration could be given of a contemporary assertion – made by the Rector of Mersham, Revd G. Brocklehurst – that occupying owners were enjoying profits 'beyond their wildest dreams'. Much the same applied, in Brocklehurst's view, to tenant farmers who were 'making enormous profits and paying low pre-war rents'; profits which, he emphasised, went largely untaxed, because farmers' income-tax payments were assessed on the basis of rentals paid.[22] His analysis anticipated the research findings of a modern scholar, P.E. Dewey, who draws attention, first, to a 242% increase in farmers' aggregate net income between 1909–13 and 1918; and secondly, on the basis of more complicated calculations, to approximately a doubling of farmers' profits considered as a percentage return on the capital involved.[23] His calculations are based on the 'national farm', but there is no reason to suppose that comparable averages for Kent would be significantly different. It was a sign of the increasing confidence of tenant farmers as a class, and of their determination to fight their corner in future, that they flocked in large numbers to join the National Farmers' Union in these years. In May 1915 it was calculated that 900 out of 3,400 Kent farmers were members, and just over a 1,000 in March 1916, while by May 1918 Mr Mainwaring, the Kent President, reckoned that member-

---

[19] A.G. Street, *Farmers Glory*, 23rd impression, London 1947, p. 142.

[20] Armstrong, *op. cit.*, p. 127. In cases such as that of E.F. Sinden of Bolsington, the likelihood is that the farmers in question were under-capitalised and quite probably on the slide before the war.

[21] CKS U1383/B1/13–20 and U1383/B3/3. Chambers' Farm Accounts.

[22] *South Eastern Gazette*, 16 April 1918 (reprinting a letter to *The Times*).

[23] Dewey, *op. cit.*, pp. 232–4.

ship had reached 2,200 and was busy taking names of more wishing to join at the end of the meeting of the Canterbury Farmers' Club, where these figures were announced.[24]

To summarise, there was an obvious element of inequity in the way in which the war impinged on the main elements of Kentish rural society, although no doubt such differences of experience pale into insignificance when the greater sacrifices of those engaged in actually fighting the war are borne in mind. In the short term, Kent had played a noteworthy part in upholding the level of national agricultural output and, in turn, this was a factor – albeit not the sole or even the most important one – in enabling the Allied cause to prevail.[25] Success in this respect had entailed a pronounced deviation from the patterns of production which had evolved over the forty years preceding the outbreak of hostilities and, as well, a degree of destabilisation of the old social order. The unexpectedly sudden signing of the Armistice on 11 November 1918 was marked by a public holiday, flags and bunting, thanksgiving services and congratulatory speeches; although for many, the wounds left by the war were too fresh to allow 'the spirit of rejoicing to reign in our hearts undisputed', even at Christmas, according to the *South Eastern Gazette*.[26] The events of the recent past were indisputably painful; what lay in the future it was impossible to foretell.

(2) Between the Wars, 1919–39

For a time, the British economy was caught up in a boom and in the circumstances prices received by farmers continued to move ahead briskly. Activity in the land market continued unabated, featuring, *inter alia*, the sale by Earl Sondes of a number of farms at Nackington near Canterbury where substantial tenants such as George Finn and Frank Goodson bought their holdings for £7,500 and £6,500 respectively.[27] During the course of 1919 the county war agricultural committees began to wind down their work. They were formally instructed in the spring to refrain from further directions over the use of agricultural land, and the horses, tractors and machinery which they operated were put up for sale: in Kent 194 tractors and 446 horses were thus disposed of, fetching prices that ran as high as £222 for a Fordson tractor and £173 5s for a grey gelding.[28] Prisoners of war were repatriated, the Women's Land Army was

---

[24] *South Eastern Gazette*, 11 May 1915; 7 March 1916; *Kentish Gazette* 11 May 1918.

[25] A. Offer, *The First World War: an Agrarian Interpretation*, Oxford 1989 argues convincingly that what was decisive was the Allies' command of the economic and human resources of the Americas and the British Dominions. The naval blockade that was imposed on the Central Powers, coupled with the failure of German agriculture and food administration (in contrast to Britain) gave rise to widespread malnutrition and low morale.

[26] *South Eastern Gazette*, 31 December 1918.

[27] CKS U1175/E34/13: Sondes Papers, Nackington Estate.

[28] CKS CC/R46: *Report on Work done by the Kent Agricultural Executive Committee from 2 January 1919 to 30 September 1920*, pp. 16, 18, 22.

demobilised by Christmas 1919 and the 1921 census would reveal that the hired labour force was returning to its normal profile, albeit reduced by some 8% from the 1911 level.[29] Farm workers' wages continued to ascend, reaching (for those aged 21 and over) statutory minima of 39s 6d. in May 1919 and 47s 6d. in March 1921, although this is not to say that they were rising in real terms, due to increases in the cost of living.[30] The County Council itself was becoming a significant landowner. Earlier legislation (in 1909) had obliged it to make a start on providing small holdings and the Land Settlement (Facilities) Act of 1919 provided central funds to assist county councils to create small holdings for ex-servicemen. In Kent, hundreds of applications were received and by 1922 the Council was leasing 318 such holdings, comprising around 5,000 acres in all.[31] Meanwhile – though not without provoking hot debate – the Agriculture Act of 1920 upheld the regime of guaranteed prices for a further four years, retained the wage-fixing machinery of the Agricultural Wages Board and made minor improvements to the security of tenants (notices to quit when a holding was offered for sale were invalidated). All in all, wrote one authority, 'optimism ruled the agricultural world at the end of the war' and another, more recently, suggests that farmers might have been forgiven for believing that *laissez-faire* had been truly reversed as a result of the war experience.[32]

Unfortunately, these conditions were short-lived. As a consequence of a world-wide glut of agricultural products, especially cereals, prices fell dramatically during the second half of 1921, a situation exacerbated by a severe slump in industry and exports. In this situation, the government, fearing the bill for guaranteed prices, repealed the 1920 Act. This step was subsequently represented as 'the Great Betrayal', though evidently it was not strongly opposed by the NFU at the time, perhaps due to the simultaneous abandonment of wage controls, and to some temporary compensation payments.[33] It represented a return to market forces, and through the rest of the 1920s and in the early 1930s, prices continued on a downward trend with temporary remissions, as in 1923–5 and 1927–9. Throughout the inter-war period, the question of what should be done to assist agriculture was a difficult one for British governments – of any political complexion – since they had to take account of the interests of the consumers (and the electorate was, after all, primarily urban), of Empire producers who expected preferential treatment, and of foreigners who might well retaliate against British exports in the event of strong protectionist meas-

---

[29] Comparing the numbers of agricultural labourers and farm servants recorded in the censuses of 1911 and 1921, the fall was from 31,591 to 28,853 in Kent as a whole.

[30] Mejer, *op. cit.*, p. 33; idem, *Agricultural Labour in England and Wales, Part II, Farm Workers' Earnings, 1917–1951*, University of Nottingham School of Agriculture 1951, pp. 12–13, 15.

[31] E. Melling, *History of the Kent County Council*, Maidstone 1975, p. 39.

[32] A.W. Ashby, 'Agricultural Conditions and Policies 1910–38' in *Agriculture in the Twentieth Century. Essays . . . presented to Sir Daniel Hall*, Oxford 1939, p. 59; S. Pollard, *The Development of the British Economy, 1914–50*, London 1961, p. 134.

[33] R. Perren, *Agriculture in Depression, 1870–1940*, Cambridge 1995, pp. 37–9; J. Brown, *Agriculture in England. A Survey of Farming, 1870–1914*, Manchester 1987, pp. 78–9.

ures. However, a short-lived Labour government restored, in 1924, the Agricultural Wages Board (though not a national minimum wage – the levels were determined county by county) and this halted the sharp fall that occurred after 1921. In the later 1920s Baldwin's Conservative government introduced subsidies in order to assist the growing of sugar-beet (1925), prohibited pork imports (overtly on sanitary grounds) in 1926, passed a measure to provide loans for farm purchase (the Agricultural Credit Act, 1928), and in the same year relieved agricultural land and buildings of all liability to rates. These steps were the harbingers of more comprehensive intervention in the wake of the 1931 crisis, by which point the price index of farm crops had fallen further, to only about 70% of its already depressed level in 1928–9. Under the auspices of the National Government, Britain introduced protection for horticultural products (December 1931), and then a series of quotas and tariffs on a range of agricultural goods from European and non-Empire countries (1932), modified at various dates by bilateral agreements with countries such as Denmark and Argentina. In 1931 the second Labour administration had already introduced an Agricultural Marketing Act which permitted a two-thirds majority of the producers of an agricultural commodity to band together and compel the rest to co-operate in regulating sales, but this measure had little success until, in 1933, it was revised in such a way as to add protection to any scheme deemed to require it. Marketing schemes were established for hops under the Labour government's Act, and subsequently for bacon, pigs, potatoes and – perhaps most notably – for milk. Finally, a variety of subsidies and deficiency payments emerged during the 1930s, notably with respect to wheat, where an Act of 1932 guaranteed prices and was financed by a levy on users of flour. The whole edifice of measures could be described as 'makeshift . . . improvised to meet a succession of particular emergencies', but in the round government assistance to farming certainly came to exceed anything that had been offered before in peacetime.[34] The overall effect was to lift the total national volume of production by one-sixth between 1930–1 and 1936–7, although prices never regained their 1927–9 level, let alone the heights of the war years, while imports in 1939, though slightly lower than in 1931, nevertheless remained above the 1929 level.[35]

This brief and simplified account of inter-war problems and policies provides a back-drop against which the successes and failures of Kent farmers can be interpreted. Reference to Table 24 shows a 52% fall in the wheat acreage between 1919 and 1929 and a minor consequence of this, perhaps, was the dying out of a number of ploughing matches by 1925.[36] There was but a modest recovery in the wheat acreage by 1939. In the county at large the barley acreage also fell considerably, except, it would appear, in Thanet where leading growers such as E. and C. Philpott, Captain Friend and E.S. Linington were producing

[34] Viscount Astor and B.S. Rowntree, *British Agriculture*, London 1938, p. 4; Perren, *op. cit.*, p. 53.
[35] *Ibid.*, pp. 60–1.
[36] Garrad, *Agriculture of Kent*, p. 194.

crops of prize-winning quality, highly regarded by brewers, from the 1930s.[37] The rest of the crops itemised in Table 24 showed highly variable fortunes. In the case of hops, the government control instituted in 1917, giving guaranteed prices and an assured market, lasted until 1925 and under this arrangement hop growers fared well.[38] Thereafter – despite exceptional protection offered by a tariff on foreign hops – prices sagged and the hop-growers' problems were not averted by the establishment of a voluntary co-operative association (English Hop Growers Ltd) which was wound up as early as 1929: 'ninety per cent of the growers joined. But the 10 per cent who didn't were quite enough to smash the whole show; which they did'.[39] Huge financial losses followed in 1930–1 until a new, and now compulsory, Hops Marketing Scheme was formulated in the wake of the Agriculture Act of 1931. From 1932 production was controlled and prices fixed in accordance with the quality of the produce and the costs of production. This arrangement was vulnerable to criticism on the grounds that it was monopolistic, conferring favours only on those already producing the crop, whose quotas soon became a saleable commodity. However, it did succeed in stabilising prices in the 1930s at around £9 per cwt, well above the level prevailing in 1927–32, and also the acreage involved.[40] Special importance attached, in the case of Kent, to fruit-growing, and Table 24 shows that the acreage given over to orchards was expanding but that of small fruit contracted, at least after 1929. In contrast to the hop-growers, Kentish fruit producers faced highly competitive market conditions: for example, the importation by jam manufacturers of foreign strawberry pulp in the 1920s, and the advent in the 1930s of Australian apples, which particularly affected small growers with no long-term storage facilities.[41] As a long-standing producer of fruit, Kent suffered to some extent from the penalties of pioneering, for large acreages had been planted before any scientific advice was available: moreover, although the orchard acreage was still increasing (relative to the western counties), ground was being lost to East Anglia in the production of soft fruits.[42] In the face of these developments, time-honoured methods of trial and error necessarily gave way to a more scientific approach. This was encouraged by experiments carried out at the internationally famous East Malling Research Station, established in 1913 and much expanded between the wars. The most successful enterprises were well exemplified in the impressive 1,000 acres of fruit cultivated by S.W. Mount of Patrixbourne, who in the 1930s engaged in extensive spraying, brought in new root stocks, and developed improved forms of controlled storage

---

[37] Quested, *op. cit.*, pp. 193–4, 222.

[38] Garrad, *op. cit.*, p. 104.

[39] E.H. Whetham, *The Agrarian History of England and Wales*, VIII, *1914–1939*, Cambridge 1978, p. 190; J.A.S. Watson, *Rural Britain Today and Tomorrow*, Edinburgh and London 1934, p. 101.

[40] Astor and Rowntree, *op. cit.*, p. 130.

[41] Garrad, *op. cit.*, p. 114; Watson, *op. cit.*, p. 100.

[42] Garrad, *op. cit.*, p. 108; Astor and Rowntree, *op. cit.*, pp. 158–9.

Table 24

Changes in the farming pattern, 1919–52

	1919	1929	1939	1945	1952
Total Area under Crops and Grass (acres) [includes:	713,768	673,665	637,570	665,526	644,075
Wheat	61,551	29,463	35,175	60,178	57,502
Barley	27,564	20,576	16,184	42,821	39,726
Potatoes	17,851	14,252	15,152	23,038	22,236
Hops	10,559	11,820	10,460	11,160	12,374
Orchards	40,993	50,881	64,831	67,041	78,157
Small fruit	15,433	16,831	11,664	6,379	9,390
Vegetables	24,876	19,922	18,858	32,337	23,737
Temporary grass/ Clover/Lucerne	35,163	30,947	23,311	69,630	76,237
Permanent grass]	383,773	396,417	383,655	211,553	210,036
Rough Grazing	(16,346)	32,385	40,993	27,852	26,566
Numbers of:					
Cattle	104,579	98,744	104,657	116,426	122,872
Sheep	756,120	754,574	788,477	439,409	462,711
Pigs	53,011	72,388	95,411	54,069	122,321
Poultry	854,823 (1921)	1,371,238	1,722,755	958,442	1,709,246

Source: Ministry of Agriculture and Fisheries, *Agricultural Statistics*, published annually.

Notes

(i) The figure for 'rough grazing' in 1919 is not directly comparable with later returns: it relates to 'mountain and heathland' only.

(ii) No separate return for poultry was made before 1921.

(iii) Land beneath orchard trees could accommodate small fruit, and such acreages are included here under the latter heading only. Other orchards stood over permanent grass and acreages are included under both headings.

and packaging.[43] The vegetable acreage remained comparatively stable across the inter-war years, and the prices received did not fall so far as did the general price index for agricultural products in the twenties and early thirties.[44] This owed much to a degree of natural immunity against imports (green vegetables, especially, perished rapidly) and, after 1932, to tariff protection, leaving British producers in possession of almost the entire market. Even so, specialist producers, that is market gardeners, were always vulnerable to competition from

[43] N.B. Bagenal, 'Fruit Farms of S.W. Mount, Patrixbourne', *Journal of the Royal Agricultural Society of England*, xcvi (1935), pp. 89–100.

[44] Astor and Rowntree, *op. cit.*, p. 133.

'general' farmers whenever prices of 'ordinary' farm produce were low. Within the county of Kent, there had arisen by the 1930s a 'vegetable area on big farms in the Isle of Grain and to the north of Rochester', while further afield the expansion of vegetable growing in East Anglia was particularly noticeable.[45] However, established market-gardening locations do not appear to have suffered unduly: on the Isle of Thanet, E.S. Linington, Eric Quested and others were paying increased attention to the growing of broccoli, and the conveyance of this and other market garden produce to Covent Garden by lorry had given rise, by 1936, to 'a very large volume of nightly traffic to London', resulting in complaints about the noise.[46]

Perhaps the most striking feature of Table 24 is a marked increase in the amount of land given over to permanent grass and rough grazing – reflecting a nation-wide trend. On the livestock side, the number of pigs recovered after the war, and, generally, moved in an upward direction, subject to the peculiarities of the pig cycle.[47] Pig producers faced various difficulties in these years, not least in the face of extensive Danish imports, especially prior to 1932, and a producers' co-operative bacon factory established at Lenham in 1923 lasted only three years before closure in the face of competition from rival bacon curers.[48] However, restrictions on imports after 1934 via quotas, and the establishment of the Pigs and the Bacon Marketing Boards at any rate helped to stabilise prices, while it suited many Kentish producers to concentrate on rearing pigs for fresh pork which found an excellent market in London.[49] Sheep farmers experienced a heavy slump in prices for both mutton and wool in 1930–2 and reduced their flocks accordingly; but as Table 24 shows, across 1919–39 as a whole flocks were well sustained. Here again, a voluntary co-operative was tried and in this case met with success: Kent Woolgrowers Ltd was formed in 1920 to grade and sell fleeces and the number handled increased steadily from 25,000 in its first year of operation to 245,000 by 1939.[50] The Romney Marsh Sheep Breeders Association, formed in 1895, continued to oversee the export of ewes of the breed to almost every part of the globe, not just to Australia and New Zealand.[51] Cattle numbers were relatively stable. By and large Kent was not a beef-producing county, but experienced a good market for liquid milk in its resorts during the summer, and in London. With animal feed prices being characteristically low, the development of this branch of livestock farming appeared relatively profitable in the 1920s, notably to small farmers in the Wealden clay where much of the land passed into permanent pasture, as well as in the estab-

45 *Ibid.*, pp. 134, 140–3.
46 Quested, *op. cit.*, pp. 222, 223, quoting *The Isle of Thanet Gazette*.
47 The pig cycle took four years to work through. It is described (by Astor and Rowntree, *op. cit.*, pp. 215–16) in these terms: pigs fetch good prices, therefore farmers go into pigs, therefore pig prices fall, therefore farmers go out of pigs, therefore prices rise, and farmers go into pigs . . . (etc.), the point being that it is relatively easy to take up, or drop pig production.
48 Garrad, *op. cit.*, p. 161.
49 *Ibid.*, p. 158.
50 *Ibid.*, pp. 154–5.
51 *Ibid.*, p. 149; Watson, *op. cit.*, pp. 103–4.

lished districts such as Thanet and around Bromley and Sevenoaks.[52] Much attention was given in the inter-war period to the establishment of pedigree herds, to the monitoring of milk yields, the cleaning up of milking parlours, and to the systematic testing of cattle for tuberculosis (TT testing).A number of Kent producers were to the fore in these developments. They included, at Faversham, Thomas Neame whose herd gave the highest milk yield in Kent in the 1920s; the Alexander family at Eynsford; and, in Thanet, Captain Friend, H.A. Smith and Eric Quested who was responsible for piloting the introduction of the Milk Marketing Board into Kent in 1933.[53] Indeed, it was one of the aims of the Board to further improvements in quality and in hygiene, although its principal objective, of course, was to put dairy farmers in a better position by upholding guaranteed prices for milk. Finally, Table 24 shows that the count of poultry in Kent doubled, reflecting the national trend. Although egg and poultry prices tended to decline, so also did the cost of feeding stuffs, and the low capital requirements and the relative ease of entering this field meant that enterprises could be built up quickly.[54] Egg imports were curtailed by quotas after 1934 and the national *per capita* consumption increased by 50%, comparing 1909–13 to 1934–5.[55] The first egg-packing stations in Kent were established at Stonegate (just across the Sussex border) in 1926 and at Wye (1933), while some Kent farmers concentrated on table fowls for the London market, fattened by the 'cramming' method. However, as the daughter of a Headcorn poultry farmer remembers from her childhood, there were 'no loathsome factory farms or battery eggs then'.[56]

This brief and necessarily selective overview of the vicissitudes of the various branches of farming suggests that the state of Kentish agriculture between the wars defies easy generalisation. Progress was real, in terms of technical and economic efficiency gains. It was exemplified in the spread of the use of tractors – it is reckoned that in Thanet 'the leading farmers probably all had one or more by about 1930' and the number of horses in use declined quite sharply; the larger dairy farms usually deployed milk lorries or motor vans by 1931, and returns gathered in 1941 attested to the existence there of about a hundred assorted stationary engines, mostly powered by oil or petrol.[57] Old fashioned and locally made implements and equipment, including the traditional Kentish plough were passing out of use, and, showing some foresight, G.H. Garrad and N. Bagenal began as early as 1922 to collect them as potential museum

---

[52] Garrad, *op. cit.*, pp. 131, 132.

[53] M. Austen, *Changes in Farming. The Last Hundred Years*, Faversham Papers, No. 38, Faversham 1994, p. 51; W.G.G. Alexander, *A Farming Century. The Darent Valley, 1892–1992*, London 1991, pp. 64–6; Quested, *op. cit.*, pp. 198, 225–6.

[54] Astor and Rowntree, *op. cit.*, p. 231.

[55] *Ibid.*, pp. 244, 246.

[56] Garrad, *op. cit.*, pp. 164, 168; East Kent Federation of Women's Institutes, *East Kent within Living Memory*, Newbury and Canterbury 1993, p. 94 (hereafter referred to as EKWI).

[57] Quested, *op. cit.*, pp. 217, 218.

exhibits.[58] This was incidental to their work as, respectively, the County Agriculture Organizer and researcher at the East Malling Research Station. The expansion of agricultural education and research, at Wye College, the Kent Farm Institute at Sittingbourne (opened in 1929), Swanley Horticultural College, and as already noted, the celebrated East Malling Research Station played a notable part in encouraging the best standards of farming practice.[59]

We are, however, speaking of progress in the face of what often seemed highly adverse circumstances, and the fortunes of individual farmers varied enormously. Much depended on their sagacity and ability to react to changing circumstances; on the extent to which they had enjoyed the opportunity to build up a strong financial position in the preceding good years; and even on whether the wife was a source of independent capital or income.[60] Insofar as any generalisation is possible, a distinction should be drawn between substantial farmers – regardless of whether they were owners or tenants – and the smaller fry. Into the former category we can place figures such as William Alexander of Eynsford, whose changing enterprise continued to expand and 'was ticking over well'; and the larger-scale farmers in Thanet who acquired cars and telephones. These typified the sort of men who were able to participate in the world of county and even national affairs, marketing boards and dinners, and who were able to send their sons to Wye College which in 1939 had fifty-two Kent students out of a total of 180.[61] At times, of course, even they could feel the pinch: Rosemary Quested records that at the nadir of prices (winter 1930) her father Eric felt obliged to take emergency measures, including the paying of her school fees in potatoes and cauliflowers and the partial laying up of the family car; however, it was the only time, fortunately, when he was 'really short of money'. Her view is that, in contrast, Thanet's small farmers and small-holders were 'trapped in a hard lot', and she notes a sharp decline in the number of holdings smaller than fifty acres, some being given over to building and others amalgamated.[62] That this trend was by no means localised is suggested by the fact that in Kent as a whole – despite the County Council's attempt to provide for ex-servicemen, already noted – holdings of 1–49 acres declined by 976 between 1914 and 1939, and in the range 50–149 by 129.[63]

One of the perceived problems of farmers, and an area where they sought to restrain costs, was in respect of labour. Wages, as we have seen, were decon-

---

58 Garrad, *op. cit.*, p. 129.
59 *Ibid.*, pp. 107–8, 178–88. See also S. Richards, *Wye College and its World. A Centenary History*, Wye 1994, who remarks on the acceptance by the mid-1920s by leading farmers of the value of the college, some of whom had earlier doubted its practical relevance (pp. 82–4, 101–2).
60 Quested, *op. cit.*, p. 195.
61 Alexander, *op. cit.*, p. 53; Quested *op. cit.*, pp. 198–201; Garrad, *op. cit.*, p. 180.
62 Quested, *op. cit.*, pp. 195, 197, 200.
63 Figures based on a comparison of Board of Agriculture and Fisheries, *Agricultural Statistics* (for 1914) and Ministry of Agriculture and Fisheries, *Agricultural Statistics* (for 1939). Note that two or more holdings might in practice be worked as a single agricultural unit, run by a single farmer, so that the number of 'holdings' need not correspond directly to the number of 'farms', or 'farmers'. See Ministry of Agriculture, Fisheries and Food, *A Century of Agricultural Statistics*, London 1968, p. 21.

trolled from 1921 and the rate applying to 'ordinary' male labourers aged twenty-one and over no doubt fell sharply in Kent as elsewhere; in Thanet it was reported that they had sunk to 30s by the following year, and sometimes less.[64] The re-establishment of statutory wage control after 1924 helped to brake their descent, although the minima applying in this county, even for 'special classes' (stockmen, shepherds, horsemen etc.), stood at 33s in 1925 and 30s in 1933, thereafter rising somewhat to reach 40s in January 1940, when the 'ordinary' wage was 38s.[65] Earnings, due to overtime etc., would normally be a little higher than these figures, but a recent recollection of a typical farm worker's wage as 'a little over £2' must be close to the mark.[66] Seen from the employers' perspective such wages seemed high in comparison to pre-war days, and indeed were, in relation to the prices they were receiving for farm products. Due to the falling cost of living, the purchasing power of wages also increased. Virtually all farmworkers now possessed bicycles, and the marriages of their daughters were beginning to be celebrated in some style, with long dresses and bridesmaids in attendance.[67] There appears to have been little resentment of employers as such. Mr Wallis who worked on a farm at Hoo recalls that the farmers in his locality 'treated the farm workers well'. He continues:

at the end of the harvest the farmer laid on a charabanc to take the entire group for a trip to the seaside. At Christmas [he] supplied each worker with a joint of meat, so being a farm worker was not a bad lot considering the rent of his cottage was 2s 6d per week, plus perks like vegetables, eggs, cheap milk and the odd bird or rabbit when the farmer had his annual shoot.[68]

Despite such considerations, farm wages remained low in relation to other manual occupations and they often had large families to support. Rosemary Quested remembers that even as a small child, she was 'uneasily anxious of the gap that separated her from the workers' children on our isolated farm'. While her clothes were usually new, theirs were rarely so: 'she had leather shoes in winter and leather sandals in summer, they had old-fashioned laced boots in winter and shabby black plimsolls in summer'.[69]

As a result of pressures on farmers to reduce their costs, and more attractive wages outside agriculture, there was a 20% decline in adult male labour, a 41% fall in males under twenty-one and a 28% decline in the employment of women and girls between 1921 and 1939 (see Table 25), and by the late 1930s the difficulty of keeping men on the land was frequently remarked upon.[70] To the extent that moves out of agricultural employment implied social as well as occupational mobility, much of it was probably inter- rather than intra-generational – as

[64] Quested, *op. cit.*, p. 209.
[65] Mejer, *op. cit.*, Part II, pp. 45, 80.
[66] EKWI, *op. cit.*, p. 128.
[67] Quested, *op. cit.*, pp. 212, 213.
[68] G.K. Nelson, *To be a Farmer's Boy*, Gloucester 1991, p. 158.
[69] Quested, *op. cit.*, p. 211.
[70] *Ibid.*, p. 213, reporting remarks made at the 1938 NFU annual dinner.

Table 25

Changes in the (Hired) Farm Labour Force, 1921–68

	1921	1929	1939	1947	1952	1957	1962	1967
Regular Workers:								
Male, 21 and over	24,705	22,989	19,855	21,609	21,229	} 19,479	15,293	11,262
Male, under 21	5,501	4,044	3,236	3,353	2,749			
Women and Girls	3,757	2,712	2,722	4,500	3,583	2,253	1,635	1,080
Others, WLA	–	–	–	1,183	–	–	–	–
Others, POW	–	–	–	2,931	–	–	–	–
Casual and Seasonal Workers:								
Male, 21 and over	4,748	3,150	2,157	3,339	4,803	} 14,544	11,769	9,834
Male, under 21	1,127	524	197	296	461			
Women and Girls	9,576	6,679	5,585	8,966	10,537			
All Hired Workers:	49,414	40,098	33,752	46,774	43,362	36,276	28,697	22,176

Source: Ministry of Agriculture and Fisheries (and Food, from 1957), *Agricultural Statistics.*

Notes

(i) In principle, these figures exclude farmers and their wives, daughters and children at school, but include other persons who may be related to the employer.

(ii) The descriptive headings used in the Agricultural Returns have varied across the period. It is here assumed that 'regular' workers correspond to 'whole-time', and that the expressions 'part-time' and 'casual and seasonal' can be treated as synonymous. They were not separately distinguished until 1955.

in the case of the three sons of Alfred Studham, a horseman of Hartsdown, Thanet, who became, respectively, a small farmer at Selling, a nurseryman at Acol and a rating officer for the Margate Corporation. More commonly, perhaps, young farmworkers or their sons achieved mobility by joining the forces as regulars, including one known to have eventually become a lieutenant.[71] For the daughters of labourers, prospects remained limited. 'Most girls went into service when they left school at 14' recalls a woman from Ide Hill, while the experience of an East Kent girl must be representative of many: 'On leaving school at Nonington at fourteen I was straight into service in a big house. There was no choice for me as it meant one mouth less to feed at home.'[72]

Along with the advance of permanent grass, the Kentish countryside saw a marked increase in the incidence of gorse and weeds, notably on the Weald.[73] Otherwise, its physical appearance changed relatively little. The construction of a number of new arterial roads, especially in the 1920s, did not compromise the

71 *Ibid.*, pp. 212, 214.
72 West Kent Federation of Women's Institutes, *West Kent within Living Memory.* Newbury and Maidstone 1995, p. 161 (hereafter referred to as WKWI); EKWI, *op. cit.*, p. 149.
73 P. Brandon and B. Short, *The South East from AD 1000*, London 1990, p. 330.

landscape as much as might have been expected, for in 1934 Kent County Council adopted by-laws to control the appearance and siting of petrol stations. Moreover the county was among the first to use powers given under the Advertisement Regulation Act of 1925 to seek to protect the scenery against unwelcome signs; among others, the *Kent Express* voluntarily removed its existing roadside hoardings in 1931.[74] The Kent coalfield – for better or worse – did not, as many had feared, give rise to a major industrial area, and the surrounding countryside remained largely untouched.[75] The threat of a major London airport at Lullingstone, first mooted in 1935, never materialised on account of the war – afterwards it was decided to develop Heathrow instead.[76] In other respects, the interpretation of rural social changes during this period is complicated – in Kent as elsewhere – by the intrusion of value judgements. Contemporary critics emphasised aspects of decline and backwardness in rural life, and, as often as not, any signs of 'modernisation' or 'progress' were the very features that they were most inclined to deplore.[77] However, their opinions, however forcefully stated, cannot be taken as representative of the mass of the rural population and the best way to proceed, no doubt, is to draw up a balance-sheet of the influences affecting the welfare of the rural people of Kent.

A prominent sign of the decay of rural England, in the eyes of its critics, was a continuing tendency for village populations to decline. This was certainly true of many Kentish civil parishes: an examination of 144 cases for 1921 and 1931 reveals that fifty-eight (40%) fell to some extent, the figures varying from only two or three persons (Frinsted, Mereworth, for example) to perhaps 100 or 200 (Marden, Staplehurst, Goudhurst).[78] Other settlements were by no means declining and some were rapidly becoming suburbanised. A case in point was Otford, once so small that 'everyone knew who everyone else was'. Here the population grew by 53% in 1921–31 and continued to do so in the 1930s. New housing was encouraged by the introduction of mains gas and electricity in the 1920s, and by the electrification of the railway. The early building of some council houses was followed in the 1930s by new suburban roads and ribbon development, some of these houses (as in Wells Road and Tudor Drive) displaying 'Tudorbethan' features.[79] And, here and there, totally new communities were established, for example at Kemsley, a model village built for Bowaters in 1925–6; the British Legion village near Maidstone featuring bungalows,

---

74 D.N. Jeans, 'Planning and the Myth of the English Countryside, in the Interwar Period', *Rural History*, i (1990), pp. 254, 255.

75 Brandon and Short, *op. cit.*, p. 305.

76 Alexander, *op. cit.*, p. 63.

77 See, for example, the works of C. Williams Ellis, C.E.M. Joad, H.W. Massingham, J.W. Robertson Scott.

78 This statement rests upon a comparison of 1921 parish population figures given by E. Minchin in *The Victoria History of the County of Kent*, vol. III (1932), pp. 356–70 with 1931 figures from *Census, 1951, England and Wales, County Report, Kent*, p. 2. My calculations exclude cases where boundary changes clearly invalidated direct comparison and the resulting summary can be regarded only as an approximation.

79 WKWI, *op. cit.*, p. 28; D. Clarke and A. Stoyel, *Otford in Kent. A History*, Otford 1975, p. 245.

verandas and sizeable gardens for ex-servicemen; new colliery villages at
Hersden and Aylesham in East Kent; and All Hallows on the Hoo peninsula,
where in the 1920s and 1930s small plots of land, ideal for seaside bungalows,
were offered for sale (a branch line was constructed, and high hopes were entertained as to its development as a major resort).[80]

The spread of modern amenities, such as those sustaining the growth of
Otford, was decidedly patchy: the steady progression of Ickham (mains water in
1913, gas 1926, electricity 1931), was probably unusual.[81] Improvements to
individual tenanted farmhouses and cottages depended on the whim of landowners who might or might not avail themselves of the modest grant aid that
became available as a result of inter-war legislation. In regard to piped water
supplies, Kentish farms by 1941 stood well in advance of England as a whole
(68%, against 50% nationally, were catered for[82]), but others still relied on wells
and even roof water, streams and ponds, and the spread of mains drainage was
even slower. Although bathrooms might appear in the homes of better-off
farmers (such as Eric Quested at Woodchurch, Thanet, after his farm was linked
to the main sewer at Manston aerodrome), many isolated rural homes lacked
such amenities.[83] A now elderly woman recalls growing up on a farm in the
Elham valley which relied upon a well: 'my father drew up the water needed in
my home, enough to last all day, with extra on Monday to fill the copper for
Mother's washday; extra on Saturday too, which was bath night'.[84] In Thanet in
1941 only thirty-six out of 116 farm holdings of over five acres had electric
light and twenty-two had power: in Kent at large the figure (for lighting) was
35% as against 30% for England as a whole.[85] This necessarily limited the use
of electrical appliances, even though they were being widely advertised in the
1930s at farm shows, but the advent of Aga or Rayburn cookers to replace open
ranges in some farmhouses was welcomed by wives and daughters as a great
advance.[86]

In inter-war Kent the offspring of the wealthy would often attend public
schools locally (at Tonbridge, King's School at Canterbury, or further afield)
and the children of the more substantial farmers and business people could
expect to complete their education at less prestigious fee-paying establishments
including the grammar schools. For the majority of rural children, schooling
began and ended in village establishments which were the responsibility of Kent
County Council. The authority formulated appropriate plans following the
Education Act of 1918 which sought to encourage higher forms of elementary
education through the provision of 'central' schools, and the Hadow Report of

---

[80] G. Darley, *Villages of Vision*, London 1975, pp. 285–6; P. McDougall, *The Hoo Peninsula*, Rochester
1980, p. 158.
[81] L.C. Coombs, *Ickham. The Friendly Village*, privately printed 1978, p. 189.
[82] Garrad, *op. cit.*, p. 10.
[83] Quested, *op. cit.*, p. 202.
[84] EKWI, *op. cit.*, p. 58.
[85] Quested, *op. cit.*, p. 202; Garrad, *op. cit.*, p. 11.
[86] Quested, *op. cit.*, p. 202; G.K. Nelson, *Countrywomen on the Land. Memories of Rural Life in the
1920s and 30s*, Gloucester 1992, p. 34 ff.

Plate 7. Posed photograph of Kent hop pickers, c.1907.

Plate 8. Hop picking at High Halden, c.1930.

Plate 9. Stilt men stringing hops at Hermitage Farm, Wateringbury, 1960
(© Topham Picturepoint).

Plate 10. Hop picking at Nettlestead Farm, Paddock Wood, 1958.

Plate 11. Outdoor staff at Eastwell Manor, c.1920.

Plate 12. Cattle market at Sandwich, 1927.

Plate 13. Horsedrawn sprayer at Bethersden, c.1930.

Plate 14. Preparing for a ploughing match with Clydesdale horses at Betsham, 1959
(© Topham Picturepoint).

Plate 15. Modern tractor ploughing at Wye, 1979.

Plate 16. Land girls being addressed by Minister of Food, Lord Woolton.

Plate 17. War damage at Smarden illustrating the risk of looting.

1926 which advocated a universal system of post-primary education with a split at age eleven. Unfortunately, financial stringencies, many of them imposed by central government, limited the progress that could be made.[87] However, a number of central schools appeared, mostly in the 1930s and in some districts began to turn village schools into 'feeder' institutions. Thus, the new school at Aylesham (1928) absorbed the older pupils from Adisham, Barham and Nonington, which ceased to be 'all-age' schools – though not without provoking what Mrs Payne recalls as some 'clannish rivalry' in the relationships between the boys.[88] Boughton Monchelsea School likewise ceased to be all-age in 1936, but elsewhere, on the Isle of Hoo, all schools remained in this category until as late as 1947.[89] A typical recollection, in this case of Herne, evokes long walks to school, toilets at the end of the yard which was composed of stones and mud; kicks under the table from the boots of children unlucky enough to live in the nearby workhouse, and the particularly effective teaching of knitting and sewing: 'I still remember the ruler across the knuckles if it went wrong.'[90] Another, more exceptional one comes from a woman who attended Ruckinge School (twenty-six children), who at the age of ten won one of a dozen scholarships to the county secondary school at Ashford: this created 'quite a stir' and was rewarded by the rector with a ride to Folkestone in his Ford car and a celebratory cream tea.[91]

Whatever their shortcomings, village schools at least completed the final banishment of illiteracy. The countryside was permeated, as never before, by the written word. A useful barometer of progress in this respect was the inauguration and expansion of the county library service. Its origins lay in an Act of 1919 which permitted county councils to set these up, with the aid of the Carnegie Trust, to cover rural areas and small towns. That for Kent was started in 1921, and by 1928 the number of books topped 100,000; there were 49,000 registered borrowers, and 348 village centres (schools, village halls and institutes). Kent was the first English county to introduce a mobile van (1924, followed by another in 1927).[92] More or less simultaneously, the coming of wireless transmissions exposed the more adventurous of the rural population to other urban-based channels of information. Mr Wallis, then a young farm worker, remembers constructing a crystal set in the 1920s, yet it was a great day when people gathered *at the Village Hall* (my italics) to hear King George V deliver the first Christmas speech. This suggests that powered sets were still far from ubiquitous in 1932, although a few years on they must have become more common possessions as the wireless 'enthusiasts' of the 1920s merged into

87 Melling, *op. cit.*, pp. 44–5.
88 Personal communication, Mrs J. Payne of Adisham, October 1997.
89 D. Tye, *A Village Remembered. Boughton Monchelsea 1900–1940*, Maidstone 1980, p. 55; McDougall, *op. cit.*, p. 171.
90 EKWI, *op. cit.*, p. 117.
91 *Ibid.*, p. 118.
92 Melling, *op. cit.*, p. 46; G.P. Hirsch, 'The Library Service in Rural Areas', *The Farm Economist*, No. 9 (1951), p. 236.

growing ranks of 'listeners'.[93] Meanwhile, attractions generated much further away, in Hollywood, were increasingly accessible to rural as well as to urban picture-goers, due in part to improved bus services which, by 1934, were said to have made even the remote village 'almost a thing of the past'.[94] As early as 1925 Canterbury and Herne Bay each supported two 'cinematographic halls' and Whitstable, three, as did Dartford.[95] The telephone, with its capacity for exchanging messages of every kind, appears to have been used sparingly. A woman who trained as an operator in 1937 at the Newington exchange (covering seven villages and 150 lines) recalls that it was used 'mainly by people in business – the butcher, grocer, garage proprietor, the doctor, the railway station, the local brick fields and most of the farmers'; it had 'little to do with the social side of the village'.[96]

Despite these novelties, which clearly had some capacity to individualise leisure or at least confine it to the family group, there remained a communal aspect to quite a wide range of activities. Some were distinctly gendered, such as sports clubs for males, and the church-based Mothers' Unions or the Women's Institutes for females. The latter movement, which had originated in Canada, first appeared in Kent at Wye in 1917 and by 1938 no fewer than 145 institutes had sprung into life, often on the initiative of the wife of the principal landowner or other women of 'quality' such as Lady Dyke of Lullingstone (Eynsford), Mrs Andrews (Stowting) or Miss Willets (Denton).[97] Often, these institutes, along with drama groups, concert parties etc. could avail themselves of new or improved village halls which were assisted in various ways – notably in their applications for grants and loans – by the Kent Rural Community Council (formed in 1923, later becoming the Kent Council of Social Service), which viewed them as 'the natural focus of all village activities'.[98] And particularly prominent among the recollections of the now elderly are vivid, even euphoric, recollections of special celebrations or events such as Jubilee Day 1935 at Godmersham where the entire village repaired to the 'Great House' – races took place on the lawns, side-shows abounded and the tea was lavish; a memorable ox-roasting at Stone for the coronation of George VI; as well as more regular events such as the hospital fêtes held at Newington, with fancy dress parades; and the Church Fête at Lydd – 'one of the great days of the year', with its marquee containing flower and vegetable exhibits, coconut shies, a small

---

[93] Nelson, *Farmer's Boy, op. cit.*, p. 150; A. Briggs, *The History of Broadcasting in the United Kingdom. Vol. II: The Golden Age of Wireless*, London 1965, pp. 3, 253, who notes that (nationally) the number of licenses held rose from 2.18m. in 1927 to 9.08m. in 1929, by which date there were 78 for every 100 households.

[94] Kent Community Council, *Voluntary Service in Kent*, 1932, p. 19.

[95] *Kelly's Directory of Canterbury, Whitstable, Herne Bay*, London 1925, p. 400; WKWI, *op. cit.*, p. 236.

[96] EKWI, *op. cit.*, p. 169.

[97] M. Leonard, 'The Women's Institutes, with Special Reference to the East Kent Federation of Women's Institutes', BA Dissertation, University of Kent, 1996, pp. 4, 6, 24, 38–9.

[98] Kent Council of Social Service, *14th Annual Report*, 1938, p. 20.

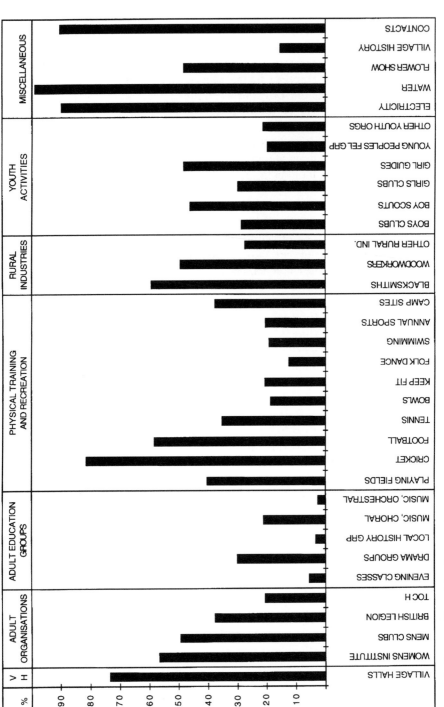

Figure 6. Survey of Kentish village activities, 1939.

Source: Based on Kent Council of Social Services, 15th Annual Report year ending 31 March 1939, p. 28. Note that village halls, as defined in this survey, include halls run by parishes, the WI, YMCA, etc., as well as those managed by village-hall committees.

merry-go-round and the day rounded off by 'young things' waltzing on the tennis courts.[99]

Perhaps Mr Wallis, the young wireless enthusiast, was also an exceptionally active participant: he remembers going to evening classes at the village school, learning to dance at WI socials in the village hall, acting in *A Midsummer Night's Dream* and *The Pickwick Papers*, and playing cricket for the local team. There seemed 'always plenty to do after work', he says – an impression supported by a Chelsfield woman: 'looking back there never seemed to be a dull moment in our lives'.[100] Rose-tinted though they may seem, such recollections are supported by the findings of a more or less objective enquiry carried out by the Kent Council of Social Service in 1939, whose main findings are summarised in Figure 6. Although we may suspect that the information is biased to some degree,[101] it covers no fewer than 257 villages, showing that more than 70% of villages possessed halls of some kind and that youth and sporting activities (especially cricket clubs) abounded in rural Kent.

This argues against the entrenched opinions of those who declared that rural life in the inter-war period was moribund. In reality, as the more perceptive commentators appreciated, village life was changing, rather than disintegrating.[102] No doubt the Church – discussed elsewhere in this volume – was losing some of its influence, for better or worse. Indeed, as an institution it faced for some years a tide of hostility from some farmers in eastern England, as small owner–farmers rebelled against the incidence of tithe-payments which in real terms became particularly onerous in the early 1930s when prices tumbled.[103] Some Kent land was tithed at as much as £1 an acre, and a passive resistance movement on the part of farmers in this county, as elsewhere, led to notices of distraint, the barricading of farm premises to keep the bailiffs out, and to the 'reclaiming' of stock sold by auction in default of payments.[104] However, as the chairman of a meeting at Sandwich in December 1930 pointed out, their quarrel was with the system and was not directed personally against members of the clergy.[105] The situation was in any event resolved by the Tithe Act of 1936,[106] and, although the episode warrants more research, it would be misleading to infer a rift between the Church and the rural community as a whole. Indeed, rural church attendances – at least by later standards – were still impressive: they were 'regular' (until 1940) at Ickham, for example, and like-

---

99   EKWI, *op. cit.*, pp. 239, 242, 248, 249.
100 Nelson, *op. cit.*, p. 158; WKWI, *op. cit.*, p. 232.
101 Because it was based on a questionnaire addressed to the head teachers of rural schools, which the smaller communities did not always possess.
102 For example, Astor and Rowntree, *op. cit.*, p. 328.
103 E.J. Evans, *The Contentious Tithe: The Tithe Problem and English Agriculture, 1750–1850*, London 1976, pp. 165–6.
104 D. Wallace, *The Tithe War*, London 1934, pp. 51, 114; EKWI, *op. cit.*, p. 132.
105 Wallace, *op. cit.*, p. 80.
106 Evans, *op. cit.*, pp. 166–7.

wise at nearby Adisham, where Mrs Payne remembers a strong male choir led by the village schoolmaster at the organ.[107]

The influence of the 'great house' on village life, though generally thought to be in decline, was by no means wiped out, much depending on their owners' individual survival powers or on the timely appearance of new buyers. Some, of course, disappeared altogether; Montreal Park (adjacent to Sevenoaks) was demolished and the land built over in the 1930s, while Preston Hall was the site of the British Legion Village near Maidstone.[108] Here and there, cases of dereliction and decay occurred, as at East Malling where Sir John Ramskill Twisden (old, blind and unmarried) allowed his house to fall into a state of near-collapse and the parkland was ruinous from neglect.[109] Others held up well. At Barham Court (Teston, near Maidstone), Colonel (later Sir) Charles Ward maintained in the 1920s twenty-five indoor and many outdoor staff and was able to engage in a major rebuilding operation after a fire in 1933; at Bramling House (Ickham), Lieutenant Colonel and Mrs Friend continued to employ about a dozen servants and gardeners; while at Boughton Monchelsea Place in the 1920s Colonel and Mrs Winch had ten inside and fourteen outside staff including two chauffeurs looking after the mechanical needs of the Rolls Royce and the electricity generator.[110] In this, as in other respects, inter-war rural Kent was a complex mosaic of mixed experiences and fortunes.

(3) The Second World War and its Aftermath

In 1939, Britain still depended on imports for some 60–65% of its food requirements.[111] In the face of predictable problems with regard to shipping space and the submarine menace, the First World War provided clear pointers as to what would be expected of home agriculture in the event of another war: indeed, two steps taken by the Ministry of Agriculture in the late 1930s anticipated what was to come. As early as 1936, an embryonic system of War Agricultural Committees had been set up, and in 1938, the year of the Munich agreement, stand-by notices were issued to chairmen and key committee members. Then, the Agricultural Development Act of 1939 – a distinctly war-orientated measure – offered a grant of £2 an acre to enable grassland of long standing to be ploughed up and either re-seeded or cropped.[112] In Kent, the first act of the chairman-designate, Lord Cornwallis, was to write to every farmer occupying fifty acres or more to discover their reactions. Fewer than a score failed to reply,

107 Coombs, *op. cit.,* p. 161; Mrs Payne, personal communication.
108 H.A. Clemenson, *English Country Houses and Landed Estates,* London 1982, pp. 184, 185.
109 M. McNay, *Portrait of a Kent Village,* London 1980, p. 47.
110 J. Severn, *The Teston Story. Kent Village Life through the Ages,* Teston 1975, pp. 6, 12; Coombs, *op. cit.,* p. 162; Tye, *op. cit.,* pp. 31–2.
111 Perren, *op. cit.,* p. 61.
112 K.A.H. Murray, *Agriculture,* History of the Second World War, United Kingdom, Civil Series, London 1955, pp. 59–60; Whetham, *op. cit.,* p. 329.

and he was encouraged to discover that 6,761 acres were in the process of being ploughed up while a further 18,039 were promised, should war break out.[113]

In the event, the adjustments of agricultural output that took place in Kent went far beyond this. As indicated in Table 24, there were huge increases in the acreages devoted to cereals, and Garrad later calculated that the rise in the production of wheat alone in Kent between 1939 and 1943 was sufficient to provide 1¼ extra loaves per head, per week, for every person in the county.[114] The output of potatoes, vegetables and sugar beet also rose sharply, and the keeping of more cattle was facilitated by increases in the output of stockfeed (e.g. mangolds) and in the acreage of temporary (rotational) grass. On the other hand, the acreages given over to flowers, small fruit and orchards (some of which were grubbed up) and permanent grass declined, as did the numbers of sheep, pigs and poultry kept on Kentish farms. This changing pattern, which marked a clear reversal of peace-time trends, entailed extensive drainage schemes and the improvement of farm ditches, notably in the Weald; while no district in the county was more affected than Romney Marsh where in 1940 the threat of invasion prompted the compulsory purchase and evacuation to inland counties of some 85,000 sheep, together with their lambs, and the preparation of plans to flood the Marsh should the enemy cross the Channel. Fortunately these plans never needed to be implemented, although increasingly the Marsh was given over to arable cultivation, despite the hazards of air raids and, later in the war, damage wrought by the disabling of flying bombs *en route* to London.[115] It was only to be expected that a minority of farmers would be unable to meet the demands made on them and the War Agricultural Committee eventually found itself farming directly about 11,500 acres in Kent, including 1,206 on behalf of the War Department on the edge of the White Cliffs of Dover where, notwithstanding the lack of cover from shell-fire, farming operations continued in a defiant spirit.[116]

The drive to increase arable output stood to be hampered by shortages of labour. However – in contrast to the First World War – the government moved swiftly to lock farmworkers into place. One aspect of this strategy entailed the setting of a (national) minimum wage of 48s in the Spring of 1940 which was thereafter regularly increased so that in 1945, the minimum wage stood at 70s; in fact typical earnings were a good deal higher than this figure.[117] Also, farmworkers were prevented from taking jobs in other sectors under the Undertakings (Restriction of Engagement) Order of June 1940. In Kent, farmers were advised by the NFU to report immediately to the local labour exchanges any cases of men leaving for other jobs when alternative agricultural employment was available; furthermore, where a worker was suspected to be leaving

113 P.W. Cox, 'Front Line Farming. Kent's War-Time Effort', *Agriculture*, li (1944), p. 119.
114 G.H. Garrad, 'Kent Farmers' War-Time Effort', *Kent Farmers' Journal*, December 1945, p. 70.
115 Garrad, *Survey*, pp. 79–80.
116 Cox, *op. cit.*, p. 122.
117 Mejer, *op. cit.*, pp. 78, 94.

farming, employers were recommended to refuse to hand over his insurance cards and to send them instead to the labour exchange.[118] Thus, in one way or another, the loss of male workers on Kent farms was held down to 5% between 1939 and 1944. Their efforts were supplemented in due course by prisoners of war, of which Kent was one of the heaviest users – some 3,000 Germans and Italians by 1946 – 'the former being much the better workers' as a Kent woman later recalled.[119]

Female, as well as male, labour was likewise strictly controlled from 1942 when the government took powers to direct women into essential war-work. One of these forms included the Women's Land Army; again Kent, with 3,968 land-girls in 1944, was one of the main users. Those employed on Kentish farms introduced some unfamiliar accents; 'it was like having three Gracie Fields in the back of the car' recalls a WLA Officer charged with transporting a group of northern girls from the station to their billets.[120] Others were Londoners, or were drawn from local sources, and it is these who remain conveniently near at hand to record their memories. 'At first the men made fun of me, all older men who had been farm workers all their lives,' recalls one land girl, but adds that 'soon they became my friends when they realised I could do the work'.[121] Indeed, the girls impressed employers too, by the way in which they absorbed new skills, not least in the handling of machinery.

> Led by twenty-six year old Mrs Olive Bass who was a dressmaker before the war, the team has operated the [threshing] set on every farm in the area . . . the sight of Mrs Bass skilfully steering the high-powered tractor, with the threshing machine, caravan, elevator and trusser along the country lanes . . . and to see her manoeuvre the outfit into the most difficult stock yards, setting it up to the stacks and adjusting it to a dead horizontal position – excites the admiration of both farmer and the general public.[122]

Without detracting from the extra efforts required of the farm labour force, and those of other auxiliaries, it is fair to say that large increases in the output of arable crops during the war could not have been achieved without major changes in the techniques of production. Substantially increased amounts of fertilisers were applied to the land and great strides were taken in the sphere of mechanisation.[123] In 1939 there were only one or two agricultural contractors in Kent, but no fewer than 196 appeared (duly registered and licensed) during the war; in addition to this the War Agricultural Committee ran fifty-eight hiring depots for agricultural implements and machines, including 238 tractors, 344 binders and 50 threshers, such as that operated by Mrs Bass. In all, by 1946 the number of

---

118 *Kent Farmers' Journal*, March 1941, pp. 80–1.
119 Garrad, 'Kent Farmers' War-Time Effort', p. 70; *idem, Survey*, pp. 14, 227; EKWI *op. cit.*, p. 222.
120 V. Sackville-West, *The Women's Land Army*, London 1944, p. 38.
121 EKWI, *op. cit.*, p. 214.
122 Cox, *op. cit.*, p. 121.
123 Brown, *op. cit.*, pp. 139–40.

tractors in use on Kentish farms had reached 7,729, now surpassing, by a small margin, the declining number of horses in use (6,999).[124]

The allocation of resources was controlled by the War Agricultural Committee, which spawned sub-committees of every kind. Farmers, while deeply conscious of their crucial role, found plenty to chafe at in a sea of wartime restrictions of every kind. The files of *The Kent Farmers' Journal*, the organ of the county branch of the NFU, evoke many of their concerns. Readers were advised, for example, how to secure the necessary permits to acquire rubber boots and reconditioned battledresses for their own and their workers' use; how to deal with the regional petroleum officers to ensure their full allocations of fuel; and reminded that as employers they were obliged to deduct tax, where appropriate, from workers' earnings. There are details of resolutions passed at the twenty-five-or-so local branches which were screened and usually supported by the County Executive, though sometimes they found it necessary to tone down their stridency before transmitting them to the NFU headquarters. No aspect was more closely watched than the regime of government controlled prices, for Kent farmers, like their counterparts up and down the country, were determined that these should rise in line with increases in costs, especially of labour.[125] The NFU was also anxious to push up its membership and was successful in doing so; from 2,592 in 1941 it had climbed to 4,170 by 1945.[126]

It is generally accepted that, for all the difficulties they faced and the hard work involved, farmers did well out of the war: nationally, the aggregate net income of farmers (after deduction of expenses) rose by 200–300% and their share of the national income doubled between 1938–9 and 1944–5.[127] There is no reason to suppose that the farmers of Kent failed to share in these gains. At present, very little direct information is available to illustrate this, although published material on the financial results achieved on the farms of Wye College (some 600 acres) gives an indication of the general direction: from an annual profit of only 6s 2d per acre in 1926–32, and £3 17s 6d in 1932–8, the figure for 1938–44 moved to £8 18s 2d.[128] How representative this was is another matter, and Kentish farmers, like their counterparts elsewhere, could argue that they were merely recovering ground lost during the depressed years of the inter-war period. At all events, the effect on the landscape was noticeable: once more, declared Lord Cornwallis in 1944, 'does the land begin to look as if it was cared for and once more really worthy of being regarded as "The Garden of England" '.[129]

---

124 Cox, *op. cit.*, p. 120; Garrad, *Survey*, p. 120.
125 *Kent Farmers' Journal*, February 1942, March 1943, May 1943, June 1943, December 1943, February 1944.
126 *Ibid.*, December 1941, December 1945.
127 Murray, *op. cit.*, pp. 279, 289–91. The precise extent of the increase depends on the years chosen for comparison: his figures suggest 303% by 1943–4 (compared to 1938–9) and 229% by 1944–5 – due to poor yields in that year.
128 *Kent Farmers' Journal*, January 1946.
129 Cox, *op. cit.*, p. 123.

It goes without saying that the priorities forced upon the nation in time of war left virtually no scope for improvements in rural amenities or services, the housing stock, or the condition of village schools which, in the early stages of the war – as at Bearsted Church School – were obliged to share their accommodation with evacuees from London, by rota; at Ickham, the arrival of eighty evacuees and two teachers from Erith, carrying small bags and gas masks, taxed the capacity of the school to its limits.[130] Though this particular problem was eased later in the war (Kent was too dangerous), the neglect was such that, in the recollections of those who attended them, in 1945 'schools had changed very little from the days of their grandparents'. They still evoked memories of the smell of 'chalk, damp clothes and plimsolls plus the occasional unwashed child or coke fumes'.[131] In other respects, despite the privations associated with the deterioration of all forms of physical accommodation, the rationing of food supplies and clothing – leading to expedients such as the making of garments from discarded Army blankets and underwear from parachute silk – the recollections of those who lived through these years are vivid, blending personal and communal memories. At Ickham, the village shopkeeper remembers, the village at the outbreak of war saw the arrival of troops housed in Nissen huts on the cricket field, and weekend visitors to these men and the evacuees ensured that the village was 'alive with parents, children and troops'.[132] Most prominent among these memories were the experiences described in graphic detail for Smarden:

> The Battle of Britain roared overhead, the skies streaked with white vapour streams from the planes. A girls' school was evacuated here from London. Refugees came in from the coast, soldiers were quartered in the larger houses. We were crowded out. . . . Before D-Day American airmen were encamped in the woods. And then . . . the buzz bombs. A number of houses were destroyed and ten village people killed . . . we had our own official W.I. work, that of jam-making and fruit-canning . . . the cans were boiled in a copper fed by billets of wood, while the planes roared and crackled over our heads . . . the village swarmed with American airmen from the Thunderbolt aerodromes round about. They appreciated the dances we organized for them.[133]

Inevitably, the time arrived when an end to war could be foreseen, and men's minds turned to the future. The case of agriculture was addressed by the Mayor of Maidstone, Alderman Sir Garrard Tyrwhitt-Drake, in his welcoming speech to NFU members attending the AGM in January 1944. He suggested that although in the past farming had been a Cinderella industry, 'in the last one or two years they had been at the Prince's Ball having a good time'. Farmers might well 'have an eye on the clock which in their case represented the end of the war

130 EKWI, *op. cit.*, p. 121; Coombs, *op. cit.*, p. 211.
131 EKWI, *op. cit.*, pp. 122, 123.
132 Coombs, *op. cit.*, p. 211.
133 P. Jennings, *The Living Village*, London 1968, p. 84.

... [but] ... he assured them that Cinderella did marry the prince and lived happily ever after, and expressed the hope that farmers would do likewise'. His sentiments were echoed by Sir George Stapledon, who spoke in favour of 'a virile and thriving British agriculture and a Rural Britain pulsating with energy and enthusiasm'.[134]

Farmers' expectations were not disappointed, for there was an all-party consensus behind the Agriculture Act of 1947, with its famous preamble, stating the government's intention to promote and maintain

> a stable and efficient agricultural industry capable of producing such part of the nation's food and other agricultural produce as in the national interest it is desirable to produce in the United Kingdom, and of producing it at minimum prices consistent with the proper remuneration and living conditions for farmers and workers in agriculture and an adequate return on capital invested in the industry.[135]

In practice, many of the details of this broadly supportive role were left to be settled by administrative action and by discussion. The price reviews of 1946, 1949 and 1950 were all contested to a greater or lesser extent and on south-eastern farms profits per acre were certainly lower in the late 1940s than in 1943–5.[136] Moreover, horticulturalists – whose products were not included in the price-review mechanism and who had to rely instead on variable general and seasonal tariffs – frequently voiced concern as they faced the same inflationary pressures as farmers in general. Nevertheless, as Table 24 shows, the output of cereals did not fall back and there were increases in most other areas of production, so that Lord Northbourne in 1949 remained optimistic about the future of farming and 'continued prosperity for all engaged in it'.[137] His confidence was presumably shared by the more progressive farmers, such as W. G. Alexander of Eynsford who bought Castle Farm, Shoreham (316 acres), in 1948, 180 acres of the Eynsford Mount Estate in 1951, and the freehold of Home Farm, Eynsford (320 acres and tenanted since 1891) in 1952. Mr Alexander also took up skiing in 1950.[138] The County Show was revived in 1947 and the *Kent Farmers' Journal* of September 1948 featured its first advertisement for new cars (the Vauxhall Velox and Wyvern), placed by Drake & Fletcher of Maidstone. Membership of the NFU continued to expand at least until November 1949, bringing the prospect of 90% membership into view.[139] Agricultural mechanisation continued apace. The Alexander enterprise acquired its first milking machine in 1947, a combine harvester in 1948, and expanded the number of tractors in use from two in 1939 to six in the immediate post-war years, together with rubber-tyred

---

134 *Kent Farmers' Journal*, January 1944.
135 Quoted in B.A. Holderness, *British Agricultural Society Since 1945*, Manchester 1985, pp. 13–14.
136 *Ibid.*, pp. 64–6; *Kent Farmers' Journal*, April 1949.
137 *Ibid.*, February 1949.
138 Alexander, *op. cit.*, pp. 107, 113.
139 *Kent Farmers' Journal*, February 1949, November 1950, December 1950, January 1951.

trailers to suit. In the county at large during the years 1946–50 the number of milking machines doubled and combine harvesters in use rose from 95 to 367. The count of tractors rose by 64% and that of agricultural horses fell by 42%, all these developments fostering a more 'modern' image of the industry.[140] Young Farmers' Clubs expanded in numbers and in the range of their activities, featuring in 1951 exchange visits between members in Kent and in Liskeard, Cornwall.[141]

Moreover, despite the disbanding of the Women's Land Army (completed in 1950), the repatriation of the last prisoners of war by 1948, and a tendency for the employment of regular women and girls to fall away, casual work on farms continued to run at levels higher than in the inter-war years. Most significantly, the number of regular male workers employed on Kentish farms in 1949 was greater than at any time since 1928. Kent at about this time featured in the aggregate more agricultural workers (excluding farmers and their wives) than any other county in England, and employed (per hundred acres of crops and grass) about twice as many as the national average figure, mainly, no doubt, on account of the importance of fruit and hop farms and market gardens.[142] Minimum wages in 1949 for ordinary adult male farmworkers stood at 94s per week, but calculations based on twenty farms in three south-eastern counties, including Kent, were significantly higher than this reaching, in 1948–9, 102s 11d for general workers, 110s 5d for herdsmen and 130s 10d for stockmen.[143] During the later stages of the war, union badges had bloomed 'like flowers in May' and, indicative of both better wages and the comparatively healthy state of the National Union of Agricultural Workers just after the war was the trip organised by the Wingham branch in October 1949 to the Southend Kursaal. Two coachloads of members and their families were mustered and a good time was enjoyed by all: 'Replete with winkles and whelks and whacking great sandwiches the homeward journey was commenced and Wingham eventually reached . . . all tired out and happy and everyone agreeing that this pleasant social venture ought to be repeated next year.'[144] Truly, as one commentator put it, there were signs that even the farmworker was bidding fair to enjoy his 'place in the sun'.[145]

The fact that most (though by no means all) Kent villages increased in population between 1931 and 1951 was another sign of rural reinvigoration.[146] There were corresponding advances in the provision of basic amenities to rural house-

---

[140]   Alexander, *op. cit.*, pp. 77, 78, 88; Garrad, *Survey*, pp. 121, 127, 128.
[141]   *Kent Farmers' Journal*, February 1949, June 1951, October 1951.
[142]   Garrad, *Survey*, pp. 11–12, 227. Note that in making such comparisons the author followed the practice of the Agricultural Returns in treating Yorkshire and Lincolnshire, in each case, as three separate counties.
[143]   Mejer, *op. cit.*, p. 94; Garrad, *op. cit.*, p. 16.
[144]   *The Hop Pocket*, February 1944, October 1949 (local newsletter of the NUAW, located in the mid 1980s at the Maidstone branch of the union, now part of the TGWU).
[145]   Mejer, *op. cit.*, p. 108.
[146]   *Census 1951, England and Wales, County Report, Kent*, London 1954, pp. 2, 6–10. The returns show population increases to a greater or lesser extent for all 18 rural districts. However, an examination of 146

holds, such that by 1951 the proportions having exclusive access to piped water supplies was much the same in the rural and urban districts (87%). On the other hand, rural households were less likely to have exclusive use of a fixed bath (56%, with the figure ranging down to 45% in Strood and Swale), compared to 66% in the urban districts. Likewise, rural households were still much more likely to depend on earth closets: the proportions with exclusive use of a water closet were 80% in the rural districts (ranging down to 68% in the Tenterden, Hollingbourne and East Ashford districts), compared with 90% in the towns.[147] 'Progress' was definitely in the air, but it was patchy and uneven.

At about this time Sutton-at-Hone became the first Kentish village to be intensively studied by academic social scientists. Situated in the Darent valley only seventeen miles from London, and four from Dartford, the village had grown considerably since 1931; and it was on the large side, with forty-eight council houses and a paper mill. Sutton was well-served by train and by bus services, which on a typical weekday carried no fewer than 440 people out of the village (principally to Dartford) in search of shops, amusements and work, while at least three-quarters of adult male villagers were employed elsewhere, again mainly in Dartford. The survey also gave useful indications of the activities and aspirations of those who lived there and these were, to a degree, ambivalent. On the one hand there were frequent calls for more urban-type amenities including a well-equipped park, more entertainments (especially a cinema), better educational facilities (the state of the school lavatories was especially criticised); for more and better shops, including a fish-and-chip shop; and for improvement of the older (as distinct from council) housing. On the other, most expressed satisfaction with their patterns of friendships and there was unanimity in wanting to remain a village though not, most children thought, a place where they would expect to remain all their lives.[148] Of course, Sutton was not a 'typical' Kent village (if any such norm could be said to exist), and it was even further removed from the mythical version which would be popularised only a few years later in the novels of H.E. Bates.[149] Nevertheless, the changes it had undergone, and the mixed reactions that these had provoked, anticipated future trends in some important respects. For, unbeknown to most who lived there, in about 1950 agriculture and rural society in Kent – as elsewhere – was teetering on the brink of changes of lightning rapidity.

(4) From c.1950 to the 1990s

While acknowledging the competition for the use of land from industry and the growth of London's suburban dormitories, Garrad in the early 1950s suggested

civil parishes where no boundary change is noted between 1931 and 1951 reveals that 40 (27.4%) show decreases, notably in the Bridge-Blean (7) and Elham (6) RDs.

[147] *Ibid.*, pp. 74–6, 82–3.

[148] C. Stewart, *The Village Surveyed*, London 1948, pp. 16–19, 55–66, 70, 75, 98, 100.

[149] *Ibid.*, pp. 17, 19. *The Darling Buds of May*, by H.E. Bates, was first published in 1958.

that 'Kent is still and is likely to remain mainly agricultural.'[150] It is certain that
Kentish agriculture is more technically efficient than ever before: the county has
shared fully in what is now seen as the true 'agricultural revolution', a transformation that has caused all earlier agrarian changes to pale into relative insignificance.[151] Rises in output and productivity are the consequence of rapid
mechanisation, the chemical control of unwelcome pests and weeds, and the
application on an unprecedented scale of nutrients in the form of artificial fertilisers to improved strains of plants. Yields from arable and livestock activities
have risen remarkably and – in contrast to the position in 1914, or 1939 – Britain
is close to reaching self-sufficiency in terms of many non-tropical food products. None of this can be understood without appreciating that 'the history of
British agriculture since the Second World War has been inextricably bound up
with government.'[152] For a generation, support for agriculture, prefigured in the
1930s and confirmed by the 1947 Act, remained firmly within the control of
Westminster. The system featured deficiency payments (i.e. price support) for
eleven major farm products, the details of which were hammered out in annual
price reviews which at times were bitterly contested by the NFU; a well developed agricultural development and advisory service (ADAS); and subsidies, or
grants to assist with the cost of farm improvements and capital or chemical
inputs. Specialists in this complicated subject note also the introduction from
1964 of import controls for cereals and livestock, which had a tendency to shift
the burden of agricultural support from the tax-payer to the consumer.[153] Entry
into the EEC in 1972 effectively removed decision-making to Brussels, but
under the regime of the Common Agricultural Policy British farmers continued
to enjoy price support and also protection against non-EEC producers, although
the benefits were certainly unevenly distributed, as has been emphasised in the
writings of Richard Body and other prominent critics.[154] From the mid-1980s,
due to their enormous and ever-escalating cost to governments and consumers,
and their tendency to generate unwanted surpluses, these arrangements came
under closer scrutiny: as Viscount Coke of Holkham, Norfolk, put it in an
address to the Canterbury Farmers' Club, farming was 'under attack'.[155] While
the Common Agricultural Policy remained intact in principle, 1984 saw the
introduction of milk quotas, and the years that followed brought a more stringent price-setting regime, with, eventually, 'set-aside' policies whereby farmers
could be compensated for taking land out of production. Against this background we can approach developments in Kentish agriculture in more detail.

---

150 Garrad, *op. cit.*, p. 1.
151 See, e.g., D. Grigg, *English Agriculture. An Historical Perspective*, Oxford 1989, pp. 2–3; G.E.
Mingay, *Land and Society in England, 1750–1980*, London 1994, pp. 253, 266.
152 Holderness, *op. cit.*, p. 12.
153 J.K. Bowers, 'British Agricultural Policy since the Second World War', *Agricultural History Review*,
xxxiii (1985), pp. 71–2.
154 R. Body, *Agriculture: the Triumph and the Shame*, London 1982, pp. 4–5, 13–14; *idem, Farming in
the Clouds*, London 1984, pp. 67, 151.
155 R. Fuller, *Farmers at the Fountain, 1793–1993*, privately printed 1997, p. 137.

'During this period', remarks William Alexander, 'we were growing up in the era of mechanisation, much as schoolchildren of today are growing up with computers.'[156] Tractors of increased size became universally used and at Monkton Court in 1973 no fewer than twenty-six were available, with a solitary horse. The use of combine harvesters continued to spread and when, in 1962, a threshing contractor at Eynsford gave up, his tractors found a ready market but the old-style threshing machines could find no buyers; they were set alight in a field, their only value being as scrap iron.[157] Mechanisation was extended also, *inter alia*, to the automatic planting as well as the harvesting of potatoes and broccoli, and nowhere with more obvious impact than with respect to hops, owing to the increasing scarcity and rising cost of hop-pickers – the result of higher wages in industry, holidays with pay and higher expectations regarding accommodation. On the Alexander farms, with only a moderate acreage of hops (eighteen), prior to 1960 it had been necessary to house up to 200 pickers for four weeks in eighty-six huts, most of them ex-army.[158] But in the last days of hand-picking, it was calculated, the cost of harvesting by hand reached 2s 6d a bushel, whereas by machine it had been reduced to 4d. By the 1960s, virtually 98% of hops were picked by machine and the seasonal appearance of bands of hop-pickers from London's East End became only a colourful memory.[159]

If mechanisation was the most striking feature of changing techniques, other aspects should not be disregarded. The increasing use of sprays is well illustrated in an account of the schedule applied to apples at Pembury where in the 1960s as many as thirteen or fourteen washes were applied during the growing season, creating a 'vision of frantic mixing up of chemicals for warfare against a vast army of pests' – in this case scab, aphids, caterpillars, canker, the red spider, mildew and sawfly.[160] Of course, spraying was by no means confined to orchard crops or fruit and the new techniques, especially the use of artificial fertilisers, had a marked tendency to render obsolete traditional patterns of mixed farming. This was a general feature of British farming and one confirmed by local experience. Mr Austen of Faversham describes his farm as still mixed in the mid 1960s (though it had recently discontinued dairying); but in the early 1970s they went out of pigs, which were losing money just then, so that there were no longer any animals on the farm. Two bad years with cauliflowers, the effect of the beginning of 'the great hop decline' (see below) and the grubbing up of half the fruit ensured that his farm was increasingly given over to cereals.[161] Greater specialisation was conducive too, to the banding together of producers, not only through their association with existing marketing boards (these had been subsumed

156 Alexander, *op. cit.*, p. 84.
157 *Ibid.*, p. 90; Quested, *op. cit.*, pp. 254–5.
158 J.A.C. Gibb and G.P. Chater, 'The Mechanization of Hop-Picking', *Agriculture*, lix (1952), p. 25; Alexander, *op. cit.*, p. 101.
159 Austen, *op. cit.*, p. 13.
160 Jennings, *op. cit.*, pp. 67–8.
161 Grigg, *op. cit.*, pp. 187–8; Austen, *op. cit.*, p. 75.

Table 26

Changes in the Farming Pattern, 1957–92

	1957	1962	1967	1972	1977	1982	1987	1992
Total Agricultural Area (acres)	641,810	642,058	618,533	605,713	591,192	651,257	643,177	614,016
Total Area under Crops and Grass [includes:								
Wheat	65,029	62,998	71,561	87,233	78,773	130,671	152,597	144,825
Barley	57,302	79,914	125,484	112,280	114,096	97,780	67,735	37,724
Rape	2,213	984	867	2,602	4,027	17,075	39,195	39,548
Potatoes	21,349	20,969	20,121	18,027	17,724	14,658	12,716	10,022
Hops	11,102	11,152	10,307	9,186	7,373	n/a	n/a	n/a
Orchards	77,556	72,622	65,293	57,449	50,811	42,869	39,022	35,602
Small fruit	7,732	8,038	5,469	5,876	5,028	5,980	5,597	5,547
Vegetables	23,665	22,266	18,513	20,238	23,756	19,864	15,048	12,076
Temporary grass/ Clover/Lucerne	86,604	95,136	70,405	78,270	79,529	60,428	49,726	46,798
Permanent grass]	216,069	217,494	188,142	175,785	166,835	155,374	147,007	145,497

	1957	1962	1967	1972	1977	1982	1987	1992
Rough Grazing	25,714	19,857	19,602	18,059	18,315	n/a	n/a	15,782
Numbers of:								
Cattle	126,804	134,589	122,222	133,877	128,671	107,614	88,523	72,164
Sheep	600,930	711,037	664,534	557,782	564,134	645,022	645,893	593,693
Pigs	139,615	128,615	127,583	137,897	124,149	106,631	81,592	52,526
Poultry	1,888,872	2,399,597	2,245,535	2,503,308	2,637,130	2,892,048	2,827,307	2,616,738

Source: as Table 25

Notes

(i) 'Total Agricultural Area', quoted from the 1980s, includes woodland and rough grazing.

(ii) From 1982 the statistics distinguish only rape grown from oilseed.

(iii) Hops were not separately distinguished from 1982.

(iv) Orchards and Small Fruit. The headings used in the 1957 and 1962 returns are comparable with earlier years and have been handled as in table 24, note (iii). From 1967 the returns distinguish instead between orchards operated commercially and small acreages run non-commercially, which are here aggregated. The acreages given for small fruit, from 1967 are 'not under trees'. This means that small fruit grown under trees cannot be detected, hence the sharp fall between 1962 and 1967.

(v) From 1977 the old distinction between temporary and permanent grasses was abandoned in favour of a new classification, distinguishing grasses five years old and over from those under five years of age.

(vi) The acreage classed as 'rough grazing' is not identifiable at county level in 1982 and 1987, but resurfaces as 'Rough Grazing (Sole Rights)' by 1992.

under the Ministries of Food and Agriculture during the War but most were subsequently revived) and some new ones, created in the 1950s, but also through the formation of private groups such as East Kent Packers, which started trading in 1949.

What Kentish agriculture produced, and in what quantities, remained largely a matter for the judgement of individual farmers and the pattern of output varied from year to year. Some of Kent's traditional specialities have experienced great difficulties, it is true. As is shown in Table 26, despite the mechanisation of picking and the liberal use of sprays, the hop acreage eventually declined to the point where, in the Ministry's view, it was no longer worth separately recording. The Hop Marketing Board was wound up in 1983 (on the grounds that it was a monopoly, not tolerable under the Common Market) and was replaced by a voluntary co-operative, English Hops Ltd, which had to compete with other co-operatives such as Wealden Hops and similar organisations in the English Midlands, as well as with continental growers whose products were well suited to the increasingly popular lager beers, while the public began to show a noticeable liking for wine as well.[162] 'The future does indeed look bleak,' wrote Mr Austen in 1994, although some hopes were entertained of a developing niche market among small brewers in the USA, encouraging the belief that the industry might not, after all, be 'on its last legs'.[163] With respect to orchard fruit, cold storage and competition from abroad, especially France, has made continuous inroads into the market for apples, and the response of Kentish growers (to move to bush varieties, easier to pick as well as to spray) enjoyed some success although it did not prevent the aggregate acreage from falling by 54% between 1957 and 1992. Cherry trees, of standard size, likewise diminished in number, not least because fewer people could be found who were prepared to climb tall ladders;[164] under the regime of the Common Market, the vegetable acreage, too, showed clear signs of falling away. By the early nineties, the historian of Thanet agriculture was impressed by 'the growing tide of vegetable and fruit imports', while at Faversham, Mr Austen was appalled at the sight of 'lorry-loads of Spanish strawberries' and apprehensive of the likely effects of a government decision to allow the sale of irradiated fruit.[165]

With respect to cereal crops, Kent shared much the same remarkable yield increases that were general in England and Wales in the post-war period: they approximately doubled between 1939–48 and 1978–9.[166] Moreover, as Table 26 indicates, vastly increased acreages were given over to cereal crops, especially from the 1960s. In 1973, McCrae and Burnham remarked on the conversion of

---

162 Austen, *op. cit.*, pp. 10, 14.
163 *Ibid.*, p. 14; *Kent View*, No. 11, 1996. (This magazine is the official publication of the Kent Agricultural Society).
164 Austen, *op. cit.*, p. 21.
165 *Ibid.*, p. 20; Quested, *op. cit.*, p. 243.
166 From 19.9 to 38.6 cwt. per acre in the case of wheat and 18.9 to 32.1 in barley (MAAF, *Agricultural Statistics* 1945–9, England and Wales, Pt I; MAAF, *Agricultural Statistics* 1978–9, converting, in the latter case, the figures stated in tonnes and hectares.)

marshland to arable on Thanet, and noted that Romney Marsh was 'now largely arable', the proportion of land given over to permanent grass having declined from 52% (1950) to 31% (1970).[167] Wheat and barley have vied for pre-eminence and another striking feature is the remarkable advance, since about 1980, in the growing of oilseed crops: the garish yellow of rape and the more subtle blues of the linseed flower became an increasingly common sight. So great was the expansion of cereal growing that the proportion of land given over to temporary and permanent grass, together with rough grazing land, declined as did the numbers of livestock kept, notably of cattle. This did not signify that milk production decreased in the same proportion, for efficient producers were securing major increases in yields: on the Alexander farms, consequent on a change to Friesians, there was a doubling of the milk yield per cow by 1972 from the 1930s level.[168] There was, however, a persistent tendency for the smaller producers to be driven out. In Thanet, Quested remarks on the tendency for many small unhygienic businesses to be eliminated quite early on, owing to the effects of the war, farm amalgamation and the activities of the Milk Marketing Board; over at Hoo, the Vidgeon family, having sold milk in jugs until 1950 when they were obliged to bottle and pasteurise it, finally gave up in 1977 when new EEC regulations demanded, in effect, bulk production. Nearly all the small local herds in the Faversham district had disappeared by the early 1990s, only a few specialised ones surviving; on Thanet even the efficient producers showed a marked tendency to retreat from dairying by the 1970s, so that by 1981 there were no cows in milk or calf left in the district: it was difficult to compete, on level terms, with the producers of western Britain with its fuller grass crops. Indeed, livestock as a whole tended to 'ebb away from Thanet' where, however, the wheat acreage more than tripled between 1961 and 1984.[169]

Through much of the period, land prices were extremely buoyant; they have been partially documented for Thanet, at least, by Quested. There, farmland was selling in 1948 at around £93 per acre, but by 1960 well-drained marshland in the vicinity could reach £625. Prices went on rising to peak at over £3,000 per acre in 1982–3. In the rather less propitious years that followed, they fell back quite considerably but remained, in 1993, of the order of £2,000 per acre.[170] Arguably, the value of agricultural land was artificially boosted, in Kent as else-where, by the system of agricultural support but, be that as it may, the price at which it changed hands was at all times governed by the extent to which existing owners were tempted to sell, and by the purchasers' ability to make new acquisitions pay. Increasingly, tenancy was giving way to owner-occupation. In a range of districts along the route of the A21 London–Hastings road, studied by Gasson in the early 1960s, there was a significant increase in owner-occupation

[167] S.G. McRae and C.P. Burnham, *The Rural Landscape of Kent* (British Association for the Advancement of Science, Annual Meeting), Wye 1973, pp. 112, 121.
[168] Alexander, *op. cit.*, p. 77.
[169] Quested, *op. cit.*, pp. 256, 261–2, 292–3; McDougall, *op. cit.*, p. 169; Austen, *op. cit.*, p. 51.
[170] Quested, *op. cit.*, pp. 237, 242.

when figures for 1941 and 1964–5 were compared: whereas in 1941 two-thirds of the land in question was tenanted, the same proportion was owner-occupied by 1964–5. Here, the process was bound up, at that period, with a marked advance in part-time, or hobby, farming by businessmen who were by no means dependent on their income from farming activities.[171] In Thanet, the proportion of cultivated land that was owner-occupied moved from 25% (1921) to 49% (1971) and 55% (1988), although some tenants, such as R. F. Linington, bought while continuing to occupy rented land. Meanwhile, the number of individual occupiers in Thanet fell quite rapidly, from 219 (1945) to 96 (36 of them full time) in 1971, and 61 in 1988, as small owners, conscious of ever-increasing costs and recognising that the optimal economic size of farms was definitely on the increase, disposed of their land to other farmers or for development.[172] These trends were fairly general: at Smarden on the Weald, when Major and Mrs Southern retired in the early 1960s after sixteen years of farming, the land was bought by a large farmer living seven miles away, who at once grubbed up the hedges and turned three fields into one.[173] At Faversham, in 1989–90 alone, no fewer than five farms were given up, three being taken over by larger neighbours.[174] Thus large-scale farming enterprises grew still bigger. In Thanet, the Tapp brothers and nephew were by 1984 farming over 2,000 acres at St Nicholas, while in the west of the county the Alexander enterprise continued to grow, adding to its already extensive holdings Ulberry Farm (1964), Eynsford Nurseries (1965), New Barn Farm, Lullingstone (1973), Ridge Farm, Shoreham (1977), and Lower Austen Lodge Farm, Eynsford (1985).[175]

As a result of such changes, there was a gradual diminution in the absolute number of identifiable farmers, partners, directors and spouses, which can be traced by comparing the figures given in Tables 27 and 28. But it was nothing like the major decline in the size of the hired labour force. From Tables 25, 27 and 28 it is clear that in the 1950s the numbers of hired workers resumed their pre-war tendency to fall, halving between 1952 and 1967 and doing so again by 1992. Over the course of forty years, approximately three out of four whole-time jobs in agriculture disappeared, though the decline in seasonal and temporary employment was less dramatic. The factors involved were of both a pull and a push nature, doubtless varying over time and between districts. In her study of the A21 'corridor' in the early 1960s, Gasson examined the rate of reduction, finding that it diminished with increasing distance from London. Farmers, she wrote, were turning to mechanisation *in response to* this situation, and some producers dropped the more labour-intensive lines (such as strawberry-growing) which had the effect of pushing them further afield, beyond a forty-mile radius

---

171 R. Gasson, *The Influence of Urbanization on Farm Ownership and Practice*, Department of Agricultural Economics, Wye College, 1966, pp. 10, 23, 70–3.

172 Quested, *op. cit.*, pp. 237, 248, 284, 285.

173 Jennings, *op. cit.*, pp. 59–60.

174 Austen, *op. cit.*, p. 36.

175 Quested, *op. cit.*, p. 265; Alexander, *op. cit.*, p. 113.

Table 27

Changes in the (Aggregate) Farm Labour Force, 1973–77

	1973	1977
Family Workers:		
Regular whole-time	1,086	669
Part-time	860	506
Hired Workers		
Regular wholetime	7,732	6,573
Part-time	3,288	2,948
Seasonal or Casual:		
(Hired or Family)	7,071	6,418
All Workers	20,037	17,114
Salaried Managers	107	393
Farmers, Partners, Directors	5,996	5,701
Total, Farmers, Managers, Workers	26,330	23,208

Table 28

Changes in the (Aggregate) Farm Labour Force, 1982–92

	1982	1987	1992
Farmers, Partners, Directors, Spouses working on holdings	6,457	6,363	5,785
Regular whole-time workers and Salaried Managers	6,259	5,481	4,615
Regular part-time workers	3,021	2,861	2,694
Seasonal and casual workers	6,944	7,637	7,533
Total labour force	22,681	22,342	20,627

Sources: as Tables 25 and 26.

Notes

(i)   Table 27 excludes spouses of principal farmers/partners (numbering in 1977, 1,270).
(ii)   Spouses are included in table 28.
(iii) 1973, rather than 1972 provides a closer basis of comparison with 1977.

of London.[176] Later, the pace of the reduction quickened across the whole county, as farmers became increasingly aware of the cost-savings made possible using the techniques of the new agriculture, coupled with recourse to specialist agricultural contractors.[177] At Street End, near Canterbury, the labour force of the Baker White partnership was reduced to four men on 630 acres, where it had once been twelve on 200 acres.[178] Much of the reduction, no doubt, took the form of natural wastage; for example, it was Mr Austen's policy not to replace men when they retired.[179] And often, ex-employees who had been laid off found good openings elsewhere. Such was the case, for example, with two long-term employees of Eric Quested when he retired in 1970: one took up a post as head cowman at Wye College and another got a good job with the Gas Board.[180] But the outcome cannot have been so happy in every case. There is no record of the consequences that followed from a 39% reduction in the hired labour force in Thanet between 1984 and 1988, which released 115 workers; or of the fate of the seven employees paid off by a young farmer in the same district in 1992, when he decided that the only way he could continue was by growing mostly corn and doing the work himself, with some help from contractors.[181]

The wages of the remaining farmworkers continued to be underpinned by national minima set by the Agricultural Wages Board. Its role was closely scrutinised by the government in 1994 at a time when similar arrangements for other workers were being abolished, but in the event, uniquely, it survived. At any point in time, farmworkers' earnings tended to stand rather higher than the prescribed minima on account of overtime, and the latest national figures to hand concerning gross earnings (for 1993) put the weekly average at around £210–211.[182] Over the years, successive wage increases – though no doubt less than employees would have preferred, even after the devising of a system of gradings in 1972[183] – have sustained obvious improvements in the farm workers' material standard of living, such as the acquisition of television sets and cars. However, their ability to build up long-term resources has always been limited. The private pension scheme operated by Alexanders from 1962 remains relatively uncommon[184] and only a small minority have ever been in a position to buy their own homes. In post-war Kent reliance on tied cottages (though they

---

176 Gasson, *op. cit.*, pp. 57–8, 60, 61.
177 By 1996–7 there were approximately 47 agricultural contracting businesses in Kent. (Information from BT Yellow Pages, directories for Canterbury, Maidstone, London South East and Tunbridge Wells, excluding some Sussex entries in the latter).
178 J. Baker White, *True Blue; An Autobiography*, London 1970, p. 48.
179 Austen, *op. cit.*, p. 23.
180 Quested, *op. cit.*, p. 249.
181 *Ibid.*, pp. 243, 297.
182 Department of Employment, *New Earnings Survey*, 1993, Parts C and D. Kent figures, were they available, would be unlikely to deviate much from these national estimates.
183 For details, see A. Armstrong, *Farmworkers*, London, 1988, pp. 228–9.
184 The pension scheme is mentioned in Alexander, *op. cit.*, p. 116. Recently an informal survey carried out by Mr R. Fuller at a meeting of the Canterbury Farmers' Club, and responded to by thirty-two of those present, suggested that seven employers had such schemes in 1960 and eleven in 1997.

gradually improved in quality) was decidedly above the national average, and in 1973 no fewer than one-third of legal actions to recover them, defended by the National Union of Agricultural Workers, took place in this county.[185] The goal for many was in preference a council tenancy, which freed a man to look for work outside agriculture; even if he stayed in the industry, such a move might well reduce the isolation of his wife from shops and other amenities, while he drove to the farm. As a Thanet incident shows, however, the problem of the tied cottage was by no means dead, even in 1993: the Union was then taking up the case of rent levels for once-tied cottages occupied by former employees of a farmer–owner who had reduced his workforce and wanted to let his property at an economic rent.[186]

Disquiet extended, at times, to the work itself. The nature of the skills involved was rapidly changing. Gone was the need for stacking, laying a hedge, mowing with a scythe or broadcasting seeds by hand – all recalled as practised within living memory. An East Kent woman remembers the career of her father (1900–72) whose lifelong vocation centred round horses: 'Poor Dad, it really broke his heart when first one then two then three tractors appeared . . . Dad was asked if he would like to learn to drive a tractor. The polite translation of his answer was, "No, thank you, you can't talk to a tractor and they don't stop if you say whoa." '[187] Once well-established ploughing matches died out at Thanet in 1973, due, Rosemary Quested thinks, to waning interest on the part of farmers, and likewise at Faversham in the 1960s.[188] While it is true that new skills – sometimes the product of formal training – replaced the old ones and were given some formal recognition, there is no escaping the conclusion that, arising from a lack of workmates, farm work in the second half of the twentieth century became a more lonely, isolated occupation.[189] The pick of the farm jobs was a (relatively) new kind of post, that of the farm manager. Such a man was F. Stanley who managed Broadwater Farm at East Malling for its owners, the Vestey family, in the early 1980s. College-trained at Wye, Stanley introduced various improvements (if the substitution of Cox's Orange Pippins by Golden Delicious is to be counted as such); lived in a farmhouse with a sitting room likened to the saloon of the *Mauretania*; was given expense-account lunches in Maidstone by the representatives of fertiliser and herbicide companies; and was a member of the Lions' Club, where he could meet other businessmen and trade experiences with them.[190]

---

[185] R. Gasson, *Provision of Tied Cottages*, Department of Land Economy, University of Cambridge, Occasional Paper No. 4, 1975, pp. 12, 90.

[186] Quested, *op. cit.*, p. 251. Note that the union referred to is the agricultural section of the Transport and General Workers' Union, which absorbed the National Union of Agricultural and Allied Workers in 1982.

[187] EKWI, *op. cit.*, pp. 131, 132–5.

[188] Quested, *op. cit.*, pp. 268–9; Austen, *op. cit.*, p. 64.

[189] See, e.g. G.E. Evans, *Ask the Fellows who cut the Hay*, London 1965, p. 16; H. Newby, *Green and Pleasant Land: Social Change in Rural England*, London 1979, p. 129. With respect to Kent, Austen, *op. cit.*, p. 1, and Quested, *op. cit.*, p. 251 hold the same view.

[190] McNay, *op. cit.*, p. 64.

Despite unprecedented attempts through the planning process to conserve and protect areas of natural beauty, wildlife and buildings of particular historical interest,[191] the Kentish rural landscape suffered considerable deterioration. One obvious contributory cause lay in agricultural progress itself. A particularly glaring case, well-documented by the author of an outstanding polemic on the subject, concerned the wholesale clearance of the natural vegetation clothing the chalk downland in the Alkham Valley by an unrepentant farmer. In 1977 the hillside was interspersed with pathways, wild roses, brambles and hawthorn and plenty of birds, flowers and butterflies: in 1978 all this had disappeared under the bulldozer and the plough, giving way to a bare chalk slope, and the villagers were greatly upset.[192] The same writer's enquiries among rural primary-school children at Minster-in-Thanet, surrounded by intensively cultivated land, revealed a keen awareness that their favourite playground, the countryside, was being rapidly eroded: 'recreation grounds' were no substitute for the disappearance of buttercup meadows, trees and marshes, under the plough, the chainsaw and drainage schemes.[193] Windmills, watermills and traditional farm buildings having an harmonious relationship with their surroundings were all threatened, and most new ones were framed in steel or reinforced concrete, clad with corrugated asbestos, the designs of Messrs Atcost of Paddock Wood being much in evidence.[194] The use of chemical sprays and the practice of stubble-burning (until it was banned in 1991) also aroused a good deal of indignation in Kent, as elsewhere. In her study of the Thanet farming community, Rosemary Quested freely acknowledges many of these problems. Her father, Eric, though he loved nature, in the 1960s ploughed up an historic right of way and decimated an ancient hedge on the advice of ADAS, 'in order to gain or improve at most two acres with grant aid': and she regrets the loss of bird life and the dawn chorus (only the most resilient species survive); of partridges, larks and hares ('victims of double and treble cropping'); of picturesque sheaves and stacks; and the deterioration of water quality due to its infusion with nitrates – in short, much of 'the agricultural beauty' has gone.[195] Latterly, however, from the 1980s there have been signs of a greater concern for the environment by farmers who have felt a need to improve their image. Partly for this reason, and partly because of the escalating costs involved, 'blanket' spraying every week or fortnight has given way to a more discriminating use of sprays, notes Mr Austen of Faversham, who also holds the view that the depredations of farmers in regard to hedgerows have been exaggerated, since conservationists tend to disregard new plantings of trees and hedges.[196] Moreover, it seems invidious to single out

---

191 McRae and Burnham, *op. cit.*, pp. 45, 95, note the existence by 1973 of five National Nature Reserves, 70 Sites of Special Scientific Interest and about 29 reserves administered by the Kent Trust for Nature Conservation, founded in 1958.
192 M. Shoard, *The Theft of the Countryside*, London 1980, pp. 71–3.
193 *Ibid.*, pp. 192–4.
194 McCrae and Burnett, *op. cit.*, p. 193.
195 Quested, *op. cit.*, pp. 262, 273–70.
196 Austen, *op. cit.*, pp. 24, 38.

farmers as environmental vandals: the pressures on the landscape come from a variety of quarters, including industrial and commercial developments, housing and, of course, roads. Indeed, it was an interesting sign of changing sentiments when, in 1993, a Kentish farmer, though conscious of the benefits derived from 'the communications revolution' since the 1960s, could write of 'the rape of our county in the so-called name of progress'.[197] Yet, for whatever reasons, the face of the county certainly changed greatly. A report published by the Council for the Preservation of Rural England in 1995 concluded that the area of Kent that could be classified as 'tranquil' had been reduced by 38%, from 918 to 568 square miles, and that the average size of these 'areas of peace' had been reduced from 46 to 8.5 square miles.[198]

To fully understand the background to these changes it is useful to take note of some significant population trends, which are not widely appreciated. In view of the changes in agriculture which have been described, particularly its decline as an employer of labour, it is at first somewhat surprising to discover from a study of census data covering 1971–91 that rural and 'fringe' districts of Kent were actually growing considerably faster than those designated as urban; that the number of job holders has risen faster in rural areas than in the towns; and that although agriculture remains important, it is now easily surpassed, even in rural districts, by a range of service activities.[199] A brief commentary on these findings can be offered as a series of numbered points.

(i)   That agriculture is still an important source of employment in rural districts is, of course, true, although the definitions employed in this study naturally include farmers, partners and directors who (as we have already seen) now account directly for a large share (at least 28% and as much as 44% if seasonal and casual workers are excluded) of the total labour force (see Table 28).

(ii)   The service functions that are flourishing are not, in the main, of a traditional kind. We may instance the disappearance of the function of the village carrier, as at Wye where the retirement of Mr Coulter brought to an end 400 years of fetching and carrying by the same family, and the closure of small brickworks by the 1970s.[200] In 1971 the wheelwright at High Halstow, Mr Plewis, retired and donated his tools to the Weald and Downland Museum at Singleton, Sussex.[201] 'Ford Cortinas don't need a wheelwright or a blacksmith' it was remarked (by the historian of East Malling), while even in agricultural engineering there was a marked tendency for small firms to disappear, with spare parts available only from centralised dealerships, producing 'a new impersonal relationship' with farmers.[202]

[197] *Kent View*, No. 4, January 1993.
[198] As reported in the *Kentish Gazette*, 20 December 1995.
[199] Kent County Council, *Report by County Planning Officer to Planning Sub-Committee, Rural Economy*, 17 October 1995, pp. 1–3. The districts referred to in this study are wards.
[200] EKWI, *op. cit.*, p. 166; McCrae and Burnham, *op. cit.*, p. 138.
[201] McDougall, *op. cit.*, p. 168.
[202] McNay, *op. cit.*, p. 130; Austen, *op. cit.*, p. 63.

Village shops likewise came under pressure, not surprisingly in view of a marked tendency for villagers to patronise town shops, especially super-markets, for their main weekly shopping expeditions.[203] The disappear-ance of the once numerous shops of East Malling was noticeable and at Boughton Monchelsea the Goodwins' butchers shop, owned for over 150 years by the same family, closed in 1980 having been run by Mrs Goodwin since the death of her husband in 1970.[204]

(iii) It was not into service activities such as these that expansion took place: the main constituents of the category in 1991 included transport; hotels and catering; business services (including banking and insurance); public administration and defence; education; and (subject to what is said above), wholesale and retail distribution.[205]

(iv) These job-holders, though residing in rural districts, tended to be commuters who, in the age of the ubiquitous motor-car, found it conven-ient and pleasant to live out of town, away from their places of work. The new rural populations were sustained in a large measure by urban jobs – especially in the west of the county where commuting to London was commonplace – but by no means confined to it.[206]

These features suggest that the pace of social change has been at least as great and possibly more far-reaching in the countryside than in the town. They are not, of course, peculiar to Kent or even to Britain, and they have given rise during the last forty years to a lively interpretative literature, much of it devoted to demolishing mythical notions about the nature of country living. Most people who live in the countryside do not now work there: indeed, according to one pioneer writer on the subject, 'there is no village population as such – rather there are specific populations which for various reasons find themselves in a village'.[207] Among the inter-related consequences that have been traced or suggested we may include the advancing view that the countryside is or should be a leisure amenity; the taking over of the countryside by a vocal and articulate 'middle class'; the creation of tensions between old and new residents, frac-turing 'true' village life, also between the invaders and the farming element, forced back on itself and becoming, in the words of Newby, an 'encapsulated community'; a loss of rural cultural identity; the urbanisation of the mind, i.e. the spread of urban influences via the media; a convergence of life-styles; loss of authority on the part of traditional rulers, notably landlords and the Church;

203 As early as 1971, three-quarters of the retail trade of East Kent was concentrated in towns of 20,000 or more (E. Mitchelhill, *Basic Data on East Kent*, Centre for Research in the Social Sciences, University of Kent at Canterbury, July 1977, pp. 69–70). At Adisham, 110 out of 150 respondents to a questionnaire carried out their 'main household weekly shop' at Canterbury, seven miles way. (*Adisham Village Appraisal*, Canterbury 1988, p. 60.)

204 McNay, *op. cit.*, p. 130; Tye, *op. cit.*, p. 30.

205 Kent County Council, *Rural Economy*, *op. cit.*, pp. 2, 3.

206 *Loc. cit.*

207 Pahl's view, stated in 1966, is quoted by A. Rogers, 'People in the Countryside' in *The Rural Idyll*, ed. G.E. Mingay, London 1989, p. 107.

and the increasing isolation of that minority who are too poor to have a car, as public transport services deteriorate.[208]

A myriad of facts and recorded opinions from Kent mirrors these concerns. Many villages have been changed almost out of all recognition by housing developments, or by new roads. Cases in point, which happen to have attracted attention, include Wrotham (with 'its heart ripped out by the motorway interchange . . . cut off from its past by everyone else's hurrying present'); Larkfield ('all new estates, 2,000 homes and 4,000 people, rising all the time'); Pembury, packed by the mid-1960s with high-density new estates and becoming 'a village which was once just outside Tunbridge Wells and is now, in terms of its many new inhabitants, just outside London'; and Otford, which saw a further seventeen new building operations between 1945 and 1973, and was plagued particularly by heavy traffic after the opening of the Dartford Tunnel in 1963.[209] A woman born at Rainham in 1944 witnessed its transformation from 'a smallish village where you couldn't walk down the street without meeting and greeting nearly every other person, surrounded by green fields, farms, fruit trees, sheep and woods . . . to a great sprawling dormitory town'.[210] The creation of a totally new settlement was a rarity, although one such was constructed as a self-consciously 'urban village' by Span, later by Bovis, on what had been strawberry fields. This was New Ash Green, whose residents turned out to be mostly 'middle-class' and very liable to move on quickly for career reasons or to achieve greater privacy.[211] Meanwhile the stability associated with great country houses, already much undermined long before 1950, was virtually eclipsed. In some cases, they were simply demolished (instances included Lee Priory at Littlebourne and Sandling Park, bomb-damaged during the war) while their sites, sometimes, were built over (for example Haste Hill House, Boughton Monchelsea, and Farnborough Hall). Other mansions happily survived and passed into the hands of the National Trust (Scotney Castle), or they changed their functions entirely. Bradbourne House became the East Malling Research Station and Linton Park a school, while Roydon Hall (East Peckham) was by 1980 the Maharishi Centre of Transcendental Meditation, and Mereworth Castle the country seat of His Excellency Sayed Mohammed Mahdi Al-Tayer, Ambassador Extraordinary and Plenipotentiary in London of the United Arab Emirates.[212] At Nonington, in the east of the county, St Alban's Court came to house, first a teachers' training college and currently the British branch of the Brud-

---

208 The chief works include R.E. Pahl, 'Class and Community in English Commuter Villages', *Sociologica Ruralis*, v (1965); H. Newby, *The Deferential Worker*, London 1977; *idem, Green and Pleasant Land*. For succinct summaries of the most pertinent literature see especially Rogers, *op. cit.*, and M. Winstanley, 'The New Culture of the Countryside' in *The Vanishing Countryman*, ed. G.E. Mingay, London 1989, pp. 142–54.

209 McNay, *op. cit.*, pp. 37, 129; Jennings, *op. cit.*, pp. 99–100; Clarke and Stoyel, *op. cit.*, pp. 250, 258, 272.

210 WKWI, *op. cit.*, pp. 106–7.

211 *Ibid.*, p. 110; Darley, *op. cit.*, pp. 259–61.

212 Coombs, *op. cit.*, p. 169; Clemenson, *op. cit.*, pp. 121, 133; Tye, *op. cit.*, pp. 55, 156; WKWI, *op. cit.*, p. 20; McNay, *op. cit.*, p. 47.

erhof, an American sect dedicated to godliness and plain living. In such cases (and the list could easily be extended) it was no longer possible to look to the great houses as sources of authority or social leadership. Nor were farmers willing to occupy this role, by and large. In Thanet, comments Quested, those who were involved in public life tended to give their time to county or national-level activities concerned with their own industry and were generally too busy to play any part in local government except, sometimes, at the parish level. And although the Canterbury Farmers' Club continues to flourish, with an increasingly regionalised membership, at a more local scale the activities of the NFU have shown some decline in vitality. Nor do Young Farmers' Clubs ('due to a dearth of young people') survive in their former numbers.[213]

By contrast, branches of the Womens' Institute remained in 1992 quite numerous in both east and west Kent, although national membership was on the decline, perhaps reflecting the proposition that there was now 'no such thing as "a rural woman" in the old sense'.[214] From work carried out on the movement, it is clear that the later-established branches tended to be in larger settlements, even in towns or suburbs, including places such as Broadstairs, Hythe, Folkestone, Faversham, Sevenoaks, Vinters Park, Chislehurst, Rainham and Bexley; and the subjects discussed were less specifically rural.[215] In regard to schools, Kent County Council was less ruthless than some authorities (e.g. Norfolk) in seeking the closure of small, uneconomic units, but, whenever it did make such a move, would encounter strong resistance from villagers both old and new. All the same, the distinctiveness of village schools became less apparent. At Pembury in the early 1960s, the children were exposed to Cuisinaire rods and the Carl Orff music system:[216] no doubt such modernity spread unevenly, but by the 1990s, certainly, the advent of the National Curriculum worked to remove any lingering differences from town schools, and concurrently the promotion of competition between them, otherwise referred to as parental choice, showed a marked tendency to disturb existing catchment areas.[217] In any event, the fact that village schools were generally 'feeders' to urban-based secondary schools must have encouraged – in Kent as elsewhere – the formation of extra-parochial friendship networks and inured youngsters to the idea of commuting from an early age.

These reflections are for the most part of a factual nature and (like others which have not been mentioned, such as the decline of rural bus services) are often amenable to measurement. Other observations on rural life lie more within

---

213 Quested, *op. cit.*, pp. 240–1, 244, 246; Fuller, *op. cit.*, p. 121, who notes a doubling in the membership of the Canterbury Farmers' Club in the last fifty years.

214 Leonard, *op. cit.*, p. 13, quoting an article in *New Society*, June 1979.

215 *Ibid.*, pp. 38–9.

216 Jennings, *op. cit.*, p. 208.

217 Thus, as the school roll expanded at Adisham in the mid-1990s, it was discovered that over half the pupils lived at nearby Aylesham, causing minor traffic congestion as parents from the neighbouring community arrived to deliver and collect their children. For their secondary education, children from both villages by now commuted to Canterbury.

the realm of opinion, sometimes, indeed, echoing the interpretations of rural sociologists. Thus, the shopkeeper at Ickham reckoned that his village was a 'perfect example' of the disruption of traditional rural life, due to the loss of its school and the almost universal ownership of cars and television sets, which 'destroyed the pleasures of making your own fun'.[218] Mr Tye, the schoolmaster at Boughton Monchelsea opined that 'to this day many of the older village families remain unreconciled to the arrival of many new families'. This, he suggested, was understandable but, as an outsider himself to some extent, he felt that the village 'needed desperately a blood transfusion' and that the newcomers had brought a new vitality and community spirit, exemplified in the building of a new Village Hall in 1978.[219] There is, too, much to be read into the recent comments of a retired farmer from Barnfield near Charing, who stresses the need to find ways of bringing work back into the villages: 'if people lived and worked in a village they would be more sympathetic to farming and country ways'.[220] And, regularly, relative newcomers seem to be prominent in leading opposition to business developments which, though intrusive, could create jobs – albeit not of the kind needed by those most actively hostile. Such appears to be the case, for example, with regard to recent plans to extend quarrying activities at Ickham, to develop a major motor-vehicle service station on Barham Downs, and to create a monster holiday village in the Lydden Forest area of East Kent.

On the other hand, the representativeness of such opinions and stances is difficult to judge and, where attempts have been made to assess prevailing opinion in a systematic way, the outcome is liable to yield few clear pointers. This was the case, for example, with the Adisham Village appraisal conducted in the 1980s, when the population stood at approximately 700 persons. A variety of 'needs' were mentioned by respondents to the questionnaire, such as 'mower for the Rec.' and 'Bottle Bank', through to a more active police presence and a surgery or clinic; but a widely agreed 'need' was to 'retain rural atmosphere', and there was a strong consensus of opinion against the building of more new houses in the village. Here, the dislikes and dissatisfactions elicited were 'of a minor sort', and the vast majority were happy to live there and hardly any would choose to move away.[221] Such evidence argues against the view that could easily be inferred from some academic writings, that the countryside is racked with bitter social tensions.

Nevertheless, across the whole period covered by this chapter, the historian cannot fail to be impressed by the comparative stability of agriculture and rural society on the eve of the Great War, and the restless and uncertain state of both in the dying years of the twentieth century. With respect to farming, Mr Austen in 1994 pointed to the fact that with fewer crops and more specialisation 'when something fails it really hurts', instancing the fact that in 1992–3 potatoes, fruit

---

[218] Coombs, *op. cit.*, pp. 161–2.
[219] Tye, *op. cit.*, p. 56.
[220] *Kent View*, No. 10, January 1996.
[221] *Adisham Village Appraisal*, pp. 53–4, 57, 61.

and vegetables 'hit their lowest prices for many a year'; moreover, many farmers had to deal increasingly with supermarket chains, with their demanding specifications and tendency to 'treat farms as factories and farmers as hired labour, under their contracts'. The future of agriculture seemed to him to depend heavily on 'the whims of faceless bureaucrats'.[222] Much the same beleagured tone was struck by other farming observers in the early nineties. 'We have been deserted by the politicians . . . and their interest in agriculture is mainly lip-service' declared the Chairman of the Kent Agricultural Society in 1992, adding that the industry was now 'in decline'; Mr Peter Mummery envisaged 'a rocky future for farming', and Jonathan Tipples, Deputy Chairman of the Kent NFU, would settle 'for survival rather than prosperity', warning that not all would succeed in even that limited aim in the face of efforts to cut down agricultural support.[223] There followed an interlude of improvement as the effects of Britain's withdrawal from the European Exchange Rate Mechanism, in Autumn 1992, began to filter through. The 25% depreciation in the value of the pound raised the sterling value of European subsidies by a roughly equivalent amount, and this was coupled with increased area payments for cereals, and good crop yields. But gloom returned with a vengeance by 1997 when the Ministry of Agriculture announced a fall of nearly 50% in farm incomes. This particularly affected cattle producers wrestling with the consequences of the BSE (bovine spongiform encephalopathy, popularly known as 'mad-cow disease') crisis and the banning of British beef; but also, more generally, there was a fall in the value of farm produce caused by a resurgence in the pound. Under the heading 'Militant farmers set to act', the *Kentish Gazette* reported in January 1998 that at least ten farmers from the Canterbury area had joined thousands of others in a parliamentary lobby over falling prices which, according to Messrs Twyman and Ash, were 'crippling the countryside'.[224]

Predictably, the NFU gave its backing to a rally held in London on 1 March 1998, which aimed, in the words of the Duke of Northumberland, to draw attention to the 'grave threat to the livelihood and way of life' of country folk and to put pressure on 'the powers that be' to understand the complexities of rural communities.[225] This demonstration was organised by a 'Countryside Alliance' and in quantitative terms was a success, for a quarter of a million marchers turned out. It received much attention in the press, although various reports pointed to the leading role played by the pro-hunting lobby (a Private Member's Bill to abolish hunting with dogs was currently being considered by Parliament), and by those who opposed the 'right to roam' across private land, another cause which was supported by the new Labour government. Moreover, there were suspicions that some tenants and estate workers had been dragooned into

222 Austen, *op. cit.*, pp. 5, 36, 79–80.
223 *Kent View*, No. 3, June 1992; No. 4, January 1993; No. 6, January 1994.
224 *Kentish Gazette*, 22 January 1998.
225 *Observer*, 1 March 1998.

supporting it ('Yeomen receive their marching orders').[226] In a judicious leader, the *Guardian* newspaper acknowledged that there were some 'genuine rural issues desperately in need of attention, including job losses, income, transport, housing, local schools and village shops', but judged the alliance to be merely 'a coalition of contradictory interests'. No wonder, it declared, that there were no speeches at the finishing point in Hyde Park, for conflicting interests would soon have emerged: 'landowners v tenants, agri-businesses v smallholders, second home-owners v workers'. The difficult bit, according to a reporter in the same issue of the newspaper, was 'deciding whose countryside it is, and what it's for'.[227]

These remarks echo the emergence – in academic circles – of a looming crisis of confidence in the very notion of 'rurality' as a distinct analytical category. This theme is explored in a recent set of essays edited by Paul Cloke, Professor of Human Geography at Bristol University.[228] In the most readable of these pieces, Cloke describes the evolution of his thoughts on such matters. Born in Enfield, he first developed an interest in rural planning at Southampton University in 1971–4 before moving to Wye College where, at the time, the figureheads of rural planning and research were Professor Wibberley and Dr Robin Best. Here, living in a village which – he soon appreciated – was not 'typical', Cloke completed a PhD thesis on empirical lines, constructing an 'index of rurality' which used principal-components analysis, and was set firmly within the positivistic and planning parameters of human geography research. Later, he worked at Lampeter in west Wales and gradually came round to the view that his initial research had been restrictive and reductionist, that the category 'rural' was increasingly an unhelpful form of spatial delineation, and that the changes occurring in rural Britain were intimately bound up with the dynamics of economic and political change, in particular those associated with the Thatcher years. Professor Cloke thus distances himself from the traditional approaches of rural geographers, but does not deny that in real life 'people do make decisions (where to live, where to set up business, where to go for recreation or leisure) which *presume* a category rural'. In short, according to this line of thought, the idea of rurality is a social construct, although 'there is no expectation here that people's constructions of rurality will all fit neatly together into a unitary thing called rural, since people are unlikely to hold clear, well-defined and well-structured images of the rural'.[229]

The style of expression which these essays (and others like them) adopt has been sharply criticised, not least effectively by R.E. Pahl, another academic with strong Kentish connections and himself a pioneer of the study of social change

---

[226] *Guardian*, 21 February 1998; 2 March 1998.
[227] *Ibid.*, 2 March 1998.
[228] P. Cloke, M. Doel, D. Matless, M. Phillips, N. Thrift, *Writing the Rural. Five Cultural Geographics*, London 1994.
[229] *Ibid.*, pp. 154–61, 164–5.

in twentieth century Britain.[230] Clearly, this is not the place to examine in depth such highly academic controversies, but their very existence, paralleling the anxieties expressed by practical farmers and some evidence of dissatisfaction, however inchoate, bears witness to ever-deepening uncertainties in the 1990s. What lies beyond the millennium cannot be prophesied with any confidence by the historian – and, probably, by no-one else either.

---

[230] R.E. Pahl, review of Cloke *et al.*, *op. cit.*, in *Rural History*, vi (1995), pp. 119–22. Pahl was, until recently, Professor of Sociology in the University of Kent at Canterbury.

4

Transport

GERALD CROMPTON

Air, road, rail and sea transport have all been relevant to the development of the Kentish economy in the twentieth century. The contribution of each mode has, naturally, varied enormously. It is also the case that the impact of each has been in part predictable on the basis of standard national trends and in part has taken forms which were specific to Kent. It is the latter which merit most attention in this context.

(1) Air and Sea Transport

One major transport mode has been distinctive because of the negligible character of its positive effect on Kent. In civil aviation the county drew a blank. Despite Kent's associations with the early days of flying,[1] and despite the military importance of its airfields during World War II, Kent missed out on all the significant developments in international air travel during the second half of the century. London's various airports were all located in other home counties. Kent's only effective contribution to the debate over a third London airport was to oppose the claims of Foulness, an option which would have brought no benefits, and some indirect environmental damage, to the county.[2] Although the successful establishment of Heathrow, Gatwick and Stansted has been an accomplished fact for some time, basic geographical factors almost invite counterfactual speculation. Kent, with its lengthy coastline and proximity to London on the eastern side, might easily in principle have been found to contain a suitable site for a major international airport. That hypothetical development would undoubtedly have entailed investment in improved land transport connections with the capital. In reality, however, Kent has possessed only a number of minor airports, of which the largest was Lydd (category 'B'). The principal service was to Beauvais in northern France, which, with additional coach journeys, offered a form of link between London and Paris. At the end of the century some hopes

[1] T. Barker, 'Road, Rail and Cross-Channel Ferry', in *The Economy of Kent, 1640–1914*, ed. A. Armstrong, Woodbridge 1995, p. 159.
[2] E. Melling, *History of the Kent County Council, 1889–1974*, Maidstone 1975, p. 122.

existed that Manston ('Kent International'), after its evacuation by the military, might have potential for growth from its initial charter flight base into an international airport. Very minor airfields (Ashford, Headcorn, Rochester and West Malling) offered general aviation services, business and air-taxi flights.[3]

In the case of sea transport, Kentish circumstances require a distinction to be made between the cross-Channel trade, with its large passenger component, which has belonged overwhelmingly to Dover and Folkestone in the south-east of the county, and the rest, which has been freight-based and has served geographically more diverse routes. Sheerness and Ramsgate have, for shortish periods, had a foot in the cross-Channel camp, which will be discussed later, but the differences have in general been clear enough. The smaller ports on the Thames estuary, Faversham, Whitstable, Ridham Dock (near Sittingbourne) and Sandwich/Richborough have shown little long term growth, but have maintained an involvement in coastal and mainly short-sea trade. Various useful specialisms evolved, such as the importation of aggregates at Whitstable and motor vehicles at Ramsgate, in addition to the handling of general cargoes. Ramsgate periodically showed promise of significant expansion, and at times had regular freight services to Emden in Germany and Flushing in the Netherlands, but eventually fell back in the face of stronger competition. The major growth point over the last few decades has been the Medway area where trade increased rapidly after investment at the end of the 1960s to establish Sheerness as a multi-purpose deep-sea port. Also Thamesport has since 1990 expanded strongly beyond its original function of serving the BP refinery on the Isle of Grain and became the British port of call for some long-distance international container freight services. Its development has been facilitated by Kent's first freightliner rail depot. It was envisaged in the 1990s that Dartford International Ferry terminal would provide another growth-point within the Crossways Business Park. Gravesend remained a minor port but was the base for the London tug fleet and the Port Control Centre responsible for pilotage on the Thames. It should be noted that none of the estuarial ports on the Kent side of the river developed on the same scale as Tilbury.[4]

(2) Road Transport

In most respects the development of road transport in Kent conformed to national trends throughout the century. The road system was progressively extended in response to rising demand. Mechanised road transport had modest beginnings, exemplified by a total number of car registrations of under 12,000 in 1914. In the inter-war period the most profound changes were in relatively short-distance travel (buses for passengers, vans and lorries for freight). After 1945 came a dramatic expansion in the use of both cars and road haulage, for

---

3 Kent County Council Transport Policies and Programme for 1978–9.
4 Kent Structure Plan, Kent County Council, Maidstone 1993, pp. 131–4.

journeys of all lengths. This growth was achieved, from the 1950s onwards, at the expense of both railways and buses, thereby expanding the private sector and shrinking the public. In national terms, by the 1990s rail and bus had 5% and 6% respectively of the passenger market, whereas cars accounted for 86%.[5] The roads had taken well over two-thirds of the freight market and railways held considerably less than one-tenth.[6] In this context Kent was distinctive only in limited respects. For example, the share of rail remained higher than the national average. Travel-to-work surveys in the early 1990s showed that 65% went by car and 11% by rail, with the latter figure rising for longer journeys. It was also true that road use increased more dramatically than elsewhere during periods of economic expansion in the south-east. Between 1980 and 1991 road traffic grew by an estimated 70% when the national average increase was 48%.[7]

The county's road pattern inevitably reflected the facts of both geography and geology and of previous economic development. The principal routes radiated from London towards the coastal towns, moving for the most part from north-west to east and south-east. The natural hindrances of Downs and Weald limited the number and quality of roads crossing these primary axes. The most fundamental barriers to transport in Kent remained, of course, London and the Channel, and the road system was unable to make much impact on these massive obstacles until late in the century. The main contribution to reducing isolation was eventually made through the provision of greatly improved direct links with areas west and north of the capital and the upgrading of roads serving the major Channel ports. In the last few decades transport demand, especially on the roads, has been intensified by the county's function as a corridor for continental traffic and by the decline of the traditional holiday trade in the coastal resorts. The former brought acute seasonal peaks, with up to a quarter of annual passenger flows to the continent occurring in the month of August, and weekend movements half as great again as on weekdays. The latter change might have been expected to ease summer traffic problems, but this has not been the case as day trippers have replaced longer-stay visitors and a higher proportion has travelled by road.[8]

The process of road improvement moved slowly in the inter-war years and several schemes, including sections of the A20 and the A2, owed something to the desire of both London and Kent County Councils to provide relief work for the unemployed. The absence of large towns and cities reduced the incentive to undertake major investments. When the Ministry of Transport assumed responsibility for trunk roads in 1937, the only road involved at that time in Kent was the A20 London to Folkestone. One inter-war project of long-term potential was the Dartford Tunnel. Kent County Council, in conjunction with its opposite number in Essex, lobbied the government on this matter as early as 1924 and

5   J. Glover, *Privatised Railways*, London 1998, p. 120.
6   T. Barker and D. Gerhold, *The Rise and Rise of Road Transport, 1700–1990*, London 1993, p. 94.
7   Kent Economic Report 1994, Kent Economic Forum, Maidstone 1994, pp. 132–5.
8   Kent County Council Transport Policies and Programme for 1978–9.

promoted legislation in 1930 and 1937. These initiatives were ill-fated and encountered lengthy postponements, first as victims of the financial crisis of 1931, and then in consequence of World War II. Although a pilot tunnel had been completed by 1939, the genuine article was not available until 1963. Other desirable measures were similarly delayed. A by-pass for Ashford on the A20 had been planned in 1929 and finally materialised in 1957. The Medway towns also had a long wait for a much-needed by-pass but their problem was spectacularly resolved when it arrived as part of the M2 motorway which opened in 1963 between a point west of Rochester and Brenley Corner, east of Faversham. At this stage Kent was briefly well advanced by national standards of motorway provision, especially as two short sections of the M20 followed soon afterwards. The case for priority for the M2 was a strong one, in terms of facilitating flows of longer-distance traffic on the London–Dover route, and also of relieving severe urban congestion in the Medway towns, Sittingbourne and Faversham.[9]

The pace of subsequent development was, however, much slower. Although the A2 was gradually widened and improved between Rochester and London, the more easterly parts of the route received much less attention and some sections remained single carriageway at the end of the century, despite the heightened economic importance of the port of Dover. Similarly the M20 remained in a fragmentary state until the 1980s, when its completion between London and Folkestone/Dover was accepted as a matter of some urgency. This transformation was brought about by the successful progress of two much larger transport schemes, the M25 London Orbital Motorway (constructed between 1972 and 1986) at the north end and the Channel Tunnel at the south. Indeed this degree of improvement in the Kent road network was one of the few planning measures undertaken by the British government as a necessary implication of the opening of the Channel Tunnel. Kent's road links with the British interior were enormously strengthened by the completion of the M25, via its intersections with the A2/M2 and the M26/M20. This had not, of course, been the principal purpose of the orbital project, but the benefits to Kent were probably relatively greater than those accruing to other areas on the periphery of the capital. The M25 originally incorporated the Dartford Tunnel (actually twin tunnels since the 1970s) which in the early 1990s became the Dartford Crossing, with the Queen Elizabeth II suspension bridge carrying the southbound traffic and the two tunnels the northbound. These positive developments still left some serious deficiencies in place. Thanet's road communications remained poor and the economic decline of this and other eastern parts of the county was likely to be accelerated by the opening of the Channel Tunnel and the concentration of ferry traffic on Dover. This problem was addressed in the late 1990s when the realignment and dualling of the A299 Thanet Way link to the M2 was undertaken. The initial submission for funding of the Thanet Way argued that it was essential to enable north-eastern Kent, with its high unemployment and weak

9   Melling, *op. cit.*, pp. 40–1, 47, 61, 102–3.

manufacturing base, both to retain existing industry and to attract new.[10] Another strategic concern in the final decade of the century was to improve west–east road links in the areas of manufacturing decline on the south bank of the Thames, where a start was made on the South Thames-side Development Route and a Medway Tunnel was opened. Before the end of the century road transport had become so important to certain economic activities that reasonable proximity to good quality roads was not necessarily sufficient if the immediate access was difficult. For example, it was always obvious that the port of Ramsgate would be handicapped by its remoteness from the major road network, but it took longer to become clear that Folkestone and even Dover Western Docks were also at a disadvantage in comparison with Dover Eastern Docks (at least after the acquisition of a direct link with the A2). Even the expansion of the county's pharmaceutical industry, which by the late 1990s included four of the world's top ten companies and employed 10,000 people, set up demands for improved transport. In particular the rapid growth of Pfizer at Sandwich put strains on the road system of the east coast.[11]

Final decisions on such matters as trunk roads, motorways, Thames and Channel crossings were, of course, in the hands of national government and were necessarily taken outside the county. Often, as with questions of priorities for road improvements, there was a clear line of pressure from County Hall, however ineffective or slow in producing results. But no definite Kentish viewpoint was discernible on some of the biggest issues, such as the various Channel Tunnel and rail link proposals. The main source of inhibition here was the sharp divisions between areas and interests which stood to gain from these developments and those which were set to lose. The County Council was accordingly restricted to a position of rather bland opportunism, of attempting to maximise benefits and minimise damage wherever either seemed likely to occur.[12] On a number of lower-level transport issues, however, policy could much more easily be resolved. An example is the County Council's desire to maintain local bus services, especially in the rural areas. For some time after demand began to fall in the 1950s, the bus operators were able to use profits from urban routes to cross-subsidise their loss makers. By the 1970s when the total annual bus journeys in the county fell below 100 million, this ceased to be a viable strategy, and the decision was taken in the mid 1970s to provide public subsidies. Kent was in no sense unusual in acting in this way and did so because it had a higher incidence than many counties of sparsely populated areas which were vulnerable to the withdrawal of bus services.[13]

[10] Kent County Council Planning Sub-Committee, 26 November 1991.
[11] Kent Economic Report 1994, pp. 132–5; *Financial Times*, 23 April 1998.
[12] I. Holliday, G. Marcou and R. Vickerman, *The Channel Tunnel*, London 1991, esp. c. 6.
[13] Kent County Council Transport Policies and Programme for 1979–80.

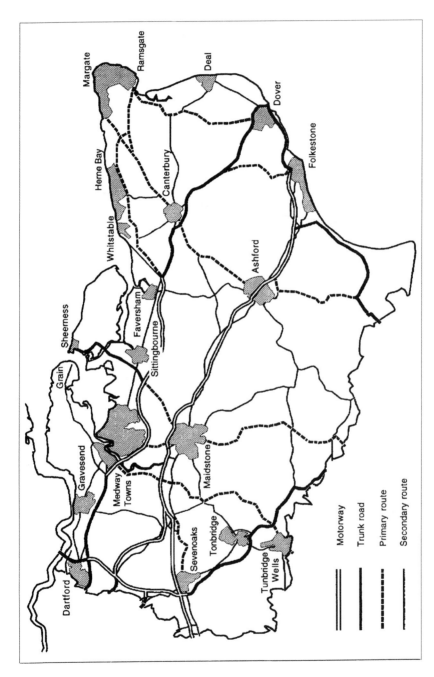

Figure 7. Kent inter-urban route hierarchy, 1996.

(3) Rail Transport

Kent's railway system had been put in place during the nineteenth century by two main agencies, the London, Chatham and Dover and the South Eastern railways. Their rivalry had attained legendary proportions before it was terminated by the merger of the two companies in 1899. The relationship between the two has been described as 'the worst case of mutually damaging competition'.[14] The expression 'mutually destructive feud'[15] has also been used to characterise their behaviour in the last third of the nineteenth century. The longer-term implications of this feuding are not entirely straightforward. What is clear is that both companies (and especially the LCDR) weakened themselves by their practice of cut-throat competition. Parts of the additional mileage added during this period were not commercially justifiable. The consequent over-capitalisation and financial enfeeblement meant that customers suffered. Charges were higher, and accommodation and services were poorer than might otherwise have been the case. Some of the results of strategies pursued during the feud were inevitably long-lasting, and in some cases are still being felt today. The 'Chatham Line' from London to Dover has always posed operating difficulties, with its 'fierce gradients and appalling curves' which were necessitated by 'construction on the cheap'. Many of the original stations were 'simple to the point of meanness', and throughout the county a legacy of low-quality rolling stock and unreliable time-keeping ensured that a 'full measure of public opprobrium' was passed on the newly formed Southern Railway in 1923.[16]

It seems obvious that in different circumstances Kent might have inherited a stronger and better-designed railway network after the First World War, and one in somewhat better financial health. The county was not in any sense unique in being subjected to a process of unplanned competitive construction of its railways. It was simply unfortunate that antagonistic competition between a pair of approximately equally matched rivals persisted for longer than was common, and left a quasi-permanent mark on the infrastructure. There were also some substantial compensating factors. However illogical it may have been, the network was certainly denser as a result of the pattern of nineteenth-century construction, and many Kentish towns were consequentially closer to a station. The thick clusters of lines in the London suburbs acquired a more rational appearance with the growth of commuter traffic and incidentally made the rail system more resistant to the effects of wartime bombing. It was once calculated that there were 128 different routes between London Bridge and Deal, none involving a reversal.[17] Very few standard-gauge routes were in fact abandoned completely. As for the financial legacy of earlier railway development, Kent ceased, from the time of the Railway Act of 1921, to be autonomous in this

---

[14] M.R. Bonavia, *The History of the Southern Railway*, London 1987, p. 9.
[15] H.P. White, *A Regional History of the Railways of Great Britain. Volume II: Southern England*, Newton Abbot 1982, p. 42.
[16] *Ibid.*, pp. 41, 52.
[17] *Ibid.*, p. 51.

respect. The county's dominant company, the South Eastern and Chatham, was merged by this legislation with the London and South Western and the London, Brighton and South Coast to form the Southern Railway.

Although it was the smallest of the four new main-line groups, the Southern, with nominal capital of nearly £150 million and route mileage of over 2,000, was a massive concern by the standards of the British economy at that time. Its territory was, of course, virtually everywhere south of the Thames, and its largest pre-grouping component was the LSWR. Kent could expect no particular priority within the new set-up, and, indeed, did not receive any. The Southern soon moved towards centralisation and rationalisation once it had a single General Manager, in the person of Sir Herbert Walker, from January 1924. The company's Eastern division, corresponding roughly to the former SECR territory, soon benefited from improvements in the quality of the available rolling stock, one of the SECR's weakest points.

Of greater importance ultimately was the question of electrification. The Southern's most distinctive strategy, and its principal claim to be the most successful of the post-1923 groups, was its commitment to a major programme of electrification of passenger services. There were some substantial reasons why electrification should have appeared a more attractive option to the management of the SR. Passenger traffic was an unusually high proportion of the total, average journey lengths were shorter than elsewhere, actual and potential commuter traffic was greater because of the company's dominance of the southern half of Greater London, and Southern territory as a whole was more prosperous than most parts of Britain in the inter-war years. Electrification was widely assumed initially to be most appropriate for handling suburban services, and two of the Southern's constituent companies (though not the SECR) had already provided solid evidence for this proposition. Furthermore during the course of a rolling programme during the 1930s it was to be demonstrated that electrification was abundantly justified also on longer mainline routes. By the end of the 1930s the Southern had transformed itself into one of the largest electrified systems in the world, with well over 600 route miles and nearly 2,000 track miles employing electric traction. Electric mileage overtook steam on passenger services in 1936, and by this date amounted to around 60% of the total.[18]

Kent naturally shared in the benefits of these positive developments, at least in respect of suburban, and, eventually, some of the shorter mainline services. Their significance was that the 'sparks effect' showed its ability to attract more passengers through better services – the improvement usually incorporating some combination of higher speed, greater frequency and reliability, with improved cleanliness. The Southern was thereby able to resist the national trend of the inter-war period by which railway passenger traffic increased only

---

[18] E.C. Cox, 'The Progress of the Southern Railway Electrification', *Journal of the Institute of Transport*, xviii (1937), pp. 108–21.

slightly, with almost the whole of the large-scale expansion of the total market being captured by the roads. Electrification increased traffic wherever it was adopted by the Southern, and the advantages were not confined, as was sometimes assumed in inter-war attempts at cost–benefit analysis, to economising on the cost of existing services. Even before 1914 the experience of the LBSCR and the LSWR had shown that when receipts were adversely affected by tramway competition, no solution was to be found by simply cutting costs (i.e. running fewer steam trains and reducing the level of service). By contrast investment in electrification allowed more trains to be run with no rise in gross current expenditure, and the enhanced receipts represented the return on the investment. In round figures the Southern gained increased revenues of around £2 million a year from electrification by 1938, for a capital outlay of about £19 million.[19] Although the Southern's management was adventurous by contemporary British standards in backing an electrification strategy, there were still many indications of caution and financial constraint. Only about £11 million of the requisite capital was actually charged to capital account, and much of this was raised via the government-sponsored Railway Finance Corporation which enabled loans to be obtained at lower rates than railway credit alone would have allowed. The rest was found mainly from various reserves, such as the locomotive renewal fund, the carriage renewal fund or the rebuilding premises fund, and by writing displaced steam traction equipment out of capital account.[20] An economical approach was apparent in the use of existing carriage bodies and under-frames. Even the virtually continuous financial success of electrification schemes could not remove all doubts about the risk element implicit in this prudent programme. The proposal to extend electrification of the Hastings line south of Sevenoaks was rejected by the board in late 1937 to the detriment of both Kentish residents and indeed of the company itself. This decision was taken despite the fact that the results of the previous extension to Sevenoaks had exceeded expectations. It may well have been influenced by the recent appearance of symptoms of an economic downturn.

The LBSCR and the LSWR had bequeathed just over eighty electrified route miles to the Southern in 1923. The SECR was equally aware of the issue, but was characteristically unable for financial reasons to respond adequately. In 1923 it was still entirely steam operated, and some of its suburban trains, for example on the North Kent lines, were illuminated by fishtail gas burners.[21] Nevertheless a plan had existed for the conversion of all the SECR's London network and for the current to be supplied by a new power station at Angerstein Wharf on the Thames. These preparations were in the hands of Alfred Raworth, who, as engineer for new works, worked closely with Walker in developing the Southern's electrification programme. Obviously a strategic decision was required as to which technical system should be used in future and whether it

---

[19] K.H. Johnston, *British Railways and Economic Recovery*, London 1949, p. 175.
[20] C.F. Klapper, *Sir Herbert Walker's Southern Railway*, London 1973, cc. 9, 10; Bonavia, *op. cit.*, c. 5.
[21] H.W.A. Linecar, *British Electric Trains*, London 1947, p. 96.

should be standardised throughout the company's territory. These were initially open questions because the Southern inherited mileage from the LBSCR which employed 6,600 volts alternating current with overhead collection, and also some from the LSWR using 600 volts direct current with third-rail collection. The SECR had selected 1,500 volts direct current, with a protected third rail, for planning purposes. However, when the Southern introduced electric traction on the eastern section, the former-LSWR mode was chosen. This was a strong signal for the final verdict. After hearing from a committee (chaired by E. C. Cox) of chief officers with strong former-SECR representation, the board ended the debate in August 1926 in favour of comprehensive standardisation on the basis of 600 V third-rail DC. Extensions to the AC overhead system in the Brighton section had been completed as recently as 1925, and some AC working continued until 1929.

Quite apart from the existence of the former LSWR installations, the Southern management had some solid reasons for selecting this path. Economy was of course a factor. Third-rail systems were cheaper than those requiring overhead structures, did not interfere with signalling, were more easily replaced in the event of damage, and the DC motors of the time produced good power output and acceleration at low speeds. Furthermore AC trains were normally heavier and tended to have higher operating costs. On the other hand the third-rail system was less suitable for freight haulage (less of a problem for the Southern than elsewhere) or shunting yards, and was vulnerable to frost. Its adoption strongly implied that the company would be committed to multiple-unit operation with no (or few) separate locomotives, with goods and inter-railway through-trains relying on steam or diesel traction. Internationally, third-rail DC was a minority system. Within Britain, different modes were favoured both by other groups and by the government. No fewer than three government committees (Kennedy in 1921, Pringle in 1928, and Weir in 1931) opted for 1,500 V DC with overhead collection as a future standard (though accepting that 750 V DC was an acceptable alternative in some conditions). A senior Southern manager served on the Pringle Committee, but refused to sign the report.[22]

With hindsight, it is clear that overhead AC traction had the higher potential for technical development in the long term. Some improvements were incorporated into DC third-rail working, such as the elimination of dependence on closely spaced sub-stations for the supply of current. But it cannot be doubted that the popularity of high tension AC overhead systems in the post-war period has been firmly based on its greater technical efficiency, especially for high-speed operation. British Railways selected 25 kV AC for the electrification of the West Coast mainline at the beginning of the 1960s, and subsequently decided to standardise on this basis. However the Southern region was excluded from the applicability of this policy – almost necessarily given the desirability of

22 Bonavia, *op. cit.*, c. 5; White, *op. cit.*, c. 9.

uniform working methods over a large territory with a high level of interlocking operations and the prohibitive cost of comprehensive conversion. Kent, like the rest of the region, has been stuck with the third rail, which continued to be used in post-war extensions of electrification long after a superior technical mode had become available. This is an unusually strong example of the complex and long-lasting, if largely unintentional, impact of institutional and technical factors, expressed in this case through the medium of the Cox committee's decision in 1926. Western areas of Kent during the inter-war years enjoyed in consequence a short-distance passenger train service of a quality which was no doubt envied in most other parts of the country. For much of the last few decades of the century many towns in Kent found themselves in the distinctly unenviable position of being at least twice as far from London in terms of travelling time as equivalent locations to the west and north of the capital.[23]

Institutional factors were also at work, though to a much more modest degree, in influencing the fortunes of Kent's single complex of railway workshops, at Ashford. The manufacture, maintenance and repair of locomotives and rolling stock, had always been the most important and direct backward linkage from railway operation. Ashford, otherwise a market town of limited significance, had acquired a locomotive works in 1847 and a wagon works in 1850, under the auspices of the South Eastern company. Following the merger, it became the principal establishment of the SECR, and both works were extended and modernised. But under the SR from 1923 Ashford took second place to Eastleigh, the former LSWR centre, which had greater capacity in both its locomotive and carriage and wagon units. Ashford concentrated far more on the repair than the construction of locomotives, finally ceasing to build in 1944. Neither Ashford nor Eastleigh built any of the post-nationalisation standard steam locomotives, and the Ashford locomotive works closed in 1962, with the remaining repair work being transferred to Eastleigh. The wagon works had more staying power, and after extensive reorganisation in the mid-1960s became one of BREL's two main wagon plants, winning some large export orders. It was finally closed in 1982, by which time the town had fortunately acquired a much wider employment base.[24]

Electrification of the former SECR parts of the Southern network was well under way by the mid-1920s. New services were opened in three stages in 1925 and 1926, including lines to Herne Hill, Orpington, Beckenham Junction and Dartford. Further extensions reached Gravesend in 1930, St Mary Cray in 1934, and Sevenoaks in 1935 by two routes. A final major tranche of electrification in the eastern section was completed in the summer of 1939, when fifty-three route miles were added in the Medway area. Thus Kent had gained during the inter-war period a fairly dense suburban network in the commuter areas nearest to London, plus conversion along the three main lines from London as far as

23 *Ibid.*, p. 210.
24 E.J. and J.G. Larkin, *The Railway Workshops of Britain, 1823–1986*, London 1988.

Gillingham, Maidstone and Sevenoaks. Even here the electric trains operated essentially in an outer suburban role, and these towns continued to rely on steam services for their longer-distance connections. Eastern Kent was largely untouched, and a glance at the map suggested that the counties of Hampshire, Sussex and Surrey had enjoyed more substantial benefits from the Southern, especially where mainline electrification was concerned. Large-scale projects completed outside Kent were the Brighton line, covering the coast to Worthing (1933), Eastbourne, with a link to Hastings and Ore (1935), Portsmouth 'number one' (1937) and 'number two', which basically served Bognor Regis and Littlehampton (1938). It may well be the case that the eastern and southern parts of Kent which remained outside the electrified area lacked towns of sufficient size to make expensive investment an attractive proposition, although the failure to make the extension from Sevenoaks to Hastings looked anomalous by the Southern's own standards. Furthermore the growth potential of cross-Channel traffic was underrated in this context.[25]

Where electrification was undertaken, however, the Southern certainly showed a well-tuned awareness of the positive relationship between railway transport and residential property development. It also, especially after the appointment of John Elliott in 1925 to a public relations position at head office, proved effective in the advertising and promotion of its commuter and other services. One atmospheric poster, by Edward Vaughan, under the heading 'So Swiftly Home', portrayed an illuminated electric train passing a signal in evening light, with track of the third rail type conspicuous in the foreground. Another, against a rural backdrop, with oast houses prominent, featured the slogan 'Live in Kent and Be Content.'[26] In more practical vein was a series of 'Southern Homes' booklets, such as 'Southern Homes in the Kentish Hills', which was published in connection with the Sevenoaks electrification, and which gave details of builders and estate agents in the area.

Before nationalisation the Southern had committed itself to the completion of electrification in its central and eastern sections, but implementation was not feasible during BR's first decade. Sometimes when modernisation occurred, steam traction gave way not to electric, but to diesel-electric. In 1958 twenty-three diesel multiple units were introduced on the Tunbridge Wells and Hastings line. As with the 'sparks effect', this change facilitated a regular-interval service at greater speed and even more importantly, increased frequency, and with comparable success. The Hastings–Ashford branch benefited from similar treatment. The first post-war extension of electrification took place in 1959 and involved seventy-eight route miles between Gillingham and Faversham and thence to Ramsgate and Dover, along with the Sheerness branch. Again the results showed that electrification, after an interval of twenty years, had not lost its capacity to generate increased traffic. A second phase followed quickly in

[25] Klapper, *op. cit.*, c. 10; Bonavia, *op. cit.*, c. 9.
[26] *Ibid.*, pp. 86–7. Klapper, *op. cit.*, p. 213.

Plate 18. Calais steamer at Dover harbour, 1910.

Plate 19. War-time bus and anti-tank blocks on Maidstone Bridge.

Ashford Station.
Boat Express.

Plate 20. Boat Express at Ashford station, c.1920.

Plate 21. Commuters at Ashford station, c.1960.

Plate 22. Aerial view of Lydd airport (© Aerofilms Ltd).

Plate 23. The Kent end of the Channel Tunnel near Folkestone, under construction.

1961 and 1962, when a further 132 route miles were converted, including Seve-noaks to Dover and Ramsgate, Maidstone East to Ashford, Maidstone West to Paddock Wood and the Folkestone Harbour branch. In early 1962 steam was eliminated from what had since 1958 been known as the south-eastern division of the Southern region.[27]

British Transport Commission statistics show that the 'Kent Coast' scheme (Sevenoaks–Dover/Ramsgate) required a net investment of nearly £29 million, which was expected to produce £2.5 million in net revenue (8.7%). As the existing assets were yielding £0.5 million (1.5%), the anticipated outcome was that just under 5% would be earned on an enlarged capital of nearly £62 million. Such results, although indicating unquestionable improvements in efficiency, were undoubtedly some way below those obtained from inter-war electrifica-tions, and the historian of British Railways has commented that 'operational advantages . . . clearly carried more weight here than purely commercial consid-erations'.[28] These advantages were essentially the removal of a steam enclave from an electrified area, a gain which may not have been fully captured by the BTC figures. A further positive dimension of the project which could not have been reflected in the measured return was the social benefit of retention of some passenger traffic which would otherwise have been lost to the roads. After the early 1960s the only additional electrification carried out (partly) in Kent was on the Hastings line in the mid-1980s (almost half a century after Walker's proposals were rejected by the Southern), and no major technical innovation was on the agenda until serious consideration of a Channel Tunnel rail link began in the late 1980s.

The problem for Kent and for much of the Southern region was that for approximately three decades after the end of the war it was considered to have reached a plateau of relative efficiency by national passenger traffic standards. The freight market, where there had been serious losses to road competition, had always been less important in the south-east. Furthermore Kent succeeded through the 1960s and into the 1970s in resisting the national downward trend in rail freight, with increased flows of trainload traffic in oil, cement, steel, china clay and motor vehicles. General prosperity, above-average population growth and the continued popularity of commuting to London ensured a level of demand for railway services which conferred a large measure of immunity from the widespread fear (and the reality) of closures which affected most other parts of the country. Commuter demand continued to rise on the longer-distance serv-ices until the mid-1970s. The Beeching Report of 1963, which contemplated the abandonment of up to one-third of the national system which was contributing disproportionately little to revenue, was obviously not aimed primarily at the Kentish lines. On the other hand, Beeching, being concerned to identify, for purposes of prioritisation, the types of traffic best suited to rail, perhaps

27 White, *op. cit.*, pp. 200–202.
28 T.R. Gourvish, *British Railways 1948–1973*, Cambridge 1986, p. 280.

signalled the beginnings of managerial disillusionment with commuter and holiday traffic, both of which had always been important in Kent, but were now seen as unprofitable. The Southern region received no infrastructure grant under the 1968 Transport Act, such as financed the Great Northern suburban electrification, though the Southern suburban services were supported *en bloc* until the change of formula in 1974. A Monopolies Commission report of 1980 largely absolved the region's management, as opposed to successive governments, from responsibility for the shortcomings of the suburban services.[29] This view was endorsed by Kent County Council, one of whose transport-policy submissions noted that 'generally the best possible level of service is provided bearing in mind the economics of a severely peaked operation and the need to provide a reasonable level of services to everyone'.[30] Overall, Kent commuter traffic was static or declining in the late 1970s and the first half of the 1980s, since when it has tended to behave cyclically, fluctuating in sympathy with employment trends.[31] But scarce investment resources rarely found their way to Kent or other parts of the region, being channelled at national level to (mainly) longer-distance lines where the need was judged more acute and the growth prospects better. There were no equivalents of the electrification of the London–Glasgow (1960s), London–Norwich (1990) and London–Edinburgh (1991) routes, with their various spurs in the Midlands and north, or the introduction of Inter-City 125 diesel services on such routes as London–Sheffield and London–Bristol–Cardiff. British Rail's 'business-led' reorganisation after 1982 created a new structure, within which Kent became part of the London and South East sector (later Network South East) which covered all the Home Counties and beyond. This did not change any fundamentals, and commuter traffic remained the principal concern of the new management set-up. The widening of the area of responsibility may actually have helped to promote useful innovations, such as the popular Network card for off-peak travel and the development of the Thameslink scheme for direct services through London.[32]

A situation of stasis gradually gave way to one of decay and decline. The last major institutional change of the century, the privatisation and break-up of British Rail under the Railways Act of 1993 brought little promise of improvement with it. For the first time since the days of the SECR between 1899 and 1923, the railway map of Kent became virtually coterminous with the territory of a single organisation, the French-owned Connex South Eastern. Responsibility for the infrastructure, with its many remaining shortcomings, passed to Railtrack, but Connex SE became the passenger-train operating company for the Kent area by bidding successfully for a fifteen-year franchise, starting in October 1996. The initial annual train mileage of around 17.5 million made it

29 White, *op. cit.*, pp. 205–13.
30 Kent County Council Transport Policies and Programme for 1979–80.
31 R. Gibb and R. Knowles, 'The High-speed Rail Link: Planning and Development Implications', in *The Channel Tunnel: A Geographical Perspective*, ed. R. Gibb, London 1994, pp. 180–1.
32 N.G. Harris and E. Godward, *The Privatisation of British Rail*, London 1997, pp. 40–59.

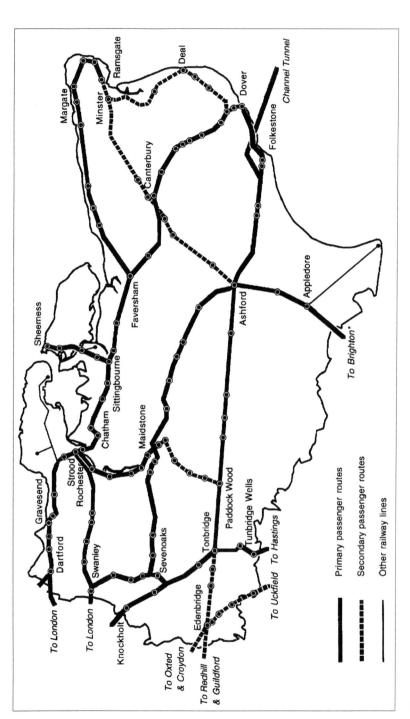

Figure 8. British Rail passenger network in Kent, 1996.

* Following electrification planned for 1995/96 this route will carry through services between Ashford and Brighton.

General notes

The route hierarchy is based on current (1996) usage, planned imporvements and KCC objectives.

Primary Route – two or more passenger trains each hour to London and/or Ashford.

Secondary Route – other route with a regular passenger service.

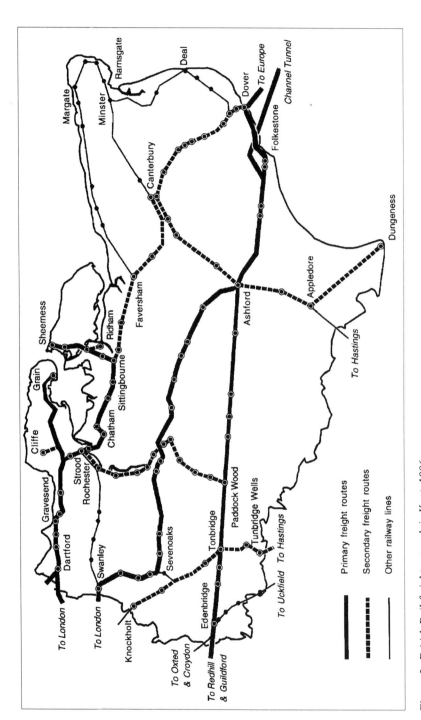

Figure 9. British Rail freight network in Kent, 1996.

The route hierarchy is based on current (1996) usage, planned improvements and KCC aspirations.

Primary Route – more than 50 freight trains per week.

Secondary Route – between 1 and 50 freight trains per weeks.

one of the largest of the new TOCs, although the average journey length of fifteen miles was one of the shortest in the system, reflecting the continuing importance of commuting in the inner Connex area. The level of public subsidy made available to the new private owners was higher than that enjoyed by BR, but was subject to a tapering principle. It began at £136.1 million a year, declined to £85.1 million by 1998–9 and was set to fall slowly to zero and actually to become very modestly negative in the last full year of the franchise. Partly for this reason, the outlook for investment and renewal was not good. Most services in the outer Connex area at the end of the century were still provided by the aged class-411 stock which dated from around 1960, with a minor contribution from a few class-365 Networker units.[33] Connex was, in common with other TOCs, widely though ineffectively criticised for unreliability and unpunctuality, especially the latter. The Rail Users' Consultative Committee, reporting a 44% rise in complaints about late trains, made the judgement in June 1999 that train services in Kent were worse than they had been under BR.[34] Connex SE had been named by the Office for Passenger Rail Franchising as a D category operator (the second lowest grade) for its performance in the last quarter of 1998. The company was anxious to transfer much of the blame onto Railtrack. Its chief executive pointed out in early 1999 that BR had invested some £400 million in lengthening platforms and other route improvements, but that progress had been interrupted by privatisation. He claimed that crucial improvements, to the track at London Bridge, to platforms at Dartford and to the network's electricity supply could be completed in about eighteen months at a cost of up to £30 million. Railtrack, however, lacked financial incentives to respond quickly. It did have plans to improve some Connex routes, but only as part of a longer-term upgrading of Thameslink services for which the earliest possible finishing date was 2006.[35]

(4) Cross-Channel Transport

The various railway companies which dominated Kent all showed an active interest in cross-Channel traffic from the mid-nineteenth century onwards, and for this reason most became closely involved in shipping activities in addition to strictly railway operations. The South Eastern had developed Folkestone as a directly owned harbour, and the port passed on this basis to the Southern. Dover Harbour Board, as a trust port, was an independent body, but the Southern inherited representation (three seats) on it from the SECR. There can be no doubt that the Southern appreciated the opportunities offered by the Channel traffic. In its first ten years the Southern constructed twenty-nine ships (ten cargo), and thus by the early 1930s had assembled a fleet of fifty-six, of which

33 Glover, *op. cit.*, p. 62.
34 *Kent Messenger Extra*, 4 June 1999.
35 *Financial Times*, 19 February 1999.

twelve were small Isle of Wight ferries. Dover and Folkestone had nine passenger and seven freight ships – more than Newhaven but fewer than Southampton. In 1929 the new 25.5-knot *Canterbury*, of almost 3,000 tons, made its first appearance and established itself as the informal flagship of the Southern fleet. Initially it catered specifically for the patrons of the recently introduced 'Golden Arrow' Pullman train between London and Paris, although this meant that only around one-third of its capacity was used.[36]

Dover also gained some business in long-distance freight, mainly fruit, and in the passenger-liner trade. In such activities Dover was, of course, overshadowed by Southampton, and indeed occupied a status which was clearly subordinate to that of Southampton in the priorities of the Southern. It was significant that two docks managers at Southampton, Szlumper and Missenden, went on to become chief executives of the Southern Railway. Sir Herbert Walker, the Southern's longest-serving general manager, called Southampton 'the jewel in the crown of the Southern Railway'.[37] The port had been a successful acquisition by the LSWR in 1892, and the SR was happy to maintain a high rate of investment in the inter-war period. The Southern committed almost as much capital to Southampton as to its entire electrification programme and enjoyed good results both for itself and for the local economy. But the last major tranche of investment, the Ocean Terminal, started by the Southern, but opened in 1950 after nationalisation, took place only just before the ocean-liner trade entered a permanent decline in the age of long-distance air travel. After World War II it became apparent that Dover, with its short crossing to the Continent, had better prospects than Southampton in passenger traffic.[38]

A small development of enormous long-term significance occurred at Dover in 1928 when a disgruntled former customer of the Southern, Captain Townsend, whose firm was in the coastal trade, introduced the first dedicated car ferry. His original, chartered, ship had the tiny capacity of fifteen cars and was intended to revert in winter to its former role as a collier. Two years later Townsend began to use a reconstructed minesweeper, the *Forde*, which carried twenty-six cars and 165 passengers. This initiative was sufficient to provoke the Southern into launching in 1931 a specially commissioned ship for the same purpose, with the unimaginative but self-explanatory name, *Autocarrier*, of just over 800 tons and with space for 35–40 cars. The company also carried cars between Dover and Calais on two other ships, both of which sailed during the night. A basic problem which was not fully overcome in the 1930s was the inevitable slowness of the crane loading procedure, but this did not prevent a steady increase, from a very small base, in the popularity of the service. From approximately 6,000 in 1928, the number of cars using Dover annually had risen to over 31,000 by 1938. At the beginning of 1938 a pooling arrangement was introduced between all the car-ferry operators, which allocated just over 53% of all

[36] A. Hasenson, *A History of Dover Harbour*, London 1980, c. 20.
[37] D. St J. Thomas and P. Whitehouse, *SR 150*, London 1988, pp. 133–4.
[38] Bonavia, *op. cit.*, c. 13; Klapper, *op. cit.*, pp. 231–5.

fares to the Southern and 28.5% to Townsends, with the remainder going to two
French companies. Passenger traffic, in contrast, was more subject to fluctua-
tion than the car-ferry business. On the Dover–Calais and Folkestone–Boulogne
routes, inter-war peaks were reached in 1926 and 1929 respectively, and the
depressed years of the early 1930s brought a pronounced trough. Dover–Ostend
passenger numbers exhibited a stronger recovery in the late 1930s, albeit from a
low base.[39]

Even in the doldrums of the 1930s there was some noteworthy innovation.
The year 1937 saw the inauguration of the first regular train ferries, which, in
addition to freight services, allowed through-passenger sleeping cars to run
between London and Paris. One possible source of inspiration for this idea was
the wartime use of Richborough as a terminal for train ferries carrying military
supplies to the Continent. The new *Night Ferry* service required three new ships,
all of which could carry twelve sleeping cars or forty goods wagons on four
parallel lines of track. These ferries offered a surprising side-line, as their upper
decks were designed to take twenty-five cars, which from 1937 could be driven
on and off the ship at Dover – a very small-scale application of the principle
which became central to the vast post-war expansion of the car-ferry trade.
However novel and however glamorous its image, the *Night Ferry* had its limitations as a luxury service. The overnight journey took a long time and the transfers were accompanied by the loud clanking of chains.[40]

After the Second World War the *Golden Arrow* resumed in April 1946,
carrying its 100,000th passenger some six months later, and the *Night Ferry* in
December 1947, only a couple of weeks before nationalisation. *Autocarrier* was
back at work by May 1946, switching from Dover to Folkestone two years later.
It was soon joined by an additional railway-owned car ferry in the form of the
converted passenger ship, *Dinard*. Other operators were soon active, including
Townsend, who introduced a former naval frigate, the *Halladale*, as a new type
of car ferry in 1950. It was the first stern-loading drive-on cross-Channel vessel,
and offered a capacity of 50–60 cars, with a turntable on board, plus 350 passengers. Townsend was actively pursuing the principle of drive-on, drive-off, and
first achieved this ambition on the French side by giving the authorities at Calais
an old military Bailey bridge, adapted as a car ramp. This was in regular use by
1951, but crane loading continued at Dover for some time afterwards. By 1953
four car ferries were operating between Dover and the French and Belgian ports,
plus the train ferries whose car capacity had, in two cases, been enhanced to
nearly 100. Even then foot-passenger traffic was still predominant. In 1952 the
1939 figure of one million passengers was exceeded, and this number more than
doubled by 1959. A process of continuous increase then saw annual totals rising
to 3 million by 1962, 5 million in 1970, over 7 million by 1976, and more than 9
million by the end of the 1970s. The number of cars passing through Dover rose

39 Hasenson, *op. cit.*, pp. 343, 376.
40 Bonavia, *op. cit.*, c. 12; Hasenson, *op. cit.*, c. 20.

even more steeply (from 31,000 in 1938) to 40,000 in 1948, almost 100,000 in 1950, over 200,000 in 1955, and more than one million by 1976. The new car-ferry terminal of 1953 had handled its one millionth vehicle by the end of the decade. There was also a steady and significant increase in general cargo, which by 1976 amounted to more than 4 million tons, hauled in about 400,000 lorries.[41]

More French and Belgian car ferries appeared in the late 1950s and early 1960s. Townsend broke new ground in 1962 with their first purpose-built car ferry, a replacement for the *Halladale*. It inaugurated a series of eight ships, introduced between 1962 and 1974, all named *Free Enterprise*, followed by the appropriate Roman numeral. Although neither its size nor its capacity was out of the ordinary (2,600 tons, 850 passengers and 120 cars), its hydraulically oper-ated stern doors, giving access to one of two vehicle decks, allowed easy drive-on conditions. The second member of the *FE* fleet, launched in 1965, was more notable still, being the first British-owned car ferry to employ the drive-through method, which allowed cars to be driven in at the stern and out again at the bows, or vice versa. The third became in 1966 the largest car ferry working in the Channel, and was specifically designed to take lorries. Another Townsend initiative was the opening of a Dover–Zeebrugge service in 1966 (previously a Belgian monopoly) using an improved permanent berth from 1970. There was no doubt that during the 1960s this company moved faster than its competitors to exploit the growth potential of the market. It was able to do so partly because of the misfortune which overtook Captain Townsend, who attempted to go public on the day the nationalisation of the Suez Canal was announced. A new group of shareholders eventually removed Townsend and his supporters from the board. The most prominent of the expansionist newcomers was an accountant called Roland Wickenden, who became managing director when George Nott Industries acquired the share capital of Townsend in 1959. From 1965, when the headquarters moved to Dover, he took over the chair of the company, which merged with the Norwegian Otto Thoresen Shipping Company in 1968. The parent company took the name European Ferries in 1971 when it absorbed the Atlantic Steam Navigation Company at a cost of £5.5 million. ASN had experience of freight operations, including early exploitation of the roll-on, roll-off principle, in both the Irish and North Seas, and was disposed of by the National Freight Corporation as part of the Conservative government's limited privatisation programme of the early 1970s. Thoresen worked more westerly routes in the Channel, but the second of their four 'Viking' ferries (three car, one freight) was adapted for relocation to Dover. The *FE* names reflected Wickenden's outlook, and his willingness to make quick decisions to implement his priorities of an up-to-date fleet of large drive-on, drive-off ships, and the development of the lorry freight business. He died in 1972 and was soon succeeded by his brother Keith, who also died relatively young in 1983. The

---

[41]   J. Hendy, *Ferry Port Dover*, Staplehurst 1998, cc. 1, 2, p. 127; Hasenson, *op. cit.* c. 23.

period of Wickenden domination was the most effective in the history of Town-send Thoresen. As the younger brother took over in 1972, he was able to recall that seven years earlier they had operated one ship on a single route, but currently boasted more than thirty on twelve routes. By the mid-1970s a strong market share and the status of Dover's principal operator had been secured. Despite this extensive expansion the company remained strongly focused for some years after the move to Dover, with a clear strategy and a heavy emphasis on the primary Dover–Calais route. There were some setbacks, such as the unsuccessful use of a former tank-landing craft in freight service to Calais. But the freight market grew, and TT obtained a rising share of it, introducing four freight ferries between 1974 and 1978, three of which were Dover-based. By 1977 freight accounted for half of European Ferries' turnover.[42]

British Railways were considerably more cautious, perhaps not surprisingly as they were subject to tighter constraints on capital investment, particularly during the latter part of this period. When the Thatcher government announced its intention to privatise the shipping and other sections of BR in 1980, the chairman conceded that investment had been 'limited' and the subsidiaries 'starved', and that the board had been considering the need for partnership ventures for the previous three years.[43] The Shipping and International Services Division had seemed to react relatively slowly to changes in the market situation and, periodically during the 1960s and 1970s, to have been more inhibited than its competitors by the danger posed to investment in shipping by the possible imminence of the Channel Tunnel. Its share of an expanding market declined sharply from a position of great initial strength. During the 1960s alone BR's share slid from around 90% to 60% of the total cross-Channel trade.[44] In 1969 the 'Sealink' consortium was formed from British, Belgian, French and Dutch public concerns. This did not, however, prevent BR from falling further behind TT in ordering new capacity. A pooling agreement between Sealink and TT survived until 1979.[45]

BR was more active in promoting the new technology of the hovercraft. The first such flight across the Channel had been completed in two hours by SRN1 in July 1959. Less than a decade later BR's Seaspeed subsidiary inaugurated the world's first commercial passenger- and vehicle-carrying hovercraft service, when *Princess Margaret* began work between Dover and Boulogne in August 1968. A second SRN4, *Princess Anne*, arrived in 1969. These craft had space for thirty cars and 150 passengers. By then competition had appeared in the form of the Swedish Hoverlloyd company which opened a service from Rams-gate (Pegwell Bay) to Calais. This new method of crossing the Channel could offer up to three times the pace of ships, but with lower capacity and greater vulnerability to bad weather. Growth was rapid in the first ten years. Seaspeed

42 Hendy, *op. cit.*, c. 2, pp. 93–4; Hasenson, *op. cit.*, pp. 386–97.
43 Hendy, *op. cit.*, pp. 95–6.
44 *Ibid.*, p. 48.
45 *Ibid.*, p. 60; M. Cowsill and J. Hendy, *The Sealink Years, 1970–1995*, Kilgetty n.d.

entered the Calais market in 1970 and by the late 1970s the two operators had gained around a quarter of the total short-crossing traffic for both passengers and cars. This proved, however, to be a peak, and subsequent technical change favoured shipping operators, as greater increases in the size of their vessels facilitated a faster reduction in unit costs.[46]

The expansion of the whole cross-Channel market would not have been possible without a corresponding enlargement of the port facilities at Dover. Most of the new investment went to Eastern Docks which by the mid-1970s had absorbed more than half of Dover's passenger trade. An exception was the construction of a new Hoverport on reclaimed land between Prince of Wales Pier and North Pier between 1976 and 1978. This had been necessitated by the decision to 'stretch' the two SRN4s by adding a 55-feet section to increase capacity to 360 passengers and fifty-five cars. They thus became the largest hovercraft in the world and outgrew their original base in Eastern docks. Some of the new installations in Eastern Docks were needed to cope with the growth of coach traffic, which first exceeded 100,000 annually in 1982. A year later, coach passengers overtook private motorists in number. An expensive and recurring item for the Harbour Board was the periodic demand for new or enlarged and re-equipped berths to handle the increasing size of ships. Perhaps the most intensive phase of such investment occurred between 1988 and 1993 when four 28-metre berths cost a total of £24 million. The DHB was able to claim in 1992, with the opening of the Tunnel imminent, that it had kept total dues below 10% of the ferries' revenues, and that it sought a reduction in this proportion to counter the competitive threat.[47] This amounted to an invaluable specialised service to the ferry business, given that a combination of rapidly rising demand and changing technical requirements had called for continual flexibility and substantial investment. The latest development schemes at Dover in the last years of the century were directed towards increasing accommodation for cruise liners and yachts.[48]

These developments, along with some associated road improvements (notably the opening in 1977 of the elevated Jubilee Way by-pass from Eastern Docks to the A2, and the extension of the M20 from Folkestone to Dover in 1993) completed the basic infrastructure with which the ferry trade faced up to competition from the Channel Tunnel.[49] The rising totals for passenger traffic had passed 10 million by 1980, 15 million by 1989, and 20 million by 1997, with the only significant interruptions to growth occurring in 1988 (a three-month strike) and 1995 (the first full year of the Channel Tunnel). The number of cars passed 1.5 million in 1981, 2 million in 1989, 3 million in 1994, and 3.5 million in 1997. By 1994 150,000 coaches were using the port, and 165,000 in

[46] Hendy, *op. cit.*, pp. 48–9; Hoverspeed website at http:/www.hoverspeed.co.uk/ENG/company/company_history.ht ml

[47] Hendy, *op. cit.*, c. 3.

[48] Port and Ferry News, on Internet at http:/www.topsy.demon.co.uk/dover/news.html

[49] Hendy, *op. cit.*, pp. 82–91.

1997. Units of freight first exceeded 500,000 in 1979, 1 million in 1989 and 1.5 million in 1997.[50] Estimated dry cargo handled in 1995 showed Dover accounted for exports of 5 million tons (third after Middlesbrough and Felixstowe) and imports of 7.2 million tons (fifth).[51] It is clear that only Felixstowe (freight) and, from a much lower base, Portsmouth (passengers) could claim faster growth. However Dover's tonnage mainly took the form of unitised freight with a higher value/weight ratio than the traditional bulk cargoes, and the steady growth of around 10% a year throughout the 1980s made Dover the busiest port in the UK in terms of value handled. This reflected a stronger long-term orientation of Britain's external visible trade on the countries of continental Europe, a trend which obviously benefited North Sea and Channel ports at the expense of older deep-sea ports.[52] Dover by 1997 had two-thirds of the total cross-Channel ferry trade of around 32 million passengers (Portsmouth came second with one-tenth of this figure). This trade had itself grown by 37% over the previous ten years, a rate of growth which was exceeded by both air and (from 1994) Tunnel crossings, which were more popular with business travellers.

This expansion was dependent on further radical changes in the size and design of ships. TT's *FE* fleet in the 1960s had inaugurated the third generation of ferries. Two more followed. The fourth was launched by TT in 1980, when three Bremerhaven-built 'Spirit' class ships (the first was named *Spirit of Free Enterprise*) arrived at Dover. Described by some as 'revolutionary', they became the first British-registered mixed ferries to allow ro–ro traffic on two continuous decks, with simultaneous loading and unloading. The new ships could also make five return Channel crossings a day if necessary. Soon afterwards Sealink made its contribution to the third generation in 1981 when it introduced two Belfast-built ferries of almost similar size though of rather more traditional design.[53] It was the second of the 'Spirit' class, the *Herald of Free Enterprise*, which achieved international notoriety in March 1987 when it sank outside Zeebrugge with the loss of 155 passengers and thirty-eight crew. The immediate cause of this disaster was undoubtedly failure to close the bow doors before sailing, an omission which was by no means unknown at that time. But the *Herald* sank in a couple of minutes once the main vehicle deck had taken in just a few inches of water through its open doors. This replicated in more extreme form a fatal accident in which six died off Felixstowe in late 1982 after the *European Gateway* sank in about ten minutes following a collision. Obviously questions of a fundamental character were raised about the safety of ro–ro ferries with uninterrupted decks and heavy superstructures. However, subse-

---

50 *Ibid.*, pp. 127–8.
51 R. Goss, 'British Ports Policies since 1945', *Journal of Transport Economics and Policy*, 32, 1 (1998), p. 53.
52 A. Spencer and M. Browne, 'The Implications of the Tunnel for Freight', in Gibb , *op. cit.*, esp. pp. 115–17.
53 Hendy, *op. cit.*, pp. 59–66; N. Robins, *The Evolution of the British Ferry*, Kilgetty, n.d., pp. 86–8.

quent official enquiries resulted in only minor modifications being required to structure and operating procedures.[54] The phrase 'bow doors open', as a metaphor for dangerous and foolhardy conduct, gained wider currency as a result of insensitive remarks at a press conference four days after the Zeebrugge tragedy by the Environment Secretary, Nicholas Ridley.[55] Another consequence of the disaster was the renaming of the TT passenger ferries, whereby the 'free enterprise' was replaced by the 'pride' theme (e.g. *Pride of Hythe, Pride of Bruges*).

The demise of the *Herald* occurred just before the onset of the fifth generation of ferries, represented in the first instance by *Pride of Dover* and *Pride of Calais*. These were characterised by greatly increased size and capacity, with a strong emphasis on upgraded comfort, entertainment and shopping facilities. The economic context was indicated by the term 'Chunnel beaters' coined by their owners. Three similar freight ships, with certificates for 200 drivers, were introduced in 1991 and 1992. A fourth was converted during construction to become a mixed car/lorry vessel, and in 1993 became the largest ferry yet to operate from Dover, the 28,000 ton *Pride of Burgundy*. This distinction passed in 1996 to the Stena *Empereur* when it was relocated from Scandinavian duties. Because of the high cost of ships of this type, a number of older ferries joined the fifth generation through a process of 'jumboisation' – being elongated or 'stretched' by having the superstructure raised and new fore parts added. Indeed Sealink provided no new purpose-built ships for the Channel services after the last of the fourth generation 'Saint' class ferries of 1981. It relied entirely on the conversion of older vessels or the redirection of ferries from Scandinavian routes (mainly too shallow in draft to carry many lorries, but offering lavish passenger accommodation).[56]

Sealink's Scandinavian connections had arisen following two changes of ownership. The Thatcher government, at that stage limiting itself to privatisation of only the non-core parts of British Rail, sold Sealink UK for £66 million in the summer of 1984 to the Bermuda-registered Sea Containers. This very low price was inevitably dubbed 'the sale of the century'.[57] European Ferries (TT) had made an £80 million bid in 1981, but this had fallen at the hurdle of the Monopolies and Mergers Commission. From 1984 to 1990 Sealink British Ferries enjoyed a disappointing period under the overall leadership of the American President of Sea Containers, James Sherwood. At least two promises of major new tonnage remained unfulfilled, and Sherwood was briefly involved in the mid-1980s in the Channel Expressway scheme for a road and rail fixed link (opening his firm to the same suspicions of divided loyalties as its British Rail-owned predecessor). Around this time he forecast that ferry services would be reduced by 75% by the time the tunnel was open. Sherwood was also drawn into a bruising dispute with the nationalised Belgian operator RMT over shares

---

54 Robins, *op. cit.*, pp. 88–90.
55 Hansard, 10 March 1987, Oral Answers, columns 145–6.
56 Hendy, *op. cit.*, pp. 67–76; Robins, *op. cit.*, pp. 91–7; Cowsill and Hendy, *op. cit.*, p. 7.
57 *Ibid.*, p. 5.

of the Dover–Belgium trade, driving RMT into a new partnership with TT. SBF did open a Dover–Zeebrugge freight service in 1987 and 1988, but this failed, partly because of lack of suitable ships to make three round crossings per day. RMT and TT were left with the bulk of the passenger and freight trade respectively between Dover and Belgium.[58]

A rather more successful move by Sea Containers was the acquisition in 1986 of Hoverspeed, the hovercraft operator formed in 1981 through the merger of Seaspeed with Hoverlloyd. This had meant the ending of the Ramsgate service and concentration on the Dover to Calais and Boulogne routes. Investment policies remained cautious and the original (albeit stretched) SRN4s were still in service thirty years later. Some innovation was, however, accommodated, such as the introduction in 1990 of the first vehicle-carrying catamaran, *Great Britain* (600 passengers and eighty vehicles), and the 'superseacat' in 1997. In 1998 and 1999 services were introduced, or restored, between Dover and Ostend, and Folkestone and Boulogne.[59]

SBF's ferries and ports division (but not Hoverspeed) was acquired in 1990 by the Swedish company Stena Line through a hostile take-over bid. This move had been anticipated by the purchase of an 8% stake in Sea Containers in 1989. Once again any optimism engendered by the change of ownership was to evaporate swiftly. The new management had been prepared to invest in order to develop 'a Scandinavian cruise-style culture', and specifically, to encourage heavier spending in the floating shops. But Sealink Stena made a pre-tax loss of £28 million in its opening year, and soon launched a major economy drive, 'Operation Benchmark'. This quickly led to the closure of the Folkestone–Boulogne service in 1991. Whereas Sealink had clearly been undervalued by the government in 1984, this time it appeared that the buyer had seriously miscalculated by paying as much as £259 million and assuming £200 million of Sea Containers' debt. It was believed that £180 million would have been close to the company's value.[60]

The TT shipping division of European Ferries had also undergone some vicissitudes. From the 1970s onwards the group diversified and began to lose its cross-Channel focus, acquiring two docks concerns and then entering the property market through Stockley in the UK and EF International in the USA. Some critics believed the group never recovered from the death of Keith Wickenden in 1983. A fall in the value of the American properties, related to the declining price of oil, aroused external interest. The P&O Group first bought a substantial stake in 1986, placing its chairman, Sir Jeffrey Sterling, on the European Ferries board, and then completed a successful £448 million take-over in early 1987, which survived a Monopolies Commission investigation. P&O European Ferries became the new organisation's trading name, replacing TT, now tainted with 'the disease of sloppiness' after the Zeebrugge disaster. Partly because of

58 *Ibid.*, pp. 53–4, 58, 62–3, 66; Hendy, *op. cit.*, pp. 96–100.
59 Hoverspeed website, *loc. cit.*
60 Hendy and Cowsill, *op. cit.*, pp. 76, 80, 83–4; Hendy, *op. cit.*, pp. 100–101.

swifter action to sacrifice labour, P&O EF was financially more successful than its principal competitor during both the SeaCo and the Stena periods (the latter, innovative in this way at least, changed its name first from Sealink Stena to Stena Sealink in 1992 and then to Stena from 1996). But the pressure of competition from the Tunnel, the need for further operating economies and a collapse of profitability for Stena inevitably produced the idea of the big merger. After previous rebuttals, and against the advice of the Director General of Fair Trading, the government sanctioned the emergence in late 1997 of P&O Stena Line, with gross assets of £410 million. It was then planned to cut about one-fifth from the combined labour force of around 5,000 and four of the fourteen ferries. By the time the joint venture began in March 1998 the fleet had been reduced to six ships, four former-P&O and two former-Stena. The only remaining competition at Dover was the new French undertaking, SeaFrance, which had two ferries, and whose predecessor had ended its co-operation with Stena Sealink at the end of 1995. SeaFrance made a promising start, claiming an initial 15% of the Dover–Calais market. In 1999 P&O Stena and Eurotunnel held a combined 90% of the short sea-crossing trade, leaving small niches for SeaFrance and Hoverspeed.[61]

(5) The Channel Tunnel

The challenge of the Tunnel, both before and after its actual opening, led to a marked concentration of cross-Channel shipping services, though not in the short term to loss of overall capacity. The Dover–Dunkirk train-ferry service ended in late 1995. It had worked on a freight-only basis since 1985, and the celebrated 'Night Ferry' train had been discontinued in 1980. The Dover Western Docks–Calais train-connected services were terminated in 1993. Sealink retired from the Dover–Boulogne route at the beginning of 1986, and P&O EF in 1993. The latter also withdrew from the Belgian passenger services in 1991, precipitating RMT's shutting down of their Ostend–Dover route in 1993 and their move to Ramsgate in partnership with Sally Line, which had been operating since 1980 from that port. Sally's principal service to Dunkirk was, however, closed in 1997, and that to Ostend in 1998. The Australian fast-craft firm Holyman had briefly worked in partnership with Sally on the Dunkirk and Ostend runs in 1996 and 1997. Many of these services had been relatively high volume at the time of their suspension. For example, Folkestone–Boulogne had in 1990 handled 1.2 million passengers, 130,000 cars and around 50,000 units of freight. Ramsgate had at that time a considerably higher share of the car trade than Folkestone. The outcome of the rationalisation was an intensive service of frequent shuttle-type crossings by large ferries focused on the Dover–Calais and Dover–Zeebrugge (freight) routes.[62] Another consequence of

[61] *Ibid.*, pp. 99–101, 111–13.
[62] *Ibid.*, pp. 73–4, 101–2, 109–10.

the merger was the ending of the protracted 30% decline in the real cost of fares between 1980 and 1998, which had culminated in a virtual price war over the last four years of that period. Prices then rose by around 20% by 1999 even before the anticipated withdrawal by the EU of duty-free concessions in mid-1999. This was likely to be a bigger problem for the ferry operators than for Eurotunnel, as they were thought to derive up to 40% of their revenue from sales on board. Both, however, were expected to raise prices further. The cross-Channel market suddenly seemed to have too little competition, rather than too much.[63]

The Channel Tunnel project was finally brought to completion in 1994 after a long string of failed ventures. These had begun in earnest with the competitive tunnelling of the 1880s (an aspect of the rivalry between the LCDR and the SER), with the two most recent episodes occurring in 1966–8 and 1973–5. Military considerations, real or imaginary, had formed a serious obstacle to success until the mid-1950s. More recently, one authoritative judgement attributed delay in renewal of the project to 'lack of political will, compounded by adverse circumstances, both economic and political, at key points in [its] development'.[64] Although several kinds of fixed link were possible in principle, the traditional favourite, twin bored rail tunnels (with road vehicles to be carried on shuttle trains, plus through-trains) reasserted itself in the early 1980s following two new reports, of which the more important was the Anglo-French study of 1982. An injection of political will was received when the British Prime Minister, Margaret Thatcher, was apparently converted to the idea at a meeting in Paris in late 1984. A competition among construction groups proposing various fixed-link schemes was held in 1985, resulting in the selection in 1986 of the entry submitted by the Channel Tunnel Group and Franche-Manche, which formed the basis of Eurotunnel. Contracts were drawn up with Trans-Manche Link as main contractors for design and construction and with British Rail and SNCF, who acquired the use of half the capacity of the Tunnel for through rail services.[65]

A crucial feature of the policy of the British government was expressed in section 42 of the 1987 Channel Tunnel Act, which excluded any element of public subsidy for international rail services. The Conservatives wished to make a virtue of the anticipated ability of the private sector to carry out major infrastructural projects without public assistance. This determination soon put the future of the Tunnel in jeopardy. Eurotunnel's attempts to raise capital encountered grave difficulties in the autumn of 1986, and only heavy pressure by the Bank of England on reluctant institutions retrieved the situation. The company's needs coincided with a shortish period when syndicated international loans were available. Much came from Japan, whose banks had contributed almost a

---

[63] *Observer*, 30 May 1999.

[64] Holliday, Marcou and Vickerman, *op. cit.*, p. 9.

[65] R. Vickerman, 'Transport Policy and the Channel Tunnel: UK, French and European Perspectives', in Gibb, *op. cit.*, pp. 217–23.

quarter of total loans by 1990. The European Investment Bank made one huge loan of £1 billion. But no income could be obtained until the project was finished. Both delay in completion and periodic upward revisions of construction costs meant further borrowings and an increasing burden of interest payments. The technical battle was virtually won at the end of 1990 when the service tunnels were connected, and the overall delay in opening the Channel Tunnel was no more than twelve months (May 1994, as against the original target of May 1993, though it was not fully operational until well into 1995).[66] But the cost of building was roughly quadruple the £2.3 billion originally estimated in the 1985 submission. At a later stage it had been hoped to open in 1993 with a bill of £5.5 billion. The out-turn saw total costs of over £10 billion. In consequence the future of Eurotunnel was placed in serious doubt at several points before and after the tunnel's physical completion. In its first full year of operation the company lost £900 million, and in the autumn of 1995 was forced to suspend debt repayment. A measure of stability was achieved through a major debt restructuring which became effective in 1998 (backdated to late 1996). The conversion of borrowings to equity clipped £1 billion from total indebtedness, which declined to £7.68 billion, and lowered the average interest rate by almost two percentage points. Even so, servicing the debt was still costing around £1 million each day in 1998, and an operating profit of £46 million in the first half of that year was transformed into an underlying loss of £130 million after interest. The venture was thought to be still several years away from regular pre-tax profits or dividend payments, and the refinancing prospectus was predicated on the need for ten years of strong growth. The new Labour government in 1997 offered further assistance to the project by extending its licence for an extra thirty-four years. Eurotunnel was, however, enjoying greater success in transport than in financial terms. In the short sea-crossing market, it claimed leadership for cars and joint leadership with P&O Stena for coaches, and 36% of the lorry market (a few percentage points behind P&O Stena). Like the ferry operators it faced the imminent necessity of a substantial increase in fares in order to maintain revenue after the abolition of duty free.[67]

Construction of the Tunnel gave a powerful short-term boost to Kent's economy in the late 1980s and early 1990s, which was particularly welcome as the second half of this period coincided with a general recession. At the height of activity in 1990, about 8,300 were employed in Kent (almost two-thirds of the total), although by no means all had been recruited locally.[68] It was apparent from the outset that the British government intended to follow up its non-involvement in the private-sector construction project with a high degree of abstention from related policy-making activity. The unavoidable contrast is with the quite different policy responses in France. Despite the disadvantage imposed

---

[66] I. Holliday, 'The Channel Tunnel: The Problems of Binational Collaboration', in *Industrial Enterprise and European Integration*, ed. J. Hayward, Oxford 1995.

[67] Eurotunnel Interim Report 1998; *Financial Times*, 23 September 1998.

[68] Holliday, *op. cit.*, p. 215.

by British insistence on private ownership of the Tunnel, French public authorities in both Paris and in the Nord-Pas de Calais region were far more positive in attempting to co-ordinate and maximise the available opportunities. Not only was railway and motorway development orientated towards the Tunnel link, but a regional economic strategy was evolved which focused on Lille as a major development axis. A TGV station was planned for the centre of the city, as was an international business centre, Euralille Metropole. The nearest British equivalent was some limited activity by the Department of Transport as lead ministry, which consisted essentially of a briefly more generous attitude towards grants for road-building in Kent. Additionally local authorities were co-opted onto a Joint Consultative Committee, which gave rise to a Kent Impact Study Team, whose report lacked the power to commit any of its sponsoring institutions and whose main recommendation (a development agency for East Kent) was not implemented.[69] These divergent national-policy processes have inspired striking generalisations, such as 'a clear focus on the Whitehall village in Britain contrasted with the developed centre–periphery linkages which are held to characterise the French politico-administrative system'.[70] Within this framework the national differences between regions may have been as salient as those between capitals. It has also been concluded that 'quite simply, Kent, *qua* Kent had no need of a Channel Tunnel, did not really want one, and certainly could not be made to benefit from one to the extent that Nord-Pas de Calais could'.[71]

The most severe consequences of the British government's attitude to the public sector were reserved for the related project of a high-speed rail link from London to the Tunnel – a distance of just under seventy miles. On the French side of the Channel, high-speed rail services, linked to the substantial existing TGV network, had been running since 1993, before the opening of the Tunnel. On the British side the situation could scarcely have been more different. As the last unsuccessful attempt to build a tunnel had foundered on the high cost of a rail link, there may have appeared to be some merit in keeping the two separate in the mid-1980s, despite their obvious interdependence. It is unlikely, however, that the government, or indeed anyone in Britain, could have contemplated the outcome without embarrassment. British Rail began feasibility studies for a London–Folkestone route in 1987, published details of four possible alternatives in 1988 (to the inevitable dismay of the thousands of Kentish residents potentially affected), and announced its preference for a South London option in 1989. Later the same year it even selected the Eurorail consortium (BICC and Trafalgar House) to build the line. The estimated cost (widely regarded as too low) was at this time £1.7 billion. BR was required by the government to act within its standard financial remit, to earn a rate of return of at least 8% on investment and to find a private-sector partner. By mid-1990 the scheme had collapsed, with Eurorail withdrawing and the government continuing to rule out

69 Holliday, Marcou and Vickerman, *op. cit.*, pp. 104–5.
70 Holliday, *op. cit*, pp. 218–19.
71 Holliday, Marcou and Vickerman, *op. cit.*, p. 109.

public funding. In the autumn of 1991 BR's southern route, on which £40 million had already been spent, was dropped in favour of a new approach to the capital via Stratford and East London.[72]

These changes reflected the unattractiveness of the original unsubsidised project to the private sector, the success of the protests mounted by residents' groups in South London and parts of Kent, and the government's attempt to combine limitation of environmental damage with economic regeneration of the east-Thames corridor. In March 1993 St Pancras was scheduled to become the (cheaper) North London terminal rather than King's Cross. In early 1996 London and Continental Railway was chosen to take over from BR with a 999 year concession. By then the government felt obliged to concede the principle of public subsidy, to help LCR cope with construction costs estimated at £3–4 billion in 1996 and £5.4 billion in 1998. The promised subsidy amounted to £1.8 billion in 1998, as stated in a development agreement. But some estimates of the total 'sweeteners' available to the concessionaire, including the assets of European Passenger Services (the operator of Eurostar through-trains to the Continent), the terminal opened in 1993 at Waterloo International, and much land along the proposed route, reached £5 billion.[73] The significance of these sums was undeniable. Had the sum later offered to LCR (on the plausible grounds that completion would be worth £6 billion in social returns) been made available to BR ten years earlier, a fast rail link would almost certainly have been in existence at the British as well as the French end of the Tunnel when it opened.[74] When the infrastructure of the whole British railway network was privatised in the form of Railtrack, no more than £1.9 billion was raised for the public revenue. Nevertheless, LCR eventually admitted its inability to fulfil the plan, after an ignominious rejected appeal for a further public hand-out of £1.2 billion in early 1998. The Labour government was not prepared to accept the abandonment of the project. The deputy prime minister, John Prescott, committed it to additional payments of £140–360 million (depending on the size of Eurostar revenues), but the Treasury was to guarantee £3.8 billion of debt and bonds. LCR was to raise the finance, but the project would be managed by Railtrack, which would buy the first stage, from Folkestone to Fawkham Junction, for £1.5 billion in 2003. It would hold an option for the purchase of the final stage to St Pancras for an anticipated £1.8 billion in 2007. Total cost was then estimated at £7.7 billion, allowing for inflation and a contingency reserve. The LCR concession was cut from 999 to a more modest ninety years. The government was thus due to acquire both the rail link and the Tunnel by 2086, and would additionally receive 35% of LCR's profits after 2020 and a small stake in Eurostar.[75] In the spring of 1999 the government took steps to underpin the second stage financially by making £277 million available to the developers for land acquisition,

[72] Gibb and Knowles, *op. cit.*, pp. 177–91.
[73] A. Barnett, 'Rail Link's Hidden Subsidies', *Observer*, 7 January 1996.
[74] V. Keegan, 'Public Taken for a Ride on Railways', *Guardian*, 4 March 1996.
[75] *Financial Times*, 4 and 5 June, 1998; *Guardian*, 4 June 1996.

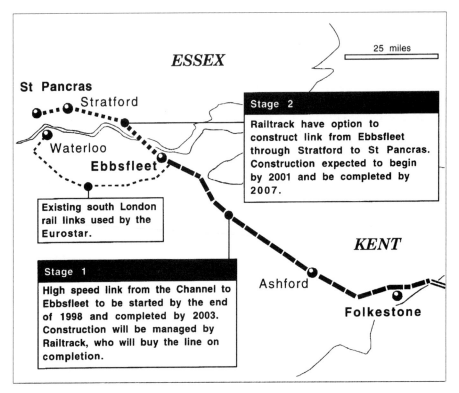

Figure 10. Final proposed route of high speed rail link from London to Channel tunnel, 1993.

design work and preliminary construction work, presumably in case Railtrack lost its appetite for the venture.[76] But the best expectation in 1999 was that by 2007 the British private sector, with state assistance, would have emulated, on a smaller scale, what the French public sector had put in place by 1993.

A major element in LCR's miscalculations was its overestimation of the growth of traffic on Eurostar, which had attracted 6 million passengers a year by 1997 instead of the forecast 9 million. These disappointing figures caused the postponement, and possibly the cancellation, of plans for through-rail services to the continent from various northern and midlands cities, although the necessary rolling stock had already been provided. They even raised doubts as to whether the large investment in the HSRL itself was justified in order to reduce the sixty-eight-mile journey time by roughly thirty-five minutes.[77] For those who took a broader and more positive view of the value of both the Tunnel and the fast rail link, such hesitancy made little sense. Their conclusion was that the

76 *Ibid.*, 28 April 1999.
77 *Observer*, 1 February 1998.

prolonged delay to the HSRL, attributable to the government's bungling and free-market dogmatism, meant 'that the cost-reducing, market-widening opportunities of high-speed through-rail services are deferred, the image of the Channel Tunnel itself is tarnished'.[78]

Whatever the original doubts about the Tunnel and its impact, there was strong support in most of Kent by the late 1990s for the earliest possible completion of the HSRL. This had come to be regarded in both Kent and Essex as vital to the longer-term prospects of the regeneration of the Thames Gateway. The main growth points envisaged were around Stratford and the Royal Docks on the north bank of the river and Kent Thameside west of Gravesend. The chief executive of North Kent Success, an organisation whose mission was to co-ordinate the Kent side of the Thames Gateway, stated its key assumption in the spring of 1999: 'The rail link is the catalyst for the whole development of the North Kent area.'[79] The Ebbsfleet station was reckoned by the County Council to be worth 50,000 jobs, many acres of commercial space for new businesses, and better services for commuters. The original centrepiece was the Bluewater shopping and leisure complex, close to the M2 and M25, which was launched successfully in early 1999 by the Whitecliff property group. Early indications suggested it might achieve its target of £650 million a year turnover, equivalent to 12% of the annual retail expenditure of people living within an hour's drive.[80] Having obtained the largest mixed-use planning consent so far granted in England, it also intended to develop up to 8.5 million square feet of office and residential space (3,200 houses), but was acutely aware that long-term progress would be faster and more assured if the rail link materialised, and sooner rather than later. Further east, the area around Ashford, which since early 1996 has had an international station with Eurostar services, has already felt some economic stimulus. It had by then developed two business parks and has become more attractive as a centre for value-added distribution by companies like K'Nex International, the American self-assembly toy operation, which packs components there before exporting to the Continent. Both the Tunnel, and to a lesser extent the HSRL, were relevant to the future of tourism, which already employed about 24,000 directly by 1996 and was scheduled for further growth. Estimated spending by UK and overseas visitors was well over £500 million a year. The largest proposed new development, Rank's £100 million Oasis Holiday Village at Lyminge, would be close to both Tunnel and ferry ports.[81] An offsetting factor here was that quicker and cheaper cross-Channel travel meant that large numbers of British day-trippers were not only attracted by the general shopping facilities of the French Channel ports, but were particularly keen to take advantage of the much lower rates of duty charged on beer in France. The resulting large-scale importation of beer had been legalised for personal

---

[78] Gibb and Knowles, *op. cit.*, p. 198.
[79] *Financial Times*, 11 March 1999.
[80] *Ibid.*, 16 June 1999.
[81] *Ibid.*, 23 April 1998.

consumption after the arrival of the Single Market in 1992, although much of it was illegally resold. The Faversham brewing firm Shepherd Neame, most of whose 360 pubs were in Kent, claimed that in 1998 cheap imports from France accounted for one-third of the beer drunk in Kent and accordingly threatened jobs and the future of many pubs. Neames sought unsuccessfully to establish the illegality of the British government's failure to harmonise excise duties with other European states.[82]

(6) Conclusion

The salience of transport and of transport related issues is not hard to explain in the case of a county such as Kent with its quasi-peninsular shape and its position between the giant poles, one natural, and the other the result of centuries of economic growth, of the Channel and London. Proximity to the capital conferred certain advantages throughout the century, especially on favoured areas of west and central Kent, and attracted both residents and companies who looked to the London market. On the other hand Kent's hinterland was in effect shrunk and its communications with the rest of the country were hampered by the size and location of the capital. Similarly, closeness to continental Europe always held promise and opportunities for Kent's economy. But until sufficient progress had been made in reducing economic obstacles and strengthening the physical links, it was difficult to take advantage. Even then, a corridor situation was not enviable for all concerned, and some of the benefits of transport improvements were more apparent to transients than residents. Furthermore, each successive advance usually implied contraction and reduced employment in some other transport mode or location, usually somewhere in the eastern half of the county. Kent may have been transformed from a buffer against invasion to the county most integrated, as part of the Transmanche region, with the continent, but there were clear limits to the extent of this tendency at the end of the century. Despite some modest progress in attracting European Union inter-regional funds, the county's economy still recognisably responded to British rather than continental rhythms. It may well be that Kent's modest level of prosperity, by south-eastern standards, is partly to be explained by transport problems or by inadequate responses to them. Here the inhabitants of Kent, some million and a half at the end of the century, have not always been well served by the various companies, institutions and government departments whose priorities have often been determined by shareholders, by more broadly defined regions, or by political assumptions which left little or no room for the planning of transport or economic development.

82 *Ibid.*, 9 October 1998; T. Barker, *Shepherd Neame*, Cambridge 1998, pp. 101–2.

5

Politics

BRIAN ATKINSON

(1) Introduction

The main feature of twentieth-century Kent politics is the continuance of the Conservative domination originally established in the mid-1870s. This was built initially upon the three pillars of the Church of England, the landed interest (and a landed interest increasingly united as erstwhile Whigs left a Liberal Party dominated, as they saw it, by Gladstone's extremism) and the licensed trade. These pillars were strengthened from the mid-1880s by opposition to Irish Home Rule and support for the Empire and further buttressed by villa Toryism and commuters in West Kent and by the dockyards and military presence, plus the cautious retired in the resorts. Thus, in 1900 the Conservatives returned fourteen MPs to the Liberals' one. This dominance was seriously challenged only in 1906, by the Liberals, and in 1945 and 1997 by Labour, but even then it was not broken. A subsidiary feature is Labour's relatively early emergence as the principal challenger to the Conservatives, replacing the Liberals in this role in most constituencies by the 1920s. These developments occurred amidst considerable changes in the political system. The introduction of universal suffrage created a vastly increased electorate which was wooed by the parties via the press, as before, and increasingly by the new media, first radio, then television, and by advertising methods pioneered in the USA. These had the effect of nationalising politics at the expense of local men and local issues. Even *local* government elections became increasingly determined by voters' reactions to the national government of the day.

(2) Conservative and Liberal, 1900–18[1]

The poor Liberal performance in Kent in 1900 was no surprise; the Liberal Party nationally was disunited and at a low ebb. Even its sole Kent MP was unseated for bribery. At the subsequent Maidstone by-election in 1901, however, a

---

[1] Unless otherwise stated, this and the following three sections are based on information derived from F.W.S. Craig, *British Parliamentary Election Results, 1885–1918*, London 1974, *1918–1949*, Chichester

tolerant electorate returned another Liberal with an increased majority. This was the harbinger of change. The Conservatives became increasingly divided over the issue of protective tariffs, the Liberals increasingly united as their nostrils smelt the scent of office. The Liberals had also done a deal with the Labour Representation Committee (LRC), a body representative of many trade unions and some socialists, to avoid splitting the anti-Tory vote. The consequences were seen in 1906 when the Conservatives nationally suffered their worst defeat since 1832. Even the Garden of England was affected by the hurricane, though less seriously. Maidstone, against the national trend, returned to its Conservative allegiance but the Liberals gained Faversham and Tonbridge for the only time ever, as well as Rochester. Dartford was won by a Liberal–Labour (Lib–Lab) candidate and, a portent for the future, Chatham by an LRC man, J.H. Jenkins, the Liberals and the LRC having done a deal whereby Rochester was assigned to the former, Chatham to the latter. The LRC now changed its name to the Labour Party: Chatham thus had the honour of returning one of Labour's twenty-nine founding MPs. Kent, though, even in 1906, returned ten Conservative MPs out of fifteen.

Despite their huge majority in the Commons, the Liberal government was unable to get cherished legislation through the overwhelmingly Conservative House of Lords. In 1909, in a bid to regain the initiative, the Chancellor of the Exchequer, David Lloyd George, introduced the People's Budget to wage war on poverty. He needed to finance the newly introduced old-age pensions and he proposed to do so in part through new taxes which the Conservatives thought discriminated against landowners. The Lords duly rejected the budget and two years of bitter political conflict, reminiscent of 1831–2, eventually resulted in the limitation of the Lords' powers under the Parliament Act 1911. Two elections were fought in 1910, in large part over the political role of the Upper House. It is said the English love a lord; Kent's devotion in January was total, fifteen Conservative MPs, and its passion only slightly cooled in the following December.

The 1910 elections in Kent merit examination. The Liberals did indeed high-light the Lords. Their candidate at Canterbury, Woodcock, declared that the question was 'whether they would be governed by the people, for the people or be content to be governed by 500 or so individuals whom hardly anybody knew but their own set, men in a position unelected by the people, from mere accident of wealth or birth'.[2] Vivian Phillips at Maidstone blamed the crisis on the Peers' House 'which the People may not elect, cannot control and cannot dissolve'. He went on to defend the record of the government ('the best we have had since the Commonwealth', according to Woodcock), its humane social reforms made possible by free trade finance, the Budget facilitating further social reform. This was the typical Liberal approach: the Budget was defended as placing the

1983, *1950–1973*, Chichester 1983, *1974–1979*, Chichester 1980, *1983–1987*, Aldershot 1989; *1988–1992* (Colin Rawlings and Michael Thrasher), Aldershot 1993.
2   *Kentish Gazette*, 6 November 1909.

burden on the shoulders of those best able to bear it, free trade was defended as the source of prosperity, and emphasis was placed on the Liberal reforms, especially pensions, though Woodcock also highlighted the Trades Disputes Act 'which safeguards the funds of our great Trade Unions and restores to the workers the right of effective combination'.[3]

The arguments of the Conservatives and Unionists, to give them their full title, contained themes that were to stand them in good stead for many years. The budget was confiscatory and socialist, indicating Liberal dependence on socialist Labour MPs. The House of Lords, portrayed as containing many of the country's greatest statesmen, was quite right to refer it to the judgement of the people (whose verdict, of course, the House of Lords would accept) at an election. In a neat touch, Akers-Douglas at St Augustine's argued that in view of Liberal losses at by-elections it was the *Commons* which was really unrepresentative of the people. The way to finance social reform was not the budget but tariffs. There was a strong Kent Tariff Reform Federation with branches throughout the county; the cause was presented as widening the tax base, increasing trade and employment, and securing a fair contribution from foreigners selling goods in our markets; the budget was derided as protecting the foreigner. Tariff reform would also strengthen the bond of union between the colonies and the mother country. The need for a strong navy and army, defence of the licensed trade and, for some, the spectre of Irish Home Rule leading to the break-up of the United Kingdom made up a heady Unionist cocktail.[4]

The *Kent Messenger's* 'Current Notes' commented on 9 October 1909: 'we should not be surprised to see the representation of the county after the contest very much what it is today'. One wonders if it was the same writer who less than four months later described the result at Chatham, where moderation was not enough to save Jenkins, as 'one of the surprises of the election'.[5] In what was described as an exceedingly heavy poll, Jenkins's 2,672 majority of 1906 was replaced by a Conservative one of 1,281. Turnout was 85.7%, up 6%. Interest was intense: the declaration was witnessed by 20,000–30,000 people, the dockyard having been closed for the event. The Conservatives benefited from the service vote which had been augmented by the transfer of several hundred navy personnel from Sheerness. The strong navy and army card played well: 'Vote for Hohler and a Supreme Navy'. It was also thought that many moderate Liberals were alarmed at what they perceived as the rapid growth of socialism and ignored the wishes of their leaders to support Labour, either abstaining (unlikely in view of the high turnout) or voting for Hohler. He also benefited from the Unionist victory at neighbouring Rochester which was known before Chatham polled, sending enthusiastic Conservatives across the border to get out the vote.[6]

---

3   *Loc. cit.*, and 18 December 1909; *Kent Messenger*, 8 January 1910.
4   *Kentish Gazette*, 2 and 16 October, 11 and 18 December 1909; *Kent Messenger*, 18 December 1909 and 8 January 1910.
5   *Kent Messenger*, 22 January 1910.
6   *Loc. cit.*, and *Chatham, Rochester and Gillingham Observer*, 15 and 22 January 1910.

Table 29

Kent Election Results, 1906 and 1910, by share of poll

		Con (%)	Lib (%)	Other (%)	Turnout (%)
Borough seats					
Canterbury	1906	63.7	36.3		89.8
	1910 J	38.8	23.0	38.2 (Ind Con)*	92.2
	1910 D	34.0	18.2	47.8 (Ind Con)*	89.2
Chatham	1906	37.5		62.5 (Lab)	79.7
	1910 J	54.7		45.3 (Lab)	85.7
	1910 D	56.4	34.7	8.9 (Lab)	78.4
Dover	1906	65.7	34.3		75.4
	1910 J	67.9	32.1		78.5
	1910 D	Con unopposed			
Gravesend	1906	57.6	26.2	16.2 (Lab)	82.0
	1910 J	55.7	44.3		87.6
	1910 D	55.4	44.6		83.4
Hythe	1906	58.0	42.0		85.8
	1910 J	65.7	34.3		87.1
	1910 D	Con unopposed			
Maidstone	1906	51.2	48.8		94.5
	1910 J	52.1	47.9		94.9
	1910 D	50.6	49.4		91.7
Rochester	1906	44.4	55.6		92.7
	1910 J	51.3	48.7		92.7
	1910 D	48.5	51.5		90.0
County seats					
Ashford	1906	51.6	48.4		83.7
	1910 J	64.3	35.7		87.2
	1910 D	Con unopposed			
Dartford	1906	41.4		58.6 (Lib–Lab)	82.4
	1910 J	52.2		47.8 (Lib–Lab)	87.8
	1910 D	49.4		50.6 (Lib–Lab)	84.4
Faversham	1906	42.4	57.6		80.9
	1910 J	58.0	42.0		87.6
	1910 D	57.4		42.6 (Lib–Lab)	82.0
Isle of Thanet	1906	51.3	39.5	9.2 (Ind Con)	84.4
	1910 J	66.9	33.1		81.8
	1910 D	Con unopposed			
Medway	1906	50.4	49.6		83.6
	1910 J	60.5	39.5		88.1
	1910 D	Con unopposed			
St Augustine's	1906	61.5	38.5		78.6
	1910 J	69.8	30.2		81.9
	1910 D	Con unopposed			

		Con (%)	Lib (%)	Other (%)	Turnout (%)
Sevenoaks	1906	51.1	49.6	0.3 (Ind Lib)	81.8
	1910 J	62.1	37.9		88.1
	1910 D	Con unopposed			
Tonbridge	1906	45.1	54.9		84.2
	1910 J	60.5	39.5		89.2
	1910 D	57.4	42.6		84.4

* This candidate was Francis Bennett Goldney whose driving political ambition split the local Conservatives. A wealthy antiquary, five times mayor of Canterbury, but with a rather dubious reputation for appropriating the possessions of others as his own, he challenged and almost defeated John Henniker Heaton, MP for the constituency since 1885. In a bitter campaign Goldney mobilised support from the poorer electors, employing, it was alleged, bribery and treating to sustain his attack on the established Conservative hierarchy. An ill Heaton took the hint and did not stand in December whereupon Goldney defeated the official Tory candidate. He sat, taking the Conservative whip, until his death in a car crash in France in 1918: see Audrey Bateman, *The Magpie Tendency*, Whitstable 1999.

The Liberal victors of 1906 were swept away; the enthusiasm, as demonstrated at the declarations and by the turnout – over 90% in some cases, nearly 95% at Maidstone (see Table 29) – was extraordinary. At times it got out of hand: after the Conservatives retained Gravesend with a reduced majority the Liberal agent's house was attacked, a large knife being thrown into the sitting room and the curtains set alight with a firework. Police intervention was needed.[7]

Kent was not representative of the United Kingdom as a whole, and at Westminster the Liberals, though with scarcely more MPs than the reviving Unionists, were able to count on the support of Irish Nationalists and Labour to remain in office. Eventually they brought forward plans to limit the powers of the Lords and fought another election in December to seek a mandate for their proposals. As is clear from Table 29 the main feature of this election in Kent was Liberal recognition of their subordinate position: five of the county seats and two of the boroughs were simply not contested. Paradoxically they made two gains, the Lib–Lab Rowlands recapturing Dartford, the Liberal Lamb Rochester, and Phillips came within seventy-one votes of unseating Castlereagh at Maidstone. Elsewhere, Chatham was rendered safe for the Conservatives by Liberal and Labour both fielding candidates, the latter coming a very poor third. At Gravesend the Liberal again reduced the Unionist majority; no knives were reported this time. Turnout was slightly down, inevitably so on an older register where deaths and removals had taken their toll.

Arguments were similar to earlier in the year. For example, the Liberal at Gravesend stressed free trade, social reform and restriction of the powers of the Lords, while Castlereagh replaced the socialists as the bogeymen with the Irish Nationalists. In a lurid address he blamed the election's being held at such an inconvenient time of the year on the Nationalist Leader, Redmond, flush with

---

[7] *Kent Messenger*, 22 January 1910.

funds from hostile American sources, being in a position to dictate terms to the 'Radical' government. For Castlereagh the whole structure of the constitution was at stake: will you be governed by two chambers 'as in the case of all civilised countries' or only one? The government plan leaves the Lords with only sham powers in order to accede to Redmond's demands for the disintegration of the United Kingdom through Home Rule to which Castlereagh, of course, was opposed. He did favour reform of the Lords, Tariff Reform, Naval Supremacy and the Licensed Trade; this heady brew was just about sufficient to save his electoral skin.[8]

Nationally the result in December was not markedly different from January and the Liberals remained in office with Irish and Labour support until the Great War, continuing their programme of social reform which laid the foundations of the future welfare state.

The Great War affected all aspects of British life, including, of course, politics. The Liberals suffered badly. Liberalism and war were uneasy bedfellows. Peace had been one of the party's most cherished principles and war severely restricted basic Liberal freedoms: of the individual with the conscription of adult men in 1916; of the press and of speech, with censorship; free trade also suffered. To these strains were added personal conflicts, especially after 1916 when Lloyd George, with Conservative support, replaced Asquith as Prime Minister. Labour was also divided by the war but gained respectability and valuable experience as some of its leaders were brought into the three-party coalition government formed to maximise the war effort. The Conservatives were the principal beneficiaries. Always seen as the 'national' party and the party of the armed services, they had little difficulty coming to terms with the demands of total war.

The war had another major political effect. One of its casualties was the property franchise which had denied the vote to perhaps 30% of men and all women. It became difficult to argue that survivors of the trenches were not fit to exercise the franchise because they lacked the property qualification. The acceptance of adult male suffrage removed an important barrier against the enfranchisement of women whose role in key areas of the war effort further strengthened their claims. So in 1918 the right to vote was extended to all men aged twenty-one and over and to women aged thirty and over, subject to a residence qualification and being placed on the register. In 1928 the vote was extended to women on the same terms as men and in 1970 the voting age was further reduced to eighteen.

(3) The Inter-War Years: Conservatism versus Labour, Round One

The enlarged electorate necessitated changes in constituency boundaries. Canterbury, Dover, Gravesend and Maidstone were extended to take in parts of the surrounding countryside (a move which undoubtedly benefited the Conser-

---

8 *Kent Messenger*, 26 November, 3 December 1910.

vatives) and joined Ashford, Dartford, Faversham, Isle of Thanet, Sevenoaks and Tonbridge as county constituencies. Medway and St Augustine's were abolished but this was balanced by the creation of a new county seat at Chislehurst and a new borough seat at Bromley. Hythe continued as a borough seat while the Medway conurbation was divided into Rochester, Chatham and Rochester, Gillingham (henceforth Chatham and Gillingham). Kent thus retained fifteen MPs as shown in Table 30.

Table 30

Size of Kent electorates, 1910 (December), 1918 and 1935

	1910 (D)	1918	1935
County			
Ashford	14,202	32,349	48,910
Canterbury	3,836	31,453	55,417
Chislehurst	–	26,801	85,028
Dartford	21,398	45,666	106,043
Dover	6,247	35,170	58,183
Faversham	14,649	37,478	56,664
Gravesend	6,733	31,070	50,300
Isle of Thanet[9]	12,588	31,767	60,716
Maidstone	6,260	30,747	50,334
Sevenoaks	19,035	30,189	48,559
Tonbridge	17,116	37,448	56,106
Borough			
Bromley	–	40,709	90,532
Chatham	15,799	31,000	43,573
Gillingham	–	27,899	40,271
Hythe	6,541	19,896	35,205

All the Kent constituencies, apart from Chatham and Sevenoaks, at least doubled in size between 1910 and 1918 and the process of expansion continued in the inter-war years when the electorates of most constituencies increased by between a half and two-thirds except for those responding to the growth of London: Dartford and Bromley more than doubled, Chislehurst more than trebled.

The first general election fought under the new arrangements on 14 December 1918 (unlike before the war all constituencies now voted on the same day) was a confused affair. The Coalition continued in office, though Labour withdrew, and Lloyd George issued a letter of support, the so-called coupon, to

---

9   The figures for Thanet are for 1919 and 1931.

candidates expected to back the government in a bid to avoid contests between fellow coalitionists. Naturally, Kent being Kent, the Conservatives made an almost clean sweep, winning fourteen seats, the exception being Dartford, where the sitting Coalition Liberal was allowed a free run. All seats save Thanet were contested, principally by Labour, which fielded nine candidates. The size of the Labour vote is shown in Table 31.

Table 31

Labour share of the Vote in Kent Constituencies, 1918

Constituency	%	Number of candidates
Canterbury	19.2	2
Dartford	28.6	2
Faversham	31.8	2
Gravesend	21.5	5
Maidstone	34.5	2
Tonbridge	23.3	3
Chatham	22.5	3
Gillingham	25.9	3
Hythe	28.0	2

The first impression is of obvious Labour weakness: only in Maidstone was more than a third of the vote secured (no Liberal stood). Yet looked at from another angle, Labour came second in each of the seats it contested, beating Liberals at Chatham, Gravesend and Tonbridge, in the last two of which the Liberals lost their deposits. The disappointing Liberal share of the vote is shown in Table 32; for them, with the artificial exception of Dartford, 1918 was a disaster.

Table 32

Liberal Share of the Vote in Kent Constituencies, 1918

Constituency	%	Number of candidates
Dartford	71.4	2
Dover	31.3	2
Gravesend	8.4	5
Tonbridge	8.6	3
Bromley	20.5	2
Chatham	15.1	3

Conservatives ruled the roost: their MPs secured over 80% of the vote at Ashford and Canterbury, over two-thirds at Chislehurst, Dover, Faversham, Sevenoaks, Tonbridge, Bromley, Gillingham and Hythe. Even at their lowest, in

Gravesend, they polled over 50% of the vote. Eleven MPs were survivors from before 1918: McNeill at Canterbury (previously at St Augustine's), Rowlands at Dartford, Viscount Dungannon at Dover, Wheler at Faversham, Richardson at Gravesend, Craig at Isle of Thanet, Bellairs at Maidstone, Spender-Clay at Tonbridge, Rt Hon. H.W. Forster at Bromley (previously at Sevenoaks), Sir Philip Sassoon, Bt, at Hythe and Hohler at Gillingham (previously at Chatham). The four newcomers were Steel at Ashford, Smithers at Chislehurst, Bennett at Sevenoaks and Moore-Brabazon at Chatham, the last being the sole non-Coalition Conservative MP. Of the survivors, only Forster went back much beyond 1910, having represented Sevenoaks since 1892.[10] Those old stagers, Hardy at Ashford and Warde at Medway, both like Forster first elected in 1892, retired from the scene.

Opinion soon turned against the Coalition as perceived election promises were not kept: the Kaiser remained unhung, Homes Fit for Heroes were slow to materialise, and economic conditions worsened. The principal beneficiary was Labour. In March 1920, on Rowlands' death, J.E. Mills captured Dartford with over 50% of the vote, the Liberal came second (16.8%), the Coalition Conservative third (15.5%). As the electoral situation continued to worsen, many Conservatives began to fear that Lloyd George would destroy them as he had the Liberals. At a meeting of Conservative MPs on 19 October 1922 a clear majority resolved to withdraw from the Coalition, precipitating its downfall and the formation of the first Tory government since 1905. At the resultant general election on 15 November 1922 Kent bestowed its seal of approval, returning fourteen Conservative MPs, the exception being Dartford where a Constitutionalist (nominated by both the Conservatives and National, i.e. Lloyd Georgite, Liberals) defeated Mills: the Independent Liberal lost her deposit. Labour fought ten seats, but came nowhere near winning, though polling 40% of the vote at Dartford, Faversham and Gillingham, at the last two benefiting from the absence of a Liberal. As for the Liberals, they put up eight candidates, two lost their deposits and at Tonbridge they were beaten into third place by Labour. But there were encouraging signs for them as well: Labour was pushed into third place at Bromley, at Chatham they secured 48.5% of the vote in a straight fight, and at Maidstone a Liberal standing as an Independent lost to the sitting Conservative by a mere thirty-three votes with Labour some 900 further behind.

After 1922 the Liberals reunited, with Lloyd George accepting Asquith's leadership of the party and Asquith hoping that the party would be able to benefit from the money in Lloyd George's political fund. Liberal union was further aided by Prime Minister Baldwin's decision to dissolve parliament in 1923 to seek a mandate to introduce protective tariffs in a bid to reduce unemployment; the sacred cause of free trade was a powerful rallying cry for Liberals. They did indeed win a Kent seat in 1923, in the unlikely territory of Sevenoaks,

---

[10] Forster had a distinguished career: junior Lord of the Treasury 1902–5, Conservative whip 1905–11 (continuing a good Kentish whipping tradition), Financial Secretary to the War Office 1915–19 when created Baron Forster, Governor-general of Australia 1920–5.

which they had not contested since January 1910 and which failed to return a Conservative for the only time in its history. At Thanet, again in a straight fight, the Liberal came within forty-nine votes of unseating the sitting Conservative. The party polled strongly at Bromley, pulling away from Labour, and pushed Labour into third place at Tonbridge, though still nowhere near winning. In Medway, unlike the previous year, Liberals fought Labour, coming second in Chatham and third in Gillingham, leaving the Conservatives in safer possession of the seats. The big disappointment was Maidstone where the near-victor of 1922, standing as a Liberal this time, was over 2,000 votes behind the Conservatives.

Like the Liberals, Labour fought nine seats. Mills regained Dartford from the Constitutionalist and G.A. Isaacs captured Gravesend from the sitting Conservative MP by 119 votes with the Liberal a distant third. The party polled strongly at Faversham in a straight fight, but was nowhere near winning. Labour now had two MPs in Kent for the first time, the Conservatives were reduced to twelve and a few of these had had a nasty shock.

The 1923 election left the Conservatives the largest single party in the Commons but with no overall majority. Clearly they had no mandate to introduce tariffs – Labour, like the Liberals, was committed to free trade – so Baldwin resigned and James Ramsay MacDonald, as leader of the second largest party, formed the first Labour government. A minority administration, it was inevitably vulnerable and lasted less than a year before the Liberals combined with the Conservatives to turn it out. At the resultant election Kent gave an unequivocal verdict, a plague on both Labour and Liberal houses. The Conservatives won all fifteen seats, polling over 65% of the votes at Canterbury, Chislehurst, Dover, Maidstone and Thanet (what a difference a year made). Sevenoaks was triumphantly regained by the Conservatives with 62% of the vote as was Gravesend with 58%. The only close contest was at Dartford where Mills was narrowly beaten.

Labour had put up more candidates in the county, twelve, than ever before. It was a chastening experience. In the county constituencies, apart from the two they were defending, their best performance was at Maidstone, where they obtained one-third of the vote. Nowhere else did they get 30%, at Ashford, Chislehurst, Dover and Thanet not even 20%. The boroughs were little better: 37% at Chatham, 35% at Gillingham, a derisory 16% at Bromley. The only consolation was that of the eight seats where Labour fought Liberals, the former were second in five and the latter in only three.

The Liberals, if anything, had even less to show for their efforts. They too, put up more candidates, ten, than at any time since the war. Apart from Sevenoaks, no Liberal polled 30% of the vote in a county constituency; in the boroughs, that figure was just reached at Bromley, but 11% at Chatham and 12% at Gillingham were disastrous.

The Conservatives were now securely in power but, after seeing off the threat of the General Strike in 1926, their popularity soon began to wane. The vindictive Trade Union Act of 1927 sat uneasily with Baldwin's image as the Man of

Peace, and the government seemed to have no answer to the continued problem of unemployment. By contrast, Labour claimed to have a solution in a socialist reorganisation of society, and a resurgent Liberal Party, led by Lloyd George after Asquith's retirement in 1926 and benefiting from a well-financed series of policy initiatives, also presented a dynamic image. The Conservatives' slogan in the 1929 election, 'Safety First', seemed by contrast unimaginative.

The 1929 election was highly significant. Labour, for the first time, contested every Kent seat, as did the Liberals. These massive efforts yielded no more success than in 1923: two Labour gains (Dartford and Chatham), one Liberal (Ashford, the only time the Conservatives lost it). One result of three-cornered contests was, of course, to reduce Tory majorities but even so they polled over 50% in Canterbury, Chislehurst, Dover, Sevenoaks, Thanet and Hythe, and only Faversham, where the challenge was from Labour, could be remotely considered marginal. In the battle for runner-up the Liberals beat Labour 8–7 though in the aggregate vote it was the other way round: Labour 145,525, Liberal 142,449. The Conservatives, with 255,580, were not that short of out-polling both combined.

Labour was now the largest single party in the Commons and MacDonald formed his second government, though still without an overall majority. He was soon buffeted by the effects of the Wall Street Crash and the Great Depression. Faced with a financial crisis in 1931 the government split, MacDonald leaving with three colleagues to join the Conservatives and a section of the Liberals in a National Government. Manoeuvred into an election against his former party, he saw Labour smashed as its candidates faced, usually, a single government candidate. Not surprisingly, Kent returned fifteen Conservative MPs as it did again in 1935. By contrast, only two Liberal candidates appeared in 1931 and six in 1935: throughout the 1930s Canterbury, Dartford, Dover, Faversham, Gravesend, Maidstone, Chatham and Gillingham were Liberal-free zones. The Conservatives regained Ashford in 1931; even though Kedward stood as a National Liberal, i.e. a supporter of the government, he was soundly beaten. In 1935 Ashford was the only constituency out of the four they contested in Kent where the Liberals beat Labour. As for Labour, in 1935 only at Dartford did they press the Conservatives at all closely and it was at Dartford that Labour set a portent for the future, capturing the seat at a by-election in 1938. Their candidate was Jennie Adamson, Kent's first woman MP.

(4) The Second World War and Post-War Consensus, 1939–79: Conservative versus Labour, Round Two

Unlike the First, the Second World War did not benefit the Conservatives. Despite the leadership of Winston Churchill, people blamed them for the unemployment of the 1930s and the appeasement of Hitler, notably at Munich in 1938. People wanted a better, fairer Britain and Labour captured this mood, especially in its response to the Beveridge Report which envisaged the construction of a welfare state. The party manifesto in 1945, *Let us Face the Future*, encapsulated this as well as recalling the failure of the Conservative-dominated Coalition to deliver on its promises after 1918. Nor could Labour be tarred with the communist brush; the Soviets were our heroic allies and socialist planning appeared the way forward in peace as well as in war. Moreover, Labour's leaders, particularly Attlee and Bevin, were prominent members of the war-time coalition, experienced and respected. The 1945 election produced a Labour landslide. It almost produced a Labour majority among Kent MPs.

There were seventeen Kent constituencies, Dartford giving birth to Bexley, both being reclassified as boroughs, Chislehurst spawning Orpington, both county seats. Labour retained Dartford and won Bexley, Chatham and Gillingham among the boroughs and gained Chislehurst,[11] Dover, Faversham and Gravesend among the county constituencies; Kent thus returned eight Labour to nine Conservative MPs. In terms of the aggregate poll the positions were reversed, Labour winning 314,101 Kent votes, the Conservatives 305,129. As for the Liberals, they put up ten candidates, all came third behind the major parties, and only at Bromley did they get as much as 20% of the vote; four candidates lost their deposits. Still, they did better than the Communists whose sole candidate, at Sevenoaks of all places, got 1.6%. Mrs Adamson, who had moved to Bexley, remained Kent's sole woman MP. Apart from those constituencies noted in Table 33, most had electorates within the range 50,000–60,000.

Table 33

Size of Kent constituency electorates differing from the norm, 1945

Above norm		Below norm	
Bromley	81,938	Chatham	48,270
Dartford	71,591	Dover	45,279
Chislehurst	71,246	Thanet	44,745
Tonbridge	63,441	Gillingham	39,765
		Hythe	23,525

Clearly, given such disparities, most notably between Bromley and Hythe, some redistribution was going to be necessary, and this took place before the next general election. Turnout was almost everywhere in the range 68–75%, only Bexley slightly exceeding this.

Labour had reached its high-water mark; thereafter the tide began to recede, despite the fact that the government was a great reforming ministry. Building upon the work of the Liberals before 1914 and the report of another Liberal, Beveridge, it fulfilled its election promises, creating the welfare state and the

---

[11] Waldron Smithers was rewarded for his foresight in choosing Orpington rather than Chislehurst which he had represented since 1924.

National Health Service. It nationalised key sectors of the economy, granted independence to the countries of the Indian sub-continent and inaugurated what became the bipartisan foreign policy which operated throughout the Cold War of allying with the USA to forestall further Soviet encroachment in Europe. This foreign policy contributed to the government's fall, as it felt obliged to join the USA in resisting the communist incursion into South Korea, leading to disadvantageous economic consequences and internal party division. Even before this, economic difficulties had meant hardship and austerity which cost the government support. By 1950 Labour seemed to be running out of steam but the election still gave it a wafer-thin majority of seven. The following year, however, saw the return of the Conservatives even though they polled fewer votes nationally than Labour.

Labour, of course, lost support in Kent. Although it managed to retain Bexley and Gravesend in by-elections in 1946 and 1947, it was with reduced majorities, and in the 1950 election it lost half its Kent seats: Bexley, Chislehurst, Dover and Gillingham. The victorious Conservative at Bexley was a certain E.R.G. Heath, whose long career was launched on a slender majority of 133 votes. He may have owed his seat to the intervention of a Communist named Job, most of whose 481 votes would otherwise presumably have gone to Labour. Job could thus be said to have been Heath's comforter! The margin of victory at Chislehurst was also very narrow, 167, Miss Patricia Hornsby-Smith thereby becoming Kent's first Conservative woman MP. Since the Tories also won the new seat of Beckenham, created to cut the previously gross Bromley down to size (by a similar token Folkestone and Hythe replaced previously puny Hythe) they now held fourteen Kent seats to Labour's four. No seats changed hands in 1951, the general picture being of increased Conservative majorities and reduced Labour ones, almost terminally so at Faversham. The Liberals fought every seat in 1950 except Chatham and Gillingham. With monotonous regularity they came third, losing every single deposit save at Canterbury where they managed to achieve 13.3% of the poll. Certainly cash-strapped and, no doubt, disheartened, they contested only Canterbury in 1951 and proceeded to lose that deposit as well, polling only 7.9%. Turnout was remarkably high in both elections, over 80% in every case save Folkestone (79%) and Thanet (78%) in 1951. The highest, 88.7%, was at Bexley in 1950.

The incoming Conservative government accepted much of Labour's achievement. The welfare state was not dismantled, indeed in some ways it was enhanced. There was little denationalisation; the policy of full employment and good relations with the trade unions was maintained; so were decolonisation, the transformation of Empire into Commonwealth and the bipartisan foreign policy. With growing prosperity as the ravages of war receded and Britain enjoyed favourable terms of trade with her partners abroad, the Conservatives were returned with increased majorities in 1955 and (despite the Suez fiasco of 1956) 1959, on the latter occasion under the urbane premiership of the MP for Bromley, Harold Macmillan. In Kent, Tory majorities increased as did Labour difficulties: Gravesend was lost in 1955, though this was balanced by victory at

Erith and Crayford, created out of the populous Dartford. Chatham was lost in 1959 but Percy Wells hung on heroically at Faversham, with majorities of fifty-nine in 1955 and, against the trend, 253 in 1959. The Liberals put up only two candidates in 1955, at Chislehurst and Orpington: both lost their deposits. There was, however, a modest revival of Liberal activity in 1959: seven candidates put up and all came third, but only two lost their deposits. Their best performance was 21.2% at Orpington, fewer than 500 votes behind Labour.

The most interesting development of the 1959 parliament was Macmillan's decision to despatch Heath to negotiate British entry into the then infant European Common Market in 1961. The attempt foundered on the veto of the French President de Gaulle but it was a portent for the future, both Heath's and the country's. The Conservatives were running into trouble and it was in this context that a Kent constituency captured the national attention as never before: the year was 1962, the constituency Orpington.

Orpington had been solidly Conservative ever since its inception in 1945. The by-election was caused by the appointment of the sitting MP as a judge in 1961. With the government in trouble, Liberal support had been growing at several by-elections without the victory breakthrough being achieved. In Orpington itself an active Liberal Association had been setting up ward committees and fighting local Urban District Council (UDC) elections since the mid-1950s; by 1961 they held twelve of the thirty-three council seats. The Tories delayed the by-election for several months during which the Liberals got off to a bad start: their candidate of 1959, who had run Labour close, encountered personal problems and was, rather messily, eventually persuaded to stand down. It was not until November that the Liberals adopted a local, family man, aged thirty-three, UDC councillor and engineer, Eric Lubbock, grandson of Sir John Lubbock, Bt, who had held Maidstone for the Liberals from 1870 to 1880, being subsequently elevated to the peerage as Lord Avebury. The Conservatives, perhaps unwisely, chose an outsider, Peter Goldman, a Jewish-born party researcher.

At the climax of the campaign the Liberals flooded Orpington with party leaders and activists and on 14 March 1962 won one of the most sensational by-election victories of the century: a Conservative majority of 14,760 less than three years earlier had been replaced by a Liberal one of 7,855. Labour lost their deposit. The 80% turnout was only slightly down on 1959. The question posed by the *Daily Mail* the previous December: 'will the word Orpington be engraved on the coffin of the Macmillan government?'[12] had been decisively answered. *The Times* more prosaically proclaimed on the morning after that Orpington was 'the most severe blow the Conservatives had suffered since they returned to office in 1951'.[13]

Such a seismic event had profound consequences. Psephologists and sociologists read the runes and 'Orpington Man' was revealed: young, middle class,

[12] Quoted in C. Cook and J. Ramsden, *By-elections in British Politics*, London 1973, p. 203.
[13] Quoted *Ibid.*, p. 214.

professional, with family, the sort of person who had been flooding into the rapidly expanding constituency over the past decade, for Orpington was really part of metropolitan suburbia and was soon to be electorally recognised as such. Lubbock was able to appeal to such people: he was one of them but also had the aristocratic connections to appeal to any subconscious feelings of deference. The Liberal activists, furthermore, gave the party an image of youth, a new way seemed to have been found between Socialist–Labour and Capitalist–Conservative. The established parties responded: Macmillan sacked one-third of his Cabinet, provoking the observation from the future Liberal leader, Jeremy Thorpe: 'Greater love hath no man than this, that he lay down his friends for his life';[14] Labour under Harold Wilson stressed their appeal to the classless meritocracy by emphasising the white heat of the technological revolution rather than class war.

Orpington, however, was a singular success. With the approach of the general election, the established parties, enjoying greater resources, were able to appeal to the rising professional classes. This emphasises the factors peculiar to Orpington, party activity at local level over a period of years, the strength of Lubbock's candidacy and an effective campaign, factors which other Liberal associations were eventually to build upon.[15] But at general elections the efforts of leaders and activists cannot be so focused on a single seat. Orpington thus failed to fulfil the predictions of the *Daily Mail* that if Lubbock won it 'would become the beacon to set the Liberals alight all over Britain',[16] but it did form part of a series of by-election victories in the 1960s and 1970s which may well have saved the party from terminal decline. After all, there were only six Liberal MPs until Orpington added a seventh, making it that little bit more difficult for the Liberal Party to comply with the old jibe that it went to Westminster in a taxi.[17]

Orpington, therefore, proved a false dawn for the Liberals though they did retain it in 1964 and 1966. It was Labour, however, who benefited from Conservative disarray to win power in 1964, albeit with a mere four-seat overall majority. Kent made its contribution, Labour holding its existing seats and doubling them by winning Chatham, Dover (narrowly) and Gravesend.[18] Defeat led the Conservatives to change their leader, and Edward Heath was elected to the post in 1965. This had little initial effect and Wilson was able to secure a majority of almost 100 in 1966. Labour made only one gain in Kent, Chislehurst, where the defeat of the by-now Rt Hon. Dame Patricia Hornsby-Smith halved the county's number of women MPs.

[14] Quoted in D.E. Butler and Anthony King, *The British General Election of 1964*, London 1965, p. 16.
[15] Not always successfully. For the struggles of Tonbridge Liberals in the late 1960s, see below, pp. 181–2.
[16] Quoted in Cook and Ramsden, *op. cit.*, p. 203.
[17] There are two studies of Orpington, one by Ken Young, 'Orpington and the "Liberal Revival" ', in Cook and Ramsden, *op. cit.*, pp. 198–222, the other a not-unbiased account by a Liberal active in the constituency, Donald Newby, *The Orpington Story*, London 1963.
[18] Chatham added Mrs Ann Kerr to the as yet small band of Kent women MPs.

The Liberals contested seventeen Kent seats in 1964, coming third in all save Orpington, but saving their deposits except in five seats where the prospect of close contests between the major parties squeezed their vote, a fate which befell Labour at Orpington. In 1966 they put up fifteen candidates, withdrawing from Faversham and Maidstone, but only succeeded in increasing their lost deposits to seven.

The Labour government struggled against various economic problems but by the time of the 1970 general election most pundits, to say nothing of most opinion polls, Harold Wilson and, some believe, Edward Heath,[19] expected it to secure re-election. In the event it failed to do so. It suffered particularly badly in Kent. Faversham finally fell as did Chislehurst (to a resurgent Dame Patricia), Dartford (Labour for over a quarter of a century), Dover, Gravesend and Chatham where in a straight fight between two women, Mrs Peggy Fenner ousted Mrs Ann Kerr; Kent once again had two women MPs. To complete Conservative delight Orpington returned to the fold. It was just like old times; only Erith and Crayford prevented a clean government sweep. Nor, except at Dartford, where the majority was 560, were the gains narrowly achieved: over 5,000 at Chatham, over 3,000 at Chislehurst and Faversham. Kent's prime minister could revel in his county's endorsement, though Labour apathy may have played a part, whether through disaffection or complacency: turnout was down everywhere. Nor did the Liberals benefit; they failed to contest Dover, Faversham, Folkestone, Erith, Chatham and Gillingham, though they did reappear at Maidstone; everywhere their vote was down, five deposits were lost and Orpington was the only constituency in which they came second. It must have seemed a long way from the 1962 'revival'.

The Heath government started out with radical intentions but it was forced into a series of U-turns. It faced severe problems in Northern Ireland, with the miners and with inflation, accentuated by the massive hike in oil prices organised by OPEC. In February 1974, during a miners' strike, Heath called an election, the main issue perceived as being 'who governs the country?' The country decided it was not to be him, and Wilson returned to office, dependent on the Liberals. In October he in turn went to the country and gained a narrow overall majority of six. Conservative leaders who lose successive elections do not usually last long, and Heath was duly replaced by Margaret Thatcher in 1975. However, the Heath administration had been responsible for one of the most momentous decisions in modern British history, the application to join the European Economic Community which was carried through to fruition, Britain becoming a member on 1 January 1973.

Time caught up with several Kent constituencies before the 1974 elections. In 1965 London had gobbled up various parts of the county, and now these areas were formally recognised as Greater London constituencies, namely Beckenham, Bexley (renamed Sidcup), Bromley (renamed Ravensbourne), Chislehurst, Erith and Crayford, and Orpington, plus the newly created Bexleyheath,

---

19 See, for example, John Campbell, *Edward Heath: A Biography*, London 1994, p. 282.

though we shall still keep an eye on them under the designation Kentish Greater London (KGL). Within Kent proper there were also changes to take account of population movements. The Isle of Thanet became Thanet East and Thanet West, Dover became Dover and Deal, Tonbridge was divided into Tonbridge and Malling and Royal Tunbridge Wells. Kent proper now returned fifteen MPs, Kentish Greater London seven.

Kent contributed but marginally to Labour's return to power. In February the party regained Dartford and Gravesend and in October added Chatham while in KGL James Wellbeloved retained Erith and Crayford but four seats out of twenty-two was an unimpressive achievement. There were two new developments: in February, in nine of Kent's fifteen seats (Ashford, Canterbury, Folkestone, Gillingham, Maidstone, Sevenoaks, Thanet West, Tonbridge and Malling and Tunbridge Wells) the Liberals pushed Labour into third place, though in all but Folkestone, Maidstone and Tunbridge Wells Labour regained second place in October. Nowhere did the Liberals come anywhere near success. The second development was the appearance of the right-wing National Front at Canterbury, Chatham (October only), Dartford, Gillingham (October only), Gravesend and Thanet East (October only). All their candidates lost their deposits, the highest poll being 2.4% at Gravesend in February. Turn-out was up; in February over 80% at Ashford, Canterbury, Dartford, Dover, Faversham, Gillingham, Gravesend, Maidstone, Sevenoaks, Thanet East, Tonbridge and Malling, and Tunbridge Wells, though falling back below 80% in every case in October. Considerable variation in constituency size had reappeared. Maidstone had over 88,000 electors, Gravesend 87,000, Canterbury 85,000, contrasted with Thanet, which had fewer than 48,000 electors in East and 44,000 in West. A vote in Thanet West was worth two in Maidstone.

The Labour government's position became increasingly vulnerable as it quickly began to lose by-elections and became dependent on the Liberals. Finally, the winter of discontent, 1978/9, suggested to many that trade-union power had become excessive, a feeling that was bound to damage Labour. The 1979 election returned the Conservatives to power under the leadership of Mrs Thatcher. Kent was in the van, giving them all fifteen seats in Kent proper, which was to be a Tory fiefdom for the next eighteen years. The verdict was decisive: despite the presence of three, and sometimes more, candidates, the Conservatives won over 50% of the votes in every seat save Chatham and Dartford (both captured from Labour, the former by Mrs Fenner). The Liberals were back to square one: third place everywhere except Folkestone and Maidstone, and six lost deposits. The National Front contested every seat except Thanet West and contributed fourteen lost deposits to the national coffers, in every instance where the comparison is possible falling back from their 1974 performance.

As for KGL, this was once more a Conservative clean sweep save for Erith and Crayford, the Tories polling over 50% in all their seats, with the Liberals third everywhere except Orpington, losing two deposits to the National Front's seven.

(5) The Thatcher–Major Years: 1979–92. Conservative versus Labour, Round Three: No Contest

Labour celebrated loss of office by tearing itself apart. The Left sought to move the party in a more socialist direction, sections of the right, increasingly alienated, departed to form the Social Democratic Party (SDP), among them James Wellbeloved, MP for Erith and Crayford. The SDP allied with the Liberals, the majority eventually merging with them in 1988 to form the Liberal Democrats. The Conservatives benefited from divisions among their opponents but they also benefited from the resolute, forceful, populist leadership of Mrs Thatcher who, unlike Heath, refused in the face of initial unpopularity to be deflected from her radical approach: 'the lady's not for turning'. The aim was to reduce the role of the state (and hence taxation), privatising its industries and reducing people's dependence on welfare, thus encouraging enterprise and initiative, and to curb the power of the unions, thus allowing employers to deploy their powers of enterprise and initiative. The way to prosperity was through market forces and monetarism. Further buoyed by the Falklands War, Mrs Thatcher won a great victory in 1983, with an overall majority of more than 140. Kent did its bit: boundary changes had given it an additional constituency, Mid-Kent, and Kent duly returned sixteen Conservative MPs. Only at Dover (48.3%), Gravesham, formerly Gravesend (47.0%), and Medway, formerly Rochester and Chatham (48.9%), did the victor receive less than 50% of the vote: none was remotely in danger. The Liberals pushed Labour into third place at Canterbury, Folkestone, Gillingham, Maidstone, Mid-Kent, Sevenoaks, Thanet South and Tunbridge Wells (now shorn of its Royal); the SDP did likewise at Ashford, Faversham, Thanet North (there had been a geographical revolution in Thanet, North and South replacing West and East) and Tonbridge and Malling. Labour's highest share of the poll was at Gravesham, at 31.7%, and it lost four deposits: the Liberals and SDP lost not one. The worst electoral imbalances had been ironed out: Thanet South had the fewest voters (62,000) and Faversham the most (76,000).

The picture was similar in KGL: seven seats, seven Tory MPs; all but one with over 50% of the vote, the figure rising to 60% at Old Bexley and Sidcup (the constituency of Edward Heath) and 63% at Ravensbourne. The exception was Erith and Crayford where the Conservative defeated the SDP's James Wellbeloved by under 1,000 votes (37.1% to 34.9%) with Labour third (27.3%). The Liberals came second in five seats, the SDP in two; Labour was third everywhere, with two lost deposits and, apart from Erith and Crayford, nowhere attaining as much as one-fifth of the vote.

Although the Conservatives nationally lost some support in 1987, their majority declining to 102, in the Garden of England they suffered not. Their share of the poll slipped slightly in seven seats and rose slightly in the other nine, including Gravesham and Medway, which joined everywhere else except Dover in giving their MPs over 50% of the vote. In the battle for the minor placings, the party which had finished second in 1983 did so again in 1987. As for KGL, the Tory share of the vote was up marginally in four seats, identical in a fifth, marginally down in a sixth. Erith and Crayford was the only seat where Labour managed to regain second place, pushing the by now less Wellbeloved into third place; it was the only seat where the Conservatives increased their share of the poll markedly, from 37.1 to 45.2%. Thus the Conservatives held all 'Greater Kent's' twenty-three seats, all save Dover (46%) and Erith and Crayford with over 50% of the votes.

Significant changes occurred before the next election. Mrs Thatcher seemed to lose touch with important senior colleagues and back-benchers, the newly introduced community charge or poll tax proved unpopular, unemployment and interest rates were rising, Conservative popularity falling. In November 1990 she was driven from office and replaced by the more emollient John Major. Labour began to revive and, like the recently formed Liberal Democrats, went into the 1992 general election with high hopes. They were dashed, Major returning to power with an overall majority of twenty-one. 'IT'S THE *SUN* WOT WON IT,'[20] according to the *Sun*, but as usual it was the South of England, including Kent, where confidently predicted opposition gains failed to materialise. The Conservatives retained all their seats in Kent, usually with a slightly reduced share of the poll (though Ann Widdecombe at Maidstone, Dame Peggy Fenner at Medway, Andrew Rowe at Mid-Kent, and John Stanley at Tonbridge and Malling managed to increase theirs), but even so only Gravesham joined Dover in giving its MP less than half the vote, and then only just (49.7%). Dover, which Labour had expected to win, was the only close contest, 44.1 to 42.6%. Labour however re-emerged as the principal challenger to the Conservatives, adding second place in Faversham, Gillingham, Mid-Kent, Thanet North and Thanet South to its existing holdings, but the essential modesty of this achievement may be illustrated by the fact that only at Dover, Gravesham (40.4%), Dartford (34.7%) and Medway (34.6%) did it manage to attract more than a third of the vote. Some disparity in electoral size had reappeared, the 62,000 votes of Medway and Thanet South contrasting with 82,000 at Faversham.

The Conservatives were similarly successful in KGL, actually increasing their share of the poll, marginally at Beckenham, Bexleyheath, Chislehurst and Ravensbourne, slightly more substantially at Erith and Crayford, despite the fact that a Labour recovery was turning this into a marginal (46.5% to 41.5%), the only seat in KGL where the Tories won less than half the vote. Labour recaptured second place at Beckenham, Bexleyheath, Chislehurst and Old Bexley but still polled less than a quarter of the vote. There was little indication in the 1992 results to prepare one for the Conservative Armageddon five years later. Before examining that, however, we need to consider the major personalities of Kent politics, the role of the political parties and local government.

---

[20] Quoted in David Butler and Dennis Kavanagh, *The British General Election of 1992*, London 1992, p. 180; the *Sun*'s claim is refuted on p. 209.

(6) Political Personalities[21]

Pride of place among Kentish politicians of the twentieth century must surely go to Sir Edward Heath, prime minister from 1970 to 1974. Born at Broadstairs, the son of a carpenter who managed to establish himself as an independent builder and decorator, he was educated at Chatham House, Ramsgate, before going to Balliol College, Oxford. Heath was the first ex-grammar school boy to become Conservative Party leader. Widely talented as a musician and yachtsman he was something of a loner, awkward in company and frequently rude to colleagues, defects which helped to bring about his removal from the leadership and his replacement with another outsider, a grocer's daughter from Grantham. Bitterly disappointed that his own, largely unsuccessful, period as prime minister suffered by comparison with the rule of the Iron Lady, Heath, now knighted, became largely estranged from the Conservative Party. However, he remained implacably loyal to his vision of Britain in Europe, and he retained his seat in the Commons long enough to become Father of the House and see the successor he hated replaced by a prime minister whose Conservatism was more in keeping with his own.[22]

Ironically, although the voters of Kent showed their support for the policies of Heath's successor, they had earlier rejected her personally. As Margaret Roberts she was defeated at Dartford by Labour in 1950 and 1951 and she failed to secure the Conservative candidacy at Orpington, Beckenham and Maidstone before being adopted for Finchley, where she was first elected an MP in 1959. Dartford, however, had left Miss Roberts with more than memories of rejection: at her selection there in 1949 she met a successful North Kent businessman, Denis Thatcher; they married two years later.[23]

Another leading politician to be personally rejected by a Kent constituency was Hugh Gaitskell, the Labour leader tragically robbed by death in 1963 of the almost certain prize of the premiership. Educated at public school and Oxford, his experience of the 1926 General Strike led him to the cause of democratic socialism. Gaitskell was selected as Labour candidate for Chatham in 1932, and fought his first parliamentary contest there. His commitment to socialism was unequivocal: 'the time has come when the Labour Party must go straight out for socialism when it is returned to power'. He described socialism as 'the destruction of inequality, the creating and maintaining of a society in which it cannot exist'.[24] He gained some Liberal support – indeed, as J.H. Jenkins had done in 1906 and 1910, he had Liberals sign his nomination paper – but he still lost in 1935 by nearly 6,000 votes. Chatham bid him a fond farewell: 'the whole of the

---

21 Unless otherwise indicated, this section is based on material in M. Stenton and S. Lees, *Who's Who of British Members of Parliament. Vol II: 1886–1918*, Hassocks 1978, *Vol III: 1919–1945*, Brighton 1979, *Vol IV: 1945–1979*, Brighton 1981, supplemented by *Who's Who*, London various dates.

22 There are several books on Heath, the most comprehensive being Campbell, *op. cit.* Sir Edward has recently published his autobiography, *The Course of My Life*, London 1998.

23 Hugo Young, *One of Us*, London 1990, pp. 34–5, 39.

24 Philip M. Williams, *Hugh Gaitskell: A Political Biography*, London 1979, pp. 40–1

Plate 24. Cartoon by Emmwood in *The Daily Mail* showing Edward Heath having dreamed he had won the general election, 1966 (© Trevor York, 49–53 Kensington High Street, London W8 5ED; caption reads: 'I had a terrible night, Iain, I dreamt we won.').

LADY M: "INFIRM OF PURPOSE! GIVE ME THE DAGGERS."

Plate 25. Cartoon by Garland in *The New Statesman* of Margaret Thatcher supplanting Edward Heath as leader of the Conservative Party, 1975 (© Ewan MacNaughton, 6 Alexandra Road, Tonbridge, TN29 2AA).

"Women and elephants never forget an injury." (Saki)

Plate 26. Cartoon by Garland in *The Daily Telegraph* of Edward Heath maintaining his dislike for Margaret Thatcher, 1981 (© Ewan MacNaughton, 6 Alexandra Road, Tonbridge, TN29 2AA).

LEADERSHIP STAKES

Plate 27. Cartoon by Peter Brookes in *The Times* showing Ann Widdecombe destroying the hopes of Michael Howard to lead the Conservative Party, 1997 (© Peter Brookes).

Party in Chatham would be pleased if you were offered a "safe" seat in the near future'. He found his Finchley in Leeds South.[25]

Heath was not the first twentieth-century prime minister to represent a Kent constituency. Harold Macmillan was rescued by middle-class, suburban Bromley, having been rejected by the voters of Stockton in 1945. Aided by the good offices of that well-known Kent resident Winston Churchill and, no doubt, by the fact that he was the son-in-law of the Duke of Devonshire, Macmillan was selected to replace the sitting member who, in the curious circumstances of that election (to allow the armed services' votes to be apportioned to the appropriate constituency three weeks elapsed between the poll and the count) had been re-elected without knowing it: he died before the result was declared. Macmillan represented Bromley until he retired from the Commons in 1964: interestingly, when he finally accepted the earldom to which ex-prime ministers are customarily entitled, he chose to become Earl of Stockton, which had always meant more to him politically.[26]

A number of Kent MPs reached the lower ranks of government as Parliamentary Private Secretaries (PPS) to ministers or Parliamentary Under-Secretaries of State, but few made the highest offices of state. Sir Patrick Mayhew, MP for Tunbridge Wells from 1974 until he retired in 1997, progressed through various offices to become Solicitor General (1983–7), Attorney General (1987–92) and finally Secretary of State for Northern Ireland (1992–7), a vitally important and demanding post. He was joined in the Cabinet by Michael Howard, who started out as his PPS in 1984, rising through a number of positions to Home Secretary (1993–7), and Jonathan Aitken, MP for Thanet South, Chief Secretary to the Treasury 1994–5. If one adds the Canterbury-born and educated John Redwood, who sat in the Cabinet as Secretary of State for Wales from 1993 to 1995, clearly Major's government had strong Kent connections. Common representation of Kent constituencies did not necessarily breed comradeliness, however. In the Conservative leadership election which followed defeat in 1997, the chances of the member for Folkestone (Michael Howard) were dealt a severe blow by the member for Maidstone (Ann Widdecombe) who declared (in the context of the breakdown of relations between them when she had served under him at the Home Office) that there was 'something of the night' about him.

Conservative ministers from earlier days included Sir Edward Hilton Young, MP for Sevenoaks and newspaper editor, Minister of Health from 1931 to 1935 when he was created Baron Kennet. Of similar, but longer-lasting, vintage was Lt Col. the Rt Hon. John Moore-Brabazon, pioneer motorist and aviator, who was appropriately Parliamentary Secretary to the Minister of Transport (1922–3, 1924–7). Although losing his seat at Chatham in 1929, he went on to become Minister of Transport (1940–1) and of Aircraft Production (1941–2)

[25] *Ibid.*, pp. 49, 50–2, 72–5; the quotation is on p. 75.
[26] Macmillan's official biography is Alistair Horne, *Macmillan, 1894–1956*, London 1988, *1957–1986*, London 1989.

before being raised to the peerage as Baron Brabazon. Hythe had a strong ministerial tradition. Sir Philip Sassoon, Bt, was Under-Secretary of State for Air
(1924–9, 1931–7) and First Commissioner for Works (1937 until his death in
1939). He was succeeded at Hythe by Commander Rupert Brabner, who, after
continuing the good old Kent Tory tradition of serving as a government whip in
1944, also became Under-Secretary of State for Air: he died in a plane crash in
1945. He in turn was succeeded at Hythe by Sir Henry Mackeson, Bt, who lived
at Barham. He too served as a whip (1947, 1950–2), then as Secretary for Overseas Trade (1952–3). He was also President of the Kent Football Association in
1949 and of the County Cricket Club in 1951.

Labour ministers were naturally fewer in number but they did exist. George
Isaacs, son of a printer who became a union general-secretary, during his brief
tenure of Gravesend from 1923 to 1924 served fellow union secretary J.H.
Thomas, as PPS in the first Labour government, later becoming Minister of
Labour in Attlee's administration. Arthur Bottomley (Chatham 1945–59), a
former railwayman, educated at elementary school and Toynbee Hall, was
Secretary for Overseas Trade (1947–51) and, like Isaacs, again held office after
his Kent links were severed, becoming a member of Wilson's cabinet in 1964.
David Ennals (Dover 1964–70) became Minister of State at the Department of
Health and Social Security (1968–70) and, like Isaacs and Bottomley, survived
defeat in Kent to hold office again. A contemporary, Albert Murray (Gravesend
1964–70), educated at elementary school, printer's assistant, was Minister of
State at the Board of Trade (1967), transferring to Technology (1968) and to the
post of Parliamentary Secretary to the Minister of Transport (1969–70). Finally,
Terry Boston (Faversham 1964–70), educated at Woolwich Polytechnic and
King's, London, a barrister, served as PPS to several ministers before becoming
a government whip (1969–70). He was ennobled as Baron Boston in 1976 and
later became Minister of State at the Home Office.

Turning from ministers to members, twentieth-century Kent MPs were not as
socially prestigious as their nineteenth-century predecessors. The grandees
faded away early on. Hart Dyke was defeated at Dartford in 1906; Akers-
Douglas, Viscount Chilston, retired in 1911; Cranborne became Marquess of
Salisbury in 1903, Castlereagh Marquess of Londonderry in 1915. The old
Kentish families were conspicuous by their almost total absence: only Knatchbull and William Deedes, both MPs for Ashford, revived memories of the past.
Knatchbull became a PPS before making his mark on India as Lord Brabourne:
Governor of Bombay (1933–7), of Bengal (1937–9), acting Viceroy (1938).
Deedes attained ministerial office (without Portfolio 1962–4) but arguably
enjoyed greater influence as editor of the *Daily Telegraph* (1974–86), and
greater fame as the recipient of Denis Thatcher's 'Dear Bill' letters in the
columns of *Private Eye*, than he ever did as a minister. He received a peerage in
1986. A few members of the aristocracy do appear. Angus McDonnell, son of
the Earl of Antrim, was elected for Dartford but served only one term before
retiring, perhaps finding his duties with bankers Morgan Grenfell more congenial. Thanet was graced by a son of Lord Carson for eight years from 1945,

but an earlier Thanet MP had carried greater weight: Hon. Esmond Harmsworth, member from 1919 to 1929, was the son of Lord Rothermere and succeeded to the title in 1940; he was Chairman of Associated Newspapers (1932–71) and of the Newspaper Proprietors' Association (1934–61).

Another press magnate with aristocratic connections represented Dover from 1922 to 1945, J.J. Astor of London and Hever Castle, son of the first Viscount Astor and brother-in-law of Nancy Astor, the first woman to take her seat in the Commons. Astor married the daughter of an earl, was chairman of *The Times* publishing company (1922–9), director of banks and insurance companies as well as of the Great Western Railway, and president of the MCC (1937–8); he was ennobled as Baron Astor of Hever in 1956. Two sons of baronets who duly inherited the titles were also returned, Sir Adrian Maxwell Baillie (Tonbridge 1937–45) and Sir Richard Acland (Gravesend 1947–55). Acland was unique among those recently mentioned, as he was a Labour MP. A west-countryman and former Liberal MP for Barnstaple, he had earlier founded the Common Wealth Party and given his estate to the National Trust.

Kent MPs were drawn from a wide variety of backgrounds. Conservatives were often educated at public school and Oxbridge and came from the realms of the armed services, commerce, industry, law and the media. Many were London-based. Labour MPs broadened the social and educational range. Mills at Dartford was an engineer and chairman of the Woolwich shop stewards: he was a PPS during the first Labour government. Another Dartford MP, Norman Dodds, Dartford resident, educated at elementary school, was a PPS in 1951 and survived to fill a similar position in the 1964 Labour government though by then he had transferred to Erith and Crayford. Elementary school, work in a trade, the union movement was the background of a number of early Labour MPs, though with time this broadened: Bob Bean (Chatham 1974–9), for example, son of a dockyard worker, educated at Rochester Mathematical School and Medway College of Technology, became a Polytechnic lecturer. Bean illustrates another tendency common to all parties during the latter part of the century, service on a local council as an apprenticeship before being selected as a parliamentary candidate, much as in the nineteenth century eldest sons of peers spent time in the Commons before being summoned to the House of Lords. This was made possible by the increasing politicisation of local government and also meant that the MP was more likely to have roots in the constituency, as in the case of Eric Lubbock at Orpington.

Only five of Kent's some 140 MPs up to 1992 were women. Two were Labour, Jennie Adamson, who was Parliamentary Secretary at the Ministry of Pensions from 1945 to 1946, resigning to become deputy chairman of the Assistance, later National Assistance, Board, and Ann Kerr, a member of the actor's union, Equity. The other three were Conservative: two became Dames, Peggy Fenner, who did two stints as Parliamentary Secretary at the Ministry of Agriculture in the 1970s and 1980s, and Pat Hornsby-Smith, who held minor ministerial office in the late 1950s and early 1960s before being elevated to the peerage in 1974. The third, Ann Widdecombe, has represented Maidstone since

1987 and, at the time of writing, is becoming a figure of growing importance in the Conservative parliamentary party, being appointed shadow Home Secretary in 1999.

(7) Political Parties

Party formed the vital underpinning of politics throughout the twentieth century at constituency, and increasingly at many local, levels, the crucial link between government and people. To begin with the newcomer, Labour, formed as the Labour Representation Committee in 1900: in fact, Labour parties existed in Kent (as elsewhere) before the national party was born. The London Dockers' Union, formed in 1889, organised in the Medway Valley and one of its officials, Arthur Field, who lived in Maidstone, organised a branch there of the National Labour Electoral Association in 1889. Closely linked to Maidstone Trades Council, most of its members were unionists: paper-makers, engineers, tailors. The main aim was to achieve the eight-hour working day by lobbying candidates of the existing parties. Field was also instrumental in forming a Labour Party in Gillingham in 1891, in conjunction with Chatham Trades Council. Its executive was dominated by dockers. Gillingham was one of only two Labour parties outside the North of England to send delegates to the Bradford conference of 1893 which led to the formation of the Independent Labour Party (ILP), a socialist society which affiliated to the LRC in 1900. The ubiquitous Field set up the Kent ILP in 1893, and a branch of the intellectual Fabian Society was established in Maidstone in 1895. After 1900 Maidstone responded to national developments by transforming its organisation into a local LRC but it was to Gillingham, then part of the Chatham constituency, that the honour was to fall of returning Kent's first Labour MP.[27]

As for the Labour programme, initially it scarcely differed from the Liberals'. J.H. Jenkins began his address at Chatham in 1906 by pointing to his credentials as a working man and trade unionist but then went on to express his support for such Liberal nostrums as free trade ('the noble principle which has done so much for the welfare of this country'), free, unsectarian education, and temperance. He even made play for Conservative votes by linking the national problem of unemployment and the need to find jobs with expansion of the dockyard: 'it is a duty which I shall endeavour to faithfully carry out to see that they are kept in a proper state of efficiency and that they receive their full share of national work which is necessary to be executed for the safety of our country'. Indeed, he was not above playing the national card: after expressing hearty approval of Liberal prime minister Campbell-Bannerman's comments concerning Chinese labour in South Africa he went on to urge its total removal 'so that Britishers may enjoy

---

27 Peter Clark and Lyn Murfin, *The History of Maidstone*, Stroud 1995, pp. 182–3; Rod Helps, 'The Founding of Gillingham's Labour Party', *Byegone Kent*, vol. 8, no. 6 (1987), pp. 323–5.

the land for which so much British blood was shed and so much money paid'. He then expressed support for what was to become a staple of Labour addresses, social reform, specifically, on this occasion, trade-union law, old-age pensions, taxation of land values, railway nationalisation (the one socialist measure and the only one which might have troubled Liberals), housing and employers' liability, promising to work with Labour and Progressive forces to bring them about.[28]

Four years later Jenkins was, if anything, even more liberal. Railway nationalisation disappeared. At the top of his address was an attack on the House of Lords, followed by a strong defence of his record concerning the dockyard where he claimed to have increased employment and improved working conditions. He then took credit for Labour for social reform: old-age pensions, Trades Disputes Act, Trade Boards Act, Coal Mines (Eight Hours) Act, medical inspections of schoolchildren, feeding of necessitous children, and labour exchanges. He foreshadowed the National Insurance scheme which was to become law in 1911, defended the People's Budget, opposed Tariff Reform, repeated his education and temperance pledges of 1906, before ending where he had begun, with the Lords whose removal was necessary 'for the march of the people to a happier England'[29]

Labour's adoption of the 1918 constitution with its commitment to the nationalisation of the means of production, distribution and exchange, raised the profile of socialism. An advertisement for the Maidstone Division Labour Party, 'The Party of the Workers by Hand or by Brain', urged people to read *Labour and the New Social Order*, price 2d. The candidate at the 1918 election, a Maidstone railway guard, portrayed himself as a working man and proud of it, and defended the quality of Labour's leaders which had been recognised by their membership of the Coalition. He argued for social reform, claimed Labour as the women's party and was not above a bit of anti-German zeal – in the style of his opponent: referring to the Kaiser, 'personally he would like to give him and those responsible for the war a taste of the poison gas and all the diabolical things done to our men, and he emphasised the fact that it was the Labour Party who first demanded that these men should be brought to justice'.[30]

Maidstone Labour's next standard bearer came from a different stable. Hugh Dalton was one of 'the workers by brain', son of a Canon of St George's, Windsor, educated at Eton and Cambridge, becoming a socialist at the latter, a qualified barrister and future Chancellor of the Exchequer in the Attlee government. Dalton advocated a capital levy which would enable reductions in indirect taxation, including the beer duty, which played well in the hop-growing areas, but in a bid to win Liberal support he confined nationalisation to coal, railways,

---

28 *Chatham, Rochester and Gillingham Observer*, 6 January 1906.
29 *Ibid.*, 8 January 1910.
30 *Kent Messenger*, 23 November, 14 December 1918. The Conservative put it more bluntly, describing the Kaiser as 'nothing but a glorified murderer . . . [who] should be put to death (applause)', *Ibid.*, 7 December 1918.

land, liquor and armaments and, as he himself put it later, kept it 'quite in the background'. Dalton came a good third and thought he had won in Maidstone itself but done badly in Lenham, Staplehurst and Headcorn where there was no Labour organisation 'and feudalism was still strong'.[31]

The main pattern was set. Labour candidates with varying degrees of enthusiasm committed themselves to socialism (see Gaitskell at Chatham above), usually of a gradualist nature, to social and welfare reforms, to combating unemployment and, abroad, to peace and international organisation and to relations with Soviet Russia, in part to further employment.

This provided Conservatives with easy targets. Nationalisation was attacked as inefficient and leading to higher taxes; the way to prosperity and *affordable* social reform was through private enterprise and lower taxes. Abroad, Conservatives were the party of national security and, while it lasted, Empire. Few opportunities were missed to tar Labour with the Soviet communist brush or with association with strikes by its trade-union affiliates.

As for the Liberals their problem was that, like their organisation, their programme was disappearing. Free trade, though it helped reunite the party in 1923, was becoming less viable amidst the economic traumas of the inter-war years and was anyway less popular in Kent. Their Irish policy lapsed with the treaty of 1922 which set up the Free State. Religion was declining as a political determinant which left middle-class nonconformists easier prey for the Conservatives. As for social reform, Liberals were outbid by Labour.

Maidstone in the 1920s provides a case-study of Liberalism's difficulties. It was a seat where before the war the Liberals had polled strongly. After it, they suffered a number of disadvantages. Boundary extension brought in rural areas (by 1920 there were 16,615 voters in the borough, 14,604 in the countryside), franchise extension brought in women (13,172 of the voters in 1920); both factors worked against the Liberals, the Conservatives having greater resources to deploy to woo the female electors.[32] The Liberals also disadvantaged themselves. In 1918 the leadership agreed loyally to support the sitting Coalition Conservative, Bellairs, though by only a small majority. A Liberal duly seconded Bellairs' nomination. Subsequently, angered by Coalition treatment elsewhere of Phillips, the 1910 candidate who remained popular in Maidstone, John Potter, chairman of the Liberal and Radical Association, and Kent's first working-class JP, attempted to withdraw Liberal support from Bellairs, a move countered by that gentleman's seconder. In 1922 a prominent local custard manufacturer, Foster Clark, known to be a Liberal, came forward, but as an Independent, claiming support from Conservatives as well as Liberals. This caused one old Liberal to come out in favour of Labour. The following year, as a loyal free trader, Clark stood as a Liberal, but the Tory majority increased and in

31 Hugh Dalton, *Call Back Yesterday: Memoirs, 1887–1931*, London 1953, pp. 136–7. See also Ben Pimlott, *Hugh Dalton*, London 1985, pp. 128, 134.
32 Centre for Kentish Studies (CKS), Maidstone Division Conservative and Unionist Association Minute Book (esp. agent's report for 1920), U 1634 A 3/1/1.

1924 neither Clark nor the Liberals contested the seat. In 1929, clearly galvanised by the Lloyd George-financed programme, the Liberals reappeared, standing for peace abroad via the League of Nations and the conquest of unemployment at home via a vast building programme of houses and schools. Defeat, followed in 1931 by the absorption of some Liberal leaders into the National Government, had a demoralising effect, and in 1935 the Conservatives were able to praise 'the assistance given by prominent members of the Liberal Party' to the victorious 'Conservative and National Government Candidate'.[33]

The basic problem facing the Liberals was that their wealthier supporters, businessmen, manufacturers, prosperous shopkeepers, were alienated by Labour's socialism and increasingly comfortable with the Conservatives with whom they co-operated in local elections. Other Liberals, as at Chatham in 1935, were attracted by Labour promises of social reform. In such circumstances a Liberal Party with no chance of electoral success came dangerously close to withering away.

Even after the revival in the 1960s, associated with Orpington, based on hard work and fostering local issues, the way forward remained hard, as the experience of the Tonbridge Division Liberal Association reveals. Its constitution proclaimed among its objects 'continuous educational and propaganda work' and helping 'all citizens, without regard to party, race or creed, to secure their rights and to protect them against oppression'. There was provision for local branches as well as branches of the Women's Liberal Association, the Young Liberals and Liberal Trade Unionists. The reality was a few dedicated, sometimes argumentative, activists keeping the faith alive in financially-strained circumstances: in November 1970 there was £39 in the funds and some outstanding loans to be met; it was hoped the proceeds of the Christmas Draw would resolve these financial problems. Membership in August 1966 stood at just over 500 spread over nine wards. Membership might not mean much, however. A damning analysis of Tunbridge Wells North Ward commented:

> Section membership is 58. Total inactivity pervades some 30 of these, whose contribution . . . consists solely in voting at Parliamentary (though not necessarily local) elections and paying their annual subscription – though a few have been known to make modest financial contributions when confronted with the conscience blackmail of a personal visit.

Even among the active:

> the preferences shown do not give any encouragement at all, since apart from those who came to the Wine-and-Cheese Party (hardly an arduous task) the only activities at all popular seem to be the non-effort, stay-at-home ones, like addressing poll cards or giving something to a stall.

---

[33] *Ibid.*, U 1634 A 3/1/2; *Kent Messenger*, esp. 23 and 30 November and 7 December 1918, 4 and 11 November 1922, 17 November 1923, and 25 May 1929.

The author would probably have been surprised had he been told that some thirty years later Tunbridge Wells would have, briefly, a Liberal Democrat council.

The minute book comes to an end in 1971 when the Association was replaced by separate bodies to take account of the creation of the constituencies of Royal Tunbridge Wells and Tonbridge and Malling. The last entry reads:

> *Minute Books* For historical and political reference these books are to be kept and it was suggested that they be kept altogether, whether in a Research Library or locally.
> This ended the meeting.[34]

This historian is duly grateful.

The Conservatives presented a marked contrast. Maidstone is the exemplar here. Its Conservative and Unionist Association was constituted on 23 March 1918 responding to the constituency changes resulting from the extension of the franchise. It had a full-time secretary/agent and, the following year, a full-time Women's Organising Secretary. Her efforts bore fruit: there were soon branches of the Women's National Association in thirty parishes and Maidstone set up its own Women's Branch. All this cost money: £885 was budgeted for in 1921 towards which Bellairs' annual subscription of £300 (often quarterly in arrears) made the largest contribution.

In March 1935 a new constitution was adopted. At the apex was the General Council, beneath were various committees, of which the Executive and Finance and General Purposes Committees were the most important. There were separate local branch associations for men and women in each parish in a county polling district, and in each ward in the borough of Maidstone itself. Unlike Labour and the Liberals, subscriptions were voluntary but, to encourage them, all who gave five guineas or more became vice-presidents. All subscribers and branch officers were members of the General Council to which branches sent delegates, one for every 200 electors from the men's, one for every 400 from the women's. As a counterpoint to this differentiation, half the members of the Finance Committee had to be women. Women also had a Central Advisory Committee. By 1937 there were nearly 6,000 female members, among whom the publication *Home and Empire* circulated. The latter theme was also reflected in a thriving Junior Imperial League. Income frequently reached £500 a quarter and when a new agent was appointed in 1936 he could be paid £400 p.a. plus £75 expenses for a car.

This was the sort of organisation to which Kent Liberals after 1918 never, and Labour but rarely, could aspire: a constituency party with a plethora of branches (and clubs) professionally organised and well-financed, though it is worth noting that even Maidstone Conservatives suffered at the outbreak of war

---

34 CKS, Tonbridge Division Liberal Association Minutes (the quotation is from 2 March 1971), U 1702 A 1/1. A 2/1 and A 2/2 contain miscellaneous material including the constitution and membership analysis from which the other quotations are taken.

in 1939 as staff joined up and buildings were requisitioned.[35] Nor was Maidstone necessarily typical. For an interesting insight into the weakness of Conservative organisation at Bromley, a seat so safe before the Second World War that canvassing was deemed unnecessary, Macmillan's comments are illuminating.[36]

As for the Labour Party, the 1918 constitution established the basic structure which operated for the rest of the century. Individual membership was instituted and divisional parties were envisaged with, beneath them, local branches bringing together party members and (this differentiating Labour from the other parties) members of affiliated societies such as the ILP and trade unions. Parties were quickly set up in the industrialised areas, growing out of existing organisations, and even Thanet had a divisional party by May 1919, formed at Ramsgate with branches at Margate and elsewhere.[37] By contrast, at Canterbury Labour's gestation was difficult. The ILP had been active before the First World War, a branch being formed in 1907 with an energetic secretary in Walter Speed who also initiated a branch at Folkestone and, possibly, Whitstable, before transferring his energies to Chatham, whereupon the Canterbury branch promptly collapsed.[38] Another ILP branch appeared in Canterbury in 1920 but that also folded in less than a year.[39] Yet another branch was formed, for on 26 May 1927 it disbanded to reconstitute as the Canterbury and District Labour Party, affiliated to the national body. Local union branches were contacted in a bid to secure their affiliation; some, including miners, railwaymen, carpenters, painters, farm workers and asylum workers from Chartham did so. Feelers were put out in the neighbourhood; there was known to be a branch at Herne Bay, possibly one at Whitstable. The aim was to expand until the formal structure of divisional party with local branches became feasible. The minutes reveal the usual small number of enthusiasts and a by-election in 1927 came too soon for a candidate to be fielded.

This failure stimulated the formation of a Divisional Party in March 1928 by delegates from parties at Canterbury, Herne Bay and Whitstable and from the National Union of Railwaymen (NUR), Carpenters and Painters. Colonel Maurice Spencer, JP, was elected president: there seem to have been ten people present. It appears that a previous divisional party had existed but folded, leaving debts. Attendances were usually under twenty but by March 1929 the party had its own headquarters at 7 Church Street, St Paul's, sometimes referred to as Keir Hardie Hall. (It was destroyed by enemy action in the 1942 blitz.[40]) Elections were fought unsuccessfully: £290 was spent in 1929, £204 in 1931. By 1937 the divisional party was supported by branches at Canterbury, Whitstable,

---

35 Maidstone Conservative and Unionist Association Minute Books, *loc. cit.*
36 Harold Macmillan, *Tides of Fortune, 1945–1955*, London 1969, pp. 285–6.
37 *Kent Messenger*, 30 March 1956.
38 Sadly, Speed died in 1911, aged only twenty-eight, leaving a widow and year-old son.
39 *Labour Leader*, 20 and 27 September 1907, 3 October 1911, 24 June 1920, and 16 March 1921. I am indebted for this information to Fred Whitemore of the School of Politics and International Relations at the University of Kent.
40 *Kent Messenger*, 30 March 1956.

Herne Bay, Littlebourne and Chartham, there was a Women's Section and the Transport Workers, Agricultural Workers, Carpenters, NUR and Railway Clerks were affiliated. Respectability was being attained: both the secretary and treasurer had joined Spencer on the magisterial bench. When one considers that each branch had its own general council, executive committee, women's section and ward committees the impression is gained of a party putting down roots even in unfavourable soil.

Though differences occurred (see, for example, conflicts between workers-by-hand and workers-by-brain at Chatham in the 1930s[41]), Labour's structure proved resilient enough to survive often generations of defeat, aided by two factors: Labour never, unlike the Liberals, succumbed to the Conservative embrace and, secondly, Labour was able to achieve some success in certain areas of local government.[42]

(8) Local Government

There was a whole host of local authorities in twentieth-century Kent, all elected. At the top stood the County Council; beneath were the one county borough, boroughs, Urban District Councils, Rural District Councils and Parish Councils, to say nothing of the Boards of Poor Law Guardians until 1929. In the nineteenth century, party politics had dominated some of the borough councils, Canterbury and Maidstone for instance, but in the early twentieth century passions seem to have cooled and most local bodies were not permeated by politics. Local political leaders often sat upon them by virtue of their prominence in local affairs but even committed partisans would claim that when they entered the council chamber they left their national party allegiances outside. A retiring councillor seeking re-election in Maidstone in 1923 promised 'faithfully [to] serve your interests independent of Party politics which in my opinion in municipal affairs should never exist'. Nor was this simply for public consumption: the minutes of the Conservative Central Committee for Maidstone Borough record on 23 May 1919: 'several members spoke against the introduction of Party politics into local elections' and the Chairman stated that it would not be in the town's interests to oppose an effective councillor 'because of his political bias'.[43]

Increasing Conservative domination as Liberalism declined permitted a continuation of this relaxed attitude and endowed Conservatives and Liberals (and Independents) with a degree of moral superiority when fighting the one party which believed that politics *had* a role to play in local government, namely Labour. The pattern seems to have been that Labour was able to gain a foothold

---

41 Williams, *op. cit.*, pp. 50–1.
42 The minute books of the Canterbury Divisional Labour Party (1928–37) and the Canterbury Branch (1927–30) are in the Centre for Kentish Studies, U 1760 A 1/1, A 2/1.
43 *Kent Messenger*, 20 October 1923; CKS, U 1634 A 3/3/1.

in urban and industrial areas such as Ashford, Maidstone, the Medway Towns, even Thanet, but no more than that. At Maidstone, for example, Labour managed to control North Ward but never had more than four councillors before 1939 (though this was more than the Liberals who declined from six in 1936 to three two years later). Labour was contained as Conservatives, Liberals and Independents ensured that the anti-Labour vote was not split. The lack of bitter party feeling is evidenced by the election of two Labour mayors in the 1930s.[44]

The occasional Labour member was also returned to Kent County Council before 1939. The first was William Ling, a carpenter, who was elected for Erith in 1907. He fell out with his local party and did not stand in 1910, but Labour representation was maintained as Gillingham sent Alf Tapp, a shipwright, to County Hall. Tapp served as a County Councillor for a total of twenty-two years between 1910 and 1938, at a time when the landed interest was still strongly represented on the County Council.[45]

After the Second World War local government became more politicised. In March 1946 Labour increased its representation on the County Council from five to twenty-six, a quarter of the council, a third of the elected representatives (there were seventy-seven councillors and twenty-five aldermen). Most Labour gains were in the urban areas but with even Tenterden and Sevenoaks Rural South falling to 'the Reds' the situation clearly called for desperate measures.

Valuable information on the response to the Labour presence is contained in a collection deposited in the Centre for Kentish Studies. Labour, of course, acted as an organised group or, as the chairman of the Conservative Party on the council put it in his annual report dated 5 October 1949, 'a raucous, confident and very influential element'. The fear was that Labour would be able to exploit the lack of cohesion among the Conservative and Independent members.

The threat was soon countered. On 10 April 1946 a meeting took place of 'ANTI-SOCIALIST MEMBERS' in order 'to protect the interests of Independent Members following the methods employed by the Labour Group at the last meeting of the County Council'. There were twenty-five present, fifteen more supported the meeting but apologised for absence, two declined to attend. A sub-committee was appointed to consider a constitution and name; the first suggestion, 'The KCC Political Emergency Committee', gives a sense of the atmosphere in which they felt they were operating. The title eventually chosen, however, was the Independent Members' Group since it was thought that this would maximise its appeal. The annual subscription was fixed at a guinea, a committee and officers were elected and the chairman and vice-chairman were given power to call a group meeting prior to that of the Council if any item on the agenda seemed to require it. It was also recognised that future action would

---

[44] Clark and Murfin, *op. cit.*, p. 232; *Kent Messenger*, 4 November 1922.
[45] Elizabeth Melling, *History of the Kent County Council, 1889–1974*, Maidstone 1975, p. 163. See also Prudence A. Moylan, *The Form and Reform of County Government, Kent 1889–1914*, Leicester 1978, pp. 42–3. Dr Moylan casts useful light on the early years of the Council and its leading councillors.

largely depend on what Labour did, not that Labour was the title to be accorded to their political opponents: 'it was agreed that in future when referring to the Labour Group it should on all occasions be termed the Socialist Group'.

This was linked to the Independent Group's aim, to oppose socialism, the only issue on which all Independents, inside or outside the group, could agree. This was spelled out in a letter dated 28 June 1946, sent to possible new members. Group membership was said to be forty, of whom fourteen were aldermen. Some thirty council members belonged to no group; if they voted with the socialists, they would prevail. The Independent Group therefore sought a dozen extra members to gain the security of an absolute majority, but in vain. At the Annual General Meeting, on 29 May 1947, there were said to be forty-three members of the group. Nonetheless, the mood was one of self-congratulation. The committee report commented:

> Its success must be measured by the knowledge that the Socialist Party has not diverted by one iota the measured progress of the County Council. . . . On the other hand it should be recognised that the Socialist Party has 'dug itself in' and consolidated the position it won in 1946.

The report went on to point out the importance of the 1949 elections when twelve gains would be enough (aldermen also coming up for election) to give the socialists control of the council and added that the election would be won not in the Council Chamber but in the constituencies. This paved the way for the next dramatic development.

The Conservatives had been active. Independents, both members and non-members of the Group, had been invited to a meeting on 12 March 1947 addressed by Henry Brooke, leader of the Conservative opposition on the London County Council. Brooke

> advised the Kent County Council Conservative and Independent members, who had only recently experienced a Party challenge on the County Council, to heed the experience of London and not to awaken too late to the power of Labour's election-winning machine.

Brooke's seed fell on fertile ground. A debate at the Annual General Meeting mentioned above made it clear that the Independent Group

> neither possessed not could creat [sic], an electioneering machine which could compete with that used on behalf of Labour candidates throughout the County Council elections. Such a machine is however at our service.

That machine was the Conservative Party and the meeting resolved 'that the group allies itself, officially, with the Conservative and Unionist Party and shall henceforth be known as the Conservative Party of the Kent County Council'.

The meeting then adjourned to allow a letter to be sent out on 1 June, over the signature of the Group Secretary, E. S. Oak-Rhind (from which the above quotations are taken) to members asking if they would transfer to the Conservatives:

'It is felt that the decision now taken is the only wise one in the circumstances as the experience gained during the past year show [sic] conclusively that only in this way can we successfully combat socialist domination'.

The adjourned meeting on 25 June ratified the decision and transformed itself into the Conservative Group. There were only fourteen present, with nine apologies. A committee and officers were elected, Sir Henry D'Avigdor-Goldsmid becoming leader. A list exists giving the membership of the Independent Group. Sixteen of the twenty-four Independent councillors joined the Conservatives. Of those giving reasons for not so doing, the most common was election pledges. Of the twelve aldermen, only five transferred: perhaps they felt less need of the election machine.

D'Avigdor-Goldsmid reported to a committee meeting on 17 September 1947 that the party had twenty-eight paid-up members. He tirelessly sought out new recruits and by 4 February 1948 his group stood at thirty-eight, fifteen aldermen and twenty-three councillors, of whom the most socially distinguished was Lady Violet Astor of Hever Castle. Labour numbered twenty-eight (including two aldermen), the Independents eight aldermen and twenty-four Councillors, Lord Northbourne being their aristocratic counter to Lady Violet. Pencilled alterations and deletions hint at the continued seepage of Independents to the Conservatives. D'Avigdor-Goldsmid continued to press as the elections drew nearer, writing to all Independents to enquire under what label they would stand: seven replied Conservative, six Independent, three were standing down, one 'will not state his views', six had not replied. Further pressure was applied to persuade Independents to stand as Conservatives 'as recent elections showed Independents were losing seats when opposed by Conservatives'; 'or Socialists' was subsequently added in pencil.

These tactics bore fruit. By 29 July 1948 a Conservative committee member was able to refer to his party as the Majority Party on the Council. Even so, D'Avigdor-Goldsmid was not satisfied, moaning to a committee on 3 November 1948 about his 'difficulties in regard to Conservatives who still wished to stand as Independents; he felt every endeavour should be made to persuade Members to accept the responsibility of a party vote'. The responsibility of a party vote, indeed! A far cry from the spirit of Independence and an eloquent comment on the extent to which Labour views concerning the role of party on the Council had been accepted.

The Conservatives continued their predecessors' practice of meeting an hour before the Council – indeed it was stated in their constitution that they should do so – to discuss Council business, but within a year they had decided to meet the day before, one hour, presumably, being insufficient for group discussion. Group members were expected to support the recommendations of the party meeting. The Committee was the key body, responsible for policy inside and outside the Council chamber. As early as November 1948 it was engaged in preparing the programme for the 1949 elections.

The policy statement was issued in April 1949:

In 1949 for the first time in its history, the Conservative Party is fighting the County Council elections in Kent; it is doing so in order to preserve the old tradition of independent judgement in local affairs now in danger. Labour spokesmen have declared that it is their object to ensure that Labour representation throughout the county should work as one unit; only by returning Conservative candidates will the Kent electors get the truly local government that they undoubtedly want.

The appeal to 'the old tradition of independent judgement' was, however, somewhat at variance with the role of the party meeting described above.

The policy document went on to make specific commitments in the areas of finance (economy, efficiency, value for money), education (the spirit of the 1944 Act, shhool [sic] health and meals services) and social services (the use of local experience and voluntary effort 'to combat the deadening influence of the remote and bureaucratic control that the Socialists prefer').

It seems that this indeed was what the electors of Kent undoubtedly wanted, for Labour was annihilated at the polls, losing almost three-quarters of its seats, returning only seven candidates. The group leader and secretary were among the casualties. One of only three Labour members of the old council to be returned was, in the words of the *Kent Messenger*, 'Kent's veteran Socialist, the Revd Stanley Morgan, who, with the prescience born of long political experience, resigned his aldermanic seat and stood for his old division'. The Conservatives did not oppose him and Morgan secured victory over an Independent. Another Labour veteran, Basil Noble, who had represented Ashford ever since 1919, chose this election to retire, possibly another example of prescience.

Of the new councillors, fifty-eight were Conservative, nine Independent, seven Labour, and there were three Ratepayers. The Conservatives had gained fifteen seats from Labour and, nominally, fifteen from Independents, but many of these gains were illusory, the same candidates now standing as Tories. What could happen to an Independent who proved obdurate was illustrated at Gravesend East, where the retiring councillor, standing as 'Non Party', came a bad third behind the victorious Conservative and Labour.

Polling was described as unusually heavy, over 50% in some divisions, averaging out at 44%. Only thirty-eight former members came back. The new councillors included ten women. The *Kent Messenger* described the new Conservative group as 'a strong team of many and varied talents and listed two retired major generals, an ex-ambassador (Sir Hughe Knatchbull-Hugesson), two retired brigadiers, a retired wing-commander, four retired majors, two solicitors, a doctor, a surveyor and an undertaker. The funeral was undoubtedly Labour's.

The Conservative chairman's annual report, on 5 October 1949, was understandably euphoric. Including aldermen, the party now numbered seventy-eight.

Last year we were a minority of elected members and our task was to protect against the inroads of the Labour party. . . . Today we are in an overwhelming majority and great possibilities of constructive activity lie before us.

Generous tribute was paid to the old independent members' group, 'the chrysalis from which the Conservative party on the Council emerged'.

In the heady aftermath of victory the Conservatives were initially disposed to generosity. The party meeting on 13 April 1949 included Morgan on the list of nominations to the aldermanic bench. Second thoughts soon set in, however, and at the next meeting, on 4 May, despite a Churchillian appeal by the chairman, 'in victory magnanimity', by a large majority Morgan's name was deleted and replaced with that of a Conservative.

In keeping with the national trend, the pendulum swung back to Labour in 1952: they gained sixteen seats from the Conservatives and seven from Independents to bring their total number of councillors to twenty-nine, three more than in 1946. Unlike 1946, however, they were outnumbered by forty-three Conservative councillors who, with their aldermen, formed a disciplined and controlling group. The once-dominant Independents now had a mere five councillors. Nevertheless, D'Avigdor-Goldsmid was clearly surprised: 'the extent of the Socialist reaction has come as a shock', and he went on to refer to 'the restoration of an effective socialist party to the Council'. However, three years later, again in keeping with the national trend, the pendulum swung once more. In a council expanded to 106 members, of the eighty councillors, exactly three-quarters (sixty) were Conservative, Labour had seventeen, Independents three.[46]

The same politicising process seems to have occurred in at least the larger second-tier local authorities. We have already noted Liberal efforts at Orpington from the mid-1950s to build a presence on the local council, to strengthen party support and facilitate a bid for the parliamentary seat, and the trend for an increasing number of future MPs to find in the local council chamber a training school and power-base on the road to Westminster. Another modern process began soon after the war: punishing an unpopular government by rejecting its local councillors. Thus, at Maidstone in 1947 all the Labour candidates were defeated, even in North Ward, the first time it had fallen in twenty years. The same thing happened on the County Council in 1949 (as noted above) and in 1967, when the Conservatives reduced Labour to a mere two councillors (plus three aldermen); all the rest were Tory.[47]

Generally in the boroughs Conservatives and Independents remained in control, though there were exceptions, one being Canterbury where, as a result of a well-organised campaign mobilising council-house tenants and students at

---

[46] Conservative Papers (from which, unless otherwise stated, the quotations are taken), CKS, U 2805 A 1 (Independent Members Group KCC Letters, 1946–9), A 2 (Minute Book, 1947–9), A 3 (Conservative Party Kent County Council, 1949–52); *The Times*, 5 and 6 March 1946, 11 and 12 April 1949, 7, 8 and 12 April 1952, 25 April 1955; *Kent Messenger*, 14 April 1949. There is a sympathetic and balanced entry on D'Avigdor-Goldsmid in the *Dictionary of National Biography, 1971–80* (edited by Lord Blake and C.S. Nicholls), Oxford 1986, by a fellow member of the Jewish community, Keith Joseph, who refers to his subject's 'swift changes of mood: he could be impatient, he could not tolerate fools, he was easily bored' (p. 218). He later served as Conservative MP for Walsall South from 1955 to February 1974. His father, the first baronet, was also a member of Kent County Council, from 1910 to 1936: Melling, *op. cit.*, pp. 152, 159.

[47] Clark and Murfin, *op. cit.*, p. 232; Press Cuttings, CKS, U 1702 A 2/2.

the newly founded University of Kent, Labour gained control in 1972. The last twenty-two months of the old cathedral city's independent existence were thus spent under a Labour council, its last mayor being Labour for the one and only time. In 1974, with the expansion of the council's area, the Conservative eighth cavalry rode in from Herne Bay, Whitstable and the villages to put an end to the socialist experiment.

The expansion was part of a national reorganisation of local government which greatly reduced the number of authorities and thereby greatly simplified the task of the historian (though this was probably not among its objectives). At the bottom, parish councils remained but they were hardly ever politicised. Kent County Council remained at the top with beneath it fourteen second-tier district councils. Aldermen were abolished; all councillors were elected. District councils could choose to have roughly one-third of their members elected annually, but in Kent most of the districts elected the whole body every four years, and the County Council was elected in the same manner.

Conservative dominance was initially overwhelming. They took the County Council in 1973, with sixty-three seats to thirty-one Labour, seven Liberals and two Independents.[48] They controlled most of the district authorities, the sole exception being Labour Dartford, and even this had fallen by 1983. The only blot now on the Tory escutcheon was Maidstone which – and this was a harbinger of future change – because of increasing Liberal strength, was generally under no overall control. Where Maidstone led, Gillingham, Gravesham and Swale soon followed. The process was facilitated by two factors, the eventual emergence in 1988 of the Liberal Democrats after the messy demise of the SDP–Liberal Alliance and the introduction of the poll tax in 1990 to replace domestic rates as a major source of local-government finance. The consequences were seen in Kent in 1991 when Canterbury, Dover and Rochester joined the no-overall-control camp and Shepway gave the Liberal Democrats their first major Kent council. The Conservatives now controlled fewer than half of Kent's district authorities. This did not, however, prevent them from sweeping to power in Kent's constituencies at the general election barely more than a year later.

(9) Conservative Armageddon, 1992–7

The Conservatives soon ran into trouble after their surprise victory in 1992. On 16 September that year the government was forced, humiliatingly, to withdraw Britain from the European Exchange Rate Mechanism. Its prestige never recovered. Europe remained a constant source of division in the party and, indeed, in the Cabinet, leading to the prime minister, John Major, appearing a weak and ineffectual leader. Furthermore, having won the election by implying that they

---

[48] *The Times*, 13 April 1973.

would not increase taxes, the state of public finances led the government to backtrack, imposing VAT on domestic fuel, for example. The mishandling of the crisis associated with BSE in cattle was another blow as were a whole series of 'sleaze' cases, two of which involved 'Greater Kent' MPs. Jonathan Aitken resigned from the Cabinet to fight a libel case against *The Guardian*, which he subsequently dropped, leading to a charge of perjury, to which he eventually pleaded guilty. Piers Merchant (Beckenham) was revealed in the *Sun* as having an affair with 'a teenage night-club hostess'.[49] Meanwhile Tony Blair, who became Labour leader following John Smith's untimely death in 1994, set about modernising his party, employing sophisticated presentational techniques to project the image of 'New Labour'.

In Kent, as elsewhere, Conservative difficulties were soon highlighted in local-government elections. In May 1993 'a century of unbroken Tory rule in Kent came to a dramatic end when they lost overall control of the Garden of England', i.e. the County Council.[50] This was the culmination of a process going back to 1985 and 1989, the Conservative majority having been reduced in each of these years. One of the fourteen seats lost this time was Tunbridge Wells Central, a Tory stronghold ever since 1889, which returned a Liberal Democrat with a comfortable majority. This was a hint of things to come: the following year in the district council elections, the Conservatives appeared to lose Tunbridge Wells itself; in fact they were able to retain control on the mayor's casting vote.

Another form of local election took place in June 1994, that for seats in the European Parliament; it produced another first as the Conservatives lost Kent's two seats. The beneficiary was Labour, the first indicator that they rather than the Liberal Democrats would provide the main challenge to the Tories in the future. Admittedly turnout was low as usual in non-parliamentary elections, 40.3% in East Kent, 37.3% in West, and Labour majorities were not large, but the message was clear, for the Liberal Democrats as well as the Conservatives, as shown in Table 34.[51]

Table 34

Kent Euro-Election, 1994: Major Parties' Share of the Vote.

	Labour	Conservative	Liberal Democrat
East Kent	34.4%	34.2%	22.1%
West Kent	41.0%	32.1%	17.9%

[49] For Aitken and Merchant, see David Butler and Dennis Kavanagh, *The British General Election of 1997*, London 1997, pp. 15–16, 96 (from which the quotation is taken).
[50] *The Times*, 7 May 1993.
[51] *Ibid.*, 14 June 1994.

May 1995 marked Kent Conservatism's *annus horribilis*. This was a year when all the district councils saw elections (only Gillingham, Maidstone, Swale and Tunbridge Wells chose a proportion of their councillors annually). When the votes were counted, the Conservatives controlled not a single Kent district council. This time there was no reprieve for Tunbridge Wells. By contrast Labour controlled five: Dartford (gained from the Conservatives), Dover, Rochester, Thanet (gained from no overall control) and Gravesham (held). The Liberal Democrats gained Gillingham from no overall control but lost Shepway to it. The rest were no overall control. Table 35 gives a detailed breakdown of the composition of these councils.

Table 35

Composition of Kent District Councils after the Elections of May 1995

	Con	Lab	Lib Dem	Ind	Other
Ashford	18	13	15	1	2
Canterbury	10	15	24		
Dartford	10	36		1	
Dover	13	39	4		
Gillingham	8	9	24	1	
Gravesham	10	34			
Maidstone	17	15	17	5	1
Rochester-upon-Medway	1	44	5		
Sevenoaks	17	11	20	5	
Shepway	19	13	21	3	
Swale	14	14	20	1	
Thanet	3	45	4	2	
Tonbridge and Malling	23	11	21		
Tunbridge Wells	19	5	23	1	
Kent total	182	304	198	20	3

Perhaps an even more astonishing statistic than who controlled (or did not control) the councils is this: only at Ashford and Tonbridge and Malling did the Conservatives form the largest single group. At Rochester, where they lost twenty-one seats, and Thanet, where they lost twenty-three (Labour gained thirty-one, Independents being the other principal sufferers), the Tories were almost wiped out. The Liberal Democrats now had more Kent councillors than the Conservatives, even though they had none at all at Dartford or Gravesham. That once popular breed, the Independent, still maintained a modest presence on all but five councils.

1995 was Kent Conservatism's Armageddon. It was part of a national phenomenon and was clearly directed against the government, as local Tory leaders were quick to point out. Nationally it was a foretaste of what was to come in 1997. It says a lot for Kent Conservatism's strength that 1997 represented something of a recovery even though in the intervening year they suffered the final indignities of seeing the Liberal Democrats take control of Tunbridge Wells, sinking to third place at Maidstone (Lib. Dem. 21; Lab. 18; Con. 11; Ind. 5) and being reduced to two councillors at Gillingham.[52]

There were considerable changes to constituency boundaries to correct the imbalances in size which had emerged by 1992. Chatham was allied with Aylesford, Maidstone with The Weald; Faversham lost its historic links with Sittingbourne and Sheppey (which became a separate constituency), and was joined with Mid-Kent. The county thus returned seventeen MPs, but the gain of one here was balanced by the loss of one in KGL. Here Erith was divorced from Crayford (which was lumped in with Bexleyheath) and wedded to Thamesmead, an event so seismic in its implications that this new constituency would probably have gone Labour in 1992: Erith and Thamesmead was thus classified as 'Labour hold' in 1997. Ravensbourne disappeared into a resurgent Bromley and Chislehurst; Beckenham, Old Bexley and Sidcup, and Orpington survived on roughly similar boundaries.

Nationally 1997 was a Conservative disaster: according to some commentators their worst defeat since 1832. Even their grip on Kent was shaken; shaken, but not broken. Eight seats were lost, all to Labour, forming a compact group in the industrial areas along the Thames and Medway: Dartford, Gravesham, Medway, Gillingham, Chatham and Aylesford, Sittingbourne and Sheppey, plus, on the coast, Dover and Thanet South. There were some notable casualties. Sir Roger Moate had drawn the short straw of Sittingbourne and Sheppey when the Faversham spoils were divided, and was beaten, thus ending twenty-seven years in the House. Dame Peggy Fenner's chequered career at Chatham and Medway took a turn for the worse: first elected in 1970, defeated in October 1974, bouncing back in 1979, she suffered a second defeat in 1997. Robert Dunn lost Dartford after eighteen years there; Jonathan Aitken had been at Thanet South even longer, ever since the constituency had been created (as Thanet East) in February 1974. Scandal may have played a part here but it is worth noting that the swing against Aitken at 15.0% was not that much greater than the 14.1% swing in Thanet North where Roger Gale managed to ride out the storm. In defeating Aitken, Stephen Ladyman became the first non-Conservative (and of course the first Labour) MP ever elected for Thanet.

It was a great result for Labour, recalling the heady days of 1945 when they had also taken eight Kent seats to the Conservatives' nine. In addition to seats won, Labour overtook the Liberal Democrats to take second place in Ashford, Canterbury, Maidstone, Sevenoaks and Tonbridge. But a word of caution is required: Labour majorities were quite small, often just two or three thousand. Only Gwyn Prosser at Dover had over 10,000, only Chris Pond at Gravesham

---

52 *Ibid.*, 7 and 8 May 1993, 6 and 7 May 1994, 5 and 6 May 1995, and 3 May 1996.

and Robert Marshall-Andrews at Medway over 5,000. This helps to explain why, unlike 1945, the Conservatives (346,885) outpolled Labour (317,762) in aggregate Kent votes. The Liberal Democrats polled 145,896 votes. A related point is that only at Canterbury, Faversham and Thanet North did Labour get within 5,000 votes of the victorious Conservatives.

For the Liberal Democrats nationally, 1997 was their best result since 1929: Kent, however, remained a wasteland. Only at Folkestone and Tunbridge Wells did they retain second place and in neither case were they anywhere near victory.

As for Kent Conservatives, 1997 was, of course, a terrible defeat, but there were bright spots. Michael Howard retained Folkestone with a majority of over 6,000, and limited the swing against him (to the Liberal Democrats) to a mere 2.4%. His future sparring partner, Ann Widdecombe at Maidstone, had a majority approaching 10,000, the swing to Labour being 12.9%, at the lower end of the range. In these seats and at Canterbury, Sevenoaks and, to a lesser degree, Tonbridge and Tunbridge Wells, anti-Conservatives were unsure as to whether Labour or the Liberal Democrats had the better chance of beating the Tories; elsewhere the Liberal Democrat vote collapsed as Labour were perceived to be stronger. The danger for the Conservatives next time was that if voters remained unimpressed with them, they would have the result of 1997 to indicate which was the leading challenger. No Conservative MP secured 50% of the vote (in fact only Prosser at Dover achieved this for Labour). Only Sir John Stanley at Tonbridge polled more than the combined Labour and Liberal Democrat vote.

A general point to note was that turnout was in the range 71–76%, save at Dover (78.9%), Gravesham (76.9%) and Thanet North (68.8%), markedly down on 1992.[53] The swing from Conservative to Labour ranged from 10.0% at Gravesham to 16.0% at Gillingham. With Dame Peggy Fenner's defeat, Ann Widdecombe was left as Kent's only woman MP. This was not surprising; of the fifty-one candidates put up by the three major parties a mere nine were women. Only Cheryl Hall (Canterbury) and Iris Johnston (Thanet North), both Labour, came anywhere near joining Miss Widdecombe at Westminster.

Turning to KGL, Labour duly held Erith and Thamesmead and captured its neighbour, Conservative Bexleyheath being dragged down by Labour Crayford. Further from the Thames the Conservatives held on to Beckenham, Bromley and Chislehurst, Orpington, and Old Bexley and Sidcup where Sir Edward Heath won his fourteenth consecutive victory, though with his smallest majority since 1966. Only at Bromley did the Conservative majority exceed 10,000, and even here it was less than the combined Labour and Liberal Democrat vote. The other Conservative majorities were fewer than 5,000. At Erith and Thamesmead Labour received over two-thirds of the poll. The Liberal Democrats came third everywhere save at Orpington where they came within 3,000 votes of winning.

---

[53] Turnout across the United Kingdom as a whole was the lowest since 1945: Butler and Kavanagh, *1997*, p. 295.

Turnout ranged from 74.2 to 76.4% except at Erith (66.1%), again down on 1992. Swings from Conservative to Labour ranged from 11.8% at Bromley to 15.3% at Erith and Thamesmead. The 15.0% against the scandal-engulfed Piers Merchant at Beckenham was not markedly out of line. Women were, in the main, notable by their absence, though after Merchant resigned, following renewed allegations about his private life, Jacqui Lait, late MP for Hastings and Rye, held the seat for the Conservatives at the subsequent by-election.

The Nuffield Election Study applied certain economic criteria to the various constituencies. In Kent the clearest correlation with Conservative/Labour victories lay with the proportion of the population who were employers and managers: Thanet North was the only Conservative seat where this fell below 16%; in no Labour seat did it reach that figure. On the criterion of high income (£25,000 p.a. for a household), not surprisingly Conservative seats had the highest proportions, only Ashford, Folkestone and Thanet North falling below 25%, only Dartford among Labour seats attaining that level. As for unemployment, this was normally highest in Labour territory but was highest of all in Folkestone, where Michael Howard did well, comparatively speaking, and Thanet North, both 5.1%; Dover and Thanet South came next at 4.9%.[54] Similar patterns prevailed in KGL: the proportion of employers and managers was 18% and over in Conservative seats, 16.1% in Bexleyheath and Crayford, only 11.6% in Erith and Thamesmead. Perfect correlation occurred again for high income, no Conservative seat falling below 28%, and neither Labour seat at that level, with Erith and Thamesemead as low as 18.4%. As far as unemployment was concerned, Conservative Beckenham's 3.8% was higher than that in Labour Bexleyheath and Crayford but still well short of the 7.5% in Erith and Thamesmead.[55]

(10) Whither Now?

Does 1997 represent the beginning of the end of the Conservative domination of Kent politics which has lasted for a century and a quarter? It seems reasonable to think that some of the pillars on which Conservative support was based at the beginning of the century are no longer so sound. But the Conservatives have a remarkable capacity to reinvent themselves. As Union with Ireland and Empire faded into the background and the landed interest became less significant, they presented themselves as the party of low taxation and prosperity, prosperity attributed to private enterprise and freedom from controls. For a largely prosperous county like Kent this has proved very congenial. It may well be that 1997, like 1906 and 1945 before it, will be a mere blip. Indeed there are already signs of Conservative recovery. On the same day in 1997 that they suffered

---

[54] These figures represent the registered unemployed in March 1997 as a proportion of the electorate.
[55] Butler and Kavanagh, *1997*, pp. 260, 266, 272–3. Otherwise, the electoral statistics are taken from *The Guardian*, 3 May 1997.

national humiliation, they regained control of Kent County Council. Their hold on it was inevitably strengthened by the departure of the Medway Towns to form its own unitary authority. In 1998 they recaptured Tunbridge Wells and in May 1999 they added to it Sevenoaks and Shepway and became the largest party on three of the six councils where there was no overall control (Ashford, Canterbury, and Tonbridge and Malling) They now returned more Kent district councillors than either of the other two parties. But it was an essentially modest recovery. Control of a mere quarter of Kent district councils (Gillingham and Rochester had been subsumed into the new Medway unitary authority which did not poll in 1999) was a far cry from the almost total dominance of less than twenty years earlier. They controlled no more councils than Labour (Dartford, Gravesham and Thanet). Labour satisfaction at a reasonable performance two years into the new government's term of office was, however, tempered by the loss of Dover to no overall control, and this might bode ill for the local Labour MP. As for the Liberal Democrats, they performed poorly, though less so than in some parts of southern England. They controlled not a single Kent district council, though they were the largest single party on two (Maidstone and Swale). By contrast they were completely unrepresented on three (Dartford, Gravesham and Thanet), had only one-quarter of the councillors at Tunbridge Wells, which they had controlled from 1996 to 1998, and fewer than one-quarter at Shepway, which they had likewise controlled as recently as 1995.[56] The details are given in Table 36.

Table 36

Composition of Kent District Councils after the Elections of May 1999

	Con	Lab	Lib Dem	Ind	Other
Ashford	24	11	10	4	
Canterbury	18	14	17		
Dartford	14	28		1	4
Dover	26	28	1	1	
Gravesham	15	29			
Maidstone	15	13	22	5	
Sevenoaks	33	9	9	2	
Shepway	30	13	13		
Swale	9	17	23		
Thanet	16	35		3	
Tonbridge and Malling	27	7	21		
Tunbridge Wells	28	7	12	1	
Kent Total	255	211	128	17	4

[56] *Ibid.*, 9 May 1998 and 8 May 1999.

Liberal Democrat weakness may work to Conservative advantage at the next general election, and, as memories of sleaze and arrogance dim and New Labour runs into difficulties, some Tory recovery at constituency level seems likely. The one danger on the horizon is Europe: if their traditional business supporters deem further integration necessary to ensure future prosperity, this may conflict with Conservative nationalism and enable New Labour, and indeed the Liberal Democrats, to appear the safer option. Yet it is not beyond the bounds of possibility that Europe may work to the Conservatives' advantage. Benefiting from popular hostility to replacing the pound with the Euro, they performed well in the final major test of electoral opinion in this century, the elections for the European Parliament held in June 1999. Given the poor turnout – fewer than one voter in four bothered to go to the polls in the south-east, as in England as a whole – the political century may be said to have ended not with a bang but with a whimper. That did not trouble the Conservatives; for them it was the return of the good old days as the map of Kent turned into an unbroken sea of blue with their 'recapture' of the eight constituencies lost to Labour in 1997.

One aspect of these elections may be a pointer to the future rather than a reversion to the past. For the first time a system of proportional representation was employed. As a consequence, Kent was subsumed into a vast South-East England European Parliamentary Electoral Region ranging from Thanet to beyond the Isle of Wight before sweeping north as far as Oxfordshire, running in an arc around Greater London. The Conservatives won it easily with 44.4% of the vote. Labour took 19.6%, the Liberal Democrats 15.3%, the United Kingdom Independence Party 9.7%, and the Greens 7.4%, the rest being shared among a number of minor parties. This translated into five seats for the Conservatives, two each for Labour and the Liberal Democrats, one each for the UK Independence Party and the Greens.[57] If proportional representation is indeed to be the system for the new millennium, it means that the Conservatives will be unable ever again to enjoy the almost total dominance they achieved over Kent politics for much of the twentieth century. However, the Conservatives will have at least three chances in the new millennium to benefit from the first-past-the-post system which has served them so well in the past: it has already been decided that the existing parliamentary voting system will be retained for the next parliamentary election, and it is almost certain that there will be no changes to the voting system for local elections before the next set of elections for Kent County Council in 2001 and the non-unitary district elections throughout Kent in 2003.

[57] *The Times*, 15 June 1999.

6

Housing

MICHAEL RAWCLIFFE

The development of housing in both Kent and England and Wales in the twentieth century has been much affected by the two World Wars. The First World War accelerated the search for solutions to already emerging and well-documented problems, the Second resulted in much war damage precipitating an increased housing shortage after six years of virtually no building. War has been said to be the accelerator of social change and certainly the respective post-war governments came increasingly to involve the state in social problems and their resolution. 'Homes fit for Heroes' was both a political initiative and a response to the rising expectations of the people as well as a desire not to return to the poverty of the Victorian and Edwardian world. Equally the consensus after the Second World War had a similar determination not to go back to the past.

From the latter part of the nineteenth century overcrowding and the housing of the working classes had become a political issue, and the 1891 and 1901 censuses added new questions for families occupying fewer than five rooms. Overcrowding in the 1911 census was defined as two or more persons per room. In 1961 this was decreased to 1½ and in the 1981 census to one person per room, reflecting the increasing standard of living.

Whilst the overall improvement is clear one must bear in mind throughout this discussion definitions of what constitutes a family, a household and a dwelling, and the accuracy of the actual returns. Whitehead warns us that as late as 1981, a post-enumeration survey revealed that 28.6% of households gave the number of inhabited rooms incorrectly.[1]

The most important aspect of the relationship between population and housing is that between the housing stock and the number of families to be housed. In contrast to the population boom of the nineteenth century the period since 1914 has seen a much reduced birth rate. In addition the death rate has not returned to its earlier high levels. Thus there was a lower rate of natural increase in both Wales and England, including Kent. Population, then, is clearly a major

---

[1] F. Whitehead, 'The GRO Use of Social Surveys', *Population Trends*, xlviii (1987), pp. 46–57; quoted in E. Higgs, *A Clearer Sense of the Census*, PRO Handbooks, no. 28, London 1996, p. 26.

factor affecting housing, but in a county as large and diverse as Kent, internal migration has also played its part, leading to commensurate building growth in north-west Kent and the Medway towns in particular.

However, there are important social trends which have brought pressures on the housing market. These relate to the nature of the family itself. First families have become smaller. The one- or two-child family is now more common than the earlier three-child or more. Also there are fewer families where three generations live together. In an ageing population, more pensioners live together or singly, often occupying the house in which they brought up their children. In addition the increase in divorce rates has split households and an increase in one-parent families amongst the divorced and in single-parent families has led to further pressure on housing. The housing stock is rarely suitable for the changing needs of society.

In 1921 the phrase 'structurally separate dwelling' was introduced, being defined as 'any set of rooms having separate access either to a street or to a common landing or staircase accessible to visitors'.[2] This meant that a large house-conversion into flats would contain several separate dwellings, whereas an undivided large house in multiple occupancy would not. In Kent in 1921 there were 233,707 separate dwellings. Whilst this was an increase of 8% over 1911, the number of private families was 252,936, though many of these might comprise only a single lodger. Allowing for the 7,530 dwellings vacant, there still remained a deficit of 950. Significantly the largest increase had been in families of two, three and four, which now represented 63.8% of the whole, nearly 5% more than in 1911. The average rooms per family in 1921 in Kent was 5.6, and all save 6.8% of families in Kent occupied a two- or more bedroomed dwelling with one or two living rooms and a kitchen.[3] By the prevailing standard for overcrowding in 1921, there were considerable regional variations in Kent, as shown in Table 37. The majority of dwellings in Kent were individual private houses, but the size varied considerably between areas.

Table 38 brings out the type of housing predominant in selected areas of north-west Kent, north Kent and the coastal resorts. Beckenham, Bromley and Chislehurst had developed as prosperous suburbs in the late Victorian period, and a significant part of the development was of large detached houses which could accommodate both family and domestic servants. Conversely, Crayford and Dartford contained a majority of four- or five-roomed dwellings. These were likely to be terraced houses containing two bedrooms, a kitchen and living room. Many were built for Thameside industrial workers. Another feature was that the other areas which contained many-roomed, larger houses were in the coastal resorts, which also contained the greater range of housing.

It was the Victorian suburbs of north-west Kent and the seaside resorts which had the highest number of rooms per dwelling. Beckenham UD had 6.8, and

---

2   *Census of England and Wales 1921: County of Kent*, London 1923, p. xii.
3   *Ibid.*, p. xiv.

Table 37

Overcrowding in Private Families in North Kent, 1911–21

	1911 (%)	1921 (%)
Bexley UD	3.7	7.3
Cheriton UD	9.6	6.5
Crayford UD	*	8.9
Dartford RD	*	7.8
Erith UD	5.5	8.8
Hoo RD	6.0	8.4
Northfleet UD	7.4	8.5
Penge UD	5.2	6.8
Strood RD	4.7	6.1

* Boundary changes. Details not available.

Table 38

Housing According to Rooms per Dwelling in Selected Areas of Kent, 1921

| | Number of rooms | | |
Area	4–5 (%)	6–8 (%)	9 and over (%)
Beckenham UD*	28.5	46.6	23.0
Bexley UD	63.3	27.4	–
Bromley MB	47.9	33.7	15.6
Chatham MB	58.8	37.3	–
Chislehurst UD	49.9	33.0	14.4
Crayford UD*	83.2	11.0	–
Dartford MB*	71.2	21.7	–
Erith UD	57.7	36.8	–
Folkestone MB	34.6	43.0	19.8
Herne Bay UD	20.3	62.5	14.9
Hythe MB	46.0	36.8	12.6
Maidstone MB	63.5	27.5	–

* Ten years later, in 1931, Sandgate and Beckenham UDs had the highest average rooms per dwelling in Kent, whilst Crayford UD (4.8), Swanscombe UD (4.9) and Dartford MB (4.9) had the lowest.

Herne Bay UD, Penge UD, Sandgate UD and Sidcup UD all had 6.6. With the exception of Penge UD, these areas have retained their character. Penge, adjoining London, had many of the capital's characteristics. With the railway it had developed as a suburb, but by 1921, although it had many large houses, originally built to accommodate single families, only 49.2% of families were in individual occupation of separate dwellings. On average there were 1.4 families per dwelling. Many new migrants were moving from London into Penge and so there was pressure upon housing exacerbated by many large houses, and increasingly smaller families, without domestic servants. To meet their needs Penge had 12% of its housing in either flats or tenements. This contrasts with the county average of 1%.[4]

In 1921 91% of the houses in Kent were privately owned, either by owner-occupiers or by mortgagees. This compared with a figure of 77% in Penge. Crayford, with a larger percentage of smaller houses, had a larger percentage of privately owned houses (96%). Crayford also had the lowest average of rooms per person at 0.99.

The 1931 census reflects the growth of house-building since 1921, stimulated by the subsidies given to builders by the 1919 Housing Additional Powers Act and the 1923 and 1924 Housing Acts. The Housing Act of 1919 led to a rise in the number of council houses built by local authorities. In Maidstone, council houses were built in the outskirts of the town, and by 1929 a thousand had been built on five sites. After the 1923 and 1924 Housing Acts, minimum building standards were lowered, and houses became smaller. For a brief period, houses on the Coombe Farm Estate in Maidstone were built without bathrooms. This practice was outlawed in 1925. The level of rents was a continuing problem to the tenants. In 1928 they were lowered to between 8s. 9d. and 12s. 3d. per week, including rates, to try to forestall tenants who were taking in illegal lodgers.[5]

In spite of a 23.9% increase in structurally separate dwellings in the county between 1921 and 1931, and a 57.8% increase in vacant ones, the gain was offset by a 22.6% increase in the number of private families, whilst the population within private families had only increased by 9%. Family size in Kent had fallen from 4.1 to 3.6 by 1931, an 11% reduction. The effect of the declining birth rate was reflected in a fall of 9.3% in the number of families of five and over. Conversely, between 1911 and 1931 there had been a growth in three-person families from 37.2% to 40.1% in 1921 and to 48.1% in 1931. This had an effect upon housing as larger families are easier to house.

Between 1921 and 1931 the population of the county rose by 6.8% (natural increase 5.1%, migration 1.7%). Not all areas increased uniformly. For example, whilst all areas expanded their housing stock, north-west Kent and the Thameside area saw the greatest increase. Bexley and Sidcup saw rises of 85% and 67%. Bromley RD saw the greatest increase of 86%. Houses were built in rural areas accessible to rail communication to London, though more remote areas within Bromley RD such as Downe still only had a density of 0.43 per acre.

So whilst the rate of house-building was impressive, reductions in the size of the family and the increase in the number of private families meant that overcrowding remained constant at 1.6% in the county between 1921 and 1931. In suburban Bromley MB we see the following in 1931:

4　*Ibid.*, Table 10, p. 19.
5　P. Clark and L. Murfin, *The History of Maidstone*, Stroud 1995, p. 224.

Plate 28. Aerial view of Downham Estate on the boundaries of Bromley and Lewisham, c.1925–30.

Plate 29. Aerial view of Shepway Estate, Maidstone (© Aerofilms Ltd).

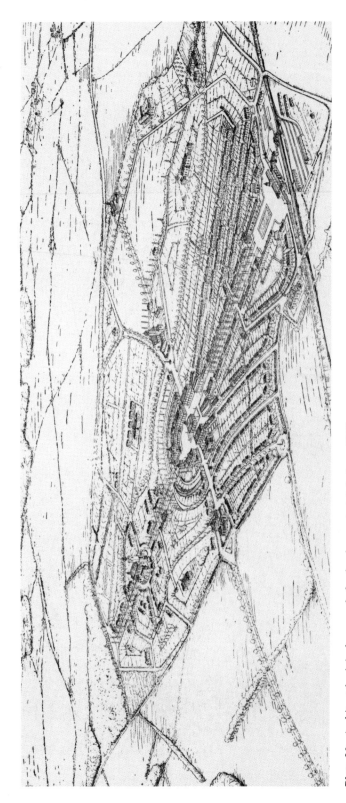

Plate 30. Architects' original proposals for development at Aylesham, 1943.

Plate 31. Building plots at Kings Road, Biggin Hill, 1925.

Plate 32. Bombed properties in St John's Lane, Ashford, 1943.

Increase of 3,364 in occupied dwellings   45.5%
Increase of 3,557 in private families   42.4%
Increase of 198 in unoccupied dwellings   1.8%[6]

Thus, in spite of the increase in house-building, the decreasing size of the family unit and the number of new migrants meant that the overall provision was scarcely above demand, in spite of 3,364 new dwellings.

Between 1919 and 1939 3,998,000 houses were built in England and Wales. Burnett[7] has estimated that by 1939 one-third of all houses were new, and that another third were old, basic by-law housing, and a further third were sub-standard slum dwellings. By far the greater part of the new houses had been built by the private sector, of which nearly 10% had received grants towards building.

During the Second World War little or no building took place and many areas were subject to German bombing. The damage was not evenly spread but Kent suffered more than most. Thameside Kent, the Medway towns, north-west suburban Kent, the coastal resorts, and Canterbury and Maidstone all suffered heavily in damage to property and also loss of life. Equally areas around the many airfields and military bases were also affected.

Consequently the 1951 census incorporates a twenty-year period in which 1931–39 had seen substantial building and 1939–45 one when the housing stock had been diminished through war damage and during which no new residential building had taken place. The 1945 election saw the return of a Labour government which pledged itself to reconstruction and which was committed to a philosophy of planning. Nevertheless the 54.3% increase in dwellings between 1931 and 1951 was largely achieved before 1939.[8] In Kent, as elsewhere, the demand for large Victorian and Edwardian properties for family use continued to fall. The diminution in the size of families and the dramatic fall in the number of domestic servants allied with economic pressures led to many of them being converted into flats. Thus we see a fall in the relative number of dwellings with six rooms or more from 40% in 1921, to 36% in 1931, and to 22% in 1951.[9] Two-thirds of Kent's houses now contained four or five rooms and reflected the building of two- or three-bedroomed houses. The three-bedroomed houses now comprised 44% of Kent's housing stock, an increase of 11% since 1931. Significantly whilst there was a rise from 7% to 10% between 1931 and 1951 in one- to three-roomed dwellings it was probably accounted for by flats. By contrast the London County Council area saw an increase from 18% to 32% during the same period.

As we have noted, the number of dwellings in Kent had increased by 54.3% between 1931 and 1951 but the number of households had also increased by

6   *Census of England and Wales 1931: County of Kent*, London 1933, Table VII, p. xvi.
7   J. Burnett, *A Social History of Housing, 1815–1985*, 2nd edn, London 1986, p. 226.
8   *Census of England and Wales 1951: County of Kent*, London 1954, p. xviii. Dwellings in Kent occupied by private households were 459,622 in 1951, an increase of 161,792 over 1931.
9   *Ibid.*, Table B, p. xix.

51.3% so building seemed to be keeping pace with need. However, by 1951 96% of dwellings were occupied by one household only, and the number in each household had continued to fall from 3.64 in 1931 to 3.16 in 1951. The population in private households only rose by 31.5%, with its implications for housing. Now nearly 40% of households comprised one to two persons. By 1951 there were more than twice the number of one-person households as in 1931 and nearly twice as many two-person households.[10]

The post-war housing crisis can be illustrated by Maidstone. Clark notes that in spite of post-war council building, Maidstone in September 1951 still had 2,083 people on the housing list and 176 pensioners waiting for old-people's flats. By 1961 2,049 houses had been built on the post-war estate of Shepway which had a population of 15,337.[11]

(1) The Quality of Housing

Overcrowding, defined as two persons or more per room, in Kent continued to fall between 1931 and 1951 from 1.6% to 1.1%. However, the 1951 census for the first time asked questions about the single or shared use of five essential household facilities. The questions asked posed problems about exactly what was meant by the term 'shared', but the trends were clear and they give a good indication of those areas of Kent which were without one or more of the basic facilities. These five questions were about a fixed bath, piped water, cooking stove, kitchen sink and a water closet.

The lack of certain facilities in Kent between the Wars is illustrated by the following brief oral-history extracts:

> I lived in Wouldham in the 1930s. There was no electricity in the Village so we used lamps and candles. Lavatories were sited at the bottom of the garden and buckets were emptied at midnight by a man with a horse and cart.[12]

> I was born in Gravesend in 1919 . . . in a three-storey house at the end of a terrace of six, with gas lighting on the two lower floors but oil lamps or candles for the bedrooms.[13]

> We lived in an old Elizabethan house in Wye which was a jumble of rooms, passages and inside steps. A pump in the scullery gave a water supply and lighting was by candle or oil lamp. The only lavatory was about thirty yards up the garden, and with no flushing. We had a bucket of soil in order to add some after every major use.[14]

---

[10] *Ibid.*, p. xxi.
[11] Clark and Murfin, *op. cit.*, p. 246.
[12] *West Kent within Living Memory*, Newbury 1995, p. 64.
[13] *Ibid.*, p. 15.
[14] *East Kent within Living Memory*, Newbury 1993, p. 46.

John Edwin Smith who lived in a new council house on the Downham Estate recalls

> We were allowed one bath a week . . . the bath was upstairs and we would have to pump up the hot water from the coal fired copper in the kitchen. . . . Each pump would send up about two cup-fulls of water so by the time the bath was full enough, it had become cold. In the end my parents finished up by carting the water upstairs in a bucket.[15]

In 1951 61% of Kent households had exclusive use of all five listed facilities, increasing to 74.3% in 1961, and to 85% in 1981. In one-person households, 67% had all five facilities in 1951. In 1951 13% of households were without piped water, compared with 31% in London and 17% in the whole of England and Wales.[16] Ten years later this had fallen to 1.7%. This was a great improvement, and in 1971 the question was changed to the use of hot water; 91.4% claimed to have exclusive use, with owner-occupiers at 95.2%. Only 73.9% in property rented from private landlords had exclusive use of hot water. In 1951 95% had exclusive use of a cooking stove, 94% of a kitchen sink, 88% of a WC, and 70% of a fixed bath. By 1991 only 1.4% were without, or sharing, the last two facilities. Interestingly, no question was asked on heating until 1991, and then it referred to central heating, 82.7% answering in the affirmative.

In each sector improvement had taken place between 1951 and 1991 but there were wide differences between types of tenure – owner-occupiers being most likely to have 'exclusive use'. In addition there were also wide variations between different areas of Kent. Generally speaking urban areas scored higher than rural ones. Almost all urban areas had exclusive use of piped water, but many in rural areas had to share. Also, seaside resorts scored highest in exclusive use of WCs, rural areas the lowest.

In 1951 urban areas generally scored highly in terms of exclusive use of all facilities, though again there were significant variations, as shown in Table 39. The anomalies are probably explained by the fact that in areas where the most recent building had taken place, there were more owner-occupiers, and the houses were built to higher standards. Conversely Gillingham and Chatham and many rural areas had much older properties. Housing in the RDs was also more dispersed making the supply of the utilities more difficult.

The 1961 census showed a 21% increase in the number of the county's structurally separate dwellings, the total being 556,010.[17] It also showed that 89.2% of Kent households had sole occupancy. As in 1951 five- and six-roomed houses were the most common, at 62.3%, and many of these had probably been built since the 1930s.

Family size continued to fall from 4.1 in 1921 to 3.16 in 1951 and 3.02 in

---

[15] *Just Like the Country, Memories of London Families who Settled on the New Cottage Estates, 1919–1939*, London 1991, p. 35.
[16] *Census 1951 Kent, op. cit.*, pp. xxv–xxxiii.
[17] *Census of England and Wales 1961: County of Kent*, London 1963, Table 11, p. 38.

Table 39

Exclusive use of all Basic Housing Facilities by Selected Areas, 1951

	%	Highest	%	Lowest	%
Kent	61	Chislehurst and Sidcup UD	82	Chatham MB	45
MBS and UDs	64	Orpington UD	82	Holling-bourne RD	46
RDs	53	Crayford UD	80	Malling RD	46
		Bexley MB	79	Cranbrook RD	47
		Beckenham MB	76	Gillingham MB	56

1961. Thus whilst there was an increase in the population of households of 10.5% since 1951, there was an increase of 15.7% in the number of private households. This was a much smaller increase than that over the period 1931–51, but still maintained pressure on housing provision.

In 1961 overcrowding was redefined as 1½ persons per room, and the figures show a dramatic fall between 1961 and 1971. The county average fell from 3.1% to 1.5%, the MBs and UDs from 2.9% to 1.6%, and the RDs from 3.9% to 1.4%. However, there were considerable variations between and within areas. For example Chislehurst and Sidcup UD averaged 4.6%, but the wards of Mottingham South and St Paul's Cray had figures of 10.5%. As might be expected the biggest range was to be found between wards in RDs.[18]

The greatest growth in the number of houses built had been in the area of north-west Kent under the influence of London. Here the housing stock had doubled between 1931 and 1951. The greatest expansion had been in Chislehurst and Sidcup UD (276%), through a combination of private and council building; in Bexley MB expansion was 212%, in Orpington UD 192%, and in Crayford UD 107%. The majority of these houses had married heads of household and were self-contained units, with little sharing. However, some areas closer to London continued to share many of London's characteristics, with a higher density and many shared properties.

Two other areas which had continued to expand their housing stock were the dockside towns of the Thames and Medway, which had more than the average numbers of smaller dwellings, and households which were generally larger than in other parts of the county. Thirdly, there were the seaside resorts, where the dwellings were more substantial, containing many Victorian and Edwardian houses, and where the households were small. Here the proportion of households with non-married heads was smaller than elsewhere, and many householders were retired.

[18] *Ibid.*, Table 3, p. 2.

With the creation of the GLC in 1964, and the London Boroughs of Bexley and Bromley, 503,287 people were taken from Kent's population. Much of the newer housing stock in suburbia was removed and so direct comparisons become difficult. Still, certain trends are discernible. The percentage of owner occupiers continued to grow, as shown in Table 40. In 1971 there were 473,960 households living in 478,885 dwellings, and 96.4% of households in Kent were private ones. The 1981 census demonstrated how overall housing standards had improved. By the new standard for overcrowding of one or more per room, the numbers overcrowded in Kent had fallen from 4.2% in 1971 to 2.5% in 1981. There were still wide variations. For example the districts of Canterbury and Thanet had only 2% of households overcrowded, contrasted with Rochester-upon-Medway with 3.3%. Other substantial gains were for those lacking or sharing the use of a bath. This was reduced from 10.5% of households in 1971 to 3.7% in 1981. Sevenoaks District had the lowest percentage (2.2%) and Tunbridge Wells the highest (5%).[19]

What was of continued importance was the size of the family and its effect upon housing supply. In Kent and elsewhere the majority of new houses contained three or more bedrooms. In fact there is a continued demand for detached houses which accounts for many of the new houses in the last decade. This must be set against the ageing of the population. In 1981 18.4% of Kent's population was of pensionable age,[20] rising to 19.3% in 1991. The district variations were considerable. In the younger populations of Gillingham and Rochester-upon-Medway there were only 14.1% and 13.4% respectively of pensioners in 1981.[21] This contrasted with Shepway at 25.2% in 1981 and 24.7% in 1991, and Thanet's respective 28.2% and 27.7%. The ageing of the population and the decreasing size of the family unit are major factors in the ability of Kent to house its population.

If we look at the composition of various households (as shown in Table 41) the problems become evident. The demands upon the social services especially in Thanet must be considerable. Over 30% of people are living alone, over 35% of these are pensioners. Significantly, Thanet also has the highest percentage of single-parent families in Kent. The figures for 1981 and 1991 demonstrate the upward trend, although there has been a slight reduction in two-pensioner households.

One new innovation in 1991 was a question relating to house type. The difference in types of property between districts is considerable. Over a third of the dwellings in Sevenoaks are detached, compared with just over one in ten in Rochester-upon-Medway. Gillingham has only 39.4% detached and semi-detached houses, whilst Dartford, Gravesham, Rochester-upon-Medway and Thanet have less than half. This is in contrast to Ashford (61.2%), Canterbury (63.3%), Sevenoaks (61.4%) and Tonbridge and Malling (66%). There is a 30%

---

19 *Kent County Monitor,* 1981, Table H, p. 7.
20 *Ibid.,* Table C, p. 5.
21 By 1991 they had risen to 14.5% and 14.4% respectively. *Kent County Monitor,* 1991, Table E, p. 19.

Table 40

Selected Tenure in Kent, 1961–91 (%)

Type of tenure	1961	1971	1981	1991
Owner occupiers	51.4	56.9	64.5	73.9 (26.7% owned, 47.2% buying)
Rented from Local Authority* or New Towns	45.4	22.5	22.0	11.8

* General consent had been given in 1952 and 1970 for the sale of council houses, but it was not until the Housing Act of 1980, which gave all tenants the right to buy on generous terms, that the sales rapidly increased, and many local authorities decided to transfer their remaining housing stock to housing associations.

difference between Gillingham and Sevenoaks in relation to terraced housing. The figures illustrate the broad differences between the prosperous Kentish commuter suburbs and the Medway towns with their many smaller properties, a younger population profile and a higher percentage of migrants. Thanet and Shepway have a significant number of purpose-built flats, many of which were built for the newly retired at the seaside resorts. The rise in owner occupiers between 1981 and 1991 was nearly 9%, with Gillingham having about 80% in this category. The rise is largely accounted for by the continuation of 'the right to buy' for council tenants and the opportunities given by low mortgages against a background of a decreasing amount of furnished rented accommodation. Equally the various Housing Associations, which had taken over much local-authority housing stock, having thus become the new private landlords, maintained their position. One other interesting statistic which affects housing location is the number of cars per household. The number of households without cars decreased between 1981 and 1991 from 33.7% to 26.7%. Sevenoaks had only 17.8% without in 1991, whilst Thanet had 38.4%. In 1991 28.2% of households had two or more cars, an increase of 10.6% over 1981. Sevenoaks had 40.1% of its households in this category and Thanet 17.6%.[22]

(2) Housing and Planning in Kent

The desire for town and country planning called for by late nineteenth-century reformers was a response to the rapid and indiscriminate growth of Britain's towns and cities in the Victorian era. Ebenezer Howard[23] believed that this had

[22] *Kent County Monitor,* 1991, Table G, p. 22.
[23] Ebenezer Howard's book *Tomorrow,* published in 1889, called for planned towns where there would be a blend of housing and industry. They were to be surrounded by green fields which could not be developed. The book inspired the formation of the Garden City Association. Letchworth and Hampstead Garden Suburb were early examples of the application of Howard's ideas.

Table 41

Households – Selected Types in Relation to Highest and Lowest
in each Category by District, 1981–91 (%)

Area	Living alone		1 adult person and 1 person 0–15		1 pensioner alone		2 or more pensioners living together	
	1981	1991	1981	1991	1981	1991	1981	1991
Kent	20.5	24.7	1.8	2.9	14.5	15.0	11.0	10.7
Rochester-upon-Medway					11.2	12.1	7.9	7.8
Sevenoaks			1.5	2.4				
Thanet	26.6	30.5	2.4	3.9	20.3	20.2	16.3	15.0
Tonbridge and Malling	17.0	21.3	1.5	2.3				

been carried out without any overview and 'without any consideration for the common interests of the people'.[24] However, pressure for housing in 1919 led politicians to believe that planned development would cause delay and that this would bring political unpopularity. Thus whilst the Housing Act of 1919 stated that housing should be well planned and sited, little else was done. In the following years both council and private housing was supported by government subsidies under the 1919, 1923[25] and 1924 Acts. In 1924 the LCC began a council estate at Downham on agricultural land on the Lewisham–Bromley border. This was to develop into one of the largest of the LCC estates. Many of the early residents came from Bermondsey and moved into purpose-built housing with all essential facilities.

The inter-war period eventually saw the acceptance of the planning concept. At the national level, the Local Government Act of 1929 authorised county councils to co-operate officially in planning with others. Prior to the Act Kent was not a Town Planning Authority but it co-operated with the East Kent Joint Planning Committee which had been established in 1923. The problem which had led to the committee's formation was the plan for the further development of the east Kent coalfield. Collieries had already been established at Chislet (c.1917), Snowdown (1913) and Tilmanstone (c.1914). The coalfield covered an area of 190 square miles from Sandwich to Dover, and inland about twelve miles to the east of Canterbury.

Naturally the local authorities in east Kent welcomed new industry, but were also determined that the future expansion would be planned. More houses would

[24] R. Unwin, *Town Planning in Practice*, London 1909, p. 2.
[25] Under the Act Welling Council borrowed £400,000 in 1920 for the construction of 426 council houses. The scheme was completed in 1926; M. Barr-Hamilton and L. Reilly, *From Country to Suburb: The Development of the Bexley Area from 1800 to the Present Day*, Bexley 1996, pp. 55 and 59.

be needed, but this was not to be at the expense of the countryside. The wish was to produce guidelines which would lay down principles for the future. Thus, in the Final Report zoning was recommended to control the type of residential building and to prohibit noxious industries in the vicinity of housing. The Final Report advocated that 'houses, . . . must be grouped into a few large communities which can pay for a favourable drainage system'.[26] This was seen as essential, not only for the benefit of the countryside, but also because of possible drainage problems on the chalk, if the development was widely dispersed.

Twelve collieries were envisaged, with approximately 12,500 miners and their families per pit. New towns were to be sited at Aylesham, Elvington and Chislet where 2,000, 640 and 350 houses respectively were to be added to the existing villages. Plans were also made for development at Woolage, Snowdown and Betteshanger. In all it was envisaged that 28,000 houses would be needed within ten years, assuming a density of five persons per house. However, since the first report in 1925, houses had only been built at the rate of 300 a year.[27] By 1928 the coal industry was in a difficult position, industrial relations were strained and by the 1930s Britain was in the throes of a depression. By 1948 only four collieries were still active. Despite this, the planning process had been a necessary exercise, the authorities had co-operated effectively and voluntarily and they had made early comments on zoning and on the preservation of the countryside.

The next report of relevance to Kent was the *North East Kent Regional Planning Scheme*, published in 1930.[28] A committee had been constituted in February 1926 for the purpose of preparing an advisory regional plan for the local authorities of north-east Kent – six municipal boroughs, one county borough, four urban districts and six rural districts. Significantly, the area under study was between the rapidly expanding Greater London area and the newly developing east Kent coalfield. The primary purpose was to retain the 'Garden of England' whilst at the same time providing economic opportunities for the people. To this end, regulated development was seen as imperative. The major considerations were centred in the first place on zoning residential, business, industrial and agricultural areas;[29] secondly, on improved communications and the introduction of new transport routes; thirdly, on the creation or preservation of open spaces for present and future needs; and finally, on the preservation of amenities in both urban and rural areas. To this end advertising hoardings and petrol stations were to be regulated and existing ancient monuments and historic buildings protected.

The report must be seen against the background of the petrol engine, ribbon development, indiscriminate building and the fear that town and country would

[26] P. Abercrombie and J. Archibald, *East Kent Regional Planning Scheme: Final Report*, Canterbury 1928, p. 4.
[27] *Ibid.*, p. 47.
[28] By Adams, Thompson and Fry, Town Planning Consultants, Westminster.
[29] The Report was published two years before the Town Planning Act of 1932 which introduced zoning.

soon become one. Significantly, the report contained photographs of congested main streets in Chatham, Maidstone, Rochester and Sittingbourne, and called for bypasses. Each town was on either the A2 or A20, the main east–west arterial roads. Bypasses, however, were not to be achieved for many years. The report envisaged the expansion of selected existing towns and villages, largely as a result of the continued 'decentralisation and the gradual redistribution of the population of London'.[30] Thus, ordered development was the theme of the report, and to this end it was suggested that ideally rural and urban densities be advocated of four houses per acre in rural areas, and twelve, or exceptionally sixteen, on urban sites.

The third and fourth reports of importance to Kent were produced by the Greater London Planning Committee. This had been constituted by the then Minister of Health, Neville Chamberlain, in November 1927. Its forty-five members were drawn from the LCC, the City Corporation, the Home Counties, the Standing Joint Committee of the Metropolitan and County Boroughs and 126 other boroughs, urban and rural districts. It covered an area of twenty-five miles radius from Charing Cross, which included suburban north-west Kent and the Thameside towns. All local authorities in Kent inward from Gravesend MB, Northfleet UD and Dartford RD were included.

The committee produced its First Report in December 1929.[31] Its major concerns had been fourfold. The first, the decentralisation of industry, was soon seen to be too large a topic and was left to a later report. Thus it was to concentrate on open spaces, a green belt, or belts, around London and ribbon development. Each had immediacy. Indiscriminate building and ribbon development along roads were both regarded as unsightly and dangerous. The report contained many poignant photographs of countryside ruined in this way, not only by housing, but by petrol stations and advertising hoardings. Ribbon development was not new. The New Kent Road, for example, had been laid out in 1819, and in the early part of the twentieth century electric tramways had had the same effect. The extensions of the tramway to Welling in 1903, for instance, led to housing along it, and culs-de-sac off the main roads. However, in the inter-war years ribbon development had advantages for many. With a depressed agricultural sector, land was readily available at an attractive price. Developers found it easier to build along an existing highway and new householders welcomed access to transport at the front and green fields behind.[32] It was all made easier by weak or non-existent planning controls.

The report urged the buying of land parallel to main roads to provide service roads and parking areas. This, the committee felt, would enhance safety. Traffic was not only increasing for leisure, but the new roads were enabling people to travel further to work. Raymond Unwin expressed it thus:

---

30 *Ibid.*, p. 46.
31 *First Report of the Greater London Regional Planning Committee*, London 1929.
32 See A.M. Edwards, *The Design of Suburbia*, London 1981.

The new roads have also offered well advertised frontages which have in too many cases been occupied by an ill-regulated assortment of residential, commercial and industrial buildings. . . . This unsuitable ribbon development along main roads, and the general sporadic building . . . is spoiling the countryside.

Unwin felt that development was growing apace whilst the means and powers to regulate it were inadequate:

the lands which are urgently needed for playing fields and other open spaces are being rapidly overrun or disfigured by sporadic buildings; the traffic efficiency of main roads is being depreciated and their amenities destroyed by unsuitable marginal development.[33]

As with the report for north-east Kent, both regional committees felt that more planning powers were necessary. The preservation of open spaces was seen as essential because of the dispersal of population into the Outer Ring from Inner London. Here was an early call for a green belt, which was not to be achieved until the Green Belt Act of 1938.

Overall the 1929 report was most concerned with sporadic building and its consequences:

It is not reasonable that individual owners as developers should be able to build wherever they like, regardless of the cost to the community or of the injury which they do to the beauty and amenity of the countryside. Such an unregulated right to build anywhere, is quite inconsistent with any system of planning.[34]

Kent contained many examples of the problems faced by unchecked development. Biggin Hill not only saw ribbon development along the Bromley to Westerham road, but also sporadic building in the valley below. Land had become available on the Aperfield Court Estate and had been subdivided into 250 freehold building plots. The plots were auctioned on 8 April 1901 with prices ranging from £10, for a twenty-foot frontage, to £35.[35] Some were purchased by speculators, others by families for weekend, holiday or even permanent use. Over the next few years a variety of small, often weatherboarded bungalows were built. Some were no more than small wooden sheds with a corrugated iron roof. Building came before roads, and the unmetalled tracks were soon potholed in winter. By 1939 the valley had been 'developed' by speculative development. With rising land values in the 1970s, and the shortage

---

33 Greater London Report, p. 27.
34 Ibid., p. 32.
35 West Kent within Living Memory, pp. 30–2. The down-payment was £1, with the remainder repayable over nine years. The plots were often difficult to sell because of the cost of transporting building materials to them along the unmade 'roads'.

Table 42
Families per Dwelling in 1931 (%)

	Families in single occupation of dwelling	Two families per dwelling	Three or more families per dwelling	Over two persons per room (over crowding)
London	36.7	31.2	32.1	7.5
Kent	85.5	11.8	2.7	1.6

of building land, many of the properties were demolished and new estates built.[36]

The *Second Report of the Greater London Regional Planning Committee* was published in March 1933. Pressure from this and other similar groups had resulted in the Town Planning Act of 1932. The main concern of the report was the decentralisation of London and its impact on the Home Counties. Between 1911 and 1921 Kent had gained 13,942 persons by internal migration, and between 1921 and 1931 another 19,583. During these two periods the LCC had lost respectively 397,023 and 326,037 people. Nevertheless the differences between London and Kent in terms of housing remained (as shown in Table 42). The problem appeared to be that whilst substantial building had taken place and significant numbers were leaving London for the Home Counties, many new migrants were coming from elsewhere to replace them. Pressures on land and the environment were increasing, and the report urged that planning and zoning under the 1932 Town Planning Act should be introduced either to prohibit or to regulate future building. The report once more denounced sporadic building and urged the adoption of better-planned, compact units; it was strongly against the continued encroachment of the built up areas into the surrounding countryside. Preference was for a girdle or green belt as close as possible to the existing completely urbanised area of the County of London. Outside this would be planned development.

The report which carried this suggestion further, and had a considerable effect upon the Home Counties including Kent, was *The Greater London Plan 1944*.[37] Its author was Patrick Abercrombie whose brief was to consider an area of thirty miles around London. This included much of north-west Kent. Abercrombie divided London and the surrounding area into four concentric rings.

1. *The Central Area.* The centre of London and the nearby built-up areas. The only part of Kent in this section was part of Penge.

2. *The Suburban Ring.* This was twelve miles from Charing Cross, beyond the central area. This included the remainder of Penge, and parts of Beckenham, Bexley, Bromley and Erith and the Urban Districts of Chislehurst and Sidcup

---

[36] J. Nelson, *Grandfather's Biggin Hill*, Biggin Hill 1982, contains a splendid collection of photographs of the early development.

[37] P. Abercrombie, *Greater London Plan, 1944*, London 1945.

and Crayford. This area was regarded as 'a static zone'.[38] No decentralised population or industry was to be received, except a small amount in Erith.

3. *The Green Belt*. This extended to the southern slopes of the Greensand ridge bisecting Sevenoaks RD, and to an irregular line north to south bisecting Swanscombe UD, Sevenoaks UD and to include the Darenth Valley and some of the hills beyond, with the towns of Sevenoaks and Dartford. This area comprised much open country, but Abercrombie stressed that it should not be used for further housing but as a Green Belt.[39] The area already contained established towns such as Sevenoaks, 'situated in country of great charm and now a high class dormitory town'. The ring also contained Crayford, 'another industrial centre, whose natural beauty has been spoiled by bad siting and lack of control'.[40] Also in the area were unspoilt villages whose character had remained, such as Farningham, Otford and Shoreham in the Darenth Valley. However in the half-ruined Cray Valley to the west lay the once rural and peaceful hamlets of St Mary Cray, St Paul's Cray and Foots Cray. Abercrombie put their condition down to the fact that many features of villages are unsuitable as a basis for urbanisation. In the case of the Crays he believed that it had potential for limited new industries. The valley already had a major north–south road dividing suburban Orpington to the west from the Cray villages. The parallel old north–south road linking the villages became very run down, until in the 1990s a regeneration scheme was implemented to renovate many of the older houses which remained along the road. The banks of the River Cray have also been restored and a continuous park area opened up alongside it. Abercrombie suggested that to the west of the Cray Valley an estate for 10,000 people might be built by the LCC at Scadbury in Chislehurst.[41] This was opposed by Kent County Council. Later an estate was built on the fringes of the Scadbury Estate, but the central core of the Scadbury estate was retained, and the London Borough of Bromley has converted it into a nature reserve.

4. *The Outer Country Ring*. This was seen as 'the chief reception area for overcrowded London'.[42] Kent had very little land in the Outer Ring, but Abercrombie believed that Gravesend, Northfleet and Swanscombe could expand by 8,200.

The Greater London Plan also affected Kent's development beyond the four rings, for Abercrombie recommended the dispersal of London 'wholly outside

---

[38] *Ibid.*, pp. 5–6. One of Abercrombie's assumptions was that the 'total population of the area will not increase, but on the contrary will be somewhat reduced'. This was not to be the case. Essentially the *Plan* was for the better redistribution of the population, not planning for more.

[39] The effect of the Green Belt can still be seen on the southern boundary of Orpington, where the suburban development ends and fields begin. See *ibid.*, pp. 8 and 24.

[40] *Ibid.*, p. 25.

[41] *Planning Basis for Kent*, Kent County Council 1948, p. 29, incorporates reports upon the County Planning Survey and the County Road Plan. This document contains Kent County Council's response to the *Greater London Plan*.

[42] *Greater London Plan, op. cit.*, p. 8.

the Metropolitan influence'.[43] This was about fifty miles from London, and Ashford was seen as capable of taking an extra 30,000 people. Kent County Council was in general agreement, preferring the expansion of existing towns to the creation of new towns in the countryside.

By 1944 there were several examples of wholly planned new towns, such as Letchworth and Welwyn. However, the only site suggested in Kent was on the chalk belt between Longfield and Meopham, where a town of 40,000 was recommended. Kent County Council objected, arguing that it would destroy good agricultural land, and that it was too near both London and Gravesend. This would preclude its becoming self-sufficient, and the County Council felt that it would develop into a predominantly dormitory town. The proposal was successfully rejected, but twenty years later, in 1965, planning permission was given to build 2,000 houses at New Ash Green, forty-five of which were to be for GLC overspill. By 1968 the first neighbourhood had been built. The development was undertaken by Span and their architects. It was to be a self-contained town for 5,000 to 6,000 people with houses which were to create 'a maximum of variety'. It was seen as less destructive of the environment than the newly developed sprawl of Hartley, Longfield and New Barn to the north of Meopham, and West Kingsdown, along the A20 to the east: 'If the planners make New Ash Green their model there may still be some country left in north-west Kent in twenty years time.'[44] However, Span went bankrupt within a year, largely because of a credit squeeze. Two-hundred and twenty-six people who had put down deposits for properties in New Ash Green had to withdraw because they were unable to sell their own homes. The final straw came when the GLC withdrew its support in 1969.[45] Newman[46] believed that, whilst the later houses built by Bovis Holdings were not as innovative, the essential planning concept had survived. Today New Ash Green is essentially as Kent County Council foresaw, a dormitory with no industries of its own, except services. Nevertheless it has fitted well into the surrounding countryside.

Abercrombie had singled out Ashford for expansion because it was a good distributive centre. The other towns such as 'Rochester, Gillingham and Maidstone are already sufficiently large and are industrially congested.'[47] Ever since the South Eastern Railway had opened its repair yards and works at Ashford in the 1840s, and built Ashford New Town for its workers, it had been an important railway town. It was rapidly becoming a prominent market, distribution and commercial centre. It is not surprising that it is now developing further since it is the international station on the rail link between London and Brussels and Paris.

The 1948 Kent Report made an interesting comment on Aylesham. The Kent coalfield had not developed as anticipated, new industries had not been

43 *Planning Basis for Kent*, p. 30.
44 J. Newman, *West Kent and the Weald*, 1st edn, Harmondsworth 1969, p. 413.
45 Edwards, *op. cit.*, p. 192.
46 Newman, *West Kent and the Weald*, 2nd ed., Harmondsworth 1977, pp. 429–30.
47 *Planning Basis for Kent*, p. 130.

attracted by cheap coal and electricity, consequently Aylesham was now seen as an unbalanced community, in that it comprised only miners and their families. In March 1945 the Kent Coalfield Regional Report recommended that there should be no further expansion to the existing mining village system. Aylesham was said to have suffered 'from arrested development, with many of the sites in the centre of the town rough grassland'.[48] The Kent Report suggested that, in order to create a more mixed community, Aylesham should accept a number of families from the London overspill.

The 1947 Town Planning Act gave councils more powers to stop ribbon development and to safeguard agricultural land. Thus, the 1948 Kent Report laid down plans for the limited expansion of certain areas in the Kent Green Belt, among them being Biggin Hill, Dartford, Crayford, Stone, North and Foots Cray, Orpington, St Paul's and St Mary Cray, Farnborough and Sevenoaks. In the outer ring Gravesend, Northfleet and Swanscombe were to be developed.[49] In 1962 a further Town Planning Act required all local planning authorities to prepare plans for their own area to show intended land use over the next twenty years. When this had been approved by the Ministry of Housing and Local Government there was a statutory obligation on planning authorities to control all new development in accordance with their plans.[50] To this end Kent drew up its revised plan in 1967.

Many speculators, before and after the First World War, had taken advantage of the popularity of the Garden City concept and 'the rural arcadia' outside the cities and towns. This had appealed particularly to ex-servicemen after the 1914–18 war who did not wish to return to industrial jobs but were tempted by a place in the country with a smallholding. Others simply sought a rural weekend or holiday retreat, such as at Biggin Hill. Hardy and Ward[51] have describe these plotlands. One such in Kent was on a 415-acre estate at Walderslade, south of Chatham, which came on to the market. It was largely bought cheaply by speculators who subdivided the land into plots. No services were provided, neither were roads laid. Soon many of the initial weatherboarded single storey structures fell into disrepair, but some remained after the Second World War. By this time building land was scarce and a decade later much of the land was acquired to relieve the housing problems of the Medway Towns. Armed with its new powers under the 1967 Act, Kent County Council started buying up plots and laying down services.[52]

In other areas of Kent, when land was cheap between the wars, similar plotlands had sprung up. In time some plots were used as caravan sites. The problem was made worse by the fact that several of the areas were now either in the Green Belt or in areas of designated natural beauty. By the 1970s district coun-

---

48   *Ibid.*, p. 32.
49   *Ibid.*, p. 37.
50   *Traffic in Towns*, London 1963, p. 173.
51   D. Hardy and C. Ward, *Arcadia for All: The Legacy of a Makeshift Landscape*, London 1984.
52   *Ibid.*, p. 230.

cils were able to use their new powers to restrict further urban-type developments and were able to apply tree-preservation orders. Hardy and Ward use the
Knatts Valley and East Hill plotlands as an example.[53] In 1920 Homesteads
Limited had bought 547 acres on the East Hill Estate in the parishes of Kingsdown and Shoreham. Plots were offered at £15 an acre. Publicity suggested their
use for poultry farming or fruit growing, or as holiday homes. Two years later
another firm, Ideal Home Estates, offered a further 330 acres on the same estate
in 156 plots. Before 1939 only a few houses and smallholdings had been developed. In 1967, under the Kent Development Plan, the area was designated as
part of the Kent Downs Area of Outstanding Natural Beauty. It was also by this
time in the Green Belt. Under the new powers, future development was only to
take place in the existing villages, and only forestry and agriculture was allowed
outside them. A survey conducted by the Sevenoaks District Council in 1980
found that of the original 156 plots, forty-eight were now vacant, eight had been
amalgamated, and five were caravan sites.[54]

Recent demand for building land has brought renewed pressure on the
countryside and the Green Belt. Now existing farms or outbuildings can be
extended or converted to provide more economic use. Also unused land can be
used for leisure pursuits such as golf courses. Thus we see renewed demand by
those with means, or builders, to seek out buildings for conversion. Kent
provides many examples of oast- and barn-conversions, and the transformation
of a row of one-time labourers' cottages into handsome period homes. Some of
these have become permanent homes, others weekend retreats. In many cases
this has transformed plain working villages, but its side effect has been to put
pressure on the young indigenous population who find employment increasingly
difficult and the rising house prices beyond their means.

Technology has brought opportunities for work in the home, just as in earlier
centuries each village contained its domestic weaver. Information technology, or
the demand for high-quality crafts, have enabled many to establish their home as
a place of work. However, many of these are incomers. Thus in many parts of
Kent, either in rural or semi-rural areas, the population has stabilised but many
rural inhabitants now commute to work, work from home, or have chosen to
retire to the country. Thus, housing needs have changed, and as the amount of
land available for infilling decreases, older properties are being transformed and
occupied by those who can afford to bring these houses up to date.

The time of cheap land for future plots is over. The end of council building
and the paucity of new small affordable homes has caused problems in both
urban and rural areas. In the latter the elderly without private transport find
increasing problems as the post office and village shop may have disappeared,
whilst public transport is dear, sparse or both. The irony is that so long as agriculture is in depression, green-field sites will remain attractive to the developer,

---

[53] *Ibid.*, pp. 233–4.
[54] *The West Kingsdown Draft District Plan*, quoted in *ibid.*, p. 234.

the owner of land, and government seeking to meet the country's housing needs. Thus, the very legislation designed to protect the countryside is itself in ever-increasing danger of being circumvented.

(3) Three Contrasting Suburban Developments

(a) Petts Wood, Orpington – A Planned Estate

Basil Scruby, an Essex property developer, bought 400 acres of land at Petts Wood, Orpington, in the mid-1920s. His intention was to create a garden suburb, which would attract those who worked in London. The purchase was a speculation dependent upon a railway station. At the time the nearest stations were at Chislehurst and Orpington, but the line between them went through his newly acquired land. In February 1928 he reached an agreement with the Southern Railway Company. Scruby was to provide the land both for a station and a goods yard, and also contribute £6,000 towards its construction.[55] The station opened on 9 July 1928, perhaps the first example of a station being built in anticipation of demand. It was set amongst fields and at first was very basic indeed. Nevertheless Scruby was delighted. The line had recently been electrified and served Bromley, Victoria, and Holborn Viaduct. It was an ideal site for City commuters, and the all-night service to Blackfriars made it attractive to Fleet Street printworkers.

Scruby set out to create an attractive, low-density estate. The restrictions laid down by Bromley Rural District Council for no more than eight houses per acre were less severe than Scruby's own requirements. Scruby created the plan, laid out the roads and arranged for drains, gas, water and electricity. He then sold off plots to speculative builders, who after building and selling them, renewed the process. Scruby was determined to have a development of quality, with well-built houses in attractive settings. Old trees were to be preserved wherever possible and new plantings took place. Many of the houses were in the Tudor style, with internal and external beams, stucco and stained glass. Inside were oak panelled hallways and ingle-nooks. In all some forty-five builders were involved, and each had to meet Scruby's strict specifications. An estate office was built in the newly created square by the station. Today some of the most sought after houses are those by Noel Rees. One of his roads, The Chenies, comprising twenty-eight contrasting 'period' houses surrounded by mature trees, is now a conservation area.

The more expensive properties were four-bedroomed houses in Wood Ride, selling at £2,200, but more common were the semi-detached houses in Tudor Way, where prices started at £795, and detached houses in Ladywood Avenue at £925. Later, cheaper housing was built to the west of the railway, with higher

---

55   This section owes much to P. Waymark, *A History of Petts Wood*, 3rd edn, Bromley 1990, p. 37.

densities. At the time the railway line created a social divide, but today both developments are in high demand. The popularity of Scruby's development can be judged by increased ticket sales. In 1934 Petts Wood Station sold 320,597 ordinary tickets as well as 13,049 season tickets.

(b) West Wickham – A Development Adjoining an Established Settlement

A contrasting and less coherent development is seen at West Wickham. Here development had been taking place around the village nucleus, and by 1931 the population had reached 6,229. Unlike Petts Wood, this had placed severe strain on existing services, for until 1928 drainage had been by means of cesspools. However, the railway had been electrified in 1925[56] and four years later a Residents' Association was formed. Their first demands, for the watering of unmade roads in summer and for better gas pressure, tell us much about the rapid and indiscriminate development which was taking place. To their credit they managed to achieve the planting of 500 trees along the new roads. Many of the original inhabitants found it difficult adjusting to West Wickham's rapid development. By 1935 there were 10,080 inhabitants living in 3,360 houses.[57]

To the south of the parish, away from the village centre, building had been taking place since 1929. Unfortunately, no shops were opened until 1936, and the roads were so bad that London Transport refused to run a bus service along them to the railway station. The builder Morrell, who had begun to build in the area in 1933, provided a free bus service to Hayes Station so that potential buyers would not be discouraged. Morrell's cheapest houses were £479 with a deposit of £1. The area was known as Coney Hall. In 1938 the Coney Hall Residents' Association supported 400 residents who refused to pay their mortgages. They argued that their houses were defective and not up to the standard outlined in the builder's brochure.[58] The case had originally been brought by a Mrs Borders in 1934 on a £690 semi-detached house with a £40 garage on which there was a 95% mortgage. Within a few months defects had appeared and payments were withheld.[59] The case eventually went to the House of Lords which found in favour of the building society. Whilst the case was lost, building societies were to be much more careful in future. The strike had caused divisions amongst the residents and also drew comment from the *Beckenham Times* of 7 August 1937:

> Coney Hall folk were different from Wickham folk. Black-coated workers largely and in the other, more of the artisan class.[60]

Coney Hall was not alone in suffering from builders' shoddy work and the breach of by-laws. Jackson recounts how at Dartford Police Court in 1933 a

56 P. Knowlden and J. Walker, *West Wickham: Past into Present*, West Wickham 1986, p. 170.
57 *Ibid.*, p. 176.
58 *Ibid.*, pp. 178, 181.
59 A.A. Jackson, *Semi-Detached London*, London 1973, pp. 197–9.
60 Quoted by Knowlden and Walker, *op. cit.*, p. 178.

builder was prosecuted for not informing Bexley Council of the completion of houses. The houses were part of a 900-house estate at Welling. Council inspectors gave evidence of work being covered up before inspections could be made. The builder was found guilty and was fined.[61]

(c) Bexley – A Mixed Suburban Development

Whilst Beckenham and Bromley saw their greatest growth in the nineteenth century, with the coming of the railway, Bexley's rapid growth was a twentieth-century phenomenon, as shown in Table 43. Bexley[62] is some fifteen to twenty miles from the centre of London. Unlike Bromley it adjoins the more densely populated Thameside industrial areas of Woolwich and Plumstead where many of the first wave of migrants to Bexley worked.

The Second Boer War had brought employment and prosperity to Crayford, in the northern part of the area, with the production of the machine-gun by Vickers. Production was boosted by the First World War, and at its peak Vickers employed 14,500 workers in Crayford. Erith, Dartford and Woolwich also prospered, and the resulting housing shortage was met by temporary huts at Eltham, and at East Wickham in Bexley.

The impressive Well Hall Estate at Eltham was built for Woolwich Arsenal workers, while Vickers built the Barnes Cray Estate at Crayford. The intention was to match Well Hall, and Gordon Allen was employed to design the houses. Each house had both hot and cold water, and half of them were built with experimental concrete walls. Thus, Crayford developed as a working-class suburb drawing workers from the nearby Thameside factories and yards. The population doubled between 1911 and 1921, and by 1939 there were 25,200 inhabitants.

As we have seen, the First World War produced a housing shortage, and the northern parts of Bexley faced increased pressure from the higher-density areas of Thameside. Many workers preferred to take advantage of the tram, bus or train to travel to work each day. With the various post-war Housing Acts, subsidies became available to enable the low paid to rent a self-contained council house. The 1923 and 1924 Acts sought to encourage the more affluent worker to buy their own homes, and many did so through taking out council mortgages. These new houses, both council-owned and private, proved very attractive to incomers from Inner London and Thameside, where many had rented old properties in which the facilities were often shared.

In order to qualify for a subsidy, the builder had to build to a density of twelve houses per acre, and a maximum size and price was also stipulated. House prices in the 1920s were much higher than in the 1930s, and builders often found it difficult to keep below the maximum price. With the local-authority mortgage, the deposit on a £650 house was £65 and repayments at £1 a

61 Jackson, *op. cit.*, p. 155.
62 The area under consideration covers the boundaries of the present London Borough of Bexley and includes areas such as Crayford, Sidcup and Welling.

Table 43

Population Growth in Bexley and Selected Suburbs, 1921–39

	1921*	1931	1934	1935	1936	1937	1938	1939
Bexley	21,104	32,626	51,930	59,970	69,000	74,380	77,020	80,110
Chislehurst and Sidcup UDC	8,981	27,182						63,140
Crayford UDC	12,295	16,229						25,200
Orpington UDC	18,628	25,858						

* Census figures for 1921; later figures from *London Statistics*, vol. 41 (LCC 1939) adjusted to 1938/9 areas. Full set of figures only available for Bexley.

week over thirty years. A skilled worker on £4 a week could thus afford to buy. The unskilled worker on £3 a week would have to rent, and new council house rents were from 12s. to 14s. per week.[63]

By contrast, council rents in Maidstone were 10s. to 12s. per week plus rates, but were regarded as beyond the means of many: 'not for the people who must get out of the slums'.[64] Bexley's advantage was that unlike Maidstone it did not have slums to clear and their inhabitants to rehouse. In Bexley those moving into rented or mortgaged properties were in work. In Maidstone those who were able to afford to rent a council house had their furniture fumigated by council officials before occupation, if they were rehoused from slum properties.

In 1929 Bexley produced its Town Development Plan in which various zones were identified. The first was the area under discussion, the working-class area to the north, where a density of twelve houses per acre was laid down. By this time the area was attracting not only Thameside workers, but also City clerks and their families from the inner suburbs. The electrification of the railway in 1926 and 1930, low down-payments on affordable housing, and effective advertising all played their part. New Ideal Homesteads developed estates at Falconwood Park and Westwood Farm and soon the area was all but urbanised.

The 1929 plan placed a lower housing density in other parts. Around Bexley Village, six to eight per acre was laid down, whilst densities as low as three per acre were laid down in areas of more affluent development. Thus between 1930 and 1939 the number of houses in Bexley increased by 269% and the population by 189% from 28,120 to 80,110.

After 1932 many of the houses built were for private sale, and prices were much lower than in the 1920s. Interest rates were now lower and real incomes

---

[63] M.C. Carr, 'The Development and Character of a Metropolitan Suburb: Bexley, Kent', in *The Rise of Suburbia*, ed. F.L.M. Thompson, Leicester 1982, p. 231.
[64] Clark and Murfin, *op. cit.*, p. 224.

were rising. Consequently more of those who had previously rented could afford to buy. The lower middle class were now able to become home owners: 'the social revolution gave the family a house in the suburbs'.[65]

For the majority, houses were purchased from the large developer, who with economies of scale was able to offer very competitive deals. A £5 deposit was not uncommon, with reasonable payments over twenty years. Both Stevens and Ideal Homesteads were completing a hundred houses a week in the early 1930s. This was mainly housing built to standard designs,[66] through the bulk purchase of materials with workers on piece rates. Whilst land remained available, cheap development surged ahead.

By 1936 most of the available land had been built on and the creation of the Green Belt enabled Bexley, in co-operation with the Greater London Regional Planning Committee, to purchase the Hall Place Estate as part of the Green Belt Girdle.[67] Also, land around the Cray was preserved and residents' groups successfully resisted further building development around old Bexley village.

Since 1945, and especially since the 1970s, new building has taken the form of either redevelopment of older properties or infilling. In the main this has been for purchasers in the higher income brackets. For those who could not afford to buy there were council houses, but in the 1980s the right to buy was accelerated, and fewer were available for rent.

Thus, Bexley emerged before the Second World War as a metropolitan suburb. Most of the houses, especially in the north of the area, were occupied by the lower middle class. In 1951 60.1% of males over the age of fifteen were in Social Class III – skilled and non-manual. Only 4.1% were in the professional Class I.

Today the London Borough of Bexley incorporates Thamesmead which was designed by the GLC in 1967, when part of the Erith marshes were drained to become fields and parkland, alongside the new town of Thamesmead. This is a development far in excess of what Abercrombie considered for Erith in the Greater London Plan.

(4) Conclusion

The inter-war housing boom may be illustrated by one Gravesend family.[68] Husband and wife had moved from Bristol to Gravesend where the husband, a window dresser, took a job at Bon Marché. After the birth of their first child they moved locally to a new three-bedroomed terraced house in an unmade road

[65] Carr, *op. cit.*, p. 238.
[66] In the more exclusive areas, the plots would be larger, an architect might be employed, and a greater number of fittings and features made available.
[67] Carr, *op. cit.*, p. 241.
[68] I am indebted to Mrs J. Abdallahi for giving me the opportunity to read her mother's extensive and detailed diary and other family documents.

in Laurel Avenue, Gravesend. Theirs was the sixth house built on a plot of 238' × 97' on which six more houses were later erected. The house was purchased from Gravesend Council under the 1923 Housing Act. The mortgage was £400 on which they repaid £2 9s. 6d. a month over twenty years. The deposit was larger than most as the house cost £535. The mortgage agreement laid down various regulations such as that the house must be insured and 'maintained in good sanitary condition and in good repair'. In 1985 the house was put on the market for £26,000.

The wife was clearly pleased by the space provided by the new house: 'we are loving our new little house more than ever' was the comment three days after moving in. There were also comments on the garden, a third bedroom for the child and the new Jackson electric stove. This, along with the Sadia water heater, were innovations much appreciated. However, there were faults. Within a short time cracks in a ceiling led to its collapse and after much chasing the builder repaired the damage.

The various planning documents of the 1980s and 1990s have emphasised the fact that much of Kent is protected by Green Belt legislation. Thus the Kent planners believe that housing development should be concentrated where possible on damaged land, and through reinvestment within the existing urban areas. Nineteen urban areas are identified in the 1996 County Plan.[69] As in the earlier reports, they argued that the separation of towns from their rural setting should be preserved. The character of the areas for housing expansion vary widely. With the M2, M25 and the High Speed Rail Link, a Thames Gateway has been identified incorporating both southern Essex and north Kent. In this area economic development is seen as necessary in reusing derelict land, both in town and country.[70] Equally derelict urban sites within such towns as Rochester and Chatham should be improved for both new industry and housing.

Thus, housing development is seen as essential to meet the needs of business and the people of Kent. Bearing in mind the rise in the number of smaller households, it is recommended that a significant amount of the new building should be non-market social housing. In the 1996 Plan it is calculated that 116,000 houses will need to be built between 1991 and 2001. The bulk of these will be in Dartford (10,500), the Medway towns (16,000), Swale (13,200), Ashford (13,900) and Canterbury Districts (10,300). Interestingly, in the search for building land which is not Green Belt, the now defunct East Kent coalfield and redundant aerodromes such as that at West Malling have been identified as suitable.

As we have seen, housing provision is not an exact science, and planning for future needs in a county as diverse and large as Kent poses problems. The *Householder and Commuter Surveys*[71] showed that migrants were influenced by the availability of housing stock in particular areas. For example London was

69 *Kent Structure Plan, 1996*, p. 22.
70 The Bluewater site to the east of Dartford is an example.
71 *Household and Commuter Survey of Mid and North Kent, 1989–90*, Kent County Council 1991.

not providing sufficient appropriate accommodation; 48% said their reason for moving to Kent was better and affordable housing, and more dwelling space.[72]

As might be expected, only a minority of migrants from London were moving for jobs. However, if one looks at migrants from outside Kent, London jobs account for 31% in Dartford/Gravesham and 60% in mid-Kent. Many of these new migrants are commuters; 38% of heads of household in each of the study areas commuted to London, and the majority of these were owner occupiers.

Thus, at the end of the twentieth century, Kent's population no longer has the high decennial growth rates of former years (as identified in Chapter 1). Moreover family size is continuing to fall, whilst the population ages. Migration has been shown to be subject to economic circumstances, house prices and employment being major determinants. Whilst east Kent is not so subject to the influences of London, certain areas of the county such as Ashford and the Medway towns/Maidstone corridor are likely to expand due to transport developments and closer ties with Europe.

The planners and citizens of Kent clearly wish Kent to be economically prosperous and to provide for its indigenous population. Equally, growth will require continued in-migrants, many of whom may be attracted by the provision of quality housing and the environment which the planning reports are seeking to preserve. It is a difficult and unenviable balancing act.

[72] *Kent Structure Plan*, 3rd review, technical working Paper 1/92, Kent County Council 1992, p. 9.

7

Health and Social Welfare

PAUL HASTINGS AND NIGEL YATES

The transformation that has taken place in the provision of health and welfare services, not just in Kent but throughout the United Kingdom, during the twentieth century, has probably had a greater impact on the lives of ordinary people than any other development in the same period. Most of this transformation has been the result of government legislation. At the beginning of the century much of the framework for the provision of health care or support for those in need had not changed fundamentally since the second quarter of the nineteenth century. Access to medical services depended on a person's financial situation. The provision of relief for those in need was dependent on private charity or on the Boards of Guardians set up under the Poor Law Amendment Act of 1834. These boards were not finally abolished, with the provision of welfare services then taken on initially by County Councils, until 1929; some were subsequently transferred to the National Assistance Board in 1934 and 1948. Major reforms in social welfare were undertaken by the Liberal Government of 1905–15, which introduced the first, fairly limited, scheme for old-age pensions in 1908, followed by a much more extensive National Insurance Act in 1911. The most dramatic changes to the provision of health and welfare services were those recommended by the report of Sir William Beveridge, published in 1942, and implemented, together with the introduction of a National Health Service, by the Labour Government of 1945–51. Throughout the 1950s, 1960s and early 1970s there was a strong consensus across the political spectrum in support of what became known as the Welfare State. It was only with the election of Margaret Thatcher to the leadership of the Conservative Party in 1975 that this consensus began to break down, and the Conservative Government of 1979–97 introduced a series of measures which, whilst they did not undermine the principles on which the Welfare State had been constructed, nevertheless put far greater emphasis on individual initiative and the roles of both the private and the voluntary sectors in the provision of health and welfare services. This chapter will consider all these developments and analyse their impact on the people of Kent over the past century.[1]

---

[1] Newspaper references in this chapter have been abbreviated as follows:
CN Chatham News; *CO Chatham Observer*; *KE Kentish Express*; *KH Kent Herald*; *KM Kent Messenger*;

(1) The General Health of the Population

It is hazardous to generalise about the living standards of the bulk of the population in the early twentieth century. There was some improvement, particularly among urban workers, as real wages rose, diet improved and the adulteration of food decreased. In the rural areas wages varied considerably and depended on the type of farming practised, the individual skills of labourers, local perquisites and opportunities for supplementary work being available to the families of labourers. Conditions in Kent remained poor for agricultural labourers, with many still living below the poverty line. Malnourishment was commonplace since bread, potatoes, tea and cheese remained the mainstays of an unhealthy diet, in which meat was a rare luxury and there were insufficient proteins, fats and iron.[2]

Although adulteration of food was decreasing, it was still estimated in 1906 that 47% of milk suppliers in the Dartford district were practising it. Two years later the County Analyst reported that in one-quarter of that year fifty-seven samples of food, out of a total of 849 tested, were impure; impure foodstuffs included tea, sugar, cornflour, cocoa, preserved peas, margarine and 18.5% of all samples of milk.[3] Particular concern was expressed about the health of children. A report of 1904 stated that it was 'the height of cruelty to subject half-starved children to education', and resulted in the passing of the Education (Provision of Meals) Act 1906 and the Medical Inspection Act 1907. The former empowered local authorities to add a maximum of one halfpenny in the pound to the rates to provide free meals for children unable to benefit from their schooling because they went to school without breakfast. There was little support for this legislation, which was permissive and not mandatory, in Kent, where the voluntary principle was strongly entrenched. The East Ashford Guardians, supported by the local MP, protested that the state was taking over the duties of parents and throwing the burden on the ratepayers. At a meeting of the County Council's Education Committee in October 1908 a proposal that the legislation should be implemented could not even find a seconder. 'Private charity has hitherto fed hungry children,' stated Councillor Frederick Wingent, 'and I believe it will continue to do so. Once the rates are used private charity will dry up.' Next month the full council agreed in principle to fund the free school meals, while hoping that voluntary provision would remain sufficient. By January 1909 Erith was feeding 120 needy children. Dover and Gravesend still left winter provision of meals to private effort. The County Council, as it made clear when Northfleet UDC claimed that private charity had been exhausted by three years' industrial depression, refused to help 'until every effort had been

---

MKJ Maidstone and Kentish Journal; *SEG South Eastern Gazette*.
References follow a standard format giving day, month and year numerically (e.g. *KE* 26.12.1860).
2   E. Royle, *Modern Britain: A Social History, 1750–1985*, London 1987, p. 159; J.F.C. Harrison, *Late Victorian Britain, 1875–1901*, London 1991, pp. 68–9; M.J. Winstanley, *Life in Kent at the Turn of the Century*, Folkestone 1978, pp. 24–5; F.B. Smith, *The People's Health, 1830–1910*, London 1979, p. 215.
3   *KE* 6.1.1906, 23.5.1908; Smith, *op. cit.*, p. 214.

made to meet the need from voluntary resources'. A request by Tonbridge UDC for Kent Education Committee to adopt the Act in May 1909 met the response that 'winter distress does not now exist'. The following November, however, the Education Committee finally agreed to provide the equipment and premises to feed 350 undernourished Tonbridge schoolchildren. The cost of the food was still met by a Tonbridge Canteen Committee.[4]

In contrast Gillingham adopted the Act in February 1907. Head-teachers, the School Attendance Officer and the Mayoress's Relief Committee provided the names of 351 children 'in necessitous circumstances' and on 2 December 1907 the first free meals of pea soup and rice pudding were served. Irish stew, potato pie, stewed mutton, suet pudding, and bread and jam subsequently appeared on the menu. During this first winter the contractor and seventy-five female volunteers served 17,191 dinners costing the ratepayers 2d per meal. The only concern arose from the failure of Chatham and Rochester to adopt the Act. This created the danger 'of the loafing class migrating from over the hill . . . to get their children fed here for nothing'. Next year Gillingham Education Committee supplied second-hand boots and clothing to their needy youngsters – a venture not terminated until 1948.[5]

More influential in Kent than the Education (Provision of Meals) Act 1906 was the Medical Inspection Act 1907, also introduced by the Liberal Government spurred on by the emerging Labour Party. It was not permissive but imposed on education authorities the duty of providing for the medical inspection of schoolchildren, and gave them power to provide remedial treatment. Kent County Council had not appointed a County Medical Officer under the Local Government Act 1888. Fears that a highly salaried officer could become 'their master rather than their servant' were still strong in the minds of some county councillors. Nevertheless it was now decided to appoint one at £800 a year plus expenses for travel, a laboratory, an office and two clerks. The first county medical officer, appointed in 1908, was Dr W.J. Howarth, formerly medical officer at Bury and at Derby, who had public health as well as medical qualifications. His appointment was preceded by the selection of medical officers at Maidstone and Folkestone. Canterbury and Gillingham quickly followed suit. Gravesend did not appoint until 1909, when one man was appointed to the offices of town medical officer, public analyst and schools medical officer for £250 a year.[6]

The worst fears of some councillors were rapidly realised. At Dover, where pupils were examined when they entered and left school, the town was divided into four school districts, each supervised by a doctor who was paid the standard

---

4   J. Burnett, *Plenty and Want: A Social History of Diet in England from 1815 to the Present Day*, Harmondsworth 1968, pp. 212, 271–2; *KE* 12.5.1906, 28.3.1908, 31.10.1908, 21.11.1908, 30.1.1909, 1.5.1909, 20.11.1909, 27.11.1909; *KM* 9.1.1909.

5   J. Fox, *Education in Gillingham, 1893–1974*, Gillingham 1974, pp. 16–17.

6   E. Melling, *History of Kent County Council, 1889–1974*, Maidstone 1975, pp. 16, 19–20; *KE* 8.2.1908, 22.2.1908, 25.7.1908; *KM* 4.12.1909, 19.3.1910; Fox, *op. cit.*, p. 18.

remuneration of 1s. 0d. per child. The total cost was estimated at £150–200. Frank Wacher, the medical officer for Canterbury, told the Education Committee that he would be examining some 600 children between January and June 1909. Sanitary inspection of the schools would follow. Children with defects would be re-examined and their parents informed. In cases of defective eyesight the Education Committee might be asked to consider the purchase of spectacles.[7] When Howarth revealed his plans for the county there was widespread opposition. He proposed that children should be inspected during their school lives between 3 and 5, and at 7 and 10 years. Part-time medical officers were to be appointed for each district under his direction entailing some fifty part-time appointments. Weighing machines, measuring equipment and screens would be required at each school. The total cost of the scheme, estimated originally at £800, would be in the region of £3,000 while a series of conferences would be staged to better inform doctors, school managers and teachers. Lord Northbourne had already queried the cost. 'The medical examination of children may be essential,' commented the *Kentish Express*, 'but when will this addition to expenditure cease?' When medical examinations began, one school doctor was met by representatives of the local Ratepayers' Association protesting at the cost. Howarth had not only to contend with the objections of ratepayers but with the Kent Association of Teachers, which welcomed the medicals but objected to the excessive unpaid clerical work they imposed. Many small schools lacked the space to hold medicals or the playgrounds for summer teaching. Only a handful of school managers supported him 'for taking a leaf from Germany's book'. Nonetheless his scheme was accepted and the County Council even appointed two additional full-time 'lieutenants' to inspect schools in the outlying districts of Ashford and Tonbridge bringing the full-time staff of his expanding department to four doctors and two female inspectors of midwives by 1910.[8]

School medicals were rigorous and included the child's general state of cleanliness including the head. Early examinations uncovered some horrifying facts: 'dirt and vermin abound . . . in those districts inhabited by casual labourers and the unemployed', read the first report upon medicals in Gravesend, 'the necessity of washing undergarments seems to have escaped parents . . . Boots are woefully defective . . . Dullness of intellect goes with the generally dirty condition.' Howarth's report in 1909 reiterated the presence of vermin, poor personal hygiene, variable cleanliness and deficient footwear in the case of many county children. He also emphasised the need to control infectious disease, with ringworm in epidemic form. Twenty per cent of the 31,000 children examined had enlarged tonsils or adenoids. Many suffered from ill-health through dental neglect. Seventy-three per cent of 1,206 Maidstone children examined in 1911 had gross, visible, dental defects. Almost half had more than three teeth decayed. Many possessed no toothbrush. Over-anxious mothers

7   *KE* 23.5.1908, 26.12.1908.
8   *KE* 31.10.1908, 14.11.1908, 28.11.1908, 5.12.1908, 26.12.1908; *KM* 2.1.1909; Melling, *op. cit.*, p. 19.

frequently clothed children in as many as ten layers of garments making them prey to infection of all kinds. Nearly one-fifth of children examined were recommended for further treatment.[9]

Even when defects had been diagnosed the problem lay in remedial work. Poor children, requiring the removal of tonsils and adenoids, could seek help from their Poor Law doctor. Otherwise parents sought hospital 'tickets' or children were treated by mothers and neighbours. Gravesend hospital, like many others, was by 1909 overburdened by children referred for treatment. Early reports on school medicals emphasised the need for school nurses to treat children at home. Gillingham appointed a nurse in 1908 at £80 per year but Gravesend councillors vehemently opposed an appointment, maintaining that treatment was a parental responsibility. Advice could be provided by the voluntary Kent Nursing Association but its nurses were few for so large a county.[10] School medicals also systematically revealed the insanitary condition of many Kent schools. In October 1909 the 'offices' of Chart Sutton School were condemned as 'regular death traps' and the sanitary arrangements at Langley School described as 'a disgrace to the parish'. At Swanley Junction School an overflowing cesspit deposited 'a foot of liquid sewage on the surrounding ground which, besides being dangerous to the children, constitutes a nuisance to the neighbourhood'.[11] At first school medicals in Kent revealed more problems than answers. Defectiveness was appalling by modern standards. The scale of these difficulties had been systematically disclosed for the first time but solutions were a long time in coming.

The problem posed by insanitary and overcrowded housing was even more difficult to solve. In 1911 Kent's rural cottages were condemned as 'little dens which are incubators of immorality and disease'. At Gatehouse Farm Cottage, Kilndown, nine persons occupied two bedrooms, one of which was 'little more than a landing'. The roof was defective, the windows broken, the dwelling filthy and without sanitation. Water was obtained from a well containing excessive organic matter. Two children had recently died there. Councils and medical officers were reluctant, however, to interfere with private property. Desperate cases of overcrowding were reported in Hawkhurst, Sandhurst and Aldington. The cottages of the poor were 'unfit for habitation' at Sandway, Lenham and Stockbury, but little was done other than to report the matter to the property owner. The demolition of ten houses in Wye, condemned by East Ashford RDC, was unusual as was a systematic inspection of houses, parish by parish, by the same council's sanitary inspector under the Housing and Town Planning Act in 1911. This legislation rebounded on Wrotham UDC, where families were turned out of overcrowded, insanitary housing, only to be forced into the workhouse by housing shortage.[12]

9 *KM* 3.7.1909, 19.3.1910, 4.6.1910, 8.6.1912.
10 *KM* 20.11.1909, 19.3.1910, 2.4.1910, 4.6.1910, 28.5.1910; Fox, *op. cit.*, p. 18.
11 *KM* 9.10.1909, 30.10.1909.
12 *KE* 17.2.1906, 1.9.1906, 21.11.1908, 6.5.1911, 14.10.1911; *KM* 16.1.1909, 8.6.1912.

The epidemic diseases which had predominated in the last quarter of the nineteenth century still took their toll. West Ashford isolation hospital was filled with patients suffering from scarlet fever in the epidemic of 1906, and scarlatina remained the most prevalent disease at Erith and elsewhere in 1909. The year 1906 saw an outbreak of whooping cough at Charing. Two years later a measles outbreak spread from Canterbury throughout much of Dover RDC. There was a further measles epidemic at Maidstone in 1911. Diphtheria, another omnipresent complaint, erupted at Herne Hill and Bethersden in 1908, at Swanley in 1909, and at Ashford in 1913. An outbreak of typhoid at Snodland in 1910, where sewage disposal was primitive, twenty-seven typhoid victims at Lenham the following year, and a major epidemic with over fifty cases at Strood in 1912 were salutary reminders that inadequate sewerage and lack of clean water were still commonplace in Kent. These diseases still brought fatalities but mortality was by no means so high as in the great epidemics of the previous century. The exception was the great influenza pandemic of 1918–19, the virus being carried to Europe by American soldiers in the closing stages of the Great War. With the retreat of cholera and smallpox, tuberculosis, consumption or phthisis as it was variously known, reasserted itself in the public eye. Although recognised as a disease from the earliest times it did not become notifiable until January 1909. There were constant allegations that it was conveyed from country to town by means of milk. Rural dwellers on the other hand alleged that the towns were 'factories of consumption'. In 1911 there were estimated to be some 5,000 cases in the county, of which half required treatment. Over 10% of Kent's death rate was attributed to tuberculosis.[13]

An outbreak of enteric fever among hop-pickers at Chilham in October 1907 led to a bitter dispute between the medical officers of East Ashford RDC and Ashford UDC. While the latter attributed the outbreak to a farm's drinking water, which he claimed was polluted by sewage from Ashford and Wye, the former blamed the pickers' lodgings in Ashford. The importation by hoppers of infectious disease into Kent had long been recognised and was re-emphasised by Howarth in 1908. His claim that the risk had been much reduced by by-laws was over-optimistic. Efforts had been made to improve hoppers' horrific sleeping and sanitary conditions with model by-laws in the last decades of the nineteenth century. In 1883, however, only six of the thirteen districts used these by-laws. By 1906 they had been adopted by Maidstone Council, two urban district councils and eleven rural district councils.[14] A review of hoppers' conditions for the Local Government Board in 1907 found most of Kent's 74,000 'foreign' pickers housed in purpose-built wooden or corrugated iron hopper huts. Some, however, were still housed in overcrowded farm outhouses and old War Office tents

---

13 *KE* 24.11.1906, 4.1.1908, 7.11.1908, 30.11.1908, 2.1.1909, 21.1.1911, 11.2.1911, 15.4.1911, 20.5.1911, 13.12.1913.
14 *KE* 4.1.1908, 22.2.1908; N. Yates, R. Hume and P. Hastings, *Religion and Society in Kent, 1640–1914*, Woodbridge 1994, pp. 193–7, 209; A. Bignell, *Hopping down in Kent*, London 1977, pp. 62–7.

whose sanitary condition and lack of decency left much to be desired. Only straw was provided for bedding. Serious fires were still common. Some farms, particularly in the area of the Mid-Kent Water Company, had a supply of clean water, but there were many where the supply was limited or seriously polluted. In numerous instances privy accommodation was absent. Nevertheless conditions, although giving grounds for concern, were regarded as improved compared with thirty years previously. When the Malling District Medical Officer visited Crowhurst Farm, East Peckham, in 1909 he found twenty tents, half of which were 'worn and riddled with holes'. In some tents he discovered 'hundreds of small holes and in others openings as big as a man's hand'. In Faversham RDC, where 9,200 hoppers occupied 2,550 hopper huts and seventy-five bell tents during the 1911 season, the Local Government Board Inspector reported a great improvement since 1906. In 1913 the Local Government Board suggested that local medical officers should make a detailed inspection of camps before hopping began. Changes could be made before the hoppers arrived and infringements reported.[15]

The First World War brought changes in hop-picking. The outbreak of hostilities meant that there was a shortage of pickers as men joined the armed forces and women secured more profitable employment in war work. They were replaced with students and other volunteers, thus making the pickers more socially acceptable. Between the wars conditions improved with greater cleanliness, toilets and communal cookhouses on some sites. Missionaries were to be found in the larger hop gardens and from 1923 the Red Cross camped among the hoppers. The County Medical Officer was, however, still critical of sanitation, fire risk and infection. In 1924 the Medical Officer for the South-West Kent United Health area commented:

> I have seen the slums of Dublin and Salonika . . . conditions here put these in the shade . . . The latrines . . . had not been emptied for three seasons. Small wonder epidemics broke out . . . All credit is due to the voluntary workers, many of them trained nurses with war service, who have worked in such conditions.

A party of Ministry of Health doctors, who spent twelve days among the hoppers in the same year, found conditions a good deal better than this, noting that 'the lot of the Kentish hop pickers has greatly improved during the past two years. Public opinion is helping local health authorities . . . to raise the general standard of camp conditions.' In 1926 the Ministry of Health issued new model by-laws governing hopper encampments. The final outbreaks of smallpox among hoppers occurred at Marden in 1928 and Hawkhurst in 1930. By 1931 South-West Kent alone had 11,548 purpose-built 'hopper huts', some constructed of brick, on 386 farms. Mains water was available at 296 of the

---

[15] R. Farrar, *Report to Local Government Board on the Lodgings and Accommodation of Hop Pickers*, London 1907, pp. 15–25; Bignell, *op. cit.*, pp. 70–1; *KM* 16.10.1909; *KE* 14.10.1911.

farms. This was a higher proportion than in the cottages of many rural districts. Moreover, 309 camps were served by two hospitals and forty-seven dispensaries. The Rural Water Supplies Act 1934 gave local authorities an additional reason for enforcement and some camps in Maidstone District improved beyond recognition. In 1936 conditions at Whitbreads' Beltring Hop Garden were described as 'ideal' with hot and cold water in the huts, excellent sanitation and a surgery nearby. Furthermore the hoppers were expected to behave and, until they were replaced with machine picking in the 1950s, hopping became more of a working holiday than the earlier annual incursions when 'the undesirable visitors from London' brought poverty and disease to the Kent countryside.[16]

The days of large-scale epidemics were also now largely over. In 1920 the county death rate from diphtheria was higher than in any year since 1914. There was another serious outbreak in Dartford in 1921. By 1937 the medical officer for Northfleet UDC reported a complete absence of diphtheria which had been endemic for many years. Periodic typhoid outbreaks were still reported in schools, but swabs were immediately taken from all children in the schools affected for examination in the bacteriology laboratories. Whereas 6,500 specimens were examined in 1913, 36,000 were analysed in 1930. Tuberculosis, on the other hand, remained in 1931 'one of the greatest health problems in Kent'. It was exacerbated by budget reductions during the Great Depression. These created long waiting-lists for the sanatoria upon which the victims' lives depended. The disease was still increasing alarmingly in 1946. The death rate from the new scourge of cancer, increasing in 1920, reached record proportions in 1928. In 1939 the total number of cancer deaths in Kent was 2,344 growing to 2,829 by 1948.[17]

The crude death rate throughout Kent continued to fall. In 1919 it was 12.7 falling to 11.4 by 1920. This compared with significantly higher rates in many parts of Kent before 1914. By 1936 it was 11.3 and in 1948 stood at 10.7. Part of the fall was the result of lower infant mortality which dropped steadily from 109 per 1,000 in 1911 to 69 per 1,000 in 1919, 47 per 1,000 in 1936, and 26 per 1,000 in 1948. In part these figures could be attributed to improvements in midwifery, infant welfare and maternity services. They were also the result of progress in public health and general medical advance. The County Medical Officer for Schools Report in 1922 indicated the advances made in health care among elementary schoolchildren since 1907. Medical examinations of 142,620 children had been performed during the year. Almost 7% of these were found to be verminous and 1,922 had been excluded from school for treatment. Operations on tonsils or adenoids had been performed on 1,104 children, 729 had been seen at TB clinics and 423 cases of ringworm had been treated. The value of early diagnosis was becoming accepted: the School Medical Officer for

---

16 Bignell, *op. cit.*, pp. 71–4, 76–7, 79, 85–6; R. Filmer, *Hops and Hop Picking*, Aylesbury 1982, p. 47; *KM* 19.8.1922, 28.12.1929; *KE* 20.9.1930.
17 *KM* 5.2.1921, 7.12.1929, 26.6.1937; *KE* 15.8.1931, 29.8.1931; Kent County Council, *Annual Report of Medical Officer of Health*, Maidstone 1948.

Chatham noted in 1933 that 'children are better developed and cleaner than they were in the early days of medical inspection'. Among adults the National Insurance Act 1911 entitled only a limited number of men to medical treatment from a 'panel' doctor. Wives, children, the elderly and self-employed still had to pay for a consultation and for medicines. By 1936, however, the Kent Insurance Committee was reporting substantial increases in the number of prescriptions and the frequency of prescribing per person. Prescriptions had grown from 1,557,606 in 1934 to 1,734,950 in 1936, while chemists had dispensed for 379,697 persons in 1934 compared with 408,257 in 1936, suggesting that more drugs were becoming available to more persons who had previously depended on proprietary medicines.[18] By this time medical research had furnished vaccinations against typhoid, diphtheria and tuberculosis, and further advances were to come.

(2) Drainage, Sanitation and Water Supply

The last decades of the nineteenth century had seen some piecemeal improvement in drainage, sanitation and water supply in both urban and rural Kent. In the countryside much depended upon local initiative. Improvement was slow. Sanitary progress was reflected in an overall fall in mortality rates, but in 1900 barely half of twenty-year-olds nationally could expect to survive to the age of sixty-five. Most adults experienced a life of debilitating manual labour in the workplace or at home.[19]

The decade after 1890 had also seen a piecemeal acceleration in the provision of clean water, particularly after the Maidstone typhoid epidemic of 1897–8. Milton UDC completed a new waterworks for the Sittingbourne area in 1906 and another new waterworks opened at Hythe in 1908. An enlargement to Dover Waterworks in the latter year created additional storage for 57,000 gallons of water and an extra pumping capacity of 8,000 gallons an hour. The Metropolitan Water Board took over the supply for Dartford in 1904. By 1909 Gravesend was the only major Kent town lacking piped water. In rural Kent, the Mid-Kent Water Company was authorised in 1906 to supply Stalisfield and a number of other parishes in Faversham Rural District, while the extension of mains water from Smarden to Headcorn and from Charing to Ashford proceeded satisfactorily. The Mid-Kent Water Company also accepted terms to supply the villages of Borden, Bredgar, Milsted, Kingsdown and Tunstall, and to extend its mains from High Halden to Bethersden, connecting with the Pluckley supply. New Romney's Medical Officer reported that the town was provided with 'as good and safe a supply of soft water as could be wished for', whilst two-thirds of Willesborough houses were also connected to the mains, and the hamlets

---

[18] *KM* 1.1.1921, 16.7.1921, 3.12.1921, 12.5.1923, 26.5.1923, 8.4.1933, 15.7.1933, 12.6.1937; *KE* 26.12.1931.
[19] Yates, Hume and Hastings, *op. cit.*, pp. 210–24.

surrounding Headcorn supplied.[20] Water projects met comparatively little opposition. Even so water supply in many parts of rural Kent was still critical. Pond water, unfit for drinking purposes, was the only water available at Egerton and Bethersden. Shadoxhurst, Kingsnorth, Elham, Dymchurch, Challock, Shottenden, Bapchild, Iwade, St Nicholas-at-Wade and Bilsington were but a few of the many rural communities cited as lacking clean water in 1906–8. At Dymchurch, even after a Local Government Board Enquiry, progress foundered on the quarrel between the Rural District Council and Parish Council over who should bear the cost. Residents continued to drink from a condemned pump. At Newchurch, where the water supply failed in summer, the only suggestion of the district medical officer was that water should be gathered from the church roof and stored.

Chilham Lees, Molash and Shottenden, whose 123 dwellings were visited by the Medical Officer of East Ashford RDC, already relied on rainwater kept in tanks. Bilsington, too, obtained its water from rainwater tanks and contaminated wells while Leeds' water supply left the Local Government Inspector fearful that 'an outbreak of serious illness might be expected at any time'.[21] A correspondent to the *Kentish Express* summarised the position:

> In some villages the want of water is pitiable. . . . Many cottagers are dependent on small water tanks. . . . In the long, dry summer these fail them. . . . In the few existing wells little more than a chalky deposit remains. . . . Women have remained unwashed for several weeks because they could barely get sufficient drinking water having to pay threepence for a small pailful. If the cottager complains he gets notice to quit.[22]

The County Medical Officer, in his first report, made no serious complaint about the quality or quantity of water in urban districts and noted 'evidence of considerable activity in rural districts although the supply in some areas is not what it ought to be. . . . Better provision in this respect represents the most urgent sanitary reform.'[23] Nevertheless a high proportion of Kent rural parishes still depended on ponds for drinking water in 1913.[24]

Despite constant pressure from the Local Government Board, sewerage schemes made even slower progress. The pace of drainage had quickened in the 1890s, but effective sewerage was dependent upon good water supply and local authorities were held back by the cost and uncertainty of success. Of Kent's towns, Gravesend, which also lacked piped water, Chatham, Rochester, Cranbrook, Tenterden and Whitstable were still without mains drainage at the turn of

20 *Ibid.*, p. 219; *KE* 13.1.1906, 3.2.1906, 10.2.1906, 10.3.1906, 14.4.1906, 16.6.1906, 10.11.1906, 1.8.1908, 12.12.1908; *KM* 18.12.1909; A. S. Wohl, *Endangered Lives: Public Health in Victorian Britain*, London 1983, p. 63; G. Porteous, *The Book of Dartford*, Dartford 1979, p. 79.
21 *KE* 18.8.1906, 8.9.1906, 15.9.1906, 28.3.1908, 20.6.1908, 18.7.1908, 12.9.1908, 24.10.1908, 21.11.1908, 8.12.1908; *KM* 20.11.1909, 4.12.1909, 8.7.1911, 7.10.1911.
22 *KE* 3.11.1906.
23 *KM* 4.12.1909; Centre for Kentish Studies, CC/ R 17/1.
24 Yates, Hume and Hastings, *op. cit.*, p. 209.

the century. Gravesend, a town of 30,000 inhabitants, was 'in the same elementary sanitary condition as when it secured its charter in 1562'. There were 6,000 cesspools in the borough. Some had remained unemptied for thirty years. Others had never been emptied. Many lay beneath the houses. When the pools were full they were emptied into discontinued wells. The cost of mains drainage was estimated at between £50,000 and £100,000 in 1909, the year that Gravesend Corporation was sued by the Thames Conservancy Commission for pouring liquid sewage into the Thames. Three years later a special committee of the Borough Council was still trying to decide upon the best drainage scheme to adopt.[25] At Cranbrook, where the town sewage had been polluting the Crane for many years, the goodwill of the owners of land through which the river passed was exhausted by 1909. Under pressure Cranbrook Parish Council determined to implement the cheapest of three drainage schemes prepared by the RDC surveyor rather than await intervention by the Local Government Board 'who would saddle the parish with debt for many years'.[26] At Whitstable, where the system had been taken from the Commissioners of Sewers in 1902, the UDC considered four schemes in three years to replace sewerage 'unworthy of even the nineteenth century'. The fourth scheme was rejected by the Local Government Board after Whitstable's own Medical Officer claimed it was 'rash, quixotic and impossible' and would ruin the public health of the town and its oyster fishery. Even the ratepayers were totally opposed to it.[27]

The experience of towns which had adopted drainage schemes also caused others to hold back from 'the financial abyss of sanitary engineering'. In 1909 only 1,200 of 1,800 houses on the line of Sittingbourne's main sewer had been connected. Connection of the remainder was being undertaken by the Urban District Council at the ratepayers' expense. Maidstone, which had been striving to perfect its sewers for half a century, opened a new sewerage works at Aylesford, costing £80,000, in June 1909 to prevent pollution of the Medway:

> Maidstone has at last done all that is scientifically possible to dispose of its sewage. . . . No expense was spared and the ratepayers are entitled to hope they have the best value for their money.[28]

Three months later the residents of Aylesford, Eccles, Ditton, Larkfield and New Hythe were vehemently complaining of the 'abominable stench' given off by the works which prevented them from opening windows and forced them to walk the streets 'holding camphor and disinfectant to their noses'. An enquiry by the Local Government Board in 1910 revealed that the million gallons of sewage per day was still inadequately treated. A year later, with the problem still unsolved, Kent County Council was considering asking for a second enquiry.

25 Ibid., pp. 202, 219, 223; KM 12.6.1909, 26.6.1909, 2.10.1909, 13.1.1912.
26 KM 4.9.1909, 18.11.1911.
27 KE 3.6.1911, 19.8.1911, 26.8.1911.
28 KM 26.6.1909, 24.7.1909; Yates, Hume and Hastings, op. cit., pp. 221–2; J. Hilton, Maidstone: An Outline History, Maidstone 1978, p. 35.

Ashford, like Maidstone, spent much time and money improving its sewerage, but in 1913 was still polluting the Stour as Maidstone was the Medway.[29]

Howarth's first annual report claimed optimistically that 'efficient sewage disposal was more or less solved in many districts' and 'in others was receiving careful consideration'. Herne Bay adopted a drainage scheme in 1906; Sheppey RDC opened a sewerage works at Minster in 1911; in 1912 a new plant at Tonbridge replaced the original one of 1873. Kent, however, was a county of over four-hundred parishes, many containing several small communities with inadequate sanitation. Refuse at Dymchurch, without sanitary provision, was thrown into the sea whence it washed back onto the sands. Sewage at Saltwood overflowed into the Royal Military Canal at Hythe. At Lenham, the sewer, 'no more than an elongated cesspool', discharged into the vicarage pond which was the source of the Stour running through Ashford and Canterbury. Sewage found its way into the cellars of houses in the square, and many dwellings were supplied from water mains 'in dangerous proximity to cesspools and privy pits'. At Harrietsham and Halling sewage was directed into the highway drains while Wrotham's sewage flowed untreated down the Ivy Hall Farm Estate. The sanitary condition of Leeds, where overflowing cess pools stood adjacent to a baker's shop, was described as 'disgusting' and 'a disgrace to Hollingbourne RDC'.[30] The populous village of Rainham required a drainage system as did Sandwich and Wye. At the former, where population was growing with the Kent coalfield, improvement had been recommended for some years. The latter became the subject of a Local Government Board enquiry only after questions were asked in Parliament.[31]

The sewage of many parishes was cleared only by scavengers appointed by contract. These would only accept a contract if the principal farmers guaranteed that the sewage could be deposited on their land as fertiliser. An even greater obstacle to progress was the obdurate opposition of ratepayers. Wingham ratepayers rejected a proposal for draining their village made by the RDC Medical Officer in 1908 on the grounds that his report 'did not warrant such a costly scheme'. At Lenham, a local Ratepayers' Protection Association proposed an alternative scheme to that put forward by Hollingbourne RDC since 'they were anxious that drainage should be provided at the least possible expense'. When this was ignored they memorialised the Local Government Board. When Strood RDC adopted a sewerage scheme at Halling, costing £10,700, the largest ratepayers, the cement manufacturers, threatened to close their works unless the Council reconsidered the scheme.[32]

Even after the First World War the provision of pure water and adequate

29 *KM* 18.9.1909, 18.12.1909, 29.1.1910, 18.11.1911; *KE* 4.1.1913, 9.8.1913; Yates, Hume and Hastings, *op. cit.*, p. 223.
30 *KM* 3.4.1909, 6.11.1909, 4.12.1909, 20.4.1912; *KE* 6.1.1906, 2.6.1906, 1.12.1906, 21.11.1908, 15.4.1911, 24.6.1911.
31 *KE* 11.2.1911, 8.3.1911, 20.5.1911, 19.8.1911.
32 *KE* 7.11.1908, 1.4.1911, 15.4.1911, 11.11.1911; *KM* 9.1.1909.

sanitation for individual communities proceeded piecemeal and slowly. A £15,000 scheme to provide mains water to eight parishes east of Ashford in 1929 was regarded as dual purpose by East Ashford RDC because it also absorbed the unemployed. The pace quickened a little after the Rural Water Supplies Act 1934 encouraged schemes for rural water supply. Projects received government grants if the county and the relevant rural district councils also contributed. In this way Cliffe, Frindsbury, Meopham, Luddesdown, Grain and Cooling obtained piped water in 1937. Piped water did not fully reach some villages, like Boughton Monchelsea, until after the Second World War.[33]

Progress in relation to drainage was equally slow. Of Kent's major towns, Gravesend was still polluting the Thames in 1921, a year in which the Council emptied some 3,712 cesspools at a cost of £7,945. In all, the Borough Surveyor estimated there were 5,600 cesspools, 700 of which discharged directly into the Thames. Even so many councillors considered improvement an unnecessary luxury. A mains drainage scheme was finally sanctioned in 1922 and a grant of £100,000 made from the Government Unemployment Grants Committee. Prevarication occupied a further ten years before a final loan of £15,000 was secured to replace the last cesspools. A year later, in 1933, Gravesend finally lost the stigma of 'a cesspool town'.[34] Chatham and Rochester were also considering a joint scheme for mains drainage and unemployment relief work in 1922. After six months debate they were no further forward. A new sewerage works opened at Cranbrook in 1930 and a mains drainage scheme was accepted for Rainham in the same year. At Erith, where the sewerage system built in 1898 for a population of 15,000 now catered for 33,000, the Council proposed in 1931 to borrow £87,000 under the Unemployment Grants Scheme to install an improved system. Northfleet, where drainage plans were rejected in the depression of 1921–3, eventually began a scheme in 1930. This was scheduled for completion in 1934 at a cost of £98,000.[35]

While the larger towns could attract government grants to meet the unemployment of the depression years, it was much more difficult for the rural villages. Malling RDC did not even try to get financial assistance in 1921 for the insanitary village of Wouldham. Instead, half-hearted attempts were made to improve the existing system. Cesspools were emptied and disinfected more frequently and pail closets replaced middens as they fell out of repair. Wrotham UDC, where drainage was 'most unsatisfactory', simply accepted in 1922 that 'the district is not capable of paying for mains drainage under present financial conditions', and proper sanitation was delayed for another ten years. Tenders were accepted for the sewerage of Barming Heath and for Darenth in 1922. Bearsted, still on cesspools in 1922, secured sewerage and a sewage disposal works in 1930. Marden, Bapchild, Borden and Tunstall had schemes agreed the

33 Melling, *op. cit.*, p. 59; *KM* 5.10.1929, 9.1.1937; *A Village Remembered*, ed. D. Tye, Maidstone 1980, p. 15.
34 *KM* 10.12.1921, 7.1.1922, 17.1.1931, 7.5.1932, 21.10.1933.
35 *KM* 11.2.1922, 24.6.1922, 12.8.1922, 22.3.1930; *KE* 30.8.1930, 31.1.1931.

following year when work began on a new sewerage works for Sittingbourne UDC.[36] An outspoken editorial in the *Kentish Express* in March 1930 indicated that much still remained to be done:

> In our county there are large villages with such bad drainage that a terrible epidemic . . . may occur at any time. . . . Insanitary conditions are producing illness when it might be avoided. . . . The remedy is to . . . spend less on education and transfer it to . . . the provision of proper drainage in every town and village. . . . Demolish the slums and build houses for the poor.[37]

In some communities local ratepayers blocked progress when it was offered. At Loose, which lacked mains water or refuse collection, 'it was no uncommon sight to see a cesspool flowing before a house'. Parish councillors were alarmed in 1932 by the news that Maidstone RDC was considering a sewerage scheme for their parish. They believed it was a covert plan to incorporate the parish into Maidstone Borough! Mains drainage in the remaining villages was further delayed by the Second World War. Cesspools at Boughton Monchelsea still gave cause for complaint in 1961. It took questions in Parliament before sewerage was finally installed in 1965.[38]

(3) Hospitals and Medical Care

Kent hospitals had developed only in the late eighteenth century. The Kent and Canterbury was opened in 1793, serving the needs of in- and out-patients. Others, like the Margate Seabathing Infirmary, quickly followed. Established as charities, they were not always accessible to the poor who had to obtain a note from a subscriber before treatment could be obtained. By 1900 many were unable to meet the growing demands upon them. West Kent Hospital had fifty-six surgical and nine medical cases waiting for one of its sixty-five beds. The report of the Governors of Gravesend Hospital, which in 1909 had to cope with 662 in-patients, 7,454 out-patients and an adverse balance of £485, argued the need for state or municipal aid.

Equally important were the public dispensaries founded in a number of Kent towns in the first half of the nineteenth century. These were based, like the hospitals, upon charitable subscriptions carrying the right to recommend, and still played an important role at the beginning of the twentieth century. Otherwise, medical assistance in 1900 rested largely with the Poor Law authorities. In 1842 district medical officers had been appointed by Boards of Guardians to treat sick paupers referred to them by relieving officers. They also treated paupers in workhouse infirmaries. Guardians, however, kept expenditure to a

---

36 *KM* 7.5.1921, 4.3.1922, 8.4.1922, 2.9.1922, 4.11.1922. 21.6.1930, 10.1.1931, 29.8.1931.
37 *KE* 15.3.1930.
38 *KM* 14.7.1923, 28.5.1932, 10.9.1932; Boughton Monchelsea Parish Council Minutes, 13 March 1961 and 13 July 1965.

minimum, and sick wards were often rudimentary and the service basic. The building of specialised isolation hospitals gathered momentum in the 1880s and 1890s as a result of epidemics and pressure by the Local Government Board. In North Kent, however, the authorities still brought the old convict 'hulks' into temporary service when required. East Ashford Guardians, like other Boards, subscribed to the Kent and Canterbury, the Maidstone Ophthalmic and the Brompton Cancer hospitals, but in remote villages cottage hospitals provided the only nursing and medical care.

Trained nurses and midwives were in short supply. Wye Nursing Association provided a trained nurse 'to give the poorer classes some idea of nursing' in 1906. Maidstone appointed two nurses for the poor in 1909 on the initiative of its Mayor and West Kent Hospital. The nurses were at the disposal of the town's doctors but they were pitifully few for a population of 35,000. When the Midwives Act was introduced in 1910, barring untrained midwives from practice, Kent County Council already had two female inspectors in place. A special appeal was necessary, however, by the Marchioness Camden, President of the Kent County Nursing Association, to raise money to train the large number of unregistered midwives which resulted from the legislation.[39]

From the second half of the nineteenth century the larger friendly societies provided sick members with the free services of a doctor, but for the poor, who could not afford membership, medical treatment was prohibitively expensive. The only alternatives were the aid of neighbours or self-medication. Consumption of patent medicines had been increasing since the 1870s. Local newspapers contained advertisements for them, obtainable by post. These ranged from Venos's Lightning Cough Cure, 'the most efficient remedy for Coughs, Influenza, Catarrh, Bronchitis, Asthma, Weak Lungs, Croup and Whooping Cough', to Dr Davis's Famous Female Pills, 'the best known cure for Anaemia, Giddiness, Swelling after Meals, Loss of Appetite, Hysteria, Palpitation, Debility, Depression, Irregularities and all female complaints'. 'In seven years Venos has found its way into nearly every home in Great Britain and the Colonies,' boasted the manufacturers; 'upwards of two million bottles are sold annually'. Dr Williams's 'Pink Pills for Pale People' claimed, even more amazingly, to have 'totally banished' the 'Great National Scourge' of consumption, while the ointment Zam Buk, was hailed by its makers as 'the descendant of those herbal balms by which the athletes of Ancient Greece and the gladiators of Rome ensured the . . . ready healing of their skins'.[40] Satisfied customers, such as Mrs Taryman of Northgate, Canterbury, testified weekly to the efficacy of their patent medicines without embarrassment:

For . . . seven years I suffered with protruding piles; at times the pain was torture and I had to have a specially-prepared chair. . . . The only remedy

[39] Yates, Hume and Hastings, *op. cit.*, pp. 191–2, 212; *KE* 26.12.1860, 1.8.1908, 15.5.1909; *KM* 2.4.1910, 4.6.1910.
[40] *KH* 6.1.1906, 10.3.1906.

which did me any good was Doan's Ointment. . . . After a few weeks I was cured.[41]

In an age when the average general practitioner, trained before 1914, had scarcely heard of proteins or vitamins, and nutrition and its relationship to disease was unrecognised, there was perhaps some truth in Mr W.F. Warren's claim that Venos's Seaweed Tonic 'did me more good than six weeks' medicines from my club doctor'. While some proprietary medicines were harmless quackery, others were damaging to health.[42]

Further medical progress was curtailed by the Great War, though three significant developments had taken place in the years immediately before its outbreak. The first was the opening of a County Bacteriological Laboratory in 1911, which came to be increasingly used by both district medical officers and local general practitioners. The second was the opening of the first dispensaries for the treatment and prevention of tuberculosis required by the provisions of the National Insurance Act 1911. The third was the appointment of a County Sanitary Officer in September 1914, to investigate housing conditions in rural areas, following continual criticism by district medical officers. The National Insurance Act had set aside £15 million for the establishment of sanatoria for the benefit of all and not just those who were insured. In 1912 Kent was divided into five districts, each with a central station and subsidiary stations throughout the area. By mid-1914 eighteen dispensaries had been opened and five full-time Tuberculosis Medical Officers appointed. By 1915 the number of dispensaries had increased to twenty, and by 1918 there were also ten health visitors to oversee the care of mothers and young children, and three maternity and child-welfare centres had been established, financed by government grants. Midwifery services, particularly in the rural areas, had also been expanded by means of government assistance. Government pressure had also brought about increasing activity in another sphere of public health. The appointment of a female police inspector and constable had been the initial county response to 'the large number of undesirable women drawn to Folkestone by Shorncliffe Camp'. By 1918 the County Medical Officer had arranged for a different form of preventative medicine, and five venereal-disease clinics for out-patients had opened in Kent hospitals.[43] These developments, helpful though they were, were small for such a large and populous county.

Some of Kent's voluntary hospitals were in financial difficulties. With a growing population they could never hope for financial stability, since they were entirely dependent upon bequests and voluntary contributions. The Great War brought renewed pressures, and by 1922 the West Kent General Hospital had a deficit of £3,000 and a rising number of in-patients. The Kent County Ophthalmic Hospital, which also had long waiting-lists, was forced to make a

41 *KE* 13.6.1908.
42 *KH* 6.1.1906; Smith, *op. cit.*, pp. 343–5; Burnett, *op. cit.*, p. 273.
43 Melling, *op. cit.*, pp. 20, 30–1; *KM* 29.6.1912; *KE* 18.12.1915.

public appeal for £20,000.[44] Hopes of improvement in the provision of medical and public-health services, encouraged by the replacement of the Local Government Board by a Ministry of Health in 1919, were short-lived. Throughout the inter-war years progress was hampered by the government's requirements for financial stringency, which included putting pressure on local authorities to keep their expenditure to a minimum, particularly during the depression of 1921–3 and the world-wide economic crisis of 1929–33. The County Sanatorium at Lenham, erected during the Great War and then used as a hospital, returned to its original purpose in 1919. By 1920 there were twenty-two tuberculosis clinics in Kent, and the number of venereal-disease clinics had increased to eleven to deal with the aftermath of the war. High infant mortality necessitated a reorganisation of the county's nursing service: by 1929 there were more than thirty full-time health visitors, sixty-three county and sixteen voluntary maternity centres, all of which were heavily dependent upon volunteers for their operation. Whilst the County Council was prepared to give financial assistance to the voluntary nursing associations, it took ten years for the County Medical Officer to secure the appointment of a full-time woman doctor to supervise the maternity and child-welfare services. One was finally appointed in 1930.[45] By 1931 there were 234 trained midwives in Kent, and only a handful remained untrained. It was, however, not until 1937, when the Midwives Act 1936 required the operation of a salaried midwifery service, that a fully professional service was put in place across the county. Even then the County Council continued arrangements in some areas whereby midwives were employed by local nursing associations grant-aided by the County Council. This was the situation at Tunbridge Wells; in the urban districts of Ashford, Sevenoaks and Sheerness; and in the rural districts of Dartford and Tonbridge. In other parts of Kent the County Council employed over one-hundred midwives directly. The only other major County Council project in the inter-war period was the purchase of Leybourne Grange in 1927 and its adaptation to serve as a hospital for mental patients.[46]

By January 1931 the depression, and the economies which accompanied it, had forced the Governor of the Gravesend and North Kent Hospital to suggest that friendly societies should endow its beds. Pressure, however, was somewhat eased by the transfer to the County Council of Kent's twenty-five Poor Law Unions and their various buildings by the Local Government Act 1929, which came into operation on 1 April 1930. The nineteenth-century workhouses of Kent were, in many cases, in poor repair. Romney Marsh, lit by naked gas burners, was closed immediately, but West Ashford (Hothfield) and others became Public Assistance Hospitals for the chronically sick. East Ashford (Willesborough), Sevenoaks (Sundridge), Tenterden and Eastry were converted into institutions for the mentally ill. Blean, whose infirmary building was

[44] KM 4.3.1922, 27.5.1922.
[45] Melling, op. cit., pp. 41–2.
[46] Ibid., pp. 43, 58; KE 28.8.1931; KM 30.1.1937.

considered to be 'generally satisfactory' became a hospital for epileptics. Four workhouses, which were already providing general hospital facilities, namely Dartford, Pembury, Chatham and Bromley (Farnborough), were expanded, together with Sheppey, which became a maternity hospital. All five were redesignated County Hospitals in 1935, and over £500,000 was spent on capital improvements between 1930 and 1939. Farnborough was considered the best 'Poor Law Hospital' in the county. Despite the appointment of consultants and the development of pathology laboratories, X-ray, surgical and ambulance facilities, together with the opening of new nurses' homes, they had great difficulty in shaking off the Poor Law stigma. The voluntary hospitals, too, had previously undertaken the most surgical work and feared the increased competition. The total number of beds increased in the county from 3,441 in 1929 to 5,089 in 1938. Surgical operations more than doubled, but the County Medical Officer had the greatest difficulty in persuading the two sectors to co-operate, especially when he suggested the removal of patients to the ex-Poor Law hospitals, which had empty beds, for post-operative care.[47]

Pressures of population on hospital accommodation led to the acquisition of yet another 860-bed hospital at Orpington in 1935, but by November 1937 the Public Health Committee of the County Council was pressing for the adoption of a scheme over a period of years to provide improved and new hospital accommodation for a comprehensive, modern hospital service. Hospital provision, it was claimed, was not only unworthy of the county but had not improved over the last twenty years nor kept pace with population growth. The tuberculosis scheme was unchanged since 1912. Improvement planned in 1929 had been postponed by the depression. The proposals included the erection of three new hospitals and the extension of five others at a capital cost of £1,250,000 exclusive of sites and equipment. These were opposed by the Finance Committee, which described the Council's financial position as 'alarming'. Ultimately the improvements were accepted 'in principle only' and to be made 'at appropriate stages'. The Chairman of the Finance Committee estimated their completion by 1950![48] Further discussion was postponed by the Second World War.

During the war, Kent's county and voluntary hospitals came under the direction of the Ministry of Health. The Ministry not only stipulated the number of beds to be kept free for casualties but, after a survey of hospital accommodation showed an overall deficiency of about one-third nationally, provided the additional beds. Operating theatres were installed where required. Some patients were transferred elsewhere and other hospitals evacuated completely. In June 1940 the Royal Victoria Hospital, Folkestone – a voluntary hospital in financial difficulties – was taken over by the Ministry and administered by the County Council, thus foreshadowing future events. By 1945 the County Council was running ten hospitals with over 4,000 beds. Wartime preparation had, however,

47 *KE* 17.1.1931, 29.8.1931; Melling, *op. cit.*, pp. 52–8; J. Moss, *Public Assistance in Kent, 1930–1948*, Maidstone 1951, pp. 17–28.
48 *KM* 20.11.1937; Melling, *op. cit.*, p. 57; Moss, *op. cit.*, p. 37.

revealed the need for a full-scale state health service both locally and nationally.[49]

In a 'front-line county', vulnerable throughout to aerial attack and cross-
channel shelling, and a reception area for the Dunkirk evacuation and the casualties of D-Day, Kent hospitals played a vital role in the Second World War. Dover
County Hospital alone dealt with some 400 Dunkirk wounded in nine days and
many more during the air raids and shelling in the years which followed. As the
war progressed it became increasingly difficult to provide the nursing and domestic staff to run Kent's hospitals. By 1946 the hospital service, which had
worked under extreme difficulty throughout the war years, had reached crisis
point.[50]

(4) The Relief of Poverty

Poverty was created by sickness, unemployment and old age. In the early twentieth century it was not uncommon for elderly Kent women to beg used tea
leaves from more wealthy neighbours or for the very poor to subsist upon soup
made from potato peelings.[51] Provision of temporary relief work for the unemployed became official policy at the close of the nineteenth century, when there
was an attempt to reinstate the local relief work which had disappeared in 1834.
Local Government Board circulars in 1886 and 1893 encouraged local authorities to provide work for 'deserving' workmen left jobless by the trade cycle, and
after the slump of 1903–5 the Conservative Government passed the Unemployed Workmen Act 1905. This empowered local authorities to establish
distress committees and labour exchanges, and to create public relief works,
where possible, through voluntary subscription or else at the ratepayers'
expense, but outside the deterrent aegis of the Poor Law. Emigration could also
be arranged. The distress committees, representing the local authorities,
Guardians and 'other persons experienced in the relief of distress', were to separate the worthy unemployed from the idle. The latter were to be consigned to the
Poor Law.[52]

Kent, as a basically agrarian county, did not normally suffer severely from
industrial depression. The years which followed, however, saw a considerable
increase in unemployment locally as well as nationally, particularly in the
cement, brickmaking and building trades. Early in 1906 some Kent workhouses
noted large increases in vagrants. 'Quite 90% are men really seeking work,'
reported the West Ashford workhouse master as he purchased an extra five

---

[49] Melling, *op. cit.*, p. 72.

[50] *Ibid.*, p. 70.

[51] *KM* 2.1.1909, 12.2.1910.

[52] E.P. Hennock, 'Poverty and Social Reform', *Twentieth Century Britain: Economic, Social and Cultural Change*, ed. P. Johnson, London 1994, pp. 87–8; B.B. Gilbert, *The Evolution of National Insurance
in Britain*, London 1966, p. 242; Royle, *op. cit.*, p. 200.

stone-pounders. With the increase in vagrancy came the customary, grim catalogue of suicides. Sidney Bell, an unemployed Cranbrook carter, hanged himself
in March 1906 'depressed through continued lack of employment'. Emma
Milgate drowned herself in the Medway in October 1908 rather than enter the
workhouse, while Harry Paine, a Northfleet docker 'out of work for six months',
was among the suicides in 1909.[53]

The onset of depression provided an opportunity to put the 1905 Act to the
test. Distress committees were established at Chatham, Gillingham, Dartford,
Erith and Northfleet in February 1906. At Maidstone in August 1908 the
Guardians also requested the borough council to establish a labour exchange
and distress committee under the 1905 Act. During the first three months 1,180
unemployed applied for work at the labour exchange. Between December 1909
and February 1910 1,136 further applicants registered. Most were provided with
relief work. Unemployment remained high throughout 1910. Between January
1909 and December 1910 only 391 registered unemployed were found work
with private employers. Public relief work in the county town was provided for
1,377 while 1,162 were found temporary work such as hop-picking.[54] Among
the public relief work given was the construction of Loose Road tramway and
snow clearance during the heavy snowfall of January 1909. The Borough
Council was authorised to spend a halfpenny rate appointing an employment
officer to bring employers and unemployed together, while the Guardians sent
fifty-three men, women and children to Devon and Cornwall to seek work at a
cost of £100.[55]

Other local authorities, with or without distress committees, resorted to
similar expedients. Sandgate began alterations to dangerous parts of the Dover
Road. Two gangs of thirty, each working three days per week, began relief work
for Folkestone Corporation making Dover Hill safer for traffic. Other unemployed were set to work constructing a pathway across the Warren and building
a new bowling green at Radnor Park. Hythe Borough Council found temporary
work for 'unemployed painters and other ratepayers' restoring and painting
borough property. The Act, however, did not lessen appreciably the hardship of
the unemployed. Although remaining in force until the Great War, relief work
clearly failed in Kent as it did elsewhere. A Folkestone Charity Organisation
attempted to raise funds to provide work, but, in general, money and work from
voluntary sources were not forthcoming. Commitment of public funds by local
authorities was inadequate. Often the work was unsatisfactory and uneconomic.
£1,500 spent at Dartford on a labour yard for stone-breaking realised £130 for
the sale of broken granite and the experiment was terminated. Two-hundred
workless longshoremen and cement workers applied daily at Rochester relief

53 *KE* 10.3.1906, 28.4.1906, 5.5.1906, 12.5.1906, 16.5.1908, 10.10.1908, 3.7.1909; *KM* 22.5.1909,
9.3.1910.
54 P. Clark and L. Murfin, *The History of Maidstone: The Making of a Modern County Town*, Maidstone
1995, pp. 162–3; *KE* 24.2.1906, *KM* 20.2.1909.
55 *KE* 8.12.1906, 22.8.1908; *KM* 2.1.1909.

works but only thirty could be employed at a time filling in the foreshore near the Esplanade. The massive subsidies needed to make the Act a success were not forthcoming from central government although henceforth unemployment came increasingly to be seen as a national rather than a local responsibility.[56]

As the failure of relief work became apparent, some sections of the unemployed turned to direct action. Kent, in the winter of 1908/9, experienced its first hunger-marches and demonstrations. At Chatham, where there were almost 1,000 out of work, hunger-marchers in October 1908 marched first to join a demonstration at Woolwich and a week later advanced on Medway Union workhouse to demand the establishment of public works. A further meeting at Rochester Esplanade on 24 October was again addressed by their leader, John Long, an unemployed mechanic. In Maidstone, protests were centred around Maidstone Trades Council and the local branch of the ILP which organised collections for the unemployed. At Tunbridge Wells a march on Pembury workhouse was led and organised by a 'Right-to-Work Committee' under the leadership of a Mr Bullen. There were also marches at Bexley Heath and Gravesend. 'Kent has been . . . perambulated . . . by hunger marchers,' commented the *Kent Messenger*, warning of the dangers of 'a permanent relief work class'. The short-lived protest, however, was soon over. Violence had been avoided but distress was real.[57]

Perhaps the most important result of the Unemployed Workmen Act was the creation by the Labour Exchanges Act 1909 of permanent labour exchanges, where both employers and workers could register their requirements. Labour exchanges were common in Germany. The 1905 Act had already empowered its distress committees to establish them in Britain using rate aid. Folkestone Corporation established a 'Labour Bureau' at which over 200 unemployed registered in November 1908. A second Kent forerunner was created at King street, Maidstone, in February 1909. Here 'artisans and labourers of every kind may be . . . engaged free of cost' with a registration officer 'to assist employers in town and country offering . . . work of any kind'. The Act authorised the Board of Trade to establish exchanges in places that needed them. The unemployed renewed their registration weekly. The labour exchange department of the Board of Trade, with the young civil servant, William Beveridge, as its first director, took over the sixty-one existing exchanges in February 1910. This number had doubled by the end of the year.[58]

In Kent new exchanges were opened at Dover, Chatham, Erith, Gravesend and Woolwich. The Maidstone exchange was finally taken over from the distress committee in 1911. The improvement in economic conditions in the

56 *KE* 8.12.1906, 15.12.1906, 22.12.1906, 14.3.1908, 5.9.1908, 19.12.1908; Gilbert, *op. cit.*, pp. 238–44; *KM* 20.2.1909, 22.5.1909.
57 *CN* 12.9.1908, 17.10.1908; *CO* 12.9.1908, 17.10.1908, 24.10.1908; *MKJ* 8.10.1908, 15.10.1908; *KM* 17.10.1908, 23.1.1909, 30.1.1909, 6.2.1909, 20.2.1909, 13.3.1909; *SEG* 3.11.1908, 10.11.1908. Most of these references were kindly supplied by Bruce Aubry.
58 Gilbert, *op. cit.*, pp. 245, 260–5; *KM* 27.2.1909; *KE* 7.11.1908.

years prior to the Great War make assessment of the impact of exchanges difficult. The Chatham Exchange registered 500 unemployed in its first two days,
but had few situations to which it could direct them. The exchanges created no
extra jobs. Yet they established a national network, in touch by telephone,
through which the unemployed could seek work, and they abolished the need for
tramping fruitlessly in search of employment.[59]

(5) Old Age Pensions and National Insurance

If the relief of unemployment still had a long way to go, the introduction of
old-age pensions in 1908 provided the first state payments for the relief of
poverty from central resources, and it represents in a small way the first truly
nation-wide social service and, in effect, the beginnings of a welfare state. Old
age had long been recognised as a major cause of poverty. The idea of state
pensions had been discussed in Britain since their introduction in Germany in
1889. Charles Booth first proposed universal, tax-financed pensions in 1891. A
Royal Commission on the Aged Poor, reporting in 1895, took evidence from
John Ladd of Sellindge in Elham Union which gave outdoor, aged pauper couples
only 2s. 6d. a week. Ladd, an auditor for the London and Counties Labour
League, argued persuasively that double that amount should be granted to
'deserving . . . persons of old age . . . so that they might live with their children
instead of being compelled to enter the workhouse'. The strongest argument for
pensions was that they would reduce pauperism among the aged and provide an
alternative to the degradation of the Poor Law, while transferring the cost of
parochial relief to central government.[60] Pensions had already been discussed by
some Kent Guardians before the end of the nineteenth century. Added impetus
was given to the movement for pensions by their introduction in New Zealand in
1898. Tunbridge Wells Corporation adopted an old-age pensions scheme for its
workmen towards the end of 1906, and Folkestone Corporation, where the
Borough Surveyor claimed that by ceasing to employ old men he would save
£2,000 a year, was producing a similar scheme for its employees by 1908. In
vain Lord Northbourne, addressing Canterbury Farmers' Club, described the
proposal for old-age pensions as a return to the situation before the 1834 Poor
Law Amendment Act. In the 'Liberal landslide' of 1906 a substantial body of
Liberal and Labour MPs were returned pledged to old-age pensions. Back-
bench pressure induced Asquith to commit the Government to a non-
contributory Pensions Bill and to set £7 million aside for the purpose. The Bill
became law in August 1908 and the first pensions were paid on 1 January 1909.

59 *KM* 15.1.1910, 5.2.1910, 26.2.1910. 28.5.1910, 15.10.1910, 10.12.1910; *KE* 7.1.1911; Clark and
Murfin, *op. cit.*, p. 162.
60 Royle, *op. cit.*, p. 201; Hennock, *op. cit.*, pp. 82–3; *Parliamentary Papers* (1894), vol. xvi (i), Royal
Commission on the Aged Poor, Evidence of John Ladd, Questions 14344–502, pp. 786–92; Gilbert, *op.
cit.*, p. 228.

They were very restricted. Shortage of funds entailed a harsh means-test. At the last moment the qualifying age was set at seventy rather than sixty-five, which was regarded as crucial for old-age pauperism, thus ignoring the original intention of saving the deserving aged from the Poor Law stigma. Moreover, in an attempt to identify the deserving, the Act disqualified anyone who had received poor relief during the previous year, although receipt of Poor Law medical relief did not bring disqualification. Other grounds for disqualification were nationality, habitual failure to work, lunacy, and imprisonment during the previous ten years. For anyone over seventy and not disqualified, whose annual income was £21 per year (8s. 0d. per week) or less, the pension was 5s. 0d. per week (7s. 6d. for married couples). Thereafter the pension was reduced on a sliding scale to nothing for those whose income was around 12s. 0d. per week. Claimants were advised to complete their applications four months in advance to allow time for investigation.[61] The basic pension was raised to 10s. 0d. per week in 1919.

Some Kent Poor Law Unions endeavoured to secure deletion of the disqualification through receipt of out-relief but without success. Sevenoaks and Faversham Unions even attempted unsuccessfully to devise a scheme whereby charitable relief was given parochially to persons on out-relief but otherwise entitled to receive a pension. The Act set up a pensions committee for every county council. Kent County Council then delegated its powers to fifty sub-committees – twenty-three for the rural districts, nineteen for the urban districts, and eight for the small boroughs – to administer pensions. Committee memberships ranged between seven and nine persons. Because of the volume of business, persons appointed as committee members were not necessarily county councillors but a county councillor was appointed to each committee. Members were expected to possess a sound knowledge of those selected to receive pensions. The composition of pensions committees in the larger boroughs varied. At Maidstone and Canterbury, all town councillors automatically became committee members. Faversham appointed its Estates and Finance Committees *en bloc*. Folkestone chose sixteen members of its Corporation plus representatives of the town's friendly societies, a member of a charitable society, and three 'ladies'. At Deal, Alderman Hayward objected to the inclusion of women since 'they would introduce an element of undesirable hysterical sentiment'. Nevertheless there were female members of many sub-committees including those at Bridge, East Ashford and Tenterden.[62]

Attempts in some Unions to increase outdoor relief to 5s. 0d. per week in line with pensions came to naught. When the day of the first payment came, 'long delayed and long deferred', a large number of pensioners attended on the Isle of Sheppey despite a blizzard. To the aged poor it seemed unbelievable that a

61 Yates, Hume and Hastings, *op. cit.*, p. 188; Hennock, *op. cit.*, pp. 83–6; *KE* 29.12.1906, 8.2.1908, 11.4.1908; *KM* 2.1.1909.
62 *KE* 6.6.1908, 4.7.1908, 15.7.1908, 15.8.1908, 22.8.1908, 29.8.1908, 5.9.1908, 12.9.1908, 21.11.1908.

pension could be collected by attending at the post office on a given day. At Gravesend there were 261 pensioners

> mostly respectable old folks . . . who had worked hard throughout their lives and through no fault of their own at the eventide experienced some difficulty in making ends meet. Many smiled blandly at post office officials as they exchanged their oblong green notes for cash and many grateful words were expressed.[63]

At Maidstone an early recipient was an eighty-year-old widow who stated that 'she would no longer have to stint herself of light and firing'. Many of these first pensioners were said to be so overcome with emotion that they could hardly sign their names. In Northfleet UDC area pensions were described as 'a great boon not only to the old people themselves but in many cases to their relatives'. At Gravesend, Northfleet and Dartford the first payment was celebrated by a tea and entertainment for the old people, but at Folkestone only three members of the Pension Committee favoured such action. Opponents claimed that pensions imperilled thrift and were a reward to those who had saved nothing. The pension alone was hardly sufficient to live on without family support but important in that it helped to lift the burden of helplessness and insecurity from the aged, and for many it represented the difference between degradation and self respect. The statistics suggest that initially few applicants were unsuccessful. In Rochester, Chatham and Gillingham between 91% and 97.5% of claimants were awarded a pension. The figure fell to 89% at Maidstone and 86% at Malling. In Kent as a whole pensions committees disallowed 10% of all applications during the quarter ending 31 December 1908 and granted some 6,921 pensions at a cost of £83,170.[64] There are no statistics for those who were disqualified by receipt of poor relief.

To this extent the 1908 Act marks the beginning and not the end of a process of reform. In 1911 most paupers over the age of seventy on out-relief became able to opt out of the Poor Law and obtain an old-age pension instead. In Maidstone Union 149 recipients of outdoor relief were entitled to a pension, saving the ratepayers £1,200 a year. £1,500 was saved at Dover Union. Ninety-six paupers were removed from the relief lists in Cranbrook Union and forty at Romney Marsh Union. Far fewer at first gave up the security of the workhouse. Only 23 of 194 inmates initially left Medway Union workhouse; 44 of 118 left Maidstone and 12 of 190 left Thanet Union workhouse. In 1911 a correspondent from Ivychurch pointed out that, while pensions in the antipodes began at ages sixty-five and sixty for men and women respectively, 'the days of our age are three score and ten. . . . You must . . . work until you die . . . then you can apply for your old age pension.'[65]

63 *KM* 2.1.1909, 9.1.1909, 21.6.1909.
64 Gilbert, *op. cit.*, p. 226; Clark and Murfin, *op. cit.*, p. 163; Hennock, *op. cit.*, pp. 85–6; *KM* 2.1.1909, 9.1.1909, 20.2.1909, 22.5.1909, 21.6.1909.
65 Hennock, *op. cit.*, p. 85; *KE* 14.1.1911, 21.1.1911, 28.1.1911, 11.2.1911, 24.6.1911.

Plate 33. Victoria Home and Hospital, Broadstairs, c.1900.

Plate 34. Oakwood Hospital, Maidstone, c.1904.

Plate 35. The County Sanatorium at Lenham opened in 1919.

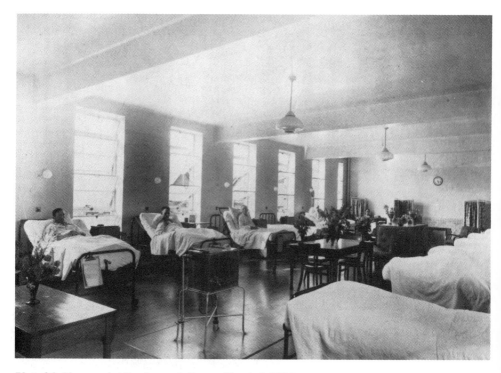

Plate 36. New ward at Farnborough County Hospital, 1936.

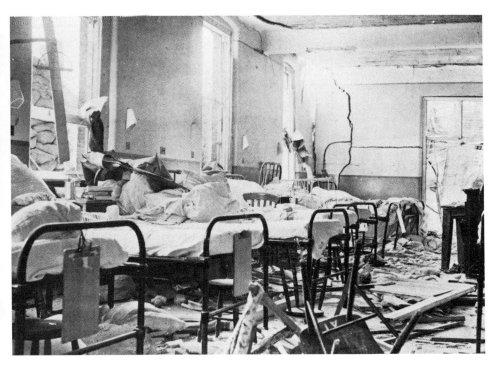

Plate 37. Air-raid damage to Dartford County Hospital, 1940.

Plate 38. Pembury Grange Old People's Home, 1949.

Plate 39. Playing croquet at Medway Old People's Home, 1952.

Plate 40. The dining room at Stanley Morgan House Old People's Home, Dartford, 1960.

The Old Age Pension was entirely funded by the state and initially cost the Liberal Government £1½ million more than anticipated. Thus warned of the high cost of welfare, it adhered to self-help when devising its climax to welfare reform in this period, the National Insurance Act 1911. Personal insurance against sickness was already provided by friendly societies and trade unions. Lapsed policies, however, were frequent; some organisations were unsound; and insurance of any sort was beyond the means of many. The Act was in two parts. Part I provided compulsory health insurance for all workers earning below £160 a year against sickness, disablement and maternity, but not death, which remained a matter for private insurance. Every worker contributed 4d. per week, the employer added a further 3d., and the Treasury 2d. In return there was to be a sickness benefit of 10s. 0d. a week (7s. 6d. for women) falling to 5s. 0d. after thirteen weeks. Free medical treatment was to be given by doctors on the 'panel' system, the panel being the list of insured patients who were the doctor's responsibility in addition to his private patients. The provisions did not cover the worker's family nor extend to hospital, dental or ophthalmic treatment. Only 15 million workers were covered.

Although the purpose of Health Insurance was to prevent the poverty caused by a worker's illness and inability to earn, the proposals met with widespread hostility in Kent as elsewhere. They not only spelt the end for village 'share out' and benefit clubs but, at first, appeared to be a threat to the friendly societies of long standing, who feared much of their business would be lost and their funds appropriated. Meetings of Kent Friendly Societies resolved that those of over five years' standing should press for exemption. Doctors were equally concerned about reduced incomes and loss of professional independence. The British Medical Association at first maintained that workers earning over £2 a week should be ineligible for medical attendance; that patients should have a free choice of doctor and that doctors should receive whatever fees they considered adequate. A mass meeting of East Kent doctors at the Kent and Canterbury Hospital only agreed to work within the scheme under conditions accepted by the BMA. Maidstone, Rochester, Chatham, Ashford and Dover doctors resolved to boycott the legislation in its present form. Farmers complained that since farm labourers were more healthy than town labourers their contributions should be reduced. It was also argued that women and child casuals should be exempt. Hop- and fruit-growers, heavily dependent on casual labour, argued similarly. One Tenterden farmer was keen to explain his position:

> I pay poor rates and insure my men against accident. . . . My men belong to a benefit society and take care of themselves and their families in sickness. The farmers will discharge their men in winter time. Then how will the labourer pay insurance?[66]

---

[66] *KE* 10.6.1911, 24.6.1911, 1.7.1911, 8.7.1911, 15.7.1911, 25.11.1911, 9.12.1911, 23.12.1911.

One of the loudest outcries came from employers of domestic servants:

> Compulsory insurance will destroy good feeling between mistresses and maids. Mistresses nurse maids in illness and pay for their doctors. . . . Leave the mistress alone and she will . . . treat her sick maid with consideration and generosity. Politicians do not understand the sympathy in Kent . . . between mistress and maid, master and man. We like to feel employers and employed can trust each other.[67]

A meeting of 'influential ladies' at Folkestone chaired by Mrs Penrose Fitzgerald, wife of Admiral Penrose Fitzgerald, determined to stage further protest meetings and to petition against the 'Servants Tax'. Many ladies declared they would refuse to lick the insurance stamps. The petition gained some 2,200 signatures while the MP for Ashford received 3,000 letters of protest and his Dover counterpart 1,000. Faced with this well-orchestrated campaign, the statement of a 'Kentish Servant' that '. . . we do need the Insurance Bill as much as any class of workers' seemed a voice in the wilderness.[68]

While some felt that state insurance was 'a gross interference between master and workman', others feared the Bill could only result, like club dispensing and Poor Law practice, in 'cheap and poor medicine'. One correspondent even called, interestingly, for 'a National Board of Health as we have a Board of Education'. Ultimately Lloyd George triumphed. The Act was administered by approved societies selected from friendly societies and insurance companies. 'The only way to obtain full benefit . . . is to join an approved society', read an advertisement for the Kent Friendly Society. The organised resistance of the BMA collapsed although the medical care provisions were supervised by local insurance committees upon which doctors were heavily represented. Health insurance would later be criticised for its narrow range of medical provision and lack of attention to the wider aspects of health. In contrast Part II of the Act, providing unemployment insurance, attracted little attention after the violent parliamentary struggle over health insurance, beyond the inevitable complaint that it was antagonistic to thrift. It applied to only a few 'precarious' trades. Employer, worker and government paid 2½d. each per week. In return the worker, when unemployed, could draw 7s. 0d. per week for up to fifteen weeks a year. The scheme was again operated through approved societies. The Act was described as 'the most complicated measure framed for upwards of 100 years'. Many working men did not understand it despite the efforts of touring lecturers from the Board of Trade. Nevertheless it did something to reduce the crisis caused by unemployment or illness in working-class families even if it did not relieve hardship entirely.[69]

67 *KE* 25.11.1911.
68 *KE* 2.12.1911, 9.12.1911, 16.12.1911.
69 *KE* 1.7.1911; *KM* 13.1.1912, 3.2.1912, 15.6.1912; Gilbert, *op. cit.*, pp. 283, 315; Royle, *op. cit.*, p. 201; R.C. Birch, *The Shaping of the Welfare State*, Harlow 1974, p. 31.

(6) Public Works Schemes for the Unemployed

The National Insurance Act 1911 made no provision for the relief of long-term unemployment or for dependants. The scheme was extended in 1920–1. By the end of 1921 it provided against long-term and short-term unemployment for some 11 million workers and their families and included all earning below £5 a week except agricultural labourers and domestic servants. A wife was allowed 5s. 0d. and each child 1s. 0d.[70]

After the Great War, Kent underwent a short-lived boom. By early 1921, however, the Government was proposing short-time working in the dockyards at Chatham and Sheerness; a relief fund was created for 200 Dartford schoolchildren whose fathers were unemployed; the *Kent Messenger* had reduced its advertising rates for the unemployed requiring jobs; and Kent was in an industrial recession which lasted until the end of 1923. The recession was general but it affected in particular Kent's manufacture of cement, bricks and paper. By the end of February there were 1,200 unemployed at Gravesend and Northfleet, and large numbers of cement workers were discharged at Swanscombe, Greenhithe and Burham. At Snodland over 800 were workless by 1922. A number of cement-works had closed and the remainder were working half time. Output of the Medway works, normally 15,000 tons occupying 2,000 men, had fallen to 10,500 tons employing only 1,700 workers. By January 1923 the total workforce in the Kent cement industry, which had been 10,000 before 1914, had been halved. Northfleet had lost 75% of its jobs through closures and four out of six cement-works were shut in Snodland where a third of the insurable population of Halling, Burham, Cuxton and Wouldham were unemployed.[71]

In 1913, Britain had been the world's biggest cement producer, with a large export trade. Now, with improvements in manufacture, one man did the work of four, cement was made almost anywhere in the world and was exported to Britain by European competitors. To make matters worse, most paper mills, which were also working short time, were concentrated in the Thames and Medway valleys, at Dartford, Northfleet, Gravesend, Maidstone and Sittingbourne. Some 900 men and women were unemployed at Maidstone, increasing to 1,300 by 1923. In Dartford the unemployed were increasing at a rate of 200 a week while 450 brick- and paper-makers were registered as unemployed at Sittingbourne. Elsewhere in Kent there were 500 unemployed at Sheerness; 1,500 at Dover; 300 at Ashford; 350 at Bexley Heath; and over 400 in the Sevenoaks area.[72]

The new system of unemployment insurance was based upon the expectation that no more than 4% of those insured would be unemployed at any one time. The depression of 1921–3 introduced into national social policy a new factor.

---

[70] C.L. Mowat, *Britain Between the Wars, 1918–1940*, London 1968, p. 127.
[71] *KM* 1.1.1921, 8.1.1921, 12.2.1921, 19.2.1921, 26.2.1921, 5.3.1921, 12.3.1921, 30.7.1921, 17.9.1921, 2.10.1921, 31.1.1922, 7.10.1922, 27.1.1923.
[72] *KM* 12.3.1921, 11.10.1921, 22.10.1921, 26.11.1921, 31.1.1922, 1.4.1922, 9.5.1922, 18.8.1923; *Tuesday Express*, 10 January and 2 May 1922.

By 1922, 1.5 million men were out of work. Thousands of workers had exhausted their fifteen weeks of benefit without any sign of a job, and a hard core of unemployed, long out of benefit, had to be sustained from taxation or from the contributions of those outside the depressed areas who still anticipated a reasonably secure job. In its attempts to help the unemployed, the Government, instead of restructuring the National Insurance scheme, which would have been required if the jobless were to be kept off the Poor Law, merely adjusted it throughout the 1920s in the hope that the crisis would soon be over, thus making an unpremeditated advance towards the Welfare State. By a series of Acts passed in 1921–2, the Government extended the period during which benefits could be drawn, altered the benefit rates and increased the contributions. This was done randomly in response to the continuing unemployment, the demands of the unemployed and pressure from the Poor Law Guardians and local authorities on whom the burden of relief fell after benefit was exhausted. In March 1921, two periods of extended benefit were introduced separated by gaps during which no benefit could be drawn. This 'uncovenanted benefit', beyond what the unemployed were entitled to from their contributions, became quickly known as the 'dole'. To limit the numbers, these payments were made only to those who could convince the labour exchanges that they were 'genuinely seeking work'. Uninsured families, those for whom insurance was sufficient, or those between benefit, had to resort to the Poor Law for outdoor relief.[73]

Some relief works were undertaken by the County Council and other local authorities in Kent, using government grants or loans. Road improvement and the building of new roads were the principal means of providing work. The road pattern of the county was drastically altered in the 1920s and early 1930s. Much work, however, was undertaken by the Ministry of Transport and London County Council to provide work in Kent for the London unemployed. Its impact on Kent unemployment was, therefore, limited. Nevertheless provision of materials, and sometimes unskilled work, was carried out by men from the local labour exchanges or boards of Guardians. Road construction also increased the demand for cement. By 1923 the MPs for Gravesend and Dartford were pressing the minister to build concrete roads in an effort to revive the cement industry.[74]

In January 1921 the County Council obtained ministry sanction for improvement of the Ramsgate road with a government grant and treasury loans. Next month the ministry approved schemes for the Canterbury to Sarre and Dartford to Erith roads. The latter immediately, however, ran into difficulty. The Dartford District rate of pay was 1s. 11d. per hour, but the County Council would pay unemployed labour only the agricultural rate of 1s. 2d. Bexley, too, refused to pay trade-union rates for relief work, while men on relief work at Wouldham and Aylesford were paid only 8¾d., which was insufficient to maintain them and their families. The many Kent highways to benefit from relief work included the roads from London to Folkestone, London to Dover, London to Maidstone,

---

73   Mowat, *op. cit.*, pp. 127–9; Birch, *op. cit.*, p. 37.
74   Melling, *op. cit.*, p. 40; *KM* 8.1.1921, 10.12.1921, 27.1.1923.

Farningham to Wrotham, and Malling to Strood. At the end of the financial year 1922/3, the County Council had ten road schemes under way using grants and loans worth £85,614. Other Kent local authorities resorted to relief works more sparingly. Rochester Borough Council used grant aid to employ fifty men to widen the Burham road. Margate corporation engaged ninety-three men on relief work of its own. Tonbridge unemployed were used to clean out the Medway, while 200 men were engaged on repairs to the sea walls at Elmley, Iwade, Tonge, Hoo and Minster. Relief works at Chatham included a ten-acre extension to the cemetery and the improvement of Chatham Hill. At Maidstone, where an Unemployment Relief Fund was administered by the workless themselves, there was close co-operation between the Guardians and the local council. Projects included widening of the Loose Road, employing sixty people. Wrotham UDC occupied forty unemployed 'grubbing stones', as they had done under the Poor Law a century before. Snodland, Wouldham and Burham were accepted by the Government as being distressed areas, but no special grant was ever received.[75]

The miseries of the unemployed were widespread. At Folkestone they were claimed to be 'more acute than at any time in the history of the town'. At Maidstone, there were households with half their furnishings pawned or sold and children 'hungry and shoeless'. The greatest hardships were experienced in the areas of highest unemployment within the Dartford, Gravesend and Strood Poor Law Unions. The Guardians at Dartford, chaired by Revd Stanley Morgan, who became a Labour county councillor, were sympathetic. Initially they fixed their relief scales at £1 for single men, £1 plus rent for married couples and 7s. 6d. for each child. By April 1921 their generous payments of relief had put them in deficit. In July, with applicants increasing, the deficit had reached £18,000 and the Board was obliged to adopt the Ministry of Health scales, cut the rent allowance and request the minister to sanction an overdraft. In response, a procession, estimated at 4,000 strong, from Erith, Belvedere, Bexley Heath, Crayford and Dartford, accompanied a deputation to Dartford Guardians, demanding restoration of the earlier rates and a cwt of coal per week. The marchers carried red flags and were organised by the newly-formed, Combative National Unemployed Workers' Movement (NUWM) under Wal Hannington, a Communist toolmaker connected with the wartime shop stewards' movement in London. There had been unemployed demonstrations in Kent earlier in the century but these were different. The marchers were largely militant, well-disciplined, ex-servicemen who understood the force of numbers. In London they demanded 'work or full maintenance'. From there their message was carried into the metropolitan districts of Kent. When Dartford Guardians explained their predicament, the marchers decided to send representatives with a Guardians' deputation to the Ministry. If the scales were refused Dartford unemployed were to demand entry to the workhouse with their wives and families to challenge the

---

[75] *KM* 8.1.1921, 19.2.1921, 23.7.1921, 5.11.1921, 19.11.1921, 26.11.1921, 10.12.1921, 17.12.1921, 24.12.1921, 28.1.1922, 18.2.1922, 20.1.1923, 27.1.1923, 24.2.1923, 17.3.1923, 7.4.1923, 11.8.1923.

workhouse test. When the minister rejected the scales, the Guardians nevertheless created an improved scale which meant increasing the rates. By November their overdraft had grown to £50,000 and would only sustain them until March. When yet another set of marchers from all parts of the Union, supported by contingents from Eltham and Woolwich, arrived and entered the workhouse demanding food, those who came from a distance were fed. A month later, marchers again occupied the workhouse, imprisoning the Guardians, to protest against children's meals being deducted from relief. The Guardians remained sympathetic but the building was cleared by the police. Five-hundred marchers again occupied the workhouse in February, their spokesman, Mr Straker, organiser of Erith's unemployed, demanding that the Board should emulate Poplar and concede the scales sought by the NUWM in defiance of the Ministry of Health. When the demonstration failed the marchers left, singing the Red Flag. By the end of February 7,134 persons were receiving relief at a cost of £1,800 a week. By April, numbers had spiralled to 10,332 and the cost to £3,120. In May, relief was cut by 5s. 0d. despite a noisy demonstration outside. Maximum relief was again reduced in September, by which time Dartford Union had a deficit of £96,000.[76]

If Dartford Guardians did what they could to help the unemployed, the Gravesend and Strood boards refused from the outset to deviate from Poor Law regulations, despite the same pressure from organised demonstrations and deputations which was applied at Dartford. In consequence a bitter struggle developed. Gravesend Guardians, who disapproved strongly of their Dartford counterparts, refused monetary out-relief since it would require an additional rate and insisted that the able-bodied, particularly single men, should enter the workhouse if they refused relief in kind. Gravesend Council at first denied that distress existed, and organised only limited schemes of relief work in the hope that the town could absorb surplus labour when its new mains drainage project began in 1922. Both bodies felt that responsibility for the unemployed lay with the other. No fewer than seven unemployed demonstrations and deputations to both bodies were made throughout 1921. The workless, with Revd John Lewis as their spokesman, eschewed violence but made little headway. In vain Lewis spoke of the 'terrible destitution' in the town and quoted households without coal, furniture or bedclothes and where even wedding rings had been sold to buy food. Little attempt was made to alleviate poverty once private charity was exhausted and in mid-1922 Gravesend Guardians reduced relief by 12.5%.[77]

The attitude of the Strood Guardians was similar. In Northfleet District, where unemployment was most acute within the Union, there was an energetic unemployment committee which wanted the Guardians to bring the 'dole' up to

[76] Clark and Murfin, *op. cit.*, p. 219; *KM* 22.1.1921, 2.4.1921, 14.6.1921, 23.6.1921, 14.7.1921, 10.9.1921, 17.9.1921, 24.9.1921, 1.10.1921, 26.11.1921, 10.12.1921, 7.1.1922, 4.2.1922, 18.2.1922, 13.5.1922, 27.5.1922.
[77] *KM* 12.3.1921, 19.3.1921, 26.3.1921, 2.4.1921, 9.4.1921, 16.7.1921, 16.9.1921, 24.12.1921, 31.12.1921, 3.6.1922.

the Dartford level. By August 1921 there were 1,519 on Northfleet's out-relief list as compared with ninety-two at Strood. Strood Guardians decided to discuss the application of the workhouse test to all able-bodied, unemployed males while still relieving their families outside. On the day of their meeting, eighty Northfleet unemployed marched to Strood workhouse led by G.H. Baker, secretary of the unemployed committee, to show their opposition. The Guardians decided to continue the grant of provisions to the Northfleet unemployed and their families, but Northfleet's relieving officer, Miss Carey, was instructed to exercise discretion. It was also claimed that her assistants 'shadowed' claimants to verify whether they used public transport or even entered public houses. A second deputation a week later was refused an interview, while a deputation to the local council to press for relief work was equally abortive. Northfleet UDC was more sympathetic. A plea for coal and lighting in November produced the establishment of a fund and the promise to press for mains drainage to create work. In February 1922 Baker again occupied Strood workhouse with a party of unemployed. The Guardians refused to meet them and they sat singing the Red Flag. When police reinforcements arrived they left without resistance. Relief was still given in kind. Rents were paid directly by the relieving officer. In March, Strood RDC was paying the unemployed 9d. an hour for work that in an industrial area merited 1s. 3d. an hour. Three-hundred unemployed surrounded the council offices protesting that they were receiving only agricultural wages. The protest was led by Holmer from Crayford and Baker, who refused the relief work at 9d. an hour as a matter of principle, although he had just been fined 5s. 0d. for keeping his children from school since they were without boots. He refused second-hand boots on grounds of hygiene, and relief was stopped entirely for himself, his wife and his family of four children. In his support 200 unemployed blockaded the relieving officer and her staff in their office on 'relief day', refusing relief themselves since Baker was denied. This peaceful 'siege' began at 9.30 a.m. and only ended with the arrival of a strong force of police from Chatham at 8.30 p.m. The Guardians responded by cancelling the relief of those involved since they 'had refused to work'. The relieving officer was sent on a month's sick leave.[78]

The Guardians' attitude was that their function was to relieve destitution not unemployment, which was a burden put on them by the government. The unemployed responded that they could not live upon 9d. an hour. The trial of strength continued with the balance weighted on the side of authority. After nine weeks Baker, an unemployed boilerman, whom Revd John Lewis described as 'a victim of persistent persecution' was still without benefit and all relief and only sustained by the generosity of his friends. Strood Guardians, who claimed that they had run out of money with relief still rising and some parishes withholding their rates, refused relief in July to single men who were not ex-servicemen. In August relief was reduced by 40%, despite continued depression in the cement

[78] *KM* 19.3.1921, 26.3.1921, 30.7.1921, 20.8.1921, 27.8.1921, 16.9.1921, 19.11.1921, 11.2.1922, 18.2.1922, 11.3.1922, 18.3.1922, 25.3.1922, 15.4.1922, 6.5.1922.

trade, and rent allowances were withdrawn. Dartford Guardians had industrial and rural scales of relief but Strood Guardians based their decisions on Ministry of Health advice that 'relief should be for relieving distress on a lower scale than the earnings of the lowest paid worker', which for them was the agricultural labourer.[79]

While protest was concentrated in these three Unions most affected by the depression, there was also unrest in the Maidstone, Medway, and Malling Unions. In the first a muted protest was centred around Maidstone Trades Council and Labour Party. A deputation to the Board of Guardians in September 1921 brought little improvement. Similar deputations from Chatham and Snodland, Burham and Wouldham marched to the Medway and Malling workhouses respectively. While Medway Guardians appealed to the government, a representative of the Gillingham Unemployed Workers' Committee was allowed on to the Unemployment Relief Sub-Committee of Gillingham Borough Council.[80] When hunger marches switched from a local to a national strategy, some 150 Kent unemployed reached London on the first national march in November 1922. One group marched from Dover; thirty-five men from Ramsgate; and thirty from Maidstone. Their banner read 'In the Trenches Yesterday, Unemployed Today'. Instructions from the Ministry of Health were that they should be treated as vagrants in the workhouses *en route*. Dartford Guardians, however, repaired the boots of, and provided a meal for, some 200 who began the march. On 7 January 1923, 'Unemployed Sunday', Kent marchers gathered again at Mount Pleasant, Dartford, from where some 500 marched to Crayford and Dartford Heath to meet contingents from Abbey Wood, Belvedere, Erith and Bexley Heath before proceeding to London to demand the recall of Parliament and action on unemployment. A last recruiting drive was planned in early February to mark the opening of Parliament. A column from London divided at Brighton and returned to London via Dover, Canterbury, Chatham, Strood, Gravesend and Dartford. Numbers, however, were fewer than anticipated. Government instructions were more stringently enforced. Marchers had to sleep in 'doss houses', in disused casual wards or with the Salvation Army. They were fed by the Co-operative Movement.[81] The depression, however, was slowly lifting and it was to be seven years before marching resumed in Kent.[82]

[79] *KM* 15.4.1922, 27.5.1922, 22.7.1922, 29.7.1922, 5.8.1922, 26.8.1922.
[80] *KM* 24.9.1921, 1.10.1921; *SEG* 4.10.1921, 11.10.1921; *CN* 16.9.1921, 23.9.1921, 30.9.1921, 7.10.1921; *CO* 23.9.1921, 7.10.1921, 5.5.1922, 2.6.1922, 12.1.1923, 9.2.1923, 16.2.1923. Most of these references have been kindly supplied by Bruce Aubry.
[81] P. Kingsford, *The Hunger Marchers in Britain, 1920–1940*, London 1982, pp. 43, 47–8, 65–71; *KM* 11.11.1922, 9.12.1922, 13.1.1923, 10.2.1923, 17.2.1923.
[82] *KM* 26.5.1923, 2.6.1923, 4.8.1923.

(7) The End of the Poor Law and the Great Depression

The financial strain of the depression and the refusal of some Boards to conform to regulations led, in 1929, to the end of the Poor Law. Certain Boards, like Poplar, had paid relief to whole families and not only destitute dependants during the General Strike. Outdoor relief had also been paid above recommended rates as many Guardians refused to use their workhouses for the unemployed. The government responded by abolishing the Guardians and disbanding the 635 Poor Law Unions by the Local Government Act 1929. This transferred responsibility for the able-bodied unemployed to Public Assistance Committees of the counties and county boroughs. The workhouse test was abolished in 1930. Former workhouses passed to local authorities as hospitals or survived as Public Assistance Institutions used largely to house the 'feeble minded' poor unable to support themselves.

In Kent the twenty-five Unions were superseded in April 1930 by the Public Assistance Committee of the County Council. To ensure local interest, the county was divided into eleven areas, each with its own Guardians' Committee. Of the 372 members of Guardians' Committees, sixty-two were county councillors, 191 were nominated by district councils and 119 were persons appointed by the County Council but not members of it. Many members of Guardians' Committees had previously served on Boards of Guardians. Each area had an area office supervised by an Assistant Public Assistance Officer. The unifying of members of several boards of Guardians into one Guardians' committee created some immediate uniformity in administration. In the longer term it also established some uniformity of practice. At first there was considerable resentment among former members of the old boards. The ex-chairman of Dover Guardians complained openly that the new system would not make for economy. Thus a new system was fashioned 'which no one wanted but the Government'. The Kent press were still excluded from meetings as they had been before. The old idea of 'less eligibility' persisted while the need for economy kept benefits to a minimum level. The Public Assistance Committee, however, also became responsible for care of the young, the old and the mentally ill. Fifteen children's homes were taken over from the Poor Law while some former workhouses became institutions for children. A beginning was also made upon old people's homes. Two were inherited from Dartford Institution and a third was created at Pembury Grange in 1937.[83] Thus an act of reorganisation established the foundations from which the future social services would grow.

The reorganised system was soon tested as the second great depression of the decade hit Kent in 1929–33. The severe check to American business activity in October 1929 was followed by a tremendous rise in world-wide unemployment. By the close of 1929 £89,000 had been paid out by Chatham employment exchange alone and concern was spreading throughout Kent.[84] Eight-hundred

[83] Moss, *op. cit.*, pp. 118–20; *KM* 11.1.1930, 8.2.1930, 15.11.1930, 29.11.1930, 21.2.1931; Melling, *op. cit.*, pp. 52, 57.
[84] *KM* 22.3.1930; these figures included Gillingham where there was no employment exchange.

were unemployed in Gravesend District. At Canterbury an unemployed deputation, led by W.E. Andrews, waited upon the mayor. In Maidstone, where 7% of the insured population was jobless, the council sent a telegram to the Minister of Health. An advertisement for a waggoner brought a response from between thirty and forty men, some of whom walked a dozen miles. As Kent farmers made grim predictions if poor agricultural prices continued, the number of suicides increased.[85] The *Kentish Express* commented:

> The unemployed . . . increase by the day and the only cure seems to be the making of roads. Ratepayers of Kent are already finding the burden more than they can bear. A great number of people find it impossible to pay the rates[86]

Registered unemployed at Kent labour exchanges which were 15,867 in 1929 had increased to 24,526 by the close of 1930. Only the army recruiting sergeants were able to offer security of tenure. 'Assured employment is . . . offered . . . in HM regular army,' read an advertisement for the Kent regiments.[87]

Table 44

Unemployment as a Percentage of Insured Workers throughout the British Isles

Region	1929	1932	1937
London and S. E. England	5.6	13.7	6.4
S.W. England	8.1	17.1	7.8
Midlands	9.3	20.1	7.2
North, N.E., and N.W. England	13.5	27.1	13.8
Wales	19.3	36.5	22.3
Scotland	12.1	27.7	15.9
N. Ireland	15.1	27.2	23.9

Source: C.L. Mowat, *Britain Between the Wars, 1918–1940*, London 1968, p. 464

London and South-East England was nevertheless in a much superior position to the other regions of the British Isles, particularly the old industrial areas of primary production, as Table 44 shows. By mid-1930, while 56% of insured workers were said to be unemployed in Lancashire, 8% were jobless in Kent. Even the editors of the *Kentish Express* and *Kent Messenger* agreed in 1931 that:

> We in the South of England have no idea of the terrible state of industrial Britain. . . . Farming is not paying, some of our local enterprises are suffering

---

85 *KM* 7.12.1929; *KE* 11.1.1930, 1.2.1930, 22.3.1930.
86 *KE* 29.3.1930.
87 *KE* 15.11.1930, 10.1.1931.

but the number of persons unemployed is so small compared with the factories of the North that we cannot realise the position.[88]

Kent has not suffered as severely as some parts of Great Britain from the wave of industrial depression which has overwhelmed the country during the past year.[89]

In industrial Kent the cable trade was 'doing well' as was the Ashford Railway Works. The dockyard programme promised better times for the Medway towns while Short Brothers viewed the year with optimism. A £705,000 contract from the Portuguese government meant work for Vickers armaments factories at Erith, Dartford and Crayford. On the other hand there were pockets of unemployment, some of which were short term and others longer. Agricultural labour was scarce in East Kent while many farm workers were unemployed in the north of the county. In the Medway valley some cement-works stood empty. Snodland, Wouldham and Burham were again 'distressed areas' and 350 were workless at Swanscombe and Greenhithe. Other cement manufacturers, like Portland Cement and British Portland Concrete, despite severe foreign competition, were employing more workers than hitherto. In the paper industry, while Hawley's Mill, near Dartford, and Little Darenth Mill were closed, Northfleet's four mills, employing over a thousand workers, remained busy since they had easy access to London, one of the largest markets for paper. Timber and wood pulp could be easily imported. Much of the newsprint for the London press was made by Lloyds at Sittingbourne, Bowaters at Northfleet, Reeds of Aylesford, and the Imperial Paper Mills at Gravesend.[90]

Signs that the depression was lifting at the end of 1931, with increased orders to paper- and cement-works, proved deceptive. Hitherto help had been offered to the unemployed in the form of local public works schemes assisted by government grants as in 1921–3. Thus Margate, with nearly a thousand unemployed, set about building a new sewer and promenade. Maidstone also determined to implement a drainage scheme and received the sanction of the Electricity Commission to borrow £14,371 for schemes which would employ fifty men for five months. Gillingham determined to undertake a scheme for mains drainage costing £225,000, and all three Medway towns decided to spend money on the removal of tram tracks. A new customs shed costing £96,000 was projected for Dover pier and improved facilities were considered at Dover docks. Kent County Council announced considerable expenditure on roads, schools and housing programmes and an ambitious scheme to level the thirty-eight-acre Crimean Fort Pitt in order to build Medway Technical College.[91]

The drain on public resources, however, was immense. By spring 1931 almost

[88] *KE* 14.6.1930, 20.9.1931.
[89] *KM* 30.3.1931.
[90] *KM* 24.1.1931, 31.1.1931, 7.2.1931, 28.2.1931, 11.4.1931, 23.5.1931, 15.8.1931, 22.8.1931, 29.8.1931.
[91] *KM* 24.1.1931, 31.1.1931, 14.11.1931, 21.11.1931; *KE* 8.10.1930, 1.11.1930, 29.11.1930.

3 million men were out of work nationally and the insurance fund was in debt by £100 million. Ramsay Macdonald, the Labour prime minister, was warned that the entire economy was at risk and was advised by his own and foreign bankers to introduce economies if the necessary foreign loans, to balance the budget and save the pound, were to be attracted. Finding his Cabinet divided, he resigned to form a National Government, its policy for recovery being to keep government spending to a minimum. To meet the immediate crisis stringent economy orders were applied. Normal benefits were cut by 10% and 'transitional benefits' for those who had been unemployed for over six months, were paid only after a searching family means-test. The bitter depths of the depression had arrived.

In Kent, as elsewhere, local authorities suspended projected relief schemes. Tunbridge Wells postponed building a new town hall and boys' school. Maidstone shelved a new housing and drainage scheme and Northfleet a new public library. West Ashford UDC scrapped urgently needed village housing and plans for a rural water supply while an extensive drainage scheme was deferred in West Kent. Kent County Council cancelled schemes for eighteen new buildings and improvements to forty school sites. Teachers' salaries were reduced by 10%, and spending on roads was cut by £4 million leaving only £6,000 for road improvement. The rates were reduced by 8d. in the pound. Registered unemployment throughout Kent rose to 31,401 by December, an increase of 6,000 in two months. Of these, 4,942 were transitional cases which were subjected to a means-test. The test for transitional benefit or the 'dole' was destitution. If the applicant had in the bank more than the £10 necessary for a burial fee he got no assistance. Pensions, health insurance and sick pay counted as income and were deducted from benefit. Details of his total family income were required before the Public Assistance Committee decided how much he needed. The test was, therefore, frequently responsible for family tragedies and encouraged informers. It was described as 'an abomination' by one Tonbridge councillor.[92]

Since the press were not admitted to meetings of either the Public Assistance Committee or Guardians' Committees until 1933, and then only if the Guardians desired it, decisions seemed secretive. Injustice appeared to be compounded by the disparity of relief in different districts. Parsimonious Guardians dealt with cases as if they were always dealing with the able-bodied unemployed and in the same way that their Poor Law predecessors had done before them. They also frequently appeared not to be allowing the maximum benefit to which applicants were entitled. In the Gravesend and District Committee area a single man entitled to a maximum of 15s. 0d. a week received just over 7s. 0d. A married man, formerly granted £1 11s. 3d. unemployment benefit, had it reduced after the means-test to £1 8s. 0d. A man with seven children, previously receiving 36s. 0d., got a transitional benefit of 31s. 0d. The test was hated by the unemployed and the bitterness it created lingered on into the post-war years.[93]

92 *KM* 5.9.1931, 12.9.1931, 31.10.1931, 21.11.1931, 12.12.1931, 6.2.1932, 13.2.1932, 20.2.1932.
93 *KM* 13.2.1932, 15.2.1933.

There were other human consequences of unemployment. The helplessness and hopelessness of long-term unemployment destroyed the spirit. 'Men have been following each other around trying to get work,' wrote an unemployed father of five, 'in the district around Maidstone no labourer is wanted. . . . Last month I visited twenty employers every day without result.'[94] 'A man can practically go without but how does it make him feel to see his wife and children have bread and marg. every day including Sunday?' commented another victim.[95] In these circumstances suicides increased, particularly among older men who felt they would never work again. A sixty-one-year-old from Yalding jumped under a train. A sixty-six-year-old Burham man hanged himself, while a jobless man from Bexley Heath cut his throat with a razor.[96]

The allegation made at Dover that unemployed men on 'test' work at a corporation tip were eating the rotten food created a sensation, but unemployment impacted on physical as well as mental health.[97] The question of how far unemployment led to a deterioration in the health of the unemployed and their families has generated a fierce debate. While the government's Chief Medical Officer at the time maintained there was no clear evidence of deterioration, more recent historians have argued that unemployment did have a profound effect on health not reflected in official statistics. This deterioration was particularly pronounced in the case of children.[98] In Kent medical opinion was contradictory. For Dr H. T. Sells, Medical Officer for Northfleet UDC, 1930 'was an exceptionally healthy year' while 1931 'exceeded all expectations'. The crude death rate of 6.29 per 1,000 was the lowest within his recollection as compared to 12.3 nationally. Similarly, Dr J. Holroyde, School Medical Officer for Chatham, reported in 1932 that 'there was no evidence of any material lowering of the standard of health in school children and on the whole general nutrition remained good'. On the other hand the school medical officer for the county reported that:

> . . . in the county generally children and young people are affected by the unemployment problem, more particularly by the general lowering of the family standard of living. After care work and general supervision are more than ever necessary.

Despite this fact County Council grants to provide meals for necessitous children showed a steady decrease after 1924. No grants were made in 1931, although 9,310 free meals were provided as opposed to 9,949 in 1930. In 1931 free meals were provided from voluntary sources.[99]

[94] *KM* 24.10.1931.
[95] *KM* 13.8.1932.
[96] *KE* 22.3.1930; *KM* 7.3.1931, 21.3.1931, 14.11.1931, 28.11.1931, 11.6.1932.
[97] *KM* 28.11.1931.
[98] See B. Harris, 'Unemployment and the Dole in Inter-War Britain', in Johnson, *op. cit.*, pp. 213–19; C. Webster, 'Healthy or Hungry Thirties', *History Workshop Journal*, x (1982), pp. 110–29; and C. Webster, 'Health, Welfare and Unemployment during the Depression', *Past and Present*, cix (1985), pp. 204–30.
[99] *KM* 26.3.1932, 4.6.1932, 8.4.1933.

As the depression intensified, the hunger marchers reappeared. In some ways they were less effective than in 1921–3. Their ranks were divided. The NUWM was resurrected but its effectiveness was blunted by the attacks of its Communist leaders upon the Labour party and the Labour Government. In October 1931, the Chatham branch was considering nominating Will Hannington, the national organiser, as a candidate for the parliamentary seat but was thwarted by his imprisonment. The NUWM's local organiser, Charles Mathews, had already stood as a municipal candidate for St John's ward in 1929. The more orthodox, pro-Labour Party unemployed organisation was the Kentish Unemployed and General Workers' Association, centred on Maidstone, whose local organiser, T.D. Watkins, was anti-Communist. A former artillery lieutenant, Watkins was spokesman for a number of unemployed deputations to Maidstone Borough Council before a prison sentence for bigamy removed him from the scene, leaving the way clear for the NUWM.[100]

Historians have differed in their assessment of the work of the NUWM, but its marches and demonstrations against government policy at least ensured that unemployment stayed to the fore in national debate. Some 200 Kent hunger marchers slept at the Unitarian Church, Chatham, before continuing via Gravesend and Northfleet to a London demonstration against the means test in October 1932. A second demonstration, organised to coincide with a meeting of the Kent Public Assistance Committee in December, was joined by only fifty marchers from Chatham and a few Maidstone unemployed.[101] The seeds of recovery had been apparent at the beginning of the year. 'Industries in Kent which have been paralysed . . . are awakening. . . . Fresh industries are springing up . . .,' noted the *Kent Messenger*, '1932 is a year of opportunity.'[102] There were 2,858 persons still on the register of Gravesend Employment Exchange, and a further 6,681 were unemployed at Rochester and Chatham, but two new paper mills were announced in May at Dartford and St Mary Cray. The depression in Kent agriculture began to lift with the spread of canning factories. This meant more prosperous times for the Kent fruit and vegetable grower. One Kent factory turned out 5 million cans in under a year as the demand grew for peas and soft fruit. Wisbech Produce Canneries, Paddock Wood, used 15,000 tons of fruit, 3 million packing cans and 1 million bottles in under a season.[103] The *Kent Messenger* commented:

Few counties have experienced the national depression to a lesser degree. Each Kent industry has felt the pinch but . . . not nearly . . . so hard as in the Midlands and the North. The climb to prosperity has, we believe, begun.[104]

100 *KM* 1.2.1930, 1.3.1930, 19.4.1930, 10.10.1931; *CN* 1.11.1929; *SEG* 4.2.1930, 4.3.1930, 22.4.1930. 8.7.1930, 15.7.1930.
101 *KM* 29.10.1932, 10.12.1932; *CN* 21.10.1932, 28.10.1932.
102 *KM* 2.1.1932.
103 *KM* 5.3.1932, 28.5.1932, 12.11.1932.
104 *KM* 19.3.1932.

By 1933 factories and machinery were being extended. The Southern Railway inaugurated a train–ferry service from Dover to Dunkirk. Four oil-powered coasters were under construction at Faversham. Ashford Railway Works had a large programme for the year and Chatham dockyard could guarantee employment. Kent paper mills were busier than for years. Most of their coal came from the Kent coalfield. Short Brothers were looking forward to their best year since the armistice, and there was a great deal more work available in building and construction as North-West Kent rapidly became a suburb of Greater London. As houses multiplied unemployment fell and there were boom signs in the cement industry. Chatham's workless dropped from 7,204 in January to 5,718 in May. At Maidstone there were 1,340 unemployed as compared to 2,718 in 1932. Gravesend and Northfleet exchanges had fewer registered unemployed than at any time since January 1931.[105]

In 1934 the 10% reduction in benefits made in 1931 was restored and the transitional payments scheme was replaced by unemployment assistance which took relief of the unemployed out of local hands. Insurance, based upon contributions, was separated from assistance. The Unemployment Insurance Statutory Committee, which Sir William Beveridge chaired until 1943, was designed to make the insurance plan solvent. It achieved this by devising a scheme which would break even at an unemployment rate of 16.75%, the rate existing in 1934. This rate was never reached again. Therefore the fund never again ran into debt. All unemployed who had exhausted their right to benefits came under an Unemployment Assistance Board funded from national taxation. This virtually completed the destruction of the Poor Law and brought about a common level of supplementary aid, recognising that a locally administered scheme of poor relief was inequitable. To qualify for assistance workers had to prove that they were willing to find employment. The amount of assistance still depended upon a means test, although a less severe one. The board had offices throughout Britain to relieve the overworked labour exchanges, and was also responsible for training centres to teach the unemployed new skills.

(8) The Beveridge Report and the Creation of the Welfare State

In June 1941 the wartime coalition government set up a Committee of Enquiry, chaired by Sir William Beveridge, to undertake a thorough investigation of the existing 'social security' arrangements. Beveridge took the opportunity to propose a complete system of social insurance covering all citizens whatever their income. Everyone of working age would pay a single weekly contribution, recorded by a stamp on a single card. Employers would continue to pay part of the cost of their employees' stamps. Flat-rate benefits would be paid to all citizens on 'interruption of earnings' by reason of sickness, unemployment or

---

[105] *KM* 7.1.1933, 22.4.1933, 8.7.1933, 26.8.1933, 4.11.1933, 11.11.1933, 2.12.1933.

retirement. Benefits would be based upon a 'national minimum' below which nobody would be allowed to fall. There could be extra benefits for those 'normal incidents of life' such as maternity. No means test would be necessary since all citizens were to be equal members of the scheme with equal rights. The whole scheme was to be based on the principle of insurance. The government would therefore, overall, be spared enormous expense but would have to stand the full cost of family allowance to be paid weekly to parents for each dependent child. Beveridge also proposed the creation of 'a national health service for prevention and comprehensive treatment . . . available to all members of the community', which was a considerable advance on the promise made by the Minister of Health 'that after the war the government would establish a comprehensive hospital service'.[106] The Beveridge Report therefore became not only the 'blueprint' for post-war reconstruction but the greatest single influence in the creation of 'the cradle to the grave' welfare state in place by the late 1940s.

Accepted by the House of Commons in February 1943, the key welfare and medical recommendations of the Beveridge Report were implemented by the Labour Government in 1946. The National Health Service Act created, from 1948, a free medical service for all, partly funded by national insurance but mainly out of general taxation. The National Insurance Act 1946, despite protests from the friendly societies whose role in government social-security schemes was terminated, provided large subsidies from general taxation to fund old-age pensions and sickness, unemployment and death benefits for all insured women, and for insured men and their wives.[107] National insurance was compulsory for everyone of working age except married women. The Act differed from the Beveridge proposals in that it was not based upon any 'national minimum' standard of living. Instead the government preferred to fix benefit rates by Act of Parliament and review them periodically, a strategy which was to cause problems in the future. In 1948 the Unemployment Assistance Board of 1934 was replaced with a new National Assistance Board which provided a needs-tested safety net for those not adequately covered by the new legislation, such as the blind, deaf, physically and mentally handicapped, and deserted or unmarried mothers. To some this was a disguised descendent of the Poor Law providing a safety net for those whose needs were not fully met by national insurance benefits.

The vesting day for most social service proposals was 5 July 1948, which was also the implementation day for the National Health Service. On the 'appointed day' most of the public assistance functions which Kent County Council had exercised since 1930 passed to the National Assistance Board. This became responsible for out-relief and the maintenance of vagrants, although, in the case of the latter, the County Council continued to act as an agent for the Board. Eleven former general public-assistance institutions, used mainly by the chronically sick, passed from County Council control to be administered for

106   C. Webster, *The National Health Service: A Political History*, Oxford 1998, p. 7.
107   *KM* 15.2.1946, 22.2.1946, 31.5.1946.

joint use by the South-East Regional Hospital Board. The five local authority old people's homes were retained by the county as were eleven children's homes and nurseries.[108] With many functions now removed, the County Council was able to concentrate more effort on those health, or health-related, services for which it still retained responsibility, especially the ambulance and domestic help services. In 1948–9 the Kent ambulance service, which brought together a number of separate operations covering different areas of the county, had 150 vehicles which carried 283,691 patients in a full year. By 1952 the number of vehicles totalled 228, of which 212 were new or replacement purchases, and by 1964 the number of patients carried in a full year had nearly trebled to 804,417. There was a similar expansion in the provision of domestic help for the aged and infirm, with demand far outstripping the budget provision which the County Council had made for the service. Within six years the number of families receiving domestic help had increased from 1,295 to 4,300.[109]

The National Health Service was one great pillar of the post-war Welfare State. Its beginnings in Kent could scarcely have been less auspicious. On 23 January 1946 John Moss, the Public Assistance Officer, presented to the County Council's Public Assistance Committee a damning report in which he revealed that hospital organisation for the chronically sick had all but collapsed. Nurses were too few and accommodation totally inadequate. New admissions were restricted and there was a waiting list of 650 persons. People were dying unattended in their homes. The example was cited of a man, desperately ill from tuberculosis, who, evicted from his lodgings, spent two nights on the beach. A female cancer victim living alone had been without food for several days. The County Medical Officer re-emphasised the desperate need, stating that the only beds which became available in the Public Assistance Institutions were those in which patients died. Staff shortages had forced Cranbrook Institution to close. At Milton Institution it had been impossible to guarantee a duty nurse throughout the day. Catastrophe had only been averted at another establishment by the office staff volunteering for ward duties. In vain Moss urged that soldiers and members of the ATS should be made available as ward orderlies. 'We are within virtual cessation of admissions to public institutions,' stated Dr A. Elliott, the recently appointed County Medical Officer. Political opponents of the ruling Conservative majority on the County Council were less charitable, complaining that thousands of pounds have been spent annually on making the former workhouses 'reasonably habitable' when they 'should have been demolished years ago'. 'They are a relic of days when poverty was criminal,' stated Alderman the Revd S.J.W. Morgan, 'I have heard many applicants say "I would rather go to prison than to any institution." '[110]

As the crisis deepened it became clear that it was not only Public Assistance Committee institutions which were affected. By February, as the waiting list of

108 *KM* 6.4.1948.
109 Melling, *op. cit.*, p. 83.
110 *KM* 25.1.1946.

chronically sick rose to 700, Alderman Morgan alleged that 900 hospital beds throughout the county lay empty through staff shortages, and the medical authorities warned that an epidemic would be catastrophic. Forty beds closed at Lenham Sanatorium and more lay empty at Orpington. The bed-linen stock at Gravesend Hospital was almost non-existent. Bexley Cottage Hospital was closed. The Children's Hospital at Sevenoaks, where the matron and her secretary were doing the cooking and kitchen work, announced it would shut by the end of July. At Dover, the voluntary Royal Victoria Hospital merged with the municipal Dover County Hospital on 1 January 1947. 'The voluntary system has broken down,' stated Councillor E.W. Higgs of Bexley. In vain the County Council sought the aid of the churches in attracting young women into nursing. A full-time Nursing Training Officer was appointed to visit secondary schools. Girls entering nursing went largely, however, to the London hospitals. Only a third of those needed sought work in Kent. A belated bid was made to improve living conditions. £4,500 was spent upgrading nurses' accommodation at Orpington Hospital where twenty to thirty nurses shared the same room and several the same wardrobe. Kent's formerly large civil nursing reserve had been uncalled upon throughout the Second World War and had now disappeared. In May 1948, 776 beds in county hospitals still stood empty through lack of staff.[111]

Against this background the establishment of the National Health Service was greeted by a storm of protest from protagonists of the voluntary hospitals and strong opposition from the doctors themselves. Cdr Norman Woodcock, Chairman of the Board of Gravesend and North Kent Hospital, deplored an NHS bill which 'would destroy the good feeling between patients and staff in voluntary hospitals' and leave them 'administered by long distance control as opposed to the intimate interest of local committees'. Lord Harris was even more eloquent:

> If you do away with voluntary work you will kill the soul of England. The greatness of this country has been built up by those people who give their services voluntarily. . . . What . . . sort of race shall we raise up if from childhood our people are taught to look to the state for everything.[112]

'It is wrong that the sick should be dependent on the takings of flag days,' retorted a Labour councillor.[113]

The traditional individualism and conservatism of the medical profession made it a natural opponent of the NHS proposals. Few doctors objected to the principle of a free health service. Many were dissatisfied with 'Robin Hood medicine', overcharging the rich to cover the treatment of the poor, but they

---

111 *KM* 25.1.1946, 8.2.1946, 22.2.1946, 17.5.1946, 7.6.1946, 19.7.1946, 26.7.1946, 13.9.1946, 27.12.1946, 7.5.1948; Kent County Council, *Annual Report of the Medical Officer of Health*, Maidstone 1945.
112 *KM* 22.3.1946, 12.4.1946, 2.7.1948.
113 *KM* 2.7.1948.

objected to becoming full-time salaried servants of the state or local authorities and were anxious to retain 'freedom of action, judgement, speech and publication'. Some feared the loss of lucrative private practice. 'Private practice will inevitably disappear. . . . This smacks of Hitler,' wrote one West Malling GP. Others feared 'direction' to undoctored areas. The viewpoint of most patients was put by Violet Russell, a working-class housewife from Kemsing, and strongly supported by Dr Gordon Ward, elected representative of all panel practitioners on the Kent Panel Committee:

> We shall no longer fear to send for a doctor because we cannot pay. . . . Most doctors do come . . . despite accounts unsettled. We want to see men and women with skill and high ideals unhampered by want of cash in the medical and dental professions. We welcome the possibility of a specialist not miles away but at our local hospital. . . . Many deaths can be avoided by preventive treatment could we afford it. . . . We want the best for victims of past wars, for the children and for the aged.[114]

With less than two months remaining before 'the appointed day', 5 July 1948, only 197 of the 800 Kent doctors had registered with the NHS and two-thirds of all members of the British Medical Association had voted against joining. The president of the Kent branch stated that

> It appears that very few doctors look forward to 5 July; many feel apprehension – if not desperation – and the few who have willingly joined the service have grave objections.

John Simons, Chairman of the Kent and Sussex Hospital Board and himself a surgeon, was more positive: 'we must be firm in our resolve that this must work – much as we hate it'.[115]

In the end the latter view, plus the diplomacy of Aneurin Bevan, Minister of Health, prevailed. Bevan, whilst refusing to concede on major issues, made sufficient minor concessions for an uneasy truce. By the appointed day 782 Kent doctors and 193 chemists had entered the new health service which began with over a million inhabitants enrolled.

(9) The National Health Service

The effect of the NHS Act was to reduce and simplify the many agencies which had hitherto provided health care. Henceforth Regional Hospital Boards and their management committees provided, on behalf of the Ministry of Health, all forms of hospital and specialist services. Kent's hospitals and other institutions for the treatment of the physically and mentally ill including maternity, TB, VD,

[114] *KM* 22.3.1946, 29.3.1946, 2.7.1948.
[115] *KM* 14.5.1948, 2.7.1948.

dispensary and clinical patients passed, along with the voluntary hospitals, to the government. Many of the buildings, particularly the former Poor Law infirmaries, were in poor repair owing to pre-war or wartime difficulties. An Executive Council provided domiciliary medical, dental, pharmaceutical and supplementary ophthalmic services to practically the entire population. Kent County Council, as the local health authority, was left to furnish all other domiciliary, preventive and school health services. These included absorption of the maternity and child-welfare services, previously undertaken by the twenty-four District Councils, together with responsibility for the domiciliary midwife service throughout Kent. The county became responsible for 95 ante-natal clinics, 16 post-natal clinics, 251 child welfare centres and 26 day nurseries; an extended health visiting service; a home nursing service; domestic help to sick households; vaccination against smallpox and immunisation against diphtheria; and the creation of a county-wide ambulance service. The County continued its laboratory service but the bacteriological service, controlling the spread of infection, became the responsibility of the ministry.[116]

The 'appointed day' was welcomed in Kent by the newly elected member for Gravesend:

> Never again will a harassed mother have to count the coins in her purse to see if she can call the doctor to her sick child. No more will high-priced specialists and front-rank surgeons be available only to the wealthy and for the poor the best that the panel doctor or outpatients' department can provide. . . . In future all men will, in sickness, be equal.[117]

On the other hand Sir Edward Hardy, Chairman of the County Council, speaking of the shortage of nurses and accommodation, warned that 'there was no magic way to a land of promise'. The 'family doctor' service, so long beyond the reach of many, was at last a reality for everyone and they rushed to make use of it. Doctors were all but overwhelmed. 'One would think the people saved up their illnesses for the first free day,' commented one GP. Another young Kent doctor could not understand the heavy demand for cotton wool until it was realised that some poor patients were using it to stuff their children's toys! Less opulent practices could only buy the more expensive drugs, like the tetracyclines, with difficulty. By October ophthalmic applications in Kent had reached a massive 6,000 a week. Many applicants had previously tested their eyes and bought sixpenny glasses in Woolworth's. Kent dentists, who had initially refused to join the NHS, changed their minds as their patients dwindled and soon were greatly in demand. 'I have been rushed off my feet . . . during the past five weeks,' stated one Thanet dentist. 'Many of my patients have been elderly people . . . who have had fittings for dentures for the first time.' While critics claimed that taxpayers' money was being needlessly squandered, the govern-

---

116 *KM* 13.12.1946, 23.1.1948; Melling, *op. cit.*, pp. 80–3; Kent County Council, *Annual Report of the Medical Officer of Health*, Maidstone 1948.
117 *KM* 26.7.1946.

ment countered that the pressure on the new service resulted from pre-war neglect. At first the Kent and Canterbury Executive Council dismissed 'the stampede to get something for nothing' as 'a passing phase'. Chemists were bound to provide a fresh medicine bottle with every prescription but, as a shortage of bottles developed, the Health Minster was obliged to appeal to the public to use the service sensibly. Health centres, intended to be at the heart of the new service, were still a rarity twenty years later, and from the outset the waiting factor became acute.[118] By 1951 the Labour government, which had been responsible for creating a free national health service, had been obliged to introduce charges for dental and ophthalmic services, and only narrowly avoided having to introduce charges for prescriptions. These were introduced by a Conservative government in 1952, and increased in 1956 and 1961.[119] The political debates over the future of the Welfare State in general, and the health service in particular, since 1975, have tempted many people to see the early years of the National Health Service as some sort of 'golden age', but it is an image which recent research has shown to have been far from reality. In the words of one commentator:

> The establishment of the new health service is often thought to have marked the beginning of a long period of tranquillity. . . . For the most part, the situation between 1948 and 1964 was characterised by resource starvation and policy neglect.[120]

In no area was this more true than in the case of the NHS hospitals, both nationally and locally in Kent.

During the 1950s most hospital funding was directed at the improvement of existing hospitals, including those inherited from the Poor Law, rather than the building of new ones. Work did not begin on the construction of a new hospital (in Swindon) until 1957, and the first new hospital to be completed was one to serve two Hertfordshire new towns, Welwyn and Hatfield, in 1963.[121] Endeavouring to work within the constraints of inherited hospitals, at a time when the creation of the National Health Service had raised expectations among patients of a greatly improved hospital service, caused severe problems. At the Kent and Canterbury Hospital there was a 50% increase in out-patient attendance during the initial years of NHS operation which exposed the need for both additional medical staff and extensions to the existing hospital.[122] However, nothing was done until June 1961 when it was decided to double the capacity of the hospital from 251 to about 500 beds, to provide an accident centre – an NHS requirement which the hospital could not offer – and to upgrade the existing wards. All this

---

118 *KM* 9.7.1948, 27.8.1948, 15.10.1948.
119 Webster, *op. cit.*, pp. 36–7.
120 *Ibid.*, p. 30.
121 *Ibid.*, p. 41.
122 F.M. Hall, R.S. Stevens and J. Whyman, *The Kent and Canterbury Hospital, 1790–1987*, Canterbury 1987, p. 127.

work was expected to cost something in the region of £5 million pounds, which was simply not available, so only minor improvements were made to the hospital.[123] The delays were in fact fortuitous. In 1965 money was made available to begin work on a completely new replacement hospital, which was built in stages and finished in 1972, when it was officially opened by HRH Princess Alexandra of Kent.[124] This story of frustration leading, after several false starts, to complete rebuilding programmes was replicated at many other hospitals in Kent. The major push for improvements to the National Health Service, and particularly for investment in new hospitals, was begun by Harold Wilson's first Labour government of 1964–6 and continued until the fall of the Callaghan government in 1979,[125] though some of the programmes initiated were not fully implemented until the 1980s. This included the completion of the new Maidstone Hospital. The efforts of successive Conservative governments after 1979 to reduce the escalating costs of the National Health Service, as the expectations of patients continued to rise, resulted in the closure of some older hospitals and the temporary suspension of services at some of the newer ones. Economy drives at Maidstone Hospital led to a reduction in the availability of surgical beds and the cancellation of operations, thereby increasing waiting times for patients, and the hospital had to embark on the sort of fund-raising efforts previously associated with private charities to raise money for new initiatives, such as a new diabetes centre.[126]

The pressure on hospitals and other parts of the National Health Service led to calls for the reorganisation of the service. The Redcliffe-Maud Commission on English local government, which reported in 1969, recommended making all health services the responsibility of the new unitary authorities proposed in the report, but the medical profession, which had seen itself as escaping from local-authority control with the creation of the National Health Service in 1948, was strongly opposed to returning to such control and lobbied against it.[127] In 1974 the service in England was reorganised, outside the remit of local government, into fourteen regional health authorities, ninety area health authorities and 207 community health councils.[128] This reorganisation even deprived the new local authorities, created at the same time, of the community health services they had run since 1948. Local-authority medical officers of health transferred to the new community health councils as community health physicians. The only health responsibility retained by local authorities was that for environmental health. The resulting fragmentation between the responsibility of local authorities for the monitoring of public establishments and that of the community health councils for responding to local health emergencies was seen as a major cause of

---

[123] *Ibid.*, pp. 129–30.
[124] *Ibid.*, pp. 135–41.
[125] Webster, *op. cit.*, p. 65.
[126] *KM* 10.10.1997.
[127] Webster, *op. cit.*, pp. 88–9.
[128] *Ibid.*, p. 108.

subsequent public-health scares;[129] this fragmentation has not, however, been addressed in the reorganisations of the National Health Service which have taken place since 1974. The main advantage of the 1974 reorganisation was that it brought together all other aspects of health-care provision, from community health services to hospitals, dentists and general medical practitioners, into a single unified service.[130]

A major area of national concern from the late 1960s was the treatment of mental patients, and a number of high-profile cases were revealed which led eventually to a major, but not wholly satisfactory, reassessment of mental-health provision in the 1980s. One of the hospitals accused of ill-treating patients was St Augustine's, Canterbury, where an enquiry into local conditions was carried out between 1972 and 1975 and a report published in 1976. The report concluded

> that, taken as a whole, St Augustine's was not a bad hospital. The critique related to the long-stay wards and these had tended to be neglected by the medical staff as a result of a policy of concentrating resources on acute cases, and on developing a psychiatric service in the community.[131]

The main complaint at St Augustine's was not that patients were being positively ill-treated but that staff were unwilling to accept any new ideas about patient care or better ways of doing things. Senior staff were unwilling 'to act positively when confronted with weakness in their organisation' and concern was expressed about 'a small group of senior staff whose concentration of power tended to destroy initiatives from below'.[132] There was specific criticism that 'people were promoted or given responsibilities for which they were unfitted'; one nurse left in charge of a ward 'was unable to deal with any of the difficulties, and difficulties arose daily'.[133] Staff made derogatory remarks to or about patients, and some patients were called 'dumbos' to their faces.[134] The prime fault, however, lay with management:

> A person charged with monitoring is responsible for devising a system which provides him with reliable information. . . . Far too much monitoring consists of waiting to be told, and then of taking no effective action when information does come.[135]

Nevertheless the report was strongly criticised by most of the staff at St Augustine's who 'felt very badly let down'.[136]

---

129 *Ibid.*, pp. 124–6.
130 M. Brown and S. Payne, *Introduction to Social Administration in Britain*, London 1990, p. 74.
131 J.P. Martin, *Hospitals in Trouble*, Oxford 1984, pp. 32–5.
132 *Ibid.*, pp. 86, 88–9.
133 *Ibid.*, pp. 94–5.
134 *Ibid.*, p. 100.
135 *Ibid.*, p. 203.
136 *Ibid.*, p. 66.

(10) The Creation of Social Services Departments

The third part of the National Assistance Act 1948 had placed a duty on county councils to provide residential accommodation for old people needing care and attention, and also to make provision for the welfare of the handicapped. Initially this had been restricted to promoting the welfare of the blind, but in 1951 this was extended to cover the deaf, and in 1960 further extended to cover all handicapped people.[137] The legislation had, however, been relatively vague in its expression and most provision was discretionary. In 1948 Kent County Council had only five old-people's homes which between them provided only 168 places, though it also had access to nearly a thousand places for old people in hospitals as a result of joint-user agreements between the County Council and the Regional Hospital Board. Gradually the County Council built more homes for old people and was able to reduce its dependence on joint-user agreements. By 1964 the number of beds provided under joint-user agreements had fallen to 619. The County Council acquired eight new old-people's homes between 1949 and 1952 through the purchase and adaptation of existing large houses. These provided, with extensions to some existing homes, an additional 674 places for old people at a total cost of £368,250. It was not, however, until 1956–7 that Kent County Council opened its first purpose-built old people's homes at Bexley Heath and Hildenborough. The minimalist approach of the County Council to the provision of social welfare replicated its pre-war attitudes and was reflected in its failure to follow the example of other county councils and set up a separate Welfare Department. In an attempt to keep down the rising costs of having to build and maintain old people's homes the County Council offered financial assistance to other local authorities in Kent to provide sheltered housing for old people and to Old People's Welfare Committees to provide lodgings for old people that did not require the facilities of a residential home. County Council provision for the handicapped was similarly slow and minimalist.[138]

A major reform of welfare services nationally was instigated by the report of the Seebohm Committee which was published in 1965. Under the provisions of the Local Authority Social Services Act 1970 all county councils were obliged to set up social-service departments and appoint directors of social services. The new departments brought together responsibility for the provision of services for the elderly, physically disabled, deprived children and the mentally ill or handicapped.[139] Kent County Council had appointed its first children's officer in 1948, as a result of the passing of the Children Act that year, and a separate Children's Department had been set up in 1950. By 1963 the department ran thirty-two residential establishments but even here there were attempts to reduce the costs of residential provision by boarding out children wherever possible. In 1964, of the number of children in care, which fluctuated between 2,000 and

137   Brown and Payne, *op. cit.*, pp. 233–4, 258–9.
138   Melling, *op. cit.*, pp. 84–5.
139   Brown and Payne, *op. cit.*, pp. 175–6.

2,500 a year during the 1950s and 1960s, 46.1% were boarded out and 53.9% were in residential establishments.[140]

After many years of lagging behind much of the rest of Britain in the provision of personal social services, the creation of the new Department of Social Services by Kent County Council, on 1 April 1971,[141] was to provide the catalyst for a series of radical experiments in the provision of such services in the 1970s and 1980s. Part of the reason for this was the appointment of two somewhat unorthodox Directors of Social Services between 1974 and 1991, neither of whom had a professional background in local-authority social work. Nicolas Stacey (1974–85) was an Anglican priest who, after eight years as Rector of Woolwich, had become Deputy Director of Oxfam in 1968 and Director of Social Services for the London Borough of Ealing in 1971. Norman Warner (1985–91) had had a distinguished civil-service career which had included short breaks to take up fellowships at the University of California in 1971–3 and Nuffield College, Oxford, in 1983–4. He was later to become a policy adviser to the Home Secretary and Chairman of the Youth Justice Board for England and Wales, and was made a life peer in 1998.[142] The first major social-services experiment in Kent was to increase the numbers of children in fostering. The project was set up immediately after Nicolas Stacey's appointment as Director of Social Services and was a collaborative effort between the County Council, the University of Kent and the Gatsby Charitable Foundation. The project organiser was made a Senior Research Fellow at the University of Kent with a salary paid by the Gatsby Foundation, and the other project expenses were met by the County Council.

> The scheme was an attempt to discover whether it is possible or desirable for England to develop a community-based placement policy – an attempt, in other words, to show that adolescents with severe problems, who would formerly have been considered 'unsuitable for fostering', could be placed and maintained in families in the community and that these placements could reduce or solve their problems.[143]

Stacey had 'inherited a department which', less than three years after its creation, 'was far from problem free'.[144] Kent had a particularly low rate of fostering, and relied heavily on long-established and poorly maintained children's homes. It was, therefore, ripe for experiment and similar schemes had been shown to work successfully in Belgium, Sweden and the United States.[145] Most parts of the United Kingdom had only provided fostering for children with less severe problems. The only local authority to have gone beyond this was

140 Melling, *op. cit.*, p. 87.
141 *Ibid.*, p. 118.
142 Entries in *Who's Who*, London 1999, pp. 1899, 2099.
143 N. Hazel, *A Bridge to Independence: The Kent Family Placement Project*, Oxford 1981, pp. 1–2.
144 *Ibid.*, p. 7.
145 *Ibid.*, pp. 17–23.

Reading, where the pre-1974 county borough council had 'placed older children with severe difficulties with salaried foster parents'.[146]

Over a five-year period the County Council placed almost two-hundred children with foster parents. It was discovered that 70% of these placements had been successful; the behaviour of children placed with foster parents had improved, whereas in the residential homes children with different problems simply made each other worse. Foster parents were paid a professional fee; those with one placed child were considered the equivalent of a half-time social worker, those with two placed children that of a full-time social worker. It was argued that one beneficial side-effect of the scheme was that 'the creation of a new "cottage industry" helped women to stay at home while earning and remaining professionally active'. There were some placements which were not successful:

> Some arsonists and some children with acute forms of mental illness needed more security and specialist help than a family could offer. Some very delinquent boys did not respond to family placements – but they did not seem to respond to anything else either.

The Kent experiment was eventually copied by thirty other social-services departments in the United Kingdom.[147] Although it helped to reduce the number of children in residential establishments, and thus the costs of maintaining these, it was not simply an economy measure; it helped to produce responsible adults. The success of the fostering scheme led to other initiatives in community-based care for those in need. In the early 1980s Kent County Council pioneered several such initiatives in its Kent Community Care Project,[148] ideas that were strongly supported by an incoming Conservative government dedicated to a radical overhaul of welfare provision.

(11) The Thatcherite Revolution in Health and Social Welfare

The election of Margaret Thatcher to the leadership of the Conservative Party in 1975 led to the first breakdown in the national political consensus about health and social-welfare provision since the publication of the Beveridge Report and the subsequent creations of the National Health Service and the Welfare State. The party's thinking was based on a belief that the machinery for providing these services was bureaucratic and inefficient, and the reforms introduced after the Conservatives were returned to power at Westminster in 1979 were part of a much wider reform of the public services and the privatisation of nationalised industries. It is, however, significant that popular attachment both to the

---

146 *Ibid.*, p. 26.
147 *Ibid.*, pp. 158–60, 162–3.
148 *Implementing Community Care*, ed. N.A. Malin, Buckingham 1994, p. 106.

National Health Service and to the concept of the Welfare State made the Conservative government proceed fairly cautiously. Attempts had been made by right-wingers in the Conservative party to persuade the Heath government of 1970–4 to extend private health care and to adopt compulsory health insurance, but they had been resisted.[149] After 1979 both ideas were back on the agenda. It was pointed out that Britain was the only country in Western Europe to have a health service financed wholly out of national taxation. Once again, however, fear of public hostility persuaded the Conservative government not to introduce compulsory health insurance, but from 1980 encouragement was given to individuals, through tax concessions, to take out private health insurance. By 1990 only 12% of the total population of the United Kingdom was covered by private health insurance, compared with 6% in 1980, and a further tax concession to encourage greater uptake was offered in the 1989 budget. Attempts to increase the direct financing of the National Health Service were made by significantly raising prescription charges, which were increased by 500% between May 1979 and December 1980, and by introducing, from 1989, charges for eye tests and dental inspections, which had previously been free, despite widely expressed fears that such charges would constitute a deterrent to early detection and treatment especially among the poor.[150]

In its first years the new Conservative government concentrated on attempting to reduce the costs of the National Health Service through reorganisation and strict cash limits. In 1982 the ninety area health authorities and 207 community health councils, created in 1974, were reduced, in what was described 'as a piece of fine-tuning rather than a major shake-up', to 192 district health authorities. All health authorities were obliged to contribute efficiency savings of at least 0.5% of their annual budget for 1981/2, and most achieved this 'by cuts in services and reductions in standards of care, rather than in such areas as fuel efficiency, as was intended'. Pressure was also put on health authorities to contract out services to save money and to identify surplus land and property for disposal.[151] In 1989 it was decided that further savings could be achieved by promoting an internal market within the National Health Service by forcing hospitals to restructure their management so that one group of staff (the purchasers) entered into a formal transaction with another (the providers) for the delivery of services at an agreed cost. Hospitals were permitted to opt out of district health-authority control and to form self-governing NHS hospital trusts, and general practitioners were allowed to become fund-holders, buying 'a selected range of non-emergency services for their patients from providers in the public and private sectors'. By 1997, when the Conservative government was replaced by a Labour one, there were 429 NHS hospital trusts, with only 5% of hospitals directly managed by district health authorities; 13,423 out of 31,748

---

[149] Webster, *op. cit.*, p. 69.
[150] *Ibid.*, pp. 154–8.
[151] *Ibid.*, pp. 160–1, 165–6.

general practitioners were registered as fund-holders.[152] The election of a Labour government did not mean an immediate reversal in health-service policy but it did lead to a distinct change of rhetoric and, in the case of mental-health care, some change of direction.

The Mental Health Act 1983 had aimed 'to provide treatment and care of the mentally disordered on an informal basis and in the community wherever possible'.[153] Over the next five years there was a dramatic

> decline of beds in long-stay hospitals. . . . However, in many instances hospital beds are being lost whilst the corresponding level of support outside the hospital is not being provided. Many mentally ill and handicapped adults are forced to live in hostels for the homeless, and many more are simply sleeping rough.[154]

Towns in Kent which had not seen beggars in their streets since the 1950s began to find that they had a significant homeless population forced to support themselves by begging. When the incoming Labour government announced that 'seriously disturbed psychiatric patients must be kept in secure units', even some of the most solidly Conservative newspapers admitted that their previous Conservative government, despite its good intentions, had made a serious error of judgement:

> A sad and sorry episode in the history of British social theory is drawing to a close. The policy known as care in the community, which plucked the mentally ill out of huge Victorian asylums and sent them to live, often alone, in towns and villages is to be reversed. . . . The experiment went wrong from the beginning. All too often, there was no care and minimal community. Vulnerable individuals, a high proportion of whom had no experience of living on their own, were cast adrift. . . . The government deserves congratulations for taking the difficult decision to admit that a whole generation of liberal social engineers were mistaken.

This was, perhaps, a somewhat simplistic analysis. The Conservative reforms had been influenced at least as much, if not more, by the financial benefits of closing institutions as by 'liberal social engineering', the validity of which, with some modification, the new Labour government accepted. There was to be no return to the 'huge Victorian asylums', those 'large and unfeeling institutions whose failings provided the original impetus for the experiment'. The new Health Secretary, Frank Dobson, described them as 'clapped-out old motor coaches', which needed to be replaced with 'custom built vehicles', defined as small residential units 'staffed by specialist doctors and nurses'.[155]

The 'care in the community' approach to mental health was to be adopted by

---

152 *Ibid.*, pp. 189, 191–2, 198–9.
153 Brown and Payne, *op. cit.*, p. 274.
154 *Ibid.*, p. 288.
155 *Daily Telegraph*, 17 January 1998.

the Conservative government towards many areas of the personal social services, thus encouraging other parts of the United Kingdom to emulate some of the pioneering work undertaken by a Conservative County Council in Kent since 1974. In 1986 a committee was set up to review personal social services under the chairmanship of Sir Roy Griffiths; when its report was published in 1988 it was entitled *Community Care: An Agenda for Action*. It recommended a 'mixed economy' approach to social-service provision, involving private, public and voluntary sectors, but it was felt to be too favourable to continued public provision by some in the Conservative party. In the end the government somewhat reluctantly implemented its main provisions through the White Paper *Caring for People*, published in 1989, and subsequent legislation. The White Paper stated that the aim of the legislation would be to enable social-services departments to design 'care packages to meet individual needs, in consultation with clients and other professionals, and within available resources'.[156] The changes led to a massive reorganisation of social-services departments. In Kent a department which had a director, deputy director and six divisional directors was restructured in 1991 to become a department with a director and three assistant directors. One of the assistant directors was responsible for purchasing care packages; the service was administered by two senior members of staff responsible for East and West Kent respectively, and by sixteen local managers. A second assistant director was responsible for staff providing care packages to specific groups of people: children and families, those in need of domiciliary services, the elderly and physically disabled, people with mental health and learning difficulties. A third assistant director was responsible for overall strategy and quality assurance with section heads for information and communication, finance and strategic planning, quality assurance, human-resource planning and capital projects. The reorganisation was described as 'early and dramatic. Officers, jobs and systems were changed over one weekend and 1200 staff were transferred to new posts.' Some staff considered the whole exercise 'total confusion'. This was despite the fact that the County Council had been moving since the late 1980s 'towards decentralised, localised cost centres and devolved budgetary responsibilities' and had previously reorganised several other departments:

> The Conservative-controlled County had seized on a radical enabling model of local government that involved 'externalising' what had hitherto been in-house services such as highways and planning, property services and the treasurer's department. This involved setting up these services in a trading relationship with the 'client'.[157]

There was a widely held view that the reorganisation in Kent, as elsewhere, was not assisted by the government's not having put in place proper arrangements

---

156 Brown and Payne, *op. cit.*, pp. 191–2; Malin, *op. cit.*, pp. 6–7.
157 J. Lewis and H. Glennerster, *Implementing the New Community Care*, Buckingham 1996, pp. 45–51.

for 'funding or planning the changes adequately'.[158] Kent County Council received an extra £6 million for the first year of the restructured social-services provision in 1993/4 of which £1.5 million was for 'transitional administrative costs'. £3.5 million of this had to be spent in the private or voluntary sectors, mostly on providing residential care for the elderly. The County Council took the view that its settlement was £1.3 million short of what it actually needed. They had to spend 85% of the 'new money' in the independent sector, 'but the independent sector did not offer good quality home support services. . . . They could not spend the grant on the council's own services which were well developed and respected for their high quality.' The 'new money' did not recognise the growing pressures for expenditure on services for children – which had been increased from 21% to 30% of the social services budget between 1987/8 and 1992/3 – or for those with learning difficulties. The County Council was forced to manipulate its budget in order to make the provision it considered necessary to maintain services at a reasonable level whilst at the same time trying to meet government targets for spending in the private and voluntary sectors.[159]

The changes to the health and social-welfare services which had been implemented by the Conservative governments of Margaret Thatcher and John Major between 1979 and 1997 had been dramatic and had led to some of the hostility to the government which resulted in the Labour victory in the general election of 1997. The weakness of the reforms was that they were, like much else of the Conservative programme, primarily motivated by ideological considerations: a belief that the private or voluntary sectors were almost always more efficient than the public sector, and a complete unwillingness to recognise circumstances in which this was not the case; a distrust of what was dismissively described as bureaucracy; and an unshakeable belief in 'market forces' as a recipe for 'best value'. On the other hand there is no doubt that there was bureaucracy and inefficiency in the provision of health and social-welfare services and that decisions were all too often made less in the interests of those who used the services than of those who ran them. Although there were times in the 1980s and 1990s when the health and social-welfare services 'appeared locked in an almost Maoist state of permanent revolution with no-one clear of what the final outcome would be', these services had by 1997 'arguably more coherence' in their aims and objectives 'than for many a year'.[160]

---

[158] Malin, *op. cit.*, p. 8.
[159] Lewis and Glennerster, *op. cit.*, pp. 32–7.
[160] N. Timmins, *A History of the NHS*, London 1996, p. 38.

8

Popular Education

IAN COULSON

(1) Education in Kent before 1900

At the beginning of the twentieth century Kent County Council inherited an education system that had grown piecemeal over the course of the previous hundred years. By 1914 a rudimentary form of education was available for young people up to the age of thirteen. The 1870 Education Act had ended the indirect involvement of the state in education, and established schools in areas where there was no provision for elementary education by the voluntary societies. It marked the acceptance that a national system of elementary education could not be provided solely by the voluntary sector. It was not however a system without its flaws: the curriculum was crudely constructed; compulsory attendance for all children between the ages of five and thirteen was not introduced until 1880, and it remained possible for children, from the age of ten, to attend only part-time if they reached a certain standard of attainment.

Secondary education was even more underdeveloped and haphazard. At the end of the nineteenth century there was no systematic and effective provision of secondary education in Kent and this was only partly resolved in 1902 by an Act that devolved responsibility for education into the hands of the counties and the county boroughs. In Kent in 1914 many of the deficiencies of the previous two centuries, noted by Hume,[1] remained unresolved.

Throughout the nineteenth century the provision of popular education was dominated by religious competition and animosity. In Kent the dominant voluntary body was the National Society which represented the interests of a Church of England that considered education to be one of its prime duties. In competition there were the voluntary societies of the free churches including the British and Foreign Society. The nonconformist societies feared the domination of the established church and the bitter debates between the voluntary societies created a political stalemate that restricted the development of elementary education in Kent, as in the rest of the country, during the nineteenth and early twentieth centuries.

---

[1]   N. Yates, R. Hume and P. Hastings, *Religion and Society in Kent, 1640–1914*, Woodbridge 1994, pp. 103–11.

The most significant turning point for popular education in the nineteenth century came in 1870 when the government passed the Elementary Education Act. This forced the establishment of elected school boards where there was inadequate provision by the voluntary societies. The 1870 Act created a dual system of elementary schools in the county that continues, somewhat altered, to this day. The voluntary denominational schools were endowed or relied on subscriptions, fees and government grants, and they often had great difficulty raising money within their own communities and parishes.[2] The new school boards were non-denominational and were funded from the rates and government grants as well as by fees. By 1900 the board schools in Kent tended to be larger with better resources and in many cases had more pupils who stayed on beyond the age of eleven. The voluntary schools, which dominated education in the rural areas, were smaller and often very poorly resourced. They too had to rely on local support for their day-to-day maintenance. From the 1880s there was pressure from the voluntary-society managers for some access to funding from the rates. The Church of England felt that there was 'unequal competition'[3] with the school boards because the voluntary schools had no right or access to public funds, and in 1888 this view was expressed in the majority report of the Cross Commission. In 1902 the Conservative government supported this movement by abolishing school boards and giving church schools support from the rates.[4]

In 1900 the elementary school system was well established, although attendance was very poor by modern standards. The rationale and the curriculum were laid down in practice and statute. Schools were intended to educate the lower classes but not to provide an extended education. The curriculum aimed to give pupils only the basics of reading and writing. The standards in many Kent schools were pitifully low, and arithmetic was regarded by some as an extension subject. Moral education, a feature of most schools, focused on obedience, patriotism and duty, and was reinforced by stern discipline. Much of the curriculum was taught by rote-learning. Discipline was often maintained through the fear of punishment for the slightest misdemeanour and for what was sometimes called 'wilful ignorance'.

The most significant influence on the curriculum in Kent schools from 1862 was the revised code. This provided a common syllabus that could be easily inspected. Schools were inspected once a year and the results of the pupils in the examination, and the number of pupils in attendance on that day, determined the grant for the following year. Not surprisingly the teachers taught to the code and the results in educational and teaching terms were low standards and a restricted curriculum. By the middle of the 1890s the code had been partially relaxed. In a small number of schools ideas from abroad were being adopted. On the continent, the new Kindergarten teaching methods of Froebel emphasised the importance for infants of learning by doing. The approaches of Pestalozzi were also

2   *The First Annual Report of Kent Education Committee*, Maidstone 1904, p. 427.
3   S.J. Curtis, *History of Education in Britain*, London 1967, p. 307.
4   B. Simon, *Education and the Labour Movement, 1870–1920*, London 1974, p. 159.

becoming more popular. This was a philosophy that believed in training rather than rote learning, with discipline based on respect rather than unquestioning obedience. The ideas of the American John Dewey about child-centred teaching and an education for life were becoming increasingly well known[5] but were accepted only slowly in Kent. It was infant teachers who adopted the ideas with the greatest enthusiasm. The curriculum in the vast majority of elementary schools remained narrow, and progress was particularly ponderous in the development of art, science and technology.

Not surprisingly, attendance in elementary schools was always a problem. It was not until 1880 that elementary education became compulsory. This compulsion was seen by many as an intrusion into the independence of the individual. Pressure for attendance was brought to bear by the school boards or, in areas where there were no school boards, attendance committees. The effectiveness of this system in Kent varied and there continued to be opposition to compulsory education, especially where the potential earnings of a family were threatened. In rural areas there was often an indifference to popular education and the preference of both farmers and parents for the employment of children continued well into the twentieth century.

At the end of the nineteenth century, the government provided no state secondary-school system. The extension of school beyond the age of eleven was left to the individual school boards who had the financial independence of being able to use money from the rates to support older pupils. In Kent the development of secondary education was very slow. There was a lack of political will and a belief that the lower classes would not benefit from education beyond the elementary phase. There was also the potential cost of establishing such a system. In some towns and cities, especially in the northern industrial areas of the country, higher elementary schools had been established to provide the sort of basic education required by industry. For example, in Bradford in the 1870s three-quarters of the timetable in the higher elementary schools was devoted to science. There was no equivalent type of school with these priorities in Kent until the 1890s.

Concerns about technical and scientific education were raised throughout the nineteenth century. They were encouraged by the realisation that the relative performance of British industry was falling behind many foreign competitors. In Kent the first co-ordinated response came from the newly formed County Council when the Local Taxation Act of 1890 released 'whisky' money. This duty was raised on alcohol and was passed directly to the new local authorities to either help develop technical education or supplement the rates.[6] This legislation had a real impact on the movement towards secondary education and the Kent Technical Education Committee (KTEC) was established in July 1891 to administer the funds from central government.[7]

5   J. Dewey, *School and Society*, London 1899.
6   PRO, HLG 29/31.
7   P.A. Moylan, *The Form and Reform of County Government in Kent, 1889–1914*, Leicester 1978, pp. 54–6.

Grants for buildings, salaries and equipment were administered by the KTEC, which was dominated by Alderman George Arnold, who was chairman from 1891 to 1902.[8] The committee was financially independent of the County Council, although on several occasions this independence was challenged, albeit unsuccessfully, as in 1893 and again in 1897. The annual grants of between £22,000 and £31,000 per annum were distributed mainly to the established grammar schools and the technical institutes in towns. Expenditure was low at first and then rose as demand increased. A limited number of scholarships were also offered by the Committee for pupils to continue on to secondary education, for women to go on to higher education, and for courses in 'domestic economy, agriculture and nursing'. Assistance was also given to the Southeast Association for the Provision of University Teachers to promote further education for adults. The lectures supported by KTEC included a range of subjects from wood-carving to demonstrations using a migratory dairy. 'Domestic economy' was promoted extensively through lectures on hygiene, cooking and needlecraft. Initially, the lectures were very successful but by the end of the 1890s the number of people attending had declined and the Committee devoted a greater percentage of its finances to schools, colleges and institutes.

The money was also used to support two agricultural colleges, one at Wye and the other, a horticultural college, at Swanley.[9] The South Eastern Agriculture College at Wye was opened in 1894 and reflected the importance of agriculture in the county. This was the most ambitious foray by the Committee into further education. Originally the KTEC investigated the possibility of sharing the project with Sussex, Surrey and Hampshire. When this proved impractical the college was established as a joint affiliation with the University of London to create its School of Agriculture. Funds were also provided for a girls' school of domestic economy in Maidstone. This was one of the few schools where girls had an opportunity to receive any form of secondary education. Unfortunately the curriculum and teaching was limited and was encouraged to be 'lucidly supplied and kept well within elementary limits'.[10]

(2) The Education Act of 1902

In 1899 the government created the Board of Education 'to supervise, to promote harmony and cooperation, but not to control'. The Board was formed from four government departments and took over the educational roles of the Education Department, the Science and Art Departments, the Board of Agriculture and the charity commissioners. This rationalisation was extended in the 1902 Education Act to encompass the creation of local education authorities, of

---

[8] E. Melling, *History of the Kent County Council*, Maidstone 1974, p. 12.
[9] The college was originally privately run. It took charitable status in 1897 and was purchased by KCC in 1947.
[10] G.M. Arnold, *Education under the Kent Technical Education Committee*, Maidstone 1903, p. 15.

which Kent was one of the largest. The administrative changes were driven by Robert Morant, a determined junior official in the Board of Education. He pushed for a test-case that challenged the right of any elementary school board to use money from the rates to fund secondary education. Morant believed very strongly in the value of maintaining the grammar-school system which in many parts of the country was competing unsuccessfully with the technical institutes and the secondary departments in board schools.

In 1899 the Cockerton judgement denied the London School Board the ability to finance secondary education from the rates. This forced the government to consider the whole administrative basis of secondary education and its financing. In Kent there was no overall strategy for secondary education. The new act was welcomed by the County Council because it continued the support for the grammar schools, which was favoured by the majority of members, and it offered support from the rates for the voluntary schools.

The 1902 Education Act abolished the school boards and created 140 Local Education Authorities (LEAs) that were to be run by county and county borough councils, and which took over the functions of the school boards and the school-attendance committees. The board schools became known as county schools.

The Kent Education Committee was established from a Special Sub-Committee of the Kent Technical Education Committee which reported on the financial implications of the 1902 Act. From these proposals the Kent Education Committee (KEC) was formed on 16 February 1903. The school boards in Kent were abolished and the pattern of local educational administration was established that was to last throughout the rest of the century. The dual system of county schools and the voluntary schools continued with KEC providing at least partial funding for all elementary schools. This posed a series of immediate problems as it became very clear that the voluntary schools were much less well resourced and maintained than the old board schools. The school boards fought to resist their abolition because they feared that the new system would result in the loss of local participation in the management of the schools[11] and certainly there were fewer opportunities for independent action as a result of the increased centralisation.

The councillors who were members of KEC were also concerned about the new system and their workload.[12] In 1907 there were 135 meetings of KEC, and some members were spending almost half their working week on council business. The deluge of requests and questions on school repairs, school cleaning and the payment and appointment of teachers resulted in the establishment of a range of new county services run by KEC. Many councillors considered this bureaucracy was unnecessary and extravagant[13] but the practical tasks before

11   J. Lawson and H. Silver, *The Social History of Education in England*, London 1973, p. 379.
12   Melling, *op. cit.*, p. 16.
13   In 1903 there were ninety employees working for the Kent Education Committee, the largest department in KCC.

the Education Committee were daunting and could only be performed with the assistance of professional officers.[14] Twenty-one local sub-committees were established to help with the workload. The co-ordination of higher education was delegated to Local Sub-Committees of the County Committee in the main urban areas. This allowed for more efficient use of scarce resources. For example, in Rochester, Chatham and Gillingham the higher-education needs of the Medway towns were catered for by a single Local Sub-Committee.

The 1902 Act made KEC responsible for secondary education throughout the county except in Canterbury where the City Council retained control. Two types of secondary school were supported by the new legislation. The endowed grammar schools were now supported by LEA grants, and new county secondary schools were financed wholly by the KEC.

Two particular problems faced the Education Committee. The first was the lack of secondary places for girls, Faversham Girls' School being the only girls' secondary school in the county.[15] This problem was partially remedied in 1904 and 1905 when eight new secondary schools and two pupil–teacher centres for girls were opened. In 1907 the total number of new secondary schools that were maintained by the committee rose to thirteen, although many were housed in temporary accommodation and were short of resources and well-trained staff.

The second major problem faced by KEC was the shortage of teachers and the need to establish a revised system of teacher training. Pupil teachers had previously been trained in pupil teacher centres and in some rural areas they had remained in the elementary schools. As part of the 1902 Act, KEC was given the responsibility for training teachers and followed the recommendations of the Board of Education by sending candidates through secondary school. This avenue for training took several years, and without financial support few candidates were recruited. Faced with a serious shortage of teaching staff, the County Council introduced a scholarship system for prospective teachers. There was, however, some concern from members that the bulk of the funds for scholarships were going to future teachers rather than to other scholars. This was certainly the case, but without this support there would have been an acute shortage of teachers. In a joint effort to increase the supply of graduate teachers, Kent combined with Middlesex, Surrey, Croydon, London County Council and London University to establish a teacher-training college at Goldsmith's. This provided up to fifty places for Kent students each year, although it did not guarantee fifty new teachers for Kent schools because the qualified teachers were free to take up posts anywhere in the country at the end of their training.

For many of the grammar schools in the county the 1902 Act brought financial security. In 1896 Dartford Grammar School had thirty-five pupils, and this had fallen to twenty-five in early 1902. Not surprisingly there were discussions about the amalgamation of the school with the Dartford Technical Institute.

---

[14] *The Second Annual Report of Kent Education Committee*, Maidstone 1905, p. 19.
[15] *The Second Annual Report of Kent Education Committee*, p. 7.

There were lively public meetings and a decision on the proposal was delayed pending the passage of the Education Act. The proposals for amalgamation were dropped once the intentions of KEC were known and it was seen that the grammar schools would benefit financially. A new head-teacher was appointed and for the first time in many years it was clear that the school had a more secure financial future.

The curriculum in the grammar schools in the county was based on the classics with, in some schools, the reluctant inclusion of science. When the new head-teacher was appointed at Dartford Grammar School in 1902, the job description required 'the Classics, Holy Scripture and the Church Catechism to be taught to the scholars who desire it', and that 'the rest of the curriculum, which should be that of an Endowed School', is arranged by the headmaster. Also mentioned was the fact that the county council made 'the teaching of science subjects obligatory for earning the grant from them'.[16] In 1904 the Board of Education urged secondary schools to broaden their curriculum up to the age of sixteen by including modern languages, history, science and mathematics as well as the classics core. Specialisation was encouraged for those who stayed on after the age of sixteen. This pattern set the mould for the rest of the century. It was unfortunate that technical education was not as well supported. For the remainder of the century the encouragement of technical and vocational education lacked continuity and profited only from intermittent bursts of enthusiasm and financial support.

An elementary-school education was compulsory in 1902, but the extension of that education beyond the age of twelve depended on the financial support of parents, the LEA paying fees or providing access to scholarships.[17] In 1907 the government gave larger grants to those grant-aided secondary schools that offered more than 25% of their places free to the winners of scholarships. To put a limit on the middle class playing the system, any pupils admitted on a scholarship had to have spent at least two years in a state elementary school. The scholarships worked well for a small number of pupils, but some were not able to take up the opportunity because they could not afford the additional costs or persuade their families that education was an investment.

The new county secondary schools were wholly supported by the County Council and offered a secondary education that was of a lower standard than that of the grammar schools. A place in these schools was not determined by a scholarship examination and was free up to and beyond the age of compulsory attendance. The average number of pupils in secondary education in the county was similar to the national averages with 1.98 per 1,000 in 1902 and 4.83 per 1,000 in 1906. Despite this increase, the figures represent a very small percentage of pupils staying on at school beyond the age of fourteen.

With its newly accepted responsibilities, KEC faced a number of pressing

---

[16] R. Hudson and D. Patterson, *Dartford Grammar School History*, Dartford 1997.
[17] Education Act 1902, Section 23(2).

financial problems.[18] The first was the backlog of repairs and the lack of resources in the voluntary schools. An HMI visit to Chilham reported

> The Infants school has been in difficulties during the past year and was found to be in a poor condition when visited in November last. The present Mistress is improving matters and will do well I hope. The small baby room with no fireplace, but with a poisonous stove, is unfit for children. The offices are altogether unsatisfactory and should not be used.[19]

At Seal and Underriver National School another HMI reported

> The physical exercises cannot be well done in school owing to the want of space. The room is dark and crowded with children and furniture. The playground should be properly drained. At present the rainwater runs to the doors, where it forms large ponds through which the children must pass.[20]

In the County Council regular concerns were expressed about the costs of running education. The rates increased from 7¼d. in 1902 to 1s. 0¾d. in 1904 with the education rate increasing from 8d. in 1905 to 11¼d. in 1914. In November 1907 an independent accountant was employed to enquire into the efficiency of the Education Committee and its work. The result was some minor savings, a few salaries were lowered and there were staff reductions through 'natural wastage', but essentially the conclusion was that the work of the Education Committee was performed economically and efficiently.

From 1894 the KTEC had met in London. This continued to be the venue for the meetings of KEC when the KTEC was dissolved and the new Education Committee was established in 1903. The choice of London as a venue was largely for the convenience of the members many of whom worked in the City. In 1910 the Education Offices moved from London to the new County Hall in Maidstone where the work of the Committee and the offices of the professional staff could be kept under one roof. The move was completed in November 1913.

The changes during the first decade of the century were a small step towards providing a structured education system for primary and secondary pupils. The Board of Education and the new Local Education Authority created a system that was streamlined and where the political power had moved from the school boards to the LEA. The politics of the Education Committee came to dominate the education system, with support for secondary education being concentrated on the largely middle-class grammar schools. The Act of 1902 reinforced the nineteenth-century curriculum in the elementary schools and promoted the public-school model in the grammar schools. The perception remained that elementary education was for the lower classes and that they were unable or unlikely in most cases to benefit from anything more than a rudimentary educa-

---

[18] The cost of providing elementary education rose steadily from £171,000 in 1904 to £300,000 in 1914. Just over half of these figures was received in the form of government grants.
[19] *The First Annual Report of the Kent Education Committee*, p. 152.
[20] *Ibid.*, p. 331.

tion in the basics. This was a major loss to the economy and failed to push the debate about education on towards one focused on a relevant secondary education for all. In turn, the class-based presumptions upon which education policy was based put a major block on changes in the curriculum. The much-vaunted scholarships did not offer a ladder to higher education for any but a tiny minority; indeed this was the intention. Both Morant and Balfour were opposed to a broad secondary education for the majority of the population but did believe in, and give their support to, the ailing grammar schools.

(3) The Impact of the First World War

From the start of the War in 1914 the education services in Kent were in some disarray. There was a clear determination throughout the conflict to keep the service running, but the administration was seriously dislocated by both changes of staff and the war effort. Added to this, from the middle of the war there was a national movement to plan for post-war reconstruction.

One of the most significant effects of the war on education was the change of staff in both the schools and the administration of the service. Forty per cent of the administrative staff joined up during the first few months of the war and this rose eventually to a figure of 65%. Special training for former employees and women supplied many of the replacement staff that were necessary to keep the service running.[21] In the schools 249 teachers joined up, of whom 207 had returned to their posts by February 1920. Not surprisingly, all building projects were halted in 1914, and from 1915 onwards only emergency repairs took place. Unlike London, there was no damage to Kent schools from enemy action and only a few buildings were commandeered for military use during the conflict.

Throughout the conflict there were numerous initiatives to support the war effort. The number of elementary-school gardens increased from 110 to 169. Five secondary schools had Cadet Units at the beginning of the war, and by 1918 there were eleven units in the county.[22] Many schools were involved with voluntary work, including raising money and materials for the services and prisoners of war. School-based saving schemes raised upwards of £150,000 from children and their parents. At one point, schools were even involved in the collection of horse chestnuts for processing into material for gas masks.[23]

A comment on the impact of the war hinted at the growing interest in extending further the reforms of 1902: 'an added sense of social solidarity and the widening of the boundaries of citizenship have been amongst the results of the war. At the same time there has been developed a better understanding of the importance of education in relation to national life and national development.'[24]

[21] *The Twelfth Report of the Kent Education Committee*, Maidstone 1914–19, p. 67.
[22] *Ibid.*, p. 38.
[23] *Ibid.*, pp. 10–13.
[24] *Ibid.*, p. 67.

(4) The Education Act of 1918

The momentum for educational change that eventually resulted in the 1918 Education Act had its origins in the proposed increases in spending on education by the Liberal government in 1914. Unfortunately that expenditure was 'arrested by the outbreak of war' but it remained a priority for the future.

The resurgence of this interest in education came towards the end of the First World War. There was increasing public pressure for education to be extended beyond the elementary level and there was a 25% increase in the number of pupils attending secondary schools in Kent.[25] There was also considerable concern expressed about the morality of juvenile employment between 1914 and 1918, and it was this that motivated a considerable number of politicians. Throughout the war there had been pressure for increased industrial and agricultural production. At the same time large numbers of men had left their jobs and joined the army leaving a desperate shortage of labour. This resulted in the employment of large numbers of young people.

Many employers supported the use of this source of cheap labour. There had always been a strong lobby in rural Kent for school attendance to be relaxed at important times in the farming calendar.[26] The view that for some pupils, 'education was no good for them at all; it unsettled them and they were much better off on the farm' was not unusual.[27] Even before the war some boroughs in South London were sympathetic to the requirements for seasonal labour and turned a blind eye, by not prosecuting families that went hop-picking during term time. From late 1914 there was also the financial pressure from within families which had lost the income of the main breadwinner. Those who had volunteered or were conscripted to the forces often left behind a family in financial difficulties. The attraction of well-paid employment also drew many children out of school at the earliest opportunity. The result was that children in Kent were being put prematurely to work.[28] It is impossible to assess the number of under-age children who were in employment in the county. Nationally it was estimated that in 1917 600,000 children were at work and employed in 'excessive hours of strenuous labour' before they had reached the school leaving age.

A government departmental committee met to consider 'juvenile education and employment after the war'. It recognised that very few teenagers had any experience of secondary education: 'public education after the elementary school leaving age is a part-time affair. And there is very little of it.' The response to the report also illustrated a change in contemporary thinking about the education system.

---

25 *Ibid.*, pp. 21, 273.

26 Several schools recorded in their logbook entries like this one from Boughton Monchelsea: 'June 29, 1917, School closed for fruit-picking holiday. Owing to abundance of fruit and scarcity of labour the holiday is extended to three weeks.'

27 Comment by the Chairman of Ashford branch of the National Farmers Union recorded in *South-Eastern Gazette*, 2 February 1915.

28 From March 1915, twelve-year-old boys were allowed to leave school to work in agriculture. By 1918, 4,000 boys were licensed to work on the farms in Kent.

Plate 41. Pupils at Sundridge School, c.1910.

Plate 42. Boy's gardening class at Boughton Monchelsea School, c.1910.

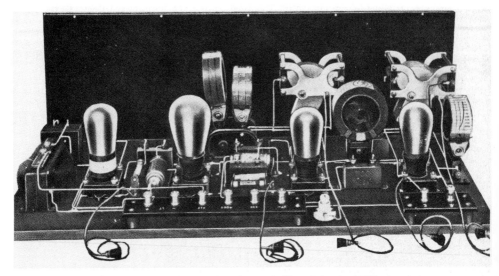

Plate 43. Standard four-valve wireless receiver for use in Kent Schools, 1927.

Plate 44. Pupils at Rolvenden School, 1931.

Plate 45. Book-binding class at Stelling Minnis School, 1936.

Plate 46. School dinners, c.1960.

Plate 47. School sports hall, 1974.

Plate 48. Pupils at Singlewell County Junior School, Gravesend, 1974.

Plate 49. School pupils using computers, 1986.

It is framed to repair the intellectual wastage which has been caused by the war; and should it pass into law before peace is struck it will put a prompt end to the evil which has grown into an alarming proportions during the past three years – I allude to the industrial pressure upon the child life of this country – and it will greatly facilitate the solution of many problems of juvenile employment, which will certainly be affected by the transition of the country from a basis of peace.[29]

The response from the government was to invite H.A.L. Fisher from Sheffield University to frame a new education act. As the debate about the proposed act developed, KEC created a sub-committee to prepare policy guidelines for Kent. The committee later became permanent and co-ordinated the promotion of the Education Act in the county through conferences and public meetings.

The Education Act of 1918 attempted to draw together the haphazard organisational structure of the education system, but the government was unable to provide the necessary resources for counties like Kent. The Act required local authorities to provide a scheme 'for the progressive development and comprehensive organisation of education in respect of their area', and such a scheme was duly submitted by KEC.

The ambitions of H.A.L. Fisher and the KEC plans were commendable. The Act proposed the establishment of nursery schools, an increase in the number of secondary places, the establishment of Central Schools to provide advanced courses for elementary school pupils over the age of twelve, and the creation of 'central tops', extra classes in elementary schools, where the building of separate central schools would be un- economic. The Act also encouraged the creation of Specialist Subject Centres, the provision of schools for handicapped pupils and compulsory continuation classes for part-time wage earners up to the age of sixteen.

Such ambitious proposals dominated KEC business during the period 1918–21. Unfortunately there were delays and the scheme submitted by KEC[30] was not received back from the government until February 1921,[31] two months after a Government Order stated that 'excepting with fresh cabinet authority schemes involving expenditure not yet in operation are to remain in abeyance.' The preparations by KEC came to a halt and were further complicated by the economic depression in Kent in the early 1920s. Gradually KEC abandoned the proposals in the Act. In 1921 the Education Committee discarded the plans for nursery education and compulsory continuation classes. None of the new central schools for secondary education were built. Once again the permissive legislation of 1918 and government retrenchment led to the cancellation of plans for a system that desperately needed an overhaul.

In Kent a piecemeal reorganisation of elementary and secondary schools took place over the next two decades. The continued centralisation of education in the

---

29 *House of Commons Debates*, 10 August 1917.
30 KEC Draft Scheme for Education in Kent under the Education Act 1918, PRO ED 120/416.
31 Draft Scheme of Education for the County of Kent, Kent County Council, 1921.

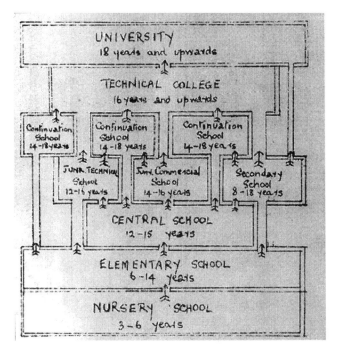

Figure 11. Diagram illustrating the correlation of education in Rochester, Chatham, Gillingham and District, c.1920.

hands of KCC caused friction between several districts and the LEA. This antagonism was longstanding and had its origins in the clashes between the school boards and the Kent Technical Education Committee in the 1890s. This had been made worse when the school boards and the voluntary schools lost control to the new LEA in 1902. The desire for local control of education remained very strong, and by the end of the Great War there had been several conferences held to discuss the devolution of some of the powers of the KEC. The plan was to create District Education Boards that would control their own local educational districts with divisional education officers. Their main functions were to be a responsibility for higher education, further education and the work of the School Attendance Committees. Agreement was reached in 1918 to create twenty-four Boards. The Medway Education Board was the first to be established in February 1919.[32] Within two years eleven of these Boards were operating and plans were in progress for the others to be established when the economic depression forced a review of expenditure. After the economic

---

[32] 'A county such as Kent with its varied population, industry and diversity of character is too large a unit for perfect and sympathetic educational control from one centre. The vitalising and stimulating effect of personal contact is lost for the members of the County Education Committee, however willing, cannot possibly make themselves acquainted with the multifarious needs, interests and difficulties of the various different localities.' *Twelfth Report of Kent Education Committee*, p. 6.

depression of the early 1920s only the Medway Board survived and District Committees replaced the rest of the Boards.

The expansion of secondary education proposed in the 1918 Act did not take place as planned. The legislation imposed a school leaving age of fourteen, but, with the economic constraints and various government economy measures, the building of the secondary schools progressed very slowly. In 1903, Kent provided 2,036 places in secondary schools; by 1929 this had risen to 12,263.[33] A similar increase had taken place in the art and technical schools where the numbers had risen in the same years from 8,743 to 15,465. The increase in numbers reflected a changed attitude to education by many parents. Where once the pressure would have been to leave school at the earliest opportunity, by the 1920s a significant minority was looking to extend their children's education. Although the proposals of 1918 did not come to fruition in the 1920s, the whole secondary curriculum and its organisation was beginning to offer a wider range of opportunities. Provision and opportunities varied across the county and access to the system was still largely defined by social class. It was a system that did not give access to a good education for the majority of the population.[34]

The structure of secondary education in Kent in the 1920s was different in each district. The 'correlation of education' for Medway was produced in diagrammatic form (see Figure 11) as evidence to the Hadow report, and shows the provision for secondary education in the early 1920s.[35] The system was structured to produce a number of pathways through secondary education with a minority going to university. The different types of secondary school had had their origins in a piecemeal pattern of development over the previous thirty years. What is not shown is the complex movement of the different types of school from one set of premises to another. As the demand for secondary education increased, new sites had to be purchased. For example, nine acres at 'Holcombe' were bought for a Junior Technical School in 1922. This eventually became the secondary school for boys. Once the Junior Technical School moved onto this site its premises were taken over by the Junior Commercial School for Girls, which became known as the Day Technical School for Girls, providing 220 places. The whole system was very complex and was tied together with a web of scholarships and bursaries.

The Hadow Report on the Education of the Adolescent in 1926 proposed a simplification of the elementary- and secondary-school systems. An examination at eleven would divide the primary schools from the secondary schools. The report also suggested the creation of secondary 'modern' schools for pupils who did not go to the grammar schools. The hope of the report was that standards would be raised in the modern schools and that the system of secondary educa-

---

33 *Education in Kent, 1928–1933*, Maidstone 1934, p. 65.
34 *Secondary Education for All*, ed. R.H. Tawney, London 1922, p. 37. This was a policy statement by the Labour Party that described the scholarship system as providing 'slender hand-rails' rather than a bridge to a good secondary education.
35 PRO, ED 10/147.

tion would be simplified. The report suited KEC because it supported the development of the grammar schools. Unfortunately Hadow did not take account of the place of the technical schools. The report also supported county control of the grammar schools and maintained the freedom of district authorities to control the other secondary schools. This allowed towns like Gillingham some independence. In 1928 a conference was hosted by Gillingham Education Committee and included head-teachers, HMIs and representatives of the churches. The result was a major reorganisation with the creation of infant, junior and secondary schools. In Gillingham most of the schools were affected by the reorganisation. Some of the changes were innovative, for example a consultative committee of parents was established in 1934. Special classes were also provided for pupils with special needs, described at the time as 'dull and backward children and high grade defectives.'

The 1930s began much the same as the previous decade with the 'shadow of financial stringency' falling across the three-year development plan issued by KEC in 1930.[36] The reorganisation of the elementary schools and the establishment of the new central schools were started only to be stopped once again by government restrictions on spending. It was not until financial controls were removed between the end of 1936 and the early months of 1939 that a substantial building programme began again. By the end of this short period 'forty three new school departments and six enlargements had been provided.'[37] These developments still did not satisfy the ambitions of the 1918 Act and were not established long enough to have any significant impact on standards.

There were three areas where the reorganisation of elementary education was completed before the start of the Second World War. The first was in North-West Kent where between 1933 and 1938 the population rose by 150,000. That translated into an increase in the school population of 11,074 pupils. Here the authority was able to build schools despite the government restrictions because of the rapid increase in house building.[38] Several of the schools in this area were badly built, with the result that it was necessary to make good at considerably greater cost at a later date.[39] The second area where the reorganisation was completed was in the Kent coalfield district that covered Sturry, Hersden, Nonington, Aylesham and Sandwich. In this area new communities grew rapidly around the recently opened mines. The only rural area where the reorganisation was completed was in Ashford where the central schools were also built. The rural areas posed special problems with their preponderance of voluntary schools[40] that did not have to, and often could not afford to, comply with the recommendations of the Hadow Report and the support given to the report by

---

[36] *Education in Kent, 1928–1933*, p. 22.
[37] *Education in Kent, 1933–1938*, Maidstone 1939, p. 9.
[38] Of the thirty-eight central schools in the county, twenty-four were in this area, *ibid.*, p. 23.
[39] *Ibid.*, p. 7.
[40] There were 276 voluntary elementary schools in Kent in 1933; this fell to 244 in 1938.

the Board of Education.[41] As well as building, extending and adapting schools the authority continued to purchase land for future developments, especially when the government reintroduced the proposals for raising the school leaving age to fifteen.

During the 1930s the total number of pupils in the county remained fairly stable with the population increase in the north-west balanced by a decline in the birth rate in the rural areas. This caused KEC financial problems because the reduction of numbers in rural areas could not be reflected in the reduction of the number of schools and teachers. There were very few school closures.[42] Pupils at the age of eleven in rural areas had limited choices. Many had to travel considerable distances to get to any of the various types of secondary school. For many the cost of travel was an insuperable barrier. The government recognised the problems of educating a widely dispersed population, and in 1937 raised the grant for transporting pupils from 20% to 40% of the cost.

The curriculum in the elementary schools in the 1930s changed slowly. There had been a general increase in the amount of practical work in domestic economy and handicrafts. Science was promoted but was related to the limited spheres of domestic science and the other practical subjects. Gardening continued as a subject in the curriculum and some of the central schools had up to two acres of gardens.[43] Physical training was a government priority and several advisers were employed by KEC. There was, however, still a great shortage of facilities, gymnasia were rare, and schools had to rely on portable equipment where it was available.

For the vast majority of the population in the county it was still not possible to acquire anything more than a rudimentary education. Lindsay estimated that just under half of the school population were significantly underachieving nationally because the system denied them educational opportunities.[44] Some scholarships were available, but these did not pay for many of the extras required for a pupil attending a grammar school or a technical school. The representation of the scholarship system as a ladder leading eventually to a university place was misleading for all but a very small percentage of pupils. In Kent in 1938 only 1,412 scholarships were awarded to ex-elementary school pupils out of a total of 9,126 ten- and eleven-year-olds who were on the roll across the county.[45]

During the late 1930s, changes were made in the methods of selecting scholarship pupils in Kent. An intelligence test was added to the arithmetic and English tests. This change reflected the national trend towards the use of intelligence tests. The use of intelligence tests was not, however, universally

---

41 *The New Prospect in Education*, London 1928, chapters 1–2.

42 One such closure was Kilndown Infants, *Education in Kent, 1933–1938*, p. 31.

43 *Ibid.*, p. 26.

44 K. Lindsay, *Social Progress and Educational Waste: Being a Study of the 'Free Place' and Scholarship System*, London 1926.

45 *Education in Kent, 1933–1938*, p. 88.

supported, and the Board of Education in 1930 commented that 'a general use of these tests in making awards would be premature'.[46]

The grammar schools across the whole county fared better than other secondary schools during the 1920s and 1930s.[47] Several new schools were built and a number of extensions were completed. In 1923 the new Gillingham Boys Grammar School was opened and by the end of the decade new buildings were provided for Borden Grammar School at Sittingbourne and Maidstone Boys Grammar School. Sixth forms in grammar schools continued to expand and their specialist curriculum developed further. The introduction in 1917 of the school certificate and higher school certificate qualifications provided a traditional structure for the curriculum. Numbers increased after special grants became available in 1918, and the proportion of pupils staying on at school in Kent beyond the age of sixteen continued to grow.

Provision for pupils with special educational needs in Kent was very poor. In the mid-1930s it was openly stated that accommodation for mentally defective children was inadequate[48] with only thirty-four children attending day schools in the county. Other children were catered for by the Kent Voluntary Association for Mental Welfare. 'Crippled children and delicate children' continued to be sent to schools outside the county. There was a great reluctance to spend any money in Kent, and the Voluntary Community Council of Kent was relied upon to supervise many of these 'delicate children'.

By the end of the 1930s there was a huge backlog of work for KEC. The Board of Education had promoted reorganisation and a review of the curriculum in both primary and secondary schools, but the results of all these proposals was a haphazard and inefficient range of provision. Standards were low, and access to a challenging secondary-school education was still denied to the majority of the population. In Kent, as elsewhere in the country, the Education Committee did not have the resources or the will to establish a common effective system of education.

(5) The Impact of the Second World War

The threat and then the contingencies of war stretched KEC to its limits. Preparations for the war began in earnest in May 1938.[49] A Special Sub-Committee was formed to plan air-raid precautions and the use of school premises in the event of war. Three months later the government requested Kent's plans for evacuation. Schoolchildren were the largest single group of evacuees, and they were conveniently organised in their existing schools with their own staff to

[46] Board of Education, *Supplementary Memorandum on Examinations for Scholarships and Special Places*, London 1936, p. 7.

[47] *Education in Kent, 1933–1938*, pp. 68–72.

[48] *Ibid.*, p. 50.

[49] The Air Raid Precaution Act of 1938 provided funds for the necessary civil-defence arrangements.

supervise them.[50] During the Munich crisis, in September 1938, instructions were issued to schools, and emergency meetings were held by the County Council, to plan how Kent would receive 153,950 people who were due to be evacuated from London. It was also planned to move an additional 50,000 out of the Medway towns where the population was thought to be at risk from heavy bombing. In many schools pupils were evacuated by their parents with the remainder relying on the official evacuation. At Chatham County School for Girls, 100 pupils were evacuated privately, and 198 were evacuated officially to Faversham, with the remainder attending school in Chatham. After the fall of France in May 1940, and with the threat of invasion, the school was evacuated to Pontypridd.[51]

There were several phases of evacuation during the war. At first Kent was a recipient of evacuees. In 1939 towns like Folkestone and Dover took in large numbers of evacuees from London. Kent expected 136,502 when war was declared; 47,330 arrived, but by Christmas only 29,653 were left, the remainder having returned home. As the conflict unfolded those organising evacuation became adept at moving thousands of people quickly and efficiently. On 2 June 1940, 20,000 children and 1,800 adults were evacuated from the county after the fall of France. This figure included resident Kent children and the re-evacuation of many Londoners. A commentary on the diverse experiences of evacuation was recorded openly in the Kentish press.[52]

Throughout the war there was constant disruption of pupils' education. The number of hours that were spent at school was reduced considerably. There are no detailed attendance figures for 1940, but the school log books illustrate very low attendance during the worst crises, and regular periods of part-time schooling. Teaching for large numbers of pupils was seriously disrupted because many schools had dual functions and were used as rest centres in the event of heavy bombing. In Medway there were 133 rest centres, most of them schools.

The last major phase of evacuations took place in July 1944 when the V-1 and V-2 rocket attacks began. These attacks came as a surprise, and many of the arrangements for evacuation had to be improvised.[53] Secondary schools were evacuated as units and they re-established themselves in their host community. The pupils from primary schools were often not so lucky and had to join classes in the schools in their host areas or share the use of the buildings. The impact on the education of pupils during the war is difficult to assess accurately but standards fell noticeably.[54]

The work of KEC during the war was essentially a task of coping with one crisis after another and at the same time trying to maintain the administration of the system of education. The problems faced were colossal, and the difficulties that were recognised at the end of the 1930s, such as the shortage of secondary

---

[50] Accounts of evacuation are often vividly recorded in the school log books.
[51] Log book of Chatham County School for Girls (Medway Archives).
[52] See *Kentish Express*, 2 August, 22 September and 22 October 1940.
[53] 22,615 unaccompanied children were evacuated with 44,665 adults.
[54] *Education in Kent, 1938–1948*, Maidstone 1949, p. 99.

accommodation, trained teachers and low standards, were further compounded by six years of war. The most significant achievements during the war were the maintenance of the system, the successful evacuation and reception schemes and the work done by the youth service.

In both world wars pressure for change accelerated. The war accentuated the weaknesses and injustices of the existing education system. These in turn became the issues for debate in a society that in both wars was looking towards victory, reconstruction and the creation of a new world for future generations. During the 1939–45 war there was a feeling that it was a people's war, 'but the big drive for change came later, influenced by the length of the war and the great numbers of people involved in it. The war had to be made worthwhile.'[55] It was the Butler Act of 1944 that offered a chance to reform the education system.

(6) The Education Act of 1944

The Act of 1944 created the Ministry of Education with a Minister who had powers to compel local authorities to follow government policy. The Act specified that the system of education should be organised in three stages, primary, secondary and further education. The government also required all authorities to submit development plans following local consultations. All schools came under KCC control except those that could provide 50% of the cost of additions and repairs; these were given status as aided schools. The dual system of controlled schools and voluntary schools in Kent continued and this provided the compromise that satisfied the churches: they received financial support but maintained a degree of independence. Religious education, which had proved a stumbling block to progress in the previous hundred years, now had a compromise solution. To satisfy the churches, religious education and daily worship became obligatory, but parents had the right to withdraw their children. Agreed syllabuses for religious education were required in each authority,[56] and in Kent the Sunderland agreed syllabus was used for several years until a Kent syllabus was written. The government insisted that fees were abolished as a recognition of the policy of secondary education for all, regardless of the means of the pupils.

The area that continued to provide the most vigorous debate was the freedom that the Act gave to authorities to decide their own secondary system of education. Kent followed the most popular option, the creation of the tripartite system of grammar schools, technical schools and secondary-modern schools with selection at the age of eleven.[57] Not all authorities created a tripartite system; Anglesey was the first completely comprehensive authority in 1953, and London moved towards a comprehensive system from 1946. The 1944 Act was a

---

55 T. Harrison, *Living Through the Blitz*, London 1976, pp. 11–17.
56 Cambridgeshire wrote the earliest agreed syllabus in 1926.
57 This system was promoted by the Norwood Report and reinforced by the White Paper on Educational Reconstruction of 1944.

series of administrative compromises that were to prove longstanding but by no means perfect and it did not address the issues of standards and the curriculum. It was in these crucial areas of standards and the curriculum that the Act failed to provide a clear sense of direction.

The preparation of the development plan for the government forced KEC to take stock of educational provision in the county.[58] The audit revealed a situation 'where some schools would sooner or later have to be discontinued; new schools would have to be built to take their place, as well as meet the demands arising from housing developments and the increase in the child population'.[59] The fact that the plan was 'so huge' illustrated the desperate state of the existing system. The Kent plan, put forward in July 1946 and approved by the minister in February 1949, covered the next fifteen years and planned for the provision of nursery schools and the separation of the three phases, primary, secondary and further education. It also outlined the proposals for special schools. The problems anticipated by KEC were the difficulties of reorganising the secondary schools, coping with the problems of small rural schools, and the anticipated changes in population distribution. There were also the longstanding issues of teacher shortages and low standards.

The priorities for the Kent plan were threefold. The first was to build new schools where there was war damage or new housing estates, such as those at St Paul's Cray.[60] Modern schools were to be built where the existing primary schools were especially overcrowded, and, finally, the worst school facilities would be replaced. There were several constraints faced by KEC. Most notably, there was not enough money in the system and Kent had the particular problem of needing to balance the inequity of the provision for secondary schooling across the county. Where new building did take place it was often at the expense of maintaining the existing building stock. Five-hundred schools needed some form of repair as a result of war damage. Added to this was the neglect of the 1930s when many schools had been inadequately maintained. There was also the new responsibility of maintaining the voluntary schools that had not been able to keep up with their own maintenance and the extension of their own buildings in previous decades. Large sites also needed to be purchased[61] for the new schools, especially where bilateral schools were proposed.[62] The plans for one division illustrate the extent of the task that faced KEC as a result of the 1944 Act:

58 A full summary of the plan can be found in *Education in Kent, 1938–1948*, pp. 70–5.
59 *Ibid.*, p. 66.
60 *Ibid.*, p. 88.
61 It was estimated that KCC needed to purchase about ten square miles of land for new buildings.
62 KEC debated the merits of multilateral schools, where the grammar, technical and modern schools were all on the same site. This was rejected because of the size of the joint schools. Instead a combination of two of the types of school was favoured. The purchase of land for these schools represented a substantial investment in the post-war period.

Division 6 (Maidstone). The number of pupils at grant aided schools in autumn term, 1945, was 13,547. Fifty-two existing primary schools (twenty-seven county and twenty-five voluntary) will be continued, at least twenty-two of them will require new buildings. Seven existing secondary schools (five of them county and two voluntary) are to be continued, four of them being provided with new buildings. Twenty-one primary schools and two secondary schools are scheduled eventually to be discontinued. There will be twenty-five new primary schools (two voluntary, the rest county schools) and ten new county secondary schools. One nursery school is proposed in Maidstone and there will be nursery classes attached to a number of primary schools.

The same story is told in the primary and secondary plans for the other sixteen county divisions. There was no more crushing indictment of the education system in Kent as it existed before the war than this list of necessary improvements. As in the 1920s and 1930s the implementation of the Kent plan was hindered by economic crises but also by the 'innate conservatism' within the local political administration and the educational establishment in the county. Dent when referring to the national picture observed, 'the almost universal fear, usually not overtly expressed but always there, of revolutionary change, of going too far, or too fast, or both. This led inevitably to a tendency to hedge, to compromise . . . to delay, even to oppose.'[63] This was a fair reflection of the situation in Kent.

(7) Primary Education, 1944–88

After the war the primary-school system was clearly defined in terms of infant and junior schools. The use of the term elementary school was abandoned after 1944, although some older pupils continued in extension classes in primary schools until the early 1960s. To compound the post-war economic crises and the scarcity of resources there was a 'baby boom' with the birth rate reaching a peak in 1947. The bulge in school numbers, which was up by about 25%, caused enormous problems and was at its highest in the infant schools in 1954 and in the junior schools in 1956.

To help cope with the rise in numbers temporary buildings were extensively used. New schools were also built with the largest sums expended in 1955 and 1956 when £347,000 was allocated to new school buildings. This figure fell to £181,000 in 1958 and 1959 when the focus of KEC expenditure turned to cope with the impact of the 'bulge' on the secondary schools.

The pressure on school accommodation continued throughout the 1960s. Despite some new construction, the old building stock was often unsuitable and

63 H.C. Dent, *1870–1970: Century of Growth in English Education*, London 1970, p. 123.

there was a constant backlog of repairs. Mobile classrooms became permanent features on many school sites with 150 in use in 1968[64] and 288 in 1974.[65]

During the 1960s there was a change in the curriculum with a movement towards child-centred learning. The Plowden report in 1967 examined primary education 'in all its aspects'. It supported child-centred teaching methods, a broader curriculum and increased parental involvement. The report recognised many of the problems that existed in Kent primary schools at the time: a limited curriculum; very little science and technology teaching; too few graduates applying for jobs in primary schools; not enough male teachers; the failure of the LEA to recognise the importance of nursery education and the dreadful state of some of the school accommodation.

As a consequence of an upsurge in curriculum research, some teachers around the county introduced new ideas and effective methods of teaching, though this was by no means universal. Much of the work was left to the individual school as there was no national curriculum or set of standards. Changes in the curriculum relied on individual teachers trying methods promoted through individual initiatives, some of which came from the government, some from the county and some from publishers. A number of schools used the Initial Teaching Alphabet in the mid-1960s in an effort to raise reading standards. Foreign languages were introduced into some schools in Dover and Tunbridge Wells[66] and 'Missionaries for Maths' involved 500 teachers in a drive to improve the standard of maths teaching in the county.[67] The Kent Maths Project promoted individualised programmes of learning, and reading centres were set up and staffed by educational psychologists.

At the beginning of the 1970s some of the same problems dogged the primary education system that had caused concern consistently throughout the century. Nursery-school education remained underdeveloped with very few children having access to early-years education. Throughout the twentieth century, nursery education was the ghost service until the proposals for the ill-conceived voucher scheme in the mid-1990s led to funded provision. In 1998/9 Kent had one nursery school and thirty-four nursery units attached to infant and primary schools. There were 2,100 places for all 4-year-olds and some 3-year-olds.[68] In Kent in 1974, the situation was far worse, with only one county nursery school. There was more extensive private provision, but this varied in quality and geographical distribution. Classes in primary schools remained oversized, with 6.7% in Kent having over forty pupils and a quarter of all classes having more than thirty-five pupils in 1969.[69] There was also the problem of substandard and poor accommodation.

---

[64] *Education in Kent, 1963–1968*, Maidstone 1969, p. 17.
[65] *Education in Kent, 1968–1974*, Maidstone 1975, p. 26.
[66] *Education in Kent, 1963–1968*, p. 23.
[67] *Education in Kent, 1958–1963*, Maidstone 1964, p. 22.
[68] *1999–2000 Education and Libraries Directorate Plan, Summary*, Maidstone 1999, p. 22.
[69] *Education in Kent, 1968–1974*, Maidstone 1975, p. iii.

The shortage of teaching staff in primary schools in the 1940s and 1950s was acute. The population boom and the poor working conditions further compounded the dislocation that the service had suffered during the war years. The profession had never attracted large numbers of high-flying graduates, but after the war emergency training brought in many new recruits. Some of these new entrants to the profession were trained at the KCC Emergency Training College at Eversley College in Folkestone between 1947 and 1950.[70]

The shortage of teachers continued until the late 1960s. In 1957 KCC took over the College of Physical Education at Nonington. This originally ran a three-year course for women but in the 1960s and 1970s it expanded to train a broader range of teachers for schools in the county. To alleviate the shortage of teachers in North Kent, the former grammar school and agricultural college at Borden became Sittingbourne College. It admitted about 110 mature students a year. Between 1947 and the late 1960s, about 2,300 teachers were trained, many of whom took jobs in the Medway area. The shortage of teachers was compounded by a rapid turnover of staff in schools; 27% of men and 65% of women changed jobs or left the profession every five years in the late 1960s. Kent relinquished its role in undergraduate teacher training in the early 1970s. Stockwell College in Bromley, the former British and Foreign Society College, was closed as were Nonington and Sittingbourne. Eversley College survived for in-service training until the late 1980s when it too was closed at the same time as the network of Teachers' Centres.

(8) Secondary Education, 1944–88

In 1944 KEC decided to adopt a tripartite system and maintain selective education. The argument was that the choice had to be made of 'the well tried bases of existing school types'. This relied on a belief in the effectiveness of the grammar schools rather than the success of the central and technical schools. KEC was ideologically opposed to comprehensive schools and was also suspicious of large schools. It rejected the idea of multilateral schools where grammar, technical and modern schools were administered separately but all built on the same site. The cost of paying for pupils to travel across large catchment areas was also a concern. There were even doubts about the abilities of head-teachers to cope with the running of such large schools. The decisions made in 1944 were essentially based on the assumption that the grammar schools, whose academic standards had risen steadily during the 1920s and 1930s, did provide a measure of success for the secondary system. This did not, however, override the failure of the system to provide equality of opportunity with the right of education for all.

The grammar schools themselves changed little after the 1944 Act. The abolition of fee paying had an immediate impact on school rolls; it meant that

---

[70] *Education in Kent, 1938–1948*, p. 98.

more pupils went to grammar school and more stayed in the sixth form. For financial reasons many fee payers in the 1930s often left school before the sixth form whilst the scholarship pupils stayed on. With a free grammar-school system there was no longer this financial pressure, and pupils started to stay at school longer and the sixth forms of the grammar schools expanded rapidly. The academic standards also rose when entry to the grammar schools was strictly by selection through the 11+. The grammar schools continued to be well funded, well staffed and in many areas very successful. Throughout the 1950s and 1960s KEC continued to build and re-house grammar schools.

In 1944 the junior technical schools became independent of further education. The Balfour Act had downgraded the status of the technical schools, but the need for Britain to compete in international markets had not gone away. The new technical schools continued to admit pupils at thirteen, and by the 1960s there was a network across the county. The spectrum of ability was more mixed than in the grammar schools, and it became clear that this second tier of selected pupils did not automatically fall into the category of being orientated towards practical subjects. The growth of sixth forms and the loss of ties with further education loosened the connections with industry and commerce. Gradually the curriculum of the technical schools became broader and driven more by examination syllabuses, thereby creating a second tier of grammar schools. What emerged from this organic growth was that a wider ability range of pupils could benefit from a broad range of educational opportunities, from CSEs to A-levels. It also provided opportunities for pupils to stay at school longer because the accreditation brought more opportunities for employment and further education. The technical schools altered their names as gradually their curriculum changed and became the same as the grammar schools.[71] By the 1990s these schools were indistinguishable from the older grammar schools.

The secondary-modern schools established by the 1944 Act in Kent had their origins in the central schools, but such was the increase in the numbers of places that many new sites and buildings were acquired after 1944. Resources were limited in the years that followed the war, not just for the new secondary schools, but also for the new year group that were added to the school role when the school leaving age was raised to fifteen in 1947. HORSA huts and SFORSA furniture became enduring features of the period. KEC did not specify the curriculum for the new secondary-modern schools and it was left to the staff. The consequence was a curriculum that was a patchwork where expectations were generally low.

In the late 1950s and the early 1960s, educating the whole of the ability range became a greater priority. The Crowther report made recommendations for the education of boys and girls between the ages of fifteen and eighteen. It recognised that

---

[71] E.g. Maidstone Technical School for Boys became Oakwood Park Grammar School, and technical subjects had largely disappeared from the curriculum by the late 1980s.

even in the education of our brightest children – which is what the English system does best – there is still a grave waste of talent through too early abandonment of formal education. We do not think that the figure of 12 per cent of the age group still in full time education at the age of 17 and 6 per cent at the age of 20 is nearly good enough. The education that is provided for the great mass of children is inadequate both in its quality and its duration.

Unfortunately the only immediate impact of the report was the abolition of Christmas leaving for fifteen year olds. Five years later CSEs were introduced to offer accreditation for the work of the majority of the school population, but other than that the Crowther recommendations were not acted upon. It was not until the late 1980s and 1990s that an adequate 'alternative road' was found for supposedly 'non-academic' pupils.

In the 1960s and 1970s some high schools began to introduce O-levels in a limited number of subjects, but there was often opposition from within the schools themselves. Many governors and staff were convinced that their pupils were not capable of achieving passes in the examinations. In the event they were proved wrong. The introduction of GCSEs in 1987, where the CSE and O-level accreditation was combined, meant that there was no false ceiling on the potential exam results of the pupils. The new examinations also brought with them a review of marking, consistency within schools and between schools, and in Kent an inclusiveness that had not previously existed. As the GCSE examinations became established, it was possible to compare results in similar types of schools and establish averages to measure performance.

In the early 1960s a new debate took place about the tripartite system and the methods of selection in the county. The assumptions that the tripartite system was appropriate were, according to many, flawed. There was an acceptance by some that selection was not an appropriate means of assessing future performance and as a consequence there was 'not the complete acceptance of the tripartite system, which their once was'.

In the early 1960s KEC began to look at alternatives to the 11+. In Dover a scheme was introduced where parents and the primary head teacher decided the best option for the child at the age of eleven. In Swanley a new comprehensive school was built with a junior school for 11–13-year-olds and a senior school for older pupils. The Thames-side scheme was first tried in the Gravesend area where there was a massive increase in the population and a need to provide new schools. Here pupils all moved from their primary school to the local high school. At 13+ they were selected, without a test, to go to either a grammar school or to stay in the high school. There was also the encouragement for pupils to transfer at sixteen to the grammar school sixth forms, but this was always easier to offer on paper than put into practice.

The 1960s saw an experiment with the three-tier system similar to the one first introduced into the West Riding of Yorkshire. In this, pupils remained in their first school till the age of nine. They then transferred to a middle school before moving on to an upper school at the age of thirteen. The upper school offered a curriculum up to eighteen, including A-levels. The system was a response to much of the research that was promoted by various reports in the early 1960s and predated the government circular 10/65 that proposed a national system of comprehensive schools. The National Curriculum with its key stages ending at seven, eleven, and fourteen put pressure on Kent to reconsider this system. By the end of the 1990s the only middle-school system to have survived was on the Isle of Sheppey, but even here the system was compromised by the selective system where a number of pupils changed school at eleven and went to grammar schools off the island.

These experiments in secondary reorganisation were in the process of implementation when the government required KEC to prepare plans for a comprehensive system. KEC opposed this reorganisation and favoured the retention of the grammar schools, but was convinced that the different areas of Kent needed their own particular systems. By the end of the 1970s Kent had a comprehensive school, grammar schools, high schools, technical schools, wide-ability schools, bi-lateral schools, middle schools, church schools, and selection at both eleven and thirteen. The only system that had not been tried was that with sixth-form colleges; this was rejected because they would have competed with grammar school sixth forms.

(9) The Education Reform Act of 1988

The flurry of government reports and initiatives in the 1960s provided a revision of some of the detail of the 1944 Act. Butler had left the administration of the system as the responsibility of the local authorities. He also left LEAs with the freedom to pick and chose from a menu of ideas, policies and practice. By the end of the 1970s the very slow pace of educational reform and change was glaringly evident. An attempt to review the curriculum through the Schools Council in the 1960s and 1970s failed because there was no overall sense of direction or co-ordination at either national or local level.

In Kent, apart from regular administrative changes, the school system remained largely unaffected by the great wave of comprehensivisation when Margaret Thatcher was Minister for Education in the early 1970s. There were still the well established concerns: standards in both primary and secondary schools were difficult to analyse; in the primary schools the topic approach combined with the teaching of literacy and numeracy was carried out according to the preferences of the individual teacher and school; accommodation was poor, and, most important of all, there was no sense of accountability for standards. At secondary level as late as the mid-1980s a significant proportion of the school population in Kent did not enter an examination at sixteen. The county had no statistical picture of standards except those from the performance of pupils who were entered for examinations at sixteen and eighteen. Few Kent schools had written aims and objectives or policies about teaching methods. The polarisation, both socially and educationally, was stark between many Kent schools. The contrast between some high schools and the grammar schools was Dickensian, and in terms of expectations and standards the gulf was huge.

By the 1980s the Butler political compromise of a national system locally administered was clearly not working in the county. Major elements of the 1944 Act had filtered away. Technical and vocational education had been absorbed by the narrow examination-orientated grammar-school curriculum. More importantly, there were questions about standards and the need to decide upon a curriculum that was relevant to all pupils. Following the horrors revealed by the inquiry into the William Tyndale School in London, there was also increasing pressure to establish clear accountability within local education administration.

The Education Reform Act of 1988 changed the educational landscape of Kent, ended the life of the 1944 Act, and began a period of change that was sometimes practical and reasonable and, on other occasions, nothing less than bizarre. It created an open market in education with the local financial management of schools, where 85% of funding was given directly to schools.[72] Funding was by a formula according to the number of pupils. The Act also encouraged open enrolment, which was intended to allow popular schools to thrive and unpopular schools to close. KCC reacted like all other authorities to the changes for which there was little consultation and no consensus. National administration replaced local administration. It had been difficult to tell the difference between the various political parties on education policy for twenty years after the Butler Act. The issue of selection then defined the divisions in the 1960s and 1970s. After the 1988 Education Act, both the county and national policies of the political parties became polarised over the reforms until the Dearing Report in 1995 introduced a new pragmatism and removed excessive prescription.

The Education Reform Act of 1988 presented a series of solutions to long-running problems, and applied them to issues of standards, curriculum change and accountability. In Kent the requirements were applied according to the time-tables and criteria set down by national government. This was very different from the way that educational change had previously been managed. Behind the changes was the distrust of local authorities, especially the professional officers, and a belief that market forces could regulate both change and improvements in standards and accountability. The hope of central government was that this would encourage diversity and competition between schools for pupils, and a national return of the grammar schools. In Kent the impact was somewhat different from that of those authorities that were comprehensive. A significant number of high schools opted out of LEA control to mitigate the effects of the selective system, offer sixth-form provision and a more comprehensive intake. The enthusiasm for opting out was encouraged by financial incentives and promoted as a major issue in the 1992 election. City Technology Colleges (CTCs) were also established at vast expense with the original intention of being funded by industry. Leigh City Technology College, Dartford, was one of the twenty CTCs established nationally.

The third element of the 1988 Act was the introduction of the National

---

[72] The first trial of Local Financial Management took place at The Towers School, Ashford in 1989.

Curriculum, ten subjects plus religious education. The National Curriculum was implemented rapidly, but it was done without the attention to detail that was essential for it to work. There were problems with testing at seven, eleven, and fourteen, especially in English. The curriculum for 14–16-year-olds was eventually dropped and the whole structure had to be reviewed by Sir Ron Dearing in 1993 to remove what was described as 'excessive prescription'. Oversight of the changes was led by central government and delegated to local authorities and the Office of Standards in Education (OFSTED). OFSTED carried out the inspection of every school in Kent between 1993 and 1997, and during this time league tables, statistics, inspection reports and results became areas of major interest and importance. The impact on Kent secondary schools was to exacerbate the differences between schools and to reinforce the already divisive hierarchy in each area between the selective schools and the non-selective schools.

The examination system in Kent schools reflected the national developments. GCSE was introduced in 1987, combining O-level and CSE. In 1985 only one-quarter of pupils left school with the equivalent of 5 GCE passes. In one move, by introducing GCSE, the vast majority of pupils had, for the first time, the opportunity to gain credit for their abilities. This was one of the great successes of the 1990s. In 1998 one wide-ability school in Kent gained better average GCSE results than one of the grammar schools in the county.

A-level results in Kent schools also improved in parallel with the GCSE results but there has been increasing pressure to alter the 16–19 curriculum and adapt it to the needs of the twenty-first century rather than preserve the academic character of a system created in the 1950s to feed universities. Vocational qualifications were introduced with a common framework codified by Dearing in 1996. In 1999 this was still an area of debate with many Kent schools concerned about the post-sixteen curriculum due to be introduced in September 2000. The sixth forms in grammar schools are on the whole able to cater for pupils in the new system, but many sixth forms in the high schools are too small to offer the new curriculum. Once again high school pupils find themselves without adequate provision and choice.

The statistics collected during the 1990s were extensive, and for the first time allowed schools and government to track progress and specify performance in the curriculum with a fair degree of accuracy. Expectations and averages were set to establish standards in subjects and different aspects of the work of schools and the local education authority so that schools and the authority could have development plans with priorities, reasons for the identification of those priorities, action and costings. In 1998 evidence from the national performance measures showed that overall performance by Kent schools was about average and by implication showed that the selective system in Kent offered pupils in the county no advantage over those in areas with comprehensive schools.

In 1997 came a new Labour government, whose policies were built on the same priority of accountability and pragmatism that had been evident since 1993. The new priorities worked on the evidence thrown up by the changes since 1988. Raising standards was the main focus, and a drive to improve literacy and numeracy was planned and implemented in 1998–2000. Performance data were used to measure the success of schools. Greater attention was also given to the evidence provided by OFSTED about failing schools, and swift action was required by the LEA to turn around failing schools. In Kent in 1998, sixteen schools were judged by OFSTED to require special measures, with 'a considerable number of schools' requiring substantial improvement.[73] The pressure on schools to improve standards became intense.

The LEA survived its inspection by OFSTED in 1998 and a revisit in 2000[74] with mixed reports that stated that 'there are strengths in the LEA and also signs of continuing improvement'. Improvements were noted in the LEA management of an excessively complex pattern of school organisation. Pupil performance at 11 and 14 was assessed as being above the national average. The results at 18 remained average and this, with comments on delays and inconsistency in the eleven plus selection procedure, continued to fuel the debate about selection.

Popular Education at the beginning of the century was a haphazard affair for children of all ages. Progress towards an effective and accessible system was painfully slow throughout the century. Kent was a mirror of the national trends and it was not until the end of the last decade of the century that the ambitions of the previous hundred years were achieved: nursery education for all four-year-olds; a sound primary education based on agreed national standards; access to qualifications for all pupils up to the age of 18 and an increase in funding for schools.

The price was that the pressures on the system in 1999 were considerable. Pupils were working harder, teachers were under increasing pressure, school management was challenging and the role of the LEA was increasingly in question. Schools were given greater financial independence and the replacement of the role of the LEA by regional government was discussed. With the government promise of three priorities 'education, education, education', the culture of change showed no hint of slowing down. Nevertheless, for the vast majority of the children in Kent schools the learning revolution, promised so often during the twentieth century. seemed to be well underway.

---

73 LEA Statistical Profile 1998, Kent LEA Annual Report 1998.
74 Inspection of Kent LEA, OFSTED, August 2000.

9

Religion

ROBIN GILL

Throughout the twentieth century, Kent, like other parts of the country, has seen a sharp decline in churchgoing. This decline has not been spread evenly over all denominations, and there are distinctive features to the overall pattern in Kent. Nevertheless decline in regular churchgoing, and indeed in most other visible forms of participation in religious organisations in Kent, has been a dominant feature. Unlike London, the relative absence of ethnic minorities means that there is little evidence in Kent of any compensating participation in non-Christian religious organisations. In contrast, tourist visits to churches, and especially to Canterbury Cathedral, have shown an increasing popularity. There are now almost as many visitors to this cathedral (over 2 million in 1995) as there are attendances in all of the other Anglican churches in Kent in the course of a year.

This chapter will focus upon the visible features of religious participation in Kent. (There are, of course, many more elusive ways in which individuals may express their religious beliefs and feelings.) Nation-wide research[1] suggests that most people still believe in God (although not necessarily in a personal God), pray on occasions and even have moments of religious/spiritual experience. Committed secularism, although clearly growing, remains a minority position. In the sociology of religion, the study of implicit, unofficial or 'folk' religion is widely recognised as important but elusive.[2] In the absence of any national map, it is still too early to chart the distinctive features of such forms of religion in Kent. Instead what can be depicted are the visible features, such as changing patterns of regular churchgoing during the twentieth century, comparing Kent with other parts of the country.

---

[1] See my *Churchgoing and Christian Ethics*, Cambridge 1999.
[2] See P.H. Vrijhof and J. Waardenburg, *Official and Popular Religion: Analysis of a Theme for Religious Studies*, The Hague 1979; E. Bailey, 'Implicit Religion: A Bibliographical Introduction', *Social Compass*, vol. 37, pp. 499–509.

(1) Bromley Churchgoing: A Case-Study

Obtaining accurate figures for regular churchgoing across denominations which cover Kent for the whole of the twentieth century is probably impossible. The Church of England has kept average Sunday attendance figures[3] only since 1968, and few other denominations have recorded such figures for even that length of time. MARC Europe censuses[4] across denominations were made only in 1979, 1989 and 1998. The only other comparable data is from the nineteenth not the twentieth century, namely the 1851 Religious Census.[5]

Bromley, however, is an exception. Fortunately R. Mudie-Smith's invaluable census of London churches[6] in 1903 extended just as far as Bromley. As a result, it is possible to make some useful comparisons in this area of solid middle-class, suburban Kent churchgoing. Unfortunately there are some caveats to be made. The census of Bromley churches on 11 October 1903 was made on a wet day. It was also a census made by enumerators standing outside church doors rather than by asking ministers and church officials to make estimates.[7] And, crucially, it largely ignored Sunday-school attendances. These factors may well have suppressed the figures in 1903 compared with 1851 or 1993. This makes it diffi-cult to know the exact change between 1851 and 1903, but it cannot disguise, even if it may underestimate, the manifest decline between 1903 and 1993.

In 1851 morning and evening attendances combined (including Sunday schools) across denominations in Bromley[8] amounted to 40.6% of the local population. This population rose from 17,637 in 1851 to 27,292 in 1903. Morning and evening attendances combined (but not including Sunday schools) for 1903 amounted to 37.9%. The addition of Sunday-school figures for 1903 is likely to have taken these attendances at least to the level of 1851. Of course, some of those attending in the morning may have attended again in the evening (the 1903 census estimates that in Greater London 36% of morning attenders went again in the evening) so attendances cannot be equated with attenders. However, if morning attendances alone are taken, then at least the very minimum numbers of attenders can be established. On this basis, 28.8% of the population were present in Bromley churches and chapels in 1851, but only 19.0% in 1903 (although, once again, the first figure includes Sunday schools

---

3   All Church of England national statistics, unless otherwise stated, are taken from annual *Church Sta-tistics: Some Facts and Figures about the Church of England* (Central Board of Finance of the Church of England, Church House, London).

4   These are mostly contained in *Prospects for the Nineties: Trends and Tables from the 1989 English Church Census*, ed. P. Brierley, London 1991. Some information has also been taken from his *Prospects for the Eighties: From a Census of the Churches in 1979*, London 1980. Where 1979 figures were revised in 1991 the latter have been used.

5   *1851 Census Great Britain: Report and Tables on Religious Worship England and Wales*, ed. H. Mann, British Parliamentary Papers, Population 10, 1852–3 (reprinted by Irish University Press 1970).

6   *The Religious Life of London*, ed. R. Mudie-Smith, London 1904.

7   For the effects of weather and census method, see Table 8 in my *The Myth of the Empty Church*, London 1993.

8   Proportionate estimates have been included in these calculations for four Anglican churches and one Independent church missing from the original returns.

and the second does not). As happened elsewhere in the country,[9] two factors contributed to this apparent decline: a sharp decline in Church of England morning attendances (from 21.5% to 10.6%) and an increase, perhaps resulting from the introduction of street lighting, in overall evening attendances (from 11.8% to 18.8%).

Compared with most other urban areas, Bromley was evidently a place of fairly high churchgoing in 1903. Data from many other urban areas show that Anglican churches generally started to decline from the 1850s, and Free churches from the 1880s. If 37.9% represented the combined morning and evening 1903 attendances in Bromley, the comparable figures without Sunday-school attendances[10] were: for Inner Greater London 22.4%; for Liverpool 29.4% (even with its massive Roman Catholic population); and for eight[11] large towns 26.6%. In Greater London, only places which were not wet had substantially higher attendances.[12]

The population of Bromley[13] rose again by 1993, reaching 44,146. However, churchgoing declined sharply in both proportional and absolute terms. The relative absence of evening services in many churches today makes it more difficult to compare churchgoing on the same basis as 1851 and 1903. In addition, attendance figures in many denominations are collected only on the basis of separate attenders rather than attendances. However, using the 1903 estimate of Greater London 'twicers', it is possible to produce some broad comparisons. Keeping in mind the three factors of weather, enumeration and Sunday schools, on this basis 31% of the Bromley population were in church in 1903 but only 10.5% by 1993. Thus a threefold decline, and perhaps in reality a fourfold decline, seems to have taken place in these ninety years. Or, to express this differently, there were some 8,472 attenders on that Sunday in 1903 but only 4,631 on an average Sunday in 1993 despite a greatly increased population.

Stated so baldly, these figures disguise some more subtle changes between denominations in Bromley during the twentieth century. The Roman Catholic Church has increased both proportionately and absolutely, whereas the United Reformed Church has literally been decimated. Anglicans and Methodists have both declined sharply, whereas Baptists have increased in absolute but not in proportionate terms. The Salvation Army now has one of its strongest congregations in Greater London at Bromley. There is also considerable fluidity between House Churches and the evangelical congregations of the Baptists and the

9   See my *The Myth of the Empty Church*, chapter 6.

10 *Ibid.*, chapter 7.

11 *Ibid.*, Table 16. The eight towns were: Chester, Hull, Lincoln, Middlesborough, Wallasey, Whitehaven, Workington and York.

12 *Ibid.*, pp. 174f. High Barnet (60%), Ealing (51%) and Woodford (50%) all had remarkably high attendances in fine weather in 1903.

13 As defined in the 1903 survey by the Anglican parishes of St Peter and St Paul, St Mark, St John, St Luke, Holy Trinity, St George, Christ Church, and St Mary. I am most grateful to the Revd Richard Freeman for supplying me with their population figures.

Anglicans. So, although Bromley churchgoing during this century is down by at least two-thirds, relative balances between denominations are still shifting.

The Anglican churches also suggest that balances are still shifting within denominations. In 1903 the 4,620 estimated attenders represented 16.9% of the Bromley population. The 1,312 attenders in 1993 represented just 3.0%. This 3.0% is still higher than the 2.6% for the Rochester Diocese as a whole, and higher still than the national 2.2% figure (although nothing like the 4.2% for the more rural Hereford Diocese). In 1903 the parish church of St Peter and St Paul had congregations more than twice the size of most other local churches (619 in the morning and 898 in the evening), St Luke's Church had the next largest congregations and Christ Church the smallest (80 morning and 67 evening). By 1993 the parish church remained strong, but the evangelical Christ Church was now the strongest and St Luke's the weakest.

In 1903 there was a single Roman Catholic church in Bromley with 177 attenders (0.6% of the population), whereas by 1993 there were two churches with a combined 1,450 attenders (3.3% of the population). As elsewhere in the country, although not in Kent as a whole, Roman Catholics are now the most numerous regular worshippers in Bromley. St Joseph's Church today has six masses on a Sunday, drawing people from a wide radius. Replicating a pattern that can be found throughout urban England, two Roman Catholic churches serve the same area and slightly more worshippers as eight Anglican churches. Not surprisingly, all the Anglican churches, except Christ Church and St Peter and St Paul's, appear thinly attended in comparison. Ironically, in 1903 it was only Christ Church that had a thinner congregation than St Joseph's.

The Baptists in Bromley have shown remarkable resilience in the twentieth century. In 1903 they had four churches with an estimate of 748 attenders. By 1993 there were five Baptist churches in Bromley (one of them Strict Baptist) with a total of 926 attenders. The earlier figure represented 2.7% of the local population and the later 2.1%. The central Baptist Church today has much the largest congregations, with 350 adults and 70 children typically present in the morning, and 200 adults in the evening (half of the latter having already attended in the morning). It is hardly surprising that some of the smaller evangelical congregations felt the draft both from this congregation and from that at Christ Church. One chapel, currently with an attendance of just 15 adults, reported that until a few years ago it had a congregation of 100 which has now been largely 'fed' to other churches. Churchgoers with young children not surprisingly find the central Baptist Church more appealing than this thinly attended chapel with an entirely adult congregation. As happened at the turn of the century in some towns when the Salvation Army became popular at the expense of local Baptists, and in the previous century when Primitive Methodists benefited from defecting Wesleyan Methodists, so in the 1990s a similar process apparently continues in Bromley. This time around such transfers benefit the Baptists.

Finally, Bromley Methodists, Congregationalists and Presbyterians have all experienced severe decline. In 1903 there were five Methodist chapels and missions with an estimated 1,244 attenders, representing 4.6% of the Bromley population. By 1993 there were three chapels, but now with only 245 attenders, representing 0.6% of the local population. Congregationalists and Presbyterians, each with their own church that is now a part of the United Reformed Church, had congregations representing 4.0% of the local population in 1903. Ninety years later their two congregations represented just 0.4%. Like most of the Anglican churches they have found it difficult to recruit new members in an area with an array of active Baptist and evangelical churches. Alongside these established Free Churches there is also a small Society of Friends. It too makes little numerical impact upon local churchgoing.

The institutional weakness of many of the churches in Bromley today is underlined by the relative absence of children within them. In the Anglican churches only 252 children were recorded as usual Sunday attendances in 1993. In contrast, in 1903 there were 878 children present at the morning services alone. At that time at least twice that number of children might be expected to attend Sunday school in the afternoon (the census recorded such attendances only in Chelsea). It seems likely, then, that the rate of decline in attendance is higher within these churches amongst children than amongst adults. In Rowntree's surveys of churchgoing in York,[14] a relative absence of children proved to be a dangerous indicator for churches. Poor attendances amongst children bodes ill for churches in the future.[15] Even Roman Catholic attendances of young people in Bromley are little better. Within the Methodist and United Reformed Church attendances of young people are considerably worse.

Bromley is still an area of relatively high churchgoing. It also differs from the county as a whole in a number of respects. In the county of Kent there has been an Anglican dominance throughout the twentieth century. In Bromley the strong presence of Roman Catholics, who are comparatively few elsewhere in Kent, and of Baptists curtails this dominance. However, in other respects Bromley and Kent are similar. Both have an array of small independent congregations, without having strong ethnic minorities. In both there is evidence of fluidity amongst these independent congregations. Each of these factors needs to be considered separately.

(2) Anglican Dominance in Kent

In 1851 Kent was still a predominantly Anglican county with Anglicans representing 62.7% of all attendances (in contrast to a national figure of only 52.1%). By 1989 this balance had changed somewhat, yet with Anglicans in Kent still representing 45.0% of attenders, in contrast to a national figure of 30.1% and a London figure of just 16.7%.

---

[14] B. Seebohm Rowntree, *Poverty: A Study of Town Life*, London 1901, *Poverty and Progress: A Second Social Study of York*, London 1941, and *English Life and Leisure: A Social Study*, London 1951 (written with G.R. Lavers).
[15] See my *The Myth of the Empty Church*, chapter 8.

Even in 1851 Anglican dominance was uneven. As sometimes happened elsewhere, the cathedral city of Canterbury had some very strong Free Church congregations. Anglican attendances there amounted only to 50.9% of all attendances. Thirteen Anglican churches shared these attendances, with mean attendances of 140 in the morning and 98 in the evening. In contrast the Wesleyan Methodist Church in Canterbury had a morning congregation of 510 and an evening congregation of 828 and the Independent Church there had congregations of 537 and 600 respectively. Even the Chapel of the Countess of Huntingdon's Connexion Chapel had congregations of 280 and 220. Clearly the citizens of Canterbury were not over-awed by the Church of England.

In deeply rural parts of Kent, Anglican dominance in 1851 was much more apparent. For example, on the Romney Marsh 69.0% of all attendances were Anglican, and afternoon attendances in Anglican churches there amounted to a remarkable 31.2% of the population. Thirteen of the twenty churches on the Marsh were Anglican, five small chapels were Wesleyan Methodist and two Baptist. Mean attendances at the Anglican churches were 66 in the morning and 131 in the afternoon. Wesleyans had 34 in the morning, 63 in the afternoon and 99 in the evening. Baptists had only 15 in the morning, 17 in the afternoon and 53 in the evening. Since there were no evening services in the Anglican churches it is possible that here, as elsewhere in rural areas,[16] some of the population went to an Anglican church in the morning or afternoon and to a Wesleyan or Baptist chapel in the evening. At the end of the twentieth century many deeply rural areas are experiencing a rather different form of ecumenism. Free Churches are increasingly withdrawing from rural areas altogether, leaving those who still go to church with little option but to attend an Anglican church. Anglicans, in turn, in areas such as the Romney Marsh, cluster ever larger groups of churches together into a single charge.

In 1968 there was still a clear difference between the more rural Canterbury Diocese and the Rochester Diocese. Both had levels of attendance above the national mean of 3.5%. In the case of Rochester, attendance at 3.7% was only slightly higher than this mean, but in Canterbury it was distinctly higher at 4.5%. To set these figures into context, the most rural diocese, Hereford, had an attendance of 6.5%, Bath and Wells 6.4%, and Exeter 6.0%. London and Birmingham, in contrast, had only 2.1%. Another clear indicator of rural/urban differences is Easter communicants. In Hereford in 1968 these amounted to 13.4% of the population aged over fourteen, Bath and Wells 10.8%, and Exeter 10.2%. However, in London they were 2.8% and in Birmingham only 2.7%. Thus a rural area might expect twice as many communicants as usual at Easter, whereas an urban area might expect less than a third more. Canterbury, with Easter communicants at 6.8%, was still clearly different from Rochester at 5.1%. However, by 1993 these differences had narrowed. With a national rate of usual attendance of 2.2%, both dioceses now recorded 2.6%. Easter communi-

---

[16] Cf. James Obelkevich, *Religion and Rural Society: South Lindsey, 1825–1875*, Oxford 1976.

Plate 50. Charabanc outing for the parishioners of Elmsted and Hastingleigh in the 1920s.

Plate 51. Large crowd outside Ruckinge church for the institution of the new rector, 1935.

cants had also fallen to 4.0% in Canterbury and to 3.4% in Rochester, compared with a national rate of 3.3%.

The indication here that the Canterbury Diocese is declining faster than the Rochester Diocese is confirmed by electoral-roll statistics. In 1962 these amounted to 76,400 for Canterbury and 68,200 for Rochester. By 1973 both figures had declined drastically, but now it was Rochester which had the higher figure of 50,068 and Canterbury only 48,154. After the transfer of the Croydon Deanery from Canterbury Diocese to that of Southwark, the Canterbury electoral-roll figure dropped further to 23,700 in 1988, with Rochester declining only to 39,300. Both dioceses have also seen a radical decline in infant baptisms, although in this instance Rochester has declined slightly faster than Canterbury. In 1968 Canterbury's baptism rate per 100 live births was 53.4, and Rochester's was 53.2; by 1994 this had declined to 30.4 and 24.1 respectively.

Another area which shows a sharp decline, especially in the Canterbury Diocese, is the number of stipendiary parochial clergy. In 1933 there were 403 stipendiary clergy in the Canterbury Diocese: this declined to 307 by 1963, and to 179 by 1995. Some allowance must be made in the final figure for the transfer of the Croydon Deanery, but it is clear that the overall number has virtually halved over the six decades. In Rochester there has also been a decline, but it has not been so dramatic: moving from 296 in 1933, to 277 by 1963, and to 226 by 1995. Lying behind these different rates of decline are shifting concepts of viable livings. In 1963 in Canterbury, 26.4% of incumbents were in livings of fewer than 1,000 people: in Rochester it was only 15.5%. Not surprisingly Canterbury's 179 stipendiary clergy now have 329 churches to look after, whereas the 226 clergy in Rochester have 264 churches. The problems facing the Canterbury clergy are not as difficult in this respect as those facing the 121 Hereford clergy looking after 425 churches, yet they are problems that are likely to increase over the years ahead.

However, there is one important area which does show a steady increase, namely weekly giving in church collections. If such giving is measured per electoral-roll member (a measure which, of course, favours Canterbury), then it has increased from 2s. 5d. for Canterbury and 2s. 9d. for Rochester in 1962, to £1.75 and £1.72 respectively in 1988, and to £4.30 and £4.11 in 1994. Thus, even before the results of the unwise investment policies of the Church Commissioners became widely known, weekly giving had risen significantly in Kent parishes. Indeed, the rise in Kent has been faster than the national mean of 2s. 7d. for 1962, £1.45 for 1988, and £3.42 for 1994.

(3) Relative Absence of Roman Catholics in Kent

Another distinctive feature of religion in Kent is the relative absence of Roman Catholics. Bromley is sufficiently near to London which has for long had a higher concentration of Roman Catholics. In other parts of Kent there are surprisingly few Roman Catholics. This appears to be a phenomenon with a long history.

In the *Recusant Returns* of 1676 only 0.2% of the population of Kent was returned as 'Papist'. Nationally the figure was 0.5%, and in London it was 0.7%. In the 1851 Religious Census only 1.4% of attendances in Kent were by Roman Catholics, whereas in the country as a whole it was 3.5% and in London 6.6%. Kent in 1851 had only thirteen Roman Catholic churches, largely in the north of the county. In the MARC Europe Survey of 1989 Roman Catholic attenders amounted to 18.5% in Kent, compared to a national figure of 34.8% and to a London figure of 39.2%. By 1989 there were 129 Roman Catholic churches in Kent. Of course there are caveats to be made about each of these sets of figures. For example, the 1851 Religious Census tended to underestimate attendances at multiple morning masses.[17] And even today estimates of congregation sizes are often given to outside researchers in very 'round' numbers. Nevertheless, they suggest a very consistent overall pattern.

Indeed, the comparatively small Roman Catholic presence in Kent makes overall churchgoing rates appear rather small. So in the 1989 MARC Europe Survey, Kent had an adult attendance rate of 8.0%, whereas the national figure was 9.5%, simply because in Kent only 1.6% of the adult population attended a Roman Catholic church but nationally it was 3.4%. Even the average size of Roman Catholic attendances per church in Kent, namely 162, is rather small compared with the national mean of 355.

Another feature suggested by the MARC Europe research is that Roman Catholic attendances both in Kent and in the country as a whole may be declining faster than those of any other major denomination. Until about 1970, Roman Catholic statistics rose compared with those of other churches in Britain. However, since then Roman Catholics nationally have shown a very sharp pattern of decline.[18] MARC Europe argues that it is indeed sharper than other British churches, with a decline from 36.0% of adult churchgoers in England in 1979 to 34.8% in 1989. The average size of Roman Catholic attendances per church also shrank in that decade from 412 to 355. It is possible that by the turn of the century the Roman Catholic share of churchgoers will differ very little from that of the Church of England or the Free Churches. Michael Hornsby-Smith[19] shows that mass attendances in England and Wales declined from 1,934,853 in 1970 to 1,461,074 in 1985. Hornsby-Smith also produces the interesting statistic that in the 1930s 72% of Catholics married other Catholics, whereas in the 1970s only 31% did. In other words, Catholics are copying the same non-churchgoing habits of other people in Britain and are becoming more 'mixed'. Specifically in Kent, MARC Europe suggests that Roman Catholic adult attenders have declined from 2.4% of the adult population in 1979 to 1.6% in 1989, and, more speculatively, that in the course of fifteen years from 1975, attenders declined by a third from 29,400 to 19,500.

---

[17] See my *The Myth of the Empty Church*, chapter 6.
[18] *Ibid.*, chapter 8.
[19] M. Hornsby-Smith, *Roman Catholicism in England*, Cambridge 1987.

(4) Changing Balances amongst Other Denominations in Kent

Changing balances amongst the smaller Christian denominations in Bromley have already been noted. A comparison between the 1851 Census and the 1989 Survey helps to put these changes into a broader map of Kent. It is always risky to make projections for the future, but some speculations will also be attempted.

As in Bromley so in Kent as a whole, it is the Methodists and United Reformed Church which have declined fastest relative to other Free Churches. In 1851 Methodist attendances at all services in Kent (i.e. including afternoon services) amounted to 14.2% of all denominational attendances. By 1989 Methodist attenders in Kent represented just 6.9% of all attenders. Thus, at the two ends of a period when all denominations, except the Roman Catholic Church, drastically declined overall, Methodists declined at twice that rate. Congregationalists and Presbyterians, who eventually constituted the United Reformed Church, declined at three times the rate. In 1851 Presbyterian attendances represented 0.5% of all attendances and Independents/Congregationalists 9.2%. By 1989 United Reformed Church attenders represented only 3.2% of all attenders. The somewhat speculative 1975 figures recorded by MARC Europe suggest that the combined Methodist and United Reformed Church adult attenders declined from some 11,000 then to 9,400 in 1989. Less speculatively, by 1989 the mean attendance for each congregation was only 65 adults and 20 children. Thus individual congregations typically appeared thin and the proportion of children (24%) was considerably less than that recorded in 1903 at Chelsea (43%). If similar losses are sustained uniformly in the twenty-first century, neither denomination may survive in Kent much beyond its mid-point. More likely, perhaps, is that a small minority of congregations may survive, and even thrive, but the majority (especially in rural areas) will disappear. In either event, it will be difficult in the twenty-first century for these denominations to match their presence in the nineteenth century.

In contrast, Baptists in Kent, although sharing in the general decline of other denominations, have maintained their relative position well. In 1851 Baptist attendances amounted to 9.4% of all denominational attendances: by 1989 they still had 9.7% of all attenders. The latter is about twice their national rate, but still represents only 0.8% of the population of Kent. In 1989 they had a slightly higher proportion of children (27%) than the Methodists or United Reformed Church, and their mean attendance for each congregation was 88 adults and 33 children. Nevertheless, MARC Europe suggests that even they declined from 10,300 attenders in 1979 to 9,700 in 1989 and, more crucially, child attenders declined from 4,500 in 1985 to 3,600 in 1989. However, these figures probably have to be set alongside those categorised by MARC Europe in 1989 as 'independents'. The survey records an increase of children in this category from 5,200 in 1985 to 6,500 in 1989 and of adults from 5,400 in 1979 to a remarkable 10,600 in 1989.

Some of these latter figures do need to be treated with considerable caution since the 1979 survey of smaller denominations contains many estimates. Nevertheless, as in Bromley, they do suggest a situation of some considerable fluidity in these denominations. Figures for adult Pentecostals in Kent, dropping from 4,400 in 1979 to 2,800 in 1989, is certainly in line with this fluidity. But will the growth, if accurate, of independent churches be sustained into the twenty-first century? MARC Europe projects a continuing decline in the Roman Catholic Church, United Reformed Church, Methodist Church and in the Church of England. Indeed, the relative rates of decline may be in that order, with the Roman Catholic Church declining fastest and the Church of England least. The MARC Europe projection for the new independent churches is for a considerable increase – although not an increase which will actually offset the overall decline caused by the other denominations. My own assessment else-where[20] is more cautious. Looking at national data over a sufficient time-span, there is a long-established pattern of short-term growth in newer/smaller denominations. On the other hand, taking a single fixed point, in Kent in 1989 it was the independent churches which apparently had the highest rate of children present (38%), a higher rate even than their national one (31%). If that can be sustained into the twenty-first century, it would augur well for their survival in Kent.

Finally, Kent has no strong visible presence of non-Christian religions. In 1851 Jewish attendances at synagogues in Kent represented 0.1% of all church attendances, whereas in London they represented 0.3%. Even today it is difficult for an Orthodox Jew to live in East Kent. Within the University of Kent at Canterbury some Orthodox Jews choose instead to live near a synagogue in London or Rochester, since there is no longer one in Canterbury itself (the syna-gogue there had just 53 seats which were only half full in 1851). Some 400 Muslim students and Muslims spread more widely in East Kent have their own service every Friday in the University. Whereas the followers of almost any faith can find a place of worship in London, choice is much more restricted in Kent. Even the attempt to build a Multi-Faith Centre in the University finally faltered in 1996 through lack of general support, and this despite the presence of a small department of theology and religious studies there.

(5) Canterbury and the Future

This chapter has so far focused upon measurable features of religious institu-tions in Kent in the twentieth century. Of course the generally bleak picture that emerges from this says nothing about the spiritual vitality and commitment of religious institutions, their members, or of the wider public beyond them. And it says nothing about the unique and continuing attraction of Canterbury itself as the home of Archbishops of Canterbury and of Canterbury Cathedral. In addi-tion, church leaders in Kent as elsewhere do seem to be increasingly aware of the need for change. The Diocese of Canterbury, for example, is currently in the process of radically changing its management structure, with parishes becoming

---

[20] In my *The Myth of The Empty Church*, pp. 218f.

more directly in charge of their own funding. Each parish now has a ministry team in which stipendiary clergy are only a part. It is still too early to know whether or not these changes will help to reverse the patterns of churchgoing decline in Kent (and elsewhere) that have characterised the twentieth century. There is, however, a greater awareness that this is a problem which does need to be addressed more vigorously by churches.

In the latter part of the twentieth century Canterbury has hosted the Lambeth Conference of Bishops. This meets every decade and came to the new University of Kent campus for the first time in 1978. On the third visit to this campus in 1998 some 800 Anglican bishops from around the world attended the Conference. For the first time this also included eleven women bishops. Together with spouses and advisers, some 2,000 people attended this three-week Conference. The worship at this was quite outstanding. The opening service in the cathedral, which was televised live, included African drums and South American dancers, and daily worship using a wide variety of liturgies was held in the transformed sports hall on the university campus. Many bishops commented upon the unique fellowship and daily Bible study that they shared together during the course of this Lambeth Conference. Even some of my more secular colleagues in the university took more than a passing interest in this unique gathering of Anglican bishops.

Canterbury Cathedral continues its highly distinctive role of attracting visitors, pilgrims and academics from around the world. It has a very active programme and has been at the forefront of developing effective techniques for 'shepherding' large parties around the cathedral in an orderly and meaningful way. In addition, using lottery funds, a new education centre is currently being built on the south side of the cathedral. A new visitors' centre and gift shop has already been opened. Together these should be able to serve new generations of visitors coming to this unique cathedral.

Another important development has been the increase of younger Anglican scholars coming from overseas to study for a postgraduate degree in theology at the university. When Archbishop Michael Ramsey died in 1988, the then Archbishop, Robert Runcie, appealed for money from around the Anglican Communion to establish a chair of modern theology at the university in his honour. His vision was that the holder of this chair should spend a part of each year lecturing in different parts of the Communion and attracting scholars to come to Canterbury to study theology. I was the fortunate person to be appointed to this Michael Ramsey Chair of Modern Theology. To date, younger scholars have come from South Africa, India, Australia, New Zealand, Korea and Hong Kong. In turn some of these students attended the 1998 Lambeth Conference as advisers and helpers. A new, international network of younger Anglican theologians is beginning to be formed from this initiative.

Taken together these distinctive features of Canterbury may be pointers to the future. Even though institutional churchgoing is likely to remain a minority activity in most parts of Britain for the foreseeable future, a much wider interest in and concern about religious issues remains. Sometimes this takes the form of a passion for ancient churches. Sometimes it is a continuing interest in the perennial questions that theology raises. Evening classes in theology for the wider public remain very popular in Canterbury. And sometimes it takes the form of occasional acts of public ritual, such as those which surrounded the death of Princess Diana. At the close of the twentieth century, the British are not very ardent churchgoers, but neither are they ardent secularists.

10

Culture and Leisure

NIGEL YATES

'Most of today's leisure habits and expectations remain staunchly Victorian . . . there is scarcely a single modern recreation that is not based on a prototype which dates from before the First World War.'[1] This comment is as true for Kent as it is for the rest of Britain, and this chapter will begin by looking at the cultural and recreational developments during the second half of the nineteenth century and the practical implications of those developments for Kent, in terms of cultural and leisure provision, on the eve of the First World War. Thereafter we shall consider, in turn, developments during the rest of the twentieth century in respect of adult and further education, public libraries and museums, Kent's seaside towns and watering places, tourism, popular entertainment and physical recreation. A very important aspect of these developments was the developing role of local authorities in the financing and management of cultural and leisure projects; this was a role that increased enormously during the inter-war period and that expanded even further in the 1950s and 1960s. The final section of this chapter will look at the changes that have taken place in the provision of cultural and leisure facilities by local authorities in Kent since 1970, and the impact of government legislation on patterns of service delivery. In a sense, the wheel has turned almost full circle in the space of little more than a century, with local authorities being obliged to take a much lower profile in the direct provision of public amenities, and to accept a more significant involvement in such provision by private benefactors and commercial entrepreneurs, that is the mixed economy of cultural and leisure provision that had characterised this aspect of life in Britain in the late nineteenth century.

(1) The Victorian Legacy

The last sixty years of the nineteenth century saw a considerable transformation in the provision of facilities for both the profitable and the pleasurable use of increased leisure time for a growing number of people. To some extent this was

---

[1] J. Lowerson and J. Myerscough, *Time to Spare in Victorian England*, Hassocks 1997, p. 1.

concentrated in London and the larger provincial towns, so that Kent, with no single large town and within close proximity to the capital, shared only partly in these trends. By 1901 two Kent towns had populations in excess of 40,000 (Dover and Gillingham), five towns of more than 30,000 (Chatham, Folkestone, Maidstone, Rochester and Tunbridge Wells), and a further eight of more than 20,000 (Beckenham, Bromley, Canterbury, Erith, Gravesend, Margate, Penge and Ramsgate).[2] There was, however, a wide disparity in their facilities for entertainment and recreation in the years just before the First World War. The Medway Towns were among the most poorly provided. Chatham had a library and a theatre; there was a park and recreation ground in Gillingham; Rochester had a library, museum, public baths and two parks, one of which had a band-stand; most of these facilities were of comparatively recent origin. This was remarkably poor provision for an area that by 1911 had a combined population of 125,886. At the other end of the scale, the seaside resorts of Folkestone, Margate and Ramsgate and the inland spa of Tunbridge Wells had a much wider range of facilities catering for both residents and visitors. Folkestone could offer a public library and museum, three bathing establishments, a racecourse, golf links, tennis courts, an ice rink, pleasure gardens, exhibition halls, a theatre and a gymnasium. Margate had six theatres or concert pavilions and facilities for bathing and golf. Ramsgate also had six theatres, cinemas or concert halls; Ellington Park had been laid out in 1893 and a public library opened in 1904; the Granville Hotel had both Turkish and electric baths, an Italian garden and a croquet lawn. At Tunbridge Wells an opera house had been opened in 1902; there was no public library but three subscription librairies; there were also three concert halls, two cricket grounds, swimming baths and four parks or recreation grounds in addition to the open space on the Common; a museum had been opened by the Natural History and Philosophical Society; the Spa Hotel had sixty-five acres of gardens with a golf course, tennis courts and croquet lawn. The two administrative and social centres of the county, Canterbury and Maid-stone, also made reasonable provision for the leisure time of their inhabitants. Canterbury had its cricket ground, theatre, St George's Hall for musical enter-tainments and dancing, swimming baths, a long-established public park at Dane John, and a library and museum in the Beaney Institute. Maidstone had a museum, art gallery, library, theatre, swimming baths, athletic ground and facili-ties for concerts and balls in the Corn Exchange.[3]

These local developments, the majority of which dated from the last quarter of the nineteenth or first decade of the twentieth century, were wholly in line with national developments. The most significant changes in cultural and leisure provision in Britain date from the middle years of the nineteenth century. Fifty years earlier Britain was still experiencing the traditional pattern of work and festivals which had survived, with appropriate modifications, from the late Middle Ages, and which were characterised by drunkenness, rowdy behaviour

2   *The Economy of Kent, 1640–1914*, ed. W.A. Armstrong, Woodbridge 1995, pp. 281–2.
3   Details from *Post Office Directory of Kent*, London 1913.

and cruelty to animals. From the early part of the nineteenth century there had been a determined attempt, linked with changes in the economy, to abolish traditional festivals and the way in which they had been observed. In 1761 the Bank of England had been closed on forty-seven weekdays each year, but this had been reduced to four by 1834. Measures were taken to abolish cruel sports, and the Society for the Prevention of Cruelty to Animals was founded in 1824. By the 1840s there was, however, a recognition that this over-emphasis on work at the expense of leisure was not entirely healthy, and attempts were made to reduce the working week and make suitable provision for leisure time. The major difference between the leisure pursuits of the later nineteenth century and those that had preceded them was that the former were 'organised'. There was also a strong emphasis on 'improvement' with the foundation of working men's clubs, institutes and friendly societies for the purpose of providing 'serious' entertainment, such as concerts and lectures, to encourage reading and to promote 'respectable' games such as billiards.[4] Of the many traditional sports involving animals, only hunting and racing survived the campaigns against cruel sports, the former appealing particularly to wealthy city-dwellers with weekend homes in the country.[5] The growth of organised leisure and the development of 'improving' methods of using free time was much encouraged by making weekly half-holidays compulsory for women and children working in factories in 1850, and the four annual bank holidays introduced by Sir John Lubbock's parliamentary measure in 1871.[6] It was also greatly assisted by the rise in real wages and the improvement of living standards.[7]

The two areas in which the changes were most dramatic were in sport and popular entertainments. Before the late nineteenth century 'the staple diet of the poorer citizens . . . in recreation and entertainment centred on drink, informal activities in the streets, and irregular visits from commercial entertainers, particularly circuses'. Street entertainers included 'organ grinders with monkeys, . . . musicians, ballad singers and the bands which accompanied the processions undertaken by all kinds of different groups', frequently to advertise such events as circuses. From about 1860 these entertainments were being moved away from the streets and into the 'rapidly increasing number of public halls available for hire by enterprising entertainers'.[8] Another important trend was for breweries to acquire possession of formerly independent public houses, putting in tenants, thus gradually reducing their rowdiness and making them respectable, though public houses still 'tended to be bunched in their greatest numbers in working class communities. . . . The better the social tone of a district, or even a street, the less likely you were to find a pub.'[9] Although 9% of

4   Lowerson and Myerscough, *op. cit.*, pp. 8–18.
5   *Ibid.*, pp. 116–17.
6   J.A. Patmore, *Land and Leisure in England and Wales*, Newton Abbot 1970, p. 23.
7   J. Walvin, *Leisure and Society, 1830–1950*, London 1978, pp. 62–3.
8   H.E. Meller, *Leisure and the Changing City, 1870–1914*, London 1976, pp. 209–10.
9   Walvin, *op. cit.*, p. 41.

average personal expenditure was still being spent in the purchase of alcohol at the end of the nineteenth century, this was considerably less than it had been before 1870, and showed that the campaigns of temperance organisations were not without success.[10] It was the public houses that provided premises for most of the early music halls. There were twenty-eight of these in London by 1868 and about three-hundred in the provinces.[11] By the 1890s most of the tavern music halls had been replaced with much larger variety theatres, many of which, in order to attract a more respectable clientele, refused to sell alcohol.[12] Music halls were at their peak between 1890 and 1912, and encouraged music-making in the home, with an enormous increase in the sale of both pianos and sheet music.[13] There were hardly any theatres presenting 'straight drama' in the late nineteenth and early twentieth centuries; most 'concentrated on melodrama, or mixed programmes of drama interspersed with variety',[14] and were therefore little different, except in their status, from the more popular music halls. The other popular diversion, especially in the seaside resorts, was the open-air band concert: 'no self-respecting resort could be without its orchestra or band; some possessed several, . . . when an Englishman paid a visit to the summer resorts, he assumed that music would be a basic ingredient of the entertainment'. Local orchestras, like theatres, tended to present mixed programmes: 'Beethoven, Haydn, Mendelssohn and Berlioz were played side by side with ballads, polkas, quadrilles and musical comedy'.[15] The growth of theatrical and musical entertainment resulted in employment in the arts and entertainment industries increasing from 0.8% to 4.7% of total employment between 1871 and 1911, with 16.6% of average personal expenditure being devoted to leisure pursuits in 1907.[16] Not all theatrical and musical entertainment in the late nineteenth and twentieth centuries was professional. There was a notable growth in the establishment of amateur dramatic societies in the 1890s, and many towns had amateur choral and orchestral societies.[17]

The revolution in sport was enormous. It was encouraged by the public schools, which supplied the rules of play, and taken up by local clubs:

> One change was the reduction of violence. The ancient riotous game of football, where matches were little more than ritualised fights with no written rules or external authority other than local customs, was transformed with laws appropriate for play in urban areas, and consistent with the rhythm of industrial life that required the completion of matches within relatively short time spans.[18]

10 *Ibid.*, p. 38; Lowerson and Myerscough, *op. cit.*, pp. 70–3.
11 Walvin, *op. cit.*, p. 109.
12 Meller, *op. cit.*, pp. 212–13.
13 Walvin, *op. cit.*, pp. 107–8, 110.
14 Lowerson and Myerscough, *op. cit.*, pp. 79–81.
15 Walvin, *op. cit.*, pp. 105–6.
16 Lowerson and Myerscough, *op. cit.*, pp. 21–2.
17 *Ibid.*, pp. 83–4, 86–7, 93–4.
18 K. Roberts, *Leisure*, 2nd edn, London 1981, p. 29.

Many organisations and commercial undertakings had established their own football teams by the second half of the nineteenth century, though football was less popular in the south of England than it was in the north or the Midlands.[19] Professional football teams followed, and the Football Association Cup was established in 1872. Cricket was not much played outside the rural areas for most of the nineteenth century, but had begun to appeal to town dwellers by the last quarter of the century, with large crowds attending inter-county matches. Although cricket had been played in Kent since the mid-seventeenth century, it was not until the late 1870s that the County Cricket Club established its position as one of the most successful teams in Britain. From the 1860s individual, as opposed to team, sports, such as cycling, golf, swimming and tennis became popular, with cycling and tennis appealing particularly to women, other sports being primarily the preserve of men.[20] Golf courses were laid out, in Kent, at Folkestone and Littlestone in 1888, at Canterbury and Eltham Warren in 1890, at Rochester and Sidcup in 1891, at Bromley and Deal in 1892, at Chislehurst in 1894 and at Maidstone in 1897. At Sandwich the Royal St George's Golf Club had established itself as one of the half-dozen leading golf clubs of the British Isles.[21] The way in which sporting organisations developed in one Kent town has been usefully chronicled for Ashford. The first football team was founded in about 1880, most of the members being railway employees. This and another team formed shortly afterwards merged to form Ashford United in 1891. A seven-hole golf course was laid out in 1904, and increased to nine holes in 1905. A bowls club began in 1909 but there was no cricket club until 1921.[22]

An important feature of the development of facilities for culture and leisure in the late nineteenth century was the role of the local benefactor and, especially from the last quarter of the century, that of the local authority. Most early parks and pleasure grounds were provided by local benefactors, as they were at Folkestone, where Radnor Park was leased to the community at a peppercorn rent by the local landowner, Lord Radnor, and laid out as gardens, incorporating a bowling green, in 1885.[23] Parliamentary legislation permitted local authorities to spend money on facilities for educational improvement and serious recreation: the Museum Act of 1845, the Baths and Wash-Houses Act of 1846, the Town Improvement Act of 1847, the Public Health Act of 1848 and the Public Libraries Acts of 1850 and 1855.[24] Progress, however, was fairly slow. Only twenty-four public libraries were opened between 1851 and 1867. Thereafter an

[19] Kent, for example, has only one club in the Football League, Gillingham, though Maidstone United was sufficiently successful in the 1980s to have a brief career in the league, terminated largely through its failure to build a new stadium consistent with its professional standing.

[20] Lowerson and Myerscough, op. cit., pp. 120–8; Walvin, op. cit., pp. 85, 88, 92–4; R.L. Arrowsmith, A History of County Cricket: Kent, London 1971, pp. 11, 75.

[21] R.H.K. Browning, Golf in Kent, London n.d.

[22] A.W. Ruderman, A History of Ashford, Chichester 1994, pp. 98–103.

[23] C.H. Bishop, Folkestone: The Story of a Town, London 1973, p. 118.

[24] H. Cunningham, Leisure in the Industrial Revolution, c.1780–c.1880, London 1980, p. 151; S.G. Jones, Workers at Play: A Social and Economic History of Leisure, 1918–1939, London 1986, p. 88.

average of three or four public libraries were opened every year until 1886, and an average of sixteen or seventeen between 1887 and 1900. Ratepayers were often hostile towards local authorities spending money on cultural or recreational projects. Many public libraries were wholly or partly financed by the Scottish philanthropist, Andrew Carnegie. This was the case at Sevenoaks where the urban district council had decided to open a library in 1901. Funds for a suitable new building, opened in 1905, were provided by Carnegie and a local benefactor on land purchased by the council.[25] Decisions about the facilities to be provided by local authorities tended to be made on cost grounds. By the late nineteenth century it was estimated that a new library could be built and stocked for a capital outlay of £2,000 to £3,000 'at a minimal level', whereas a new park required a capital outlay in the region of £30,000 to £40,000. Councils were slow to adopt the powers given to them under the Baths and Wash-Houses Act 1846, since swimming was not taken seriously until the end of the century, when local swimming clubs began to be formed. Swimming baths were, in any case, expensive to build. A modest one in Bristol cost £14,000; the much more ambitious Victoria baths in Manchester, opened in 1906, cost £59,000. Even quite significant towns, like Cheltenham, Exeter and Southampton, managed without public baths until the 1880s or 1890s.[26] It was therefore all the more surprising that Maidstone should have opened a swimming bath as early as 1852; this was partly to dissuade people from swimming in the polluted River Medway. It was replaced with a larger pool in 1895.[27]

(2) Adult and Further Education

Provision for adult and further education in England and Wales was, until the last quarter of the nineteenth century, significantly poorer than in most other parts of Europe, including Scotland. Until the 1820s the only universities were the ones founded in the Middle Ages at Oxford and Cambridge. The first new universities were those founded at Lampeter (St David's College) in 1822,[28] Durham in 1832, and London in 1836. The last two of these established outstations at, respectively, Newcastle in 1852 and Manchester in 1851, which later became independent universities. The University of Wales was founded in 1893, but without incorporating the college at Lampeter, and between 1900 and 1909 further independent universities had been founded at Birmingham, Bristol, Leeds, Liverpool and Sheffield. The lack of facilities for formal higher educa-

---

[25] Cunningham, *op. cit.*, p. 153; Lowerson and Myerscough, *op. cit.*, pp. 105–13; Meller, *op. cit.*, pp. 100–2; J. Dunlop, *The Pleasant Town of Sevenoaks*, Sevenoaks 1974, pp. 187, 191.

[26] Meller, *op. cit.*, pp. 112, 114–15.

[27] P. Clark and L. Murfin, *The History of Maidstone: The Making of a Modern County Town*, Stroud 1995, pp. 199–200.

[28] For the unusual conditions surrounding the foundation of Lampeter and its subsequent history, see D.T.W. Price, *A History of St David's College, Lampeter*, 2 vols, Cardiff 1977 and 1990, and his brief summary *Bishop Burgess and Lampeter College*, Cardiff 1987.

tion led to demands that existing universities should provide extension lectures in those parts of England remote from a university, but the universities were slow to respond. Cambridge agreed to support extension lectures 'for an experimental period' in 1873, and a permanent 'Syndicate for Local Lectures' was established in 1875. The London Society for Extension of University Teaching was launched in 1876. Oxford set up a 'Delegacy for External Lectures' in 1878, but a Secretary was not appointed until 1885. In 1887 the colleges that formed the Victoria University in the north and the Midlands began to make provision for extension lectures. There was considerable support for university extension from two quarters: women, and those who were keen to found new colleges in areas remote from an existing university, 'an ideal which combined educational concern with civic pride'. In 1888/9 it was estimated that 'two thirds of the students in the Oxford Extension Courses were women; and this is confirmed by most of the early lecturers' reminiscences'.[29] Those who owed their initial interest in possibly obtaining a university education to the role of university extension lecturers in firing their enthusiasm for further academic studies have acknowledged that fact in their memoirs.[30] A number of local colleges were permitted to prepare students for degrees awarded by the University of London, and these eventually became independent universities: Reading (1926), Nottingham (1948), Southampton (1952), Hull (1954), Exeter (1955) and Leicester (1957). A further impetus was given to adult education by the establishment of the Workers' Educational Association and the National Federation of Women's Institutes. The WEA specifically sought to extend university education to working people, rather than middle-class women, the first four local branches being established in 1904–5. The first Women's Institutes had begun to appear in rural areas on the eve of the First World War, and by 1953 the National Federation had over 8,000 branches and nearly 500,000 members.[31] Its educational role in the early days was considerable, though it later concentrated more on domestic and craft topics. A number of Kent Women's Institutes have compiled extremely useful histories and surveys of their own villages.[32] Formal university extension lectures in Kent were the responsibility of the University of Oxford rather than that of London, and this tended to restrict the number of classes offered. The gap was to some extent filled by the County Council which, from its establishment in 1889, had been empowered to contribute to the costs of providing technical education. Through collaboration with the South Eastern Association of University Teachers it was possible to provide lectures on scientific topics at seventy-seven village centres in Kent during the winter of 1891/2.

29 J.F.C. Harrison, *Learning and Living, 1790–1860: A Study in the History of the English Adult Education Movement*, London 1961, pp. 221, 223, 231–2.

30 E.g. V. Brittain, *Testament of Youth*, ed. with preface by her daughter Shirley Williams, London 1978, pp. 59–63.

31 Harrison, *op. cit.*, pp. 264, 319.

32 Centre for Kentish Studies at Maidstone has copies of these studies for several villages in Kent. See also M. Leonard, 'The Women's Institutes, with Special Reference to the East Kent Federation of Women's Institutes', BA Dissertation, University of Kent 1996.

Towns which had established their own technical colleges also used these to provide a wide range of adult education. In 1948 the County Council established one of the first adult-education centres in the country at Lamorbey Park, Sidcup, and further centres in the county's larger towns were established thereafter.[33]

University education, however, had to wait until well after the Second World War for a major expansion. Between 1961 and 1967, as a result of the recommendations of the Robbins Committee, no fewer than sixteen new English universities were established.[34] Some, like Loughborough, were former technical colleges; another, Keele, had been founded as a university college sponsored by the existing universities of Birmingham, Manchester and Oxford in 1949; others, like Kent, were totally new foundations. The first suggestions that a university should be established in Kent had, however, been made as early as 1947 when the County Council asked its 'Education Committee to consider what steps could be taken to establish a university in the county'.[35] The proposal was speedily quashed by the University Grants Committee, which felt that the funding could not be found for this or a number of other universities proposed at the same time, to provide higher education for the large number of men and women released from service in the armed forces after the end of the Second World War. The proposal was resurrected in 1959 when the County Council appointed a group of members to consider whether a university should be established in Kent, and the most appropriate location for it. The short-listed locations were at Ashford, Canterbury – three possible sites being considered – and in Thanet. Canterbury had been the favoured location in 1947 and it was the final choice on this occasion. The new university received government approval for its establishment in 1961, the first vice-chancellor was appointed in 1962, and the first students admitted in 1965. Whereas some of the new universities established at the same time – for example Bradford, Salford and Surrey – decided to specialise in a smaller number of academic disciplines than the older British universities, Kent decided that it would include most of the main disciplines in three faculties: Humanities, Natural Sciences and Social Sciences. An unusual feature of the new university, though one replicated at the new university in York, was that it adopted a system of colleges which provided both residential facilities for students and accommodation for the academic departments. It was a controversial decision which some of the senior figures in the university were later to regret. The University of Kent had, like the University of Sussex, a certain social cachet in the 1960s and 1970s which enabled it to attract a significant number of applicants for its available places. It was, however, less successful academically in the long term than some of its contemporaries, with considerably poorer research and teaching ratings in the 1990s than the universities at Warwick and York. With individual exceptions, the University of Kent has

---

33 E. Melling, *History of the Kent County Council, 1889–1974*, Maidstone 1975, pp. 12–13, 98, 118.
34 Aston, Bath, Bradford, Brunel, City, East Anglia, Essex, Keele, Kent, Lancaster, Loughborough, Salford, Surrey, Sussex, Warwick and York.
35 Melling, *op. cit.*, p. 98.

also failed, as an institution, to match the commitment to regional historical studies shown by some of the other new universities, notably East Anglia, Lancaster and Sussex. It has, however, established a close and beneficial relationship with the city of Canterbury, occupying a spacious and attractively designed site on its northern fringes.[36]

(3) Public Libraries and Museums

Nineteenth-century reformers and philanthropists had seen the establishment of public libraries and museums as one of the most effective ways of providing knowledge and self-improvement to the mass of the population. A few places had established embryonic public libraries in the seventeenth and eighteenth centuries, one of them being Maidstone.[37] The earliest museum in Britain was the Ashmolean at Oxford, founded in 1683, and about a dozen more had been founded by 1800. By 1850 there were nearly sixty public museums in Britain. The Museums Act of 1845 permitted the councils of towns with a population in excess of 10,000 to establish public museums. Similar powers were given to local councils of towns with a population in excess of 5,000 to establish public libraries under the Public Libraries Acts of 1850 and 1855, though expenditure on their maintenance was limited to the product of a penny rate. Between 1850 and 1914 a further three-hundred public museums were established, the majority of these by local councils.[38] In many cases public libraries and museums were established, frequently under a librarian–curator, in the same building, and in Kent this was the case at Canterbury, Folkestone and Maidstone. At Canterbury a museum had been established in 1825; in 1896–7 the museum and a public library were incorporated in the new Beaney Institute. At Folkestone the museum was founded by the Folkestone Natural History Society in 1868; twenty years later it was accommodated in the newly erected public library.[39]

At Maidstone a local physician, Dr Plomley, had in 1853 offered his collection of stuffed birds as the nucleus of a museum collection, but a public meeting voted against the expense of establishing a museum. In 1855 this decision was reversed when Thomas Charles of Chillington House offered that building to the town to house a museum, together with his large collections of antiquities, books, manuscripts and paintings. The new museum was opened in 1858, and in 1870–3 the collections were further augmented by the impressive ethnological material acquired by the local explorer and traveller Julius Brenchley. In 1889–90 an art gallery was added to the museum at the expense of a local

---

[36] See G. Martin, *From Vision to Reality: The Making of the University of Kent at Canterbury*, Canterbury 1990.

[37] See W.N. Yates, 'The Parochial Library of All Saints, Maidstone, and other Kentish Parochial Libraries', *Archaeologia Cantiana*, xcix (1983), pp. 160, 166–70.

[38] R. Hewison, *The Heritage Industry: Britain in a Climate of Decline*, London 1987, pp. 86–8.

[39] W.N. Yates, 'Museums in Kent: An Historical and Contemporary Survey', *Archaeologia Cantiana*, cxi (1993), p. 204.

leather merchant, Samuel Bentliff. Although the municipality was clearly very proud of its museum it was much more ambivalent about expenditure on a library. The collection of books housed in the museum operated as a reference library with some 8,000 books by the 1870s, but with no facilities for public borrowing. A lending library was eventually established in 1890, but it only had 1,500 volumes of which 400 were fiction or 'light literature':

> Books were not on open access but had to be selected from a purchased cata-logue, while borrowers needed to be ratepayers or to be guaranteed by rate-payers – in 1893 they numbered only 687 . . . it was evidently a fairly exclusive club.

In 1897 it was agreed to extend these facilities and to add a room in which the national and local newspapers could be read. A juvenile library was added in 1906.[40] The books were not, however, placed on open access until 1921, and the number of borrowers remained low, 'many people preferring to take out books from the commercial library in Boots the chemists'. The number of borrowers rose slowly from 2,250 in 1923/4 to 3,093 by 1931/2, but this latter figure still only represented 7.3% of the population, 'the lowest percentage recorded in a sample of fifteen Kent towns', a situation probably 'not . . . unconnected with the fact that spending on books and periodicals . . . was low in comparison with other Kent towns'. In the late 1930s expenditure on the public library in Maid-stone was still less than £150 per annum.[41] By contrast there was significantly more support for the public library in Folkestone. The local council had been pressured by the Folkestone Natural History Society to adopt the Public Libraries Acts and to open a library in 1879. Temporary premises in the Harveian Literary Institute were replaced by a purpose-built library and museum in 1888. In the first year 16,335 books were issued, but this had increased to 57,811 books a year in 1900, and 795,555 in 1970.[42]

Maidstone Museum was also the headquarters of the Kent Archaeological Society, founded in the same year that the museum was opened, and one of seventy-eight county or sub-county antiquarian, archaeological or architectural societies founded in England between 1834 and 1886. Like many of these socie-ties it had a high proportion of clerical members, local clergy forming nearly a quarter of its membership at its foundation in 1858.[43] The society published a journal, *Archaeologia Cantiana*, maintained a separate library and collected both artefacts and manuscripts. The collections of artefacts were eventually integrated with those of Maidstone Museum, and in the 1950s the society trans-ferred its collections of manuscripts to the recently established Kent Archives Office: 'after more than a century without any serious competition the Kent

[40] Clark and Murfin, *op. cit.*, pp. 169–71.

[41] *Ibid.*, pp. 234–5.

[42] Bishop, *op. cit.*, p. 123.

[43] P. Levine, *The Amateur and the Professional: Antiquarians, Historians and Archaeologists in Victor-ian England, 1838–1886*, Cambridge 1986, pp. 181–5.

Archaeological Society . . . remains the only voluntary body dedicated to promoting and publishing historical studies in Kent'.[44] In 1896 Major P. H. G. Powell-Cotton of Quex Park, Birchington, opened a private museum attached to his house in which to display his collection of African and Indian fauna and ethnographic material which he had acquired during a series of big-game hunting expeditions. The museum was notable in that it pioneered the use of dioramas, showing stuffed animals in natural settings, a method of display that was subsequently copied in many other national and local museums.[45]

Public libraries, and to a large extent museums as well, were confined to the larger towns in Kent until the second quarter of the twentieth century. Even a large town like Tunbridge Wells did not have a public library until as late as 1922; this, together with a new museum and art gallery, were incorporated in the new civic centre, begun in the 1930s but not completed until 1952.[46] In 1920 the County Council took advantage of the provisions of the Public Libraries Act 1919 to establish a library service for those parts of the county which had no public libraries. Initially the books were stored centrally and loaned out through centres in schools and village halls, but the County Council quickly adopted a scheme whereby it sought to establish permanent libraries in the smaller towns, usually in association with the local borough or urban district council, beginning with Ashford in 1928. In some cases, notably at Gillingham in 1952, Orpington in 1957 and both Chislehurst and Sidcup in 1958, these libraries were subsequently taken over by borough or urban district councils. By 1974 the County Council administered thirty-two full-time and twenty-two part-time branch libraries, compared with only eighteen in 1946/7. Not all of these were in purpose-built buildings. In 1964 a headquarters building and central store was opened at Springfield, Maidstone, to replace the huts and stables in which the library service's book stock had been stored. The stock itself increased from 635,840 books in 1946/7 to 1,196,065 in 1964/5 and roughly 1.75 million in 1972/3.[47] The book stock was further increased after 1974 when the county library service absorbed, as a consequence of local-government reorganisation, the formerly independent library services in the county's larger towns. At the same time the County Council appointed a Museums Officer to manage some of the museums attached to libraries, which the new district councils did not wish to administer, and to develop support services for other museums in the county. The new service had only a limited success and it was greatly reduced in size and scope following a comprehensive review in 1990–1. Most of the major local-authority museums in Kent, such as those at Canterbury and Maidstone, continued to be managed by those districts that succeeded their respective

[44] W.N. Yates, 'Kent', *English County Histories: A Guide*, ed. C.R.J. Currie and C.P. Lewis, Stroud 1994, pp. 211–13.

[45] Yates, 'Museums in Kent', p. 206; C. Powell-Cotton, *Quex Museum, House and Gardens*, Birchington 1990.

[46] A. Savidge, *Royal Tunbridge Wells*, Tunbridge Wells 1975, p. 200.

[47] Melling, *op. cit.*, pp. 46, 99–100.

borough councils in 1974, and this was a major factor in reducing the potential effectiveness of the new county museum service.[48]

There have been significant developments in public libraries and museums, both nationally and in Kent, since 1970. A major trend in libraries has been the move away from the loan of books to that of non-book materials. In Kent there was a deliberate policy to encourage this trend following the reorganisation of the county library service in 1990:

> The provision of leisure and entertainment videos and compact discs was extended and increased in all main libraries, partly in response to the growing customer demand. . . . The growing demand for audio-visual items seems to reflect national changes in the use of leisure time, with a wide variety of other activities now competing with leisure reading for people's attention.

The loan of non-book materials, 'including music and spoken word cassettes as well as videos and compact discs', almost doubled, from 488,534 to 944,601 items, between 1991/2 and 1994/5, whereas the number of book issues declined. In 1996/7 the total number of library book issues had dropped by just over 7% compared with those in 1995/6.[49] The major national development in museums was a significant expansion in the number and variety of museums and the opening of heritage centres. A survey by the Museums Association in 1987 recorded that half the museums included had been founded since 1971. In addition a total of forty-one heritage centres had been established in Britain.[50] In Kent new open-air museums were established in the former naval dockyard at Chatham and just outside Maidstone, where the Museum of Kent Life was created on the site of a former farm from 1983. Heritage centres were also opened in the Poor Priests' Hospital at Canterbury, the Archbishops' Palace at Maidstone, and at Tonbridge Castle. Even more commercially orientated ventures were those managed by Heritage Projects using a similar formula to the pioneering Jorvik Viking Centre in York: 'The Canterbury Tales' in a redundant church at Canterbury, 'The White Cliffs Experience' at Dover, and 'A Day at the Wells' at Tunbridge Wells.[51] Kent County Council appointed its first county archivist in 1933, and was one of the first counties to erect a purpose-built store for the county's archives in 1937–8. From the 1950s there was a significant expansion in the archives service, which developed programmes for exhibitions, publications, the management of semi-current records and the use of archive material in schools. Between 1976 and 1989 the county archives service set up

---

[48] Yates, 'Museums in Kent', pp. 204–6. In 1990 the County Council administered museums in libraries at Ashford, Deal, Folkestone, Herne Bay, Hythe, Ramsgate and Sevenoaks, and a free-standing museum at Gravesend. District councils administered the museums at Canterbury, Dartford, Dover, Maidstone, Margate, Rochester and Tunbridge Wells. The County Council and one of the district councils shared the management of the Museum of Kent Life at Maidstone until 1993, when it was transferred to an independent trust.

[49] Kent County Council, Arts and Libraries Reports 1994/5 and 1996/7.

[50] Hewison, *op. cit.*, p. 24.

[51] Yates, 'Museums in Kent', pp. 207–9.

branch repositories in libraries at Folkestone, Ramsgate and Sevenoaks; made agreements with district and town councils for the management of local records at Hythe and in the Medway Towns; and established a partnership with the cathedral chapter and the city council for the management of the important collections in the cathedral library at Canterbury.[52]

(4) Seaside Towns and Watering Places

Kent had long been well known for the number and importance of its resort towns. Tunbridge Wells had been a fashionable spa since the late seventeenth century. Deal, Dover, Gravesend, Margate and Ramsgate had all developed as seaside resorts in the eighteenth and early nineteenth centuries. Broadstairs, Folkestone and Herne Bay had followed them in the mid-nineteenth century, succeeded by Birchington, Westgate and Whitstable in the two decades before 1900.[53] To some extent, however, resort activity in Kent had peaked in the last quarter of the nineteenth century. Gravesend had more or less ceased to be considered a seaside resort by 1900, and the famous gardens at Rosherville, immortalised in Gilbert and Sullivan's *The Sorcerer*, had closed. Deal and Dover were also in their last days as seaside resorts and had ceased to be regarded as such by the inter-war period. No substantial new resorts were built to replace them, though half-hearted attempts were made at both Leysdown and Little-stone. In 1851 four of the ten largest seaside resorts in England had been in Kent: Dover, Gravesend, Margate and Ramsgate. By 1881 Margate was no longer in the list of the ten largest English seaside resorts, and by 1911 only Dover was left.[54] Since the First World War the importance of the seaside resorts in the overall Kentish economy has significantly diminished. Of the major resorts only Folkestone has retained a reasonable range of good quality hotel accommodation, and none of the resort towns has developed facilities for conferences comparable with those in Bournemouth or Brighton, Eastbourne or Torquay. This pattern of decline is, however, more complicated than might at first appear and disguises the fact that many of Kent's seaside resorts made strenuous efforts both before and after the Second World War to halt their decline and to attract new visitors.

At Folkestone the Earls of Radnor continued to maintain a direct interest in the development of the resort throughout much of the twentieth century, even though they no longer lived in the town. The sixth earl served as mayor in 1902, and in the 1890s the Leas had been 'laid out with lawns, pavilions, bandstands and shelters as a high-class recreation area . . . the private policeman employed

---

[52] Melling, *op. cit.*, pp. 55–6; Yates in Currie and Lewis, *op. cit.*, pp. 212–13.

[53] F. Stafford and W.N. Yates, *The Later Kentish Seaside (1840–1974)*, Maidstone 1985, pp. 2–12.

[54] J.K. Watson, *The English Seaside Resort: A Social History*, Leicester 1983, pp. 53, 60, 65.

by His Lordship to patrol the Leas was a constant reminder of his presence'.[55] A switchback railway was opened in 1891, and in 1902 the Leas Pavilion opened a 'tea room' with a ladies' string trio. In 1924 Lord Radnor gave the East Cliff Gardens and the Warren to the town 'to extend the amenities of the resort', and this was later developed to provide facilities for campers.[56] However, like many other aristocratic and gentry landowners, the Radnors felt that economic and political trends were hostile to traditional patterns of land ownership and it was wiser for them to transfer their assets from land to 'less risky' and 'more remunerative' investments. The family ceased to reside in Folkestone, and, whilst continuing to retain an interest in the resort, began systematically to sell off parts of their seaside estates from 1920.[57] Gradually the responsibility for resort development shifted from the Earls of Radnor and their agents in Folkestone to the town council, though expenditure on the requirements of visitors was strongly opposed by some ratepayers. The zigzag path on the Undercliff only went ahead in 1920–1 after a public enquiry had been held to consider the objections of ratepayers to the expense involved. Between 1924 and 1927 the council spent over £100,000 as its contribution to the costs of the East Cliff and Marine Gardens pavilions and the Leas Cliff Hall. The last of these, designed as a venue for concerts, dancing and variety shows, was to cause the council financial headaches for many years. An attempt to provide the hall with a resident orchestra resulted in heated debate in the council chamber over the costs that this incurred, and by 1940 an orchestra of twenty-five musicians and a conductor had been reduced to 'a Dance Band of five and an organist'.[58]

Most of the larger resorts in Kent were determined to maintain their share of the visitor market, in competition with both other British seaside resorts and, eventually, the growing cheapness of foreign travel. They took advantage of the Health and Watering Places Act 1921 to publicise their attractions through guidebooks and railway posters. They catered for the inter-war cult of sunbathing by opening new open-air swimming pools. Margate did this in 1927, Folkestone in 1936, and Ramsgate in 1938. These were used as a venue for 'physical culture classes' and 'mannequin parades of bathing belles'. The difficulty for Britain's seaside resorts was that patterns of holidaymaking were changing. People no longer wanted a week or fortnight in a hotel or boarding house, but preferred camping, caravanning or self-catering. At many seaside resorts the percentage of holidays spent in residential accommodation had dropped from nearly 100% to under 40% between the late 1940s and the early 1960s. At Margate, three of the resort's largest hotels were sold to Billy Butlin to provide a slightly more up-market version of the more informal accommodation already available in his holiday camps. Four of the largest hotels in

---

[55] D. Cannadine, *Lords and Landlords: The Aristocracy and the Towns, 1774–1967*, Leicester 1980, p. 64.

[56] Bishop, *op. cit.*, pp. 117, 136.

[57] Cannadine, *op. cit.*, pp. 418, 421.

[58] Stafford and Yates, *op. cit.*, pp. 118–19, 136–8, 140–7.

Folkestone – the Metropole, the Majestic, the Queen's and the Grand – closed between 1959 and 1973. The closure of hotels and the decline in the number of resident holidaymakers, as opposed to excursionists, in resorts such as Folkestone and Margate, forced the local councils to review their policies for resort development and to curtail expenditure on entertainment for visitors.[59] The fact that Kent had been so extensively developed with traditional seaside resorts in the eighteenth and nineteenth centuries meant that there was little room left to develop the coastline with facilities for the more informal patterns of holiday-making that had begun to develop in the inter-war period. Attempts were, however, made at Leysdown and Littlestone. At the latter the idiosyncratic 'Maddy' Maddeson set up one of his pioneering holiday camps in the inter-war years, which proved so popular that he was obliged to publish notices advising potential customers that the camp was now 'booked up from July 9th to August 27th. We have a little accommodation before the 9th and after the 27th but please write us straight away if you are wishing to come.' The owner himself took an active part in the life of the camp, 'organising games and competitions, getting to know . . . visitors, and generally keeping a watchful eye on what went on':

> Leysdown-on-Sea attracted hustlers and cowboys and provided apprentice-ships in mild crookery for generations of school leavers who, in the 1950s, 1960s and early 1970s went 'down Leysdown' to work as cheap labour, cleaning the chalets in the holiday camps, serving in cafés and bars and minding stalls and machines in the fairground and amusement arcades . . . fiddles could be perpetrated all summer; prices could be exorbitant; and high labour turnover prevented possible protest but spread bad practices.[60]

Whilst the seaside resorts of Kent are still providing opportunities for entertainment and recreation for the day visitor, mostly from London or the inland areas of the county itself, their days as bases for family holidays are very definitely over and they have not yet established themselves as centres for conferences and tourism in the way that several of their competitors, further along the south coast, have managed to do.

(5) Tourism

As the popularity of seaside resorts has declined, so the other aspects of holiday-making have developed and flourished, greatly assisted by the Holidays with Pay Act 1938.[61] Tourism has had a long history in Britain, but it has only devel-

[59] *Ibid.*, pp. 109–11, 116–18, 123–6, 133–4, 165–71. For a more detailed survey of resort publicity since 1921 see W.N. Yates, 'Selling the Seaside', *History Today*, xxxviii (August 1988), pp. 20–7.
[60] C. Ward and D. Hardy, *Goodnight Campers: The History of the British Holiday Camp*, London 1986, pp. 27–8, 78.
[61] For a brief discussion of this topic, the background to it and useful references, see H. Cunningham,

oped into a major industry since the Second World War. Until the second half of
the nineteenth century, tourism was something that could only be indulged in by
the leisured and wealthy classes. The number of British tourists remained small,
though there was an increasing number of foreign tourists, especially Ameri-
cans. In 1820 there were only 1,926 recorded American visitors to Britain. This
had risen to 8,000 by 1840, 26,000 by 1860, and over 50,000 by 1880.[62] Kent
was well placed to benefit from tourism as it was on the direct route between
London and the channel ports. Its proximity to the capital also meant that it was
easily accessible to large numbers of people able to use the new forms of transport – railways, bicycles and eventually motor cars – for day excursions or long
weekends in the countryside. Deliberate attempts to preserve the countryside
had begun in the late nineteenth century with the foundation of the Commons,
Open Spaces and Footpaths Preservation Society in 1865 and that of the
National Trust for Places of Historic Interest and Natural Beauty in 1895. Local
preservation societies were brought together under the protective umbrella of the
Council for the Preservation of Rural England in 1926. Tourism in the countryside was encouraged by the Cyclists' Touring Club, founded in 1878, which had
over 60,000 members by the end of the nineteenth century.[63] During the
inter-war period there was a significant rise in the membership of various
organisations promoting internal tourism, particularly that of the Youth Hostels
Association, which was founded in the late 1920s 'to provide cheap holiday
accommodation for young people'.[64] The trend continued after the Second
World War. There was a 41.9% increase in the number of craft using rivers and
canals between 1967 and 1971. Membership of the Ramblers' Association rose
from 11,000 in 1963 to 25,000 in 1975, and that of the Caravan Club of Great
Britain from 41,000 in 1965 to 143,000 in 1974.[65]

As the numbers of tourists grew so did the number of attractions for tourists
to visit; 'by the late 1920s, well over 230 abbeys, castles, gardens and country
houses in England . . . were open to the public on a regular fee-paying basis'.
One of those open to visitors in Kent was Penshurst Place, which could be
visited before the Second World War for a shilling.[66] These developments were
not without precedent. It had been possible to visit some stately homes since the
late eighteenth century, and excursions to ruined abbeys and castles had been
stimulated by the publication of volumes such as Francis Grose's *Antiquities of
England* in 1773–6. Such tourism had, however, been confined to 'the respectable traveller'.[67] By the second half of the twentieth century anybody willing to
pay the admission fee was able to visit the significant number of historic

'Culture and Leisure', *Cambridge Social History of Britain, 1750–1950. Vol. 2: People and their Environment*, ed. F.M.L. Thompson, Cambridge 1990, pp. 279–89.

[62] Walvin, *op. cit.*, p. 30.
[63] Patmore, *op. cit.*, pp. 27, 37, 39.
[64] Jones, *op. cit.*, pp. 64–5.
[65] K. Roberts, *Contemporary Society and the Growth of Leisure*, London 1978, p. 21.
[66] A. Tinniswood, *A History of Country House Visiting*, Oxford 1989, p. 157.
[67] I. Ousby, *The Englishman's England: Taste, Travel and the Rise of Tourism*, Cambridge 1990, p. 66.

Plate 52. Sissinghurst Castle, one of the earliest properties in Kent to be acquired by the National Trust; the former home of Harold Nicolson and Vita Sackville-West.

Plate 53. Mobile library van, c.1925.

Plate 54. Sir Garrard Tyrwhitt-Drake with his female Indian elephants, Gert and Dais, named after two popular radio performers, in the 1950s, at his zoo near Maidstone.

Plate 55. Stewart caught by Fagg in the cricket match between Kent and Surrey at Blackheath, 1956.

Plate 56. The new leisure centre at Maidstone, 1991.

buildings open to the public. Some of these were ancient monuments acquired by the state which in 1985 were vested in a government funded body, English Heritage.[68] Others were administered by the National Trust, but many remained in private ownership. In 1937 legislation was passed which set up the Country House Scheme, whereby owners could give or bequeath their houses to the National Trust but be allowed to continue living in them. By 1945 the trust had acquired seventeen such properties including, in Kent, Knole, the seat of Lord Sackville, where the negotiations for transfer had been concluded in 1943. By the late 1950s the National Trust was responsible for ninety-eight houses and gardens open to the public.[69] By the 1990s there were twenty-four properties open to the public in Kent which were the responsibility of English Heritage and seventeen belonging to the National Trust. Five of these – Dover Castle, Sissinghurst Castle Gardens, Chartwell, Ightham Mote and Rochester Castle – were among eighteen tourist attractions in the county which had more than 100,000 visitors annually. The others were the privately owned Leeds Castle, Hever Castle and Penshurst Place, the cathedrals at Canterbury and Rochester, Aylesford Priory, the Eurotunnel Exhibition Centre, the Whitbread Hop Farm, Howlett's Zoo, Bewl Water, and three heritage exhibitions: the White Cliffs Experience, Canterbury Tales and Chatham Historic Dockyard. Of more than 8 million visits to attractions in Kent in 1993, over 50% were to historic buildings, compared with only 12% to museums and art galleries, 7% to zoos and wildlife collections, 6% to gardens and less than 1% to vineyards.[70] It was estimated that overall the number of visitors to stately homes in England 'comfortably passes the 16 million mark each year'. The majority of owners tried to balance the admission of the public with the maintenance of a private life, though others, led by the Duke of Bedford at Woburn (Beds.) and the Marquess of Bath at Longleat (Wilts.) – those 'enfants terribles of the stately homes business – were ushering in a new age of fun-fair attractions'.[71] In Kent there was a significant contrast between the fairly 'low key' visitor attractions of Penshurst Place and those of Hever or Leeds Castles. At Penshurst the house had been reopened to the public in 1947 and the gardens were extensively redeveloped between 1970 and 1990. Ancillary attractions were limited to a museum of toys, restaurant, 'venture' playground, nature trail and arboretum.[72] At Leeds Castle significant developments took place after it was opened to the public by the trust in which it had been vested by its then owner, Olive Lady Baillie, the trust having become

[68] Comparable bodies were established for Scotland (Historic Scotland) and Wales (Cadw).

[69] Tinniswood, op. cit., pp. 179–80.

[70] English Heritage Properties, London 1994, pp. 86–93; The National Trust Handbook, London 1998, pp. 98–149; Kent County Council, Top Visitor Attractions and Summary of Visitor Attraction Attendance Figures, 1993.

[71] Ousby, op. cit., p. 59.

[72] Penshurst Place and Gardens, Tonbridge n.d., pp. 30, 41–2, end map. The present Viscount De L'Isle, in a letter to the author dated 24 February 1998, described Penshurst Place as 'the largest family home in private hands in Kent, which is visited, and not an attraction in which we live. Therefore we have ruled out many activities which we consider unsuitable for the image which we wish to present.'

operational in 1974. By 1980 there was a museum of dog collars and a herb garden. A maze and grotto followed in 1987 and an aviary in 1988. The castle was used as a venue for conferences and special events, such as open-air concerts, flower festivals, vintage car rallies and international ballooning. A nine-hole golf course was also available for public use.[73]

(6) Popular Entertainment

In no respect has there been greater change in the cultural and recreational history of Britain in the twentieth century than in the field of popular entertainment. These changes began in the first decade of the century with the invention of the cinematograph. This was followed by the introduction of radio in the inter-war period and the development of television after the Second World War. All three inventions have revolutionised many aspects of British life and have helped to stimulate the consumerism within British society which had begun in the late nineteenth century. Between the wars there was a phenomenal rise in the sale of luxury items such as vacuum cleaners, three-piece suites, radios, gramophones, cameras and bicycles, and this trend was accelerated by the increasing availability of hire-purchase arrangements and, after the Second World War, by the dependence on American aid both during and immediately after the war. Hugh Gaitskell, the newly elected leader of the Labour Party, commented with distaste on the growing Americanisation of British society in 1955. The British public was much influenced by the romantic image of the United States shown in American films, and younger women did their best to imitate the leading American film actresses in the style of their clothes and in the way they did their hair.[74] It was, in essence, a lack of confidence in the role that Britain was now playing in the world, increased by the disintegration of the British Empire; this lack of confidence did not really begin to be reversed until the 'Swinging Sixties'.

The history of cinema in Britain had been one of spectacular rise between the first cinematographic performances, as part of the programme in music halls or as simple shows of short films in public halls, at the beginning of the twentieth century, until immediately after the Second World War. Thereafter there was an equally dramatic decline – from an audience of 1,635 million to one of only 64 million by 1982 – since when there has been a slow but steady rise in the number of cinema attendances. It is, however, unlikely that Britain will ever again see a situation in which 76% of its population were regular cinema-goers, which was the position in 1946. The early cinemas, of which there were 3,000 by 1914, brought about the closure of many music halls or, in some cases, existing music halls were converted into cinemas. Cinema appealed much more

---

[73] *Leeds Castle*, London 1989, pp. 15, 17, 49.

[74] P. Addison, *Now the War is Over: A Social History of Britain, 1945–51*, rev. edn, London 1995, pp. 200–201; Walvin, *op. cit.*, pp. 134, 152.

to women than the very definitely male-orientated music halls had done. It also appealed to all social classes, whereas music hall had not been seen as entirely respectable. By 1919 half the population went to the cinema at least twice a week.[75] Cinema-going in Kent followed the national trends. Most of the large towns in Kent had a cinema by the outbreak of the First World War: the Electric in Canterbury opened in 1911 and the Palais de Luxe in 1913; Shanly's Electric Theatre in Dover in 1911; the Gem in Gravesend in 1910 and the Plaza in 1911; the Empire Electric in Maidstone in 1910. Medium-sized towns such as Ashford, Deal, Herne Bay and Whitstable also received their first cinemas between 1910 and 1912. In smaller towns the pattern of development was more mixed; the Cinema Palace in Tenterden opened in 1910, but there was no proper cinema in Sandwich until 1937, though films had been shown in the Assembly Rooms from 1911. Every town in Kent eventually acquired a cinema in the inter-war period, and several large villages, such as Aylesham, Borough Green, Cliffe-at-Hoo, Hawkhurst and Snodland, also had one.[76] Not all these cinemas were considered to be unmixed blessings by local residents. At Sevenoaks

> The Royal Crown on the London Road was sold, soon after the First World War, to make way for the Odeon Cinema. This was a sad loss to the town. The ballroom of the Royal Crown was the social centre of the early twentieth century. . . . The well-kept gardens, now submerged beneath the Odeon car park, were a favourite resort for visitors. Tea there, on a summer afternoon, would have the added advantage of a lovely view across to the North Downs.[77]

Most of the early cinemas in Kent, as in other parts of the country, were cramped and uncomfortable, the 'fleapits' of popular folk memory. From the late 1920s many of them were replaced by much more palatial buildings, which frequently housed bars and restaurants, and were usually provided with an organ, that rose as if by magic from the front of the stalls, and was played in the interval between the main film and the supporting programme. Over 1,000 new cinemas were built in Britain between 1924/5 and 1931/2. There were 4,305 cinemas in Britain in 1934 and over 5,300 by 1939. The largest ones could seat more than 3,000 people.[78] Many Kent towns acquired these new, much plusher, cinemas in the decade before the Second World War, and some acquired more than one: the Friar's and the Royal at Canterbury were both opened in 1933; the Majestic at Gravesend opened in 1931, followed by the 954-seat Super in 1933. One of the most spectacular of these new luxury cinemas was the one that formed part of the Dreamland complex at Margate, begun in 1933 and completed in 1935. This included, as well as the 2,200-seat cinema, a ballroom for 1,500, saloon and public bars 'decorated in a modern version of the Tudor

[75] *Ibid.*, pp. 133–4, 150.
[76] See M. Tapsell, *Memories of Kent Cinemas*, Croydon 1987, which is a very detailed account of cinema in Kent.
[77] Dunlop, *op. cit.*, p. 185.
[78] Jones, *op. cit.*, p. 44.

style', and four restaurants with a total seating capacity of 3,500. 'Attached to the auditorium' of the cinema were 'two huge lounges some 70 feet long by 45 feet wide, one for the Stalls level, and one for the Circle. . . . In addition to the lounges, the Entrance and Booking Halls cover 2,500 square feet.'[79]

The national decline in cinema-going from its peak in 1946 was mirrored in Kent. Maidstone had had its first permanent cinema, the Empire Electric, opened in a converted shop, in 1910. Within a year there were two and by 1920 there was a third. In 1934 the Granada Cinema was opened in Lower Stone Street. It had a 'grandiose Corinthian portico [designed by Cecil Masey], spacious restaurant, air-conditioned auditorium and organ which ascended from the depths between films'. By 1945 there were five cinemas operating in Maidstone, but this was gradually reduced to four in 1954, three in 1957, two in 1961 and one, the Granada, in 1974, this being subsequently divided into a bingo hall and a much smaller three-screen cinema.[80] This pattern of growth and decline was repeated everywhere in Kent. The only cinemas that survived were the larger ones that were capable of being divided into more than one screen and auditorium to cater for the much smaller audiences attending what was still a significant number of new films being distributed in the 1980s and 1990s. Nearly all the surviving cinemas were in the larger towns, though Dover lost its last cinema in 1971. Of the medium-sized towns only Ashford, Deal and Herne Bay managed to retain their cinemas, and one small-town or village cinema, the Raymar at West Malling, opened in 1951, managed to buck the trend and remain open. Since 1980 a major development has been the multi-screen cinema and leisure complex, of which there are Kent examples (both of very recent establishment) at Dartford and Maidstone.

Cinema was not the only new popular entertainment in the inter-war period. Another was dancing, which became increasingly popular, especially with women. Immediately after the Second World War there were some 450 dance halls in Britain and three million tickets, costing between 1s. 6d. and 2s. 6d., sold each week. British dance bands were much influenced by American ones, such as those led by Tommy Dorsey and Glenn Miller, and the singers attached to them modelled themselves on their American counterparts Bing Crosby and Frank Sinatra. Young women went to dances as a socially acceptable way of meeting young men without a chaperone. There were, however, social divisions in dancing in the way that there were not at the cinema, the upper classes dancing in clubs and restaurants and the lower classes in the large, purpose-built, dance halls.

The impact of radio was enormous. When the British Broadcasting Corporation first launched its radio service in 1922 there were only 35,744 receiving licences. This had increased to more than 2 million by 1926 and more than 9 million by 1939. The corporation employed only 773 people in 1927 but over

[79] Stafford and Yates, *op. cit.*, pp. 120, 149–51; see also J. Walters, *Dreamland Cinema and Entertainments Complex*, Margate 1976.
[80] Clark and Murfin, *op. cit.*, pp. 197, 236, 249.

5,000 by 1939. Most homes had a wireless. Radio broadcasts of orchestral concerts helped to stimulate an interest in classical music and increased the sales of gramophone records. The Second World War did not have a detrimental effect on any of these popular entertainments, which helped to bolster morale at a time when most families lost either members or friends in the armed forces or in air-raids. Average expenditure on entertainment increased by 120% between 1938 and 1944; this included a large increase in the number of cinema attendances.[81]

Other uses of leisure time, such as seaside holidays and sporting fixtures, had been seriously affected by the war, but they recovered very quickly once hostilities were over. At Folkestone about half the pre-war hotels and boarding houses had been reopened for business by 1946, and the town was able to host conferences once again from 1947.[82] Test matches had resumed by 1946. Football matches achieved their highest ever attendances, 41 million, in the 1948/9 season. There was such an enormous boom in betting on sporting events – £400 million to £450 million on horse-racing, £200 million to £300 million on greyhound racing, and about £70 million on football pools – that the post-war Labour government set up a Royal Commission on Gambling in 1949. Social commentators have, however, emphasised the pervading air of innocence and naïveté of the post-war era compared with the decades to follow:

> The leisure pattern of the post-war years bespeaks a healthy, wholesome, orderly and somewhat repressive society. Young people knew nothing then of the deadly cocktail of drugs, demoralisation and unemployment, so freely available to them in the 1980s. The main solvent of the old order was consumerism, bringing with it a passion for private pleasures, a high risk of dissatisfaction and a temptation to consume things that were harmful as well as things that were good. In the 1940s pleasures were unsophisticated and the boundaries of rebellion were set by under-age drinking, pre-marital sex and a sweaty night out at 100 Oxford Street [a post-war jazz club opened by Humphrey Lyttleton].[83]

Within a decade this scenario had changed. How far the change was the result of the twentieth century's third most important innovation in popular entertainment is still the subject of acrimonious debate. Television had begun briefly before the war and was restarted in 1946, but initially transmissions were confined to the London area, and few homes possessed a television set. Within a decade the influence of television had permeated every aspect of British life even more effectively that the cinema and radio before it:

[81] Walvin, *op. cit.*, pp. 136–40, 146.

[82] Bishop, *op. cit.*, p. 137.

[83] For a good overview of British culture and leisure in the late 1940s and early 1950s, see Addison, *op. cit.*, pp. 113–39.

One product more than any other epitomised the change in leisure patterns; the TV set came to dominate both the front room and also the nation's wider recreation habits. After the initial establishment of ITV . . . most other forms of recreation were obliged to use television advertising to promote their interests. . . . TV hastened the decline of the cinema and drove entertainment away from the public place back into the home.[84]

Cinema audiences continued to fall until the mid-1980s, but have since begun to recover. The number of cinemas in Britain fell from 1,420 to only 707 between 1971 and 1983, and the number of cinema attendances from 2.74 million in 1974 to 1.26 million in 1983. Another casualty has been football matches, falling from a peak attendance of over 40 million a year in the late 1940s to an attendance of about 25 million a year in the mid-1970s. As colour television was developed in the 1960s so people changed their sets so that they could receive programmes in colour. The number of television licences issued in 1984 was only 18.681 million compared with 17.435 million in 1974. However, whereas more than 60% of these were still for black-and-white sets in 1974, by 1984 fewer than 20% of the licences issued were for black-and-white sets. In 1971 it was estimated that the average person in Britain over the age of five watched 18.6 hours of television a week in the winter and 15 hours in the summer. By 1984 the average adult male watched 21.75 hours of television and the average adult female 25.5 hours. This increase, particularly for female viewing, had resulted from the substantial increase in the number of daytime programmes available to watch. The impact of video was even more spectacular, the number of video recorders in Britain increasing from 110,000 in 1978 to 685,000 by 1980, and to 6,285,000 by 1983.[85]

By the mid-1960s watching television had become the most popular leisure pursuit in Britain. In 1965–6 it involved 20–25% of both men and women, scoring significantly higher than gardening (10–15% of men, 5–10% of women), physical recreation (10–15% of men, less than 5% of women), excursions (5–10% of both men and women), or country walks and visits to parks (less than 5% of both men and women).[86] A growing leisure occupation was eating out. Before the 1960s many towns had few, or any, cafés and restaurants, but over the last thirty years the number and variety of both has greatly increased.[87] Public houses also adapted to changing leisure styles by selling food and wine in addition to the more traditional beers and spirits, by promoting live entertainment, or by installing juke boxes.[88] The long established brewing firms, who had dominated the public-house trade through their tied houses, have in recent years begun to receive serious competition from a number of independent chains of public houses, which sell a wide range of beers from different

84 Walvin, *op. cit.*, p. 153.
85 Jones, *op. cit.*, pp. 200–201.
86 Patmore, *op. cit.*, p. 50.
87 Walvin, *op. cit.*, p. 158.
88 Roberts, *Leisure*, p. 41.

breweries, many of them converting redundant shops, cinemas or public buildings into public-house restaurants. One of these firms, J.D. Wetherspoon,
founded in 1979, had established 194 new public-house restaurants in Britain by
1997, including four in Kent: the Thomas Ingoldsby at Canterbury, the Eight
Bells at Dover, the Muggleton Inn at Maidstone and the Opera House at
Tunbridge Wells. The most ambitious of these projects has been the restoration
of the former opera house of 1902 at Tunbridge Wells, latterly used as a bingo
hall, to something like its original internal ambience, earning in the process a
conservation award from the Tunbridge Wells Civic Society.[89]

(7) Physical Recreation

The foundations of facilities for physical recreation had been firmly laid in the
second half of the nineteenth century, and the patterns of development then
established were carried on until the Second World War. Provision of facilities
was, however, patchy, and many towns spent the first three decades of the twentieth century trying to catch up with their neighbours in which there were better
recreational facilities. Maidstone, for example, had had a public swimming
baths from 1852 but even in the inter-war period it 'still lacked a filtration
system; the water was merely changed twice a week and the ticket price was
highest on the days when the water was clean'. There was also a serious deficiency in the provision of playing fields and public open space which was not
satisfactorily resolved until 1928 when the borough council decided to purchase
Mote Park from Viscount Bearsted for £50,000. When the park was opened in
1929 it provided 'facilities for boating, fishing and tennis, as well as a large area
of open fields, trees and a lake'.[90] Whereas the long-established team games
remained popular, a number of middle-class sports, such as golf, tennis and
yachting, attracted more participants as a result of the increase in the number of
private motor cars. There were only 314, 769 of these in 1922 but this figure had
risen to 1,834,248 by 1937.[91] One of the most traditional of English country
sports, which survived the attacks on cruelty to animals in the nineteenth
century, was hunting. From the last quarter of the nineteenth century, however,
hunting had ceased to be the preserve of the country landowners but was
attracting increasing interest from urban businessmen who had homes in the
country or who became members of hunts. Similar trends could be observed in
the growing number of rich town-dwellers who took up shooting. These trends
continued throughout the twentieth century to the point where, 'today, the
majority of enthusiasts who go hunting [or shooting] are middle class town
dwellers – who may own a weekend cottage, or who just drive down to the
countryside in their Range Rovers for the fun of it'.[92] It was part of a movement,

[89] J.D. Wetherspoon plc, *Annual Report*, Watford 1997, pp. 2, 37–9.
[90] Clark and Murfin, *op. cit.*, p. 235.
[91] Jones, *op. cit.*, p. 195.
[92] D. Cannadine, *The Decline and Fall of the British Aristocracy*, rev. edn, London 1992, pp. 360–6, 690.

aided by the continued expansion in car ownership, that turned most parts of 'the countryside into a mass playground'.[93] Kent, with its easy access from London and with significant urban communities within the county itself, found itself very much a victim of this situation, and it required the vigorous imposition of planning controls by local authorities to ensure that rural communities were not damaged by the increasing demand for access to the countryside for a wide variety of recreational pursuits.

In the years since the Second World War the most significant trend in physical recreation has been the decline in the popularity of spectator sports, at least as far as attendances at sporting events are concerned, and a corresponding growth in individual sports, and in indoor as opposed to outdoor sports. Between 1946 and 1972 attendances at greyhound tracks dropped from 36 million to 7 million a year, and there were only 250 professional boxers in 1973 compared to 1,500 in 1952. In marked contrast to this, the number of golf balls sold increased from 13 million to 20 million a year, and the sale of fishing tackle increased by 66%, between 1971 and 1973.[94] Whereas attendances at football matches declined by 28% between 1973 and 1977, participation in billiards or snooker increased by 293%, and in darts by 272% in the same period. Much of this was the result of television, which both encouraged an interest in indoor sports by including it in its sports programming, and also allowed those who had previously attended football or boxing matches to watch them in the comfort of their own homes.[95] A national survey of recreational activities in 1965 revealed that by far the most popular was swimming. More than 30% of the population were regular swimmers; it was popular with both sexes and over a large age range. Between 10% and 20% of the population participated in cycling, fishing, hiking, tennis, golf and camping. Less than 10% of the population were attracted by bowls, team games, hill-walking, climbing, riding or sailing. Team games were largely a masculine preserve and were still dominated by cricket and football. There were about 750,000 adult and post-school players of football, compared to 310,000 for cricket – though with a strong regional bias to the south of England – and 115,000 for rugby.[96] An analysis of regional leisure provision in 1972 shows that though the southern and western counties of England had below average provision for bowls, interest and provision was above the national average for camping, fishing, golf, hiking, hill-walking, climbing, riding, sailing, team games, swimming and tennis.[97]

[93] Roberts, *op. cit.*, p. 36.
[94] *Idem, Contemporary Society and the Growth of Leisure*, pp. 21, 38.
[95] *Idem, Leisure*, pp. 37–8.
[96] Patmore, *op. cit.*, pp. 58, 60, 91.
[97] B. Rogers, 'Regional Recreational Contrasts', *Leisure Research and Policy*, ed. I. Appleton, Edinburgh and London 1974, pp. 116–18.

(8) Culture, Leisure and Local Authorities since 1970

Although local authorities made a growing contribution to the provision of facilities for cultural and recreational activities throughout the first half of the twentieth century, their attitudes were very similar to those of the nineteenth-century philanthropists who had helped to lay the foundations of such provision.[98] Their primary aim had been to promote the better education and health of local people. They saw it as a legitimate use of ratepayers' money to fund libraries and museums which promoted education, or parks, recreation grounds and swimming baths which promoted public health. They were much more cautious in their financial support of other, purely leisure, activities which they felt ought to be left to the private sector. An exception was made in the resort towns where councils recognised, sometimes in the face of vociferous opposition from ratepayers, that it was their responsibility to ensure that their towns did not decline economically by failing to provide the facilities for entertainment and recreation that the visitors demanded. A change in the attitudes of other local authorities towards their role in the provision of cultural and recreational opportunities for local people occurred after the Second World War, stimulated to some extent by changes in legislation. The Local Government Act 1948 'empowered – but did not impose a duty on – local authorities to support the arts up to the limit of a 6d rate'. Support, however, remained patchy. In 1982 it was estimated that local authorities only spent on average 12% of their recreational budgets on the arts.[99] In Kent one of the effects of the new legislation was to encourage local authorities to establish municipal theatres to replace the older theatres which had been gradually put out of business by the cinemas. The older theatres had in any case done little to promote serious drama. Their performances had consisted mainly of variety shows – a development from the earlier music hall – and by the 1950s these had, in many cases, degenerated into shows including nude tableaux with such excruciating titles as 'My Bare Lady' or 'Strip Strip Hooray'. Even in the seaside towns it was found impossible to attract audiences to the traditional 'end-of-the-pier' shows, and theatres were forced to close.[100] The Pleasure Gardens Theatre at Folkestone, which had been opened in 1888, closed in 1960. In Maidstone the Palace Theatre struggled to survive after 1930 in desperate competition with the Theatre Royal and the Hippodrome in Chatham, with the result that eventually all three were forced to close.[101]

Public subsidy for provincial theatre, from both government agencies and local authorities, has resulted in far better theatrical provision in Kent in the late

---

[98] Cunningham, *op. cit.*, p. 323, notes that although local-authority expenditure on the provision of facilities for culture and recreation in England and Wales increased from £3.2 million in 1914 to £13.4 million in 1939, expressed as a percentage of total local-authority expenditure the increase was minimal, ranging between 1.3% and 2.2% for the whole period 1903–50.

[99] Hewison, *op. cit.*, p. 115.

[100] On changes in seaside entertainment after the Second World War, see Stafford and Yates, *op. cit.*, pp. 114–15.

[101] Clark and Murfin, *op. cit.*, p. 237.

twentieth century than at any time since theatres were first challenged by the new cinemas. In 1955 Maidstone Borough Council opened a new municipal theatre in part of the former Corn Exchange.[102] When the Central Picture Theatre in Canterbury closed in 1948, the building was purchased by the City Council and reopened in 1950 as the Marlowe Theatre, though its programme was not that different from the ones offered by the struggling private theatres: 'for 32 years the Marlowe entertained Canterbury with rep or latter-day touring companies, nude reviews and celebrity shows'. It closed in 1982 when the city council purchased the former Odeon (originally Friar's) Cinema, which had closed the previous year, reopening it as the New Marlowe Theatre, and with a more culturally ambitious programme, in 1984.[103] In 1983, under pressure from the Sevenoaks Theatre Action Group (STAG), the Odeon Cinema was divided into two auditoria, with a cinema in one and a theatre in the other, and renamed the Stag Theatre.[104] Both Canterbury and Sevenoaks now have flourishing annual arts festivals with a prestigious mix of drama, exhibitions, music and other events. The University of Kent has also made a significant contribution to arts provision within the county. In 1968 it appointed a Music Director to organise concerts at the university, and in 1969 the Gulbenkian Theatre was opened, funded by the Calouste Gulbenkian Foundation:

> the first production to be tackled was perhaps a trifle ambitious in its technical demands, and perhaps a little too *avant-garde* for the tastes of some of its first-night audience, involving as it did a modest amount of nudity. This provided the popular press with an opportunity for 'shock-horror' headlines, although several of the guests from the town (including the then Mayor and his wife) expressed themselves as quite unshocked.

The *Dover Express* was, however, enthusiastic in its praise of the new theatre's design: 'the auditorium is the most comfortable in Kent. The lighting is the best in Kent. The stage is the most open in Kent. The foyer is the most spacious in Kent, and the view from the terrace is second to none in south-east England.'[105] A theatre to rival the Gulbenkian, the Orchard, was built at Dartford, at the opposite end of the county, by the local district council. It opened in 1982. The cost to the local authority was considerable since, in addition to the capital investment, it was decided as a matter of policy to subsidise the operational costs. Actual seat prices ranged from £2.50 to £6.50 per performance in the first year of operation. Without a subsidy it was estimated that the charge would have been 'between £18 and £22 for a play'.[106] Despite relatively good seat occu-

---

102 *Ibid.*, p. 249.
103 Tapsell, *op. cit.*, p. 10.
104 *Ibid.*, p. 249.
105 Martin, *op. cit.*, pp. 188–91. The archives of the Gulbenkian Theatre are held in the University Library. The part of the play to which some of the audience took exception was when the central character was 'stripped naked by other members of the cast'; photograph and report in *Kentish Gazette*, 13 June 1969.
106 Orchard Theatre, Dartford, Gala Opening Performance Programme 1982.

pancy rates, ranging from 25% for films to 75% for the more popular live performances, the theatre required a subsidy of £569,373, representing 22% of its total expenditure, in 1996/7.[107]

The growing expenditure of local authorities on culture and leisure during the 1950s and 1960s happened in a rather piecemeal way and was spread across different departments. The desire to co-ordinate this provision led to the creation of new departments of culture and leisure during the process of local government reorganisation in 1973–4.[108] In Kent this was confined to the district councils. The County Council continued to administer libraries as part of the education department until 1990 when a new department of Arts and Libraries, encompassing libraries, museums, archives and the arts, was created. Contemporary commentators did not regard these moves as entirely satisfactory. The creation of culture and leisure departments resulted in the bringing together of a number of small specialist services that formerly had their own objectives but which were now obliged to contribute to an overall strategy for cultural and recreational provision:

> Support for sport and the arts can no longer be slipped through education and public health budgets. Recreation departments have to assess the merits of parks against museums and libraries, sports centres against arts centres. This requirement that services be justified in terms of leisure criteria is rather novel, and inevitably provokes a good deal of soul-searching. . . . There is no objective way of deciding which recreational tastes are particularly worthy and deserve support. In education and health the costs and benefits of alternative programmes can be at least roughly calculated, but this is not true in recreation. There is no inter-subjective consensus throughout the public as to which uses of leisure are particularly meritorious.[109]

The new culture and leisure departments have, however, had comparatively short lives. Many have been broken up, or merged with other departments, as a result of the 1979–97 Conservative governments' determination to force local authorities to put out to tender the running of many services which were previously provided directly by council staff. A very high proportion of council-owned recreational facilities, in Kent as elsewhere, especially theatres and arts centres, sports centres and swimming pools, are now managed by either private companies or arms-length bodies set up by local authorities which then secured the contract for providing the service.

The current situation for leisure provision by local authorities in Kent can be seen in the comparative statistics for two district councils – Gravesham and Tonbridge and Malling – as shown in Table 45. Although authorities of roughly similar size were spending more or less comparable sums on leisure provision, there were significant variations in the detail of that expenditure. Gravesham

---

[107] Orchard Theatre, Dartford, Annual Report 1996/7.
[108] Roberts, *Leisure*, p. 22.
[109] *Ibid.*, pp. 151–2, 155.

Table 45

Revenue Expenditure on Leisure Provision in the Districts of Gravesham
and Tonbridge and Malling, 1994–7

Service Head	Gravesham 1994/5 (£,000s)	Tonbridge/Malling 1996/7 (£,000s)
Management	144.4	193.4
Leisure centres	1120.6	629.1
Sports centres	44.3	494.3
Swimming pools	–	575.6
Theatres	494.6	–
Parks/Recreation grounds	1179.0	554.3
Play schemes/equipment	119.1	50.9
Community centres	12.1	–
Tourism	43.6	56.5
Sports development	–	46.4
Access to countryside	–	56.6
Heritage	–	16.6
Grants to other bodies	17.7	31.6
Total	3147.2	2705.3

Source: Gravesham Borough Council, *A Leisure Strategy for Gravesham 1994–1998*, p. 12; Tonbridge and Malling Borough Council, *Community Leisure plan 1996–2000*, p. 2

spent more than twice as much on the maintenance of parks and recreation grounds and on associated play schemes and equipment as Tonbridge and Malling. The latter, however, spent almost half as much again as Gravesham on leisure and sports centres and swimming pools, and its management costs were significantly higher. What is perhaps significant about local authority expenditure on leisure is how recent are most of the reasons for this expenditure. The borough of Gravesham, formed in 1973–4, brought together the former borough of Gravesend and the urban district of Northfleet with a number of parishes formerly in the rural district of Strood. Northfleet urban district council had built one of the first indoor-recreation centres in the country in 1968 and had opened a swimming pool in 1973. Gravesend Borough Council had developed the Woodville Halls as a theatre and entertainment complex in 1968 and had decided to build a sports centre, opened after the formation of the new district council in 1976. By the mid-1990s the Council, or its predecessors, had established two leisure centres with a mix of 'wet and dry' facilities; the entertainment complex at the Woodville Halls; six other small community arts or sports centres, some managed by voluntary bodies; Camer Country Park and a total of thirty-seven smaller parks, recreation grounds and open spaces; 108 miles of 'footpath and bridleway access to the countryside'; two pitches each for cricket and hockey, three for five-a-side football and seventeen for football; thirteen courts for tennis and three for netball; three bowling greens, a jogging track and a crazy golf course; thirty-one equipped playgrounds and a skateboard ramp and BMX track at one of the leisure centres. The Council funded holiday play-schemes and activity courses at sixteen different venues and sponsored twenty-one special arts or entertainment events.[110] With the exception of the Woodville Halls, Gravesham District Council had deliberately chosen to spread its money across a large number of fairly modest facilities giving easy access to a wide range of recreational opportunities, particularly in the urban areas of Gravesend and Northfleet. Tonbridge and Malling District Council chose to spend a high proportion of its funding for leisure provision on a smaller number of prestige projects, including the first example in Kent of the new type of leisure pool, pioneered in a number of large, mostly northern, towns in the 1970s:

> The concept of leisure pools has proved successful throughout the country . . . The 'beach' effect allows toddlers to enjoy water play with a minimum of supervision from parents, and the wave machine provides a new experience in indoor water recreation. . . . The Leisure Pool brings the outdoors indoors and often under much more comfortable conditions. The pool is irregular in shape like a lagoon – and has a high proportion of shallow water. It contains a water spout, play chute, and imitation rocks which act both as a wave break and as fun objects for climbing over. But the most exciting feature is the wave machine which sends out parallel waves . . . from the deep end to the beach which shelves gently up to the feet of people in the sitting out area. . . . Mums can watch toddlers in the shallow end without having to be in a swimsuit – just like paddling at the seaside.[111]

The Larkfield Leisure Centre, which incorporated similar features to those that have been described, was opened in 1981 in a location that could attract users not just from the Tonbridge and Malling district but also from Maidstone and the Medway Towns, which had no comparable facilities. The result was that Maidstone Borough Council, which had opened its own new, but very tradi-tional, swimming pool in 1974, felt obliged to react to the competition by opening an even larger and more up-to-date leisure centre in Mote Park, incor-porating the original swimming pool, but providing also a new leisure pool and sports hall, capable of being adapted to serve as a venue for orchestral concerts and more popular live entertainment, in 1991 at a cost of £10 million. The new leisure centre was attracting nearly a million visits each year by 1998 and required a slightly smaller operational subsidy than the swimming pool it had replaced.[112] Competition from the new leisure centre in Maidstone led to a significant decline in the number of those using the Larkfield Leisure Centre,

---

[110] Gravesham Borough Council, *A Leisure Strategy for Gravesham, 1994–1998*, pp. 9–10.

[111] *South Tyneside Holiday Guide*, South Shields 1978, advertisement feature between p. 30 and p. 31.

[112] Letter from Director of Borough Services, Maidstone Borough Council, to author, dated 5 June 1998.

and the council responded with 'a phased capital development programme' to 'enable the Centre to compete with other local facilities and recapture the market lost in the early 1990s'. The other major investments by Tonbridge and Malling Council were in the Angel Sports Centre and in the combined indoor and outdoor swimming pools, all in Tonbridge. By the mid-1990s the Angel Centre was 'experiencing a decline in overall usage' and consideration was being given to 'a fundamental review of the aims and objectives of the Centre ... and ... the potential for linkages between the centre and the new Tonbridge Swimming Pool'. Whilst the council recognised that the indoor swimming pool would be in competition with those at Sevenoaks and Tunbridge Wells it was 'anticipated that the outdoor pool will be uniquely placed in the summer months to secure the needs of both the local community and visitors to the town'. In 1992 the council decided to develop Tonbridge Castle, which it owned, as a heritage attraction, further upgrading the displays in 1995 and generating some 25,000 visits each year.[113]

A hundred years ago provision for culture and leisure within the local community, though growing, was still very limited, and heavily dependent on support from private philanthropists. A hundred years later, provision for culture and leisure is seen as essential by both government and local authorities, for the benefit of both residents and visitors alike. Provision has relied on a mix of public and private provision with the emphasis in the last quarter of the twentieth century being firmly on the role of public bodies as strategists and enablers, rather than as direct providers, and an assumption that provision will change and develop in response to demand. The mix of public subsidy and private entrepreneurship has led to a situation in which all those involved in the provision of cultural and leisure facilities are constantly reassessing the adequacy of what they are providing in an effort to ensure that both demand is satisfied and competition responded to. In that sense, although the quantity of provision is much greater than that of a century ago, the mechanics of its provision are not significantly different.

113 Tonbridge and Malling Borough Council, *Community Leisure Plan, 1996–2000*, pp. 8, 33, 40, 90.

Appendix I

The Population of the Principal Towns in Kent, 1911–91

Town	1911	1931	1951	1971	1991
Ashford	13,668	22,099	24,783	35,615	43,348
Beckenham	31,692	50,429	74,836	In Greater London	
Bexley	15,895	32,652	88,781	In Greater London	
Broadstairs	8,929	12,727	15,081	20,048	23,691
Bromley	33,646	47,698	64,179	In Greater London	
Canterbury	24,626	25,109	27,795	33,176	38,670
Chatham	42,250	42,999	44,424	57,153	n/a
Chislehurst and Sidcup	8,666	27,156	83,850	In Greater London	
Crayford	8,493	16,229	27,950	In Greater London	
Dartford	23,609	24,871	40,578	45,705	44,817
Deal and Walmer	11,295	19,665	24,309	25,432	28,504
Dover	43,645	41,281	35,215	34,395	37,826
Erith	27,750	32,779	46,270	In Greater London	
Folkestone	33,502	46,170	45,203	43,801	45,280
Gillingham	52,252	61,651	70,676	86,862	95,358
Gravesend	28,115	37,670	44,560	54,106	50,741
Herne Bay	7,780	14,533	18,348	25,198	32,773
Maidstone	35,475	44,877	54,035	70,987	71,200
Margate	27,085	40,307	42,512	50,347	38,535
Milton and Sittingbourne	15,855	20,177	21,904	30,913	36,630
Northfleet	14,184	16,223	18,821	26,718	21,389
Penge	22,330	27,771	25,012	In Greater London	
Ramsgate	29,603	34,442	35,801	39,561	38,095
Rochester	31,384	32,377	43,934	55,519	n/a
Tonbridge	14,796	16,832	19,237	31,016	30,358
Tunbridge Wells	35,697	35,839	38,400	44,612	55,145
Whitstable	7,982	13,557	17,459	25,449	29,485

Note: The populations of the following towns exceeded those of the smallest of the towns in the above list in 1911 but remained well below the populations of the smallest in 1991:

Faversham 10,619 in 1911 and 17,070 in 1991.
Sevenoaks 9,182 in 1911 and 18,130 in 1991.
Sheerness 17,487 in 1911 and 12,090 in 1991.

Sheerness and Dover were the only towns in Kent to have fewer inhabitants in 1991 than they had had in 1911.

Alison Cresswell

Appendix II

Local Government Structure and Reorganisation in Kent

The reform of local government in England and Wales had begun with the Municipal Corporations Act of 1835 but the major overhaul of local government, which laid the foundations of the system we are familiar with today, was delayed until the last two decades of the nineteenth century. The Local Government Act of 1888 created sixty-two county councils to take over county administration from the justices of the peace. Each historic county was provided with one or more county councils, as was London. A total of sixty-one larger towns were made county boroughs, exempt from the jurisdiction of county councils. Six years later the Local Government Act of 1894 created a second tier of local government comprising 270 non-county boroughs, 472 rural and 535 urban district councils, and, in the rural areas, a third tier was added by the creation of civil parish councils. In some cases the new civil parishes were coterminous with the existing ecclesiastical ones; in others, ecclesiastical parishes were either divided or united for civil purposes.[1]

The most important of the county councils created in 1888 was that for London, covering the area of the former metropolitan boards for works, but exempting the City of London which, through vociferous lobbying, managed to retain its unreformed corporation, a situation which still exists. Also retained were the existing vestries and local boards but these were abolished by the London Government Act of 1899 which replaced them with twenty-eight metropolitan borough councils. The effect of the 1888 Act was to detach a portion of north-western Kent from the historic county to make it part of the new London County Council. The areas detached were subsequently formed into the metropolitan boroughs of Deptford, Greenwich, Lewisham and Woolwich. In slight compensation, the county of Kent gained Penge from that of Surrey in 1901. Somewhat surprisingly, given its population of approaching one million, it was not divided for administrative purposes, as were the less populous counties of Lincolnshire, Suffolk and Sussex, but given a single county council and one county borough, Canterbury, which was the smallest county borough in England and Wales.

As a result of the creation of rural and urban districts in 1894 the county of Kent, excluding the county borough of Canterbury, was, after the transfer of Penge from Surrey and the formation of the municipal borough of Gillingham in 1903, divided into a total of sixty-four subsidiary administrative units:

---

1   *Modern Local Government: In Touch with the People*, London 1998, pp. 98–9.

Municipal Boroughs (18)

Bromley	Gillingham	New Romney
Chatham	Gravesend	Queenborough
Deal	Hythe	Ramsgate
Dover	Lydd	Rochester
Faversham	Maidstone	Tenterden
Folkestone	Margate	Tunbridge Wells

Rural Districts (24)

Blean	Elham	Milton
Bridge	Faversham	Romney Marsh
Bromley	Hollingbourne	Sevenoaks
Cranbrook	Hoo	Sheppey
Dartford	Isle of Thanet	Strood
Dover	Maidstone	Tenterden
East Ashford	Malling	Tonbridge
Eastry	Medway	West Ashford

Urban Districts (22)

Ashford	Herne Bay	Sittingbourne
Beckenham	Milton	Southborough
Bexley	Northfleet	Tonbridge
Broadstairs	Penge	Walmer
Cheriton	Sandgate	Whitstable
Chislehurst	Sandwich	Wrotham
Dartford	Sevenoaks	
Erith	Sheerness	

Although a few new urban districts were subsequently created in north-west Kent, as at Orpington and Swanscombe, the overall number of local authorities was reduced through mergers, the last being that of the municipal borough of Queenborough, the urban district of Sheerness and the rural district of Sheppey into the new municipal borough of Queenborough-in-Sheppey in 1968.[2] A further reduction had also taken place as a result of the creation of the Greater London Council to replace the former London and Middlesex county councils, and a reorganisation of this area into thirty-two new London Boroughs, by the London Government Act of 1963. A total of nineteen ancient parishes – those of Beckenham, Bexley, Bromley, Chelsfield, Chislehurst, Crayford, Cudham, Downe, East Wickham, Erith, Farnborough, Foots Cray, Hayes, Keston, North Cray, Orpington, St Mary Cray, St Paul's Cray and West Wickham – were trans-

---

2   The other mergers were those of Hoo and Strood rural districts, Bridge and Blean rural districts, Elham and Isle of Thanet rural districts, Faversham and Milton rural districts as the new Swale rural district, Milton and Sittingbourne urban districts, Walmer urban district with the borough of Deal, Wrotham urban district with Malling rural district, the urban districts of Cheriton and Sandgate with the borough of Folkestone, and the rural district of Medway with the boroughs of Chatham and Gillingham.

ferred from Kent to Greater London to form the new London Boroughs of
Bexley and Bromley.

Kent County Council had vigorously opposed the creation of the new Greater
London Council and the loss of areas close to London,[3] and the attitudes that
had formed its thinking on that occasion were to lead to a consistent approach to
the more general reform of local government during the remaining years of the
twentieth century: a determined effort to maintain the *status quo* whatever its
defects might be. Despite some amalgamations the number of local authorities
in England outside London still numbered 1210 in the mid-1960s: 45 county
councils, 79 county borough councils, 227 municipal borough councils, 410
rural and 449 urban districts.[4] In 1966 the government appointed a royal
commission, under the chairmanship of Lord Redcliffe-Maud, to review the
structure of English local government and to make recommendations. The
commissioners were generally not very impressed by either the two-tier structure of most local government or the division between urban county boroughs
and the predominantly rural shire counties:

> The fragmentation of England into 79 county boroughs and 45 counties, each
> with its own independent authority concerned with its own interests, has made
> the proper planning of development and transportation impossible. It is
> obvious that town and country must be planned together, as the evidence given
> to us recognised . . . Within the counties, the division of responsibility between
> county and district councils is a great weakness. The present district pattern
> is, as we have shown, irrational. But even if that were cured by the creation of
> larger districts, the weakness due to the division of responsibilities would
> remain.[5]

After discussion of the various options they concluded that:

> There is great strength in the all-purpose authority and this has been shown in
> the county borough councils. Not all of them have exploited their potential
> strength to the full, partly because their areas have been inadequate, partly
> because their organisation has been fragmented. But where a county borough
> council under strong leadership has co-ordinated its services and set out to
> achieve objectives through the use of all its powers, it has been the most effec-
> tive local government unit we have known.[6]

The commissioners thought that what was crucial was the size of such all-
purpose authorities and came to the conclusion that they should not have populations of less that 250,000. Thus, in their view, the nine county councils and
sixty-five out of seventy-nine county boroughs which had populations smaller
than this were not viable all-purpose authorities. When the commissioners

---

3   E. Melling, *History of the Kent County Council, 1889–1974*, Maidstone 1975, pp. 110–11.
4   *Royal Commission on Local Government in England*, London 1969, i, p. 21.
5   *Ibid.*, pp. 26–7.
6   *Ibid.*, p. 68.

reported, in 1969, they recommended that a series of all-purpose authorities with populations ranging from 250,000 to one million should be created in most parts of England with the exception of three areas – Merseyside, the West Midlands and parts of East Lancashire and West Yorkshire – in which they proposed a two-tier structure similar to that in Greater London. All the existing county and municipal boroughs, rural and urban districts, were to become 'local' councils, to be consulted by the new all-purpose councils and permitted, by mutual agreement, to undertake some of their functions. The report also recommended that a level of provincial government be inserted between West-minster and the local authorities. England was to be divided into eight prov-inces, the sole responsibility of the provincial government being to produce a strategic plan for the province. The report therefore proposed three levels of local government for England: (1) provincial, the primary aim of which was strategic; (2) unitaries with a two-tier structure in London and three 'metropol-itan' areas, these councils being the 'service providers'; and (3) local councils, which would be primarily consultative, but could provide services by agree-ment.[7]

Kent County Council had responded to the setting up of the Redcliffe-Maud Commission by submitting a memorandum advocating the retention of a two-tier structure of local government throughout England whilst conceding that some of the smaller boroughs, rural and urban districts should be merged.[8] Although the Commissioners were agreed on the principles of the new structure for local government, there was some disagreement over the boundaries of the new local authorities, and there were three separate proposals in respect of Kent. The majority report proposed the creation of fifty-eight unitary authorities in England with two in Kent. Canterbury and East Kent, with a total population of 499,000, would have comprised the city of Canterbury, the boroughs of Deal, Dover, Faversham, Folkestone, Hythe, Lydd, Margate, New Romney, Ramsgate, Sandwich and Tenterden, the urban districts of Ashford, Broadstairs, Herne Bay and Whitstable, the rural districts of Bridge-Blean, Dover, East Ashford, Eastry, Elham, Romney Marsh, Tenterden and West Ashford, and twenty parishes in the rural district of Swale. The commissioners thought that either Canterbury, because of its historic role, or Ashford, as an expanding community, would be appropriate administrative centres for the new unitary authority. West Kent, with a total population of 872,000, would have comprised the boroughs of Chatham, Dartford,[9] Gillingham, Gravesend, Maidstone, Queenborough-in-Sheppey, Rochester and Tunbridge Wells, the urban districts of Northfleet, Sevenoaks, Sittingbourne and Milton, Southborough, Swanscombe and Tonbridge, the rural districts of Cranbrook, Dartford, Hollingbourne, Maidstone, Malling, Seven-oaks, Strood and Tonbridge, seventeen parishes in the rural district of Swale and the parish of Frant from the county of East Sussex. Frant was to be included

---

7 *Ibid.*, pp. 28, 76, 107, 109.
8 Melling, *op. cit.*, p. 126.
9 Dartford, formerly an urban district, had been granted a municipal charter in 1933.

because it was considered to be 'so closely associated with Tunbridge Wells'. It was assumed that Maidstone would be the administrative headquarters of the new unitary authority. One of the minority reports, signed by Sir Francis Hill and R.C. Wallis, proposed the creation of sixty-three rather than fifty-eight unitary authorities in England, with three in Kent. The additional unitary authority was to be based on the Medway Towns and the south bank of the Thames and would have taken in parts of both the East and West Kent authorities proposed in the majority report. Another minority report, signed by J.L. Longland, recommended that Kent should be a single unitary authority and argued that division would destroy county loyalty since the county did 'not contain very large county boroughs which might otherwise each be a centre point for a new unitary authority'.[10] Although this argument had some validity, it ignored the fact that Kent had been divided for administrative purposes before 1814 and that the two unitary authorities proposed in the majority report had very similar geographical boundaries to the administrative areas of East and West Kent before this date. These divisions continued to be reflected in rivalry between the two halves of the county after 1814 and even when the new County Council was inaugurated in 1888–9 there were separate meetings between the representatives for the two parts of the county to discuss the nomination of aldermen.[11]

The County Council rejected all the proposals in the Redcliffe-Maud report and reaffirmed the stance it had taken in 1966: to retain a two-tier structure of county and districts, but with some amalgamation of smaller authorities. During 1970 the council entered into discussions with other local authorities in an effort to frustrate the recommendations which the Labour government had indicated it was prepared, with some modifications, to implement.[12] In June 1970 the government was defeated in a general election and the new Conservative administration was much more willing to be lobbied by the shire counties, a significant number of which were, like Kent, controlled by the Conservative Party. A new white paper advocated a two-tier structure throughout England, together with similar reforms in Wales and Scotland. County boroughs, which had been unitary authorities, were to be abolished. The two-tier structure differed in six areas of high population from that in the more rural areas. In these areas – Greater Manchester, Merseyside, South Yorkshire, Tyne and Wear, West Midlands and West Yorkshire – the counties had fewer and the districts more powers than in the shire counties, and this was also true in both Wales and Scotland.[13] Some modifications were made to the initial proposals, mostly in the number and boundaries of districts, including for Kent a decision not to include

[10] *Royal Commission on Local Government in England*, pp. 150, 154–5, 179.
[11] Melling, *op. cit.*, p. 126.
[12] *Loc. cit.*
[13] For example, metropolitan and Scottish district councils were library authorities, whereas in the English shire counties it was the county councils that had this responsibility; in Wales the county councils were the library authorities except where the districts applied to, and were granted permission by, the Secretary of State for Wales, to exercise these powers.

Gillingham in the new Medway authority, by the time the Local Government Act was passed in 1972. Kent County Council had succeeded in its primary objectives which were to retain the two-tier structure of local government which had existed since 1894, and to ensure that the historic county was not administratively divided any further than it had been by the Acts of 1888 and 1963. The County Council in fact had its powers extended as it absorbed the formerly exempt county borough of Canterbury into its jurisdiction. The one reform on which both Lord Redcliffe-Maud and the Conservative government agreed was the removal of aldermen from all local authorities apart from the City of London, which escaped all reform legislation in the twentieth century as it had in the nineteenth. Aldermen had formed a quarter of the local authorities at county-council, county-borough and municipal-borough level and had been nominated by the elected councillors. These provisions had never applied to rural and urban districts which were to provide the model for both the new county and the new district councils.

The effect of the reform of local government, fully implemented in England and Wales in 1974, and in Scotland a year later, was to produce a two-tier structure everywhere, with only five exceptions: the City of London, the Isles of Scilly, Orkney, Shetland and the Western Isles, all of which had all-purpose councils. In Wales and Scotland the changes saw the abolition of many historic counties and the creation of new counties or regions. In England most historic counties, such as Kent, survived. A few small counties, such as Herefordshire, Huntingdonshire and Rutland, were abolished, the last two surviving as district authorities. Three new non-metropolitan counties were created: Avon, Cleveland and Humberside. Some counties, such as Cheshire, Lancashire, Staffordshire and Warwickshire, lost significant areas to the new metropolitan counties, and others, such as Berkshire and Oxfordshire, had their boundaries significantly adjusted, with large parts of the former being absorbed into the latter. The main casualties were the district authorities replacing the former county boroughs. The councils of major cities such as Bristol, Derby, Kingston-upon-Hull, Leicester, Norwich, Nottingham, Plymouth, Portsmouth and Southampton were no longer to be responsible for the provision of education, libraries and social services, which were transferred to county councils, some of which only had experience of such services in rural areas. In Kent the effects were less severe. The only county borough, Canterbury, had been the smallest education authority in England.[14] The largest municipal borough, Gillingham, fought off a proposed merger with Chatham and Rochester, to remain one of the fourteen new district councils. The other thirteen districts were all amalgamations of existing borough with rural and urban district councils:

---

14 *Royal Commission on Local Government in England*, p. 22.

Ashford	Ashford UD, East Ashford RD, Tenterden MB, Tenterden RD, West Ashford RD
Canterbury	Bridge Blean RD, Canterbury CB, Herne Bay UD, Whitstable UD
Dartford	Dartford MB, Dartford RD (part), Swanscombe UD
Dover	Deal MB, Dover MB, Dover RD, Eastry RD (part), Sandwich MB
Gravesham	Gravesend MB, Northfleet UD, Strood RD (part)
Maidstone	Hollingbourne RD, Maidstone MB, Maidstone RD
Medway	Chatham MB, Rochester MB, Strood RD (part)
Sevenoaks	Dartford RD (part), Sevenoaks UD, Sevenoaks RD
Shepway	Elham RD, Folkestone MB, Hythe MB, Lydd MB, New Romney MB, Romney Marsh RD
Swale	Faversham MB, Queenborough-in-Sheppey MB, Sittingbourne and Milton UD, Swale RD
Thanet	Broadstairs UD, Eastry RD (part), Margate MB, Ramsgate MB
Tonbridge and Malling	Malling RD, Tonbridge UD, Tonbridge RD (part)
Tunbridge Wells	Cranbrook RD, Southborough UD, Tonbridge RD (part), Tunbridge Wells MB

All the new Kent districts, with the exception of Gillingham, brought rural and urban areas together in one authority, in the way that Lord Redcliffe-Maud had recommended, but on a very much smaller scale. Although it might have been the case that even in his larger unitary authorities this would have created tensions between town and countryside, it was undoubtedly so in these smaller authorities. In the case of the counties there was great resentment in the larger towns and cities that the interests of urban communities were being sacrificed to those of country-dwellers; in some of the districts where a single town or conurbation made up half or more of the area in terms of population, as was the case in Kent in the districts of Ashford, Dartford, Gravesham, Maidstone, Medway, Shepway and Tunbridge Wells, there was a strong feeling in the rural areas that they were an irrelevant appendage to that town or conurbation, contributing financially to facilities and services from which they derived little benefit.

Lord Redcliffe-Maud, and many other academic observers of local government, felt that the reforms introduced by the Local Government Act of 1972 had been an opportunity wasted. Although the number of local authorities in England had been significantly reduced to thirt-nine county and 296 district councils, 'this basic philosophy of two-tier government . . . has produced . . . a structure of local government which today bears a marked resemblance to that in existence before 1974 . . . the blurred nature of the division of responsibility for several services is all too obvious. Some like parks, museums and swimming pools, can be provided by either county or district councils.'[15] Although Kent

---

[15] J.P.R. Maud and B. Wood, *English Local Government Reformed*, London 1974, pp. 49–50.

County Council had entered into discussions with all the other local authorities in the county about the provision of services after 1974, and appropriate agency arrangements where these were permissible,[16] relations between the county and district councils after 1974 were frequently strained. There was a problem with the smaller boroughs and urban districts which had been absorbed into the new district authorities and felt themselves to be frustrated and powerless. Although these were entitled to be called town rather than parish councils, and in some cases, as at Faversham, Hythe and Sandwich, retained their mayoralties and strong civic traditions, there was a strong desire on their part to carry out more functions than they were entitled to by law, especially when many district councils declined to devolve powers that they could have done had they so wished.

By the early 1980s a political consensus had begun to emerge across all political parties at national level that local government reorganisation needed to be looked at again and that Lord Redcliffe-Maud's proposals, had they been implemented, but with somewhat smaller unitary authorities, might have worked better. The two-tier structure was criticised as inefficient and expensive, resulting in duplication and friction that might otherwise have been avoided. In the general election of 1983 the Conservatives promised, if re-elected, to abolish the Greater London Council and the metropolitan county councils in Greater Manchester, Merseyside, South Yorkshire, Tyne and Wear, West Midlands and West Yorkshire. All were controlled by the Labour Party and the Greater London Council was particularly resented because of its strident criticism of the Thatcher government. The Local Government Act of 1985 abolished all these councils, making the thirty-two London boroughs and thirty-six metropolitan districts all-purpose councils, with joint boards for services such as the police and fire prevention, where the new unitaries were felt to be too small. The fact that many of the shire counties were still controlled by the Conservative Party meant that the efforts by the Association of District Councils to persuade the government to abolish the shire as well as the metropolitan counties fell on relatively deaf ears. Successive years of poor local election results, however, resulted in the gradual reduction in the number of Conservative councillors and of councils controlled by the Conservative Party. With the change of Conservative prime minister in 1990 and the appointment of a committed local-government reformer, Michael Heseltine, as environment secretary, the outlook of the government changed. The Local Government Act of 1992 put forward proposals for the creation of unitary local authorities in both Wales and Scotland, which were imposed with relatively little consultation. The Conservatives were, however, still stronger in English local government and the Act set up a Commission to review the structure of local government in England, outside London and the metropolitan county areas, and to propose the creation of unitary authorities where there was support for them.[17] Most county councils, including Kent, opposed any changes. District councils, which had campaigned

---

16 Melling, *op. cit.*, p. 127.
17 *Modern Local Government*, pp. 98–9.

for change, began to take a different view when guidance from the Commission indicated that unitary authorities could only be recommended if they had a sufficiently large population to be viable. Although this was felt to be smaller than the 250,000 minimum recommended by Lord Redcliffe-Maud, it still meant that many existing districts would have to merge. Faced with this possibility many district councils, in Kent and elsewhere, decided they preferred the *status quo*. The Westminster cross-party consensus in favour of change was matched by a local authority cross-party consensus against change.

The Commission carried out its review of English local government on a rolling basis, county by county, producing initial and revised recommendations. What eventually emerged was relatively little change. Three county councils created in 1974 – Avon, Cleveland and Humberside – and the historic county of Berkshire were abolished. In a number of other counties certain areas were granted unitary status but not others. The criteria for making these decisions were not very clear, but the two factors that appeared to carry most weight were the level of support for the creation of a unitary authority in a particular area and whether such a creation would leave the remaining two-tier structure in that county as viable units of local government. A total of forty-five new unitary authorities was created in England. The majority of these were the larger, wholly urban, authorities that had been county boroughs before 1974. A small number were predominantly rural areas, including the former counties of Herefordshire, Rutland and (on slightly different boundaries) the East Riding of Yorkshire, which had been abolished in 1974. In some cases new unitary authorities were created for conurbations by merging existing district councils. This was the case at Brighton and Hove and in the only unitary authority created in Kent, in which the Medway towns of Chatham, Gillingham and Rochester were eventually merged into a single unitary authority with a population of 239,500. One of the anomalies of the 1973–4 reorganisation was thereby eventually rectified without seriously disturbing the viability of the county council and the remaining twelve district councils in Kent. However, the weaknesses of the local government structure as a whole, as identified by Lord Redcliffe-Maud thirty years ago, have still to be fully addressed and it is likely that further reform of local government will be contemplated in the not too distant future.

Nigel Yates

Appendix III

The General Strike in Kent, 1926

The General Strike of 1926 was a major confrontation between organised labour, whose strength had been increasing in a post-war world characterised by falling living standards and growing industrial bitterness, and the Conservative government of the day. Interpretations vary as to whether it was the inevitable outcome of growing trade union strength or a conflict engineered by hard-line members of a right-wing administration intent upon crushing the unions. The strike was precipitated by the longstanding conflict in Britain's ailing coal industry where in April 1926 the coal owners sought to solve their difficulties by increasing hours and reducing wages. This the miners rejected. The TUC saw the coal industry as a test-case for other industries and ordered a general strike in their support.

Kent in 1926 was not 'remarkable for . . . manufactures'. Dartford, Faversham, Maidstone, Northfleet, Rochester and Sittingbourne were variously engaged in the production of chemicals, bricks and cement.[1] Some large factories had grown up during the First World War in north-west Kent including Vickers' Armaments Factory at Crayford and the Wellcome Medical Works at Dartford. More than 2,000 men were employed at the Southern Railway's locomotive and carriage works at Ashford. Metropolitan Kent and the Medway Towns were more urban and industrialised than the rest of Kent which otherwise remained an essentially rural county where the majority of the workforce lay outside the manufacturing and production sector. The Kent coalfield, 'the Cinderella of the Coalfields', was uneconomic. Only Chislet and Tilmanstone collieries were working. Snowdown was closed for improvement. Sinking was still in progress at Betteshanger, while the mining villages of Nonington, Northbourne and Eythorne were not yet complete. Coalfield radicalism had yet to emerge clearly.[2] Employment in Kent was generally good. In early May Maidstone unemployment reached its lowest point since the start of the post-war depression.[3]

Politically, Kent in 1926 was a Conservative stronghold. Labour's Jack Mills, Chairman of Woolwich Arsenal Shop Stewards, won Dartford at a by-election in 1920.[4] He lost the seat in 1922, when Kent returned completely to Conservatism, but regained it the following year when Labour also won Gravesend by a

1 *Kelly's Directory of Kent* (1927), pp. 2–3, 36; F.W. Jessup, *Kent History Illustrated*, Maidstone 1973, pp. 66–7.
2 *(K)entish (E)xpress* 2.3.1926; *(D)over (E)xpress* 23.4.1926; *(K)ent (M)essenger and (G)ravesend (T)elegraph* 1.5.1926.
3 *(S)outh (E)astern (G)azette* 4.5.1926.
4 *(T)uesday (E)xpress* 15.12.1923, 8.6.1929.

majority of 119. Both seats were lost in 1924 when Kent again became solidly Conservative.[5]

Kent trade unionism was weak and lacked any militant tradition. Employees of the Maidstone and District Bus Company were almost all non-unionists. Only 20% of Maidstone's building workers were union members.[6] The rail strikes of 1911 and 1919 had had no major impact on Kent.[7] Chislet miners were involved in a disastrous six-month strike in 1924. Their defeat cost the Miners' Federation £13,000 in strike pay and saw the colliery work-force greatly reduced. A Maidstone building strike in April 1926 lasted a fortnight and gained nothing. A three-week strike by 2,000 north Kent brickmakers was more successful and 800 new members were claimed by the Workers Union as a result. Even so, local circumstances seemed against any widespread response to a major sympathetic strike.[8]

Industrial relations in Kent industries were generally good and company loyalties were strong. Lloyds Paper Mills at Sittingbourne treated the strike as their workers' annual holiday, thus avoiding loss of pay. Edenbridge farmers and season-ticket holders presented a gold watch to their stationmaster and cheques to four staff who remained at work enabling produce to be sent to market by rail. Similar presentations were made at Smeeth and Longfield. The Southern Railway Company also rewarded loyal employees.[9] Maidstone and District busmen, who maintained long-distance services, were given the proceeds of collections along their routes. Nine girls who refused to strike at Turkey Court paper mill were given silver wristlets by the management. Lloyds' claim that 'labour troubles have never . . . been known at this mill'[10] was echoed by many firms including the Eiffel Tower Printing Company at Maidstone.[11] In the absence of class conflict and strong trade union organisation, the TUC seemed unlikely to receive a strong response to its call on 4 May.[12]

When the strike call came the authorities were ready, having been preparing for eight months.[13] On the night of 30 April the Ministry of Health instructed town and county councils about the organisation of essential services under the Emergency Powers Act 1920. Kent was included in the London and Home

---

[5] *TE* 15.11.1922, 15.12.1923, 1.11.1924; F.W.S. Craig, *British Parliamentary Election Statistics, 1918–70*, Chichester 1971, pp. 79–81.

[6] *KMGT* 8.5.1926; *DE* 23.4.1926.

[7] *KE* 19.8.1911, 26.8.1911.

[8] *KE* 1.5.1926; *KMGT* 10.4.1926, 1.5.1926; *SEG* 4.5.1926; *(K)ent (M)essenger (M)aidstone (E)dition* 10.4.1926, 1.5.1926.

[9] *SEG* 11.5.1926; *KMGT* 12.6.1926; *KE* 22.5.1926.

[10] *KMGT* 12.6.1926, 19.6.1926; *(D)artford (C)hronicle* 14.5.1926; *SEG* 22.6.1926.

[11] *SEG* 11.5.1926.

[12] Rural counties have been largely ignored by researchers of the General Strike on the erroneous assumption that its impact on such counties was negligible. J.H. Porter, 'Devon and the General Strike 1926', *International Review of Social History*, 23.3.1978, pp. 333–56, and A.R. Williams, 'The General Strike in Gloucestershire', *Transactions of the Bristol and Gloucestershire Archaeological Society*, xci (1979), pp. 207–213, are the only studies of rural counties which currently exist.

[13] For examples of Government preparedness in the East Midlands, Edinburgh, and Northumberland and Durham, see *The General Strike 1926*, ed. J. Skelley, London 1976, pp. 44–5, 142–3, 174.

Counties Division under Civil Commissioner Major W. Cope MP.[14] Responsibility for recruiting volunteer labour and maintaining essential services, including coal and food supplies, was delegated to local emergency committees based on town councils and their surrounding districts.[15] At Maidstone, the emergency committee for the Maidstone, Malling and Hollingbourne district consisted of the mayor, his deputy, four aldermen and four councillors. A Haulage Committee took responsibility for transport of essential food supplies with H.T. Chapman, County Surveyor, as its Road Officer. An office for the recruitment of volunteers was created at the Corn Exchange by Colonel Sir Charles Warde, head of the Voluntary Service Committee.[16] Similar emergency committees were set up at Rochester, Gravesend, Bexley Heath, Dover, Deal and Folkestone.[17] Like Labour councillors elsewhere, Councillor W. Hyde, one of two Labour representatives on Maidstone Town Council, found himself with divided loyalties when made a member of the Emergency Committee.[18]

Manchester and Salford Trades Council had formed a Council of Action, representing over seventy trade unions, nine months before the strike.[19] In Kent the unions were almost completely unprepared. There emerged sixteen hastily formed strike committees. Some, like those at Ashford, Dartford, Margate, Tonbridge, Sittingbourne and Ramsgate, were based on trades councils and met at labour halls.[20] Others were joint strike committees created from representatives of the unions on strike. Chatham and District Central Strike Committee consisted of three members of the NUR, ASLEF and the RCA plus a member of the Workers' Union. Dover Central Strike Committee was made up of Messrs Stokes (NUR), Bass (Tramway Workers), Gooding (ASLEF), Cooney (RCA) and Newman (Miners) under the chairmanship of Mr Elks, secretary of the Kent Miners' Federation. Sidney Dye, organiser of Dover Labour Party, was also a member.[21] Ramsgate Strike Committee tried to maintain contact with the other east Kent strike committees but generally all worked in confusion and isolation.[22] At Margate, headquarters were set up in a private house. In Maidstone, when the Labour Club became too small for its meetings, the strike committee hired the Concert Hall from the Town Council.[23] No county organisation was ever formed. Northumberland and Durham Joint Strike Committee boasted the

14 *SEG* 4.5.1926.

15 See Birmingham Public Libraries, *The Nine Days in Birmingham*, Birmingham 1976, p. 1.

16 *SEG* 4.11.1926.

17 *KMME* 5.5.1926; *KMGT* 8.5.1926; *DE* 5.5.1926; *DC* 7.5.1926; *KE* 8.5.1926; *(F)olkestone (H)erald* 8.5.1926 and 15.5.1926.

18 *KMME* 12.5.1926. Alderman Percival Bower, Birmingham's first Labour Lord Mayor, found himself in the same unenviable position, Skelley, *op. cit.*, p. 209.

19 *Ibid.*, p. 160.

20 The local intelligence reports, bulletins, correspondence etc. of these strike committees are to be found in the microform of *The Archives of the T.U.C.: The Mining Crisis and the General Strike, 1925–26*, produced by Harvester Press, HD 5366.

21 *DE* 6.5.1926; *KMME* 5.5.1926.

22 TUC HD 5366 Report of Ramsgate Strike Committee to TUC 10.5.1926.

23 *Ibid.* Report of Margate Strike Committee to TUC 5.5.1926; *SEG* 11.5.1926.

support of twenty-eight councils of action and fifty-two strike committees. Ashford Central Strike Committee was composed of only eight trade-union branches, Sittingbourne nine branches, and Tonbridge Central Strike Committee twelve. All were much less effective than the local authority organisations.[24]

On the evening of 1 May naval officers and ratings were recalled to their ships at Chatham and Sheerness.[25] A destroyer anchored in the Thames off Erith Causeway and on 5 May Gravesend West Street Ferry was taken over by the Navy. Thirty armed troops were placed on guard at Dover Electricity Works. Others guarded Dover's Gas and Water works. Royal Engineers and sailors occupied the ammunition works at Slade Green, Erith, and the Bowater Paper Mills at Northfleet. The latter were commandeered by the government for making paper to print its *British Gazette*, which was transported by volunteers to London. The river frontage of the mills was protected by armed guards, barbed wire and an armed motor launch.[26] Eric Bowater was made Government Controller of Paper Supplies with considerable statutory powers. The arrival of ten tanks 'bristling with guns' in Maidstone *en route* for London on 8 May also created a stir, as did fourteen tanks and armoured cars, which passed through Swanley *en route* for the capital.[27] Generally, however, the armed forces kept a low profile and law, order and the emergency services remained in the hands of police, special constables and volunteers.

From September 1925 a number of branches of the government-encouraged Organisation for the Maintenance of Supplies (OMS) had been set up in Kent to enrol volunteers. When the strike began these handed their members to the local Emergency Committees.[28] At Hythe the OMS office was used to enrol more than 250 volunteers since the local Emergency Committee had no premises.[29] In all nearly half a million men and women volunteered throughout the country. There is no complete record of the number who came forward in Kent. The figure was, however, high. More than 500 had volunteered in Dover by 4 May

---

[24] TUC HD 5366 Report of Ashford Central Strike Committee 11.5.1926; Reports of Sittingbourne and Tonbridge Central Strike Committees to TUC 10.5.1926.

[25] *SEG* 4.5.1926; *KMGT* 8.5.1926.

[26] *DC* 7.5.1926; *SEG* 11 and 18.5.1926; *KMGT* 8.5.1926, 5.6.1926; *KE* 8.5.1926; *DE* 5.5.1926. W.J. Reader, *Bowater: A History*, Cambridge 1981, pp. 48–51. I am indebted to Alan Booth for this reference and for his comments upon the text.

[27] *(K)entish (T)imes (D)aily (B)ulletin* 10.5.1926; *SEG* 11.5.1926.

[28] *KMGT* 29.5.1926; *FH* 8.5.1926. The OMS handed over at least 2,563 personnel in Kent upon the declaration of a state of emergency. They had enrolled as follows:

Broadstairs	100	Gravesend	156	Tonbridge	205
Bromley	218	Margate	205	Tunbridge Wells	504
Canterbury	375	Sandwich	140	Westgate	238
Deal & Walmer	250	Sidcup	172		
				Total:	2,563

PRO HO 45/12336/2130 listed by Chris Wrigley, 'The General Strike in Local History, Part 1: The Government's Volunteers', *The Local Historian*, volume 16, Number 1 (February 1984), p. 44. The omission of such places as Maidstone, Folkestone and Dover suggests that the list is incomplete.

[29] *FH* 8.5.1926.

and 300–400 at Ramsgate by 11 May. In west Kent, including Chislehurst, Beckenham, Bromley, Sidcup, Orpington, West Wickham and the Crays, there were 1,714 by the same date. Five-hundred-and-nine volunteers had enrolled at Maidstone by 12 May.[30] Sixty out of 283 Sevenoaks volunteers acted as bus drivers and conductors including J.A. Rogers, Chairman of the Sevenoaks Bench, and his two sons. Maidstone's volunteers also included many drivers. At Folkestone forty volunteered their own cars for service. The volunteer drivers came mostly from the middle class, confident in its power, its social position and the rightness of its views.[31] Other volunteers served on the railways. A group of high-ranking army and naval officers under Colonel Thompson re-opened the rail service to London from Maidstone East. At Ashford an earl's son was a temporary fireman. Captain F.R. Roberts, managing director of the Aylesford Pottery Company and a member of Malling District Council, and J. Elliott, managing director of the Redcar Company at Tunbridge Wells, were other notable volunteer firemen. The Hon. G. Harris, only son of Lord and Lady Harris, served as a porter at a station near London.[32] In some places such class intervention violently polarised the two sides in the strike. In Kent the reaction to 'drivers and porters in plus fours' was one of amusement rather than anger. Whether volunteer locomotive engineers encouraged public travel is questionable, particularly after a Dover Labour Councillor issued a reminder that, during the 1919 Rail Strike, volunteer drivers had wrecked seven engines in a week.[33]

Kent, like Devon, had more volunteers than were needed. At Maidstone only thirty of the 509 volunteers were ever used. Unskilled manual workers were, however, hard to find. Some unemployed acted as 'blacklegs' but to keep the cross-channel ferries running seventy Cambridge University undergraduates and their chauffeurs worked for the Southern Railway in Dover docks. Organiser of the 'Dover Dockers' was Henry Duckworth of Trinity College who described their experiences between 6 and 14 May. Sleeping in Pullman cars at Dover Marine Station the students kept the port open, loading and unloading passenger and cargo vessels. While volunteer train drivers were received with amusement the 'Dover Dockers' were not. The docks were picketed and some of the casual 'blacklegs' were attacked.[34]

In addition to volunteers there was also a large force of special constables. By the close of the strike 1,300 had been enrolled in the Ashford Division alone. Maidstone recruited over 300 and each surrounding village had its 'specials'. Bearsted and Thurnham registered over 100 and 50 were sworn in at Malling. There were 200 at Tunbridge Wells and 42 enlisted at Folkestone on 4 May alone. Wrotham's 42 'specials' were 'chiefly prominent residents'. Four had

30 *DE* 5.5.1926; *TE* 11 and 18.5.1926; *KMME* 12.5.1926; *KTDB* 11.5.1926.

31 *DE* 8.5.1926; *KTDB* 11.5.1926; *KMME* 12.5.1926; *FH* 15.5.1926; Reader, *op. cit.*, p. 49.

32 *DE* 7.5.1926; *KMME* 8.5.1926; *KE* 22.5.1926.

33 *DE* 5.5.1926; *KE* 22.5.1926.

34 *KMGT* 15.5.1926; Porter, *op. cit.*, p. 335; K. Laybourn, *The General Strike of 1926*, Manchester 1993, pp. 55–6, 145–6. Duckworth's diary is now deposited in the British Library of Political and Economic Science.

served during the 1919 rail strike. One of the first recruits was the rector, A.S. Pascoe.[35] Gravesend's 206 special constables included retired army officers, solicitors, tradesmen and seventy-one Trinity House pilots. Even with this large force the local emergency committees on 11 May were urgently recruiting territorials and ex-servicemen for the Special Constabulary Reserve, a paid full-time force.[36] A formidable opposition thus confronted the Kent strikers.

On 1 May miners throughout Britain found themselves locked out until they agreed to wage reductions.[37] Kent's 2,000 miners had already been locked out on 30 April. The Kent Mine Workers' Association, led by F.W. Twigger of Chislet branch, had become increasingly militant after 1920. There were strikes and lock outs in 1923 and 1924. Kent miners now prepared for a bitter struggle, which was to continue until November.[38]

On the afternoon of 1 May the TUC overwhelmingly voted to strike in support of the miners on the night of 3–4 May.[39] It proposed to strike in 'waves', a strategy which it was hoped would place increasing pressure on the Government and produce a satisfactory compromise before a complete general strike was necessary. The first 'wave' consisted of transport workers, printers, building workers, except those employed constructing housing and hospitals, and iron, steel and heavy chemical workers. Electricity and gas workers were to co-operate in ceasing to supply power but not light, although this was technically impossible. Individual unions and strike committees were left to interpret these instructions in their own way and confusion reigned.[40]

The Kent papermakers' and printers' unions were traditionally strong but their response was mixed. Workers in the Snodland and Aylesford paper mills struck immediately. So, too, did those in the Imperial Mills at Gravesend. Reed's Mills at Tovil and New Hythe also closed as did the mills in the Crays. At Sittingbourne 1,300 members of the Amalgamated Society of Papermakers and the National Society of Paperworkers brought Lloyds Mills to a standstill. Many paperworkers acted on their own initiative and not on TUC orders.[41] On the other hand, at Maidstone, Springfield Mill continued with only two men on strike as did Turkey Mill where the male trade unionists stayed in and only 100 girls obeyed the strike call.[42]

In printing the same situation prevailed. Printers belonging to the Typographical Association (TA) struck at Maidstone, Ashford, Gravesend and Dover. Alabaster Passmore, the Maidstone printing works, closed, as did the Amalga-

35 *TE* 11.5.1926 and 18.5.1926; *DE* 8.5.1926; *KMGT* 15.5.1926; *SEG* 18.5.1926.
36 *KMGT* 22 and 29.5.1926; *KTDB* 11.5.1926.
37 M. Morris, *The British General Strike, 1926*, London 1973, p. 3.
38 *KE* 8.12.1923, 8.5.1926; *KMGT* 1.5.1926; *DE* 21.5.1926; *DE* 21.5.1926; R.P. Arnot, *The Miners: Years of Struggle*, London 1953, pp. 245, 328.
39 Morris, *op. cit.*, p. 4.
40 Skelley, *op. cit.*, pp. 222–3.
41 *KMME* 5.5.1926; *KE* 8.5.1926; *SEG* 11.5.1926; TUC Intelligence Report, Sittingbourne, 9.5.1926; PRO CAB 27/331 London and Home Counties, Home Office Situation Reports, 4 and 5 May 1926.
42 *KMME* 8.5.1926; *SEG* 11.5.1926, 22.6.1926.

mated Press Ltd at Gravesend. NATSOPA members shut down Buckland Mill at Dover and all printers struck at Tunbridge Wells except for a few non-union men. Maidstone's Eiffel Tower works, with only two out of ten trade unionists on strike, was unaffected. All Margate and Canterbury printers remained at work.[43]

In the newspaper industry, despite a government undertaking to protect printers against victimisation, a considerable number of TA members obeyed the strike call. At Folkestone every member ceased work except one. The response was insufficient, however, to prevent publication of more limited editions of the *Kent Messenger* (Maidstone and Gravesend editions), the *Kentish Express*, the *Tuesday Express*, the *South Eastern Gazette*, the *Dover Express*, the *Folkestone Herald* and the *Chatham, Rochester and Gillingham News*. The *Dartford Chronicle and Kentish Times* published a daily bulletin before returning to a fuller edition. Three apprentices typeset the *Folkestone Herald*. Much of the news printed came from BBC broadcasts. A powerful wireless had been installed at the *Dover Express* offices since 1922. In this way much detailed local information, often disadvantageous to strikers, continued to be read.[44]

The government also won the battle over the national press. London dailies were absent in Chatham and Folkestone on 4 May but by 5 May Paris editions of the *Daily Mail* had been dropped by aeroplane, and the government's *British Gazette* was being distributed throughout Kent by car. In west Kent alone, volunteers distributed over 8,000 copies to newsagents during the strike.[45] By contrast the TUC's *British Worker* was hard to obtain. The only strike bulletin published was the *Dover and East Kent Worker* produced by Dover Strike Committee. Attempts to produce bulletins at Chatham and Ramsgate failed. Thus, while in major industrial cities strikers were able to combat much government propaganda, except on the radio, by closing down the press, this was impossible in Kent.[46]

The response of Kent's transport workers varied as it did nationally. Erith watermen came out on 4 May. 150 Rochester stevedores also joined the strike and barge crews ceased work at the Medway cement works.[47] On the roads the situation fluctuated. In the Medway towns, where most of the 187 tramwaymen were members of the Workers' Union, the trams halted. Trams also stopped at Bexley Heath, Woolwich, Dartford, Gravesend and Northfleet. Half of Maid-

43 *DE* 5.5.1926; *KE* 8 and 15.5.1926; *SEG* 11.5.1926; TUC Intelligence Report 7.5.1926; CAB 27/331 Home Office Situation Report 4.5.1926.

44 *DE* 7.5.1926 and 14.5.1926; *KMGT* 8.5.1926; *FH* 8.5.1926 and 15.5.1926; *KTDB* 5 and 11.5.1926; J. Whyman, 'The General Strike: Its Impact on Life in the Medway Towns', *Cantium*, Volume 3, Number 4 (Winter 1971/2), p. 89.

45 *Ibid.*, p. 91; *KMME* 5.5.1926 and 12.5.1926; *FH* 8.5.1926; CAB 27/331 Home Office Situation Report 7.5.1926.

46 Reports of Gravesend Strike Committee 6.5.1926; Sheerness and District Strike Committee 8.5.1926 and 11.5.1926; Chatham and District Central Strike Committee 11.5.1926; TUC Route Report 6.5.1926; *DE* 11.5.1926; Skelley, *op. cit.*, p. 161.

47 *SEG* 11.5.1926; *DC* 17.5.1926; *KMGT* 7.5.1926; Whyman, *op. cit.*, pp. 91–2; CAB 27/331 Home Office Situation Report 4.5.1926.

stone's tramwaymen were trade unionists but only fifteen out of sixty-five left work. Threats by the Maidstone Strike Committee to call out electricity workers, if the council did not cut supplies to the trams, had no effect. Some Maidstone strikers were returning to work by 6 May. All Maidstone tramwaymen were back by 13 May. Erith tramwaymen returned later. At Dover, where tramwaymen were led by the socialist war veteran Alfred Bass, the strike was more complete and more bitter. Three inspectors and a female clerk attempted to keep a skeleton service running. An ultimatum was issued on 11 May threatening dismissal if the men did not return and a subscription was opened for loyal tramwaymen after the strike.[48]

If the Kent tramway stoppage was only partial, the response of Kent busmen was negligible. Maidstone and District services to London, Dartford, Chatham and Gravesend continued as normal. Gravesend and District buses also ran. Gravesend buses to Dartford enabled London commuters to catch the electric train. They also replaced Gravesend and Northfleet trams. Normal bus services also operated in Ashford, Cranbrook, Chatham, Folkestone, Deal and other parts of east Kent. Volunteer drivers conducted a normal Redcar and Autocar service between Tonbridge and London. 'Kent is being particularly well-served by the motor bus services which are running as usual,' noted the *Kentish Express* on 8 May. The successful maintenance of a bus service had an adverse effect upon Kent tramwaymen.[49] Apart from at Plymouth and Exeter the Devon experience was the same. While Newcastle's road-transport strike often prevented non-strikers from reaching work, Kent's road-transport strike was a failure. Moreover the government could maintain food supplies by road. By the end of the strike forty-two food lorries an hour were passing through Lenham carrying provisions from Dover and Folkestone to London and beyond.[50]

In Kent, as in Devon and Gloucestershire, it was the railwaymen, often accused of not wanting the strike, who were among its most resolute supporters. Kent railwaymen, like railwaymen nationally, were the most heavily unionised of the transport workers.[51] At an NUR recruiting campaign at the Ashford Works in February, E. Browning, the District Organiser, had promised 'if the miners have to fight the railwaymen will not be found wanting'.[52] In most Kent branches the NUR response was practically total. ASLEF members reacted similarly. 'The response of railwaymen nationally and in this district is magnificent,' claimed the Dover Central Strike Committee, 'many who did not strike when the issue was their own wages and conditions have this time answered the call'. Even thirty men at Whitstable, 'a black spot in the 1919 Rail Strike', left

48 *KMME* 5, 8 and 12.5.1926; *SEG* 11 and 18.5.1926; *DC* 7.5.1926 and 21.5.1926; *KE* 8.5.1926; *DE* 6.5.1926, 11.5.1926 and 21.5.1926.
49 *KMME* 8.5.1926; *KMGT* 8.5.1926 and 12.5.1926; *FH* 8.5.1926; *TE* 4.5.1926; *SEG* 11.5.1926; Whyman, *op. cit.*, p. 91; TUC Intelligence Report Gravesend 7.5.1926; *DC* 7.5.1926.
50 *KMME* 8.5.1926 and 15.5.1926; Porter, *op. cit.*, pp. 341–4; A. Mason, *The General Strike in the North East*, Hull 1970, p. 76.
51 Porter, *op. cit.*, pp. 336–41; Williams, *op. cit.*, p. 208; Laybourn, *op. cit.*, p. 67.
52 *KE* 23.2.1926.

work, and strike committees at Sittingbourne, Chatham, Margate, Ramsgate and Sheerness reported that the railwaymen were 'solid'. The exception was the railway clerks. At Ashford, Chatham and Dartford they responded well. At Canterbury and Hythe they did not strike at all. Clerks at Sittingbourne, Teynham and Newington, including the chairman of the strike committee, struck on 4 May but returned on 6 May.[53]

Nevertheless on 4 May at Maidstone, the Medway Towns, Ramsgate, Cranbrook, Deal, Lydd and elsewhere, stations were deserted and few trains ran. Some rural stations such as Tenterden, Hawkhurst, Smeeth and Longfield continued but the rest came to a standstill. At Ashford the stationmaster worked the signals. Only the stationmaster, chief clerk and a signalman remained on duty at Tunbridge Wells. Marden's stationmaster struck with four platelayers. Two or three trains continued to run daily on the North Kent line but no goods trains left Chatham or Gillingham in the first week of the strike. Canterbury strikers even included some non-unionists. Without rail transport hundreds travelled to London or to work locally by lorry, charabanc and car. School transport was organised by local garages.[54] The support of railwaymen also had wider ramifications. On 4 May a strike of 2,000 workers closed the locomotive and carriage works at Ashford, and Dover Packet Yard. Of 400–500 strikers at Folkestone, 300 were railwaymen who worked at the harbour.[55]

The Kent rail strike, however, was not sustained as it was in the major industrial centres.[56] Three trains ran from Folkestone to London on 5 May. The Canterbury to Whitstable service was restarted by George Pearson, a retired engine driver, on 6 May while S. Dickinson of Ryarsh, another retired locomotive engineer, recommenced the service between Ashford, Maidstone and London. Increased goods and passenger services were claimed on 6 and 7 May. On 10 May twenty-seven trains ran from Maidstone. Not all trains run by volunteers were well used. A correspondent to the *Kent Messenger*, who travelled between Maidstone and Dartford, found large crowds at Gravesend and Dartford but during the rest of the journey the train picked up only twenty passengers. In east Kent a further twenty-three passenger trains passed through Folkestone on 12 May.[57] While some were manned by volunteers it was clear that railwaymen were 'drifting back throughout Kent' and particularly to small rural stations.[58] By 10 May 150 men, one-third of all staff, had returned in the Canterbury area and Lenham, Staplehurst, Marden, Cranbrook and Paddock Wood stations were

53 *DE* 5.5.1926; *KE* 8.5.1926; TUC Intelligence Reports: Chatham and District 7.5.1926 and 11.5.1926, Canterbury 7.5.1926, Ramsgate, 10.5.1926, Sittingbourne 7.5.1926, 9.5.1926 and 11.5.1926, Margate 7.5.1926, Dartford 9.5.1926; TUC District Reports: Margate Strike Committee 5.5.1926, Sheerness Strike Committee 10.5.1926, Sittingbourne Joint Strike Committee 7.5.1926, 9.5.1926 and 11.5.1926.
54 *KE* 8.5.1926, 15.5.1926 and 22.5.1926; *DE* 5.5.1926; *KMGT* 8.5.1926; *TE* 4.5.1926 and 11.5.1926; *SEG* 11.5.1926; *KMME* 5.5.1926 and 8.5.1926; *DC* 7.5.1926.
55 *KMME* 8.5.1926; *DE* 5.5.1926; Ashford Strike Committee 11.5.1926.
56 See Skelley, *op. cit.*, pp. 134, 303–7; Mason, *op. cit.*, p. 77.
57 *KMME* 15.5.1926; *DE* 6.5.1926 and 8.5.1926; *KE* 8.5.1926 and 15.5.1926; *FH* 8.5.1926; *SEG* 11.5.1926; *DC*14.5.1926.
58 *KTDB* 11.5.1926; Home Office Situation Report 10.5.1926.

again working. An urgent message from Maidstone Strike Committee to the TUC warned of wavering unless a speaker of national importance was sent immediately to boost morale. While strikers in the railway strongholds of Ashford, Dover, Folkestone, Faversham and Ramsgate stayed out until the end, others in many rural areas had returned before the strike was over.[59]

Kent's building trade workers, as in Devon, responded variedly to the strike call. Only 'a few' at Maidstone joined the first wave of strikers. Work on the Maidstone and District Bus Company's extension ceased but continued uninterrupted at both local hospitals. In Chatham 200 members of the building workers' union stopped work. At Tunbridge Wells masons, bricklayers and some carpenters struck, but not painters. At Deal practically all union members joined the strike but they were few in number. Elsewhere in east Kent the response was poor. At Folkestone, where union membership had been falling, only thirty-seven men struck. At Hythe building work was unaffected. Canterbury and Margate building workers did not strike at all. At Ramsgate the local trade-union secretary of the Woodcutting Machinists was reported to be 'still at work'.[60]

In Kent's large factories the reaction to the strike call was stronger, since trade unionism was more deeply rooted. Workers at the Connaught Coachworks in Dover ceased work within half an hour. Two-hundred trade unionists struck at Short Brothers in Rochester and others closed the engineering firm of Aveling and Porter. It was in Metropolitan Kent, however, that the strike was most seriously felt. The ethos here was different. The Home Office reported 'nearly a thousand engineers' on strike at Dartford. At Gravesend 'a complete stoppage' was claimed 'with no factories working . . . in this Tory area'. Erith factories too were 'practically at a standstill' with few staff and apprentices at work. One source reported that 6,000 workers were on strike and that industrial Thameside was lying idle. Certainly no cement was being made at Northfleet, Swanscombe or Greenhithe while at Crayford 'a practically 100% strike' closed the Vickers' Works. Many workers from Woolwich Arsenal came out against the instructions of the Workers' Union. To the surprise of Kent's strike committees, Chatham and Sheerness dockyards were never called out although the government was landing wheat and flour at both.[61]

Events at Deptford illustrate most clearly the great difference between metropolitan and provincial Kent. The organised labour movement was deeply rooted in Deptford's community life. Deptford and Greenwich Trades Council had 14,000 affiliates. The Labour Party had 1,700 individual members plus 8,000 Co-op affiliates and received the highest poll in municipal elections throughout

[59] *TE* 11.5.1926; *KE* 15.5.1926; TUC Intelligence Report Maidstone 11.5.1926.

[60] Porter, *op. cit.*, pp. 345–6; *KMME* 5.5.1926 and 8.5.1926; *SEG* 4.5.1926 and 11.5.1926; *KE* 8.5.1926 and 15.5.1926; *FH* 11.5.1926 and 15.5.1926; TUC Intelligence Report Margate 7.5.1926.

[61] Whyman, *op. cit.*, pp. 91–2; TUC Intelligence Report Chatham and District 5.5.1926 and 6.5.1926; *DE* 5.5.1926 and 7.5.1926; *DC* 7.5.1926; *SEG* 11.5.1926; *KMGT* 8.5.1926; *KMME* 15.5.1926; CAB 27/331 Home Office Situation Report 4.5.1926; TUC Kent Area Report 6.5.1926.

London. Local dockers, railwaymen, road transport workers and most iron workers responded to the call of the Joint Strike Committee. The London district of the AEU did not wait for the TUC's 'second wave' instructions but in the large local factories struck in the first week. Mass picketing meant that by 10 May 'every industrial establishment in the borough was out'.[62] Moreover, since Deptford was one of the London Labour councils which refused to co-operate with the government's emergency arrangements, no volunteers were enrolled and the issue of permits for the movement of food and coal passed to the Strike Committee.[63] In neighbouring Lewisham the response to the strike also exceeded expectations.[64]

When the power workers were ordered to strike on 12 May, Kent's gas and electricity power supplies remained normal. Dover electricity labourers remained at work as did gas and electricity workers at Folkestone and the Medway Towns. Labourers at Gravesend power station struck but the engineers stayed on and the electricity and gas works continued production. When the men at Tunbridge Wells Electricity Works, which supplied the surrounding 400 square miles, decided not to strike they were personally thanked by the mayor. Thirty out of eighty trade-union labourers struck at Maidstone Electricity Works but supplies were unaffected. Only in Metropolitan Kent was there any disruption. There was a brief strike at Woolwich, which ran its own municipal electricity undertaking. ETU members came out at the London Electricity Supply Company's station at Deptford and at Greenwich Power station, which supplied the LCC tram system. Technical staff, however, stayed in and the government continued to operate these stations with naval ratings.[65]

The government and some trade union-leaders feared that the strike might produce a challenge to the constitution. Far from being revolutionary, Kent strike committees were anxious to keep strikers peacefully occupied. Ashford and Faversham socials were crowded with railwaymen and their families. Ramsgate strike committee organised a football match with local police. Chislet miners played cricket against Ramsgate police. Ramsgate sands, packed with striking miners and their families, bore a holiday appearance. 'Open air sports . . . are being provided. All workers involved being kept off the streets . . .,' reported Sittingbourne strike committee. Dover council provided free concerts at the Town Hall and seafront and the secretary of Dover Labour Party led the audience in the National Anthem, which was also sung by striking Medway tramwaymen. Local strike committees constantly emphasised the need for order. Chatham strike committee even 'policed' its own meetings.[66]

---

[62] Skelley, op. cit., pp. 262–4.

[63] Ibid, p. 269.

[64] Ibid. pp. 264–5.

[65] DE 10.5.1926 and 11.5.1926; KE 8.5.1926; KMME 8.5.1926 and 15.5.1926; SEG 11.5.1926; Skelley, op. cit., pp. 269–70.

[66] TUC District Reports: Chatham 5.5.1926, Ramsgate 10.5.1926; Whyman, op. cit., p. 92; TUC Intelligence Report, Sittingbourne Strike Committee 7.5.1926; TE 11.5.1926; KE 8.5.1926 and 15.5.1926; DE 10.5.1926; DC 14.5.1926.

In these circumstances violent clashes between strikers and police were much fewer than in parts of London, the Midlands and the North.[67] The Kent coalfield remained peaceful with the miners working in their gardens. Angry exchanges took place on 10 May between strikers and blacklegs, with special constables in attendance, at Folkestone Harbour Station. Violence in Kent was otherwise limited to Dover, where the 2,800 strikers included a thousand miners and large numbers of railwaymen, and to urban–industrial Metropolitan Kent.[68]

At Dover, solidarity was increased by mass meetings and a march of strikers to Folkestone on 7 May, which was returned by Folkestone strikers three days later. Conflict centred on the tramway service and the Marine Station. When volunteers attempted to run a service, one tram was disabled. The driver of a second tram ran into a third, bringing the experiment to a premature halt. At Dover Marine unemployed men had been recruited as porters. They were protected to and from work by a police escort. Continuation of a limited Cross Channel service heightened the tension. On 8 May there were scuffles between 'blacklegs' and pickets which intensified the following morning. Two men were taken to hospital but a strong police escort ensured that the casuals reached the pier. When they left in the evening they were chased and assaulted as they reached their homes. The attack led to five convictions. There were other convictions for a separate attack on a 'blackleg' railway guard and signalman.[69]

The Dover disturbances were not typical of provincial Kent. Maidstone was 'quiet and orderly'. Thanet remained 'almost normal'.[70] Only as the strike drew nearer to London did attitudes change. Maidstone lorry drivers transporting food were roughly handled by London pickets. In north-west Kent frustration at the failure of the road transport strike produced a violent attack on a Maidstone and District bus near Farningham and on another, run by volunteers, at St Paul's Cray. On both occasions police wielded truncheons. Erith strikers stopped a coal lorry destined for Crayford waterworks and there was a serious disturbance at Foots Cray. When Waldron Smithers, MP for Chislehurst, visited the latter to put the government's case, a striker drove his fist through his windscreen. His meeting at Swanley was abandoned on police advice.[71] Hubert Radford of the Marine Workers' Union was imprisoned 'for making a speech likely to cause disaffection' at Gravesend. There were, however, no widespread arrests of strike leaders as in some industrial parts of Britain.[72] The violence was not all one-

[67] See C.L. Mowat, *Britain Between the Wars*, London 1955, pp. 317–18. M. Morris, *The General Strike*, Harmondsworth 1976, p. 407; Mason, *op. cit.*, pp. 42, 66, 71–3; Skelley, *op. cit.*, pp. 115–16, 133–4, 182, 235–6, 245–6.

[68] *KE* 8.5.1926 and 15.5.1926; *SEG* 11.5.1926; *KMME* 8.5.1926; *FH* 11.5.1926; *DE* 5, 7.5.1926 and 11.5.1926.

[69] *DE* 7.5.1926, 8.5.1926, 10.5.1926, 11.5.1926 and 14.5.1926; *TE* 11.5.1926; *KE* 10.5.1926, 15.5.1926 and 25.5.1926; *KMGT* 15.5.1926.

[70] *SEG* 11.5.1926; *KMGT* 8.5.1926 and 15.5.1926; Whyman, *op. cit.*, p. 93.

[71] *DC* 14.5.1926; *KMME* 8.5.1926; *KMGT* 15.5.1926; *KTDB* 14.5.1926.

[72] *KMGT* 15.5.1926 and 22.5.1926; Skelley, *op. cit.*, pp. 205, 221–2, 305.

sided. In an attack on the headquarters of Gravesend Strike Committee, all the windows were smashed.[73]

In Deptford, clashes between police and populace were not unknown in normal times. Attempts to restart the tram and bus services caused serious rioting. On 7 May volunteers and British Fascists under police protection attempted to reopen the LCC Tram Depot at New Cross. Some 2,000–3,000 people gathered. Mounted police tried to clear the crowds but were forced to abandon the attempt. Rioting spread and lasted well into the night. No further effort was made to restart the trams until the strike was over. Next day another riot with fifteen arrests was caused by police attempts to arrest a speaker, who called on the crowd for protection.[74] Disorder reached its peak when steel-helmeted Special Reserves and mounted police tried to escort a bus driven by a university student:

> Stones rained down from . . . tenement buildings . . . Mounted . . . police were unseated. Running fights took place with foot police and a great crowd over-turned the vehicle which caught fire . . .[75]

When the strike was abandoned on 12 May, many Kent strikers had already returned to work. The exceptions were railwaymen at Ashford, Chatham, Sittingbourne, Dover and Sheerness; tramwaymen at Bexley, Dover, Dartford and Deptford; and some Maidstone and Folkestone printers.[76] Workers at the Medway Milling Company and Lenworth Mills left their union rather than join the second 'wave' of strikers. As the strike collapsed, engineers at Maidstone and elsewhere also refused to strike.[77] This situation differed from most industrial areas, where the strike was still solid.[78]

At first, the Canterbury and Ashford railwaymen thought they had won. Only when victimisation followed did the truth dawn. When the Southern Railway Company announced that at first there would be only a limited re-engagement of strikers, and decisions in many individual cases would be reserved, the rail strike resumed as the railwaymen demanded to return in a body.[79] Tramwaymen and building workers were only allowed back as required. Dover and Bexley tramwaymen were ordered to leave their union before reinstatement could be considered. Printers at Alabaster Passmore were re-engaged on a day-to-day basis. The *South Eastern Gazette* refused to employ its printers unless they

---

[73] *KMGT* 22.5.1926.

[74] Skelley, *op. cit.*, pp. 268, 273.

[75] *Ibid.*, p. 274.

[76] *KE* 15.5.1926; *SEG* 18.5.1926 and 25.5.1926; *KMME* 12.5.1926; TUC District Reports Ashford, Sheerness and Chatham 11.5.1926.

[77] *KMME* 12.5.1926; *SEG* 18.5.1926; *KE* 15.5.1926 and 19.5.1926; *DE* 12.5.1926; *TE* 17.5.1926 and 18.5.1926; CAB 27/331 Home Office Situation Report 12.5.1926.

[78] See Skelley, *op. cit.*, pp. 137, 152, 166–8, 187–8; Mason, *op. cit.*, pp. 90–1.

[79] *KMGT* 15.5.1926; *DE* 14.5.1926.

became non-unionists. One Maidstone printing works, which had been completely unionised when the strike began, was declared an 'open shop'. In contrast the Labour Council at Deptford reinstated its employees unconditionally. LCC Tramways settled with its tramwaymen on 14 May after two unsuccessful attempts to open the depot with volunteer labour had led to further rioting.[80] Only the Kent miners fought on. Despite collections for their families, Chislet and Snowdown miners resumed on the old terms in June. The remainder finally returned with the other coalfields in November, Kent coal owners having refused to negotiate.[81]

Members of Bridge Women's Institute greeted the end of the strike with the National Anthem and a minute of silent thanks. Many doubtless echoed the view of A.P. Margetts, Chairman of Maidstone Conservative Association, that during the past nine days his party had been the sole barrier 'between what amounts to revolution and properly organised government'.[82] Excluding metropolitan and north-west Kent, at a most conservative estimate there had been some 15,000 men on strike. Many others, like the Wellcome workers at Dartford, had been stood down as a result of the dispute. Yet in much of Kent there was 'little to indicate that a serious industrial upheaval prevailed'.[83] Beyond the curtailment of newspapers and public transport, most places, like Tenterden, were 'quite unaffected by the Strike'. Light and power supplies were uninterrupted. Most local industries continued under almost normal conditions. There were regular postal deliveries and places of amusement stayed open. Ramsgate trawlers were kept in harbour by coal rationing but only Sheerness reported any serious food shortage.[84] 'Economise! Food must become scarce,' warned the *Kentish Express* at the start of the strike.[85] The advice was unnecessary. Milk was brought from the emergency depot at Hyde Park to Dartford and Bexley Heath. Milk, meat and fish were landed at Folkestone and conveyed inland by road.[86]

The food shortage at Sheerness and elsewhere was in part due to the confusion created by the varying practices of strike committees over issuing permits for the transport of essentials. Dartford bakers travelled to Northumberland Heath to get permits to transport flour. Chatham Strike Committee claimed to be issuing permits 'judiciously' but at Sheerness the requests of local tradesmen were often not met at all. At Maidstone, while the strike committee dealt with local permits, more distant transport was left to the TUC. The total confusion

[80] *TE* 17.5.1926, 18.5.1926 and 6.7.1926; *DE* 28.5.1926; *SEG* 18.5.1926; *KE* 22.5.1926; Skelley, *op. cit.*, p. 274.
[81] *KE* 1.6.1926, 8.6.1926 and 6.7.1926; Arnot, *op. cit.*, pp. 493, 506; CAB 27/331 Home Office Situation Report 14.6.1926.
[82] *KMGT* 8.5.1926 and 22.5.1926; *(K)entish (T)imes* 19.5.1926.
[83] Whyman, *op. cit.*, p. 93; *KMME* 8.5.1926.
[84] *KMGT* 8.5.1926 and 15.5.1926; *KE* 15.5.1926; *DE* 10.5.1926; Report of Sheerness Joint Strike Committee 8.5.1926.
[85] *KE* 8.5.1926.
[86] *KE* 8.5.1926 and 15.5.1926; *KT* 7.5.1926.

was highlighted in a Kent Area Report of 6 May,[87] which clearly showed the TUC and NUR to be offering conflicting advice.

During the dispute the attitudes of Anglican and nonconformist clergy varied. Some, like the vicar of Swanscombe, were conciliatory. Others were more partisan. The vicar of Maidstone condemned the strike as 'the Devil's Work'. His Hythe colleague described it as 'the German Method'. The vicar of Yalding said public prayers 'for the defeat of an attempted break up of authority'. A peace formula, proposed by the Archbishop of Canterbury, was supported by the Free Churches but not the government. In view of such feelings, striking Faversham railwaymen and their families held their own service at the *Gem Picture Palace*. The lesson was the parable of the Good Samaritan since the railwaymen and others were 'acting as Good Samaritans to the miners'.[88]

There was a short-term escalation of unemployment as a result of the strike. Registered unemployed in the Maidstone District increased from 747 on 3 May to 1,291 on 17 May. By the end of the month, however, the figure had fallen to 995. Payment of relief to strikers was illegal. Dover guardians paid only £95 15s 10d to 358 members of miners' families. Nothing was paid to the men. Erith guardians, who were dealing with 1,500 cases daily by 14 May, made illegal payments to the value of £1,181 to strikers. Deptford guardians ran up an even larger bill for their generous, if illegal, relief payments. The defeat of 1926 also brought severe damage to the morale, membership and finances of an already feeble Kent trade-union movement.[89] Perhaps the most important outcome of the strike in Kent, however, was the county's participation in the short-lived, political reaction that brought the return of the second Labour Government in 1929. If only briefly, there was a transfer of some working-class votes from the Conservative Party. At Dartford, where the strike had been strong, Jack Mills again became Labour MP with a majority of 10,303. In Chatham, F. Markham was elected with a Labour majority of 786. Ashford, for the first and only time in its history, returned a Liberal, Revd R. M. Kedward. The change was short-lived. The Conservative monopoly was restored in the panic election of 1931 and remained undisturbed until the general election of 1945.[90] In Kent, as in Devon, the response of trade unionists to the strike was surprisingly good. Kent trade unionism, however, was weak and the number of strikers involved was often too small to have any major effect. 'The men are unorganised and remain at work,' reported Sittingbourne District on 9 May. In an essentially rural county the class consciousness, which brought a strong reaction, even in ill-organised

[87] *KT* 14.5.1926; Reports of Chatham Joint Strike Committee 5.5.1926, Sheerness Strike Committee 8.5.1926, Maidstone Strike Committee 10.5.1926; Kent Area Report 6.5.1926.

[88] *KMGT* 8.5.1926, 15.5.1926 and 22.5.1926; *DE* 11.5.1926; *KE* 15.5.1926; *SEG* 18.5.1926.

[89] *KMGT* 22.5.1926 and 29.5.1926; Skelley, *op. cit.*, p. 279; Letter from Ministry of Health to Clerk to Guardians, Dover, 26.5.1926.

[90] *KE* 6.6.1929; Craig, *op. cit.*, p. 84; Skelley, *op. cit.*, p. 279.

industrial areas like Birmingham, was lacking. 'There was no strong feeling about the strike in . . . places which were little touched by industry . . .';[91] the exceptions were north-west and metropolitan Kent.

Paul Hastings

---

[91] TUC Intelligence Report Sittingbourne District 9.5.1926; R.P. Hastings, 'Aspects of the General Strike in Birmingham 1926', *Midland History*, Volume II, Number 4 (1974), pp. 250–73; and R.P. Hastings, 'Birmingham', in Skelley, *op. cit.*, pp. 208–31; Whyman, *op. cit.*, p. 88.

Guide to Further Reading

This guide is designed to refer the reader to recent and useful background material on the subjects covered in this volume. It should be supplemented by the more detailed references, especially to primary sources and to local historical publications, provided in the footnotes to each chapter.

(1) General Works

The most readable and up-to-date survey of recent British history is *Twentieth-Century Britain: Economic, Social and Cultural Change*, ed. P. Johnson, London 1994; it comprises a total of twenty-seven separate essays by leading historians, grouped into three periods: 1900–14, 1914–39 and 1939–90. These essays cover most of the topics dealt with in this volume and some which have only been mentioned in passing, such as race relations, pressure groups and youth culture. Each chapter has a useful bibliographical note and there is a thirteen-page list of key dates and events. This volume can be supplemented by S. Glynn and A. Booth, *Modern Britain: An Economic and Social History*, London 1996. For more strictly political history there is K.O. Morgan, *The People's Peace: British History since 1945*, Oxford 1999, and two valuable older studies, C.L. Mowat, *Britain between the Wars, 1918–1940*, London 1955, and A.J.P. Taylor, *English History 1914–1945*, Oxford 1965. For the first half of the twentieth century there are the authoritative essays in *The Cambridge Social History of Britain, 1750–1950*, ed. F.M.L. Thompson, 3 vols, Cambridge 1991. An important sub-theme of recent British history has been stimulatingly analysed in D. Cannadine, *The Decline and Fall of the British Aristocracy*, New Haven and London 1990. Of the general studies of Kentish history in this period by far the most important is E. Melling, *History of the Kent County Council, 1889–1974*, Maidstone 1975, which throws much light on many of the issues covered in this volume, though somewhat constrained by the fact that it is the official history of an institution. P. Clark and L. Murfin, *The History of Maidstone: The Making of a Modern County Town*, provides a good general survey of people and events in Maidstone in the first four decades of the twentieth century, but covers those since 1939 in only twelve pages.

(2) The First and Second World Wars

The impact of these two events on twentieth-century history is dealt with in a number of important monographs. T. Wilson, *The Myriad Faces of War: Britain and the Great War, 1914–1918*, Cambridge 1986, now effectively replaces the older A. Marwick, *The Deluge: British Society and the First World War*, London 1965, as the best introduction to the first of these events. There is also an interesting discussion of the war's impact in J. Winter, *The Great War and the British People*, London 1986, though it has produced something of a backlash in the academic journals from historians who have challenged the optimism of Winter's thesis. The economic changes in British society brought about by the Second World War are chronicled in W.K. Hancock and M.M. Gowing, *The British War Economy*, London 1949, and the political ones in P. Addison, *The Road to 1945: British Politics and the Second World War*, London 1975. More general issues relating to the impact of this war are controversially considered in C. Barnett, *The Audit of War: The Illusion and Reality of Britain as a Great Nation*, London 1986. There are two excellent modern studies of post-war Britain and life under the Attlee government: P. Hennessy, *Never Again: Britain, 1945–51*, London 1992, and P. Addison, *Now the War is Over: A Social History of Britain 1945–51*, rev. edn, London 1995.

(3) Economic and Industrial History

As might be expected the British economy in the twentieth century has been extensively explored. A valuable perspective is provided by M. Dintenfass, *The Decline of Industrial Britain, 1870–1980*, London 1992, the series of essays *The Decline of the British Economy*, ed. B. Elbaum and W. Lazonick, Oxford 1986, and S. Pollard, *The Development of the British Economy, 1914–1990*, 4th edn, London 1992. For the economic history of the period between the two world wars, see D.H. Aldcroft, *The Inter-War Economy: Britain, 1919–1939*, London 1970. For important studies of the post-war British economy, see the essays in *The British Economy since 1945*, ed. N.F.R. Crafts and N. Woodward, Oxford 1991, and the pamphlet by B.W.E. Alford, *British Economic Performance, 1945–75*, London 1988, which contains a useful bibliography. The impact of Thatcherism on the British economy is considered in *The Economic Legacy, 1979–1992*, ed. J. Michie, London 1992. Compared with these national surveys, those of twentieth-century economic activity at the county level are almost non-existent. For Kent there is J. M. Preston, *Industrial Medway: An Historical Survey*, Rochester 1977, but this extends little beyond the 1930s and the north-western third of the county. Of the few business histories, the most impressive is that by W.J. Reader, *Bowater: A History*, Cambridge 1981. The best study of the Kent coalfield is contained, somewhat paradoxically, in R.J. Waller, *The Dukeries Transformed: The Social and Political Development of a Twentieth Century Coalfield*, Oxford 1983.

(4) Agriculture and Rural Society

Standard works dealing with agrarian developments in the twentieth century include P.E. Dewey, *British Agriculture in the First World War*, London 1989; E.H. Whetham, *The Agrarian History of England and Wales VII: 1914–1939*, Cambridge 1978; K.A.H. Murray, *Agriculture*, London 1955, in the history of the Second World War, United Kingdom, Civil Series; B.A. Holderness, *British Agriculture since 1945*, Manchester 1985; and an invaluable compilation published by the Ministry of Agriculture, Fisheries and Food, *A Century of Agricultural Statistics*, London 1968. Two studies by R. Body, *Agriculture: The Triumph and the Shame*, London 1982, and *Farming in the Clouds*, London 1984, are strongly critical of state policy before and since British involvement in the Common Agricultural Policy. Meanwhile, social change in the countryside has given rise to a limited number of historical studies, notably P. Horn, *Rural Life in England in the First World War*, Dublin 1984, and the accelerating pace of change has attracted the attention of a few sociologists, seeking to write from a historical as well as a theoretical perspective. Among these, the works of H. Newby, *The Deferential Worker*, London 1977, and *England's Green and Pleasant Land? Social Change in Rural England*, London 1979, are outstanding. W.A. Armstrong, *Farmworkers: A Social and Economic History*, London 1988, devotes several chapters to the twentieth century. Studies of twentieth-century agricultural changes in Kent are comparatively scarce. Of pre-eminent importance is G.A. Garrad, *A Survey of the Agriculture of Kent*, London 1954, which offers a detailed analysis of the position fifty years ago. W.G.G. Alexander, *A Farming Century: The Darent Valley, 1892–1992*, London 1991, looks at twentieth-century changes from the standpoint of his own family. R.K.I. Quested takes a longer view in *The Isle of Thanet Farming Community: An Agrarian History of Easternmost Kent: Outlines from Early Times to 1992*, privately printed 1996, but includes two lengthy and valuable chapters on the twentieth century experience of a community that included her forbears.

(5) Political History

All the major politicians of the twentieth century have either produced their own autobiographies, memoirs or editions of their diaries, or have acquired biographers, though such work varies greatly in quality. A useful guide to the whole topic is *The British Study of Politics in the Twentieth Century*, ed. J. Hayward, B. Barry and A. Brown, Oxford 1999. See also D. Childs, *Britain since 1945: A Political History*, London 1979, which covers the thirty-year period before Margaret Thatcher came to power. An excellent starting point for those wishing to follow both the electoral process and the internal disputes within political parties are the official histories of those parties, though they inevitably suffer from the defect of being somewhat inward looking: see R. Blake, *The Conservative Party from Peel to Major*, London 1997; C. Cook, *A Short History of the Liberal Party, 1900–92*, London 1993; and H. Pelling and A.J. Reid, *A Short History of the Labour Party*, London 1996. Pelling has also written a useful *History of British Trade Unions*, 3rd edn, Harmondsworth 1976. Each British general election since 1945 has also been analysed in a series of volumes, mostly involving David Butler, and published under the auspices of Nuffield College, Oxford; a full list of the available titles is published in D. Butler and D. Kavanagh, *The British General Election of 1997*, London 1997.

(6) Housing, Health and Social Welfare

Two fundamental studies are P.M. Thane, *The Foundations of the Welfare State*, London 1982, and D. Vincent, *Poor Citizens: The State and the Poor in Twentieth Century Britain*, London 1991. There are also important assessments of two of the leading figures in welfare reform in J. Harris, *William Beveridge*, Oxford 1977, and A. Briggs, *Seebohm Rowntree*, London 1961. There is much useful material on the Depression and consequent unemployment of the inter-war period in *The Road to Full Employment*, ed. S. Glynn and A. Booth, London 1987; S. Constantine, *Unemployment in Britain between the Wars*, London 1980; and P. Kingsford, *The Hunger Marchers in Britain, 1920–39*, London 1982. For the period since the Second World War, the best overviews are M. Hill, *The Welfare State in Britain: A Political History since 1945*, Aldershot 1993; R. Lowe, *The Welfare State in Britain since 1945*, Basingstoke 1993; and *The State of Welfare: The Welfare State in Britain since 1974*, ed. J. Hills, Oxford 1990. There are two exceptionally good books on the National Health Service: R. Klein, *The Politics of the National Health Service*, 2nd edn, London 1989, and C. Webster, *The National Health Service: A Political History*, Oxford 1998.

(7) The Quality of Life

M. Sanderson, *Educational Opportunity and Social Change in England, 1900–1980s*, London 1987, provides a useful overview of that topic and there are some important studies of the development of educational policy since the Second World War: B. Simon, *Education and the Social Order, 1940–1990*, London 1991; D. Rubinstein and B. Simon, *The Evolution of the Comprehensive School, 1926–1972*, London 1973; and J.G.K. Fenwick, *The Comprehensive School, 1944–1970*, London 1976. J. Lawson and H.

Silver, *Social History of Education in England*, London 1973, remains a useful general introduction to the subject. Higher education in the last fifty years is surveyed in W. A.C. Stewart, *Higher Education in Postwar Britain*, Lewes 1989, and there is a detailed study of higher education in Kent in G. Martin, *From Vision to Reality: The Making of the University of Kent at Canterbury*, Canterbury 1990, published to commemorate the university's silver jubilee. The decline in Christian religious observance in Britain, and the growth of both non-Christian religions and secularisation, are surveyed in *Religion, State, and Society in Modern Britain*, ed. P. Badham, Lampeter 1989; *The Growth of Religious Diversity: Britain from 1945*, ed. G. Parsons, 2 vols, London 1993; A.D. Gilbert, *The Making of Post-Christian Britain*, London 1980; and in two wide-ranging books by R. Gill, *The Myth of the Empty Church*, London 1993, and *Churchgoing and Christian Ethics*, Cambridge 1999. A wide range of statistical information for the first three-quarters of the twentieth century is published in R. Currie, A.D. Gilbert and L. Horsley, *Churches and Churchgoers: Patterns of Church Growth in the British Isles since 1700*, Oxford 1977. The best survey of Christianity in the twentieth century is A. Hastings, *A History of English Christianity, 1920–1990*, London 1991, but there is also much useful material and comment in D.W. Bebbington, *Evangelicalism in Modern Britain: A History from the 1730s to the 1980s*, London 1989. For a more traditionalist approach to recent church history see P.A. Welsby, *A History of the Church of England, 1945–1980*, Oxford 1984. One of the best introductions to developments in twentieth-century popular culture is R. Hoggart, *The Uses of Literacy*, London 1957, though it is based on the author's own experience of his upbringing in Leeds and his early career in Hull, where he lectured in the university's adult-education department. Much of the available literature on leisure and recreation is written from a sociological rather than a historical perspective but includes the following important studies: R. Holt, *Sport and the British: A Modern History*, Oxford 1989; S. Jones, *Workers at Play: A Social and Economic History of Leisure, 1918–1939*, London 1986; and J. Richards, *The Age of the Dream Palace: Cinema and Society in Britain, 1930–1939*, London 1984. The role of seaside resorts in Kent in the twentieth century is explored, with contemporary documentation and illustration, in F. Stafford and N. Yates, *The Later Kentish Seaside (1840–1974)*, Maidstone 1985.

Index